Conservation and Restoration of Glass

Butterworth-Heinemann Series in Conservation and Museology

Series Editors:

Arts and Archaeology
Andrew Oddy
British Museum, London

Architecture
Derek Linstrum
Formerly Institute of Advanced Architectural Studies, University of York

US Executive Editor:
Norbert S. Baer
New York University, Conservation Center of the Institute of Fine Arts

Consultants:
Sir Bernard Feilden
David Bomford
National Gallery, London
C.V. Horie
Manchester Museum, University of Manchester
Sarah Staniforth
National Trust, London
John Warren
Institute of Advanced Architectural Studies, University of York

Published titles:
Artists' Pigments c.1600–1835, 2nd Edition (Harley)
Care and Conservation of Geological Material (Howie)
Care and Conservation of Palaeontological Material (Collins)
Chemical Principles of Textile Conservation (Tímár-Balázsy, Eastop)
Conservation and Exhibitions (Stolow)
Conservation and Restoration of Ceramics (Buys, Oakley)
Conservation and Restoration of Works of Art and Antiquities (Kühn)
Conservation of Brick (Warren)
Conservation of Building and Decorative Stone (Ashurst, Dimes)
Conservation of Earth Structures (Warren)
Conservation of Glass (Newton, Davison)
Conservation of Historic Buildings (Feilden)
Conservation of Historic Timber Structures: An Ecological Approach to
    Preservation (Larsen, Marstein)
Conservation of Library and Archive Materials and the Graphic Arts
    (Petherbridge)
Conservation of Manuscripts and Painting of South-east Asia (Agrawal)
Conservation of Marine Archaeological Objects (Pearson)
Conservation of Wall Paintings (Mora, Mora, Philippot)
Historic Floors: Their History and Conservation (Fawcett)
A History of Architectural Conservation (Jokilehto)
Lacquer: Technology and Conservation (Webb)
The Museum Environment, 2nd Edition (Thomson)
The Organic Chemistry of Museum Objects, 2nd Edition (Mills, White)
Radiography of Cultural Material (Lang, Middleton)
The Textile Conservator's Manual, 2nd Edition (Landi)
Upholstery Conservation: Principles and Practice (Gill, Eastop)

Related titles:
Concerning Buildings (Marks)
Laser Cleaning in Conservation (Cooper)
Lighting Historic Buildings (Phillips)
Manual of Curatorship, 2nd edition (Thompson)
Manual of Heritage Management (Harrison)
Materials for Conservation (Horie)
Metal Plating and Patination (Niece, Craddock)
Museum Documentation Systems (Light)
Risk Assessment for Object Conservation (Ashley-Smith)
Touring Exhibitions (Sixsmith)

Conservation and Restoration of Glass

Sandra Davison FIIC, ACR

Glass Conservator
The Conservation Studio, Thame, Oxfordshire

BUTTERWORTH
HEINEMANN

OXFORD AMSTERDAM BOSTON LONDON NEW YORK PARIS
SAN DIEGO SAN FRANCISCO SINGAPORE SYDNEY TOKYO

Butterworth-Heinemann
An imprint of Elsevier Science
Linacre House, Jordan Hill, Oxford OX2 8DP
200 Wheeler Road, Burlington, MA 01803

First published 1989
Paperback edition 1996
Second edition 2003

British Library Cataloguing in Publication Data
A catalogue record for this book is available from the British Library

ISBN 0 7506 43412

For information on all Butterworth-Heinemann publications
visit our website at www.bh.com

Composition by Scribe Design, Gillingham, Kent, UK
Printed and bound by The Bath Press, Bath, UK

Contents

About the author   vi

Preface   vii

Acknowledgements   ix

Introduction   xi

1   The nature of glass   1

2   Historical development of glass   16

3   Technology of glass production   73
Part 1: Methods and materials   73
Part 2: Furnaces and melting techniques   135

4   Deterioration of glass   169

5   Materials used for glass restoration   199

6   Examination of glass, recording and documentation   227

7   Conservation and restoration of glass   242
Part 1: Excavated glass   243
Part 2: Historic and decorative glass   271

Appendix 1 Materials and equipment for glass conservation and restoration   345

Appendix 2 Sources of information   347

Bibliography   349

Index   367

About the author

Sandra Davison FICC ACR trained in archaeological conservation at the Institute of Archaeology (London University), and has worked as a practising conservator for thirty-five years. Fourteen years were spent as a conservator at The British Museum, and after a brief spell abroad, she has continued in her own private practice since 1984. Sandra has lectured and published widely, including a definitive work, *Conservation of Glass* (with Professor Roy Newton, OBE), of which this volume is a revised and enlarged edition.

In addition to working for museums in the United Kingdom, France, the Czech Republic, Malaysia and Saudi Arabia, she has taught glass restoration in the UK, Denmark, Norway, the Netherlands, the USA, Egypt, Mexico and Yugoslavia.

In 1979 she was made a Fellow of the International Association for the Conservation of Historic and Artistic Works (IIC), and in 2000 became one of the first conservators to become an accredited member of the United Kingdom Institute for Conservation (UKIC).

Preface

Conservation of Glass, first published in 1989, was intended to serve as a textbook for conservation students, conservators and restorers working on glass artefacts within museums, and those restoring painted (stained) glass windows *in situ*. It was written by two authors with very different, but complementary backgrounds and experience in the conservation of glass. Roy Newton, a glass scientist (now retired), has worked in glass manufacturing, on the archaeology of glass and on the problems concerned with the conservation of medieval ecclesiastical painted windows. Sandra Davison, a practising conservator for over thirty years, has conserved a great variety of glass artefacts, published and lectured widely, and teaches the principles and practice of glass conservation in many countries.

In this edition, written by Sandra Davison, the section concerning painted glass window restoration has been removed, with the intention of producing a separate volume at a later date. However, information concerning the history and technology of glass window-making has been retained as background knowledge for conservators preserving panels of glass held in collections. The revised title, *Conservation and Restoration of Glass*, reflects the closer involvement of conservators in developing conservation strategies for dealing with glass in historic houses and elsewhere in the public arena. The volume includes sections on the historical development and treatment of mirrors, chandeliers, reverse paintings on glass and enamels.

Conservation and Restoration of Glass provides an introduction to the considerable background knowledge required by conservators and restorers concerning the objects in their care. Chapter 1 defines the nature of glass in terms of its chemical structure and physical properties. Chapter 2 contains a brief history of glassmaking, illustrating the changing styles of glass decoration, and the historical development of light fittings (in particular chandeliers), flat glass, mirrors, reverse glass paintings and micromosaics and enamels. Chapter 3 consists of two parts. The first describes the use of the raw materials from which glass is made and the historical development of methods of glass manufacture; the second is concerned with the development of furnaces and melting techniques. The mechanisms by which glass deteriorates, in different environments, are described in Chapter 4, together with an outline of experiments undertaken for commercial/industrial concerns, to determine the durability of glass. The materials used in the processes of conservation and restoration of glass are discussed in Chapter 5. The examination of glass, described in Chapter 6, outlines both simple methods for use by conservators, and those more elaborate techniques which can be of use for analysis, research and the detection of fakes. Finally, in Chapter 7, the details of conservation and restoration techniques, based on current practice in several countries, are described and illustrated. Conservators/restorers should not normally undertake complicated procedures for which they have not had training or experience; but specialized areas of glass conservation are outlined in Chapter 7 in order to identify the problems that will require expert attention. Information concerning developments in glass conservation, which may also include details of treatments that have proved to be unsuccessful, can be found in conservation literature and glass conference proceedings.

Acknowledgements

There have been significant developments and growth in glass conservation. The author has attempted to reflect this by inviting comments from a number of conservators and restorers (in private practice or museum employment), conservation scientists and experts in related fields, working in Britain, Europe and North America.

In particular, the author is greatly indebted to Professor Roy Newton for undertaking the enormous amount of research for *Conservation of Glass*, of which this book is a development; and to the following colleagues for their valuable assistance (and who, unless stated otherwise, are in private practice):

Chapter 1: Angela Seddon (Professor of Materials Science, University of Nottingham). Chapter 2: Phil Barnes (enamels); Simone Bretz (reverse paintings on glass; Germany); Judy Rudoe (micromosaics; Assistant Keeper, Department of Medieval and Modern Europe, British Museum); Mark Bamborough (painted glass windows); Tom Kupper (plain glazing; Lincoln Cathedral); Eva Rydlova (Brychta glass figurines; Czech Republic). Chapter 3 part 1: Paul Nicholson (Egyptologist, University of Bristol); part 2: David Crossley (industrial archaeologist, The University of Sheffield) and the late Robert Charleston (glass historian and former Curator of the Department of Ceramics and Glass, Victoria and Albert Museum). Chapter 4: Ian Freestone (Deputy Keeper, Department of Scientific Research, British Museum). Chapter 5: Velson Horie (conservation scientist, Manchester Museum, University of Manchester). Chapter 6: Angela Seddon (University of Nottingham) and Ian Freestone (British Museum). Chapter 7: Victoria Oakley (Head of Ceramics and Glass Conservation, Victoria and Albert Museum) and Patricia Jackson (UK), Rolf Wihr (Germany), Carola Bohm (Sweden), Raymond Errett (retired) and Sharon Smith-Abbott (USA) (glass object conservators); Alison Rae and Jenny Potter (conservators of ethnographic material – beads; Organic Artefacts Section, Department of Conservation, British Museum); Annie Lord (textile conservator – beads; The Conservation Centre, National Museums and Galleries Merseyside, Liverpool).

Thanks are also due to Vantico (formerly Ciba Speciality Polymers), Duxford, Cambridge for technical advice and for a generous grant towards research. Finally to my family, T.K. and E. Lord, without whose gift of a computer this book would not have been written, to WBJH for patience with computer queries and endless photocopying, and Steve Bell for technical support.

The sources of illustrations (other than those by Roy Newton and the author) are stated briefly in the captions. Every effort has been made to trace copyright holders. The author and publishers gratefully acknowledge the kind permission, granted by individuals, museum authorities, publishers and others, to reproduce copyright material.

S.D.
2002

Introduction

The conservation of glass, as of all artefacts, falls into two main categories: *passive conservation*, the control of the surrounding environment to prevent further deterioration; and *active conservation*, the treatment of artefacts to stabilize them. A storage or display environment will consist of one of the following: (i) natural climatic conditions (especially painted glass windows and glass mosaics *in situ*); (ii) modified (buffered) climatic conditions in buildings and cases with no air conditioning; (iii) controlled climatic conditions, where air conditioning has been installed in museum galleries or individual showcases, to hold temperature and relative humidity within carefully defined parameters. Environmental control is a discipline in its own right (Thomson, 1998) and outside the scope of this book. However, conservators need to be aware of the basic facts in order to be able to engage in discussions regarding display and storage conditions, and the choice of materials for display, and packaging for storage and transport. The prevention of further damage and decay by *passive conservation*, represents the minimum type of treatment, and normally follows examination and recording. Reasons for not undertaking further conservation might be lack of finance, facilities, lack of an appropriate treatment or the sheer volume of glass, e.g. from excavation.

Active conservation, as the term implies, involves various levels of interference. *Minimal conservation* would include 'first aid', photography, X-radiography (where appropriate), a minimal amount of investigative conservation such as surface cleaning, and suitable packaging or repackaging for safe storage. *Partial conservation* entails the work above but with a higher degree of cleaning, with or without consolidation. *Full conservation* work would additionally involve consolidation and repair (reconstruction of existing fragments), supplemented by additional analytical information where appropriate. *Display standard conservation* might include cosmetic treatment such as restoration (partial or full replacement of missing parts) or interpretative mounting for display. Restoration of glass objects may also be necessary to enable them to be handled safely. It should only be carried out according to sound archaeological or historical evidence. The level of conservation has to be agreed between a conservator/restorer and the owner, custodian or curator, before work begins.

Historically, glass conservation was not as easily developed as it was for ceramics, for example. The fragile nature of glass made it difficult to retrieve from excavations, and the transparent quality of much glass posed the difficulty of finding suitable adhesives and gap-filling materials with which to work. The use of synthetic materials and improvements in terrestrial and underwater archaeological excavation techniques have resulted in the preservation of glass which it was not formerly possible to retrieve; and continues to extend the knowledge of ancient glass history, technology and trade routes. Early treatments using shellac, waxes and plaster of Paris were opaque or coloured and not aesthetically pleasing (Davison, 1984). Later, rigid transparent acrylic materials such as Perspex (US: Plexiglas) were heat-formed and cut to replace missing areas of glass. Advantages were their transparency and only slight discoloration and embrittlement with age. However, the processes were time-consuming, and the replacements did not necessarily fit well against the original glass. Unweathered glass surfaces are smooth, essentially non-porous and are covered with a microscopic layer of water, so that few materials will adhere satisfactorily to them. It was only with the commercial formulation of clear, cold-setting synthetic materials, with greater adhesive properties, that significant developments in glass conservation were achieved. Epoxy, polyester and acrylic resins could be polymerized in moulds *in situ*, at ambient temperatures with little or no shrinkage. However, restoration involves interference with the glass in terms of the moulding and casting processes (Newton and Davison, 1989). Recent approaches to glass conservation and restoration have been the construction of detachable gap-fills (Hogan, 1993; Koob, 2000), and the mounting of glass fragments or incomplete objects on modern blown glass formers, or on acrylic mounts.

1

The nature of glass

The term *glass* is commonly applied to the transparent, brittle material used to form windows, vessels and many other objects. More correctly, glass refers to a state of matter with a disordered chemical structure, i.e. non-crystalline. A wide variety of such glasses is known, both inorganic (for instance compound glasses and enamels, and even the somewhat rare metallic glasses) and organic (such as barley sugar); this book is concerned only with inorganic glasses, and then only with certain silicate glasses, which are inorganic products of fusion, cooled to a rigid condition without crystallizing. The term *ancient glasses* is that used by Turner (1956a,b) to define silicate glasses which were made before there was a reasonable under-standing of glass compositions, that is before the middle of the seventeenth century (see also Brill, 1962). In this book, for convenience, the term glass will be used to mean both ancient and historic silicate glasses. Understanding the special chemical structure and unique physical properties of silicate glasses is essential in order to appreciate both the processes of manufacture of glass objects and the deterioration of glass, which may make conservation a necessity.

Natural glasses

Before the discovery of how glass could be manufactured from its raw ingredients, man had used naturally occurring glass for many thousands of years. Natural silica (the basic ingredient of glass) is found in three crystalline forms, quartz, tridymite and cristobalite, and each of these can also occur in at least two forms. Quartz is the most common, in the form of rock crystal, sand, or as a constituent of clay. Rock crystal was fashioned into beads and other decorative objects, including, in seventeenth century France, chandelier drops. If quartz is free from inclusions, it can be visually mistaken for glass.

Sudden volcanic eruptions, followed by rapid cooling, can cause highly siliceous lava to form natural glasses (amorphous silica), of which obsidian is the most common. In ancient times, obsidian was chipped and flaked to form sharp-edged tools, in the same manner as flint (*Figure 1.1*). Other forms of naturally occurring glass are volcanic pumice, lechatelierite or fulgurites and tektites. Pumice is a natural foamed glass produced by gases being liberated from solution in molten lava, before and after rapid cooling. Lechatelierite is a fused silica glass formed in desert areas by

Figure 1.1 Since prehistoric times, obsidian has been used to fashion tools. The spearhead shown here is a modern example, made in Mexico.

lightning striking a mass of sand. The irregular tubes of fused silica (fulgurites) may be of considerable length. Lechatelierite has also been discovered in association with meteorite craters, for example at Winslow, Arizona. Tektites are small rounded pieces of glass, of meteoric origin, found just below the surface of the ground in many parts of the world, and which appear to have come through the atmosphere and been heated by falling through the air while rotating. Their composition is similar to that of obsidian, but they contain more iron and manganese.

Man-made glasses

In order to understand the nature of man-made glass, it is first necessary to define several terms for vitreous materials, some of which have previously been used ambiguously or incorrectly (Tite and Bimson, 1987). There are four vitreous products: glass, glaze, enamel and (so-called, Egyptian) faience, which consist of silica, alkali metal oxides and lime. Glass, glaze and enamel always contain large quantities of soda (Na_2O) or another alkali metal oxide, such as potash (K_2O), and sometimes both, whereas Egyptian faience contains only quite small amounts of alkali metal oxide. It has formerly been supposed, that because of the difficulty of reaching and maintaining the high temperatures required to melt glass from its raw ingredients, in ancient times, the raw ingredients were first formed into an intermediate product known as frit. However, there is limited evidence for this practice. In the fritting process, raw materials would be heated at temperatures just high enough to fuse them, and in doing so to release carbon dioxide from the alkali carbonates. The resulting mass was then pounded to powder form (the frit). This was reheated at higher temperatures to form a semi-molten paste which could be formed into objects, or was heated at higher temperatures at which it could melt to form true glass.

A silicate glass is a material normally formed from silica, alkali metal oxides (commonly referred to as alkalis) and lime, when these have been heated to a temperature high enough to form them into a homogeneous structure (formerly and ambiguously termed

Figure 1.2   A thick layer of glaze covering a stoneware bowl.

glass metal). Chemically, glass, glaze and enamel can all be identical in composition, the fundamental difference being their method of use in antiquity. The coefficient of thermal expansion of a glass was not important when it was used alone (unless it was applied on a different glass, as in the manufacture of cameo glass), whereas in a glaze or an enamel any difference in thermal expansion between them and the base on which they were fused could cause the glaze or enamel to crack or become detached from the base material. In practice, glasses and enamels needed to have a low melting point, remain plastic as long as possible while cooling and, apart from the very earliest glasses, be translucent or transparent (in contrast to the early glazing of earthenware where coloured decoration had been important).

A glaze is a thin vitreous coating applied to another material to make it impermeable, or to produce a shiny decorative appearance. Glaze was sometimes applied with the body material before firing, but more often it was applied to the object after it had received a first firing, following which the object was refired to form the glazed surface (*Figure 1.2*).

Faience is composed of fritted silica with about 2 wt per cent of lime (CaO) and about 0.25 wt per cent soda, lightly held together with a bonding agent such as water. The resulting paste was shaped by hand or in an open mould and then heated until the lime and soda had reacted enough (fused sufficiently) to hold the silica particles together. During the formation process, faience objects formed a glazed surface with a similar composition to the body, usually coloured blue or green with copper compounds. (Strictly speaking the term faience, derived from the name of the Italian town of Faenza, should refer to the tin-glazed earthenware made there.) To reduce confusion the material discussed here should be referred to as Egyptian faience, or preferably, glazed siliceous ware (see *Plate 2* and *Figure 3.2*), (Nicholson, 1993; Smith, 1996).

The pigment known as Egyptian Blue, first used in Egypt during the third millennium BC, and during the next 3000 years, in wall paintings, and as beads, scarabs, inlays and statuettes, is the mineral $(CaO.CuO.4SiO_2)$ = $(CaCuSi_4O_{10})$. X-ray diffraction analysis has shown that, in addition to this compound, the only crystalline materials were quartz and tridymite (another of the crystalline forms of silica) (Chase, 1971; Tite *et al.*, 1981).

A enamel resembles a glaze in that it is also fused to a body of a different material, in this case, metal (see *Figures 3.33–3.38, 7 57* and *7.58*); however, the term enamel is also used to describe vitreous pigments used to decorate ceramics and glass (see Chapter 3).

Chemical structure and composition

Zachariasen (1932) established that the atoms and ions in silicate glasses are linked together by strong forces, essentially the same as in crystals, but lacking the long range order which is characteristic of a crystal. Crystalline silica (quartz) melts sharply at 1720°C from its solid state, to a liquid, just as ice melts to form water at 0°C. This melting point is scientifically referred to as the liquidus. When the silica liquid (molten glass) is cooled from above the liquidus, the randomly distributed molecules will endeavour to adopt a less random configuration, more like those of crystals. However, an alternative three-dimensional structure forms because the crystallization process is hindered by the high viscosity of the glass, and the presence of the network modifiers. The melt becomes more and more viscous as the temperature is lowered until, at about 1050°C it sets to form a solid glass (a state formerly but no longer referred to as a super-cooled liquid). Moreover, the density of that glass is less than that of the original quartz

because there are now many spaces between the ill-fitting molecules.

However, in order to form a usable glass it is necessary to add certain oxides to the silica, which act as network modifiers, stabilizers and colourants, and which also have a marked effect on the structure of the resulting product. When network modifiers are added, they have the effect of considerably lowering the viscosity of the melt (see *Figure 1.8*). Thus there is the potential for a different type of crystal containing atoms from the modifiers, to form in the sub liquidus melt, provided the melt has been held at the *liquidus temperature* for long enough. Thus a glass with the molar composition $16Na_2O$, $10CaO$, $74SiO_2$ can form crystals of devitrite $(Na_2O.3CaO.6SiO_2)$; which grow at a rate of 17 µm per minute at a temperature of 995°C, the optimum temperature for growth of devitrite in that composition of glass. The total chemical composition of the glass remains unaltered (i.e. no atoms are added or subtracted from those already in the glass), although the composition will change locally as crystals of devitrite separate from the bulk glass.

Ancient glasses have such complex compositions that devitrification occurs much less easily than in modern glasses, so that if crystals of devitrite are present in a sample undergoing examination, there may be doubts concerning the antiquity of the glass. However, the enormous block of glass made in a tank furnace in a cave at Bet She'arim, in Israel, was found to be heavily devitrified (with the material wollastonite, $CaSiO_3$) as a consequence of containing 15.9 wt per cent of lime (Brill and Wosinski, 1965). The opalizing agent in some glasses may be a devitrification product itself, which forms only when suitable heat treatment is given to the glass. Devitrite does not occur as a mineral in nature.

Early historians and archaeologists have occasionally used the term devitrification in quite a different sense, meaning loss of vitreous structure to describe glass that has weathered with loss of alkali metal ions, of other constituents of the glass and probably a gain in water content. This ambiguous use of the term should be avoided (Newton and Werner, 1974).

Network formers

The principal network former in ancient glasses is silica (SiO_2). Silicon and oxygen in crystalline silica (quartz) are arranged in a definite pattern, the units of which are repeated at regular intervals forming a three-dimensional network consisting of tetrahedra with a silicon atom at the centre and an oxygen atom at each corner; all four of these oxygen atoms form bridges to silicon atoms of the four neighbouring silicon tetrahedra. Other network formers are the oxides of boron (B_2O_3), lead (PbO) (Charleston, 1960) and phosphorus (P_2O_5). The presence of boron is important for clarifying glass compositions. However, it is difficult to analyse and so might easily be missed, especially since ancient glasses typically contained only 0.01 to 0.02 per cent (whereas some Byzantine glasses contained 0.25 per cent boron). Boron entered the glass by way of the ash obtained by burning plants containing boric oxide. The mineral colemanite (hydrated calcium borate) ($Ca_3B_6O_{11}.5H_2O$) is found in western Turkey, and may have been used in glassmaking.

The concept of network-forming oxides is illustrated in *Figures 1.3* and *1.4*. Figure *1.3* shows the regular structure of an imaginary two-dimensional crystalline material. Within the broken line there are 16 black dots (representing atoms of type A) and 24 open circles (representing atoms of type O); hence the imaginary material has the composition A_2O_3 and its regular structure shows that it is crystalline. If the imaginary crystalline material A_2O_3, shown in *Figure 1.3*, has been melted, and is cooled quickly from the molten state, the resultant solid might have the structure shown in *Figure 1.4*. Here the broken line encloses 24 black dots and 36 open circles and hence the composition is again A_2O_3 but the structure is irregular and non-crystalline, representing the amorphous, glassy or vitreous state of the same compound. Note that the amorphous structure contains spaces and thus occupies a greater volume than the crystalline one, and hence the crystal has a higher density than the glass, even though the chemical composition is the same.

Network modifiers
Figure 1.5 shows a structure which is nearer to that of silicate glass. It is again a simplified two-dimensional diagram, and the key to it now mentions the word ion. Ions are atoms that have been given an electrical charge, by

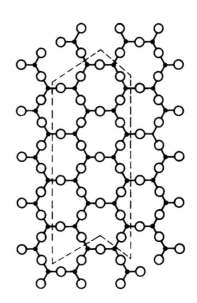

Figure 1.3 Schematic two-dimensional representation of the structure of an imaginary crystalline compound A_2O_3.

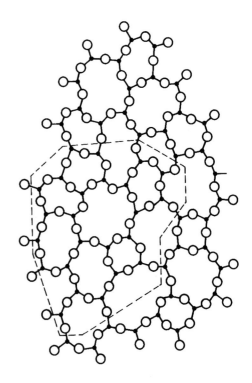

Figure 1.4 Structure of the glassy form of the compound in Figure 1.3.

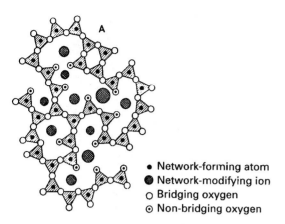

A

● Network-forming atom
◉ Network-modifying ion
○ Bridging oxygen
⊙ Non-bridging oxygen

Figure 1.5 Schematic two-dimensional representation of glass, according to Zachariasen's theory.

adding or subtracting one or more electrons; *cations* having lost electrons, have a positive charge, and *anions* having gained electrons, have a negative charge. The network-forming atoms are represented by black dots within shaded triangles (atoms of silicon), and the network modifying ions (positively charged cations) are cross-hatched circles lying in the spaces of the network. Each network-forming triangle (silicon atom) is accompanied by three oxygen atoms (shown by small circles), which can be of two kinds. There are bridging oxygen atoms (shown by plain open circles) which are shared between two triangles, thus joining them together and forming part of the network. There are also non-bridging oxygen ions (shown by circles with a central dot) which belong to only one triangle; each of these thus bears a negative charge which is neutralized by a positive charge on one of the cross-hatched circles (cations). (Strictly, the Si-O-Si bonds are 'iono-covalent'. They are not ionic enough to refer to the oxygen as ions, and the Si as a cation. In the case of the Si-O non-bridging bonds, the Si-O bond is still iono-covalent, but the negative charge on the oxygen gives it the ability to form an ionic bond to a cation in a nearby space.) It should be noted that there is a very small amount of crystalline material in the diagram, near 'A' in *Figure 1.5*, where four triangles are joined together to form a regular (hence crystalline) area. (This can occur also in ancient glasses,

where micro-crystallites can be detected.) At all other points the triangles form irregular chains, which enclose relatively large spaces (and hence the density of the glass is less than that of a corresponding crystalline form). These spaces in the network have been created by the network-modifying cations which bear one or more positive electrical charges, and which can be considered to be held, by those electrical charges, to be more (or perhaps rather less) loosely bound in those enlarged spaces.

The monovalent cations (which bear only one positive charge, having lost an electron to an adjacent non-bridging oxygen ion) are usually the alkali metal ions, either sodium (Na+) or potassium (K+), which bring with them one extra oxygen ion when they are added to the glass as soda or as potash. Because these cations bear only a single positive charge, they can move easily from one space in the network to another (loosely bound). Thus, when the glass is placed in water, it becomes less durable because the cations (the smaller of the cross-hatched circles in *Figure 1.5*) can move right out of the glass into the water, thus making the water slightly alkaline. In order to maintain the electrical neutrality of the glass, these cations must be replaced by another cation such as the oxonium ion (H_3O).

In the case of the *divalent alkaline earth* cations (the larger cross-hatched circles), each bears a double positive charge (being associated with two non-bridging oxygen ions, the circles with dots inside). These are usually Ca++ or Mg++, added to the glass as lime (CaO) or as magnesia (MgO), but other divalent alkaline earth ions may also be present. The double electrical charge on them holds them nearer (more tightly bound) to their accompanying non-bridging oxygens, making it much harder for them to move from one space to another. Thus divalent alkaline earth cations play little or no part in carrying an electric current through the glass. Because they are associated with two non-bridging oxygen ions, they strengthen the network, thus explaining why they help to offset the reduction in durability produced by the alkali metal cations. However it should be noted that in *Figure 1.5* the double ionic linkages (to circles with dots) are not immediately obvious.

It is these linkages which determine the very different effects that the monovalent and divalent cations have on the durability of glass.

Notable advances have been made in the understanding of the structure of glasses. For example, it is now realized that the network is actually loosened in the vicinity of the monovalent cations, channels (rather than merely larger spaces) being formed in which the cations can move even more easily than was formerly realized.

Phase separation

Despite the essentially homogeneous nature of bulk glasses, there may be minute areas, perhaps only 100 nm (0.1 m) in diameter, where the glass is not homogeneous because phase separation has occurred. These regions (rather like that near 'A' in *Figure 1.5*) can have a different chemical composition from the rest of the glass, i.e. the continuous phase (Goodman, 1987). Phase separation can occur in ancient glasses, and can have an effect on their durability, because the separated phase may have either a greater or a lower resistance to deterioration. The amount of phase separation can be seen through an electron microscope.

Colourants

The coloured effects observed in ancient and historic glasses were produced in three ways: (i) by the presence of relatively small amounts (about one per cent) of the oxides of certain transition metals, especially cobalt (Co), copper (Cu), iron (Fe), nickel (Ni), manganese (Mn), etc., which go into solution in the network; (ii) by the development of colloidal suspensions of metallic, or other insoluble particles, such as those in silver stains (yellow) or in copper or gold ruby glasses (red or orange); (iii) by the inclusion of opalizing agents which produce opal and translucent effects. The production of coloured glasses not only depends on the metallic oxides present in the batch, but also on the temperature and state of oxidation or reduction in the furnace. Of course the exact compositions of ancient glasses were complex and unknown, being governed by the raw materials and furnace conditions, so that the results could not be acccurately determined.

Dissolved metal oxides/state of oxidation

Coloured glasses can be produced by metal oxides *dissolving* in the glass (similar to the colours produced when the salts of those metals are dissolved in water), although the resultant colours will also be affected by the *oxidizing* or *reducing* (redox) conditions in the furnace. In the *traditional* sense, a metal was *oxidized* when it combined with oxygen to form an oxide, and the oxide was *reduced* when the metal was reformed. The position can be more complicated when there is more than one state of oxidation. For example, iron (Fe) becomes oxidized when ferrous oxide (FeO) is formed, and a blue colour is produced in the glass (because Fe^{2+} ions are present), but it becomes further oxidized when more oxygen is added to form ferric oxide (Fe_2O_3), which imparts a pale brown or yellow colour to the glass (due to the Fe^{3+} ions present). However, the situation is rarely so simple and usually mixtures of the two oxides of iron are present, producing glasses of various shades of green. When a chemical analysis of glass is undertaken, it is customary to quote the amount of iron oxide as Fe_2O_3, but that does not necessarily imply that all of the iron is in that state.

The oxidation process occurs when an atom loses an electron, and conversely, reduction takes place when an atom gains an electron. Consider the two reversible reactions set out in equations (1.1) and (1.2), where e^- represents an electron, with its negative charge. In equation (1.1) the forward arrow shows that an electron is lost when Fe^{2+} is converted to Fe^{3+}.

$$Fe^{2+} \quad Fe^{3+} + e^- \qquad\qquad 1.1$$

$$Mn^{3+} + e^- \quad Mn^{2+} \qquad\qquad 1.2$$

The combined effects of equations (1.1) and (1.2) is equation (1.3), which shows that there is an equilibrium between the two states of oxidation of the manganese and of the iron (Newton in Newton and Davison, 1989).

$$Fe^{2+} + Mn^{3+} \quad Fe^{3+} + Mn^{2+} \qquad\qquad 1.3$$

But the Fe^{3+} and Mn^{2+} are the more stable states, and hence the equilibrium tends to move to the right. Thus, when the conditions *during melting* of the glass are fully reducing (the equilibrium has been forced to the left, for example by producing smoky conditions in the furnace atmosphere) the iron contributes a bright blue colour due to the Fe_2 ions (corresponding to FeO) and the manganese is in the colourless form so that a blue glass is obtained. When the conditions are fully oxidizing (the equilibrium has been moved to the right by the addition of oxidizing agents; by changing the furnace conditions to have short, bright flames; or by prolonging the melting time), the iron contributes a brownish yellow colour and the manganese contributes a purple colour, so the glass appears brownish violet. When the conditions are intermediate, a variety of colours are obtainable, such as green, yellow, pink, etc. including a colourless glass when the purple from the manganese just balances the yellow from the iron. This is the reason why, if there is not too much manganese, it will act as a *decolourizer* for the glass which would otherwise be greenish in colour.

These conditions have been experimentally studied by Sellner (1977) and Sellner *et al.*, (1979), who produced a forest-type glass in which the colouring agents were only manganese (1.7 wt per cent MnO) and iron (0.7 wt per cent Fe_2O_3). A variety of colours was obtained, from pale blue, when the furnace atmosphere was fully reducing (with unburned fuel present and a very low partial pressure of oxygen in the waste gases) through green and yellow to dark violet when the furnace atmosphere was fully oxidizing (plenty of excess oxygen in the waste gases).

Sellner *et al.* (1979) also examined samples of glass excavated from two seventeenth-century glassworks sites, one at Glassborn/Spessart and the other at Hilsborn/Grünenplan, both in Germany. The compositions of the glasses at both sites were similar to each other, but the former factory had produced green glass and the latter had produced yellowish to purple glass. Measurements by electron spin resonance showed that the green glass had been melted under reducing conditions and the Hilsborn glass had been melted under oxidizing conditions. Thus, the colour of the glass had been determined by its having been made using beechwood ash

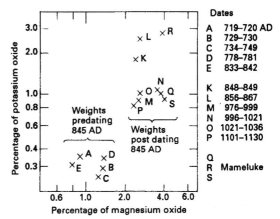

Figure 1.6 Chronological division of Egyptian Islamic glass weights into high- and low-magnesium types. (From Sayre, 1965).

(which contains both iron and manganese), and the furnace atmosphere, and not by the addition of manganese. The origin of colour in these glasses has also been investigated by Schofield *et al.* (1995), using synchrotron radiation.

Greenish colours can be obtained from copper. For archaeological reasons it may be necessary to discover whether tin or zinc is also present, because the presence of tin would suggest that bronze filings might have been added to the batch, whereas the presence of zinc would suggest the use of brass waste.

However, the presence of appreciable amounts of a particular oxide need not necessarily indicate a deliberate addition of that material. For example, *Figure 1.6* shows remarkable differences in the potash and magnesia contents of Egyptian Islamic glass weights, manufactured either before, or after, 845 AD. Brill (1971a) suggested that the earlier examples were made with soda from the natron lakes, whereas the later ones could have contained potash derived from burnt plant ash. There are still many problems and ambiguities to be solved regarding the compositions of ancient glasses, by analyses of samples from known provenances. However, there are many cases where the colouring agent is so strong that there is no problem. *Figure 1.7* shows the contents of metal ions in five kinds of ancient glass; sometimes only

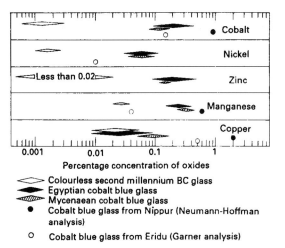

Figure 1.7 Colour element patterns in cobalt-blue glasses dating from the second millennium BC. (From Sayre, 1965).

0.02 per cent of cobalt is sufficient to produce a good blue colour. The deliberate production of an *amber* colour in ancient glass was in the form of *iron-manganese amber* described above, or *carbon-sulphur amber*. (They can be distinguished from each other because the Fe/Mn colour has optical absorption bands at 380 and 500 nm, whereas the C/S colour has its absorption bands at 430 and 1050 nm.)

The metals strontium (Sr), lithium (Li) and titanium (Ti) enter glasses as trace elements in the raw materials, in calcium carbonate for example; beach sand containing shells is high in strontium in comparison with limestone which is low in its content, and therefore the amount present in glass is an indicator as to whether shell was a deliberate addition. Strontium is a reactive metal resembling calcium, lithium is an alkali metal resembling sodium, but is less active and titanium resembles iron.

Colloidal suspensions of metals

Quite different colouring effects are obtained when the metals do not dissolve in the glass, but are dispersed (as a *colloid*) in the glass; the colour is then produced by light diffraction, and is therefore related to the size of the dispersed metal particles. For example, copper can produce red, orange or yellow colours.

The dichroic colour of the Lycurgus Cup (*Plate 4*), made in the fourth century AD, is a striking example, appearing transparent wine red in transmitted light, and translucent green by reflected light. This dichroic effect is produced by colloidal gold and silver.

The rich red colour in medieval cathedral window glass was produced by the presence of dispersed copper, but another red, with a distinct tint of purple, was produced by dispersed gold. The production of *gold* and *copper ruby* glasses is complicated because the strong colour does not develop (*strike*) until the glass is reheated (Weyl, 1951).

Copper ruby glasses have certainly been in use since the twelfth century. One problem in their use was the very intense colour produced: a piece of red glass only 3 mm thick (about the thinnest which could be used as window glass), would have appeared black instead of red. Two different techniques have been used at different times to overcome the problem. In the twelfth and thirteenth centuries, a transparent red glass was produced by distributing the red colour in a series of very many extremely thin layers. It is not known exactly how the layered effect was obtained, because the copper-containing glass had to be reheated before the colour appeared (i.e. before it *strikes*), which would have melted the glass layers together. It may have been that the multi-layered effect may have been obtained accidentally whilst trying to produce an extremely diluted copper red glass. A poor distribution of the copper in the melt perhaps influenced the *strike* of the colour in that some layers became red whilst others did not. From the fourteenth century onwards, the technique of flashing, in which a thin layer of red glass was laid on a base of colourless glass, was used to produce transparent red glass. Flashed glass appears bright red when viewed from the front, but when viewed through the edge, the layers of clear and coloured glasses can be seen.

Gold ruby glasses were probably in use from the sixteenth century, but its extensive use in the seventeenth century follows from the use of Purple of Cassius (a purple pigment consisting of a mixture of colloidal gold and stannic acid) by Johann Kunckel (1679). Kunckel evidently did not completely master the art of developing the full colour because only a small proportion of the melts seem to have been satisfactory. After Kunckel's death in 1705, the production of gold ruby glass continued in Bohemia, and certainly until the eighteenth century. The excavation of Kunckel's glassworks, on Pfauen Island, near Potsdam, caused a resurgence of interest in the work (Schulze, 1977). Neutron activation studies on the excavated samples of glass showed that the depth of colour was related to the concentration of gold, faintly coloured samples contained about 0.03 per cent gold, and the more strongly coloured samples contained 0.07 per cent, confirming data published by Kunckel (1679). In the nineteenth century the owners of glassworks had a custom of tossing a gold sovereign into the gold ruby batch. Gold dissolved in *aqua regia* would have already been added to the batch to produce the colour (Frank, 1984), and so it would seem that the custom of adding a coin was either to impress the workmen, or to confuse industrial spies (Newton, 1970).

Decolourizers

If iron is the only colouring oxide present it will produce a blue colour in its *reduced* form, but a much paler yellow is produced when the iron is *oxidized*. As seen in equation 1.3 above, manganese oxide can oxidize the iron to the yellow ferric state, and a slight excess of manganese will produce a pale purple which is *complementary in colour* to the yellow and thus effectively neutralizes it producing a virtually colourless glass. Thus, for at least the last few centuries, manganese has been deliberately used as the decolourizer for iron. There are also other oxidizing agents (such as the oxides of arsenic and of antimony) which can turn the blue from the iron to a very pale yellow, but it does not *neutralize* it in the same way that the purple colour of the manganese neutralizes the yellow of the ferric iron. Since no other colour is neutralized by this process, it is fortunate that iron is the predominant impurity in sand which produces undesired colour.

Lead glasses

Lead-rich glasses are relatively uncommon. In the West, they were used to produce red and yellow opaque glasses in antiquity, and certain transparent glasses in the medieval period. In the Far East, lead-rich glasses were produced in China. The amount of lead found in ancient glasses was probably not enough to alter their working properties or appearance, and therefore it is unlikely to have been a deliberate addition, but derived from the sand. In fact lead oxide seems to have been an unintentional ingredient of glass until Roman times. Lead-containing glasses probably existed as early as the second millennium BC, since lead was one of the ingredients mentioned in Mesopotamian cuneiform texts of that date. Analysis of a cake of red glass dating from the sixth century BC showed that it contained 22.8 per cent PbO by weight, giving the impression that 0.25 per cent of the glass composition. However, since lead is a very heavy element, the true position is seen to be quite different when the glass composition is calculated on a molar percentage, the lead oxide then being only 9.3 per cent. Thus 9.3 per cent of the molecules in the glass are lead oxide, and therefore lead glasses can be regarded as silicate glasses containing some 10 per cent of divalent network-modifying lead oxide.

Before the use of lead oxide in the making of lead glass in the seventeenth century, lead was used in the form of litharge, produced by blowing air over the surface of molten lead. When litharge is further oxidized, it becomes red lead. Its use required special furnace conditions, as its conversion back to metallic lead would discolour the glass and damage the crucibles or pots.

In the seventeenth century George Ravenscroft, working in England, produced a clear, brilliant glass by adding as much as 30 per cent lead oxide to the glass batch. Lead is so heavy that it can represent 50 weight per cent of a glass. *Figure 1.8* shows how the density of a glass is closely related to its lead content.

Opacifying agents

The most ancient glasses were opaque due to the presence of masses of tiny bubbles, or other dispersed materials within the viscous batch. Deliberate incorporation of air bubbles can be a way of producing opaque, somewhat opalescent glasses. However, the majority of opal glasses were produced by the use of relatively small number of *opalizing agents*, which form microcrystalline areas within the glass. Different opalizing agents were used in

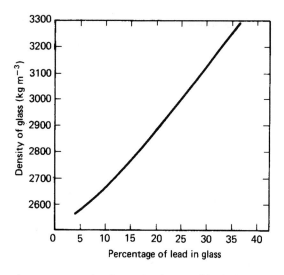

Figure 1.8 Graph relating the density of lead glass to its lead content.

present) contained calcium antimonate, whereas by the fifth century AD the opacifier in common use was tin oxide or, occasionally, calcium fluorophosphates. The use of tin oxide continued until the eighteenth century, when it was replaced by calcium fluoride or lead arsenate. Similarly, yellow opaque glasses contained lead antimonate in the early period, and a lead-tin oxide later on. It should, however, be noted that Bimson and Werner (1967) found cubic lead-tin oxide as the yellow opacifier in the rare first century AD gaming pieces found at Welwyn Garden City (Hertfordshire, UK). Thus the date for the use of this material should be regarded as being much earlier than formerly supposed. The opaque red glasses (*haematinum* or aventurine) contain copper and cuprous oxide (Cu_2O, which is always red) and they also contain tin or lead (Weyl, 1951). The origins of Roman opaque glasses, especially those containing antimony, have been discussed by Mass *et al.* (1998).

three distinct eras of glassmaking (Turner, 1957a,b, 1959; Rooksby, 1959, 1962, 1964; Turner and Rooksby, 1959, 1961).

Table 1.1 shows that Roman, and pre-Roman white opal glasses (or blue if cobalt was

Physical properties of glass

As explained at the beginning of the chapter, crystalline materials have a definite structure, whereas amorphous ones do not, and therefore only rather general statements can be

Table 1.1   Opacifying agents in glass, 1450 BC to AD 1961 (from Bimson and Werner, 1967)

Period	Type of glass	Opacifying agent	Number of specimens
1450 BC to fourth century AD	Opaque white and blue	$Ca_2Sb_2O_7$ (occasionally $CaSb_2O_6$)	15
	Opaque yellow	Cubic $Pb_2Sb_2O_7$	10
	Opaque red	Cu_2O Cu_2O+Cu or Cu	8
Fifth century AD to seventeenth century AD	Opaque white and blue	SnO_2 usually $3Ca_3(PO_4)_2.CaF_3$ occasionally	10 / 4
		Cubic Pb_5SnO_4	17
	Opaque yellow and green	Cu	
	Opaque red	$Cu+Cu_2O$ rarely $Cu+SnO_2$ sometimes	7
Eighteenth century AD to present day	Opaque white	$3Pb_2(AsO_4)_2.PbO$ (apatite-type structure)	4
		CaF or CaF_3+NaF	Many
		$(Na_2Ca)_2Sb_2O_6F$	1

made about a material which, when hot, is ductile but when cold is brittle, and fractures if there is a sudden change of temperature. The *thermal history* of glass is of particular importance, because glass that has been cooled quickly retains an imprint or 'memory' of its state at the moment before it was cooled. In the example of a viscous glass melt which is cooled *very slowly* from a temperature T_1 to a lower temperature T_2 energy available for molecular movements is gradually reduced, but (because the rate of cooling is very slow) the network has enough time to readjust itself and become more compact. (In some cases *devitrification* crystals can form when the glass is cooled too slowly at the liquidus temperature.) The spaces in the silicate network will close somewhat, and the glass at T_2 will be denser than it was at T_1 (this is quite a different process from that of thermal contraction, which also brings about a slight increase in density). If the same glass is cooled *suddenly* from T_1 to T_2, the viscous glass does not have time for the viscous network to compact, and the glass at T_2 has the lower density which would be characteristic of T_1. For this reason, T_1 is known as its *fictive temperature*, and this demonstrates the slight uncertainty about defining the properties of a glass at any particular temperature. This concept appears again, later in the chapter, under transition point (Tg).

Viscosity of molten glass

Glass is generally regarded as being a rigid material, and is recognized as such in everyday use, but depending on the composition of the glass, it becomes plastic at temperatures above circa 900°C, when it can be worked in very many ways, and into a variety of forms. The viscosity of a liquid is a measure of its resistance to flow, but compared with other liquids, molten glass has two special properties: (i) it is very much more viscous than any other liquids, and (ii) it has an enormous viscosity range depending on the temperature. *Figure 1.9* shows a plot of the logarithm of the viscosity against temperature for a wide range of glasses. Each division on the left hand scale represents a 100-fold *change in viscosity*, and the full extent of the scale represents a change of 10^{20}, or one hundred million, million, million times. Water is shown right at

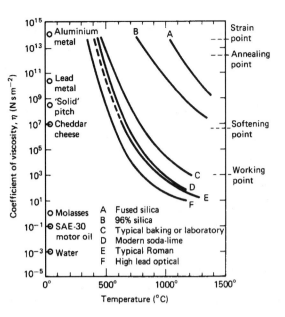

Figure 1.9 Viscosity-temperature curves for various types of glasses. (After Brill, 1962).

the bottom. Treacle (molasses) in a warm room is one thousand times more viscous, but the most fluid glass shown in the diagram (at point F) is ten times even more viscous; when glass articles are manufactured the viscosity is about ten times even greater.

The viscosity changes with temperature so rapidly that special terms are used to describe its viscosity at various stages in the manufacturing process. *Figure 1.9* shows that the *working point* (10^3 Nsm^{-2}) of a glass is at a viscosity of 1000 Nsm^{-2}, but at the *softening point* (6×10^6 Nsm^{-2}), the glass is 6000 times more viscous than that (when 'soft', it is much too viscous to be worked). At the *annealing point* (5×10^{12}) of the glass it is about a million times even more viscous and the *strain point* is about 10 times more viscous still. There is also a *transition point* which can have a viscosity as much as 1000 times higher than even strain point (5×10^{13}), and is discussed later in the chapter. The working range is the difference in temperature between the *working point* and the softening point, and thus it can be seen why neither fused silica (A), nor 96 per cent silica (B), can have a working range within ordinary furnace temperatures. (In fact special kinds of electric furnace are required to process those very hard glasses on a commercial basis, for example, in making fused silica crucibles, or other highly special chemical apparatus.) There are also marked differences in behaviour between different types of glass. Glass C (a laboratory type borosilicate glass) has a working range of 370°C, whereas glass F (high lead optical glass) has a working range of only 220°, but that is in the temperature range 580–800° and glass F will cool more slowly than glass C, which has a temperature range of 830–1220°. Glass C has a wider range in which it can be manipulated, but it also loses heat more rapidly and may therefore have to be re-heated in the furnace *glory hole* more frequently. Thus both the working range, and the actual temperature, have to be considered when fashioning glass articles. Glass C is referred to as a *hard glass* because it requires a higher temperature for working. It has been suggested that the viscosity of glass might be explained by theories of thermodynamics based on the interaction of thermally excited sound waves within fluids.

Because the viscosity increases continuously with decreasing temperature, without the discontinuity of melting which is so characteristic of crystals, it has been suggested that cold glass should show plastic flow if measured over very long periods of time. Cold glass under tension does not flow at room temperature, because irreversible flow of glass at room temperature requires a stress of at least one-tenth of the theoretical breaking strength of the glass, whereas commercial glasses have so many surface defects that they fracture under tensile stresses of only one-hundredth of the theoretical breaking strength. There is actually no evidence for the supposed cold flow of glass under its own weight, because many of the alleged examples are actually statistical (Newton, 1996).

The process of *annealing* glass (controlled cooling to relieve the internal stresses which are formed because the thermal conductivity of hot glass is low) is actually an example of slow plastic flow of glass when the viscosity is in the range 10^{11} to 10^{13} Nsm^{-2}, corresponding to temperatures of the order of 500°C. When a glass object is formed, the outside surfaces cool very rapidly, become stiff and contracts thermally, long before the inside

cools. The thicker the glass, the greater the difference in cooling rate between the surface and the interior. The subsequent internal contraction puts the surfaces into a great state of compression, resulting in a mechanically unstable condition. Thus, unless glass is cooled slowly (*annealed*), it will contain internal (frozen) strains which may cause it to shatter spontaneously (Lillie, 1936).

An extreme case of frozen strains in glass is that of Prince Rupert's Drops (*Lacymae Batavicae*; *Larmes de Verre*; or Tears Glass). The tadpole-shaped pieces of glass were named after Prince Rupert, a nephew of Charles I of England, who produced the glass drops in 1661 (Moody, 1988). They are made by dropping a gather of *molten* glass (not merely hot glass), into cold water. The sudden chilling of the glass by the water freezes the outside, while the fluid inside contracts so strongly that a space, containing a *vacuum, not an air bubble*), forms in the centre. The compressed outside will resist blows with a hammer, but the breaking of the tail, or even scratching of the surface, will cause the whole object to shatter.

Anelasticity

Glass is also described as *anelastic*, because it possesses internal friction, and absorbs energy when vibrated. Thus, when a glass vessel is lightly struck the walls can vibrate and may emit a musical note. The vibrations die away because the alkali metal ions in the spaces of the silicate network absorb energy when they jump from one vacancy in the network to another, producing internal friction. There are generally two absorption peaks, the one at the lower temperature being due to the motion of the alkali ions in the network whereas the second one, at a higher temperature, is associated with the diffusion of oxygen ions (Mohyuddin and Douglas, 1960). Different alkalis have different temperatures at which the first peak occurs; thus lithium ions have this peak at about –50° C, sodium ions absorb energy at about –20°C, and potassium ions at about +30°C. However, at room temperatures, i.e. below 30°C, potassium ions move easily and less energy is absorbed, so that the musical note can be heard for longer; potash–lead–crystal wine glasses can ring for a second or so, when lightly struck. In the case of sodium ions, the energy is absorbed at room temperature and below, so that the glass does not ring when struck.

Thermal expansion

The vast majority of materials expand when they are heated. Glasses have a somewhat small coefficient of linear thermal expansion in the range $0.5–1.0 \times 10^{-7}$ per degree C, which can actually be calculated from their chemical composition. Silica itself has the lowest expansion (with a value of only 0.05 in terms of the values given above) whereas the majority of the other constituents have values in the region of 1.7, except for the alkali oxides, which have by far the largest contribution, being 4.32 for soda and 3.90 for potash. Thus the thermal expansion of a glass depends greatly on the amount of alkali oxide in it. In theory therefore, ancient glasses will have higher rates of expansion than modern glass. In particular, the low silica, high lime, high potash medieval glasses will have about twice the expansion of modern soda–lime glasses.

Transition point (Tg)

Figure 1.10 shows a representative thermal expansion curve (curve A) for a glass which had been chilled suddenly after forming, before it had had time to adopt the somewhat more ordered structure of the glassy state. When heated, it has the large expansion value (0.8×10^{-7}) typical of a liquid (having disordered molecules), At about 500°C the molecules have achieved enough freedom to become more ordered, and the expansion falls, until the random (liquid) state has been fully reached. Curve B represents a well-annealed glass, well below the glass transition temperature (see also the discussion of fictive temperature, earlier in this chapter). It can be seen that the curve has a lower starting value (0.2) and a fairly constant slope (both characteristic of a solid) up to a temperature of about 580°C. There is then a relatively sudden increase in expansion to values that correspond to those of a liquid, as the structure becomes more random.

Optical properties

Apart from certain single crystals, such as rock crystal, naturally occurring solids are not transparent, transparency being more a characteristic of a liquid, than that of the solid state. Glass being amorphous is more akin to a liquid, which is structurally the same as an indefinite molecule. Ordinary glasses transmit visible light and also some ultra-violet and infra-red light (to which they are transparent). If the wavelengths (i.e., the frequencies) of the incoming radiation are in resonance with the frequencies of the molecular vibrations within the glass, the radiation is absorbed and the glass is said to be opaque.

Glass also has unique optical properties. For example it can transmit images in an enlarged or diminished form, or invert them. A broken or cut glass surface can reflect light in the colours of the spectrum, (when the glass causes the light to rebound from its surface). Glass actually reduces the velocity of light which travels through itself, and hence a convex piece of glass can cause the emerging light to appear as if it had come from a different direction (i.e. the light is *refracted*). This refractive effect is measured by the *refractive index* (RI) of the glass, and characteristic refractive indices are listed in *Table 1.2*. (Technically, the RI is calculated from the ratio of the sine of the angle of the incident ray to the sine of the angle of the refracted ray, when the light is refracted from a vacuum.)

The *index of dispersion* of a transparent material is a measure of the extent to which the RI changes with the wavelength (colour) of the light; for example, it determines the width of the spectrum produced by a prism of the material in question. Also, the image

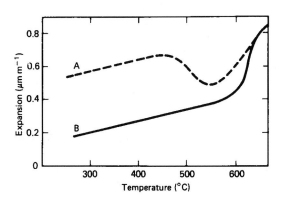

Figure 1.10 Thermal expansion of (A) a chilled sample and (B) an annealed sample of the same glass.

Table 1.2   Comparative refractive indices of some transparent materials

Material	Refractive index
Diamond	2.4173
Glass	1.5–1.7
Quartz (fused)	1.458
Ethanol (at 25°C)	1.359
Water (at 25°C)	1.332
Air (at 0°C and 760 mm)	1.000 293

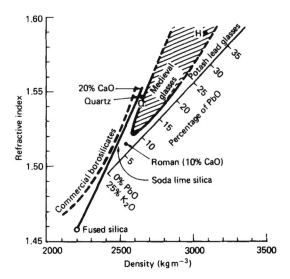

Figure 1.11 Graph showing the relationships between density and refractive index for various types of glass. Point H is the poorly durable glass H in Figure 4.18.

produced by a simple lens can be coloured because it also acts slightly as a prism, but the effect can be eliminated by making a compound lens from two pieces of glass, having different dispersions. If the composition of the glass is known, the index of dispersion can be calculated. Thus it tends to be correlated with the RI, and a cut lead crystal drinking glass is attractive because it has both high refraction and high dispersion.

A knowledge of the RI may be relevant in the conservation of transparent glasses. When joining two pieces of glass the RI of the adhesive should ideally match that of the glass, and the join would then disappear completely from view (see *Tables 1.2* and *5.2; Figure 5.1*). In the case of some ancient glasses the RI would have to be specially determined, and the cost of doing that might therefore have to be considered.

Density
The density (mass per unit volume) of glasses can fall within a very wide range, from 2400 to 5900 kg m^{-3}, depending on their composition (*Figure 1.11*), being related to the RI. Certain glasses containing lead have a very high density. SI units tend to be cumbersome, and hence it is useful to refer to the *specific gravity* (i.e., the relative density, compared to water, where the density is 1.000). Scholes (1929) lists density factors for soda–lime–silica glasses. Huggins and Sun (1946) showed how the density can be calculated from the chemical composition of the glass.

Hardness
The property of hardness cannot be defined easily, because it depends on several other properties of the material (whether it is also

brittle, elastic, plastic, etc.). A useful reference is the Mohs scale of hardness, which is based on the fact that each material is softer (and therefore scratched by) all others harder than it (i.e. having a higher number in the scale): 1, talc; 2, gypsum; 3, calcite; 4, fluorite; 5, apatite; 6, orthoclase; 7, quartz; 8, topaz; 9, corundum; 10, diamond. Depending on their composition, glasses occupy positions between 4.5 and 6.5 on the scale. The terms hard and soft can, however, be used in other ways in connection with glass. High-lead glasses are sometimes called soft because they are easier to cut and engrave. Hard glass can also refer to that which does not stain easily with silver.

Brittleness
Glass is brittle and fractures easily but, when it is newly formed, and has a perfect surface, it is extremely strong due to the nature of its inter-atomic bonding. In practice, however, defects arise very easily on the surface merely by the action of atmospheric moisture, or from extremely slight abrasion, or even by slight pressure (*Figure 1.12*). These defects concentrate any applied stress at the apex of the defect (*Figure 1.13*) in a way that is extremely

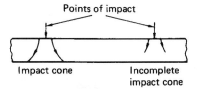

Figure 1.12 Section through impact cones on damaged glass.

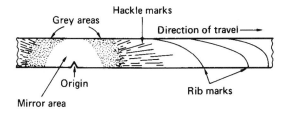

Figure 1.13 Diagnostic markings on the edges of fractured glass.

damaging. Under such stress, the strong bonds break and fracture occurs, so that the effective strength of glass in tension is only about one-hundredth of the theoretical strength. This ability of glass to fracture easily has been put to use since ancient times, by chipping and flaking obsidian and lumps of cold, solid glass to form artefacts.

Fractures on glass can be visually analysed to determine their origins and the directions in which they were propagated. Fractures that occurred rapidly, at about 2 km/s are easier to study than those that propagated at a rate of only a few millimetres per century. At the actual origin of a recent crack the broken edge bears a characteristic *mirror area* which is surrounded by *grey areas, hackle marks,* and, finally, *rib marks,* which indicate the direction in which the fracture travelled. Murgatroyd (1942) observed that rib marks are always curved, and that their convex faces show the direction in which the crack grew. If the glass has broken due to excessive heating, the rib marks are well spaced on the cold side, but are crowded together on the heated side. If the outside of a vessel has been given a sharp blow, the area which received the blow may be crushed, with a surrounding ring of cracks forming an *impact cone.*

2

Historical development of glassmaking

The natural glass obsidian occurs in all volcanic regions of the world, and since Palaeolithic times was fashioned into tools, weapons and objects of trade, by primitive peoples (see *Figure 1.1*). On the basis of chemical analysis of obsidian artefacts, and of material from volcanic flows, it has been possible to assign a provenance to many artefacts; and to determine the trade routes along which obsidian artefacts were disseminated. Obsidian is highly durable glass, and consequently does not at present pose any conservation problems.

The date and place of origin of man-made glass may never be known precisely; but it is generally agreed to have originated in northern Mesopotamia (Iraq) prior to *circa* 2500 BC. However, in ancient times, the mouth of the River Belus in Phoenicia (now the River Naaman in Israel) was associated with glassmaking for many centuries. The association of the River Belus with glassmaking, was mentioned by the Roman historian Pliny (AD 23–79), who drew much information from Greek sources (themselves a mixture of first-hand information and legend; Greek mercenaries, travellers and writers were visitors to the eastern Mediterranean from the seventh century BC). The account by Pliny (AD 77) concerning glassmaking has been so misquoted, that it is given here in full:

> That part of Syria which is known as Phoenicia and borders on Judea contains a swamp called Candebia on the lower slopes of Mount Carmel. This is believed to be the source of the River Belus, which, after traversing a distance of five miles, flows into the sea

near the colony of Ptolemais (Akko). Its current is sluggish and its waters unwholesome to drink, although they are regarded as holy for ritual purposes. The river is muddy and flows in a deep channel, revealing its sands only when the tide ebbs. For it is not until they have been tossed by the waves and cleansed of impurities that they glisten. Moreover, it is only at that moment, when they are thought to be affected by the sharp, astringent properties of the brine, that they become fit for use. The beach stretches for not more than half a mile, and yet for many centuries the production of glass depended on this area alone. There is a story that once a ship belonging to some traders in natural soda put in here and that they scattered along the shore to prepare a meal. Since, however, no stones suitable for supporting their cauldrons were forthcoming, they rested them on lumps of soda from their cargo. When these became heated and were completely mingled with the sand on the beach a strange translucent liquid flowed forth in streams; and this, it is said, was the origin of glass. (Engle, 1973a; Newton, 1985b)

According to the Roman historian Josephus, 'numbers of ships are continually coming to take away cargoes of this sand, but it never grows less'. Similar statements were made about the sand at the mouth of the River Volturnus (north of Naples in Italy).

Analysis of the sand from the River Belus have confirmed its substantial lime content (8.7 per cent CaO), which would enable stable glass to be made in the absence of any instruction to add lime, (which was not actually specified as an ingredient for glassmaking until *circa* AD 1780).

Throughout historical time man-made glass has been regarded as a special material, and it is not difficult to see why this should have been so, since glass must have seemed to have had magical origins. To take sand and plant ashes and, by submitting them to the transmuting agencies of fire, produce coloured liquids which, whilst cooling, could be shaped into an infinite variety of forms and textures, which would solidify into a transparent material with the appearance of 'solid water', and which was smooth and cool to the touch, was, and still is, the magic of the glassworker's art. Glass can be fashioned into many shapes in ways that are not possible with any other material. It has unique optical properties: for example, glass can transmit images in an enlarged or diminished form, or invert them; a broken or cut glass surface can reflect light in the colours of the spectrum. Certain types of glass are especially appealing, particularly lead crystal glass by virtue of its weight, its great clarity, its ring when lightly struck, and when cut, the sparkle and colours which arise as a result of its high refractive index and dispersion.

In consequence of the supposed magical properties of glass and the technological secrets associated with its production, glassmakers were often granted a higher social status than was given to other craftsmen; and from time to time throughout history, special legislation was passed for their benefit. In ancient Egypt for example, glass was regarded as being more precious than gemstones. During the first phase of the Roman Empire, when the best glass was being made in Syria, the Syrian glassmakers were regarded as *Cives Romani* (Roman citizen). Once glassmaking had been established throughout the Near East and the West, measures were being taken to safeguard the technological secrets of the trade. For instance, in medieval France glassmaking methods could only be passed on through the male line, and then only between members of a few specific families such as Hennezal, Thietry, Thisac and Bisseval. In 1369 Duke John I of Lorraine granted letters of privilege to glassmakers to encourage them to settle in Lorraine; and in 1448 Jean de Calabre granted a charter to the makers of glass in the Forest of Darney in the Vosges. The Italian city of Venice became an important glass centre in the middle of the eleventh century when glassmakers from Constantinople settled there to make the mosaics for San Marco. The glassmakers of Venice eventually became so powerful that they were able to form a guild in 1220; emigration of guild members was forbidden on pain of death (Forbes, 1966).

Another privilege, this time for glass vendors, existed in England in 1579, where laws were in force against rogues and vagabonds, but 'glass men of good behaviour' were exempt from prosecution if they possessed a licence from three justices of the peace (Charleston, 1967). The restriction of the secrets of glassmaking to certain specified families, or craft communities, has led to the perpetuation of glass terminology which has been handed down not merely over generations, but over centuries. Glassmakers along the Phoenician coast in the first to sixth centuries AD were using terms similar to those used in Babylonia in the seventh century BC and, following a study of sixteenth-century Italian glassmaking texts, Engle (1973b) suggested that some of the early glassmaking families of Europe may have originated in areas where Aramaic was spoken. In addition, family names in Hebrew, Flemish, French and English have been studied with a view to tracing the relationships between glassmaking families as they emigrated from Asia Minor through Sicily, Lombardy, the Rhineland and Lorraine to Britain (Engle, 1974). Freestone (1991) gives an account of glassmaking from Mesopotamian to medieval times. Histories of glassmaking have been produced by Tait (1991) and by Liefkes (1997).

The first glassmakers, 2500–1200 BC

Most authorities claim northern Mesopotamia (Iraq) as the birthplace of glass at a time prior to 2500 BC. Comparatively few glass objects have been excavated there, but this may well be due to the relative humidity of the soil, and to the rise of the water-table in historic times, causing the destruction of much of the early glass which was inherently unstable in its chemical composition (and therefore relatively water-soluble). However, it is known from objects which have survived burial, that coloured vitreous glazes were extensively used in the Jemdet Nasr phase of Mesopotamia, the Badarian civilisation of Egypt, and in the early Aegean in the fourth millennium BC, for covering steatite and sintered quartz beads in imitation of semi-precious stones such as turquoise, lapis lazuli and red jasper; later glass beads were developed for the same purpose. Small objects could be hand-formed or cast using simple tools and finished by abrading. Few glass items are known until the first core-formed vessels were made in western Asia sometime before 1500 BC. The Mesopotamian evidence was summarized by Moorey (1994).

The development of core-forming was the technological breakthrough which produced the first glass vessels, and which thereby allowed glassmaking to become an industry in its own right. This may have developed from the technique of winding glass around a core to form glass beads, but the connection is unproven. Not long after the core forming technique was discovered, polychrome vessels began to be made of mosaic glass (dating mainly from *circa* 1350–1250 BC). These were formed of pieces of monochrome opaque glass, fused together and subsequently shaped around a core or possibly slumped over or into a form. Fragments of mosaic glass recovered from a palace site to the west of Baghdad were made of sections of multi-coloured mosaic canes. Inlaid panels from the same site were formed by pressing turquoise blue and white glass into a red glass base whilst the glass was still in a pasty state, to form patterns and birds. Occasionally marbled glass was produced in imitation of veined stone.

Contemporary with the core-formed and mosaic glass vessels are a wide variety of monochrome or polychrome objects, including beads of many different types, jewellery inserts, plain and decorated pendants, furniture inlays and figurines of deities, demons and animals. Many of these were made in moulds, but there is no contemporary evidence to show whether the glass was poured into open moulds or whether moulds were pressed down onto lumps of soft glass on a flat surface.

During the later sixteenth and fifteenth centuries BC, glassmaking evolved rapidly in northern Mesopotamia. Mesopotamian glass vessels have been excavated over a wide area of the Middle and Near East: Persia (Iran), Elam and Babylonia in the east to Syria and Palestine on the Mediterranean coast; and at other centres of Late Bronze Age civilization in Cyprus and Mycenaean Greece.

During this period, the Levant played an important part in the trade in raw glass and in finished products. The Levant was the area stretching from ancient Antioch (Antakya in modern Turkey), down the coast of Syria, Phoenicia (modern Lebanon), Palestine/Israel, and included the island of Cyprus. Very few glass vessels have been found on Late Bronze Age (Mycenaean) sites in Greece. Exclusive to that area however, are ornaments of translucent glass, mainly bright blue, and normally with flat backs and suspension holes, and dating from 1400–1200 BC (Nightingale, 1998). The almost exclusive use of bright blue glass suggests that it was imported, probably from Egypt, as analysis has shown that the compositions of the Mycenaean glass is the same as the blue glass being used in Egypt at that time (Shortland, 1999). The blue glass was sometimes used in combination with gold foil. Steatite moulds in which the ornaments were made by pressing the glass into them, have been found on many sites. Glass, ivory and gold were used as inlays for luxury items of personal ornamentation, palace furnishings and weapons.

The Egyptian glassmaking industry began in the fifteenth century BC, about the same time glass starts to be mentioned in Mesopotamian cuneiform tablets. From *circa* 1450 BC the Egyptian pharaoh Tuthmosis III made military conquests in Syria and up to the Mesopotamian borders, and it is possible that as a result of this contact, Asiatic glassworkers were sent to Egypt to found the glassmaking industry there. Glassworking complexes were established at Malkat in the early fourteenth century, at Tell el-Amarna, the new capital city of Akhenaton (Amenhotep IV, *c.* 1352–1336 BC) and at el-Lisht, an early twelfth-century necropolis. Glass was not produced in any quantity until the reign of Amenophis III onwards (*c.* 1390 BC). This is far later than in neighbouring countries, which is surprising in view of the Egyptians' mastery of manufacturing techniques. Individual glass beads, probably manufacturing aberrations of glazed composition, were made a thousand years earlier, and a few scarabs are known from *circa* 1900 BC. Moreover, the basic material – an alkaline calcium silicate– is the same as that of the glaze produced in pre-Dynastic Badarian period (*c.* 4000 BC) to coat stone beads, and later in the manufacture of glazed composition. The only difference is that glass was not used to produce objects in its own right. The Egyptian term for glass was *iner en wedeh* or *aat wedhet*, both meaning 'stone of the kind that flows'.

One of the earliest glass vessels known is a small turquoise blue jug from the tomb of Tuthmosis III, with an elaborate yellow and white patterning of stylized tamarisk trees, threads, dots and scales incorporating a hieroglyphic text with the prenomen Menkheperre (British Museum, London) (*Figure 2.1*).

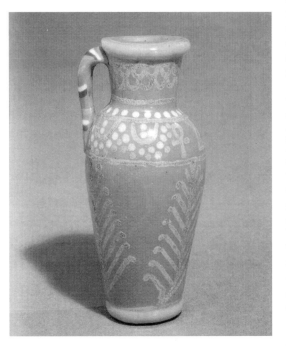

Figure 2.1 One-handled jug bearing the name of Tuthmosis III (c.1504–1450 BC). Opaque light blue, with yellow, white and dark blue opaque trails, and white and yellow powdered glass fired on. Core-formed, with ground and polished surface, on rim and underneath the base. Intact and unweathered; some bubbles and sandy impurities in the glass. H 88 mm, GD 38 mm. Second quarter of the fifteenth century BC. Egypt. (© Copyright The British Museum).

Egyptian glass is the most common type known from this period, many examples having been found in the tombs of the Eighteenth (1570–1293 BC) and Nineteenth (1293–1185 BC) Dynasties. The vessels are small and served mostly for holding perfumes and ointments or as tomb gifts and cult objects, and copy the shapes of contemporary vessels of pottery, stone and faience. These richly coloured vessels are almost opaque, due as much to the desire to imitate semi-precious stones in glass as to the technological limitations. Core-forming persisted as an important glassmaking technique for many centuries.

The glassmaking industry reached its peak in the mid-fourteenth century, both in western Asia and Egypt, but continued to flourish and spread until *circa* 1200 BC. For all practical purposes glassmaking then came to an end when Egypt and Syria were invaded by the Philistines. With the downfall of the various kingdoms under the impact of the invaders, there was no longer a market for the fine and expensively produced glass articles. There is an almost total absence of glass finds from the end of the second and the beginning of the first millennia BC.

This phase in ancient history is marked by the eclipse of the great empires and the emergence and migratory movements of new peoples and tribes, in the Aegean and Near East. Not until the resurgence of the great empires in the eighth and seventh centuries BC was there again the necessary stability and concentration of wealth and resources for the renewed production of glass. Yet glassmaking expertise must have continued somewhere, because the re-emergence of the demand in the eighth century BC, brought about the manufacture of articles by all four of the earlier techniques with increasing degrees of sophistication in Egypt, Mesopotamia and elsewhere

Western Asia and the Mediterranean *circa* 900–300 BC

The resurgence of the glass industry in the ninth century BC took place against a background of cultural revival that affected the whole of Western Asia, the Levant and the Mediterranean world. The earliest use of glass

Figure 2.2 Core-formed vessels for cosmetics and scented oils from Mediterranean workshops operating between 550 and 50 BC, together with an earlier Mesopotamian example (front). (© V&A Picture Library).

on a large scale in the Iron Age was as inlays, often in ivory plaques and panels used to decorate furniture. The glass inlays were either monochrome, different shades of blue as well as red, green or yellow, sometimes with cold painted or possible enamelled designs, or of polychrome glass forming rosettes, circles and square patterns. Glass inlays in ivory plaques were all of monochrome glass, and most have been assigned to craftsmen in Phoenicia (Lebanon) on stylistic grounds. In the tenth or eleventh century BC, glass beads were being made in the delta of the River Po, showing that glass technology had reached Italy.

Vessels, also of monochrome glass, began to be made around the middle of the eighth century BC, and were made by the lost wax method, or the technique of slumping softened glass into moulds. Polychrome glass vessels were made by the core-forming technique, but although mosaic inlays were made, mosaic glass vessels were very rare until

the late third century BC. A class of luxury vessels in greenish or yellowish or natural green monochrome glass was produced at this time, possibly in Phoenicia. Drinking vessels, mostly in the form of hemispherical bowls, were made in the eighth and seventh centuries BC. These were probably made by the slumping process and undecorated or with simple decoration of horizontal cut grooves or ridges, or rarely, with geometric patterns or glass inlays. A group of tall perfume flasks (*alabastra*) were probably made by the lost wax process and shaped by grinding and abrading; a squat example bearing the name of the Assyrian king Sargon II (721–705 BC) is one of a series which were produced during the seventh, sixth and possibly the fifth centuries.

In the mid-eighth century BC, core forming was revived in Mesopotamia, most notably in the form of *alabastra*, but the products were dull compared with those produced in the Bronze Age. Mesopotamian core-formed vessels reached other countries, notably Persia (Iran) where they seem to have led to the establishment of a local industry at Susa; the island of Rhodes (Greece); and Italy (Etruria) in the seventh and sixth centuries BC.

The core-formed products of Mediterranean workshops in production *circa* 550–50 BC were the most numerous and widespread. Shapes were copied from Greek vases in pottery and metal, the most common forms being *alabastra, amphoriskoi, araballoi* and *oinochoai* (jugs) made of dark blue glass decorated with white, yellow and turquoise glass trailed, combed into patterns of zigzags, festoons or feather patterns (*Figure 2.2*). The vessels were used as containers for perfumes, scented oils and cosmetics; and were widely traded, as far as the Black Sea, the Balkans and Gaul (France). The final flowering of the Mediterranean core-forming industry took place in the late Hellenistic period, between the second half of the second century and the mid first century BC. Only the *alabasta* and *amphoriskoi* were made and these were smaller than those produced earlier. The majority have been excavated in Syria, Palestine and Cyprus, where they were probably made. Others were imported into Egypt, where a renaissance in all branches of the arts took place during the Saite Twenty-Sixth Dynasty (c. 664–525 BC). The technique of inlaying glass into another material re-emerged during the reign of Amasis (c. 570–526 BC). During the fifth and fourth centuries BC, clear greenish or colourless glass bowls with cut decoration copying metal vessels, were made in the Persian Empire. Some may have been produced in the western provinces in Asia Minor (Turkey). In the fifth and fourth centuries BC yellowish and greenish clear glass was also being made in Greece. Excavations in Olympia in the workshop of the Greek sculptor Phidias show that glass was being cast into clay moulds.

Hellenistic glass, *circa* 325 BC to AD 400

During the Hellenistic Period (late fourth to second century BC), new shapes and decorations were introduced into core manufacture, although there was a decline in aesthetic

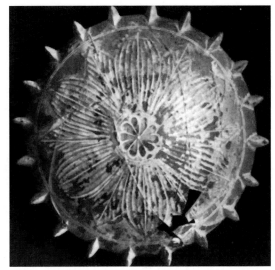

Figure 2.3 Deep bowl with band of bosses. Greenish colourless glass, now with an iridescent and flaking surface. Cast in a two-piece mould and finished by cutting and grinding; the bosses are in relief and the remainder of the design is in antaglio. H 92 mm, D 205 mm. Late third century BC. Canosa, Apulia, Italy. (© Copyright The British Museum).

quality, and in the production of glass in Mesopotamia. Contemporaneously, there were major developments in glassmaking, both from technical and artistic points of view, notably of engraved gold leaf enclosed between two layers of glass, mosaic and cameo glass techniques. In this period there appear the hemispherical mould-cast bowls made of transparent, almost colourless glass, in the Assyrian tradition. These bowls were lathe-finished and mostly decorated with moulded and/or cut ribs and lines in imitation of their metal prototypes (*Figure 2.3*). Outstanding among this type of bowl are the sandwich-gold glass vessels dating from the late third century AD (*Figure 2.4*). These were formed of two glass bowls enclosing gold leaf decoration, which were ground and polished with such precision that the outer glass fitted so perfectly over the inner that no adhesive or fusion was required to hold them together); others may have been fused at the rim. Only a few sandwich bowls have been found, and although distributed over a wide area, from the north Caucasus, central Anatolia and Italy,

Figure 2.4 A bowl of sandwich gold glass. Canosa, Apulia, Italy. Found in a tomb with seven other vessels. *Circa* 275–200 BC.

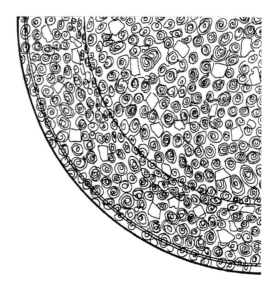

Figure 2.5 Segment of a large plate of mosaic glass, formed from sections of multicoloured canes interspersed with segments of yellow, opaque white or occasionally gold foil sandwiched between two colourless layers. H 50 mm, D 308 mm. Late third century BC. Canosa, Apulia, Italy.

it is generally accepted that they were made in Alexandria.

The technique of producing *mosaic glass* was difficult and complex, the required design being built up from canes of variously coloured glass into a slab of material (see *Figure 3.10*). When heated and pulled from both ends the slab could be drawn out into a long rod, which retained the original sectional design in miniaturized form along its whole length. The rod was then cut into small sections in which the design recurred each time. The discs were used as inlays for walls and furniture, or fashioned into beads and various kinds of jewellery. Also, as mentioned above, patterned sections were arranged in moulds and fused together. The resulting vessels, mostly small cups and bowls, transmit light with a polychrome brilliancy (*Figure 2.5*). Sometimes sections of coloured rods were fused together to create variegated patches in the body of the glass; or thin threads of glass were twisted into rods which were then fused together in moulds to form elaborate vessels of lace glass.

Vessels and plaques made by the cameo technique were composed of two or more layers of glass. The upper layers were then cut away to reveal the base colour, which then formed a background to the relief design of mythological figures, vine leaves and other motifs of Hellenistic art. However, much of the celebrated cameo glass, such as the Portland Vase and Auldjo Jug (British Museum,

London), is of the early Imperial period, dating from the late first century BC/early first century AD) (see *Figures 3.19* and *7.20*).

All the techniques mentioned above are thought to have been either invented or perfected in Alexandria, the cultural and industrial centre of Hellenistic civilization, founded by Alexander the Great in 332 BC. Despite the considerable information about Alexandria as a glass centre, only a small amount of glass has been found there. The scarcity of glass in places where glass must have been abundant seems to be due to the fact that broken glass was often collected and re-melted as cullet to form new glass batches.

There were other important glass-manufacturing centres in this period, some with long traditions of glassmaking. Those mentioned by the Roman historian Pliny the Elder include Sidon in Lebanon, Acre and the area around the mouth of the River Belus north of the Mount Carmel range in Israel, Campania in Italy, Gaul and Spain. In addition to Alexandria, the Roman historian Strabo mentions glassmaking in Rome; and the first century poet Martial refers to a hawker from across the River Tiber (in Rome), who bartered sulphur matches for broken glass.

Glass of the Roman Empire, AD 100–400

The invention of glass-blowing

Around the turn of the millennium, glass-blowing was invented, probably in the Syrio-Palestinian area long associated with glassmaking. Despite the fact that glass-blowing revolutionized the production of glass vessels, no mention was made of it by contemporary writers. Glass-blowing turned glass into a cheap commodity, which could be mass produced; and no doubt provided the stimulus for the proliferation of glasshouses throughout the Roman Empire.

At its height, the Roman Empire included the countries which are now the United Kingdom (except Northern Ireland), France, Spain, Portugal, parts of the Netherlands, Germany, Belgium, Switzerland, Eastern Europe, Greece, Turkey, the Middle East and North Africa. Thus all the major glassmaking centres came under the domination of Rome. In addition the art of glassmaking was spread and important centres established throughout the Empire. However, the glass production remained essentially Roman, with only minor regional variations until the collapse of the Roman Empire in the West soon after AD 400 (Lemke, 1998). Thus glass dating from the first to the fourth centuries AD may more accurately be described as Roman than, for instance, Spanish or Gallic (Harden *et al.*, 1968; Von Saldern, 1974, Tait, 1991). Glass ceased to be exclusively a luxury product, the styles became largely simple and functional, and in fact glass became more widely used for domestic purposes during the Roman period than at any subsequent time or place until the nineteenth century. Glass containers were particularly valued as shipping and storage containers because they were light, transparent, reusable and did not impart a taste to their contents.

Glasses were packed in straw to survive long journeys by land and sea. Some containers were square-shaped for easier packing (*Figure 2.6*). Besides the utilitarian glassware,

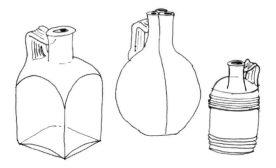

Figure 2.6   A mould-blown square bottle of the type commonly used to transport liquids, later first or second century AD; a blown triple-bodied flask, probably third–fourth century AD; and a mould-blown, barrel-shaped jug, third century AD. All made in Western workshops: the bottle and jug were found at Faversham, Kent, South Eastern England. H of bottle 20 cm.

mould-blown bottles were widely made, in fanciful shapes such as animals, human heads, fruit, sea-shells and as souvenirs of gladiatorial contests. Some glassmakers incorporated their names in their moulds, the best known being that of Ennion, a Sidonian who emigrated to Italy (Harden, 1969a). At the same time that utilitarian glassware was becoming commonplace, some of the most lavish glass ever made was being produced, for example, the gold-sandwich glasses. Many Roman glassworkers sought to imitate rock crystal with clear glass, and other semi-precious materials. Layered stones, such as those used for producing cameos, were imitated in glass and carved in high relief. Techniques of cold painting, enamelling and gilding on glass were also highly developed. Other vessels were decorated with scratched or wheel-abraded designs. Other products of the Roman glasshouses were jewellery, window-panes, lamps, mirrors, mosaic *tesserae*, cast glass panels imitating jasper, porphyry and marble, and *opus sectile* (panels made up of flat glass pieces and set in mortar). A survey of glasses taken to be lenses has shown that their focal length was too short to have improved sight; their most probable use was as magnifying aids for engravers.

In the third century, glassmaking reached a peak, both in quantity and quality of products. During the third and fourth centuries Egypt

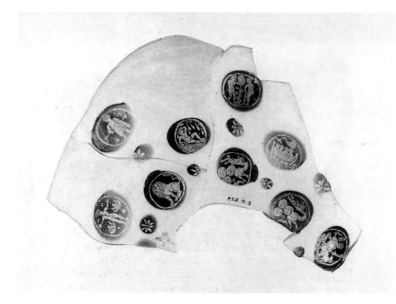

Figure 2.7 *Fondi d'oro* bowl fragment with emerald green blobs, and with gold decoration within the inner faces of the blobs and the outer surface of the colourless glass bowl. Greatest dimensions: 10 mm (smaller portion), 168 mm (larger portion). Second half of the fourth century AD. From St Severin's parish, Cologne. (© Copyright The British Museum).

also had a considerable blown glass industry, which had not existed there previously. A large number of blown glass vessels with local stylistic features such as the fashioning of the bases, was found in the excavations at Karanis (Harden, 1936). It is interesting to note that the Emperor Aurelian (AD 270–275) had imposed a duty on Egyptian glass imported to Rome, presumably to offset its cheapness. The success of the industry meant that it became subject to heavy taxation at various times. The Emperor Alexander Severus (AD 222–235) imposed taxes on all artisans. In the following century, the Emperor Constantine (AD 337) eased the burden of taxation in order that the *vitrearii* could perfect their skills and bring up their sons in the family crafts.

Until the turn of the third century AD there is evidence of strong continuous links between glassmakers in the Middle East and the West, largely formed as a result of the migration of workers, mainly in the east to west direction. Contemporary literary sources mention Syrian glass manufacturers working in the Roman provinces; and glassmakers' quarters were established in every large city. During the first century AD glass-blowing was introduced to the glassmaking district of Campania (the province around Naples); and many blown vessels have been found at Pompeii and Herculaneum, both of which were destroyed by the eruption of Vesuvius in AD 79. The accurate dating of ancient vessels is often made difficult by the fact that much of it does not have a recorded provenance and was not recovered from excavations. However, the wealth of glass objects found in use in Pompeii at the time of the eruption, shows the repertory of glass vessels current in the third quarter of the first century AD. (Much of the glass from these sites has been recovered from the cemeteries, and is therefore much older than that buried during the eruption of Vesuvius in AD 79.) New glassmaking centres arose in the north of Italy in the valley of the River Po, and at Aquileia on the Adriatic coast. From northern Italy, glass was exported as far as Britain.

A group of distinctive vessels appeared in the fourth century AD. These were the polygonal bottles (mainly hexagonal and octagonal), either without handles or with a single handle, and bearing moulded symbols on the sides. The most familiar and prominent of these symbols was the seven-branched candlestick (*menorah*) of the Jewish faith, while others were an arch supported by two columns (apparently symbolizing the Temple portals), palm trees and branches, and other designs of uncertain significance. Although the exact provenance of the polygonal bottles is unknown, it is generally supposed that they

Figure 2.8 Flask of greenish glass, with blue enamel-like weathering and flaking. On the body, three winding applied 'snake' coils, flattened and bearing a criss-cross design, ending in a triangular head. H 155 mm, D (rim) 30 mm, D (body) 81 mm. Late second century AD. Idalium, Cyprus.

Figure 2.9 Flask of greenish colourless glass, applied coloured threads on the body. Similar to that shown in Figure 2.8, but found in the Rhineland. H 213 mm. Third century AD. Cologne.

were first produced in Palestine. Bottles almost identical in shape but with Christian symbols are also known. Apparently both types of vessel were made in one workshop but provided with different symbols according to the religion of the customer.

Other glass objects with religious symbols were the gold-glass bases (Ital. *fondi d'oro*) in which a gold leaf etched or painted with a design was enclosed between two layers of glass (*Figure 2.7*). The technique was popular in Romano-Byzantine times, and was used almost exclusively for religious iconography, both Jewish and Christian. (Many gold-glass vessels were embedded in the walls of the catacombs outside Rome, where they acted as grave markers.) Religious symbols also appear on a category of objects of a personal character, such as bracelets and amulets, stamped with representations of *menorah*, lions, frogs, human masks, and also elaborate scenes and inscriptions.

Fashion and innovations spread with the continuous traffic of glassmakers with the result that types of glass originally made in the East began to be produced in the West.

Especially noteworthy are the two groups made from the second century onwards in the Rhenish centre of Cologne. One of these includes vessels with cut and engraved decoration. The other group bears the type of decoration known as snake thread trailing (*Figure 2.8*), which began to be made in Syria in the late second century and then, about one hundred years later, appeared in a somewhat altered form in the Rhineland and in Britain (*Figure 2.9*), the Western examples often bearing trailed decoration of a different colour from that of the body of the vessel (Harden, 1969b).

By the middle of the fourth century, no doubt as a result of the division of the Roman Empire, East–West contact effectively ceased, and the different glassmaking centres developed their own glass styles. Glassmaking thus became less international, and more provincial, so that regional types of mould-blown, cut- and thread-decorated glasses are found within a limited range of distribution. For example, the Syrian double unguent bottle is later than fourth century, and is not found in the West. In due course the regional styles developed into the glass types of the Teutonic north on the one hand, and the Syrian, Iranian and Egyptian styles of the Islamic period on the other.

Roman Gaul had a flourishing glass industry; some glass was already being made in Gaul before the influx of Sidonian and Alexandrian immigrants. One of the Gallic factories made cylindrical bottles, which were stamped on the base with the name Frontinius or its abbreviated form FRON. Although glass was imported to Britain during the Roman occupation, there is archaeological evidence that it was also manufactured locally at London, Colchester, Wroxeter and Mancetter, on a modest scale. Production would mainly have been of simple vessels and bottles, and some window glass. The industry may not have survived long after the Roman departure, or it may have continued in isolated areas.

Islamic countries

Gradually the prominent Mesopotamian and Syrian glassmakers established themselves throughout the Roman Empire, and were again important in the development of Middle Eastern glass, which culminated in the distinctive and sophisticated wares of Islam. With the decline of Rome, the seat of power transferred to Constantinople (Istanbul) in AD 305. Despite its magnificence and importance, Constantinople appears never to have had a tradition of glassmaking. This may be explained by the fact that since it was so close to the established Syrian glasshouses of Tyre and Sidon, there was never any great necessity to set up an independent manufacture when the best glass was so close at hand. It may also be the case that whatever glass was made in Constantinople, closely followed in the Syrian tradition and is not easily identifiable. Glass of the period is similar to that found throughout the Roman Empire, but during the Sassanian period (*c.* 100 BC to AD 600) leading up to the advent of Islam, a tradition of cut glass developed. For this purpose the glass needed to be thicker than for the earlier blown and moulded styles. Cutting generally took the form of facets or geometric patterns and was developed to a very high standard (*Figure 2.10*).

Figure 2.10   Bowl with cut decoration, of thick greenish glass with heavy iridescence. Hemispherical, with a rounded rim and base. Exterior decorated with large circular facets in quincunx; four horizontal bands on the side with one large central facet on the base, making it stable. H 75 mm, D 103 mm. Fifth to sixth century AD. Persian; said to have been found at Amlash.

Glass vessels of the Byzantine period (fourth to seventh centuries AD) demonstrate imagination and great technical skill, but the forms are rather heavy. There is an absence of clear glass, and the coloured glass was not as vivid as had previously been the case, and was generally impure. The vessels were irregular in shape and badly proportioned; the decoration is intricate and over-profuse. Cosmetic vessels in the form of two, sometimes three or even four tubes were widespread in the Near East. The majority of these vessels were found in tombs, usually with the metal spatulas for applying the cosmetics still inside one of the tubes.

Extremely common during this period are the conical cups, which were used as lamps; these were filled with water and oil on which a wick was floated. The lamps were placed in holders or suspended by a chain from the ceiling. Other lamps were in the form of stemmed bowls or cups with a hollow projection in the centre to hold the wick. Similar types, placed in metal holders, were used for lighting in the Middle Ages. Glass was an important element in mosaics, a major art of the Byzantine period. Itinerant mosaicists decorated Byzantine churches in Roman Ravenna, and in mosques in Damascus and Cordoba (Spain) with splendid wall mosaics. The synagogue mosaics in Israel included many glass *tesserae*, especially of colours not found in natural stone.

After the Arab conquest of the Middle East in AD 635, and the establishment of a capital at Damascus, there was a rapid move away from the Roman traditions of glassmaking. The change in the balance of power affected glass production, which stagnated until the rise of the Abbasid dynasty, and the transfer of the capital to Baghdad in Mesopotamia (Iraq), in AD 750, which was outside the mainstream of an area which had been unsettled for many years. By this time the whole of the Middle East had become settled under the rule of Islam and new styles in glass slowly began to emerge to suit the tastes of a new society. In the early stages of their conquest, the Arabs adopted the art of the countries over which they ruled, and had their palaces built and decorated by local craftsmen. Only at the end of the first millennium AD did Islamic art begin to assume an individual character. As with Roman Imperial art, though to a lesser degree, the development of Islamic art was remarkably uniform, whether in Persia, Mesopotamia, Syria or Egypt, centres of influence moving from country to country in the wake of shifting centres of government.

Mesopotamia, important in the ancient glassmaking world, again came to the fore; glass kilns were probably more common than pottery kilns in medieval Mesopotamia and southern Persia. Islamic glassmaking centres developed on the Euphrates river east of *Aleppo* (Syria); at *Samara* on the River Tigris (Mesopotamia); at *Siraf,* an early Islamic port on the Persian Gulf; at *Nishapur* (*Neyshabur*), an important trading centre in northern Persia; and at *Fustat* south of Cairo (Egypt) which had taken over from the Roman glassmaking centres such as *Alexandria.* There was much emphasis on mould-blown patterns and the cutting, engraving and polishing of glass, followed by pincering with tongs, lustre painting and gilding and enamelling. The most striking was the cut glass, surviving examples of which are either linear or facet cut.

A characteristic vessel of the Islamic period is the mould-blown flask with a globular body and long narrow neck. A fine group of such flasks, dating from the eleventh and twelfth-centuries AD, and typical of the Gurgan district in north-eastern Iran, is displayed in the Haaretz Collection, Tel Aviv (Israel), beside the clay moulds in which they were blown.

The relationship between Islamic cut glass and similar glass of an earlier period is not clear. The technique of glass-cutting was already known in the Late Bronze Age and much practised in Roman times, but did not reach its peak until the Islamic period. In Iran (and possibly also in Iraq) a tradition of cutting – from powerful relief work in the form of bosses, to delicate *intaglio* figural engraving – developed into a brilliant Persian-Mesopotamian school of relief cutting on glass during the ninth and tenth centuries. The glass was mainly colourless, the designs being outlined by deep, notched lines. This engraving was occasionally executed on glass cased with an overlay of emerald green or blue glass. Parallel with this luxurious relief engraving went a simpler or rougher style of *intaglio* engraving.

Lustre painting was a characteristic form of decoration from the eighth century, especially in Egypt where it may have originated. The earliest surviving example of lustre painting is on a glass bowl dated AD 773. This technique, which involved applying pigments, and firing them under reducing conditions in the kiln, to produce golden or silver iridescence, probably developed simultaneously in Egypt and Mesopotamia. The surviving examples include fragments on which different hues were obtained by repeated firings in the kiln, and vessels on which lustre spots have been applied to the interior and exterior of the glass.

The art of *gilding* glass may also have originated in Egypt. Gilding formed the basic element in the technique of gilding and enamelling glass, which developed in Syria, centred on Damascus, during the late twelfth and thirteenth centuries. The gilt and enamel glasses, largely beakers, bowls, flasks and mosque lamps, made mostly during the thirteenth and fourteenth centuries AD, are considered to be the highpoint of Islamic glass art (*Figure 2.11*). The so-called mosque lamps are in fact lamp-holders in which small glass lamps were placed. The usual shape of a mosque lamp (holder) was a large vase with a splayed neck. On the body were small glass lugs to which chains for suspending the lamp from the ceiling were fastened. Often the donor's name was included in the enamel decoration. Two main styles of glass

Figure 2.11 Mosque lamp holder of colourless glass with a yellowish tinge and containing many bubbles and impurities. Six suspension rings trailed on body. Heavily decorated in *naskh* script in red, blue, black white, green and yellow enamels (the last two badly fired). H 350 mm. Middle fourteenth century AD. Syria. (© Copyright The British Museum).

enamelling are discernible: one using enamel heavily laid on, usually in horizontal bands of intricate abstract patterns interspersed with quotations from the Koran, the other a fine linear style in red, both on a gold ground.

Glass vessels were exported from Damascus to every part of the Islamic world, and even as far as China. The beauty of Islamic glass was already appreciated in medieval Europe. In *circa* 1025 AD a ship of unknown origin and destination, carrying a cargo of approximately 1 tonne of raw and scrap glass, foundered at Serçe Liman off the south west coast of Turkey. Excavated by Bass (1980), the ship also yielded more than eighty intact engraved beakers and bottles of Islamic manufacture. These were found in the ship's living quarters, and were perhaps used by the crew, or were intended for use of items of trade. Vessels brought from Syria and Palestine by pilgrims and crusaders are now in many churches,

monasteries, museums and private collections.

Under the influence of Far Eastern Art, coming in the wake of the Seljuk and Mongol conquerors in 1258, the earlier heavier forms and styles of decoration became freer and more naturalistic, consisting of arabesque and floral designs. Enamel work declined at the end of the fourteenth century, and the manufacture of gilt and enamelled ware ceased almost entirely after the sack of Damascus by the Mongol chief Timur (Tamerlane) in 1402 during the conquest of the Middle East. The general decline in the production of Islamic glass gave Venice the opportunity to expand and to take over markets that had previously been supplied by the East.

Chinese glass

Glassmaking never achieved any great significance in Far Eastern decorative arts, possibly due to the development of other materials with glossy translucent surfaces such as jade, lacquer and porcelain. Until the end of the eleventh century the manufacture of glass in China was repeatedly stimulated by the import of glass items from Central Asia and further west. Chinese glass beads made during the fifth to the third centuries BC, whilst having a higher lead and barium content, are similar to those produced in Western Asia. During the Han Dynasty (206 BC to 220 AD), Roman glass entered China along the silk route. Han Chinese glass was treated rather as a semi-precious stone, and was often carved using jade-working techniques. The shapes of the objects were typical of those found in jade and lacquer. Glassblowing was introduced from Western Asia around the fifth century AD. The glass is found associated with Buddhism and buried in tombs of members of the Imperial family, such as that of Li Jingxub (AD 608), Li Tai (AD 631) and Li Shuang (AD 668). In the Famesi at *Fufeng* (Shaanxi province), glass is included amongst other highly prized objects in a ninth-century inventory. During the Song Dynasty (960–1279), glass was used to make egg-shaped objects of unknown use, gourd-shaped bottles and occasionally, foliate bowls (Brill and Martin, 1991).

From the Yuan period (1279–1368) onwards, the main area of production for Chinese glass was Boshan (Shadong province) in northeast China. Although excavations at Boshan have revealed furnace sites and glass rods in considerable numbers, existing glass vessels of this period, which are turquoise in colour, are rare. In the Qing Dynasty, under the Emperor Kangxi (1662–1722), a glasshouse was established in 1696 within the Imperial Workshop in the Forbidden City of Beijing. The glasshouse was supervised by a German Jesuit called Stumpf and resulted in a flourishing production which greatly increased the status of glass. However glass produced during the first half of the eighteenth century suffered from the defect of crizzling, like Western glass of the same period. The vessels were of typical Chinese shapes, often reflecting those of ceramic, jade and bronze objects. The vessels were decorated by various techniques such as moulding, incising, carving, diamond-point engraving, overlay (*cameo*) and enamelling. Glass was made as a cheap alternative to jade, and to imitate stones such as aventurine, jasper, lapis lazuli, pink quartz, realgar and turquoise. Enamelled decoration on glass was usually applied to opaque white glass which resembled porcelain or enamel. The art of enamelling glass reached its apex in the Qianlong period (1736–1797) when a number of high quality pieces were produced, undoubtedly for imperial use. They are marked with the characters *Guyuexuan* (Old Moon Pavilion). By the seventeenth century glass, in addition to its decorative use in the form of vessels, was also used for utilitarian purposes in the form of lamps and lanterns, window-panes, blinds, scientific instruments, lenses and spectacles. Occasionally glass was used for Buddhist figures and writing materials. It was used in imitation of precious stones in jewellery, hairpins, toggles and plaques. Reverse paintings on glass, produced mainly in Canton, were executed in large numbers for export to the West. The technique was paralleled by the highly skilled decorative technique of painting the interior of small snuff boxes.

Early Medieval Europe AD 400–1066

There were marked cultural changes after the fifth century, when barbarian incursions replaced central Roman imperial power. The changes were reflected in glassmaking by a general technical decline. The glass was inferior in quality and colour to Roman glass, and the vessel shapes were generally simpler. However, they were decorated with additional glass applied with considerable manipulative skill (Harden, 1956, 1969a, 1971; Henderson, 1993b).

In the northern European countries glassmaking tended to move away from the centres of population into the forests, which supplied fuel for the furnaces. It is possible that natron continued to be transported (perhaps as 'chunk glass', see Chapter 3, Part 2, and Seibel, 2000) to these countries even after the collapse of the Roman Empire in the West, by overland routes through the Brenner Pass in Switzerland, by sea around the Iberian Peninsula, or up the Rivers Vistula and Danube (Besborodov and Zadneprovsky, 1963; Besborodov and Abdurazakov, 1964). However, at some time before the tenth century, the ash produced in glass furnaces was substituted for the ashes of marine plants, which had been the almost universal fluxing agent used in Roman glassmaking. This change to potash derived from the ashes of burnt trees, especially beech, resulted in a change of both alkali and lime contents of the glass, which is known as forest glass (Ger. *Waldglas*; Fr. *verre de fougère* – fern glass). The comparisons of the locations of the northern glasshouses to the distribution of beech pollen in AD 1000 is discussed by Newton (1985b). The northern forest glassmakers, conditioned by their raw materials, produced mainly green and brown glass, and decorated it with furnace-wrought embellishments of simple rib moulding, applied trails and blobs, mostly in the same colour glass as the body of the vessel itself. The vessels fall into several categories: simple palm cups without handles, bag beakers, cone cups up to 265 mm in height and tapering to a pointed base, a variety of squat pots and bottles, and claw beakers (Ger. *Rüsselbecher*) (see *Figure 7.31*).

In the course of the later Middle Ages glass was improved to produce a substantial material of beautiful quality and a variety of green tones, used in a characteristic range of shapes of great originality and charm. Little is known of glassmaking in the Rhineland from the eighth to the fifteenth centuries. A few specimens have been found which provide enough information to show that glass was made during this period, but it appears to have been confined to small, crudely made utilitarian vessels. Two important pieces are reliquaries containing parchments dated 1282 and 1519. The former was discovered in a church at Michelfield near Hall, and is a small jar decorated with trailed threads reminiscent of the trailed-thread snake vases made in Cologne in the third century. The latter is a short parallel-sided beaker called an *igel*, with applied decoration in the form of spikes resembling those of a hedgehog (Ger. *Igel*).

The general term for applied blobs of glass is prunts (Ger. *Nuppen*); and prunts are one of the most characteristic features of northern European glass from the late fourteenth century onwards. It is possible to draw a parallel between these prunts and the projections on late Roman glass vessels, and on Seine–Rhine claw beakers (*see Figure 7.31*). Whereas in the earlier glasses the prunts were hollow blown and drawn out to form the distinctive long claws, the later prunts were restricted to solid lumps of glass, which owed their appearance and decorative effect to the manner in which the surface was finished. They were drawn out in several styles, for example to produce thin spikes resembling thorns, drawn out and folded over to form loops from which small rings of glass were suspended, and drawn into curls and pressed back onto the surface of the vessel to resemble pigs' tails. They were also flattened and moulded to produce a beaded surface, on types commonly known as raspberry or strawberry prunts.

Gradually the squat *igel* became taller whilst retaining its parallel sides until glasses were made which were in excess of 300 mm high. This type of vessel became very popular and acquired different names according to their intended use and style of decoration. One version, decorated with a row of prunts, which resembles broken-off leaf stalks, was termed *krautstrunk* (Ger. cabbage stalk). Another version was a plain glass divided into zones by horizontal trailed rings, the *passglas* (Ger.), which each drinker in turn was expected to drain to the next division in one breath.

The known glassmaking centres at this time were Cologne, Liège, Namur, Amiens and Beauvais. It seems likely that glass was exported to Britain from northern Gaul, and from the Rhineland, during the first seven centuries AD, but there was certainly some local production, at least from the seventh century. Glassmakers seem to have been working in the Kentish kingdom in the seventh century because bag beakers and squat jars are more prolific there than on the continent; moreover, a glass furnace was found in the cloisters of Glastonbury Abbey, near Bristol, beneath the medieval levels. With the spread of Christianity, the practice of burying grave goods with the dead slowly declined in Britain, northern France and the Rhineland. However, the custom continued in Scandinavia until the beginning of the eighth century so that the major source of glass from this period is from Scandinavian excavations.

There may have been no real break in the southern glassmaking tradition between late Roman times and the emergence of the Venetian glass industry in the thirteenth century, although there is as yet not much evidence of glassmaking activity in south-east Europe between the fourth and the eighth centuries. In contrast with the northern forest glassmaking sites, the manufacture of glass in southern Europe and the Mediterranean countries largely remained at sites near the coast such as Alexandria, Sidon, Damascus, Aleppo, Corinth, Aquilea, Murano, Florence and Barcelona. The towns offered many advantages: there were customers immediately at hand, especially the wealthy ones; there were churches and cathedrals with a demand for window glass; the towns provided communication and banking facilities; there was an impetus for innovation, such as the development of Venetian *cristallo*; and glassworkers' guilds could be formed to protect the interests of the industry. As a result of increasing demand, window glass was made more frequently, and many examples are now known of the early type of small crown glass window panes. The crown glass window panes in the church of San Vitale in Ravenna almost certainly came from the windows of the apse when the basilica was dedicated in AD 547. One bears an outline drawing of Christ nimbed and enthroned. Glass *tesserae* were used in wall mosaics; the mosaics at Ravenna were no doubt made locally as were those at Torcello.

Further evidence of the produce of the southern glasshouses was found in the cargo of the Gnaliç wreck. This vessel, probably the Gagiana, was on its way from Venice to the Levant, when it sank off the Yugoslavian coast in 1585. The cargo included 648 round window panes, 170 mm, 185 mm and 205 mm in diameter, and 86 types of glass objects. These included goblets, flasks, vases, pitchers, large square plates and two types of mirror, squared and round, which were obviously of Venetian origin. Some objects were of very thin transparent glass with greyish, greenish or purplish tints. Many were decorated with vertical filaments or threads of white opaque glass. There were also several small bottles of cobalt-blue glass and a group of glasses with delicate diamond-point engraving (Brill, 1973; Petricioli, 1973).

The glassmaking of southeastern Europe in the medieval period is as yet only imperfectly understood, but it is evident that good quality crystal glass had evolved by the thirteenth century at the latest. Many glasses, made of clear almost colourless glass, have now been excavated in Italy and other parts of Europe, including England, and can be dated to the twelfth to fourteenth centuries. The forms made were long-stemmed wine glasses and prunted beakers, often of considerable finesse and delicacy. Considerable use was made of opaque red glass, not only for whole vessels, but also for decoration. However, none of the glass can be attributed to the Venetian glasshouses with any confidence. Some of the clear glasses with prunts and trailed blue threads seem to have had their antecedents in the Byzantine glasshouses situated in Greece, one of which has been excavated in Corinth. It is, however, possible that a number of Italian glasshouses were involved in their production, but by the fifteenth century Venice had become the most important of these; and the eastern predominance in glassmaking was usurped by Venice. The technique of glass manufacture and its decoration had by this time largely developed, and therefore the historical development of glassmaking tends to become a list of changes in style or decoration which occurred at various times in different countries.

The pre-eminence of Venice

As previously mentioned, glassmaking in Venice may have had a continuous existence since Roman times, unless there was a migration of glassmakers from Aquilea, which is known to have had an established glassmaking tradition. Certainly a glassmaking industry was already established in Venice in the tenth century; and in records dating from 1090, mention is made of a *phiolarius*, which shows that vessel glass was being made there (Charleston, 1958). However, before the mid-fifteenth century, Venetian glassware was undistinguished and it is therefore difficult, if not impossible, to differentiate it from any other glass of the period. Whether or not there was some glassmaking on a small scale since Roman times, the pre-eminence of Venice in the glassmaking industry came about through a chain of circumstances: the accidents of geography, time, political power and the rebirth of the arts (the Renaissance) produced in Venice a standard of glassmaking both of quality and imagination which had not been achieved previously. A lagoon of low-lying swampy islands was an unlikely place to create a city. The problems of construction, communication and health would make any site on firm ground seem more favourable, but the earliest settlers were probably refugees from the effects of the barbarian invasions which swept the area after the fall of the Roman Empire in the West, for whom the lagoons may have seemed to offer security. As at various times in other countries, turbulent and troubled times had an inhibiting effect on the practice of the domestic arts and crafts. If Venice was able to establish herself while the surrounding region was in a state of turmoil, she would have offered a refuge where artisans could practise their arts with the minimum of interference.

In 1204 Constantinople fell to the Crusaders and the immediate beneficiary was Venice, whose fleets had carried them there. The glassmakers surely then obtained all the glassmaking information and assistance they required. At first, the Venetians may only have been glassmelters (i.e. not glassmakers), for masses of cullet are known to have been imported in the form of ships' ballast; and there was a law of the Marine Code, as late as 1255, which permitted *vitrum in massa et rudus* (crude lump glass) to be put on board ships as ballast.

That the glassmakers flourished, however, is certain, for by 1271 the first records of a glassmakers' guild appear; and shortly afterwards in 1291 the glass furnaces were moved to the island of Murano in the Venetian lagoon to avoid the risk of fire in a city comprised of small and densely populated islands. It may also have been that having become important and powerful enough to form a guild, it was felt that a tighter control could be maintained over the industry if the glassworkers were assembled in one locality. Glassmakers were highly regarded in Venice and the city records show that some became powerful and important men ranking with nobility in a city, which had a highly developed class system.

As communication and trade developed throughout Europe, Venice and Genoa became the natural focal points for the trade routes of the world. There was intense rivalry between the two cities but Venice eventually emerged the victor, and became the crossroads for land and sea traffic from east to west and from north to south. With this position secured, Venetian coffers swelled with the taxes and duties she levied in commercial traffic; Venice became the most powerful city in the Mediterranean. Venetian merchants travelled the trade routes of the world, and in the course of their dealings with the Middle East they would have encountered Syrian and Mesopotamian glassmakers so that the best of Middle Eastern glass would have found its way back to Venice.

During this period the trade in glassware, which of course had been taking place for some three millennia, started to be documented. Trade routes were established, for example, between Genoa and Syria, the Mediterranean countries and Asia as far east as China, and between Murano and Dubrovnik.

With the overthrow of the Middle East by Tamerlaine in 1402, the decline of the glass trade in the Middle East left a vacuum in the supply of high-quality glass. Since Venice was in control of all the main commercial routes and had established a considerable glass trade of her own, it was natural that she should step in to fill the breach. In the face of the onslaught of the barbarian hordes the local

inhabitants would flee wherever they could to find refuge, and what more natural than that the glassmakers would make for a place where, from contact with visiting merchants, they knew that there would be an opportunity to continue the practice of their skills? Thus, in addition to having new markets opened to it, Venice also had a second infusion of skills from the Middle East.

As the world once again became a more settled place, prosperity increased and there came about a rebirth of artistic endeavour and achievement – the Italian Renaissance, during which talented artists, able to satisfy the aesthetic demands of a new society, were sponsored by wealthy patrons of the arts. Glass painters are recorded in Murano as early as 1280; and colourless glass was almost certainly made there in the thirteenth century. From the middle of the fifteenth century these two branches of the arts experienced an unparalleled expansion in what was by then a highly specialized industry. Trade between Venice and the East declined after Constantinople was captured by the Turks in 1453; and the Venetians then built up an active trade with the West based on the *façon de Venise* style which enabled them to continue to dominate the glass industry.

The earliest Venetian glass vessels of any quality were goblets, usually flat-bottomed and with straight tapering sides mounted on a pedestal foot. They were made of coloured glass, usually blue or green, with enamelled decoration around the bowl (Gasparetto, 1973). Previously, stemmed glasses had been rare. At first the glass bowls were set on a plain ribbed pedestal in which stem and foot were one. Gradually the stems were made taller and were decorated with hollow blown bulbs (knops), until for the first time glasses with separate stems and feet were produced. Once the stem and foot were able to be made separately there was no limit to the ingenuity which could be used in fashioning the stem: hollow knops with moulded lion masks, stems with a central feature of glass threads drawn out in the shape of serpents or figures-of-eight, winged stems with pincered fringes, and many others (Tait, 1968, 1979). In a further development the Venetians improved their clear glass by the addition of lime to the soda–silica mixture, and purified the soda to produce a

Figure 2.13 *Millefiori* miniature ewer of opaque blue glass, with canes of purple, green, brown and blue. H 127 mm. Early sixteenth century. Venice.

Figure 2.12 Nef (or ship) ewer of colourless glass, the bowl in the form of a boat with a spout forming a prow. H 343 mm. Sixteenth century. Venice.

fine clear glass (*cristallo*), which captured the popular taste of the fifteenth century.

One of the great abilities of the Venetian glassmakers was their skill in the manipulation of the material. They acquired dexterity in controlling the molten material, which enabled glasses to be produced of a delicacy, and with a degree of elaborate decoration, which no one else could equal (*Figure 2.12*). Such glassware was made for a wealthy and sophisticated market, and outside Venice that would mean principally the European nobility. Thus Venetian glass was for a long time the prerogative of the rich and educated. Later came plates, tazzas, flasks, chalices and a wide variety of other domestic vessels in blue, green or purple glass and later in *cristallo*. The glassware was enamelled and gilded and was the

product with which Venice first entered the world market. The decorative themes were of typical Renaissance inspiration: triumphs, allegories of love etc.

Inspired by classical Rome, the Venetian glassmakers also produced mosaic, *millefiori* (*Figure 2.13*), aventurine (with copper particles) and *calcedonio* glasses, the latter in imitation of Roman agate glass produced 1500 years earlier, and which was itself an imitation of the natural stone. Enamelled glass gradually went out of favour, except for customers in northern Europe, and mould-blown or exquisite plain forms such as *aquamaniles* or *nefs* (decanters, see *Figure 2.12*) succeeded. These were sometimes decorated with bands or cables of opaque white (*lattimo*) threads, that is, *filigrana*, and occasionally by gilding, diamond-point engraving (although the thin soda glass was generally unsuited to engraving), cold painting behind glass (Ger. *Hinterglasmalerei*) (see *Figure 7.71*), or a surface *craquelure* (ice-glass, *Figure 2.14*). As the fifteenth century progressed, furnace-wrought decorations of applied threads or bosses, often of fantastic forms, became more popular, and in the seventeenth century this tendency was sometimes carried to extravagant and not always attractive lengths.

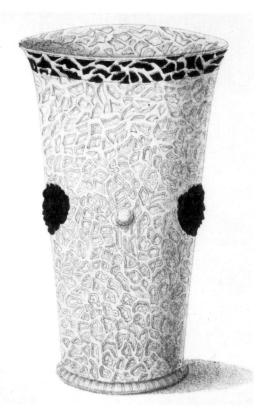

Figure 2.14 Large beaker of 'ice-glass', created by plunging the hot glass into water for a moment and immediately re-heating. The roughened surface resembling ice became popular in Venice in the sixteenth century and spread to Northern Europe, where it remained in vogue into the seventeenth century. H 209 mm. Late sixteenth century. Southern Netherlands.

Venice was jealous of her position in the world's markets, and to ensure that she kept it the Venetian Senate placed highly restrictive conditions on its craftsmen, especially the glassmakers. They were forbidden on pain of death to practise their skills anywhere outside Venice, or to impart their knowledge to anyone other than Venetians. However, the demand for Venetian glassware from the Courts of Europe was such that considerable inducements were offered to persuade Venetian glassmakers to risk the consequences and to set up their glass pots outside Venice. There are records of Venetian ambassadors using bribery and blackmail to persuade the unfortunate truants to return home. The tide could not be entirely stemmed, and slowly but

surely at other glassmaking centres throughout Europe the stylistic Venetian elements – *the façon de Venise* – were introduced by migrant workers from Venice itself, and from Altare near Genoa which was the traditional rival of Venice and where the glassmakers' corporation had a deliberate policy of disseminating workers and techniques. The Italian knowledge thus spread throughout Europe, reaching Vienna in 1428, Sweden in the 1550s and England by 1570 at the latest, so that Venice lost its supremacy in the glassmaking industry. Each country showed just a little individuality of style, which marked its product from the true Venetian glass.

Inevitably Venice made enemies who considered her power too great, or whose interests conflicted with her own. As a result there were many attempts to break her influence. When the Portuguese found a new route to the Far East via the Cape of Good Hope at the end of the sixteenth century, goods could be shipped to and from the Far East without the necessity of paying high duties to ship them through Venice. Her importance on the trade routes thus undermined, Venice started to decline, and the Republic finally collapsed in 1797. Long before this the glass trade in northern Europe had overtaken the Venetian manufacture, and from the end of the seventeenth century she had lost her important position to numerous rivals. Taste was beginning to change, looking more towards more solid, colourless crystal glass truly resembling natural rock crystal. Glass of this nature was successfully produced in Britain and Bohemia.

Europe from the Middle Ages to the Industrial Revolution

Northern European glasshouses

Bohemia

Records of glassmaking in Bohemia date from the fourteenth century, and because of the abundant supplies of wood for fuel, and of raw materials for the glass, the craft soon established itself there. Glassmaking became such an important part of the industrial life of Bohemia that, by the end of the nineteenth century, there were 56 glasshouses in opera-

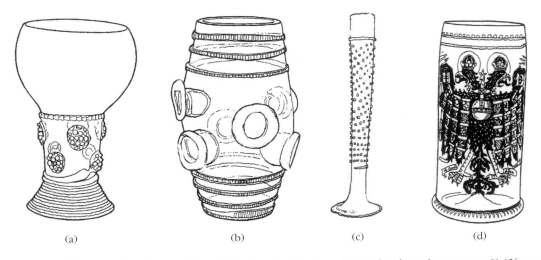

(a) (b) (c) (d)

Figure 2.15 (a) Green glass *Roemer* with a globular bowl and a stem decorated with raspberry prunts. H 156 mm. Mid seventeenth century. (b) Green glass *Daumenglas* with six fingergrips (*fingernapfen*). H 200 mm. Seventeenth century. Germany or Netherlands. (c) Greenish glass *Stanenglas* with prunted and trailed decoration. H 426 mm. First half of the fifteenth century. Germany. (d) *Reichsadlerhumpen*, pale green glass with enamelled decoration. H 290 mm. 1654. Bohemia.

tion. Several of the glass styles, the *roemer*, for example, were common to the whole of northern Europe, regional characteristics not developing until the eighteenth century. The *roemer* (*Figure 2.15*) originated as a large, cup-shaped bowl with a hollow stem, which was blown in one piece, and mounted on a long narrow pedestal foot made from a thread of glass wound round a conical pattern. The stem connection was ornamented with prunts and milled collars at the top or bottom. As time passed, the foot assumed more importance and became taller, while the bowl tended to decrease in size. In later years, the pedestal was formed in one piece with a corrugated outer surface to represent the original thread of glass. (The name *rummer*, applied to the large beer glasses made in Britain in the 1780s, may be a corruption of the word *roemer*). Contemporary with the development of the *roemer*, a number of other forms appeared: *kuttrolf, stanenglas, igel* (hedgehog) glass, *passglas, daumenglas* (or *daumenhumpen*). The *daumenglas* was a more robust, barrel-shaped vessel with a series of indentations in the sides to provide finger-grips.

During the sixteenth and seventeenth centuries, German glasses (*humpen*) became gradually taller and wider. They were usually decorated with coloured enamels, and are now classified according to the method of decoration. *Reichsadlerhumpen* bore the double-headed Imperial eagle, and on the outspread wings were painted the coats-of-arms of the 56 members of the Germanic Confederation. The thinly blown *kurfursten-humpen* depicted the emperor and the seven electors.

Although the Venetians had supplied enamelled glass for the German market, this is usually easy to distinguish from the German domestic products since these were more robust and the brighter colours more heavily laid on. Whatever it lacked in finesse, German enamelling succeeded by its sheer exuberance. *Schwarzlot* was another style of painting on glass, which gained some popularity during the seventeenth century. This consisted of outlined pictures in black with the clear areas occasionally infilled with a brown wash. Fine examples of *schwartzlot* technique were produced by Johan Schaper (1621–1670). Bohemian glass had begun to acquire its individual character in the late sixteenth century with the introduction of cutting and engraving. Glass made in the *façon de Venise* had spread northwards through Europe, and with it such techniques as the art of cutting glass as if it were rock crystal. This caught the imagination of the Bohemian glassmakers, and it was from this beginning that the great Bohemian tradition of cutting and engraving glass arose.

In the early seventeenth century another innovation by the Bohemians was combined with their skill in engraving to produce some of the most remarkable examples of this technique ever seen. This was the development of a new glass, which required the addition of lime to the potash–silica batch then in use, to produce a perfectly clear, solid crystal glass. The glass proved to be ideal for decorating by wheel-cutting and engraving; techniques which had been developed in Prague before 1600, and then transplanted to Nuremberg, where a school of engraving flourished throughout the second half of the seventeenth century. The elaborate goblets with multi-knopped stems which were made in Nuremberg copied contemporary goldsmiths' work.

A hardstone engraver, Caspar Lehman of Prague, was the greatest exponent of the revival of glass engraving in Europe. Lehman presumably used the same skills and equipment for both crafts, a tradition that was to continue until relatively modern times. When Lehman died in 1622, the patent to engrave glass was taken over by George Schwanhardt the Elder, who founded a school of brilliant glass engraving in Nuremburg, which flourished until the eighteenth century. Wheel-engraved glass was produced in Holland, shortly after the middle of the seventeenth century. The most prominent Dutch engraver was Jacob Sang of Amsterdam. English lead glass was also suitable for engraving, and blank vessels were exported in large quantities to be engraved in Holland.

Political troubles eventually led to the dispersal of the engravers throughout Germany, where engraving became a less popular method of decorating glass. Towards the end of the seventeenth century the taste for *façon de Venise* had declined and been replaced by the new style of wheel-engraving which made use of the qualities of the new glass, and which became highly developed in Bohemia and Silesia, a speciality being imposing goblets engraved in high relief (Ger. *hochschnitt*), the ground of the design being cut back by means

of a water-driven wheel (see *Figure 3.18*). From Silesia the art of engraving was transplanted to Potsdam, one of the most accomplished workers being Gottfried Spiller.

Goblets with round funnel bowls had knopped stems cut with facets, well proportioned but less ornate than the Venetian equivalent. The glass was thicker and the bowls were often cut with vertical panels and had domed covers to match. The bowl, the cover and sometimes even the foot would be profusely covered with highly ornate baroque decoration interrupted by coats of arms or formal scenes in enamel. For special court commissions gold was often applied to the surface of the glass in relief. Constant handling of such glass would quickly spoil its glory and therefore the highly burnished fired gilding of the Potsdam glasshouses, patronized by the Electors of Brandenburg, was far more practical, and rather more spectacular. Frequently the wheel-engraved decoration on Potsdam glasses is heavily gilded and the overall effect is little short of ostentatious. In the course of the eighteenth century glass engraving spread throughout Germany and Central Europe, centres of special importance being *Nuremberg*, *Kassel*, *Gotha*, *Weimar*, *Dresden* and *Brunswick*, with *Warmbrunn* and others in Silesia.

Later in the eighteenth and nineteenth centuries more naturalistic themes were introduced, which included woodland scenes with deer. So highly was this combination of glass and engraving regarded that Bohemian artists were persuaded to go to Venice and Spain to introduce the technique there. Some coloured glass was made in Bohemia, and the most important researcher connected with its development was Johann Kunckel, a chemist working in Potsdam. Kunckel (1679) produced a variety of colours varying from rose pink to purple using Purple of Cassius.

Although cutting and engraving were by far the most important of the decorative processes to be developed in Bohemia, several other techniques, well-known in antiquity, were revived and given a distinctive Bohemian quality: for example, about 1725, the art of enclosing a pattern of gold leaf and transparent enamel between two layers of glass (Ger. *Zwischengoldglas*). The inner layer of glass had a lip on the outer surface onto which the outer layer joined, thus making a close-fitting joint which completely protected the delicate film of gold leaf inside. At about the same time Ignatius Preissler was establishing a reputation for decorating glass objects with painted glass subjects of *chinoiserie* scenes enclosed in baroque scrolls painted in black enamel, frequently highlighted with gold.

In the early nineteenth century the black basalt wares of the Wedgwood factory in Britain were very popular, and this taste was reflected in black glass vessels, the *Hyalith* glass made in Bohemia from 1822 onwards. One of the manufacturers of Hyalith was Frederick Egermann, who was responsible for a number of new varieties of glassware, which imitated natural stones such as agate, jasper and marble, as well as transparent glass coloured with chemicals. In the early nineteenth century, transparent and opaque white glass, were combined to produce the overlay glass whose popularity lasted through-out the century. It usually consisted of a layer of white over a base of transparent green, red or blue glass. The white glass was then cut through to form windows through which the coloured glass underneath could be seen. The whole was then decorated with gilding or coloured enamel. The idea was taken one step further later in the century when the overlay was reduced to one or two medallions. These were decorated in coloured enamel, with portraits or with bunches of flowers, while the body of the vessel was covered with a fine meandering pattern in gilt. This style of ware was usually made as ornamental ewers or vases.

A cheaper but effective method of produc-ing coloured glass was to cover the outside of a clear vessel with a film of coloured glass. This was applied either as a stain or by dipping the gather in a pot of coloured glass. The commonest colours were fluorescent yellow produced with uranium and red, but green and amethyst examples are known. Some glasses cut with vertical panels had each panel coated with a different colour. If the vessel was embellished with engraved decora-tion the thin layer of colour was easily removed to show the clear glass underneath. Popular subjects were views of spa towns on beakers and tumblers, which were sold as souvenirs. Although they were probably not very expensive when they were made, the engraving was always of a high standard.

In the late nineteenth century when the *Art Nouveau* movement began, a Viennese, Louis Lobmeyr, established a factory to produce glass of a high artistic and technical quality employing Bohemian craftsmen. This was a reaction against the vast quantities of cheaply made mass-produced glassware which was made everywhere during the second half of the nineteenth century. This effort to revive glassmaking as an art was continued by the Loetz glassworks, where beautifully coloured iridescent glass was made.

The Low Countries

The early history of glassmaking in the Low Countries is as vague as that of the rest of northern Europe. Geographically the area comprises the country between the Rhine and the Mosel rivers (now forming part of Germany), the seven provinces of the Netherlands, and the general area of Belgium. It was rarely all under one rule at any one time, and was variously controlled by the Spanish and Austrians. Glassmaking in the Low Countries first came to prominence with the introduction of Venetian glass in the fifteenth century. The Venetian *cristallo* which was such an improvement over its predeces-sors was displayed and advertised in all the courts of Europe, and seems to have attracted particular attention in the Low Countries. There are records of glasshouses being estab-lished to make the *façon de Venise* in Antwerp (1537), *Liège* (1569) and *Amsterdam* (1597). The trade flourished, and the area became the most important in Europe outside Venice to produce the Venetian style of glassware. Its distance from Venice, however, led to slight differences in the character of the glass but it is still difficult to distinguish the glass made in local glassworks from that imported from Venice.

While the *façon de Venise* flourished, other glassworks in the principal towns as well as many others in minor centres continued to turn out masses of utilitarian wares in the traditional styles of the region. The local tradi-tion still made use of *waldglas*, but by the sixteenth and seventeenth centuries the green-ish glass had been developed further, and a whole range of blue-greens produced. The *roemer* was one of the native styles which acquired great popularity, and several types, identified by the prunts applied to the stems, have been assigned a provenance in the Low Countries. One of these employed prunts that were flattened and smoothed to the point where they blended into the wall of the vessel. This produced different depths of colour according to the varying thickness of the glass. Two other prunt variations were those moulded on the surface with a face of Neptune, and those with beads of blue glass applied to the centres. During the seventeenth century *roemer* stands were made. They were tall pedestals in precious metals designed to have a *roemer* clamped into a mounting on the top. Due to the proportions of the *roemers* then in use this had the effect of producing a tall metal goblet with a glass bowl. The total effect was reminiscent of the elaborate tall goblets made by the Nuremberg goldsmiths. Another style peculiar to the Low Countries was the tall, narrow flute. This was a very thinly blown glass up to 450 mm high and 50 mm wide. The funnel bowl was usually mounted on a single hollow knop and a spreading foot. Very few of these fragile glasses have survived.

From the end of the seventeenth century the lead glass being produced in Bohemia and Britain became increasingly popular with Dutch glass engravers, by virtue of its clarity and density. The Bohemian glassmakers had an efficient marketing organization, and set up warehouses in the Netherlands to stock their products. The Newcastle light baluster style was particularly favoured and, during the eighteenth century, British lead glass was much imitated by local glasshouses. The traffic was not all one way however; elaborate baskets and dessert services made in Liège during the seventeenth and early eighteenth centuries were popular in Britain. These vessels were made of threads of glass built up in layers to produce an open-mesh design. They stood on plain glass plates decorated with a border executed in the same mesh style.

Engraving was the only applied method of decorating glass which achieved any degree of importance in the Low Countries, and throughout the seventeenth and eighteenth centuries there were a number of artists whose work was of the highest order. The technique as developed in the Netherlands was quite different from that practised in Bohemia. Dutch engraving was carried out on the surface of the vessel with a delicacy equal to that of painting, while Bohemian engraving depended on a good thickness of glass and was more closely allied to sculpture. One of the earliest recorded Dutch engravers, Anna Roemers Visscher (1583–1651) was one of a very few women known to have been engaged in this work. She specialized in a free-flowing style of calligraphic engraving, a method also favoured by Willem von Heemskerk (1615–1692) in the seventeenth century, and by Hendrik Scolting in the eighteenth. The finest seventeenth-century work, was produced by artists such as Frans Greenwood, David Wolff and Jacob Sang. The first two specialized in stipple engraving, a method whereby the surface of the glass was marked by repeated light blows with a diamond-pointed tool. The density of the marks thus produced determined the variations in tone and shading of the completed picture. The resulting effect was rather similar to a thin photographic negative. It required a complete sureness of touch and considerable artistic ability for its success (see *Figure 7.27e*). Because of these demands on the artist, stipple engraving was never widely practised, but there are a few engravers working in contemporary Britain who can produce stippled decoration comparable in quality to that of the eighteenth-century Dutch masters. Jacob Sang specialized in wheel-engraving, and his work has a delicacy, precision and sureness of touch which few engravers have equalled. Foremost among his work are the glasses which he engraved with coats of arms.

Britain AD 1500–1850

During the first half of the sixteenth century there was an influx of French glassworkers to Britain from Lorraine. It appears that they were not popular locally and eventually they left the Weald and settled in other parts of the country. The principal cause of their unpopularity was the rate at which the forests were destroyed by use of wood fuel in their glass furnaces. Glassworkers were in competition with ironworkers for wood fuel; the latter however were static, while the glassworkers with their much lighter glass pots could move on whenever the local supplies of fuel were exhausted. Crossley (1967, 1972) calculated that the furnace at Bagot's Park in Staffordshire (AD 1535) would use *circa* 130 tonnes of wood per month (i.e. 1.6 hectares. of 15-year-old coppice) and that as a consequence the modern area of Bagot's Park would be denuded of trees in 15–20 years. This fuel consumption would correspond to about 60 Whg-1 of energy, compared with only 4 Whg-1 from coal at the beginning of the twentieth century, and less than 1 Whg-1 in the best oil-fired present-day practices. With the consumption of forests at such a rate the British government became alarmed about the loss of trees for building ships for the Navy, and in 1615 James I issued a *Proclamation Touching Glass*, banning the use of wood for making glass. Nevertheless the landowners welcomed the use for glassmaking of otherwise unsaleable timber.

By the early seventeenth century coal was beginning to be used as an alternative source of fuel. This encouraged the dispersal of the French glassmakers from the south of Britain and led them to settle in districts where coal was readily available, such as Stourbridge and Newcastle, where their influence was to be felt for two hundred years or more. Scottish coal had been used at first but Lady Mansell sent William (Roaring) Robson to Newcastle and he then found that the Newcastle coal was cheaper than the Scottish coal (Watts, 1999).

One of the Lorraine glassmakers was Jean Carré who, in 1567, obtained a licence for 21 years to set up a glasshouse in London, to produce glass in the *façon de Venise* since the Venetian product was still highly regarded in Britain. To this end Carré imported several Venetian glassmakers and was the first manufacturer in Britain to use soda instead of potash as a source of alkali, possibly as a result of his Venetian contacts.

When Carré died in 1572, one of his Venetian craftsmen, Jacob Verzelini, took over the licence and in 1574 was himself granted a 21 year licence for the making of drinking glasses, '... suche as be accustomablie made in the towne of Morano' (Douglas and Frank, 1972), but in fact the Verzelini glass was much plainer and more functional than the continental examples of *façon de Venise*. Only a handful of glasses exist which can be attrib-

uted to the Verzelini glasshouse. They are all goblets in *façon de Venise*, engraved by diamond-point and bearing dates between 1577 and 1586. Verzelini ran the glasshouse for 17 years before retiring, and he finally died a rich and respected citizen of London in 1606. With Verzelini's retirement the monopoly to make glass in Britain passed through several hands until Sir Robert Mansell gained control in 1618, having bought up existing monopolies (a history of the London glasshouses is given by Watts, 1999).

Mansell was successful as a result of the law of 1615 prohibiting the use of wood fuel for firing glass pots, since he had acquired the patents covering the use of coal as a fuel for that purpose. He established a number of glasshouses in England, which made glass using Spanish *barilla* (containing soda and lime) as a source of alkali, coal fuel and employing workmen from Altare in Italy. Mansell maintained control of the glass industry for about thirty years, but does not seem to have survived the Civil War or the Commonwealth (1640–1660). It was only on the restoration of King Charles II to the throne that glassmaking began to flourish. In 1663 George Villiers, Duke of Buckingham, petitioned Charles II for what was probably a renewal of the Mansell monopoly. With the aid of a Frenchman, Jean le Cam, Villiers opened a glasshouse at Vauxhall in London to make looking glasses and imitations of rock crystal. However, Villiers never secured the totally monopolistic power of his predecessors.

In 1664 the Glass Sellers' Company was formed, and from that date onwards the glass trade was largely dictated by that company. Two factors illustrate this clearly. First, in surviving correspondence between John Greene, a glass seller in London and Allesio Morelli in Venice, from whom he bought glass, Greene states exactly how the orders are to be executed, often complaining of the quality and enclosing sketches of the shapes and styles to be supplied. The second factor concerns the backing of George Ravenscroft by the Glass Sellers' Company to pursue research into the development of a new type of glass.

Thus the trade had changed in 100 years from an industry based on individual semi-itinerant glassmakers to a properly organized and commercial enterprise controlled by a regular trade association. This was to prove the springboard for the ascendancy of British glass over the next 150 years.

George Ravenscroft and lead glass

Venetian glass was thinly blown and delicate, and fine pieces executed for wealthy families were undoubtedly treasured and carefully preserved, so that many still survive. However, little glass made for everyday use remains. Indirectly, the glassmaker George Ravenscroft was to change this situation by producing a more robust type of glass; and thus relatively large quantities of eighteenth-century domestic glass still exist. Ravenscroft was not a glassmaker by trade, and had reached the age of 55 years before setting up a glasshouse at the Savoy in London in 1673, in order to carry out experiments to create a new type of glass.

The late seventeenth century was a period of intense research and experiment by men of culture and education, to advance scientific knowledge for the benefit of their fellow men, the Royal Society being a product of this era. Ravenscroft's early experiments were unsuccessful, the glass soon crizzling as a result of the lack of balance of constituents, but it eventually showed such promise that in 1674 the Glass Sellers' Company established him in a glasshouse in Henley-on-Thames, Berkshire, to pursue his researches in seclusion. This was on the condition that when a successful formula was achieved, the vessels would be manufactured to the Company's own specifications; however, Ravenscroft took the precaution of obtaining a seven year patent on his new ideas (Macleod, 1987; Moody, 1988).

Most early lead glass showed distinct tinges of colour, usually grey, green or yellow, which were the result of impurities in the raw materials. Undoubtedly the glassmakers endeavoured to produce a glass that was colourless, and added various chemicals to counteract the impurities. However this was very much a case of trial and error, and success was achieved more by chance than by chemical control. A more predictable result could be achieved by using purer materials, for example, sand free from contaminants could be obtained from areas near King's Lynn in Norfolk, and near Newcastle-upon-Tyne, sand from these areas

being shipped to all the British glassmaking centres.

By 1676 such progress had been made that the Glass Sellers' Company issued a certificate expressing its satisfaction with the new *glass of flint*, as it was then called, and giving permission for the glassware to be identified by means of a seal bearing a raven's head. From this badge a small number of glass vessels can be attributed to the Ravenscroft glasshouses. The secret of the glass production was the addition of lead oxide to the raw materials, which produced a soft and brilliant glass of great refractive quality. The Venetian *cristallo* had looked clear and transparent partly on account of its thinness and also on the purification of the soda which had been used, but the new lead glass remained clear and transparent when much thicker glass was blown. Lead glass did not lend itself to the extravagances of the Venetian style, but because of its lustre, plainer shapes made a display which was just as effective (*Figure 2.16*) (Charleston, 1960).

Ravenscroft terminated his agreement with the Glass Sellers' Company in 1679; and died in 1681, about the same time as his patent expired. The glasshouse was continued by Hawley Bishopp, who had worked with Ravenscroft at Henley on behalf of the Glass Sellers' Company, and who presumably knew the lead glass formula. However, before many years had passed lead glass was in common use in all the glassmaking centres of Britain.

For the first few years after the introduction of lead glass, vessels continued to be made in the Venetian tradition. Indeed, Ravenscroft had imported two Venetian glassmakers to work in the Savoy glasshouse. As early as 1670, the designs which John Greene had sent to Venice had shown a tendency to simplify the Venetian styles, and as time went by several factors combined to create a particularly British style. As the demand for glass grew, and new glasshouses opened, there could never have been enough skilled Venetian workers to staff them all. Therefore increasing numbers of British glassworkers would have had to be trained and it is unlikely that they would have acquired, and exactly imitated, the abilities of their Venetian instructors.

Lead glass became so popular that, as previously mentioned, various attempts were made

Figure 2.16   A basin and ewer made by George Ravenscroft. The basin is cloudy, having become crizzled. (©
V&A Picture Library).

on the Continent to produce lead glass in the
façon de l'Angleterre. This was not achieved
until the late eighteenth century, largely due
to the fact that in order to protect lead glass
from the effects of smoke it was necessary to
use covered pots, and this was not the practice
in continental glasshouses. The British glassmaking industry, however, was already using
covered pots before the introduction of lead
glass, as a direct result of the need to use coal
as an alternative fuel to wood (Newton, 1988).

During the period under review the various
changes of style and decoration followed each
other in a regular sequence, which has been
catalogued by Barrington Haynes (1959). The
transitional period from about 1680 to 1690 is
usually referred to as the Anglo-Venetian,
when such Venetian characteristics as spiked
gadroons, trailed decoration and pincered
stems still appeared on glassware. These
gradually disappeared to give way to the first
period which can be described as being
peculiarly British: the period of heavy baluster
stems, 1690–1725. The knop formations on the
stems of the glasses derive from the hollow

blown knopped stems of Venetian glasses, and
were the last signs of Venetian influence on
British glass. The stems of British glasses of the
period were either solid or contained air
bubbles (tears). The early baluster stems were
notable for their size and weight. The bowls
are usually solid at the base, and the knops
appear in a variety of forms with such descrip-
tive names as cylinder, egg, acorn and
mushroom knop. As time passed the proportions of the glasses became more refined; the
height increased, the weight decreased, and
where the stem had previously been made
with one knop, combinations of knops became
fashionable. This style reached its peak with
wine glasses made in the Newcastle-upon-Tyne
glasshouses in the north of England. The
Newcastle light baluster was tall with a multi-
knopped stem often containing rows of tiny air
beads, and of clear colourless glass.

One of the most famous glassmaking
families in Newcastle at this period was that
of Dagnia. The family was of Italian origin,
and seems to have arrived in Newcastle from
Bristol in about 1684. Until that time only

sheet glass and bottles had been made in Newcastle, and it is quite possible that the Dagnias brought with them the recipe for the new lead glass and began the quality glass trade which culminated in the fine wine glasses referred to above. Contemporary with the baluster period was another group of glasses, which owed their introduction to the accession of George I to the throne of England in 1714. To mark this event glasses with the so-called Silesian stems were produced. These glasses had tapering, four-sided, moulded stems, which the English glassmakers soon modified to six or eight sides.

The glasses retained their popularity along with the baluster glasses until the introduction of the *Glass Excise Act* of 1745. From the seventeenth century onwards the British Government had considered glassmakers to be a fruitful source of revenue. In 1695 William III had introduced a window tax, which greatly reduced the output of glass and caused much unemployment in the trade. The duty was subsequently repealed, but was levied again in 1745 as a duty on raw materials. As a result glassware became plainer in shape and lighter in weight to minimize the effect of the tax; and plain-stemmed glasses containing less lead were introduced (Charleston, 1959). From the mid-eighteenth century public taste changed, the more ornate rococo and *chinoiserie* styles becoming popular, and the glassmakers changed their styles to meet the demand. From 1750 onwards air-twist and opaque-twist stems made their appearance. Both these styles were suited to an art which put a premium on the amount of raw material used since they permitted decorative glass to be made without the large quantities of glass necessary for producing baluster stems. Air-twist and opaque-twist stems remained popular until 1777 when a further duty was imposed on the enamel rods used in the production of the opaque twist stems; these were then made in less quantity, and cutting began to re-emerge as the main form of decoration.

In the 1770s cutting again became popular (Bickerton, 1971), but this time as a method of decorating the glass stems with facets. The plain stems were cut with a series of scallops so that the intersecting edges formed diamonds or hexagons. The art of glass-cutting spread rapidly and from 1780 onwards a wide range of glassware was being made with more and more elaborately cut designs. Cutting was able to exploit the lustrous and refractive qualities of lead glass (see Chapter 1 for definitions of refractive index and dispersion), and for the next 50 years British glassmaking reached a peak of quality in both glass and decoration. After 1830 styles tended to become too intricate and the art of cutting generally went into decline. Throughout the period many other domestic articles, besides vessels, were made in glass, for example chandeliers, candlesticks, jugs, bowls, decanters, bottles and sweetmeat dishes. Besides cutting, other forms of decoration were employed such as engraving, gilding and enamelling, but they rarely achieved either the degree of quality or popularity which they had attained on the Continent. Engraving on glass is rare in the early eighteenth century, and when it began to make an appearance after 1730, wheel-engraving was the method of production generally preferred over hand-engraving.

In 1820 an annual licence was introduced which greatly disrupted glass manufacture. The operation of the new law was very complicated; furnaces were locked by inspectors, and 12 hours' notice in writing had to be given before a glass pot was filled. Moreover, the regulations made it virtually impossible to introduce new types of glass, such as the type required for making lenses or for bottles that would be acid-resistant (Douglas and Frank, 1972). These restrictions were lifted in 1845, and the glass industry immediately entered a period of rapid growth.

Diamond-point engraving by British artists in the eighteenth century is virtually unknown. On the other hand, large quantities of the fine Newcastle light balusters were exported and most of those which survive bear Dutch engraving, both by wheel-engraving and by diamond-point work, which is of an exceedingly high standard (see *Figure 3.16*). Gilding occurs either as oil gilding which was not permanent and became barely detectable as a result of constant handling, or as gilding which was fired onto the glass to produce a permanent decoration. James Giles, a London engraver and decorator, executed a number of glasses decorated with fired gilding, and his style consisting of sprays of flowers and insects, is easily recognizable. In the last quarter of the eighteenth century the Jacobs family in Bristol also produced a great deal of gilded glassware; unusually, many of these pieces were signed.

Enamelling was only carried out by a few artists. Most examples are attributed either to Michael Edkins or to William and Mary Beilby, although there are a few enamelled glasses, which do not conform to the style of either of these. The enamelled designs attributed to Edkins are nearly all executed on dense, opaque, white glass, which was made in Stourbridge or Bristol to resemble porcelain. Edkins is recorded as having worked in both towns, and the decorations consist of birds, flowers and *chinoiserie* designs. The Beilby family, brother and sister, worked in Newcastle from 1762 to 1778. They painted small scenes of rural pursuits or classical ruins on sets of wine glasses, usually in white enamel. The family must have been widely known and highly regarded since a small number of surviving goblets carry coats of arms in polychrome decoration, which had been executed to special orders for titled families (*see Figure 3.29*). There was also a demand for coloured glass. While early eighteenth-century pieces do exist, they are rare, and the majority of surviving coloured glass dates from the late eighteenth and early nineteenth centuries. The principal colours used were green, blue and amethyst, while amber and red are rare.

A method of dating glass of this period is by reference to the many pieces which were engraved to commemorate a person or event with a known date. Probably the best known British commemorative glasses are those relating to the Jacobite movement, from the failure of the Rebellion of 1745 to the death of Prince Charles Edward in 1788. During this period several societies sympathetic to the Jacobite cause flourished, and it was fashionable, though treasonable, to drink a toast to Bonnie Prince Charlie from glasses bearing his portrait or emblems representative of the movement. Occasionally Latin mottoes expressing hope for his return from exile were added, such as *Fiat, Audentior Ibo* and *Revirescat*.

Britain after 1850 (industrial glassmaking)

Towards the middle of the nineteenth century the orderly progression of one style to another, which had occurred during the previous 150 years, collapsed. Influences from abroad, notably Bohemia, had a marked effect on design in Britain, and the introduction of new production techniques, such as press moulding from America, led to cheaper glassware which catered for a much wider market than ever before. National and international exhibitions, culminating in the Great Exhibition of 1851, introduced many new styles to the British public. The purpose-built building in which the Great Exhibition was held, the Crystal Palace, was an enormous glass and cast iron construction. One of its principal features was a glass fountain weighing about 4 tonnes built by the firm of F & C Osler of Birmingham.

At the exhibition the finest designs and the newest manufacturing methods from all parts of the world were displayed. When it was over, glassmaking in Britain changed radically: as the Industrial Revolution gathered momentum and manufacturing units became larger; small firms using traditional hand methods became uneconomic. This led to the concentration of the glass industry into fewer companies. Glassmaking declined in areas such as Bristol and London, and became established principally in the Midlands, around Stourbridge and Birmingham, and along the rivers Tyne and Wear around Newcastle, where there was an abundance of fuel and raw materials. Whereas in earlier years every glassmaker had been content to produce what was in popular demand, after 1851 each manufacturer endeavoured to produce designs which were quite different from those of his competitors. To protect their interests designs were registered, and during the second half of the century literally thousands of patterns for glassware were registered.

Changes in style and taste were so rapid that it becomes difficult to date glass made after 1850; but attribution to particular factories is often easier, since it was the practice of some factories to mark their products with the name of the company.

The taste for continental glass was encouraged by the Great Exhibition, and Bohemian styles of coloured and overlay glass as well as the French style of opal and frosted glass decorated with coloured glass buttons became very popular.

Glass had to be manufactured to suit all pockets, and there was a demand for mass-produced wares for the working classes, as well as for high-quality glass products for the wealthy. A good example of this dual production is the difference in quality that occurred in Bohemian-style ruby glass. Expensive glass was made, by covering a clear glass vessel with a layer of red glass. Expert craftsmen would then cut through the outer layer to expose panels of clear glass. Vessels produced in this way were known as *Biedermeier* glasses. On the other hand, cheap glasses were produced by first cutting facets in the vessel, after which the surrounding areas were filled in with a ruby stain. To produce the former, foreign craftsmen were often brought to Britain to work in their own tradition, while the cheaper versions could be made with almost any class of labour.

Among the immigrant workers who settled in the Stourbridge area were several decorators who established high reputations for their skill: Frederick Kny, William Fritsche and Paul Oppitz all executed the most beautiful engraving in the Bohemian tradition, and their work was shown at many exhibitions. Jules Barbe was a gilder in the French style whose work has never been bettered in Britain. All these craftsmen worked at one time or another for the firm of Thomas Webb & Son. Webb's, which was founded in 1856, and which is still operating, is one of several firms that established the high reputation of Stourbridge glass in the nineteenth century. Others were Richardsons, Stevens & Williams, and Boulton & Mills. In Birmingham, George Bacchus & Sons, Rice Harris & Sons, and F & C Osler were well-known glassmaking firms.

These British glassmakers did not take their inspiration solely from European sources. For example, in 1885 Queen Victoria received a gift of 'Burmese' glass (which had recently been invented at the Mount Washington Glass Factory in America); and in a short while Thomas Webb & Son had agreed to make Burmese glass under licence in Britain. This unusual glass was shaded from pink to yellow, an effect which was achieved by adding gold and uranium to the raw materials.

Cameo glass was redeveloped in the nineteenth century by John Northwood, a famous Stourbridge glassmaker, who was associated with the firm of Stevens & Williams. Cameo glass was always extremely expensive since it required great skill and patience on the part of the carver. One of the best-known decorators in this field was George Woodall, who worked for Thomas Webb & Son. He specialized in carving classical figures in flowing robes; signed examples of Woodall's work command very high prices. Various methods were invented to produce glass which had the appearance of cameo glass but which could be mass-produced.

Although glassmaking largely died out in London, the oldest glassmaking firm in Britain was a London company, J Powell & Sons, which was established about 1700 under the name Whitefriars Glass (Evans *et al.*, 1995; Jackson, 1996, Watts, 1999). The firm made glass for William Morris and has been responsible for fine handmade glassware in the twentieth century. The other main centre of glassmaking in the nineteenth century was in the north of England. The area around Newcastle-upon-Tyne produced much of the cheaper pressed glass for the mass market. The technique of press moulding was developed to a very high standard, and a wide variety of goods was made. The most sought after glassware was made from slag glass. This was an opaque glass in a variety of colours, the most typical of which had a purple and white marbled effect. The three most important companies which made slag glass, and which often added their trade mark to the moulds so that their products could be identified, were Sowerbys Ellison Glass Works, G. Davidson & Company, and H. Greener & Company. In addition to moulded glass much coloured decorative glass was made in the north of Britain. It derived from the Venetian tradition with its liberal use of applied glass decoration. Coloured glass baskets, spill vases and candlesticks were also popular.

In the twentieth century several attempts have been made to establish artist-craftsmen studios in order to break away from the mass production methods of the large factories. Among the better known of these are the names Greystan and Monart.

Ireland

There is documentary evidence for glassmaking in Ireland from 1258 onwards, when

French glassmakers began to operate there. They probably made their way to Ireland from the glassmaking centres in Sussex. In 1586 a Captain Thomas Woodhouse acquired a patent giving him the sole right to make glass in Ireland for eight years. However, the venture does not appear to have been very successful, for in 1589, George Longe, a trained British glassmaker with considerable interest in the British glass trade, bought the patent. Longe is the first recorded experienced British glass-maker; until this time the glassmakers had all been French or Italian. The Act of 1615 banning the use of wood for firing glass furnaces was not extended to Ireland until 1641, so it is quite possible that there was a further influx of French glassworkers from the south of Britain after the Act was passed. After 1641 glassmaking in Ireland seems to have declined.

The first glasshouse producing lead glass was set up in Dublin in 1690 by a Captain Roche, barely 10 years after Ravenscroft's patent had expired. Roche went into partner-ship with Richard Fitzsimmons, and the company continued in business until about 1760. At the same time as the Excise Act of 1745 imposed a duty on glass made in Britain, Irish glass was exempted, but its export to Britain was prohibited. This badly affected the Irish glassmaking trade since the number of the island's inhabitants able to afford good quality glassware was too small to support any great manufacturing capacity. At the same time the effect on the Irish home trade was aggra-vated by the fact that imports from Britain were not banned. However, in 1780 the grant-ing of free trade and the lifting of all restric-tions on the industry put new life into the Irish glass trade. The art of glass-cutting was becoming fashionable in Britain at this time but, as mentioned previously, heavy duties had an inhibiting effect upon this type of decoration. The British manufacturers there-fore saw the creation of free trade for Ireland as a golden opportunity to cater for the public demand without having to pay the heavy duties they would incur at home.

The reputation of Irish glass was made between 1780 to about 1830; and glasshouses were established in Cork, Waterford, Dublin and Belfast. Those amongst them which were financed by Irishmen, such as the Penrose

brothers at Waterford, relied entirely, in the first instance at least, on imported British craftsmen to produce the glass. In 1825 the Irish free trade was ended, and the advantage of manufacturing in Ireland was lost. This, combined with an increasing floridity of style, caused a decline in the trade and the impor-tance of Irish glass.

Before the use of cut decoration, the product of the Irish glasshouses was indistin-guishable from that of the British factories. After 1780, when cutting became fashionable, the same patterns were produced in both countries, but there were certain characteris-tics, which help to distinguish the Irish product. Most important among these was the occasional practice of impressing the factory name on the base of tableware, particularly decanters. Examples are the names of B. Edwards, Belfast, Cork Glass Company, and Penrose, Waterford. Certain styles of engrav-ing are associated with particular factories, and some styles of cutting are peculiarly Irish (Warren, 1970).

Irish glass is now synonymous with the name Waterford. There is no doubt that the Waterford glass factory did acquire a very high reputation for its products, but there were other important factories also operating between 1780 and 1850: Cork Glass Company; Waterloo Glass House, Cork; Terrace Glass Works, Cork; B. Edwards, Belfast; Belfast Glass Works; Richard Williams & Company, Dublin; and Charles Mulvaney, Dublin.

The history of the Waterford Glass House is well documented by advertisements, factory records and correspondence between members of the Penrose and Gatchell families. The factory was founded in 1783, by the brothers George and William Penrose; wealthy men who knew nothing of glassmaking, but could see the opportunities which free trade offered. Initially the factory was staffed by British craftsmen under the leadership of John Hill of Stourbridge, who was an experienced glassmaker. Hill stayed for three years and then left, apparently in disgrace. Before leaving, Hill handed on his glassmaking secrets, for mixing the raw materials, to a clerk, Jonathan Gatchell. As the holder of such important information, Gatchell grew to be an important figure in the business, and in 1799, with two partners, he bought out the then remaining Penrose brother. Thereafter the company remained in the hands of the Gatchell family until it closed in 1851.

North America 1608–1940

Glassmaking in North America began in 1608, little more than a year after the first settlers had arrived. The glasshouse owned by the Virginia Company was situated at *Jamestown* (near Richmond, Virginia) and covered an area 15 m by 11 m. It was considerably larger than any of the contemporary medieval glasshouses in the Chiddingfold region of southern Britain. The furnace itself was rectangular and, like so many of the British examples, it was found to be devoid of useful fragments of the articles which had been made in it because the site would have been cleared of glass for cullet (Harrington, 1952). It seems that the Jamestown glasshouse had been set up to make use of the extensive source of fuel from the forests which were now available in the New World, and thus to provide cheap glass for use in Britain. This at a time when British glassmakers were discouraged, and eventually prohibited, from burning wood in their furnaces, and coal-firing was still in its infancy. There was however not a large local demand for glass, either as tableware or as windows, in the pioneer Colonial houses, and the project was abandoned in 1624.

During the next 150 years there were attempts to set up glasshouses, one of the longer-lived being the glassworks built in 1738 by Caspar Wistar at *Alloway*, in Salem Co., New Jersey. This began the German domination of the American glass industry that was to continue until the nineteenth century. Wistar died in 1752 and his son, Richard, managed the modest business in an effective manner until 1767. Some of the glass made there has been found to contain about 17 per cent lead oxide, which probably got into the glass from the addition of English 30 per cent lead oxide cullet in an attempt to improve the glass. A more spectacular venture was started in 1763 by a 'Baron' Stiegel, first at *Elizabethtown* (near Lancaster, Pennsylvania) and then at *Manheim* nearby. Stiegel ran the glassworks in a flamboyant manner, eventually becoming bankrupt and ceasing operations in 1774. The products of the Stiegel and Wistar glasshouses possess considerable artistic merit, but care needs to be exercised when using contemporary sources of information as evidence for the quality of the glass because, at that time, it was politically expedient to conceal from the British Colonial authorities the success which had been achieved by American glassmakers. Thus Benjamin Franklin instructed his son William, Governor of New Jersey, to report in 1768 that Wistar made only 'coarse window glass and bottles'. Stiegel imported glassworkers from Europe; and eighteenth-century American glassware was made in the German and British styles, thus making it difficult to distinguish from imported wares. Exceptions to this were the mould-blown flasks and bottles, on which the decoration was often of a commemorative nature, for example, those dating from after 1830, bearing the legend 'Union and Liberty'.

The Amelung New Bremen Glassmanufactory was set up in 1784, by Johann Friedrich Amelung, after the War of Independence (1775–1783). It was sited at *New Bremen* on the Monocasey River in Frederick County, Maryland. Amelung had previously worked at the famous Grünenplan glassworks in Germany (south of Hanover) where glass had been made since the fourteenth century. The British tried very hard to prevent Amelung from going to America to set up the glasshouse, first by arranging for the Hanoverian Government to forbid emigration and secondly by trying to capture the vessel during its passage through the English Channel, but Amelung avoided both hazards.

The Amelung New Bremen factory was burnt down in 1790 but some manufacture went on until 1795 (Schwartz, 1974; Hume, 1976; Lanmon and Palmer, 1976). The site was excavated in 1963 (see *Figure 3.70*) and analyses were carried out on many samples of the glass. Their 'fine glass' (colourless, purple or blue) was found to be a high-potash glass with a moderate lime content (16 per cent K_2O and 9 per cent CaO), but the green, aqua and amber glasses had much less potash and much more lime (5.7 per cent K_2O and 19.6 per cent CaO). Brill and Hanson (1976) suggest that a constant batch composition had been employed for both types, but purified wood ash (pearl ash) had been used in the former and the unpurified ash had been used in the latter. Other interesting features were the presence of antimony and certain trace elements; and those glasses made before 1790 contain some lead oxide (0.11–0.64 per cent PbO) while those made after 1790 contain much less (0.0–0.04 per cent PbO).

Apart from the successful Amelung Glassmanufactory, the intense demand for foreign commodities (following the War of Independence) operated as a strong deterrent to the construction of glassworks in the United States. For this, and for other reasons, such as foreign competition and local taxes, glass manufacture in the United States of America did not make much progress, but between 1786 and 1800 glassmaking was carried out in at least six New England states, and monopolies were soon granted; for example, in 1787 the Boston Glass Manufactory had a 15-year monopoly, its capital stock was exempted from all taxes, and its workmen were relieved of military duties.

The British blockade of the Napoleonic Empire brought prosperity to America, and this was reflected in an increase in the number of glasshouses, so much so that the first national survey of manufactures, in 1810, showed that 22 glassworks existed, again all on the eastern seaboard, with a total output of more than $1 million; window glass accounted for four-fifths of the total, the amount of lead glass being insignificant.

The end of the war with Canada (1812–1814), however, not only put an end to rapid expansion of the glass industry but also brought distress to many of the glasshouses that had recently begun operations. In 1817 the New England Glass Company was formed, under the ownership of E.D. Libbey. It was threatened in 1885 by a paralysing strike of workmen. Libbey, however, broke the strike and transferred his whole company across the Alleghenies to Toledo, Ohio, where he made a fresh start in 1888. The new company ultimately became the Owens-Illinois Glass Company, the largest and most influential maker of glass containers in the world (Meigh, 1972).

The Census of 1820 showed that deep industrial depression had returned to America, the total annual value of the glass output being only about $0.75 million, much less than in 1810, but 5.4 million ft^2 (5 $\times 10^5$ m^2) of window glass was made, high-quality crown glass being produced in Boston, and cylinder glass elsewhere.

Manufacturing was again concentrated in the east coast states, and an excellent source of sand was found at Milville (New Jersey), now the homes of the Wheaton Glass Company and the Kimble Glass Company. Wood was generally used as the fuel, except at Pittsburgh where coal was used, and the furnace designs were based on those of Germany, whence the migrant glassmakers had come. Some details are available about the consumption of wood in Canada, where the Ontario Glass Manufacturing Company leased 1500 acres of land in 1810. The area was richly covered in beech, hickory, oak and maple, but fourteen years later the activities of the glassmakers had cleared 200 acres; however, the owners of the land sold this cleared area as valuable farmland.

There was a resurgence in the building of glasshouses between 1825 and 1831, and a higher proportion of lead glass was made. When the fourth Census was carried out in 1850 the annual value of the glass produced had increased to $4.6 million, and then to $8.5 million in 1860. The Civil War (1861–1865) brought about a considerable increase in production. In 1860 there were 1416 workers in 13 factories but by 1870 these figures had risen to 2859 and 35, respectively.

In the early nineteenth century the even older technique of moulding glass in a closed mould was revived and improved by the process of press moulding. By this method flat or tapered vessels were formed in a two-piece mould; one half being used to compress the slug of molten glass into the shape of the other half so that at the point at which the two halves met the mould was full (and there was usually a mould-line to confirm this). With this method far more intricate patterns could be produced with much sharper definition, and perhaps even more importantly, articles could be produced at a faster rate. The earliest recorded patent for press moulding was taken out in 1829 when presses were manually operated (see also Cable, 1998).

During the next 50 years a whole succession of patents was issued covering both improvements in power presses and in moulding processes whereby several articles could be moulded at one time. Press moulding enabled a wide variety of glassware to be made at prices that put cheap copies of cut and decorative glass into every home. Similar developments took place in France, Bohemia and Canada.

In the context of the exchange of ideas between Britain and America, it is interesting to note that Harry Northwood, son of one of the greatest of the Stourbridge glassmakers, John Northwood, emigrated to America in 1885, and three years later was running his own glassworks. As well as the production of utilitarian wares, the continuing search for novelty culminated in a wide variety of flasks and bottles made to represent people, animals, birds, fruit, buildings and railway engines to name but a few. Towards the end of the nineteenth century American glassmakers became involved in the Art Nouveau movement, and much elegant and decorative glass was made in the Art Nouveau style. Louis Comfort Tiffany (1848–1933) and Frederick Carder (1863–1963) were prolific glassworkers in the style. Tiffany had a studio in New York where a whole variety of imaginative coloured glass was produced whose chief attraction was its iridescence. One of Tiffany's largest undertakings was a remarkable glass curtain for the stage of the National Theatre of Mexico, the Bellas Artes, in Mexico City. Carder learnt his skills at Stourbridge, UK, later emigrating to America and helping to found the Steuben Glassworks, Corning, New York State. Here glass artists have continued to create individual works which explore to the full the possibilities of shape and decoration.

The first use of natural gas in the glass industry (1881) gave another great impetus to glass manufacture, and there was an appreciable movement of glassworks to the gas fields of Pennsylvania, Indiana and Ohio. The total number of glassworks increased by 50 per cent between 1880 and 1890 and the first continuous-melting tank was installed at Jeannette (Pennsylvania) in 1888. Glassworkers' Unions and Manufacturers' Associations started to be formed around 1880. After that time the story is one of growth and remarkable improvements in manufacturing machinery, the Arbogast press-and-blow machine being invented in 1882, the Owens Suction machine in 1904 etc. These develop-

ments and the many others in making window glass are recorded by Douglas and Frank (1972) and, as a historical record, by Cable (1998).

Summary of nineteenth- and twentieth-century glassmaking in Europe

The second half of the nineteenth century was a period of enormous technical achievement, with Britain and Bohemia leading the field in the middle of the century, but France coming very much to the fore in artistic glassmaking towards the end of it, and the great industrial power of America gradually making itself felt, albeit mainly in styles imported from Europe. Apart from the traditional techniques of enamelling and gilding, wheel-engraving and wheel-cutting, this period saw the introduction of transfer printing and acid-etching; surface treatments such as the revived ice-glass and acid-etched satin finishes; silver and gold leaf decoration, aventurine, and an electrolytic silver deposit process; bubbles of glass trapped within the glass; glass shading from one colour to another owing to heat treatment (Burmese, Peach Blow etc.); wrought decoration of every kind, with twisted and ribbed elements, opaque and coloured twists and threads; and applied drops, and threading (by mechanical process).

From the nineteenth century, iridescent glassware was produced in Europe, and gained great popularity, e.g. Loetz; carnival glass. Opalescent glasses treated with metallic oxide were heated in a controlled atmosphere to develop the iridescent effect. It was produced commercially in 1863 by J & J Lobmeyer, and thereafter by many glasshouses under various patents.

All these methods were used in an infinite variety of combinations, reflecting the eclectic taste of the period. Of perhaps the greatest significance, however, was the perfection of press-moulding in America about 1825, for this brought decorated glass within the means of the poorer classes of society. In France in the 1870s the multiplicity of techniques was harnessed to the making of individual works of art, by Eugène Rousseau and Emile Gallé. Rousseau was greatly inspired by Japanese art; early glass pieces reflect this in their themes, forms and their decorative composition. Later, however, Rousseau developed original shapes and decorative techniques of enclosed red, green and black markings, of *craquelure* and of deep wheel-cutting. Rousseau abandoned glassmaking in 1885. Gallé had begun manufacturing glass in 1867, and after a period of experimentation with every available decorative technique in a variety of historic styles, Gallé also came under the influence of Japanese art. About 1885 Galle developed a lyrical style in which vases with mainly floral polychrome designs were made by complicated casing techniques, with much use of wheel-cutting and acid-etching. Such vases epitomize the Art Nouveau style in glass and were highly influential until the First World War (Arwas, 1977). Of equal complexity and sophistication were the glasses of the American Louis Comfort Tiffany, who used embedded drawn threads and other forms, combined with an iridescent surface treatment to produce glass objects equally characteristic of the period.

From the 1830s to the 1940s, radioactive uranium (first discovered in 1789) was widely used to produce colours ranging through yellow, green, orange-red and black, in glass, glazes and enamels on decorative objects. The most well-known colours are those in vaseline glass and fiesta red glass (Strahan, 2001).

After the disruption of the 1939–1945 war, a neutral country – Sweden – took the lead in glass fashion. Two artists, Simon Gate and Edvard Hald, employed by the Orrefors Factory, devised a variant of Gallé cased glass, Graal glass, covering the cut and coloured layers with a colourless coating, thus embedding them and imparting a smooth surface to the glass. They also produced designs for wheel-engraving on crystal glass. The general Swedish ideal was to produce well-designed goods for everyday use, apart from the luxury wares; and in this their lead was followed by other countries in northern Europe.

A more personal style of glassmaking, however, was developed in France by Maurice Marmot, a Fauve painter who not only designed, but made glass, using techniques of trapped bubbles, powdered oxides, and deep acid-etching in glass objects which recovered the forms and styles of the 1930s. This spontaneous approach to glassmaking was reflected in the work of other French contemporaries:

Henri Navarre, André Thuret and Jean Sala; and even the commercial firm of Daum abandoned the traditions of Gallé for glass made under Mainot's influence; while René Lalique applied a highly sophisticated taste to mechanical production by designing glasses with modelled decoration in high relief which could be enlivened by acid-etching and enamelling.

The northern European striving after functionalism was echoed in Murano in 1920, notably in the work of Paulo Venini, Ercole Barovier and Flavio Poli. After the decline of Venetian glassmaking in the eighteenth century, the skills and traditions were kept alive through the nineteenth century mainly by the enterprise of Antonio Salviati, and were at the service of the new style when it came. The simple shapes of Venini were often decorated by the thread and mosaic techniques in the opaque white (*lattimo*) and coloured glasses traditional to Venice, while both Venini and Barovier invented new surface treatments to give their various glass products mottled, granulated or dewy effects. The work of these masters continued after the Second World War, but this period has been chiefly characterized by the emergence of the studio glassmaker, first in America – Harvey K. Littleton, Dominick Labino and others – and then in Europe. Working single-handed, at small one-man furnaces, studio glassmakers have produced glassware in an infinite number of shapes, often non-functional and sculptural, decorated with bubbles, embedded coloured metallic powders, and other furnace-made ornaments, latterly supplemented by wheel-engraving (Charleston, 1977).

Glass micromosaics

The taste for miniatures is seen in many art forms during the eighteenth century, at the end of which, the technique of creating small-scale glass mosaics was developed in the Vatican workshops in Rome. These came to be known as micromosaics (Ital. *mosaico in piccolo*) to distinguish them from the larger architectural works. The technique was used to create portraits and pictures to embellish decorative objects such as jewellery, snuff boxes and caskets and the tops of tables (*Figure 2.17*).

Figure 2.17 Fragment of a broken micromosaic plaque, which depicts a bridge viewed from below, showing the many individual slivers of coloured glass that form the design. W of rectangular glass surround 270 mm. (© Copyright The British Museum).

Two important events heralded its beginning. One was the excavation in Hadrian's villa in Tivoli, in 1737, of the finest ancient Roman mosaic wall panel ever discovered (now in the Capitoline Museum, Rome). The panel (known as the Doves of Pliny), measuring 98 × 85 cm (38½ × 33½ in) and was composed of tiny stone *tesserae* arranged to represent doves drinking from a bowl. The second was the development of a wide range of opaque matt colours by Alessio Mattioli who was in charge of the production of mosaic *tesserae* produced for the Vatican studio from *circa* 1730 to 1750. These added considerably to the range of transparent, shiny coloured glass *tesserae* produced in Venice, and enabled mosaicists to imitate paintings more successfully.

During the nineteenth century, micromosaics gradually began to look less like the ancient Roman mosaics, owing to an increasing emphasis on naturalistic effect. In the late eighteenth micromosaics a recurring feature was the use of two-dimensional neoclassical motifs silhouetted against a contrasting background.. The next development was an attempt at greater naturalism in modelling, achieved by enhancing the effect of the graduated colours by varying the angle at which the *tesserae* were set; and by adopting a three-quarter, as opposed to frontal or profile view of the image, which was still set against a contrasting monochrome background. The

ultimate exercise in sculptural modelling was the execution of *tesserae en grisaille* in imitation of marble statues. Other highlights of the micromosaic technique were landscapes, portraits, notably papal portraits, and multi-coloured flower subjects.

As the tourist industry developed towards the second half of the nineteenth century, the production of micromosaics became a commercial enterprise, and standards inevitable dropped as easily portable souvenirs were produced. However, expensive, high-quality work continued to be produced on demand up to the end of the nineteenth century.

The glass itself was produced in the form of cakes (*smalti*) in a vast range of colours, sometimes two or more colours were blended together. The cakes were then broken, and the chips softened in the furnace-mouth whilst being held by long tongs. The glass was then drawn out to form long thin threads (*smalti filati*), which were cooled in order to harden them, and finally sliced into thin sections. The *tesserae* are so minute that some of the micromosaics are composed of more than 5000 pieces per square inch. The portrait or picture was created by placing a support covered with a slow-drying adhesive on an easel. The sections of coloured canes held in tweezers, were arranged by colour and shade one at a time. The support was usually made from a thin sheet of copper metal with a turned up rim, but slabs of marble, hardstone or glass were hollowed out to create supports for micromosaics. The adhesive was composed of lime burnt from marble and finely powdered Travertine stone, mixed to a thick consistency with linseed oil. Once the adhesive holding the glass canes in place had hardened (which might take weeks or months depending on the size of the work), any gaps in the surface were filled with wax, the entire uneven surface abraded level. This was done first with a hard stone to flatten the surface, then with emery, and finally with lead to impart a polish. Finally the surface was waxed and polished. A full description of the development of micromosaics, and an explanation of the glassmaking techniques associated with it are given by Rudoe in Gabriel (2000).

Enamels (glass fused to metal)

Objects composed of vitreous coatings fused to a metal backing are known as enamels. The technique of using enamel colours was known in Egypt from *circa* 1400 BC; it was used to a limited extent in Greece, but extensively practised in Byzantium in the sixth century, in Venice from the fifteenth century, and elsewhere in Europe from the sixteenth century. Since earliest times, enamels have been made in the form of jewellery and continue to be produced as jewellery, candlesticks, boxes, panels, dressing table sets etc., and since the nineteenth century, for commercial and industrial purposes such as signs and advertisement plaques (Maryon, 1971; Cosgrove, 1974; Speel, 1984; Wicks, 1985). There are several types, classified mainly with French terms, by the way in which the enamel frit is attached to the metal, i.e. *cloisonné, champlevé, basse taille, plique à jour* and painted (see *Figures 3.33-3.38*).

Enamel resembles a glaze in that both vitreous materials are fused to a substrate – ceramic in the case of glaze and metal in the case of enamels. However, the term *enamel* is also used to describe a colour of similar composition used to decorate ceramic and glass objects. An enamelled object is formed by applying a vitreous substance in the form of a dried frit, to a metallic surface such as copper, silver or gold. They are then fused at a relatively low temperature in an enamelling oven. Some enamelling techniques relied on a framework of metal bands or wires to contain different coloured enamels, whilst the success of others depended upon a more sophisticated knowledge of enamel composition and firing temperatures. With each colour having to be fired at a successively lower temperature, the technique was, and continues to be, painstakingly slow, and is prone to irreparable flaws. However the result are permanent brilliant colours, which do not fade.

Most early enamels failed because the highly fusible frit never actually fused to the metallic substrates. Enamels must be so formulated as to have a co-efficient of contraction roughly equivalent to that of the metallic substrate; and its melting point must be approximate to but lower than that of its backing to ensure fusion. For these reasons most enamels are a lead–soda or lead–potash glass with or without the addition of colourants and opacifiers. On very thin or extensive areas of metalwork, the contraction of the enamel on cooling might be sufficient to cause the metal to warp. To counteract this, the reverse of the object might also be enamelled, as process known as *enamel backing* or *counter enamelling*. Where necessary, the surface of the finished enamel, when cold, was made even and polished with fine abrasives. Opaque enamel usually required a lower firing temperature (*petit feu*) than translucent enamel, about 300°C. Higher temperature firing was known as *grand feu*. Translucent enamelling involves the firing of transparent layers of enamel, onto a metal *guilloche* surface, engraved by hand or engine-turned. There may be as many as five or six layers of enamel, each of which had to be fired separately at successively lower temperatures.

Sometimes gold leaf patterns or *paillons* or painted decoration or scenes were incorporated in the design. This effect was achieved, by applying and firing the gold leaf or enamel onto an already fired enamel surface, after which it was sealed with a top layer of enamel, and refired. The completed enamel then required careful polishing with a wooden wheel and fine abrasives, to smooth down any irregularities in the surface, and then finishing with a buff.

The characteristic milky quality of some of Fabergé's translucent enamels was obtained by mixing four to six parts of translucent enamel to one part of opaque enamel, producing a semi-opaque or *opalescent* enamel. Enamels were usually applied to the metal in such a way as to form a level surface with the surrounding metal, by providing a sunken area into which the frit could be fused. These areas might be provided for in the original metal casting, or cut out with scorpers, a technique known as *champlevé* (or *en taille d'épargne*). Used by the Romans, Celts and Medieval enamellers, the *champlevé* technique was perfected in Mosan enamels of the twelfth century, and used extensively in Limoges, France in the twelfth to the fourteenth centuries.

In *cloisonné* work, the enamel was placed in compartments (*cloisons*) formed by a network of thin metal bands soldered onto the surface of the metal object to be decorated. The tops of the metal bands remained exposed, defining the pattern of the cells filled with different coloured enamels. *Cloisonné* is one of the most ancient enamelling processes and is probably Near Eastern in origin. It was used by the Celts and by Byzantine enamellers. The Pala d'Oro in St Mark's, Venice, is a masterpiece of *cloisonné* work. From Byzantium the technique was transmitted to China in the fourteenth century, and eventually throughout the Orient (Cosgrove, 1974).

In *filigree* enamelling, thin wires enclose the enamel in the same manner as strips of metal in the *cloisonné* technique. It is thought to have originated in or near Venice in the second half of the fourteenth century, and is best known from fifteenth century Hungarian examples.

The technique of *plique à jour* involves supporting the enamel at the edges in a metal framework, without the support of a metal backing. The framework was produced by fretting (piercing through and removing most of) a small sheet of metal, which was then temporarily backed with a material such as sheet mica, to which enamel would not adhere. Frits formulated to produce translucent enamels, were placed in the compartments, fused and cooled. On removal of the temporary backing, light could shine through the coloured enamels, producing an effect similar to that of a stained glass window.

Apart from the use of plain, or coloured enamels, a number of techniques for enamel decoration were employed which were very similar to those on glassware, such as mosaic and *millefiore*. The metalwork itself could be decorated before application of enamel, as for example, in the technique of *basse taille*, which entailed chasing or engraving the metal surface with a delicate design in low relief, before the application of translucent enamel. The engraving could be seen through the enamel, which itself appeared lighter over the shallow cutting and darker over the deeper areas. A refinement of the *champlevé* technique, *basse taille*, was first perfected in the Paris enamels of the early fourteenth century. The Royal Gold Cup in the British Museum is a magnificent example of the technique. The cup was made *circa* 1530 in Burgundy or Paris, and depicts scenes from the life of St Agnes. An almost identical process, *lavoro di basso rilievo*, was developed independently in Italy.

The process of *en resille sur verre* entailed packing the enamel frit into gold-lined incisions engraved on a medallion of blue or green glass, to which it fused on firing. This difficult technique was only adopted during the second quarter of the seventeenth century in France, where it was mainly used to decorate miniature cases. A rich technique of covering figures or decorative devices formed in the round, with opaque enamel, *en ronde bosse*, was used in Paris at the beginning of the fifteenth century on large reliquaries, and in England, where it was known as encrusted enamelling. The Dunstable Swan Brooch in the British Museum is a fine example of this process.

Enamel colours could be applied to a metal foundation to produce a picture or painted enamel. (Glass painters are recorded in Murano, Italy as early as 1280.) The colours were formed of metallic oxides mixed with a glassy frit of finely powdered glass and suspended in an oily medium for ease of application with a brush. The object, such as a plaque or box, was first covered with a layer of white opaque enamel and fired. The design and/or inscriptions were applied in different colours, and fired in a low temperature muffle kiln (approx. 500–700°C). The medium burned out during firing. Sometimes different firings at successively lower temperatures were required to fuse different colours, in order to prevent them from running into one another. The process was invented in Limoges, France in the late fifteenth century. Led by father and son Jean and Henri Toutin, French goldsmiths developed a sophisticated technique for painting polychrome miniatures in enamel on gold. A locket bearing Henri Toutin's signature in full and the date 1636 is the earliest date to appear on one of the pieces which have survived.

In England and the Netherlands, the style of painting was copied in monochrome on the backs of many items of jewellery during the middle decades of the sixteenth century. From the mid-sixteenth century enamels were often painted on black grounds instead of white, which thus formed the basis for *grisaille* painting. If the colours were used on a black ground, thin layers of gold- or silver foil could be inserted between coats of translucent enamel to provide a warm or cold reflective tonality. Large painted enamels were produced in Limoges, including portrait plaques, platters, plates, dishes and ewers. From the sixteenth century onward, goldsmiths enriched their work with touches of coloured enamel.

In order to protect soldered joints in the metalwork, these had to be coated with rouge, whiting or plaster-of-Paris before the enamel was fired. A cheap form of enamelware made in various parts of Europe in the seventeenth century came to be known as Surrey Enamelling. The enamel was applied to brass objects, cast with recessions to hold the frit e.g. candlesticks, andirons, sword hilts and horse harness.

During the sixteenth century, painted portrait miniatures had developed in England, from a technique of illuminating manuscripts, known as limning. The technique of producing enamel portrait miniatures was introduced to England from Sweden and France in the 1680s by foreign enamellers such as Petitot, Boit and Zincke. As the technique developed, larger and more ambitious works were undertaken; for example, Henry Bone (1755–1834), made large copies of Old Master paintings.

Between 1842 and 1918, the Russian firm of Fabergé (Peter Carl Fabergé 1846–1920), produced enamelled jewellery, cases, boxes and ornaments decorated with precious and semi-precious stones, and enamels of the highest quality in terms of their evenness and smoothness of texture. The company specialized in the covering of comparatively large surfaces or fields, termed as *en plein* enamelling, since the enamel was applied directly to an object and not to plaques attached to the surface. Enamelled items continue to be produced both by individuals and in small workshops, and industrially for commercial purposes.

Pictures created on or of glass

There are many types of historical pictures created on or of glass. In the case of pictures composed of glass beads or of minute glass *tesserae* (micromosaics), conservators may be required to deal with problems of glass deterioration or of the materials used to bond the glass or *tesserae* to a substrate. In the case of pictures painted either on the front or reverse surface of a panel of flat glass, the usual damage is the fact that the glass panel has broken. However, problems associated with the paint itself will necessitate the involvement of a specialist painting conservator.

- Paintings in oil or water colours on the front of a panel of glass, which were extensively produced by amateur artists in Central Europe from the seventeenth century onwards.
- Reverse paintings on glass (commonly known by the German term, *hinterglasmalerei*), in which the design was executed in reverse order (i.e. details first, background last) on the back of a sheet of glass (see below). This group also includes reverse foil engraving (*Figure 2.18*), amelierung, *eglomisé* (sometimes referred to as *verre eglomisé*), painting combined with mirroring (mirror-painting), and mezzotints (or English glass pictures (formed by adhering prints to the underside of flat or convex glass, removing the paper whilst leaving the ink and then painting). (Silhouettes were produced by the techniques of reverse foil engraving or backpainting) (*Figure 2.19*).
- Luminaries – coloured etchings on glass.
- Photographic images on glass which are composed of different photographic materials and processes. They include

Figure 2.18 Detail of a reverse foil engraving on glass.

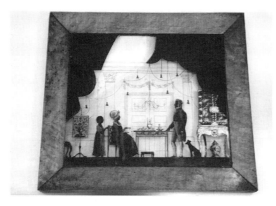

Figure 2.19 Silhouette on the reverse side of glass, paint and gilding, with a pencil drawing in the background.

lantern slides – a composite made up of a photographic image, binder and support, which are encased by a paper matt and cover glasses and bound around the edges with a gummed black paper tape; images on opal plate glass (see *Figure 7.69*) chrystoleum – hand-tinted or painted photographs adhered to the underside of slightly convex glass panels; and coloured photographic images (see *Figure 7.70*), frequently mistaken for very fine miniature paintings on glass.
- British Victorian crazes or manias, *decalcomanie*, *potichimanie*, and *vitre mania*, dating from the mid-nineteenth century. *Decalcomanie*, was the art of decorating any plain smooth surface with brightly coloured paper scraps. *Potichimanie*, was the art of decorating a plain glass or porcelain vase or jar (*potiche*) by pasting the coloured paper scraps to the interior surface. In both techniques, the entire design was then given a coat of protective paint or varnish. In *vitre mania*, decorative patterns produced as transfers were applied to window glass by a simple process to resemble stained glass windows. Around 1850, the term Pearl painting or Oriental painting was used to describe a montage of coloured tinsel and silver paper pressed on to the glass and then framed. Flower studies were painted on glass in transparent oil stains, the background filled in with opaque light tints or with the solidity of lamp-black. Tin-foil was crushed, then smoothed out and placed behind the floral forms so that it glittered when viewed through the glass.
- Architectural glass, which includes mosaics and *opus sectile*, stained glass windows and *cloisonné* glass windows and panels.
- Micromosaics, composed of minute glass *tesserae* adhered to a sheet of copper or other substrate, used as jewellery and to make small souvenirs and copies of easel paintings (see *Figure 2.17*).
- Enamels, vitreous material fused to a metal substrate and used for decorating small objects such as jewellery and boxes (see *Figures 3.4, 3.29, 7.57* and *7.58*).
- Pictures composed of glass beads adhered to a piece of flat glass or other substrate.
- Pictures composed of coloured wax on a flat piece of glass.
- Chinese nineteenth-century glass snuff boxes painted on the interior.

History and technology of reverse glass decoration with cold painting and foil engraving

As an art form, the beginnings of paintings executed in reverse on glass (*hinterglasmalerei*) can be traced back to ancient times. Painting on the reverse of colourless or tinted but transparent materials, depended on its effect on the particular material used. The materials include coloured or lightly tinted glass, rock crystal, mica, amber and tortoise shell. The earliest surviving example is a rock crystal plate dated to 1500 BC, now in the Heraklion Museum, Crete.

The technique of decorating glass objects with *cold painted designs* and *engraved gold foil* is ancient. Cold painting was known in various parts of the Roman Empire; numerous examples of polychrome images on the reverse surfaces of free-blown objects survive, but complete objects in good condition are rare (see *Figure 3.30*). Most specimens seem to have originated in the eastern Mediterranean, between the first and third centuries AD. The technique of *fondi d'oro* was being developed in the third century AD, in Rome, in Syria and other Islamic countries, mostly in the form of decorative bowls and beakers. The bases of some of these items have been found embedded in the plastered walls of Roman catacombs, where they had acted as grave markers. In late Hellenistic times, the technique of enclosing engraved gold leaf between two layers of glass (sandwich gold) and the eggshell technique were practised. The techniques of cold painting and foil engraving seem to have been forgotten after the collapse of the Roman Empire: a *vessel* with *cold painted* decoration is not known again until the sixteenth century.

The production and high quality of reverse paintings on glass was much greater than is generally recognized. In the eighteenth and nineteenth centuries it was practised at the level of folk art, which was of course much more common than the expensive commissioned pictures. Despite the enormous output, the art form has not made an impression on the history of art. Glass paintings in museum collections are not prominently displayed; most being kept in storage. Very few museums publish catalogues of their collections (Pettenati, 1978). There are some regional publications (Aigner, 1992; Schuster, 1980, 1983, 1984). Research into the art of *hinterglasmalerei* was carried out by Keiser (1937), Staffelbach (1951) and Ritz (1972). Research by Frieder Ryser in Berne (Switzerland), highlighted the range of *hinterglasmalerei* and corrected mistaken ideas concerning their technology (see Ryser in Lanz and Seelig, 1999). There have been five important exhibitions accompanied by catalogues (Corning Museum of Glass, 1992; Salmen (ed.), 1995, 1997 (Murnau); Seelig, 1999 (Munich/Zurich);

Lanz and Seelig, 2000 (Romont/Zug) and since 1998 research into Swiss *hinterglasmalerei* of the seventeenth century has been conducted by the Swiss Centre for Research and Information on Stained Glass in Romont.

Paintings produced by painting the design in reverse on glass, are generally known by the German term *hinterglasmalerei,* however the term is recognized in several other languages: reverse painting on glass (Eng); *peinture sous verre* (Fr.); *vetri dispinti* (Ital.); *pintura en vidrio* (Sp.).

Nowadays, paintings for wall-hanging are the most commonly encountered glass objects painted in reverse. However, glass vessels such as tankards and double walled bowls were also decorated in this way. Their quality and quantity was always dependent upon the availability of the glass. In times of the highest production of clear glass, it was possible to commission expensive paintings; whereas mass produced paintings were generally executed on uneven crown, cylinder or plate glass. The refractive properties of the irregular glass surface created an effect, which could not be achieved with any other material or technique. In the production of *hinterglasmalerei*, the normal process of painting was reversed. The artist began by applying the highlights and the final detail of the image, progressing by applying successive layers of paint creating the larger areas of the design, ending with the background. All the details had to be correct, as it was not usually possible to make corrections without destroying the underlying work. The painting, viewed through the clear or tinted glass acquired depth. When the painting was turned for viewing through the glass, the elements painted on the left and right of the image were reversed, an important factor to be considered when lettering was incorporated.

The technique was demanding for an artist as the work had to be visualized in its entirety before work began. Very often a drawing, engraving or print was translated into an outline pattern, (the *riss*) to be laid under the glass sheet. The outline was redrawn on the glass surface following the pattern. The mechanics of this process allowed the development of simple routines and repetitive mass production of patterns in the nineteenth century. Each colour was applied in turn by a different painter until the painting was completed. It has been calculated that in Sandl (Austria) between 1852 and 1864 the output of a single family workshop was 386,000 *hinterglasmalerei* (Eswarin, 1982; Knaipp, 1998; Ryser, in Lanz and Seelig, 1999; Bretz and Ryser, 2000).

Judging from the lack of early documents concerning instruction or recording actual experience, there appears to have been no strict rules for the choice and use of materials for the production of *hinterglasmalerei*. Many were created, by painting directly onto a clean sheet of glass. More often, the side of the glass to be painted was coated with a transparent ground. Some of the priming substances that have so far been identified include egg white, raw linseed oil, gelatin and spar varnish. In addition to oil, egg-, gum-, and casein tempera were used to produce reverse paintings on glass.

Documents dating from the sixteenth to eighteenth centuries indicate that the glass was coated with drying oils. Linseed oil and nut oil mixed with turpentine, or spike oil used as a diluent, were preferred, as these also acted as a binding medium for the paint. Fatty acids could be released from linseed oil, which would have a stabilizing effect on the paint. Certain metals (lead, cobalt and manganese) accelerated the drying of the oil. All kinds of paint available on the market were used for producing the paintings, however for commissioned paintings, only the best and most expensive were used. The poisonous nature of some pigments containing arsenic or mercury was disregarded (Wieck, 1981; and see contributions by Bretz and by Haff in Lanz and Seelig, 2000). (From about 1900, aniline dyes were used to provide colour.) Besides pigments, many other materials used to produce pictures on glass have been identified. These were used singly or in combination: bronze, silver or gold powders, mother of pearl, wax, paper, parchment, linen, silk, coloured copper engravings, painted gelatine leaves or transfers (decalcomania). After the painting was complete, it was sometimes given a protective coating of whatever material the artist had to hand, such as linseed oil and dry pigments. Other forms of backing were cloth, poor quality wood pulp paper or a wood veneer.

Reverse foil engraving

Reverse foil engraving is the decorative technique of applying gold leaf (occasionally silver leaf or both silver and gold) to a piece of glass, after which the design is engraved through the leaf with a fine needle point, and viewed through the glass (*Figure 2.18*). Great technical ability is required, for as with painting in reverse on glass, no corrections can be made. The opaque property of the foil does not permit a pattern to be copied from an outline placed beneath the glass. On completion, the back of the engraving was covered with a layer of black or coloured paint to provide contrast and protection for the gold. Most of the engravings from the Renaissance have been attributed to centres in Northern Italy, notably Padua, where an account of working on gold foil appears at the end of the fourteenth century (Cennini, *c.* 1390).

The foil engraving technique found its way to Saxony and Austria in the form of *zwischengold* beakers, goblets and decanters; to the Low Countries in landscapes and silhouettes by the Dutch engraver Jonas Zeuner (1727–1814); and into folk art in the early nineteenth century in Silesia and Bohemia. A black inner drawing and translucent paint for the shadows, etched in *grisaille* manner, were added to colourful opaque paint, or as a special feature, this kind of *hinterglasmalerei* was mounted in lead, and was often signed and dated.

By the fourteenth century, gold foil engravings were being used in Italy and France, to decorate small glass panels for religious artefacts: crosses, reliquaries and house altars. From the fifteenth century onwards, to the beginning of the Thirty Years' War in Europe, *hinterglasmalerei* were produced by highly skilled painters in Burgundy, Flanders and Lower Rhine. The same artists were producing stained glass paintings and *hinterglasmalerei*. From the fifteenth century onwards, most of the subjects were derived from contemporary woodcuts and engravings, after paintings by well-known artists, and original blocks made for producing prints. During the sixteenth century almost every reverse glass painting produced made extensive use of gold leaf beneath clear glass or transparent pigment. The refractive properties of the irregular glass surface and protection from oxidation and discoloration of the metal created an effect that could not be achieved with any other material or technique. The size of the glass panels available governed the size of the paintings which could be produced. The designs or the patterned borders were often copied from contemporary engravings. In Venice, large circular dishes of clear glass and bowls with elaborate *lattimo* cane twists were further embellished with polychrome painting on the plain base, often of a female head from a contemporary woodcut.

In the High Renaissance and in Mannerism there were two distinguishable schools of painting, to the north and south of the Alps. In Lombardy, little reverse paintings in muted colours, usually on rock crystal, were produced in the form of amulets, pictures for hanging on walls, reliquaries and small altars; and in Nuremberg paintings with etched silver- or gold leaf combined with colourful lacquers were produced for cabinets, backgammon sets, beakers, caskets, decorative mirrors, rings and thimbles. Extra sparkle was given to reverse metal foil engraving with translucent lacquers by inserting a layer of wrinkled tin or silver foil beneath them. This technique, known as *amelierung*, can be traced back to 1532 in Nuremberg, and should not be confused with *emalieren* (fired enamels). The *amelierung* achieved its high point in the Swiss art of *hinterglasmalerei* in the first half of the seventeenth century; the Swiss painter Hans Jakob Sprüngli (1559–1637) was one of the outstanding practitioners. In a deliberate deceptive technique, the naked figures in his images were painted on parchment and glued onto the reverse painting on glass.

In the Austrian Tirol and in Venice, during the sixteenth and seventeenth centuries, 3–4 mm thick glass plates, mostly with curved edges, were painted in reverse in addition to large circular dishes of clear glass and bowls with elaborate *lattimo* cane twists on the plain base. Themes were taken from mythology and from the Old and New Testaments. Tastes and fashion were beginning to change by the early seventeenth century. The stylistic and conceptual attitudes of high art were adopted, the forms became more supple, colour shades to create an illusion of depth, and the paintings executed with meticulous attention to realistic detail. From the end of the seventeenth century the gradual development of new ideas in the arts and sciences with their chief creative sources in France, Germany and England, changed popular designs from the baroque to the rococo.

There was a considerable output of reverse glass paintings in Central Europe between the middle of the eighteenth and the last quarter of the nineteenth centuries. In Augsburg, a major centre of the graphic arts and printing, accomplished individuals such as Johann Wolfgang Baumgartner (1709–1761), produced exceptional reverse glass paintings. In addition craftsmen glass artists produced multiple copies of paintings. Paintings from Augsburg (middle of the eighteenth century) influenced the development of production in the 'Augsburg style', in other localities. Because of the high demand, *hinterglasmalerei* was widely exported (to Italy, Spain, Portugal, North America as far as the West Indies) and a warehouse was established in Cadiz (from about 1750) to export paintings from the production centres in the Bavaria and Bohemia region, also the Black Forest and Alsace. In some of these areas a few painters became known by name, but the vast majority worked anonymously, turning out enormous numbers of pictures on a wide variety of subjects. Religious subjects (e.g. the names of saints who protected the household) were a favourite theme for ardent Catholic customers, as well as allegories of The Seasons or The Continents.

It is generally agreed that the Bohemian export of reverse glass paintings introduced the concept to Romania, creating a virtually individual style in the so-called Romanian icons. In southern Italy, particularly Sicily, production of reverse glass paintings flourished with other forms of folk art providing the themes. Spanish folk production seems to have been centred around the southern region of Andalusia, other areas being Barcelona and Toledo. Outside Europe, export led to the indigenous production of reverse glass paintings as far away as India, Persia (Iran), Indonesia and the Orient and North America. Production continued into the nineteenth century but was usually of inferior quality.

Around 1910, Wassily Kandinsky (1866–1944), Gabriele Münter (1877–1962) and other artists of the group *Der Blaue Reiter* in

Murnau (Bavaria) produced *hinterglasmalerei* (Eswarin, 1982; Knaipp, 1988; Ritz, 1972; catalogues: Corning Museum of Glass, 1992; Ryser and Salmen,1995; Salmen, 1997).

Eglomisé

A technique known as *eglomisé*, had developed in the Netherlands during the sixteenth and seventeenth centuries, and was also practised in Saxony, Bohemia and Austria until about 1725, to decorate small objects such as jewellery, snuff boxes and caskets. More accomplished artists painted pictures for wall decoration, using themes copied from contemporary engraved copper-plate prints of city views and landscapes.

The term *eglomisé* or *verre eglomisé* (Ital. *agglomizzato*) is derived from the name of an eighteenth-century French art dealer and picture framer, Jean Baptiste Glomy. Glomy surrounded his drawings and prints with a border of gilding and colour painted behind the glass, a technique which then became fashionable. Unfortunately, the term *eglomisé* has been and continues to be used to describe all types of painting or gilding behind glass of any age. Technically it is a layer of black paint on a glass panel etched and then gilded or decorated with translucent paint and then gilded (Steinbrucker, 1958; catalogues: Lanz and Seelig, 1999; Lanz and Seelig, 2000).

Paintings on mirrored glass

Although the technique of producing paintings on mirrored glass probably originated in England during the late seventeenth century, the best surviving examples are Chinese (see *Figure 7.72*). Trade and missionary contacts of the eighteenth century introduced the concept to the Far East. Glass panels, notably bevelled plate glass made at the Vauxhall glassworks in south London, were exported to China (especially Canton) to be decorated in this manner for the European market (until the nineteenth century), using contemporary prints as sources for subjects. An amalgam of tin and mercury was first applied to one side of the glass in order to form the mirror. The amalgam was then scraped away from the areas to be painted in oils. The best quality Chinese paintings on mirrored glass were executed in the finest transparent colours. They showed a high artistic ability. Poorer quality paintings were produced for the mass export market. (The twentieth century saw the revival of commercially produced mirror paintings in the form of advertisements.)

Mezzotints

The technique dates back to the middle or second half of the seventeenth century. *Mezzotints* were introduced to England by Prince Rupert who bought the working details from the inventor Ludwig von Giegen. The diarist Samuel Pepys mentions *mezzotints* as being new to England in 1665. The discovery of *mezzotint engraving*, and its popularity in England, would seem to be the key to the origin of reverse glass prints, since the two processes are inextricably linked. Clarke (1928), 'venture(s) to assert that the art (of applying paper prints to glass) came into being through the "call for colour" to Mezzotint Engravings'. After mezzotint engravings became firmly established in England, and after publication in 1687 of *The Art of Painting in Oyl* by the clockmaker, John Smith, prints transferred to glass began to be produced.

Tremain (1988) gives a detailed account of the history technique and conservation of reverse glass prints. There were several variants of the method for producing *mezzotints*, but the general procedure was to soak a print in water for about four hours to remove the size from the paper, and then allow it to dry. A sheet of fine Bristol glass was then covered with an adhesive (normally Venice turpentine) and the dry print laid face down upon it. When the adhesive had set, the back of the print was dampened, and the paper rubbed away with a sponge or the fingertips leaving only a thin tissue with the ink adhering to it, attached to the glass. (After *circa* 1770 the dry print was removed by the use of glass paper.) After this had again dried out, the design was coloured in, details first, background last.

The earlier, more beautiful *mezzotints* owe their brilliance to the fact that only the smallest amount of paper remained on the glass. Many display the date, a title and the name of the engraver and the painter below the painting. Later examples made by amateurs or less skilled practitioners have a much more opaque and heavier appearance, owing to the greater amount of paper remaining, the required transparency being produced by the application of a white varnish (Ryser, 1991). Back paintings were generally produced anonymously, although as suggested above, in its earlier days, the engravers of the prints probably produced the *mezzotints* themselves. During the eighteenth century portraits in *mezzotint transfers* were favoured, as well as the Four Seasons, the Months, the Four Times of Day, the Five Senses and the Elements, followed in the nineteenth century by shipping scenes.

Chinese snuff bottles

In China during the nineteenth century, clear rock crystal or glass snuff bottles began to be decorated by painting on the interior surface. The basis of the technique was similar to that used on sheet glass, where the layers of paint had to be applied in reverse order, i.e. the details first, background last, the result being viewed through the glass. However, the artist required considerable skill to create delicate designs such as portraits and landscapes, using an angled pen or brush, inserted through the tiny mouth of the bottle.

Architectural glass

Historic literary sources and archaeological evidence show that at least from Roman times, glass was used in the form of small window panes and for the decoration of walls in the form of glazed bricks, *opus sectile*, and as mosaic *tesserae* on floors, walls and ceilings. The conservation treatment of mosaic floors – lifting techniques in particular – is well covered in conservation literature (Novis, 1975; ICCROM, 1983; see also Proceedings of the Conferences of the ICOM Committee for Conservation of Mosaics).

The use of glass as an architectural medium, particularly since the nineteenth century, is outside the scope of this volume, since it is normally an architectural or building concern. Even so, a glass conservator may be consulted with regard to glass technology, deterioration mechanisms and methods of recording. Decorative glass continues to be used to form windows, wall coverings, skylights and roofs, and during the twentieth century, toughened glass has been developed for use as load-bearing walls, floors and staircases, e.g. the Glass Gallery, Victoria and Albert Museum, London, (McGrath *et al.*, 1961).

Mosaics

The architectural process of embedding small pieces of roughly squared glass fragments (*tesserae*) in floor cement to form pictures was developed from early Greek mosaics composed of coloured pebbles. The technique was extensively used in the Roman and Byzantine periods. The Roman historian Pliny records (Forbes, 1966, ref. 232) that,

> When pavimenta lost their place of honour on the ground, they took refuge in the vaulted ceilings, and glass was used for their construction. Such an application of glass is quite recent, for when Agrippa, in the baths which he constructed at Rome, adorned the terra-cotta walls of the hot rooms with encaustic paintings, and finished the other rooms in white, he would unquestionably have put glass mosaics in the ceilings if such fashion had existed, or if the glass which we have described as figuring in the walls of Scaurus' theatre had found a place in the ceilings.

There are also historical references to glass pillars (Forbes, 1966 quoting ancient sources, refs 230 and 231), which stood for instance in the temple of Aradus.

Mosaics were composed of *tesserae*, made from coloured glass, mostly about one centimetre square in cross section, which were embedded in mortar, scored with a rough outline of the design, while it remained soft (two to four days) (see *Figure 3.39*). The first mosaics were formed of brightly coloured lead glass with a limited colour range of red and yellow or intermediate hues. Later, the glass *tesserae* were formed from glass pastes, *smalti* (cakes) and metal leaf. Glass pastes appear to have been made in a limited colour range. The brightest of these were of dark, transparent homogenous glass, whilst the lighter shades were produced either by reducing the amount of colourant in the glass, and/or by the addition of a white opacifying agent. Special hues could be obtained by adding coloured crystalline materials to the molten glass, such as brownish-orange fired clay, or a vitreous opaque yellow intermediate product (*galliano*).

In Roman times the technique of adhering leaves of silver and gold and their alloys to hot glass was discovered. The metal leaf was applied to cast glass slabs 5–10 mm thick, or to a thin sheet of blown glass (the *cartellina*), less than 1 mm thick, which would protect the metal against oxidation, and add to its brilliant appearance. The two glasses were then heated in the furnace until they began to soften and were then pressed together to ensure good adhesion, and thus embedding the leaf. The final appearance of the metal-leaf *tesserae* depended upon the purity of the metal, the nature of the support and whether colour was deliberately added to the *cartellina*.

The use of the gold background in mosaic work was particularly associated with Byzantine architecture. The earlier mosaics at Rome and Ravenna generally have backgrounds of a dark blue colour, which is particularly fine at SS Cosma and Damiano in Rome, and in the tomb of Galla Placidia in Ravenna. Fiorentino-Roncuzzi has published a study of the mosaics at Ravenna in the church of San Vitale (dedicated AD 547) and the Basilica of Sant' Apollinare in Classe (*c.* AD 500). The mosaics at San Sophia in Constantinople (sixth century) had gold backgrounds, as did all the later examples in Italy from the ninth and tenth centuries only. The finest examples are at San Sophia, San Marco in Venice, and the Cappella Palatina at Palermo.

According to a twelfth-century treatise by Theophilus (Hawthorne and Smith, 1963) the Byzantines,

> made sheets of glass a finger thick (20 mm) and split them with a hot iron into tiny pieces, and cover them on one side with gold leaf, coating them with clear ground glass before firing them in a kiln to fuse the gold leaf into place. Glass of this kind interspersed in mosaic work embellishes it very beautifully.

Smalti were produced in the Murano glassworks from the fifteenth century, allowing the production of a larger range of intensely coloured glass with a greater surface brilliance,

and ease of cutting due to the high percentages of lead oxide present (producing a 'soft' glass). Vasari (1511–1571) describes the preparation of mosaic cubes. First the glass is made opaque by the addition of tin oxide, and coloured with metallic oxides. The molten glass is ladled out in small quantities onto a metal plate and pressed into cakes 20 mm in diameter, and from 10 to 12 mm thick. The cold glass was annealed and cracked into *tesserae*, the fractured surface being used to form the upper surface of the mosaic because it has a brighter surface. The thickness of the glass cake therefore determined the texture.

The production of leaf *tesserae* was extremely skilled, and in times of less technical ability, e.g. during the eighteenth century, it was replaced by cold gilding on glass. The early Christian mosaics in Ravenna (notably in the mausoleum of Galla Placidia; the Ravenna Cathedral baptistery, the basilica of Sant' Apollinare Nuovo and the Church of San Vitale), cover immense wall surfaces and vaults. Within an architectural framework highlighted by decorative design, the main areas are covered by representations of figures. Some vaults are damasked with floral motifs. The mosaics in the church of San Vitale (dedicated AD 547), and in the basilica of Sant' Apollinare in Classe (*c.* AD 500) have been published by Fiorentino-Roncuzzi (1967). In the past ten years or so, several scientific reports concerning the study and analysis of ancient mosaic *tesserae* have been published (Freestone *et al.*, 1990; Veritá, 2001). In modern times glass mosaics have been used to cover the exterior surfaces of buildings, e.g. Liverpool Cathedral, but without the same success.

Deterioration mechanisms in mosaics composed of glass *tesserae* are the leaching of alkali (sodium) by water, followed by the formation of micro-cracks. These are propagated by the crystallization of sodium (calcium) carbonate in them. In polluted environments, sodium, calcium carbonate is transformed into sulphate, which becomes acidified and hastens decay. In addition, water may penetrate metal leaf *tesserae* if the bond between the two layers of glass enclosing the leaf has not been complete. Water also penetrates between the individual *tessera* and if there are structural faults in the building, which they adorn, may penetrate behind the mosaic causing their disruption.

Opus sectile

The site of Kenchreai, one of the two ports of ancient Corinth, was excavated between 1965 and 1968, during which fragments and sections of one hundred panels of glass *opus sectile* were recovered from the sea (see *Figures 7.7a–d*). The panels are thought to have been made in the Egyptian city of Alexandria (or in Italy), and to have been stored in a warehouse when Kenchreai was destroyed by an earthquake, *circa* 365 AD, and the shoreline of the harbour was submerged. Each panel was composed of coloured fragments and moulded shapes of glass set in a rosin/marble plaster matrix to form architectural and pictorial compositions depicting buildings, human figures and Nilotic plants and birds. This was supported by a backing of thick ceramic tiles, which in addition to the cured resin, would have resulted in a heavy, sturdy construction. Because of the unevenness of this backing, the panels were packed in pairs, face to face for shipping. Immersion in salt water for just over 1600 years caused the glass surfaces to become stuck to each other; however, the natural disaster allowed the recovery of more *opus sectile* than has been found anywhere else in the ancient world.

In 1995, as a result of renewed archaeological interest in the site of Kenchreai, several of the original excavators and conservation specialists re-examined the panels and fragments. Koob, Brill and Thimme (1996) give a comparison and assessment of previous treatments applied to the *opus sectile* panels.

As was the case with so many ancient techniques, that of *opus sectile* was resurrected by Victorian craftsmen in nineteenth century-Britain. Coloured glass blown for windows was occasionally used for mosaics, and led to the 'invention' at Powell's Whitefriars Glasshouse in London of a new opaque material known as *opus sectile* and described at the time as 'standing halfway between tile painting and stained glass'. The technique was employed as a means of reducing waste: it had been discovered that fragments of flint glass contaminated with clay, and therefore

normally scrapped, could be ground to a fine powder (fritted), and baked to produce a solid, durable material with an eggshell surface and an almost unlimited range of colours. Large panels of *opus sectile* could be made from the frit, which also formed the basis of Powell's production of glass tiles. These were made by packing decorative iron moulds with powdered glass which was then fused by heating. The technique was first experimented with in the 1860s, and by the 1880s it began to be used widely to create church memorials and decorative wall effects. Many decorative schemes of *opus sectile* can be seen in churches throughout Britain. Both *opus sectile* and glass tiles continued to be made until the Second World War.

Figure 3.41 shows an example of late-nineteenth-century *opus sectile* work in a high Victorian public house, The Crown Bar (Belfast, Northern Ireland). Glass *opus sectile* panels decorate the spandrels above the bar arcade. The panels are in the design of bowls of fruit with stylized foliage formed in blue, green, deep red, purple and clear glass, attached to rough wooden backboards with putty. The putty was coloured amber, yellow or green depending upon which colour glass was to be laid on it. Some of the glass was backed with gold or silver coloured foil (which may actually be aluminium). The glass pieces were roughly cut and the edges not smoothed off. Putty either oozed up between the pieces or was deliberately applied, coloured black to resemble lead cames. Some of the blackening undoubtedly results from the smoky bar-atmosphere. It is assumed that a Belfast firm was brought in to provide all the glass ornamentation for the Crown Bar; but the source of their manufacture is unknown.

Historical development of flat glass

The methods by which glass was produced in flat, sheet form have changed considerably over the ages. Small pieces of flat glass could be produced by casting glass into open moulds or by cutting squares of glass formed by the cylinder or crown methods (see *Figure 3.43*). Syrian glassmakers were the first producers of blown glass crowns (specula) in the first century. Small windows of greenish glass, cast into wooden moulds, and bearing their imprint, are known from Roman times. Flat sections of glass cut from medieval crown and cylinder glass were termed panes. Square or diamond-shaped panes used (particularly in *grisaille* windows are called quarries (from the French, *carré*, square).

Up until the seventeenth century, broad and plate glass were produced by the cylinder method. The technique of producing plate glass by casting glass onto a flat surface was invented in France. Bernard Perrot of Orleans and Louis Lucas de Nehou, an official at the Tourlaville glassworks at Cherbourg where plate glass was already being made, both claim its invention. In December 1688, Letters Patent granted the monopoly of glass manufacture by the casting process for the French home market, and, later also for export, to several Frenchmen acting through Abraham Thevart. Following a chequered career, the factory was reconstructed in 1702, after which manufacture was concentrated at works in Tourlaville and at St-Gobain in Picardy. By 1725, the annual output had probably reached about 700 tons, by 1750 about 850 tons, and after 1760 more than 1150 tons.

Mirrors

The first mirrors were probably reflective surfaces made of obsidian, polished stone or rock crystal, and in the classical world and China, of pieces of dark glass or metal with a high tin content (speculum). The first mention of a genuine glass mirror with a reflective backing of tin is by Aphrodisias (*c*. 220 AD, Forbes, 1966). Looking glasses or mirrors formed of flat glass coated on the reverse with an amalgam (tin–mercury) came into general use in the late Middle Ages, once suitable flat glass could be produced. This type of mirror was prevalent from the sixteenth until the twentieth century, and is therefore the commonest type found in museum collections and historic buildings.

The first centre for the production of amalgam mirrors was Murano in Venice, where in 1507 brothers Andrea and Domenico del Gallo obtained a twenty-year privilege (patent) from the Ten Men's Court in Venice to make mirror glass according to a new method. Since the glass was made by the cylinder process, it was difficult to make

mirrors larger then a cylinder of one metre length. In 1687, a process of producing large sheets of plate glass by casting it onto an iron table and then rolling it flat with a metal cylinder was invented in France. The centre of the mirror industry moved from Italy to France and from there gradually spread to other countries.

Plain glass windows

The use of glass in an architectural context was relatively slow to develop. It was one of several more or less translucent materials, including alabaster, mica and shell, used by the Romans to form small windows. The materials were set into the masonry, or into decorative frames of plaster, wood or bronze. There is archaeological and literary evidence for the use of window glass throughout the Roman and Muslim worlds. Glazed windows were in use by the first century AD, particularly in the northern part of the Roman Empire. In the United Kingdom, fragments of Roman window glass have been excavated at Hartfield, East Sussex (Money, 1976), Stonea, Cambridgeshire and Caerleon in Wales (Boon, 1966). The gradual replacement of wood or plaster lattices by malleable lead resulted in a flexible and more versatile construction. When and where the use of lead began is not known, but it is possible that its use for window framing may have been suggested by the use of thin metal strips to separate coloured areas of enamel in the *cloisonné* technique.

Decorative windows appeared in Christian churches at a very early date. The poet Prudentius (348 to *c*. 410), in describing the widespread use of glass in Constantinople, wrote, 'In the round arches of the windows in the basilica shone glass in colours without number'. The windows may have been an abstract coloured mosaic as no subject matter is mentioned. Although there is much literary evidence for them, no complete windows survive from the fifth and sixth centuries.

During the Middle Ages glass was made in the forest glasshouses of France, especially in Normandy and Lorraine, the Low Countries, parts of Germany and other parts of Europe. The output would have included window glass, with a greenish caste, made by the cylinder and crown glass processes. Although the cutting of crown glass was arduous and complicated by the bull's eye, it yielded a smooth and highly polished surface. Although costly to produce, crown glass was highly favoured. Glass discs spun to a diameter of 122–183 cm (4–6 ft) and after cooling and annealing, was cut into small panes of glass, rarely more than 30×20 cm (12×8 in), and set in parallel rows. The central bull's eye formed when the pontil rod was cracked off was incorporated, the gaps between the roundels were filled with triangular pieces of cut glass. The small panes necessitated the use of glazing bars in the larger window spaces of the eighteenth and early nineteenth centuries.

The glassmaking families of Normandy and Lorraine were the finest manufacturers of window glass and their products were widely exported. In the late fourteenth century the cylinder process was refined in Lorraine by increasing the size of the cylinders to obtain large and even sheets (sometimes referred to as the *Lorraine Method*). Numerous panes were cut from the sheets and arranged geometrically (often into lozenge patterns) and held in place by lead strips. The windows were set into wooden frames ready to be installed. They were highly valued and moved with the owner when a house was sold.

With the aid of glassworkers from Normandy and Lorraine, Jean Carré established two furnaces in the Weald area of southern England, to manufacture window glass. As a result, cheaper home-produced windows could be afforded by others than the wealthy, and began to be used in carriages and ships in addition to buildings. Initially the glass was undoubtedly of inferior quality to that produced in France, however by *circa* 1580–90 its quality had substantially improved.

The French religious wars of 1560, and in England, the technical changes in glassmaking brought about by James I's proclamation of 1615, banning the use of wood as fuel in glass furnaces, had major repercussions for the way in which glass was to be developed and used. During the seventeenth to the nineteenth centuries, window tax and duty in England, through the way duty was collected, encouraged one method of production over another, and stifled creative development, giving Europe the lead in glass production techniques.

During the late seventeenth century wood largely replaced the use of lead as supports for tall windows, as it was both lighter in weight and less expensive. Timber mullions and transoms supported leaded light casements. Sash windows evolved during the neo-classical movement, with the need to let more light into buildings through the installation of larger panes of glass. In England wood was used in the manufacture of sash windows, introduced at Windsor Castle in 1686. After this date, wood framed windows became increasingly common in Europe, and after *circa* 1740, in North America. In Georgian England, the box sash window was developed with astragal divisions; and it became fashionable to insert glass fanlights above the main entrance doors. The fanlight above the main entrance door of Marble Hill House, Twickenham (built 1724–7) is amongst the first to be documented. The majority of fanlights originate between 1780 and 1830. Together with iron railings and balconies, they form the most conspicuous forms of house decoration on the late Georgian house.

The availability of sheet glass enabled large spectacular buildings to be erected, built of glass supported in a metal framework, such as the Palm House, Kew Gardens (using improved German sheet glass produced by Chance), and the Crystal Palace, both in London. The Palm House was built between 1844 and 1848, to house new plant discoveries coming into the country from expeditions around the world. Between 1985 and 1989, the building underwent major restoration work, which reduced it to its bare bones before being rebuilt. During the course of work, 16,000 panes of glass and 10 miles of glazing bars were used. The Crystal Palace was built to house the Great (Trade) Exhibition of 1851, and was later destroyed by fire.

Painted and stained glass windows

It is not known where the technique of staining on window glass originated. Staining on vessel glass was practised in Egypt in the sixth and seventh centuries. Archaeological evidence is pushing back the date of the earliest known enamelled glass. Fragments of crown glass bearing the painted outline of Christ in Benediction from San Vitale in Ravenna (Italy) have been dated to *circa* 540 AD. Silver stained (and enamel painted) glass windows flourished as a major Christian art form in Gothic Europe (mid twelfth to the sixteenth centuries), being originally made for ecclesiastical buildings (see *Figure 3.45*). Later they were also made for public buildings and private dwellings. The technique originated in medieval France at the time of the building of the great churches and cathedrals, and may have been inspired by other art forms employing similar materials and techniques: the setting of coloured glass and gemstones in jewellery, where they were held in place by metal claws over holes cut in the metalwork, the manufacture of cloisonné enamels and the use of glittering glass mosaics to cover walls and domes in early Christian churches such as those in Ravenna. In the Islamic world, coloured glass was set into a pierced marble framework to form decorative windows, e.g. Topkapi Palace, Istanbul.

The oldest surviving stained glass windows are thought to be the Prophet Windows in Augsburg Cathedral, *circa* 1065, and the Ascension window at Le Mans, *circa* 1145. These examples are so developed that there must have been precursors which have either perished or been deliberately destroyed.

Windows were produced in great quantity in France in the fourteenth century, during the period of the building of the great churches and cathedrals. The names of the medieval craftsmen remain largely unknown, but may occasionally be found in church records, e.g. John Thornton of Coventry, under whose direction the great east window of York Minster was glazed between 1405 and 1408. This window measures *circa* 23.4 × 9.8 m, and was badly damaged by fire in the twentieth century. The most renowned surviving windows are in the French cathedrals at Chartres and Le Mans, and in the Sainte-Chapelle, Paris.

Glassmaking in the medieval period was clearly dominated by the great demand for window glass for the cathedrals and churches being erected at the beginning of the Gothic era. Barrelet states that for the cathedral of Chartres alone, at least 2000 m of glass was required over a period of 30 years; this would correspond to about 8 m of glass (*c.* 20 tonnes). Large quantities of fuel might have been difficult to obtain at the best of times; it would not have been surprising therefore, if

the need for so much fuel caused a shortage at coastal glassmaking sites. Migration of the glassworkers to well-wooded sites may have been a natural consequence, especially north of the Alps where most of the new cathedrals were being constructed.

A succession of French glassmakers emigrated to Britain to carry on the glass trade; there are no records of native Britons manufacturing glass at the time. Thus from the earliest times French glassworkers acquired a widespread reputation, in particular for the production of window glass. Documents dating from the eighth century include requests for their assistance in supplying glazing for churches and monasteries in Britain. The trade would have further increased after the Norman conquest of Britain in 1066, when church building began to be carried out on a large scale. The first recorded French glassmaker working in Britain was Lawrence Vitrearius of Normandy, who obtained a grant of land at Dyers Cross in Sussex in AD 1220. In 1240 he was commissioned by Henry III to make plain and coloured glass for Westminster Abbey in London. Succeeding generations of the Vitrearius family were recorded until 1301. Then, in *circa* 1343, a John Schurterre settled at Chiddingfold in Sussex and became an important glassmaking figure. The Chiddingfold area of Sussex (in the Weald), remained the centre of British glassmaking for many years, having as it did an abundant supply of wood-fuel, and beechwood and bracken which could be burned to produce ash (alkali). A sixteenth century Venetian map of Britain shows two glassmaking sites, that at Chiddingfold, and another at Guildford in Surrey.

Medieval painted and stained windows were made of small pieces of glass, but the size of the individual pieces has increased over the centuries. The finest glass windows are those of the thirteenth and fourteenth centuries made with coloured glass; those of the sixteenth century and later were made by painting with coloured enamels, mostly on colourless glass panels.

Following the increase in realism found in fifteenth-century painted glass, sixteenth-century glass painters increasingly tried to achieve the effects of easel painting. By the seventeenth and eighteenth centuries, the leading, which had played such an important part of the design of medieval windows, was reduced to holding the large squares or rectangles of clear glass together. The entire glass surface was then painted like a canvas. By the late sixteenth century, translucent enamels were available in a wide range of colours. Their total adoption was perhaps accelerated by the increasing difficulty of obtaining coloured glass, as wars and political unrest in Europe gradually ruined or made glassmaking areas inaccessible.

The decline of the art during the second half of the sixteenth century can be attributed to a number of factors. Internal causes were technical innovation, changes in fashion and the use of new materials; external causes were the reformation, religious conflict and neglect. The rise of classicism hastened a dislike for the decorative narrative of the Gothic stained glass window in favour of smaller, simpler windows. During the sixteenth century *Biercheiben* (celebration windows) brought the ecclesiastical art of stained glass to ordinary homes. To celebrate the building of a new home or family occasion, a local artist would be commissioned to paint a suitable picture or coat of arms in transparent colours, on a small pane of glass which would then be incorporated into a window. The panels became enormously popular and were produced by tradesmen and glaziers with a flair for art, rather than by artists. Popular themes were biblical scenes and rural activities. *Bierscheiben* were exported abroad. Small leaded stained glass roundels, and panels, bearing designs executed in fired enamel pigments and – occasionally – yellow silver stain from which they derive their name, were also made for secular use.

In Venice, during the seventeenth and eighteenth centuries, small glass plaques depicting picturesque city views derived from contemporary prints and paintings were executed in cold painting and fired enamelling techniques. In Bohemia, Germany and Spain, engraved clear glass plaques depicted commemorative scenes: e.g., a panel engraved by Felix Ramos in the late eighteenth century, showing the facade of the Royal Palace of San Ildefonso (Museo Arqueologico Nacional, Madrid). In the nineteenth century *hochschnitt* plaques were produced by the German glass-

maker Wilhelm von Eiff (1890–1943) depicting figural subjects in a contemporary manner.

Stained glass window production was revived in the nineteenth century when medieval methods of manufacture were investigated and practised. One of the greatest British designers was Sir Edward Burne-Jones (1833–98), whose designs were executed by William Morris (1834–96), e.g. those in Birmingham Cathedral; by the American John La Farge (1835–1910) and others. In the twentieth century windows were designed by, among others, the artist Marc Chagall (1889–1985).

Traditional windows and panels continue to be made and restored in numerous studios. In addition new art forms have been developed, such as glass-in-concrete, appliqué glass and fused glass windows, usually but not exclusively in modern churches and cathedrals such as those at Coventry, Warwickshire (UK) and Rouen (France). Lee *et al.* (1982) published an illustrated comprehensive guide to the world's best painted glass windows.

The term stained glass used to describe these decorative, coloured glass windows, is not strictly correct, since the majority contain little silver staining, the technique only having been discovered in the fourteenth century. A technically more accurate term would be painted glass windows, since the overall colour derives from colourants introduced at the glass-melting stage, i.e. to the batch, or from the use of flashed glass, i.e. clear glass which has been covered with a thin layer of colour, e.g. ruby red; and from which the pieces of glass to form the design are subsequently cut. Onto this, details were applied in enamel colours, which were fired for permanency. Silver staining became popular during the fourteenth and fifteenth centuries, but later windows were often enamel painted with small amounts of staining on features such as crowns, rings and canopies.

In the process of creating a traditional stained glass window, the design is conceived, sketched and then a full-size drawing (*cartoon*) is produced. From this, the *cut-line*, a tracing of the lead-lines is taken. The centre of each *lead-line* is carefully drawn in order that the coloured glass pieces placed over the tracing can be accurately cut to shape. Minor adjustments may have to be made to the glass edges. In medieval times this process, termed *grozing*, was carried out using a metal tool with a hooked end (the *grozing* iron), which left the glass with a characteristic nibbled edge. From the eighteenth century, a sharp metal tool or diamond wheel was used, which created a smooth straight edge. Decorative detail is applied in the form of enamel colours and/or yellow (or silver) stain, and rendered permanent by fusing them to the glass at relatively low temperatures in a muffle kiln.

The technique of yellow staining developed in the early fourteenth century. It colours clear glass yellow (or more rarely blue glass green) by the application of a solution of a silver compound to the exterior surface and firing it. The earliest firmly dated example of the yellow stain technique is a window from the parish church of Le Mesnil-Villeman, Manche (France). Yellow stain ranges from pale lemon to orange and is produced by applying a solution of silver compound to the surface of the glass, which when fired, turns yellow. Details such as facial features can be defined with a brownish-coloured enamel made with iron oxide termed *grisaille* (Fr. *grissailler*, to paint grey). *Grisaille* was also used to create geometric patterns of regular design or of foliate design, leaded into or painted on tinted glass. *Smear shading* was a method of shading details such as drapery and facial features by applying pigment sparingly with parallel brush strokes. The technique was prevalent until the fourteenth century. *Stippling* creates the effect of minute points of light all over the glass.

The glass pieces are then *leaded-up* in a framework of lead *cames* to form panels. A series of panels is combined to form large windows. Individual small panels or larger windows are cemented into the stonework of a window aperture and supported at intervals by being tied-in to horizontal metal glazing bars (*ferramenta*).

Another type of window glass was made by the *Norman slab* (or *bottle glass*) method. A gather of molten glass was blown into a square mould. The resulting square block was then cut so that each side became a small flat piece of glass. (A modern development is the use of slab glass blocks (Fr. *dalle de verre*), cast glass pieces usually about 2.5 cm thick and 30 cm long, which are set in concrete or in epoxy resin, as opposed to being leaded-

up. Its use creates windows with a monumental appearance dominated by the dark framework; which can be load-bearing.) Traditional stained glass windows continue to be made by individuals and by small workshops. Their manufacture is not a process that can be industrialized.

The historical care of painted and stained glass windows has, as is the case with all windows, been linked with the routine maintenance of the buildings in which they were installed. During the windows' lifetime, damaged glass and lead cames have been removed and replaced by successive generations. Only a fraction of the stained glass produced during the Middle Ages has survived to the present day. Few survive intact and without considerable change in their original appearance, resulting from decay, paint loss and restoration. In some countries such as The Netherlands and Norway, the losses have been catastrophic. In Britain, during the seventeenth and eighteenth centuries, the Calvinists, fundamentalists and Cromwell's army broke as many church windows as they could, since pictorial art was then regarded as idolatrous. In France the iconoclasm associated with the French Revolution was also responsible for the loss of much painted window glass. A considerable amount of French glass was bought by patrons of the arts in Britain, and much of it was installed in British churches.

In Britain, France and Germany much more medieval glass survives, but windows have often been removed from their original settings, and some reduced to fragments. Examples of glass from the poorest to the finest buildings have found their way into auction rooms, and been sold into public and private collections. It is these smaller pieces of glass which an objects conservator might be required to treat.

Cloisonné glass

During the last years of the nineteenth century, a London company attributed to itself the invention of a decorative form of glass panel, after which it was named: The *Cloisonné* Glass Co. (at 40 Berners Street, Oxford Street, London W.) However, it is known that the company of Barthels & Pfister were also making *cloisonné* artistic windows in London at that time. The main feature of *cloisonné* glass panels was the combination of both transmitted and reflected light effects (see *Figure 7.68*).

Decorative forms do not develop in isolation, and as its name suggests, *cloisonné* stained glass derived from the techniques of stained glass and *cloisonné* enamel manufacture (and perfectly described the technique of containing coloured, tiny glass chips and globules within a framework of metal strips, between two sheets of glass). Initially, the glass was only produced in London, but later under English patent, it was produced in other European countries, notably Spain, and in the United States of America.

There is little information regarding the technique, but the following information was taken from publicity material issued by The *Cloisonné* Glass Company. The panels were made up, by first outlining the design with thin gilt or silvered metal wire secured with translucent cement (adhesive) to a sheet of clear glass (back-plate). The cells thus formed were filled with pot metal coloured glass in granular form (< 1 mm), either globules or squares, and secured in place with adhesive. The *Cloisonné* Glass Co. boasted a stock of raw glass comprising over eight hundred different shades and tints. A second sheet of clear glass was then placed over the design and sealed by binding the edges of the glass 'sandwich' with tin foil. According to the Company, the top sheet of glass was not absolutely necessary but served to give the *cloisonné* layer a smooth surface, so that it could easily be washed and kept clean. It also, of course, afforded protection to the work. Panels thus formed could be fixed in place with putty by any glazier, or by the use of wooden beading for internal decorations. They were used as windows, fanlights, door panels, lanterns and ceiling lights, window blinds, screens (including fire screens), and partitions. They were used for internal and external decorations in houses, public buildings and also in piers, yachts, liners and railway carriages, for decorative fascias, signs – illuminated or opaque, for the decoration of furniture such as cabinets, cupboards, book-cases, screens, writing desks, over-mantels and pianos etc. The panels could in fact be used as an alternative in any situation where stained or leaded glass, mosaic, fresco or tempera would be appropriate.

It was claimed that, as in the case of stained glass panels, *cloisonné* stained glass was suitable and preferable for decorations which were seen at night, when no light is transmitted through it, or where a good opaque effect was desired in addition to the transparency. It was further claimed that the double sheet of glass excluded any draughts and was absolutely water-tight. For indoor work, *cloisonné* stained glass could be supplied without the top sheet. The work was laid on a slate base and was said to be perfectly durable. The Company's description of this type of work states that the base could be gilt, thus obtaining a greater brilliancy and richness of colour as a result of the gilt layer reflecting light through the *cloisonné* layer. The panels were said to be less liable to break than ordinary window panes. The best quality window glass was used in their manufacture, in 21, 26, 32 oz weights, or plate glass, according to the required size or situation. The process of manufacture, being a cold one, the glass sheets were not subject to any strain. Panels could be made on glass varying in thickness between ¼ in and ⅜ in and also of curved glass or of plate glass between ½ in and ⅝ in. It was recommended that the panels were set in a ¼ in rebate to hide the tin foil edging, or that the tin-foil be painted a 'suitable' colour. As is the case with stained glass windows, glazing bars could be introduced to support very large panels. In the case of the front glass plate being broken, this could 'easily be replaced by any glazier'. Should the back sheet or both sheets become broken, the glass could easily be repaired at the works in a few days at small cost. If the back plate, which was always made stronger than the front, was only slightly damaged, another sheet of glass could be put behind the original to protect the work. This second sheet had to be well embedded in putty to prevent any dust entering the space between the two glass sheets.

Historical development of light fittings

Lanterns and lampshades

The first reference to glass lamps dates from the fourth century AD. Standing and hanging lamps were used for illuminating churches and other buildings. Contemporary mosaics depict various types of lamps in use, which seem to have been made of glass. The vessels are of various shapes; some were used as true lamps burning a wick, and some as candlesticks, some as single lights and some as elements in a polycandelabra. Simple glass bowls or dishes suspended from metal chains and containing oil and a wick to provide light, of a type known since antiquity, are still in use in mosques. On some much later examples of glass dish lamps, an urn-shaped reservoir was suspended centred over the dish, while on others the fixtures were equipped with three or four reservoir burners attached to and standing up from the metal rim.

So many of these devices have been converted to electricity that original metalwork does not often survive. Glass dish lights suspended from the ceiling by chains became popular in nineteenth century Europe, as they offered a practical alternative to candlelight. A wick soaked in colza oil was usually held in a central reservoir, and was gravity fed to small sumps beneath the burners which were covered with decorated or opaque glass shades.

In the earliest hand-held lanterns, a candle was protected by panels of thin animal horn (Eng. lanthorn). Metal-framed hanging lanterns became popular in the eighteenth century, when they were glazed, and when decoration of the frame and glass panels became increasingly ornate. The glass panes may be held in place with linseed putty and/or by clips incorporated in the metal framework. Checks on the metal framework, the security of any door hinges and on the fixing arrangements will need to be made. In the case of spherical lanterns, each glass panel will be curved. If one or more of these requires replacing, a complete panel can be removed and a plaster-of-Paris mould taken from the convex side into which a glassworker can heat and slump a piece of glass of the correct thickness, to form a new panel. The edges of the new panel can be chipped (*grozed*) in order to adjust it to the correct dimensions.

Following the introduction of electric lighting (the first light bulb was produced in 1879), lampshades of numerous varieties began to be made. Particularly well-known are the highly decorative lampshades produced by Louis Comfort Tiffany in the United States; and those produced by Gallé and Daum in France. Tiffany lampshades are composed of coloured fragments of glass assembled to form designs, and held in a thin copper framework, the entire effect being similar to that of a stained glass window.

Candlesticks and candelabra

Glass holders to support one or more candles (candelabra) were produced in England, France, Spain, Germany and Italy (Venice) from the 1600s onwards, then in Ireland, and by 1760 in America. Many originally followed the designs of their metal prototypes. From the mid-seventeenth century onwards it was fashionable to decorate the metal framework of light fittings with glass or rock crystal ornaments, such as pendants and facetted beads, which caught and reflected the light. In England, branched candle-holders for table use, with two or more arms for candle sockets, were commonly made of glass *circa* 1760–1880. Originally advertised as girandoles, they were known as candelabra from *circa* 1792. Early examples were plain, and again many originally following the designs of their metal prototypes. After *circa* 1714, cutting on the shaft reflected fashionable styles of contemporary wine glass stems; after circa 1765 cutting became increasingly more lavish, and the candelabra might be decorated with a star or crescent finial at the top. After *circa* 1775, many were decorated with pendant drops (lustres), which continued to feature on nineteenth-century examples.

Wall light and sconces

Wall lights and sconces were made in Venice from the early 1600s and shortly afterwards in England. Made of glass or glass combined with metal giltwood or ceramic, they had one or more branches for holding candles. One type was designed with a light-reflecting back-plate, usually of polished metal or mirror glass (the latter by the late seventeenth century), called a sconce by *circa* 1712. Their design followed the style of table candelabra of the period, and they offered a practical solution to lighting large rooms. In Ireland, cut glass was produced in Belfast, Dublin, Waterford and Cork, the Waterford factory opening in 1783. Distinctive wall lights unique to the Irish glass-making repertory combined an oval mirror-glass back-plate framed by clear and blue glass segments (and rarely, green), fitted with a metal hook on top, from which a miniature chandelier was suspended.

Chandeliers

There are few publications concerned with the historical development of chandeliers (Mortimer, 2000). Determining age can be complicated by the fact that from the end of the eighteenth century it was already fashionable for chandeliers to be dismantled and reformed to the latest fashions, including changes in the ornamentation; and that they may have begun life as gasoliers and have been converted to electricity. Thus one cannot always be certain how much alteration has taken place. The huge nineteenth-century market for lighting fixtures has furnished the restoration trade with a readily available supply of glass components, which can be used at random. Later pressed glass items may have been substituted for cut glass. It may be possible to obtain information on style from eighteenth-century trade cards of London glass dealers; or to obtain particulars of orders and invoices for purchases and cleaning, if records exist with the owner, or in a local library, museum or County Record Office.

Another difficulty arises from the use of terms to describe chandeliers (see below). Similarly, there appears to be no universally recognized terminology for describing the components of chandeliers; Davison (1988) and Reilly and Mortimer (1998) have attempted to rectify this. In the event of there being insufficient evidence to reconstruct a chandelier, a particular time period in its history will have to be chosen, in consultation with an historian of historic lighting. At some time in its life, a period chandelier should be dismantled, examined and correctly documented. Any broken, original parts that have to be replaced should be recorded, labelled and kept in a location where they will not be discarded, lost or confused with each other. This includes worn textile or *passementerie* suspension chain covers.

True glass chandeliers evolved in England and also on the Continent in Bohemia, France, Spain and Italy (Venice) early in the eighteenth century. In the twentieth century, chandeliers were produced in the USA, following the Art Nouveau style. The general use of the term chandelier to describe a freestanding light is relatively modern, being derived from the French for tallow candles (*chandelles*). Early eighteenth-century advertisements list them as *lustres* or *branches*, names also interchangeable with *candelabra*, *girandole* and *wall-light*, so that the few literature references to any of them can be misleading.

The first chandeliers, used to light churches and public buildings, were made of iron or brass. Some wealthy houses were lit with silver chandeliers, but many of these were melted down when they became unfashionable. The basic chandelier consists of a central metal support, disguised by glass globes or urns. The central support of each chandelier is normally formed over a metal pipe or rod, threaded at both ends. The metal suspension rings, receiving plates, tubes and washers are usually of silvered brass or Sheffield plate. (Sheffield or plate-silver fused onto a copper base-was a cheap substitute for solid silver. It is thought to have been discovered by a Sheffield cutler, Thomas Boulsover, in 1742. The process was used extensively from *circa* 1760.) A glass bowl at the base conceals a pierced metal disc from which numerous load-bearing glass arms (branches) radiate, each with a socket or grease-pan for a single candle (sometimes adapted for gas or electricity fittings during the nineteenth and twentieth centuries).

The general component assembly remained fairly constant, whilst incorporating structural improvements and changes in decoration. This standard framework inspired by metal prototypes was adapted widely throughout Europe and resulted in the appearance of several distinctive and readily identifiable types. Glass chandeliers may be small and simple, or large and complex in construction. In either case they are by their nature fragile.

The design of the first true glass English chandeliers, made of lead crystal, was based on early Flemish or Dutch brass chandeliers, and appeared early in the eighteenth century (the Georgian Period). They are first mentioned in an advertisement dated 1727, in which John Gumley, a London glassmaker based in Lambeth, offered 'Looking Glasses, Coach Glasses and Glass Schandeliers' for sale.

Georgian chandeliers are characterized by large baluster stem-pieces and scroll-shaped arms of glass. One of the earliest surviving examples is a chandelier made for Thornham Hall in Suffolk in 1732, and now in Winterthur, Delaware (USA). The arms of Georgian chandeliers were solid and had flattened sides with thumb cuts above and below. One end of each glass arm was formed into a combined, narrow-lipped greasepan and a tube (socket or nozzle), which held a candle. There were no canopies or dressings. The other end of the arms, were set in metal pots with plaster-of-Paris. The earliest chandeliers had square *pots*; from the mid eighteenth century round pots were made of cast brass. The earliest pots were engraved with the numbers of the arms, cast brass pots were stamped with numbers and/or letters. Corresponding numbers appeared on the circular cast brass plate (the receiving plate) cut with corresponding square or round holes into which the arms were slotted. The plate was hidden from view by a glass bowl. The metalwork was usually gilt finished, sometimes with silver-plated tubes inside the glass stem-pieces to disguise the iron shaft. Very few chandeliers survive with the combined tube/drip-pan/arms, but short examples of this type were often fitted to the aprons of pier glasses, with frames of gilt gesso, the combination being known as a sconce. These all-in-one constructions were difficult to clean, so that the drip-pans were soon made to be removable.

Famous examples of chandeliers are those made in 1771 by William Parker of Fleet Street, London, and now hanging in the Assembly Rooms, Bath (UK). In the late 1730s and 1740s, moulded chandeliers appear to have been popular. They frequently included some cutting, but were principally of reticulated glass with rope twist arms. Soon makers cut the arms to provide sparkle, and more elaborate surface treatments were devised, e.g. large flat diamonds with cross cuts, the commonest decoration between 1750 and 1770. As arms became more elaborate, curved canopies (or shades as they were then called) were added and the whole chandelier was hung with applied ornaments. By *circa* 1745, chandelier styles became even more elaborate and shallow cutting extended to cover all the glass

elements – sockets, grease-pans and branches – in diamond and star-shaped patterns. Shortly afterwards, cut glass pendant drops were introduced and applied to the framework – initially in small numbers, but by *circa* 1770 in increasingly greater numbers.

Chandeliers followed rococo, then neo-classical styles, with extensive and sophisticated cutting. Those designed by the architect designers Robert and James Adam, featured two tiers of arms with the upper tier supporting triangular spikes or spires in place of lights. The solid arms were usually ground with flat sides (hexagonal in section) with four rows of thumb cuts. Other features were top and bottom canopies, elongated and elegant urn-shaped shafts, large pear-shaped pendant drops, and smaller and pear-shaped drops wired into chains and hung between the branches in swags, each pendant facetted in meticulous detail. The Van Dyke edged drip-pans and candle nozzles were removable, the nozzles being attached to the arms with metal ferrules. By 1800, decorative ornaments had become so profuse that the underlying structure of the chandelier – the shaft and branches – was practically obscured from view.

During the Regency Period in England (*c.* 1810–1820), the country was at war with France, and harsh taxes were introduced to raise money. One of these, the Glass Excise Act, exacted a heavy tax on all glass made each day at the glasshouses. To avoid the tax, chandelier manufacturers bought crystal drops cut by garret workers from broken pieces of glass to resemble icicles. The drops were strung together and hung in tiers from the top to bottom of decorative metal frames to form tent and bag, or waterfall designs. The shaft and the branches, being completely hidden, were usually undecorated. These styles of chandelier became popular throughout Europe.

By the mid 1800s Britain was prospering. In 1832 the Glass Excise Act was repealed and chandelier manufacturers reverted to the glass arm designs. However, the chandeliers themselves became bolder and weightier with deep cutting and heavy swags of dressings. One of the most prolific manufacturers was Messrs Perry & Co., of London, many of whose products survive. The chandeliers often feature rope- or barley twist-shaped arms, those on the lower tier being S-shaped. They were heavily dressed with swags nearly always composed of button-shaped lustres pointed on either side, and with pear-shaped pendant drops. Two of the most popular cutting designs for the stem pieces were *hollow and split* and *step*. The metalwork was nearly always silver plated, and if a makers' mark was applied, the wording Perry & Co. would be stamped on the receiver plate or the top shackle.

The Birmingham Company of F & C Osler, established in 1807 by Thomas Osler and his two sons Follett and Clarkson, came to prominence in the nineteenth century, creating spectacular crystal chandeliers, fountains and furniture, much of it for export to the Indian sub-continent. The firm was commissioned to make a giant crystal fountain for the Great Trade Exhibition of 1851, held in the Crystal Palace erected in Hyde Park, London. Containing 4000 kg (4 tonnes) of lead crystal glass, the fountain stood 8.25 m (27 ft) high. The Crystal Palace was later dismantled and re-erected in Sydenham, South London, the fountain taking pride of place in the central nave. The Palace and fountain were destroyed by fire on the night of 30 November 1936.

As the popularity of chandeliers and decorative lighting began to decline, the factory continued, by cutting glass blanks supplied by local factories. The range of lighting became smaller and less ornate. In 1924 F & C Osler merged with Faraday & Son Ltd (founded by Robert Faraday in 1814) and continued to trade until 1965. In 1985 the firm of Wilkinson plc found and purchased the remnants of the Osler Company, including brass and bronze casting patterns and old working drawings, which have made it possible to restore original Osler products with confidence.

Many early chandelier styles were reproduced, for either candle or gas, during the Victorian period (1837–1901) with only slight variations in the cut decoration. Those intended to be lit by gas had hollow arms through which gas was transported to the burners. The advent of electricity brought about several changes in the style of chandeliers, which now incorporated large areas of metal, electrical wiring and glass light bulbs, which were often aesthetically unpleasing. Mehlman (1982), Reilly and Mortimer (1998)

and Mortimer (2000) give accounts of the historical changes in chandelier design, and the last two, a full glossary of terms associated with chandeliers.

Chandeliers have been and continue to be made throughout the world; the greatest producers being Germany and Bohemia, with a large export trade from *circa* 1720 to the present day. The Czechoslovakian glass industry began making Bohemian crystal glass chandeliers soon after the English manufacturers, whose designs were often copied. At present the Czech Republic is the greatest producer of glass chandeliers.

The Venetian style of chandelier has changed little over the centuries. On the earliest versions, glass arms, leaves and flowers were simply pushed into holes bored or carved into a wooden base. In later examples, glass flowers and leaves were added to decorate wooden or iron frames. Ironwork was usually painted silver. The finest Venetian chandeliers were composed of both clear and colourless glass, and were richly adorned with naturalistic motifs such as flowers, leaves and fruit.

In the sixteenth century the more elaborate types of French chandelier were decorated with rock-crystal drops, and in the seventeenth, with many-facetted pieces of crystal which reflected the light of the candles; they were called *chandeliers de crystal*. Expensive crystal was often replaced by cut glass, from the late seventeenth century, when the term lustre began to be applied (as it still is) to all chandeliers whether or not they incorporate pieces of crystal or glass. Cage chandeliers formed around a brass or bronze frame are typical of the eighteenth- and nineteenth-century production of France. Early examples were dressed with rock crystal (quartz) pendants, and later examples with less expensive glass drops.

Scandinavian and Russian glass chandeliers are difficult to differentiate from one another as they all took a similar form. They generally have light, more decorative metalwork usually with a brass or gilt finish, and small slender glass drops. Sometimes a blue glass dish or other coloured element was incorporated in the design. Sommer-Larson (1999) describes the conservation of three chandeliers, made at Nostetangen for the church in Kongsberg,

Norway. The chandeliers have iron frame-works, and glass arms decorated with glass drops and other ornamentation.

A number of flamboyant, painted glass chandeliers in the *chinoiserie* style hang in the banqueting room and the music room at Brighton Pavilion in Sussex (UK). They are more properly described as lanterns, being composed of large panes of glass held in metal ribs and similar in appearance to large inverted umbrellas. The banqueting room chandelier was created by the Regency designer Robert Jones and made by the London firm of Bailey and Saunders in 1817. The lamp itself, consisting of cut glass lustres, was created by Messrs Perry & Co. It is suspended by chains of gold radiating from the centre of a large and brilliant star, a belt of rubies, pearls and garnets encircling its base. The body represents a fountain in full play, the cut crystals forming the water being extremely realistic. Six winged dragons, each holding a beautifully shaped water lily in its upturned mouth, crouch around the base. Crystals in the form of festoons, shields and tassels are suspended from the dragons' claws. The entire chandelier is 30 ft high and weighs nearly a ton. It has undergone many changes during its lifetime. In 1999 it was surveyed and given a light cleaning by conservators (Oliver, 1999). The chandeliers in the music room were badly damaged by fire, and water from hoses, during an arson attack in 1975, and were subsequently restored (Rogers, 1980).

3

Technology of glass production
Part 1: Methods and materials

Raw materials

The materials for making ancient glasses were naturally occurring rocks and minerals: a mixture of silica, alkali and lime, which also contained trace elements. The silica was generally obtained from sea sand in which there were ground seashells, the source of lime. The alkali was natron, obtained from dried lake deposits or from ash produced by burning saltmarsh plants (containing a high amount of soda). From the ninth century AD ash produced by burning forest plants (having a high potash content) was also used as a source of alkali for glassmaking. In order to produce a durable glass, i.e. glass that would not be easily soluble by water, the raw ingredients had to be chemically balanced. In ancient times this would have been achieved by trial and error, and by the empirical knowledge thus gained. The addition of too much alkali to the glass batch had the effect of increasing the solubility of the resulting glass in water. However, other oxides such as calcium oxide (lime) acted as stabilizers, thereby to a considerable extent counterbalancing the deleterious effect, and enabling reasonably durable glasses to be made.

To produce glass, the raw materials had to be heated to about 1000°C, at which temperature they slowly melted to form a liquid and reacted together. Since it was impossible for the first glassmakers to reach and maintain high temperatures long enough to melt glass in any quantity, the melting temperature needed to be considerably lowered to around 900°C. This was achieved by the addition of alkali, which acted as a network modifier and

flux. The amount of network modifier required to lower the temperature depended on the state of development of furnace technology in any particular era. Ancient glass was unintentionally coloured by the presence of impurities such as iron in the raw materials, which resulted in the glass being yellow or green. As glassmaking technology evolved, a second group of metallic oxides, such as those of copper, iron, cobalt and manganese, were deliberately used to colour glass. The deliberate production of colours in ancient glasses was complicated since the metal oxides produced different colours depending upon the firing conditions, i.e. the oxidizing or reducing atmospheres in the furnace. Most early glasses were translucent or opaque as a result of the low fusion temperatures, which allowed microscopic air bubbles to remain in the viscous glass as it cooled.

In the production of glass one other ingredient was commonly added to the basic ingredients, that is, scrap glass (cullet), which was normally of about the same composition as the batch to be melted. The function of the cullet was purely physical, it acted as a nucleus around which the new glass formed, and helped to eliminate unevenness such as cords and *striae* in the new batch. The use of scrap glass in this way probably accounts for the lack of waste glass products on many glassmaking sites.

Apart from the raw materials, the process of making glass required a source of fuel (originally wood, from the seventeenth century, coal); a furnace; and crucibles (or pots) made from refractory (heat-resisting) materials; in practice, clay free from fluxes. The glass was fashioned into artefacts and then allowed to cool, whereupon it congealed into a solid. The cooling had to proceed slowly in an oven (later called an annealing oven, a lehr or leer), to relieve stresses set up during the manufacture, otherwise the products would shatter.

It is known that in ancient times, until at least the ninth century AD, centres of glassmaking evolved, which distributed chunk glass to other glassworking centres, which did not have the technology to produce glass from its raw materials.

Silica (the network former)

Several inorganic oxides have the ability to form vitreous materials. Of these silicon dioxide (silica) is by far the most important (although boric oxide, sodium borate, was also infrequently (accidentally) used in antiquity).

The main source of silica for ancient glass production was sand. In the Near and Middle East sands relatively pure and free from iron were widely obtainable and therefore the common source (for example, Egyptian sands contain only 1–3 per cent iron). Two other sources of sand exploited for ancient glassmaking were those at the mouth of the River Belus in Phoenicia (now the River Na'aman in Israel), which contained 87 wt per cent of lime (Turner, 1956c; Engle, 1973a, 1974), and those from the River Volturnus (the modern River Volturno), north of Naples in Italy. In the Middle Ages, when glassmaking spread to Europe, it was found that the sands in many areas were too impure to be of use in glassmaking without prior treatment, consisting of washing and then burning or being brought to red heat to remove organic matter. In Italy, for example, suitable sand could be found at the mouth of the River Volturnus; but that at the mouth of the River Tiber, and on the Italian coast above Ostia, contained large amounts of volcanic debris. Another source of silica was crushed flint or quartz pebbles obtained from river-beds. Pliny (77 AD) mentions the following ingredients of the glassmaker: soda (*nitrum*), limestone (*magnes lapis*), shiny pebbles (*calculi*), shells (*conchae*), and excavated sands and sandstones (*fossiles harenae*). In 1645 the English diarist John Evelyn was in Venice, and referred to white sand, ground flints from Pavia, and the ashes

of seaweed brought from Syria as the raw materials used for glassmaking (Forbes, 1966). In 1979, Brill filmed glassmaking in the ancient tradition in Herat, Afghanistan. The raw materials were quartz pebbles, plant ash and scrap copper. White quartz pebbles were collected from a dry river-bed, one donkey load providing enough silica for one week's glass production. Plant ash (*ishgar*) was prepared by nomads, plant twigs being heaped together in a shallow pit and burned, after which the ashes were left to cool overnight. To test its quality the glassmakers tasted the *ishgar*, choosing that which had a sweet taste. Before being placed in the furnace to melt, the quartz pebbles were broken, ground and mixed with the plant ash. To colour the glass bright turquoise, a lump of scrap copper was heated and the surface oxide scraped off and added to the batch. The furnace was fuelled with hardwood brought from the hills by donkey every two weeks; this was the most expensive commodity. A sawn-off rifle barrel was used as a blowpipe (Johnston, 1975).

Alkalis (the network modifiers)

The principal network modifiers of which ancient glasses were composed were the oxides of sodium and potassium. Until about AD 1000 the oxide of sodium (natrium – natrum in ancient times) was used universally and introduced to the glass batch either as sodium carbonate in the form of soda crystals (Na_2CO_3) or as sodium nitrate ($NaNO_3$). Sodium oxide could also be produced by burning saltmarsh plants, usually *Salicornia kali*, or seaweed. Commoner sources of alkali included natural deposits resulting from drying and evaporation of land-locked seas and lakes; arid salts obtained by deliberate evaporation of sea or river water in pans or pits. Undoubtedly natron, a natural sodium sesquicarbonate ($Na_2CO_3.NaHCO_3.2H_2O$) from the Wadi Natrun, north-west of Cairo, would have been used in the glassmaking activities there. The composition of natron is complex and variable: the sodium carbonate content varies from 22.4 to 75.0 per cent, sodium bicarbonate from 5.0 to 32.4 per cent, sodium chloride from 2.2 to 26.8 per cent, sodium sulphate from 2.3 to 29.9 per cent plus water and insoluble material. The use of sodium oxide as a modifier resulted in the production of soda glass, which remained plastic over a wide temperature range, thus lending itself to elaborate manipulative techniques (Toninato, 1984).

During the height of the Roman Empire, glassmaking had, at least by AD 50, spread from Syria and Egypt to western areas, and then northwards so that, by about AD 100, glassmakers were operating in the Rhineland. The glasses made in Europe at the time contained low amounts of magnesia and potash, and since there do not seem to have been any sources of soda with the same characteristics available in Europe, it seems reasonable to assume that the glasses were made using natron rather than the ashes of maritime plants (which contain significant amounts of magnesia and potash). The deposits of sodium sulphate in Germany, even if they had been known at the time, would probably have been too difficult to exploit, given the primitive state of glassmaking technology (Turner, 1956c). It is possible that natron continued to be transported to the Rhineland even after the collapse of the Roman Empire in the west. Although such a practice might seem to have been uneconomical, it must be remembered that the early glassmakers were extremely conservative about the use of tried and tested raw materials.

A dramatic change in glassmaking practice began to occur around AD 1000, in that potash began to replace soda as the regular source of alkali. The exact reason for this change is unknown, but it may have been the result of a greater demand for glass (and therefore fuel). Only relatively small quantities of soda would have been required for the manufacture of glass vessels and ornaments, but, with the onset of the Middle Ages, and especially after the Gothic Revolution, there would have been a large demand for window glass, first for churches and cathedrals and later for palaces. Newton (1985b) has suggested that beechwood ash was used to make coloured glass, and this would have introduced a high level of potash into the glass batch. Once it was realized that the use of beechwood ash would enable a variety of colours to be produced, the glassmakers would have moved into areas where beech forests existed, thus ensuring both a plentiful supply of fuel and alkali. Newton (1985b) has shown that there was a scarcity of beechwood south of the Alps, and has related the glassmaking centres in northern Europe to the distribution of beechwood pollen in AD 1000. Nevertheless, care must be exercised before trying to draw a picture that is too simple. Geilmann and Bruckbauer (1954) showed that the manganese content of beech wood (as with any component of any plant) depended on the place where the tree had grown, the maturity of the wood, etc.

Freestone *et al.* (1999) examined Anglo-Saxon vessel glass from south-eastern Britain, and window glass from the monastery at Jarrow (Northumbria) and identified several compositional groups. The fifth- to sixth-century claw beakers and cone beakers, and the window glass were of the low magnesia, low potash (natron) type. The sixth- to seventh-century globular beakers and palm cups were of the high magnesia, high potash ('plant ash') type. Three possibilities for these results are (i) the recycling of old Roman glass (cullet), (ii) the continued supply of chunk glass from the Mediterranean, and (iii) the use of specific raw materials. A survey of glass fragments from Hamwic (Saxon Southampton, UK) (Hunter and Heyworth, 1999) combined typological and compositional data, to suggest an emerging glass industry in middle Saxon times. The study covers the time in early Christian England, when knowledge of glass production was only slowly developing, but glass from pagan graves, the usual source of such early glass, was less commonly available. The known fragments are dominated by vessels of the palm cup/funnel beaker variety, some of them being decorated with applied coloured *reticella* rods.

Ancient soda, obtained by burning maritime or desert plants, was usually contaminated with enough lime to produce durable glass. However if the soda was reasonably pure, as was the case with some natron from some sources, it was necessary to mix it with calcareous sand in order to impart stability to the glass. The addition of too much lime, for example in ash prepared from beechwood in medieval times, resulted in the glass being less durable. Lime was not intentionally added to the glass batch in ancient times, or in fact until the seventeenth century.

Lead oxide was also an unintentional ingredient of ancient glass until Roman times. It was introduced directly to the batch, as one of the two oxides, litharge (PbO) or red lead (Pb_3O_4), or indirectly as white lead or basic lead carbonate ($2PbCO_3.Pb(OH)_2$, or as galena, the basic sulphide ore (PbS). Litharge was produced by blowing air over the surface of molten lead, an extremely dangerous health hazard. When the resulting litharge was further oxidized, it became red lead. Its use in glass-making required special furnace conditions, as its conversion back to metallic lead would discolour the glass and damage the crucible (or pot).

The high refractive index of lead glass gives a brilliance to the glass, and when the glass is facet cut, spectral colours are reflected from the facets. Lead was used with great success in the seventeenth century to produce lead (flint) glass vessels suitable for facet cutting. The usual source of barium oxide, another unintentional ingredient, was barium sulphide ore ($BaSO_4$, barytes or heavy spar). The inclusion of aluminium oxide (Al_2O_3, alumina), which occurs naturally in clays or, in a fairly pure form, as emery or corundum, and in the hydrated form as bauxite ($Al_2O_3.xH_2O$), would raise the melting point of the batch, and improve the durability of the glass. Aluminium oxide was in fact an inevitable contaminant, being introduced from the fabric of the crucibles themselves.

Colourants

Metallic oxides

The common colourants for glass were precisely the same as those used in making glazes. Unlike the potters, however, who only had to alter the atmosphere of a kiln to produce oxidized or reduced colourings, the glassworkers needed the ability to achieve these effects within the batch. Normally the colourants would be in a reduced condition, but the glass modifiers such as the oxides of antimony and arsenic could produce oxidizing conditions within the molten glass, and thus oxidized colourings were produced. Doubtless ancient glassworkers learnt this fact empirically.

Coloured glass was generally pot coloured (i.e. in the batch), but in the Middle Ages,

certain colours, especially red, were flashed, that is, clear glass was covered with a thin layer of coloured glass. To produce pot-coloured glass, metallic oxide colouring agents were added to the molten batch in the crucible. Thus, when formed, the glass artefact would be uniformly coloured throughout its thickness. In the manufacture of flash-coloured glass, a gather of clear molten glass was covered by a second gather from a pot of molten coloured glass, so that when the coated gather was blown into a cylinder, cut and flattened out, it formed a sheet of glass which was coloured on one side only, the greater thickness of the glass being clear. Flashed ruby is by far the commonest colour after the fourteenth century, but examples of others, notably blue, are known. The process of flashing glass was described by Theophilus in the twelfth century; and imperfectly flashed glasses are found in the earliest examples of glass windows. The flashed or coloured side of the sheet is generally found on the inner face of windows where it would not be damaged by weathering.

Colloidal suspensions of metals

Metals do not dissolve in glass, but exist as colloids in suspension. Gold and copper ruby glasses contain those metals dispersed on a submicroscopic scale. Other highly decorative glasses could be made to resemble the semi-precious stones agate, aventurine, chalcedony, onyx etc. by dispersing flakes of metal or metallic oxides in the glass before the artefact was formed from it. An alternative method of making onyx glass was to place two differently coloured opal glasses in the same crucible, and to make the gather before the mixing was complete. The cold glass could then be cut and polished so that the new surface displayed alternating layers of the colours.

On the whole, copper was used by the Egyptian and Mesopotamian glassmakers to produce bluish-green glass, and cobalt to produce blue or violet glass, although mixtures of copper, cobalt or manganese to produce blue glass were also common. Copper oxides may be introduced to the glass melt as any of the common copper ores, although the oxides and carbonates were the most usual. Under oxidizing conditions, copper oxide colours glass blue or green, depending partly upon which other glass modifiers are present. Thus, with lead oxide, copper oxide will produce greens; with sodium or potassium oxide the colour will be turquoise blue. Under reducing conditions copper oxide will produce a dull red colour. Copper oxide is usually present in the proportions of 2–5 per cent, above which it causes the colour to darken even to black. The Romans used copper and cobalt to produce blue glass, but were equally aware that this colour could be achieved by the use of ferrous iron, and that a reducing atmosphere in the furnace would deepen the blue colour by increasing the number of ferrous ions present. The making of blue glass continued from Roman through Islamic times and received a boost during the Renaissance when the Venetians began producing a rich blue glass. Blue glass was also made on a small scale in the northern Rhine area. It became very popular in Britain during the eighteenth and nineteenth centuries, for example the deep blue glass being made at Nailsea, near Bristol.

In ancient times, red glass was generally made, by using copper in a reducing furnace atmosphere. This resulted in a brilliant red opaque glass. A fine red glass from copper was made in Egypt from the time of the Eighteenth Dynasty. The Roman writer Pliny (AD 77) mentions an opaque red glass called haematinum, implying it was of local manufacture. In medieval times red glass was still made with copper, but manganese was used to make a pale rose red or pink glass. Manganese oxide may be introduced to the batch either as the dioxide or carbonate of manganese, and will produce purple-brown or shades of violet depending upon which other modifiers are present. For example, with iron it produces black. Manganese is generally used as about 2.6 per cent of the glass metal; and its colour fades if fired above 1200°C. It was not until the end of the seventeenth century that a clear ruby or pink glass could be made consistently. Iron in its ferric state, (i.e. fired under oxidizing conditions), can colour glass yellow or amber. Any of the ores from which iron may be smelted may be ground and added to the glass metal. When the ore is poorly ground, or when a red clay contains small nodules of iron ores, these will produce local patches of excess iron oxide in the glaze appearing as dark brown or black spots in the surface.

The Venetians made a particularly fine green glass in the Renaissance period. Copper or iron could be used to make the green colour under reducing conditions. The brownish-green colour of some English jugs made at the end of the eighteenth century is the result of iron impurities, since to avoid excess duty, the glassmaker had made the vessels from bottle glass.

The Venetians continually experimented with coloured glasses, and produced a rich purple glass, probably by the use of manganese. Venetian opaline glass of the seventeenth century was made by using arsenic and calcined bones in the batch. When heated, these materials struck an opalescent white colour. The Venetians also continued the ancient tradition of imitating semi-precious stones such as chalcedony, jasper, onyx and agate. From the late 1820s, Friedrich Egermann, working in Bohemia, made lithyalin glass in imitation of natural stones. This was a polished opaque glass marbled with red and other strong colours.

From at least the second century BC, black glass was made, by using an excess of iron oxide, that is, 10 per cent or more of the glass batch. However, an excess of any colouring oxide will colour glass so deeply that it takes on a black appearance. The only instance of black glass being produced in Britain in the first half of the seventeenth century is a fragment found adhering to part of a crucible at Denton near Manchester. A combination of iron, manganese and sulphur in the glass, coupled with a smoky atmosphere in the furnace, produced a black opacity. The next instance of black glass being produced is found in southern Bohemia, where hyalith (a dense, opaque jet-black glass) was made from 1820.

Opacifiers

Ancient glassmakers used antimony to produce a white opacity in glass. There was no great interest in opaque white glass, however, until its potential as an imitation of Chinese porcelain was seen by Italian glassmakers. Opaque white glass produced by adding tin oxide or arsenic to the batch was made at Venice before 1500 and continued thereafter, being especially popular in the eighteenth century. The products certainly had the appearance of porcelain, but feel different (cool) to the touch, and are generally considered to have none of the aesthetic qualities of either material. Tin oxide was normally added as cassiterite (SnO_2), although it could also have been added as an impurity in the raw material, for example, when calcined pewter was added to a batch to produce lead oxide. Tin oxide is not strictly speaking a colourant, but produced a white opacity in glass by existing as a colloid, that is, as a mass of minute crystals.

Modern chemistry has added a new range of colours to glassmaking, such as yellow-browns obtained from titanium, red from selenium, purple and blue from nickel and yellow-green from chromium. Chromium oxide is generally added directly as the oxide chromite, which also contains iron, or as a chromate or bichromate. It is a difficult colour to use since the result so often depends not only on the other modifiers present but also on the temperature to which it is fired. Thus with lead, chromium oxide will produce reds at low temperatures and brown or green at higher temperatures. With tin it will produce reds or pinks. Nickel oxide may be introduced from a number of sources, chiefly the mineral millerite (NiS). Alone it produces drab greens, but with iron it produces browns, and if used in great concentrations, black fluorspar and zirconia are used to produce opaque white glass.

Decolourizers

Ancient so-called colourless glasses had in fact always displayed a greenish tint due to the presence of iron from the sand, which existed in the iron (II) state in the glass. Initially, care in the selection and washing of proven materials, was probably the most common step taken to avoid the inclusion of contaminants. It was then discovered that glass containing iron oxide could be decolourized by converting the blue colour of reduced iron to the yellow colour of the oxidized state, for example, by altering the melting conditions or by adding oxidizing agents such as the oxides of manganese or antimony to the glass batch. Traces of antimony have been found in glasses dating from at least 2000 BC, probably present as an impurity in the raw materials. Colourless

glasses could well have been accidentally made, by using a raw material which, unknown to the glassmaker, contained antimony or manganese. Having obtained a desirable result, the use of the material was encouraged (Newton, 1985b). For example, the ash from a certain type of plant (one not containing antimony or manganese) might have always produced a green-tinted glass (the iron was not decolourized) whereas the ash from a different type of plant (one that did contain enough antimony or manganese) might have produced a less green or even colourless glass. For example, the brown marine alga *Fucus vesiculosus* can concentrate manganese to the extent of 90 000 ppm compared with 4800 ppm in vascular plants in general. The effect of this on the colour of the glass could well have been noticed by those who burnt the plants, or by the glassmakers. However, there is an additional technological complication because the amount of decolourization, and even the amount of opalization (in the case of excess antimony), depended upon the oxidation–reduction situation in the furnace. Geilmann and Bruckbauer (1954) studied samples of beechwood ash from different localities and from various parts of the trees, and found great differences in the manganese content of the samples.

Manganese was used increasingly from the first century AD as a decolourizer. Added to the batch as manganese dioxide, it oxidized the greenish colour of the glass, and the resultant yellow tinge was compensated for by the purple manganese. Nevertheless, the first author to mention manganese explicitly was Biringuccio (1540, translated by Smith and Gnudi, 1942).

Depending upon the firing conditions and amount added, antimony can react as a decolourizer or, as mentioned above, an opacifier. During glass-melting with antimony present in the batch, a rise in temperature will convert opaque glass to crystal clear glass. The development of colourless glass by the Romans was a gradual process; the use of antimony as a decolourizer reached a peak by the second century AD. Colourless glass formed the medium favoured by glass-cutters in the second and third centuries (Harden, 1969a). Utilitarian ware continued to be made in greenish glass.

Ancient white opaque glasses contain approximately the same amount of antimony as the colourless high antimony glasses, but those which are opaque become colourless either when melted under reducing conditions or at an elevated temperature (Sayre, 1963) Thus another possible explanation of the high-antimony situation may be that the glassmakers obtained either clear or opaque glasses depending on the type of flame in the furnace and the amount of organic matter in the batch.

Sayre (1963) also commented on two instances where parts of a glass article did not contain the decolourizer, and claimed that the examples were another indication that the antimony was added for decolouration, in the first case a colourless high-antimony glass had a blue thread decoration with a low antimony content, and in the second the body of a bead was low in manganese whereas an outer layer was high in manganese. However, the outer parts of the article might have been made from imported glass (Newton, 1971b,c).

Bearing in mind the empirical and precarious procedures of glassmaking used in ancient times, it seems unlikely that the glassmakers were knowledgeable enough to be able to add about 1 per cent of an ingredient with any confidence and also disperse such a small amount uniformly throughout the batch (which is not an easy operation even with modern techniques). Moreover, there seems to be no reason to believe that antimony was known in Mesopotamian times (Brill, 1970c), or that manganese was deliberately added to the glass batch earlier than AD 1540 (Turner, 1956a).

However, whether or not Sayre (1963) was correct about the deliberate use of antimony and manganese, the analyses have resulted in an invaluable wealth of analytical information about glasses from many different eras and geographical locations.

A clear glass luxury-ware was in production as early as the eighth century BC, the glassmakers probably being based in Gordion in Turkey and Nimrud in Mesopotamia. These glasses were mostly bowl-shaped and were ground, cut and polished with a high degree of technical skill. By the third century BC the same type of bowl was being produced in Alexandria in Egypt. However, it was the Romans who achieved the regular production of a transparent and almost colourless glass. The ancient world made a careful distinction between ordinary glass (vitrum) and crystal glass (crystallum or crystallina). The accounts by Strabo (first century BC) (Thorpe, 1938) suggest that crystal glass may have been invented between 20 and 7 BC. It had become well enough known for Pliny (77 AD) to describe the manufacture of colourless glass made from the fusion of ground sand and soda, followed by a second fusing with shells and stone referred to as 'magnum lapis', perhaps limestone or dolomite. Pliny referred to the product as 'vitrum purum' (pure glass) and remarked that the glass was colourless and transparent and as nearly like rock crystal as possible.

It was only after *circa* 1500 that the real vogue for colourless glass began, and it then became so popular that it displaced strongly coloured glass from the market.

Post-Roman glass compositions

In the Dark Ages, glass of the soda–lime type had continued to be made as the glassmakers in Western Europe were still able to obtain either natron from Alexandria or marine plant ash from the Mediterranean countries. Around the tenth century, however, European glassmakers began using ash from bracken and other woodland plants as a source of alkali thus producing green-tinted potash glass (forest glass). A different forest glass composition (high lime/low alkali) became prominent in the sixteenth century in the Eichensfeld region of Germany. Wedepohl (1993) suggested that an increase in zinc content might indicate the use of ash prepared from bracken and reeds, as an alternative fuel to beechwood. Jackson and Smedley (1999) have investigated glassmaking in Staffordshire (UK) during the fourteenth to sixteenth centuries and concluded that documentary evidence and vegetation history suggest that bracken not beechwood was the main source of alkali there.

In the fifteenth century, Venice was pre-eminent in its glassmaking expertise and therefore went to great lengths to keep glassmaking knowledge secret. Glassmakers were forbidden on pain of death to practise their skills outside Venetian territory. However, bribery and the competition of opposing glassmaking practices in Altare (near Genoa) encouraged glassmaking technology to be disseminated. Information regarding seventeenth-century batch formulations and their use in Murano (Italy) Zecchin (1987) contains a facsimile of the original notebook used by Giovanni Darduin (1584–1654), along with a transcription and modern commentary. Elsewhere in Europe glassmakers producing soda–lime glasses produced vessels in the style of those from Venice (*façon de Venise*) but without the same degree of brilliance in the glass.

Towards the end of the seventeenth century both Germany and Britain competed with Venice in producing glasses which were superior in quality to the original *cristallo*. The fourth book of *L'Arte Vetraria* (Neri, 1612) was devoted to the discussion of various lead glasses and their use for counterfeiting precious jewellery. It was translated into English by Merrett in 1662, and the work would undoubtedly have been known to George Ravenscroft, credited with the discovery of lead glass in England. In 1673, the Glass Sellers' Company had commissioned Ravenscroft to produce a substitute for Venetian *cristallo*. The first attempts using indigenous flint and potash to replace pebbles, and soda produced from the Spanish sea plant *barilla* used by Venetian glassmakers, was unsuccessful since the glass was inclined to crizzle. This crizzling took the form of a network of tiny cracks caused by the breakdown in the chemical structure within the glass due to an excess of alkali. To remedy this, oxide of lead was substituted for a proportion of the potash. Eventually this increased to as much as 30 per cent of the mix. A glass of high refractive index producing a brilliance was the result. Sand soon replaced the flints but the term flint glass continued to be used to designate Ravenscroft's glass. Lead glass was heavier and less fluid than Venetian *cristallo* but its lustrous appearance established it as the leader in the production of clear glass from the end of the seventeenth century.

The lead glass was free from seed (minute air bubbles), because molten lead glass is some 100 times more fluid than a soda–lime glass at the same temperature (see line F in

Figure 1.9); appeared very bright because it had a high refractive index (*Figure 1.11*); and sparkled when decoratively cut because of its high optical dispersivity; and had a clear ring at room temperature when struck, because its alkali (potash) ions were bound more closely to the lead–silica network than are the soda ions in soda–lime glass, and thus absorb less energy when in vibration. Lead can be introduced into the glass as litharge (PbO), as red lead (PbO_3), or as white lead or basic lead carbonate, ($PbCO_3.Pb(OH)_2$).

By 1680 Germany had established a solid clear glass, apparently first made in northern Bohemia, by adding lime to stabilize the purified potash. Potash continued to be used as a source of alkali even after the change of wood to coal as a source of fuel. The rich potash deposits at Stassfurt (in Germany) were exploited in 1861 (Douglas and Frank, 1972).

Use of cullet

A method of reducing the viscosity of molten glass was to add cullet (broken or scrap glass, either from the glassmaking sites themselves, in which case their approximate composition would be known; or obtained as an article of commerce brought from another location, and of less certain composition). Cullet is different from chunk glass, which was manufactured from raw ingredients and sold to glassmakers (Freestone and Gorin-Rosen, 1999).

Fuel, crucibles and furnaces

Apart from the raw materials for making the glass, a source of fuel was required – originally wood, or dung; and from the seventeenth century coal (in modern times, gas, oil and electricity). The glass was melted in containers made of refractory (heat-resisting) materials such as clays, which were free from fluxes. Initially these were small crucibles, and as glass technology developed, pots were used that increased in size as time progressed and higher furnace temperatures could be maintained. Furnaces are discussed in Part 2 of this chapter.

The molten glass was traditionally called 'metal', by analogy with molten metal, however the term is misleading in connection with glass. All glass artefacts fashioned from molten glass had to be annealed (cooled slowly) immediately, in an annealing oven, usually attached to the main furnace.

Crossley (1999) stressed the importance of investigating residues from glassmaking sites. Glass fragments found on site may represent glass made during the final use of the furnace, and may therefore not be representative of the earlier output. Material resembling solidified foam (spilled or ladled from the crucibles) may reveal information regarding the sources of raw materials.

Manufacture of glass

As previously mentioned, coloured vitreous glazes were used extensively in Egypt and Mesopotamia in the fourth millennium BC for covering objects in imitation of semi-precious stones. The first essential in making a good glaze was to reduce all the ingredients to a fine particle size by crushing. They were then mixed with water with or without the addition of an emulsifier to form a suspension. The glaze was applied, by brush or by dipping the object into it. The object was then heated in a furnace to distribute the glaze evenly, and to fuse the glaze particles. In antiquity the formulation of any glaze had to be arrived at by trial and error; and when one considers the cost of such experimentation to the potter it is hardly surprising that once a satisfactory glaze had been devised it remained in use, unaltered, over a long period of time. In theory it would have been possible to have produced a wide range of glazes with different melting points by altering the proportions of silica, lime and alkali (soda or potash), but in practice too much alkali resulted in a glaze prone to crazing, while too much silica resulted in a glaze with a melting point either too high for the primitive furnace or for the body to which it was to be applied; also, the coefficient of thermal expansion could become too high or too low. It was for this reason that soda–lime glazes were only used on objects of quartz, steatite or Egyptian faience (itself a soda–lime–quartz composite material) but not on pottery.

The transition from using glass for glazing to its being manufactured as a material in its own right was probably very slow. Since sustained high temperatures are required in order to melt the raw materials which produce glass, it seems likely that the art of glassmaking originated where there were closed furnaces able to achieve such temperatures, such as those used for firing pottery or smelting metal. The potter's craft was already long established by the time that glass made its first appearance, and the similarities between glaze and glass production are apparent.

Tait (1991) has published sequences of photographs of Bill Gudenrath, a modern master glassworker, demonstrating the techniques currently thought to have been used by ancient glassmakers.

In any critical discussion of the production of ancient glasses it may be necessary to distinguish between three or four different activities: glassmaking, including fritting, glass-melting and glass-forming.

Glassmaking (fritting)

Glassmaking is the preparation of molten glass from its basic raw ingredients, which in the case of most ancient glasses was calcareous sand and soda. The glass could then be fashioned into objects, or could be allowed to solidify, and then be transported as ingots or broken chunk glass, for use by glassworkers at other sites, who did not have the technical ability to melt glass.

In ancient times when furnaces could only reach the required high melting temperatures of the order of about 1000°C for short periods of time, it was extremely difficult to melt the raw materials to produce glass. The resulting product was a viscous, semi-glassy material full of air bubbles (seed) and unmelted batch materials (stones). (At higher, modern furnace temperatures, the viscosity of the glass becomes low enough for the seed to escape, and all the batch material will react to produce a good quality glass in a single operation.) Therefore, although there is limited evidence for this, it is thought that ancient glasses had to be made in at least two operations: fritting and melting. During the fritting process, the raw materials were heated to a point which allowed solid state reactions to occur between the sodium carbonate in the plant ash or natron and the silica in the sand, after which the mass was cooled and ground to a powder (frit). This process might be repeated several times to refine the frit, after which the frit was melted at a higher temperature to form a homogeneous molten vitreous material (glass melt) which could be used to manufacture artefacts (Turner, 1956c).

The fritting process was investigated by Howarth *et al.* (1934). The process was found to occur slowly at 700°C, and to increase rapidly with temperature until, at 850°C, there was a marked change in appearance of the frit, to that of partly melted sugar. This is no doubt associated with the melting of sodium carbonate (melting point 851°C; potassium carbonate melts at 891°C) (Turner, 1930, 1956c), and it indicated that the furnace temperature was too high. If melting occurs, the viscous mass causes great difficulties in handling; all contemporary sources (for example, cuneiform tablets, Pliny, Theophilus and Neri) state that only moderate temperatures should be used, and that the frit should be kept well stirred so that it should not melt and lumps should not form. Nevertheless, nearly complete glassmaking reactions can occur if heating is continued for long enough. At 750°C Howarth *et al.* (1934) obtained 98.5 per cent reaction in 15 hours, and 98.1 per cent reaction at 800°C in 10 hours, but much depends on the actual proportions of the raw materials, the reactions being more rapid when higher proportions of silica are present.

When completely reacted frit is ground and well mixed by hand, it can be melted to form a good quality, homogeneous glass at temperatures of the order of 1000–1100°C. Much of the first-quality Roman glass was no doubt made in this way, perhaps using more than one stage of quenching the melt in water, grinding and remixing by hand. This process of multiple quenching was also used to purify the glass by removing undesirable inclusions.

The subsequent melting was carried out in special kilns or crucibles, sometimes in several stages to permit unfused elements to be drawn off from the molten mixture. After the mixture had turned to glass, it was allowed to cool off in the crucibles, which later had to be smashed to release the glass ingots formed inside. The ingots were sold to glass workshops, where they were remelted and turned into finished objects.

Large quantities of a wide variety of ancient glass have been recovered by the Institute of Nautical Archaeology (Turkey) from a late Bronze Age shipwreck site (*c.* 1350 BC), and medieval glass from a wreck at Serçe Liman (*c.* 1025 AD). (The shipwrecks were named after their locations.) It is thought that both ships were carrying glass for trade.

In 1962, the late Bronze Age shipwreck was discovered less than 1 kilometre northeast of the tip of Ulu Burun, a cape near Kaş in Turkey. It lay only 50 m from the shore on a steep slope at depths ranging between 44 and 51 m. Excavated in 1984, the ship was found to have been carrying a large cargo of raw goods, amongst which were at least twelve round glass ingots, and manufactured goods including glass and faience beads. One amphora (KW8 in area J/K 12 was filled with tiny glass beads, solidly concreted together (see *Figure 7.8*). Not far from Pithos 250, lying loose under a thin covering of sand, were two glass ingots (KW 3: max. diam. 0.154; min. diam. 0.125; thickness 0.055 to 0.069; wt 2343 g) and (KW 4: max. diam. 0.156; min. diam. 0.141; thickness 0.056 to 0.068; wt 2607 g) (*Figure 3.1*). Roughly discoid in appearance, they are truncated cones with the edges of their smaller faces rounded, and their larger, flat faces of rougher texture; the faces are not parallel. They were described as cobalt blue at the time of their discovery, and chemical analysis has subsequently confirmed cobalt as the colouring matter (Brill, 1988). They are the earliest glass ingots known, and are of great interest as evidence of ancient trading in raw glass. It has been suggested that they are

Figure 3.1   Blue glass ingot, from the Bronze Age shipwreck at Ulu Burun, Turkey. (Courtesy of the Institute of Nautical Archaeology, Texas).

probably of Egyptian origin, and that they may have been made in cylindrical vessels very similar to those found at Tell el-Amarna. Further analysis will be required to prove this theory (Nicholson *et al.*, 1997). The ingots were unusually clean, with few traces of concretion or weathering layers although they were scarcely buried. Presumably they had been abraded by sea-bed action and therefore it is surprising that they are the largest and heaviest raised from the site.

About 1025 AD a merchant ship of unknown origin and nationality sank in 36 m of water within the rocky confines of Serçe Liman, a natural harbour on the southern Turkish coast opposite the Greek island of Rhodes. The wreck was excavated between 1977 and 1979 and yielded the largest amount of medieval glass yet known, having been loaded with 3000 kg of cullet in baskets, both in the form of chunks of raw glass and broken vessels, stored in the aft hold area of the ship. In addition, over eighty intact vessels, including engraved bowls and beakers, presumably having belonged to the merchants themselves, were found in the living quarters at the bow and stern (Bass, 1978, 1979, 1980, 1984).

Egyptian faience

The glazed quartz material known as Egyptian faience was, as the term suggests, first made in ancient Egypt (Peltenburg, 1987). Glazed steatite and faience beads are known from a number of Predynastic sites (5500–3050 BC). It continued to be manufactured throughout ancient Egypt into the Later Periods (1070 BC to 395 AD). The material was also produced in Mesopotamia (4300–3900 BC). It would seem that Egyptian faience was initially produced in imitation of the highly valued, semi-precious tones, turquoise and lapis lazuli. During the next five thousand years, manufacturing centres were established throughout North Africa, the Aegean and Asia, often alongside glassmaking operations (Shortland and Tite, 1998). Developments in glass technology produced an increasing range of colours.

By 2000 BC. Egyptian faience objects were transported to Europe and even to Britain by established trade routes. By the first millennium AD, the material had largely fallen out of use except in the Near East. During the twelfth century its manufacture was revived in Syria and Persia, where white faience-type bodies were produced in imitation of Chinese porcelain and stoneware.

The vitreous material Egyptian faience is not a true glass, since it is not homogenous on a micro scale. The body of faience artefacts are composed of crushed quartz or sand with small amounts of lime, metallic salts and either natron or plant ash, made into a paste with water and organic resin, e.g. gum of tragacanth. The basic mixture forming the quartz core varied in colour from white, grey to pink or orange depending on the impurities present. (Small amounts of clay were sometimes added to improve the plastic quality of the faience. However, the brown body colour was reflected through the glaze, producing a dull, muddy appearance. This could be avoided by applying a surface layer of quartz to provide a white ground for the coloured glaze.) The core was then coated with a soda–lime–silica glaze, which was generally a bright blue–green colour due to the inclusion of copper-based salts either from metal parings or crushed minerals containing copper such as malachite (see *Plate 2*). The typical faience mixture was thick at first and became soft and flowing as it began to be deformed, though it cracked if deformed too rapidly.

The earliest objects manufactured were beads, amulets and inlays, which could be hand-modelled and refined by surface abrasion. From about 2040 BC open moulds were used to make complete objects, or parts of objects, which were joined together with glaze slurry whilst still damp. Wheel-throwing was possible to a certain extent, but the resulting vessels tend to be very thick-walled. Once the required shapes had been formed, the objects were finished by grinding and smoothing, and decorated by incising the surface, and after *circa* 1782 BC, painting on details such as facial features and hieroglyphics, with a black or brown slurry, or pigment wash coloured with manganese and iron oxides. The decoration and glazed object were then glazed by one of three methods (efflorescence, cementation, application) and fired at temperatures in the range of 800–1000°C (*Figure 3.2*).

The faience paste shrank by 4–12 per cent on drying, and if clay had been added to the

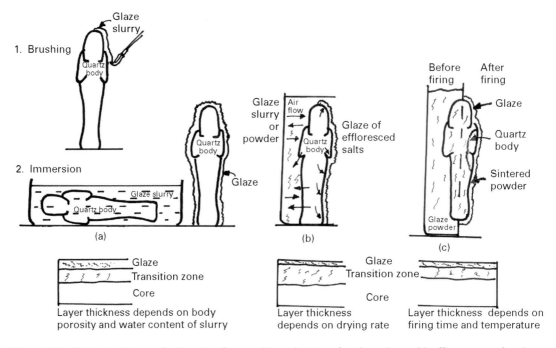

Figure 3.2   Glazing techniques for Egyptian faience: (a) application of a glaze slurry; (b) efflorescence of a glaze; (c) cementation of glaze.

mixture, differential shrinking could cause cracking and loss of glaze during firing. Cracking sometimes also occurred during the firing of objects composed of several pieces luted together.

The efflorescence technique was probably the one most commonly used by the ancient Egyptians. It was essentially a self-glazing method, in which water soluble alkali salts such as the carbonates, chlorides, sulphates of sodium (and less commonly potassium), in the form of plant ashes or natron, were mixed with the quartz material forming the core of the object. During the process of drying out, the salts migrated to the surface to form an effloresced crust or bloom. When fired, the crust melted and fused with the fine quartz, copper oxide and lime. The technique produced variations in glaze thickness, it being thickest in areas of greater evaporation and drying such as the exterior surface. Where the object had been in contact with a surface or where there had been secondary working of the object's shape by cutting away the surface, efflorescence was reduced or prevented. This glazing technique

produced the greatest amount of interstitial glass (the glassy phase in the gaps between the quartz particles), and the interface between the glaze and core is usually clearly defined.

Cementation was also a self-glazing technique, in which the unglazed but dry faience core was buried in a glazing powder composed of lime (calcium oxide), ash, silica, charcoal and colourant. On heating, the powder partially melted and that which was in contact with the quartz core reacted with and glazed it. Unreacted powder was crumbled away from the glazed object on completion of the firing. Objects produced by the cementation process can be recognized by a fairly uniform, but often thin, all-over glaze, the absence of drying marks. In the case of small objects there may also be a lack of drying marks, whereas larger examples may exhibit rough areas where they rested during firing. Occasionally the glaze may be thicker on the underside of pieces produced by the cementation technique. There is very little interstitial glass, and the interface between the glaze and core is generally well defined.

Application, as the term suggests, entails the application of a glazing powder, or slurry to the faience core, either by immersion of the object or painting it with the glaze. The powder held in the slurry may comprise quarts, lime and natron, which have been ground up together, or raw materials which have been fritted together and then crushed. The porous quartz body absorbed some of the mixture so that the mixture adhered to it on drying. On firing, the coating melted to form a glaze, which was often fairly thick. Objects produced in this way are recognized by the presence of drips, brush marks or flow lines and the greater thickness of the glaze layer. They may also have a clear edge where the application was ceased in order to enable the piece to be handled or to prevent it from adhering to the kiln supports. The amount of interstitial glass is small and the interface between glaze and core not well defined.

The forming of the body and glaze varied considerably over time. In comparison with small local workshops, those enjoying royal patronage are likely to have had access to the best materials and time to experiment. The three basic techniques of producing Egyptian faience objects are not always readily identifiable, especially since they were sometimes combined. Nicholson (1993) reproduces a table of methods of Egyptian faience manufacturing techniques by period and illustrates the techniques with diagrams and photographs taken through a scanning electron microscope. Sode and Schnell (1998) have documented techniques of faience manufacture in modern Egypt.

Faience beads

The vast majority of surviving faience objects are cylindrical beads (*Figure 3.3*). Faience beads are characteristic of the Bronze Age when bronze-melting furnace temperatures were not high enough to fuse glass satisfactorily, but from which slags were readily available as a source of colourant. The earliest examples seem to have been made in Badarian contexts (fifth millennium BC). In the Near East, faience beads may have been made in millions; hundreds of thousands have been found in one site alone, the Grey Eye Temple at Brak in the Lebanon; and a site at Nineveh

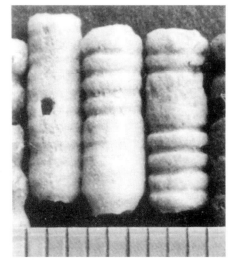

Figure 3.3 Egyptian faience beads, typical of the segmented type found in Egypt and other Mediterranean sites. Scale of millimetres below.

in Iraq yielded a layer 2 metres thick. The beads generally measure some 6–30 mm long, are 2–10 mm in diameter, have an axial hole and most are segmented.

Relatively few faience beads (some thirty in all) are quite different in shape, being either disc-shaped (quoit beads) or star-shaped, and much larger, about 30 mm in diameter. These are found almost solely in the British Isles (Stone and Thomas, 1956) and some authors (Newton and Renfrew, 1970; Aspinall *et al.*, 1972) have argued that these two types were made locally, possibly at Glenuce and Culbin in Scotland (UK). Tite *et al.* (1983) carried out extensive research, first in Iran where modern donkey beads were being made at Q'om, and subsequently in the laboratory. Briefly, the core of the bead was composed of finely ground quartzite, made into a paste with gum tragacanth, and the glaze was made from the ash of *Salsola kali* and Salsola soda, mixed with slaked lime, powdered quartz, charcoal and copper oxide. After drying, the shaped beads were embedded in the glazing powder and the whole mass was fired at 1000°C. The beads were then removed from the glazing powder (which apparently had not melted at 1000°C) and were found to have a bright, glossy blue glaze. If the firing temperature was only 900°C the glaze was coarse and pale, but at a temperature of 1110°C the glazing powder fused into a useless block. Thus the heating regime was fairly critical and it seems surprising that the plant ash did not fuse at a lower temperature.

Wulff *et al.* (1968) undertook chemical and petrographic analyses of the plant ash, the bead body and the glazing powder from beads found in Iran. It was concluded that the grains in the core had sintered together through the formation of cristobalite (a crystalline modification of silica) at their points of contact; and that the glazing action had been brought about in the vapour phase through the formation of soda (Na_2O) vapour, resulting from the interaction of the sodium carbonate (Na_2CO_3) with the slaked lime ($Ca(OH)_2$), which then reacted with copper chloride ($CuCl$) vapour formed by the interaction between sodium chloride ($NaCl$) in the plant ash and the copper oxide (CuO).

Noble (1969) adopted quite a different approach by mixing glazing material with core material before the beads were shaped. When the bead then dried out the sodium carbonate and bicarbonate ($NaHCO_3$), together with the copper oxide, had migrated to the surface as an efflorescence. Thus, when the bead was fired at 950°C, the alkali-rich efflorescence melted to form a glassy blue layer. If the copper was omitted, the resultant glaze was white but if iron oxide had been used the glaze was yellow. Manganese would give a purple glaze and Noble, in commenting on Wulff *et al.* (1968), claimed that the above process for making faience articles was correct because ancient multicoloured articles exist and these could not have been made by the vapour process. However, the natron used in Noble's experiments may not have been representative, since the material seems to have much less Na_2CO_3 and $NaHCO_3$ than the 14 analyses quoted by Douglas and Frank (1972).

Glass-melting

Glass-melting is the preparation of molten glass by the melting down of prepared frit, chunks or ingots of raw glass or of cullet (broken, waste glass). Glass-melting does not require a knowledge of or access to raw materials, and is technologically an easier

process to carry out than glassmaking. In some cases glassmaking and glass-melting were combined by adding cullet to the raw materials during the melting process, in which case, the chemical characteristics of glass melt may not be as well defined as material made by the glassmaking process, i.e. if the cullet had been imported from another geographical area. On the other hand, a long-continued re-use of cullet in one area could perpetuate a chemical characteristic of the glass long after one of the raw materials had ceased to be available. For example, such a practice might be one reason for the continual melting of soda glass in the Rhineland long after Roman glassworkers had left the area.

Glass-forming

Glass-forming is the heating and reshaping of a piece of glass without actually melting it. Many glass articles are said to have been made at certain sites whereas they were really only formed there. For example, a Romano-British purple and white glass bracelet from Traprain Law in Scotland was formed by reheating a piece of a Roman pillar moulded bowl (Newton, 1971b). Since the glass was plastic rather than molten, the purple and white layers were deformed only, and did not merge into one another.

Annealing

Annealing is a process which is applied to all glass artefacts in order to relieve stresses set up as a result of rapid cooling, or different rates of cooling of various components, for example, body, handle, foot. Failure to anneal glass in a suitable manner would leave it weak and brittle. Annealing is usually carried out immediately after the shaping process. The glass is reheated in a special annealing furnace (lehr) to the required annealing temperature (which depends upon the composition of the glass), and is then allowed to cool at a controlled rate, whilst still in the furnace. The small amount of viscous flow, which takes place during the annealing process, leads to stress relaxation within the glass which is thus rendered relatively stress-free. It is thus unlikely that conservators will encounter badly annealed glasses since these would have

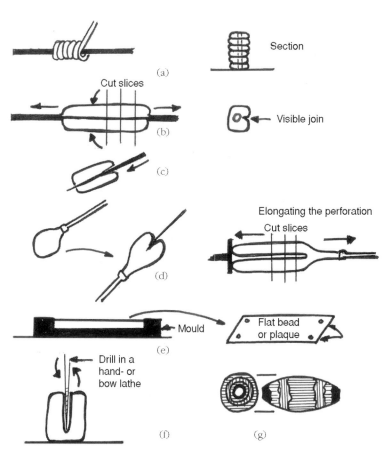

Figure 3.4 Techniques of bead making: (a) threading soft glass around a wire; (b) folding soft glass around a wire; (c) perforating a lump of soft glass; (d) perforating and drawing out a lump of glass; (e) fusing powdered glass in an open mould and drilling holes through the corners; (f) drilling through a cold lump of glass; (g) forming a mosaic glass bead.

fractured during their manufacture, or shortly afterwards during their functional life.

Shaping glass artefacts

The development of glass bead-making

The earliest vitreous material had been used in Egypt before *circa* 4000 BC, as a glaze to cover beads of stone and clay in imitation of coloured semi-precious stones. Later, *circa* 2500 BC, when furnaces were able to be maintained at temperatures high enough to soften glass, the same material was used in Egypt to make beads, which were the first objects to be made entirely of glass. Glass beads are known from Mycenae from the sixteenth to the thirteenth centuries BC. Glass paste beads made at Mycenae *circa* 1300 BC are in the form of small thin tablets of which the ends are ribbed and perforated for threading. They were circular, rectangular or triangular, and usually of blue or pale yellow glass. The beads are decorated with relief Mycenaean motifs, such as rosettes, ivy and spirals. They were formerly believed to have been used for necklaces, and as decoration on garments, but a recent view is that the beads were also used to adorn diadems and the skulls of skeletons (Yalouris, 1968).

Glass beads are found in most periods and cultures (Guido, 1977; Dubin, 1987; Kock and Sode, 1995; Sode, 1996). They can be made by at least seven methods (*Figure 3.4*): (i) winding threads of glass round a rod; (ii) drawing from a gob of glass which has been worked into a hollow; (iii) folding glass around a core, the join being visible on one side; (iv) pressing glass into a mould; (v) perforating soft glass with a rod; and (vi) blowing (though cylindrical blown glass beads are rather exceptional); (vi) drilling through a solid block of glass. The same methods of decoration were applied to glass beads as to glass vessels, that is, tooling the soft glass, thread inlay, mosaic inlay, *millefiore* etc. An agate effect was produced by casing glass tubing with layers of differently coloured glass and then chamfering down the ends of cut lengths to expose the various layers. Examples of this type are the aggry (*aggri*) beads excavated in Africa.

The early decorative patterns on beads from *circa* 1500 BC are stripes and spots; later developments are eye beads and beads with zig-zags and chevrons. Egyptian beads were exported to many countries. These early beads were normally made of opaque glass, frequently blue with decoration in yellow and white. Since the manufacture of glass beads could only be carried out in furnaces hot enough to melt iron, their production in Britain is mainly associated with the Romano-British period; although on the Continent large annular beads and armlets were made in the La Tene I period (fifth century BC). A comprehensive study of prehistoric and Romano-British beads found in Britain and Ireland (Guido, 1977) has shown that some beads were indigenous, but that many were imported. In some cases the beads or bracelets were made by reshaping fragments of Roman glass articles, and there is a strong suggestion that the highly coloured glass used for the applied decoration (spirals, eye spots etc.) was an article of trade imported from a glassworks which specialized in making coloured glass, perhaps in Gaul.

Most of the methods used in making and decorating glass beads, can be applied to the manufacture of bangles. If not cut from a solid piece of glass, however, the commonest means of producing bangles are either by bending a glass rod round and fusing the two ends together; or by first blowing a hollow glass cylinder and then cutting it into short lengths. In the latter instance it is not uncommon to find that the glass gathering has been cased with several layers of differently coloured glass.

Manufacturing glass vessels

Fourteen hundred years before the invention of glass-blowing, four very different techniques were already in use for the production of glass artefacts: core-forming; moulding; cutting or abrading (cold glass); and mosaic.

Cold, solid glass can be shaped and decorated by cold working, i.e. by glyptic techniques such as cutting and engraving. However, having the property of becoming molten (plastic) when heated to sufficiently high temperatures, means that practically all ancient (and modern) techniques of manufacture use glass in that condition and therefore can be described as hyaloplastic. Since glass can possess a remarkably wide range of viscosities (and thereby working ranges) depending on its composition and temperature (see *Figure 1.9*), glass artefacts can be made in an almost infinite variety of shapes. No other material has these properties or permits such a varied manufacture to be undertaken. In ancient times knowledge of the working ranges would have been part of the long-held secrets of the glassmaking process.

With the invention of glassblowing, new techniques of producing glass artefacts were developed, and along with them the methods of decolouration. These techniques have thus been in use for about two millennia, usually with increasing sophistication, despite the introduction of industrial mass manufacturing methods in the nineteenth and twentieth centuries. Consequently, glassmaking techniques will be described without attempting to deal with them in strict chronological order, although where possible an indication will be given of the date of their introduction. Tools for hand-working glass have remained essentially unaltered; but increased sophistication of glass designs led to changes in composition, that is choice of raw materials, and in furnace design. These will be discussed in the light of surviving ancient glass and historic glass objects, of contemporary literary sources, and modern melting trials and hypotheses on ancient glass production. Modern methods of glassworking will be mentioned only briefly, since they are outside the scope of this book.

Core-formed vessels

The majority of pre-Roman glass vessels were made by the core-forming method (*Figure 3.5*). Small vessels formed in this manner were formerly termed sand-core vessels after Petrie (1894) introduced the term, without supplying

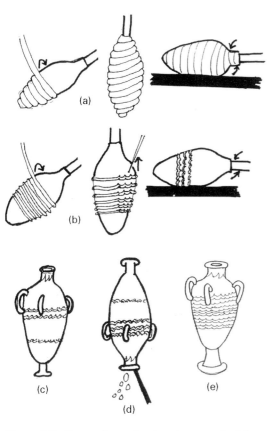

Figure 3.6 Interior of a broken core-formed vessel, showing remains of the burnt core.

Figure 3.5 Stages of core-forming glass vessels: (a) winding a soft glass thread around the core and marvering it to shape; (b) winding soft coloured glass threads around the vessel and embedding them by marvering; (c) the mouth, foot and handles are formed; (d) when cold, the core is scraped out; (e) the finished vessel.

evidence that sand had been used to form the core.

Labino (1966) carried out a series of experiments, which showed that core-formed vessels could be made by trailing glass on to an entirely organic core that had a coefficient of expansion greater than that of the glass so that the vessel would not crack on cooling. However, Labino did not disclose the exact composition of the core material in order to prevent its use in the production of fakes. Bimson and Werner (1967) examined two core-formed vessels – a Cypriot Bronze Age scent bottle and an Eighteenth Dynasty model coffin, inside which, remains of the cores were found. Both samples suggested that the origi-

nal core had been made in two layers from a friable porous mass consisting of fragments of plants (probably as dung), a highly ferruginous clay and ground limestone, the outer layer being largely ground limestone. Bimson and Werner (1969) examined a further 62 samples of core material and found that early (Eighteenth Dynasty) material did not differ substantially from the two samples mentioned above, although later material (after 750 BC) consisted of sand grains cemented together with iron oxide. Wosinski and Brill (1969) examined ten examples of core material from three basic types of core-formed vessel and found that the core materials were mixtures of sand, clay and plant material (again possibly dung), but did not confirm the presence of a surface layer of ground limestone (*Figure 3.6*).

It was formerly supposed that core formed vessels were made by dipping the core into the molten glass, but this has been shown not to be the case (Stern, 1998). A core shaped to the interior form of a vessel would be made in a soft but firm material such as a mixture of dung and sand, on the end of a wooden rod. A trail of molten glass was wound around the core and when a sufficient thickness of glass had been built up, the glass and core were repeatedly reheated, rotated and rolled smooth (marvered) on a flat stone surface. The glass could be reheated and decoration added in the form of trails of molten coloured glass. The trails could be combed into patterns such as swags and zig-zags, and embedded in the glass surface by reheating and marvering.

Additional parts such as rudimentary handles, stems and footrings might be added. On cooling, the rod was removed and as much as possible of the core picked out, following which a rim could be trailed on and shaped. The carrot and lentil shapes of the earlier vases and bottles were natural marver shapes and these vessels were usually about 80–120 mm in height, although a few larger examples exist. Core-formed vessels were mainly produced in Egypt but examples have been excavated in Mesopotamia, Cyprus, Syria, Crete, Rhodes and mainland Greece. Stern (1998) has shown that it is possible to apply finely ground glass to a wetted core, by packing it against the core with a wet brush, heating the powder to a temperature of 593°C to glaze it over, followed by a firing at 816°C.

Four distinctive types of core-formed vessels are known from the later Egyptian period (see *Figure 2.2*): *alabastron* (cylindrical or cigar-shaped); *amphorisk* (pear-shaped); *aryballos* (globular); and *oinochoe* (jug with one handle and a flat base). These containers (*unguentaria*) seem to have been luxury articles and were used for ointments, perfumes and cosmetics. Core-formed vessels continued to be made throughout the Hellenic period, slowly retiring in the face of blown glass and *millefiore*-type vessels.

Casting in open or closed moulds

Casting into open moulds was a technique already in use in the pottery and faience industry. It was used for the production of open glass vessels such as bowls, dishes and wide-necked bottles, and plaques. Three techniques were probably used: (i) fusing of powdered or chipped glass, poured or hand-pressed into a mould; (ii) direct pouring and manipulation of the glass into the mould; and (iii) the lost wax (Fr. *cire perdue*) process. The figurine of Astarte from Atchana, Turkey (*Figure 3.7*), dating from the early fifteenth century BC, was cast in a one-piece mould, the back being flattened by pressure (Harden *et al.*, 1968). Numerous clay moulds, which could have been used for moulding glazed quartz fritware, have been found in Egypt. Phidias (*c.* 450 BC) cast small pieces of glass in clay moulds *in situ* at Olympia for the famous statue of Zeus (Bimson and Werner, 1964b).

Figure 3.7 Figurine of Astarte, originally translucent greenish-colourless, now appearing opaque white. Plaque cast in a one-piece mould, the back flattened by pressure, and moulded in the front in the form of a standing figure of the goddess. L 85 mm, W 23 mm, T 16–18 mm. Fourteenth or thirteenth century BC. Atchana, Turkey. (© Copyright The British Museum).

Fusing powdered glass in situ

A closed bowl-shaped mould formed of two parts could be made of refractory clay; or by carving pieces of wood to the desired shape, and when fitted together, lining the wooden mould with clay to act as a barrier. The mould pieces were then fitted together leaving a space between them which represented the

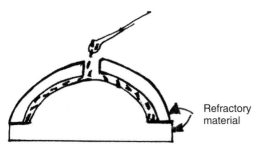

Figure 3.8   Forming a glass bowl by placing crushed glass into a mould and heating the mould until the glass fuses.

thickness of the glass artefact to be cast. The mould would then be heated to 700°C and as the temperature increased powdered or fragmented glass were dropped through an opening in the top of the mould. The glass eventually filled the mould (including the orifice which left a knob on what was to become the base of the bowl, and which had to be ground flat after the glass had hardened). When the melting temperature of 1000°C had been reached, the furnace was allowed to cool over a long period of time, and the mould taken apart to release the glass vessel (*Figure 3.8*).

Alternatively, coloured glass pastes could be placed in the mould (Fr. *pâte de verre* or *pâte de riz*). Glass ground to a powder was mixed with a fluxing medium so that it would melt readily, and coloured. It was pressed into the clay by hand and fired. Coloured glass pastes could be freely modelled like clay. The varied colouring suggested by semi-precious stones was obtained by the positioning of different powdered ingredients in the mould. Some examples were built up into polychrome high relief or figures by successive layers added to the mould, and sometimes after refiring they were refined by being carved. This process was known in ancient Egypt. It was revived in France in the nineteenth century to form artificial jewels and other decorative articles, especially by the sculptors Henri and Jean Cross. Other exponents of the technique were Albert Dammouse (*c.* 1898), Francois Decorchement (*c.* 1900–1930), Emile Gallé and Gabriel Argy-Rousseau (Newman, 1977).

The moulding operation using a two-piece mould could be hastened by pressing on the upper (male) mould if the mould material was strong enough. Such pressure will also produce a sharper impression of any pattern on the inside of the external (female) mould. During the nineteenth century and subsequently, a mechanical mould-pressing technique using metal moulds was used to provide cheap imitations of deep-cut glass. Glass made by this process bears the exact design and the contours of the two parts of the mould. Nineteenth-century glassware which has external decoration (such as raised ribbing) and corresponding internal concavities, will have been made by the blown three-mould process, or by pattern moulding also known from the nineteenth century onwards as optic moulding (Newman, 1977).

The lost wax process

Glass artefacts, such as figurines with a complicated shape with many undercuts, could be made by the lost wax process (Fr. *cire perdue*; Ger. *Wachsausschmelzfahren*). The desired object was modelled or carved in wax. The model was then encased in a mould of refractory material such as clay, incorporating airholes and pour-holes at the base. The mould was heated and inverted, so that the wax ran out and powdered glass was then introduced to the hot mould, which was reheated, thus melting the glass to form a solid artefact. Alternatively, if a hollow glass object was required, such as a pillar-moulded bowl, an internal (female) mould was made of wood or refractory clay and covered with hot wax applied with a brush (Schuler, 1959a). The wax was shaped with a template or by building up and carving the wax to form the external shape of the object. Small metal bars incorporated into the female mould and protruding through the wax into the male mould kept the mould pieces apart during the casting process. A hole was left in the base of the male mould in order for the molten wax to run out when heated. Thus the space inside represented the form of the glass object to be cast. Powdered glass was then introduced into the mould and heated in order to melt it. On cooling, the moulds were removed and the result was a hollow glass object (*Figure 3.9*).

Mosaic glass

Mosaic glass is composed of thin sections, cut from plain or coloured glass rods. The

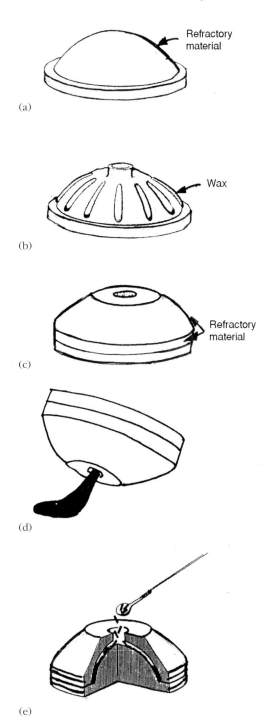

(a)

Refractory material

(b)

Wax

(c)

Refractory material

(d)

(e)

Figure 3.9 Casting a glass bowl by the lost wax (Fr. *cire perdue*) process. (a) The material used for the mould was refractory clay. After the core was formed it was dried in air, (b) hot wax was applied and shaped with a template. Ribs of wax were shaped and applied, and a lump of wax was applied at the top to form a cavity for holding glass. (In a two-part mould clay can be used instead.) (c) The wax was covered with more refractory clay and left to dry. (If the mould was two-part, the join between the pieces was coated with a thin wash of clay.) (d) The wax was melted out with the mould inverted. (If the mould is two-part, the parts are separated, cleaned of clay and reassembled, using refractory clay to seal the joint.) The mould was placed in a furnace and heated slowly to 700°C. At this point small pieces of glass were placed in the hollow part of the top of the mould. The temperature was gradually increased, and as the glass melted down, more was added. (The temperature might have been held at 800°C if the process were to take longer.) The glass flowed down and filled the space in the mould; eventually there was excess glass in the hollow space at the top. When the temperature reached 1000°C and glass was observed at the top, the mould was assumed to have completely filled, and the furnace was cooled. When cold enough to handle, the mould was taken out and broken apart.

simplest way of producing a fine, short glass rod was to pour the molten metal very slowly from the crucible or ladle so that as it fell it cooled and solidified. In the same way a glass rod can be formed by dipping a *bait* into the surface of molten glass and then slowly raising it. The molten glass adheres to the bait and behaves rather like treacle, necking in rapidly to form a thin stream. Treacle will continue to run back from the bait but glass will soon freeze and stiffen (depending upon the rate at which the bait is raised, the temperature above the glass and the composition of the glass). A rod of surprisingly constant thickness can be made by this method, thicker rods being obtained with a slower rate of draw.

At a much later date, longer and more even lengths of rod could be made, by fixing a gathering of molten glass metal to an iron post or a plate on a wall and pulling out a length of rod with the aid of a punty by walking away from the gather. Much later again glass tubing was produced in the same way except

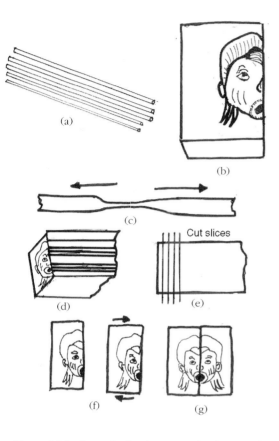

Figure 3.10 Stages in forming a mosaic plaque with a design of a mask. (a) Pre-formed coloured glass canes assembled to form half of the mask, in large section (b). (c) The assemblage is drawn out to the desired size (d), from which thin slices are cut (e). (f) Two slices are placed face-to-face to form (g) a complete mask.

Figure 3.11 Fragments of mosaic beaker, composed of circular sections of white, red, yellow and dark brown opaque rods, set in horizontal zig-zags to form the whole vessel in a pattern which has the same aspect inside and outside. Built on a core, covered with an outer mould and fused, exterior ground and polished. The colours are often obscured by enamel-like deterioration. L of largest fragment 77 mm, W of largest fragment 60 mm, average T 4 mm, average D of sections 2 mm. Fifteenth century BC. Tell al Rimah, Iraq. (© Copyright The British Museum).

that the glassworker drew out the gather with a blow iron, walking backwards and blowing gently down the iron at the same time in order to maintain the cavity in the tube. Needless to say, this operation required considerable skill.

Monochrome rods of different coloured glass were then sliced into sections which could be placed adjacent to one another and fused to form a pattern by heating (*Figure 3.10*). The technique was used to form plaques in which the mosaic slices were adhered to a backing with bitumen. In the case of a face, the image was formed as one half only, two slices from the same rod being placed side by side, one being turned over so

that a completely symmetrical face was produced (Schuler, 1963).

The mosaic technique was also used to form glass vessels. A group of vessels dating from the late fifteenth to the early thirteenth centuries BC from Tell al Rimah, 'Agar Quf and Marlik in north-west Iraq were made by the method, the different coloured sections being arranged in patterns or in zig-zag bands (*Figure 3.11*), probably on the outer surface of a circular mould having the interior shape of the vessel to be produced. The sections of rod may have been fixed to the mould with an adhesive, which burnt out during firing or, in some cases, an outer mould may have been used to keep the sections in place. The mould was then heated sufficiently to soften the sections with the minimum amount of distortion required to fuse them together to form a mosaic vessel. In some cases the glass rods were multi-coloured in concentric rings. When the mosaic was properly fused, and the article

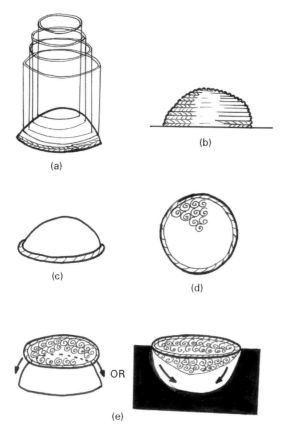

(a)

(b)

(c)

(d)

OR

(e)

Figure 3.12 Stages in the formation of a *reticelli* bowl (multi-cane), and a mosaic (cane-sectioned) bowl with a *reticelli* rim. (a) Rings of *reticelli* canes are placed over a former. (b) When the former has been completely covered, the whole is heated until the canes fuse. (c) A *reticelli* rod is formed to a similar diameter to that of a mould. (d) This cane is used as an accurate perimeter within which to fuse sawn cane sections to create a flat disc for sagging. (e) The disc is softened over, or into a mould to create a bowl, which is then finished by cutting and polishing.

had cooled, it was removed from the mould, ground smooth and polished internally and externally (*Figure 3.12*). Mosaic bowls such as those mentioned above were the prototypes of the mosaic glassware of the late Hellenic and later periods.

The distinction is not always made between true mosaic and mosaic inlay, although the two are quite different. In true mosaic the coloured glass pieces formed the entire thickness of the article, whereas in mosaic inlay thin sections of glass rod were backed by a glass of uniform colour. In Venetian *millefiori* glass, which sought to imitate true Roman mosaic, the sections of coloured glass were embedded in clear glass and then blown to the final shape of the vessel. *Millefiore* is often incorrectly used to describe any type of mosaic inlay.

The making of *millefiori* artefacts required great skill and patience, especially when complicated rod patterns were involved. The rods were produced by first casing a glass cane or tube with several layers of coloured glass on an appreciably larger scale than that which was finally required. Each layer could be reheated and shaped by marvering (round), pressing on the marver (square) or rolling on a corrugated surface (flower shape). (Later iron moulds were used to produce these shapes.) When the design was complete, the glass rod was reheated to its softening point and drawn out so that its diameter decreased, the design decreasing proportionately until it was about 20–30 m in diameter. The rod was then sectioned, the slices placed adjacent to one another, sometimes embedded in clear glass and fused by reheating (*Figure 3.13*). As a variation, sections of more than one *millefiori* rod or slices cut at an angle instead of transversely across the rod could be fused together, the latter producing elongated stripes of the design.

In AD 1495, Marc Antonio Sabellico, the librarian of San Marco in Venice (Italy), wrote of the inclusion of, 'all sorts of flowers, such as clothe the meadows in Spring, in a little ball' (of glass). The objects described, sound remarkably similar to the paperweights which were made in Murano in Italy and Baccarat, St-Louis and Clichy in France, and which were to become fashionable in the nineteenth century. Paperweights often had thin designs such as

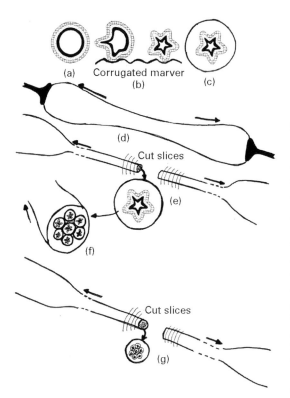

flower petals (*millefiori*) incorporated in the body of coloured glass by picking up a thin section of glass on a gather and then taking another gather over the top (Newman, 1977). *Figure 3.14* shows a piece of jewellery with a decorative centre made in the same manner.

Cutting, grinding and abrading

Cutting or grinding glass is the only technique involving removal of glass from a cold mass, which was used to produce a complete vessel. Techniques for stone- and gem-cutting were well established before the advent of glass-making, and it was natural that they should be extended to cutting glass once this material could be produced in massive form. On the Mohs scale of hardness, cold glass has a scratch hardness between 4.5 and 6.5 depending on its composition, and it can be cut or ground by harder materials such as quartz or flint (scratch hardness 7.0). Cold-cutting or grinding were used at an early date for finishing glass objects or vessels which had been cast (Harden, 1968).

The head-rest of the Pharaoh Tutankhamun (1352 BC) (Cairo Museum) was cut from two blocks of glass, the join between them being covered by a gold band. A much later example of glass abrasion, an alabastron bearing the name of King Sargon of Assyria (772–705 BC) (British Museum, London), bears internal spiral grooves and an internal knob at the bottom, which are the result of its having been cold-worked (*Figure 3.15*).

Figure 3.13 Stages in the formation of *millefiore* objects. (a) A cane is formed of concentric layers of coloured or patterned glass. (b) The soft glass cane is rolled over a corrugated surface to shape it into a flower. (c) The flower shape is embedded in clear glass. (d) The rod is drawn out and cut into sections, which (e) are fused together and encased in clear glass. (f) The rod is again drawn out, and (g) cut into slices.

Figure 3.14 Silver cross with a central design in *millefiore*, and a group of drawn *millefiore* glass canes.

Figure 3.15 Glass vase engraved in cuneiform script with the name of King Sargon II of Assyria. The interior grooves show that the vessel was ground from a solid block of glass. H *c.* 150 mm. Nimrud, 722–705 BC. (© Copyright The British Museum).

In general, the techniques of casting glass into moulds, followed by the discovery of glassblowing replaced the production of glass vessels by abrasion of solid glass blocks. However, the technique continued as a means of further embellishment as, for example, in the production of *diatreta*, as a means of surface decoration (cutting and engraving) or simply for finishing off cast glassware (Harden, 1968).

Good glassware was often (and still is) given a final polish using fine, hard abrasive, and where this was well carried out, much or all of the evidence that would suggest how the vessel had been made was removed – for example, the casting flashes which remained on the glass at the junctions of the mould-pieces.

The process of cold-cutting glass was brought to an extremely fine art in making *diatreta* (cage cups). As the name suggests, the cups bear a pattern which stands out from the (moulded) cup as an open network or cage. The majority of the pattern was completely undercut so that it stood free from the main vessel (the cup), being held to it by a small number of glass bridges. For many years there was speculation as to how cage cups were made, and it was not until 1880 that the glasscutter Zweisel succeeded in reproducing an example. Fremersdorf (1930) correctly described how the diatretarius had produced cage cups; and finally in 1964, a German glasscutter, Schäfer (1968, 1969), made a perfect copy of the cage cup from Daruvar (Zagreb, Yugoslavia). The illustration of a cage cup by Brill (1968) also makes it quite clear that a cutting technique had been used in the example shown.

Two outstanding examples of cage cups are a virtually complete *diatreta* in the Romisch Germanisches Museum, Cologne; and the Lycurgus Cup in the British Museum, London (*Plate 4*). The latter was skilfully carved in high relief, the backs of the major figures being hollowed out in order to maintain an even translucency. At one point (behind a panther), the vessel wall was accidentally pierced (Harden and Toynbee, 1959; Harden, 1963).

Surface decoration by cutting glass

Abrasive techniques for the decoration of glassware have as long a history as glass-making itself; there is evidence for glass engraving in Egypt as early as the sixteenth century BC. Engraving probably developed from the stone- and gem-cutting trade, being executed with the same pointed instruments. Harden (1968) drew attention to simple forms of incised decoration in three different eras. Cut or engraved patterns were rare in the pre-Roman period; during the Roman period good engraving declined in Egypt but excellent work was produced in Syria (Harden, 1969a); and in the post-Roman era, engraved Christian motifs began to appear on glassware (Harden, 1971).

Diamond-point engraving is, as its name suggests, the technique of using a diamond-point to scratch the glass surface. Early examples are said to date from Roman times, although it has been argued that these were executed with pointed flint tools. Diamond-point engraving was used to decorate Islamic glass. In the sixteenth century the technique was used by glass decorators in Venice (*Figure 3.16*), and in Hall-in-Tyrol (Austria), where an glasshouse under the patronage of the Archduke Ferdinand produced a great deal of diamond-engraved Venetian glass; and by German, Dutch and British engravers, firstly in the *façon de Venise* and subsequently in local styles.

Diamond-point engraving was first used in Britain on glassware made in the glasshouse of Jacopo Verzelini. In Holland, during the seventeenth century, diamond point engraving was mainly used by amateur decorators, especially for calligraphy (Tait, 1968). The technique was superseded in the eighteenth century by wheel-engraving and by

Figure 3.16 Detail of a diamond-point engraved dish, with the arms of Pius IV. (c) V&A Picture Library.

enamelling. However, it continued to be used to produce stipple engravings from the 1720s to the late eighteenth century, and in Britain for producing Jacobite and other commemorative glassware. In the technique of stippling, grouped and graded dots were engraved with a diamond-point on the surface of the vessel. These represented the highlights of the design. The diamond-point was set in a handle, which may have been gently struck with a small hammer to produce a single small dot on the glass. In the best examples of stippling the decoration can be compared to a delicate film breathed upon the glass (see *Figure 7.27e* for a nineteenth-century example). Frans Greenwood, a native of Rotterdam, brought the art of stippling to its greatest height in the first half of the eighteenth century. In the last forty years of the eighteenth century, stippled engraving was practised by numerous artists, the most famous being David Wolff in Holland.

Formative and decorative wheel-cutting and wheel-engraving

Wheel-cutting and wheel-engraving of glass are basically the same technique in which a rotating abrasive wheel is used to cut into the surface. In early times the same equipment would have been used for both methods: rotating wheels of various sizes propelled by a bow lathe. Gradually cutting came to be carried out with large wheels and was characterized by large-scale geometric designs, usually relatively deeply incised (see *Figure 7.26*); whereas engraving was executed with small wheels and was usually the method used to produce fine or pictorial work since it was possible to achieve great detail (*Figure 3.17*; Charleston 1964, 1965). Rotary abrasion (using emery powder or perhaps powdered quartz sand) had been carried out as early as the Third Dynasty (*c.* 2100–1800 BC), and engraving tools of that date have been excavated, but firm evidence for the rotary wheel-cutting of narrow lines seems to be scarce. It is not known what type of abrading equipment was used to decorate glass in Roman times. There is a suggestion that an all-purpose tool could have been used, which would be adapted as a lathe, drill or cutting or engraving wheel as required. The Romans used abrasives such

Figure 3.17 Detail of a wheel-engraved design on a Jacobite wineglass bowl.

as emery for cutting and pumice stone for polishing glass.

With the decline of the Roman Empire in the West, glass engraving died out, principally because there was no fine quality glass made after this time which was suitable for engraving. In the East the technique never ceased, and glasses with cut decoration can be traced in continuity through Sassanian to Islamic times. In the ninth and tenth centuries a school of relief cutting flourished in Persia and probably also in Mesopotamia, which was not rivalled until the end of the seventeenth century in Europe.

A description of wheel-engraving dating from AD 1464 states that a diamond-point was used, 'and with wheels of lead and emery; and some do it with little bow (archetto)'. By the fifteenth century gem-cutting wheels of lead, pewter, copper, steel and limewood were being used to engrave and polish glass. By the sixteenth century the principle of continuous rotary movement had been established. A drawing dating from 1568 depicts a foot-operated treadle with a large flywheel. Wheel-engraving was to reach its greatest heights once Bohemia and Germany produced a potash-lime glass suitable for this technique in the early seventeenth century.

Intaglio decoration (Ital. *cave relievo*; Ger. *tiefschnitt*) was created by engraving or cutting below the surface of the glass so that the apparent elevations of the design were hollowed out, and an impression taken from the design produced an image in relief. The background was not cut away, but was left on the plane of the highest areas of the design (see *Figure 3.17*). *Intaglio* work was carried out on rock crystal and other semi-precious stones and on glass by wheel-engraving in medieval Rome, but more particularly in glass in Germany and Silesia from the seventeenth century. For greater effectiveness the design was left matt or only partially polished.

The opposite decorative technique was cameo work (Ger. *hochschnitt*; Eng. high engraving) which involved the formation of a design in relief by cutting away the ground (*Figure 3.18*). The cameo technique, a combination of wheel-cutting and engraving, was used in Roman times. Cameo carving of layered stones seems to have originated in Ptolemaic Alexandria; and since Alexandria was also one of the most important centres of ancient glassmaking, it is reasonable to suppose that cameo glass was an Alexandrian invention in imitation of gem-stones. Cameo effects simulating agate and other similarly multi-coloured stones were commonly produced by casing, for example, a coloured glass with a white one, followed by cutting away the white glass in low relief.

The earliest known example of cameo glass design points to the same conclusion. This is a fragment of a plaque in the Department of Egyptian Antiquities of the British Museum, which shows a man's leg and part of a bull in a purely Egyptian style, which cannot be later than the third century BC. The white-on-blue blank for the plaque must have been moulded, since glassblowing had not been invented; but the relief was unquestionably carved. However, cameo glass that can be

Figure 3.18 An early eighteenth-century Silesian goblet and cover with an acanthus design cut and carved in high relief (*hochschnitt*). (© V&A Picture Library).

certainly ascribed to pre-Roman times is rare, and the bulk of that which has survived probably dates from the early Roman Imperial period. Two of the most notable specimens, the Blue Vase (National Museum, Naples) and the Auldjo Jug (British Museum, London – see

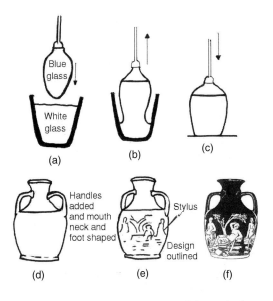

Figure 3.19 Stages in forming a cased (cameo) glass vessel. (a,b) A gather of transparent blue glass is blown and dipped into molten opaque white glass. (c) The vessel is shaped. (d) The mouth, foot and handles are formed. (e) The design is engraved through the white glass. (f) The Portland Vase. Late first century BC or early first century AD. H 245–248 mm.

Figure 7.40), were found in Pompeii and therefore pre-date the volcanic eruption of Mount Vesuvius, which destroyed the city in AD 79.

The first step in the manufacture of a cameo glass vessel such as the Portland Vase, was to blow the blue glass body and to coat it with a layer of white glass reaching up to a level just above the shoulder of the vase (*Figure 3.19*). To achieve this the glass-blower may have dipped a partially inflated paraison of blue glass into a crucible of molten white thus gathering a white layer over the blue; or a cup of white glass may have been formed and the blue glass blown into it. Having cased the blue glass with the white, the body was formed by further blowing and marvering. The average thickness of the blue glass is 3 mm.

Considerable manipulative skill was required to blow a two-layered vessel, but the glassworker's chief difficulty was to prepare two differently coloured glasses with the same coefficient of thermal expansion (and therefore also contraction) as an essential condition if

they were not to crack or split apart on cooling. The annealing process itself would have had to be carefully controlled. When the glass body was complete, the handles were formed from glass rods and attached, their lower ends to the white glass covering the shoulder, and the upper ends to the blue glass of the neck. The vessel was then handed to a glass engraver to carve the frieze, cut the ornament of the handles, and bring the whole to a finish. No doubt the frieze was copied from a model in wax or plaster, and the engraver would have begun by incising the outlines of the design on white glass, then all the white glass would have been removed from the background in order to expose the blue glass, and lastly the figures and features thereby left in block relief would have been modelled in detail.

The grooved treatment of the drapery and rocks reveals the use of engraving wheels, which were probably used for grinding away the background and other relatively coarse work; but for the more intricate and delicate details, small chisels, files and gravers would have been required (Haynes, 1975).

It was not until the nineteenth century that a glass cameo vessel such as the Portland Vase was produced again. (The Portland Vase is such an exceptional work of art that considerable effort has been devoted to making a copy.) In 1786 Josiah Wedgwood made a ceramic copy in Jasper ware; and in the early 1830s a prize of £1000 was offered for a copy in glass. This was achieved in 1876 by John Northwood Senior, but, even using nineteenth-century techniques of glassmaking, there was an expansion mismatch between the blue and white glasses, and the vase cracked after three years' work had been spent on it (Northwood, 1924). Other cased articles made by Northwood have also shown evidence of strain between the layers of glass. However, cameo glass was popularized to such an extent that its production became commercialized by the end of the century. In order to increase production cameo workers worked as teams rather than as individuals; and the larger areas of unwanted overlay were removed by dipping the vessel into hydrofluoric acid, having first covered the areas to be retained with a protective acid-resistant material such as wax.

Allied to cameo-cutting was the work of the *diatretarius* previously discussed, in which a glass blank was almost entirely undercut by lapidary means to produce the delicate decorative cage.

Cutting in high relief was used by the Chinese on scent and snuff bottles, and in the nineteenth century for the decoration of glass in the Art Nouveau style which arose in the 1930s, the name being derived from that of a Paris gallery devoted to interior decoration. Art Nouveau was adopted as a movement in Britain by William Morris (1834–1896) and his contemporaries. The style was adapted for glassware by Emile Gallé (1846–1904) in France and Louis Comfort Tiffany (1848–1933) in the United States, much of the decoration resulting from cane cutting.

Facet cutting

It is evident that ancient glass-cutters knew how to exploit the refractive effects of glass by cutting facets in addition to engraved lines. Harden (1969a) illustrates facet-cut bowls from the second century AD but states that by the fourth century the art of facet-cutting had degenerated to a mere abrasion of the surface both in the East and in the West. Some two hundred years later, in the Sassanian area of eastern Iraq and western Iran, bowls were produced with regularly spaced deep circular or hexagonal facets. Another 600 years later in the twelfth century, the Hedwig glasses (Pinder-Wilson, 1968; Harden, 1971), possibly produced in Russia, portray animals most effectively with large sweeps of the cutting wheel. In contrast with the cutting of fine lines with a narrow wheel, the use of a large and wide wheel seems, not surprisingly, to have been established much earlier.

It is only towards the end of the seventeenth century that a genuine distinction between glass cutting and glass engraving can be made. For the first time it is obvious that different types of equipment for cutting and for engraving were being developed. The glass engravers' equipment was light enough at this period to be carried, and resulted in a number of travelling glass engravers who would engrave any design on the spot for customers. The most famous of these was Georg Franz Kreybich who travelled Europe at the end of

Figure 3.20 Glass cutting and engraving. An engraver holds a goblet beneath a copper wheel powered by a treadle (omitted from the print). On the table are several other wheels, and bowls of abrasive paste. (© V&A Picture Library).

the seventeenth century engraving glass. On the other hand, the glasscutters' equipment used for facetting, intaglio, deep cutting, or roughing out for finer engraving was hardly portable. The large interchangeable wheels were rotated on a heavy, hand-turned cutting machine, a form of equipment, which survived until the modern period (*Figure 3.20*).

By the end of the seventeenth century water-power was in use for turning the wheels to cut glass. Water-power was probably used to enable all-over facetting to be carried out as an obligatory prelude to the engraving of potash glasses in Bohemia and Silesia in the eighteenth century. The highest development of facet-cutting, to produce designs in colourless glass, occurred with the cutting of full lead crystal glass. Cut glass has become synonymous with the deep wheel-cutting used on Irish glass from the late eighteenth century onwards, and also on modern cut wine glasses and decanters (Warren, 1981). Cut glass products enjoyed great popularity in Britain in the later nineteenth century. In this style of glassware angular cuts were made into the vessel which, when polished, act as prisms with adjacent cuts, producing a brilliant effect. The glass blank would first be marked with the pattern using a mixture such as white lead and gum water. Following the design, deep cuts would be roughed in against an iron wheel fed with abrasive such as sand. For coarse work, overhand-cutting where the vessel was pressed down onto the wheel from above was usual, whilst underhand-cutting where the vessel was pressed up onto the wheel from below was used for more delicate work. After the initial design had been cut, fine-grained, water-cooled stones, which required no abrasive, were used to smooth the first cuts and to add finer lines. (Besides water-power, steam-powered cutting mills were in existence by the beginning of the nineteenth century.) Finally the cuts could be polished with lead or wooden wheels or with rotary brushes charged with tripoli or putty powder. After the second half of the nineteenth century a method of plunging the glass vessels into a mixture of hydrofluoric and sulphuric acid was used to polish cut glassware.

Two techniques related to engraving are sand-blasting and acid-etching.

Sand-blasting

The technique of decorating glass by sand-blasting was invented in 1870, by the American Benjamin C Tilghman. Some early sand-blasting was steam-powered, but this was soon superseded by compressed air power. Parts of the glass to be left plain are covered with a stencil plate of steel or an elastic varnish or rubber solution painted on to form a protective shield. A stream of sand, crushed flint or powdered iron is then directed onto the surface of the glass in a jet of compressed air. The type of finish is varied by altering the size of the nozzle directing the abrasive, the size of the abrasive, or the pressure of the air. Sand-blasting is normally carried out in a closed circuit in a cabinet which can be sealed. The technique has rarely been applied to vessel glass except for lettering on mass produced items. The main use of sand-blasting has been on glass panels for decorative architectural use.

Acid-etching

The effects of abrasion can be duplicated, by etching glass with hydrofluoric acid (HF). A 90 per cent solution of HF possesses the unique property of dissolving silica:

$$SiO_2 + 4HF - SiF_4 = 2H_2O.$$

The effect depends greatly on the strength of the acid, and whether sulphuric acid is also present since some combinations of the acid mixtures polish the glass instead of producing a rough-etched surface (Schweig, 1973). Hydrofluoric acid is both difficult to prepare and extremely dangerous to use from the health point of view. It seems that the earliest example of acid-etching was made by Schwanhardt at Nuremberg in 1670. This example has been the centre of much speculation in the past since it was not until 1771 that Scheele discovered hydrofluoric acid. However, it appears that the Nuremberg article was treated with a mixture of calcium fluoride and sulphuric acid which produced hydrofluoric acid. The method of acid-etching generally employed was to coat the glass with wax after which the design was scratched through the protective layer onto the glass. The glass was then placed in a bath of hydrofluoric acid and was only etched in the areas from which the wax had been removed. In France, Gallé, Daum and Marmot used the technique to produce deep bold patterns on glass. Acid-etching is now used mainly to produce interesting surface textures and patterns on architectural glass. Glass can also be polished with a mixture of demineralized water, sulphuric acid and hydrofluoric acid.

Glass-blowing

It is remarkable that none of the contemporary Roman sources give any indication of a fundamentally important occurrence in the field of glassmaking, namely, the invention of glass-blowing; nor of the great increase in output of glass vessels which was brought about by its use. Later authors (Augustinian and Tiberian) refer to the use of glass-blowing without saying when it was invented (Harden, 1969a). Literary sources have traditionally given the birthplace of glassblowing as the Phoenician coast. However, on archaeological evidence it seems more likely that the invention took place in the Aleppo-Hama-Palmyra area of Syria, or in Israel. Grose (1977) reviewed the evidence for the introduction of glass-blowing, and concludes that discoveries made in Israel in 1961 and 1970 point to glass-blowing having been invented there sometime in the period 50–40 BC.

Despite the fact that there are no examples of blown glass earlier than this date, an ancient Egyptian wallpainting depicting workers blowing into tubes, was cited as evidence of glass-blowing. The depiction in fact shows Egyptian metallurgists blowing a charcoal fire with reed tubes ending in clay nozzles. Harden (1969a) suggested that solid metal rods had long been used for gathering molten glass from crucibles to introduce it into moulds, and that it was but a short step to using a hollow tube to inflate the glass into a mould by blowing. Schuler (1959b), however, believes that free (off-hand) blowing preceded mould-blowing since more skill was required to handle a blowpipe in the vertical position required for mould-blowing.

Remains of glasshouses have been uncovered at Rishpon near Herzlia, Tiberias, Sussita (Hyppos) and in several places along the sea-shore in Israel. During the excavation of a first century AD cemetery at Acre a group of glasses (mainly piriform *unguentaria*) were found. These may have been the product of a local factory using the glass sand of the Belus district, which is known to have been shipped south, even to Alexandria. At Bet She'arim (Sheikh Abreiq) near Nazareth a glasshouse was found which was working as late as the second and third centuries AD, and which produced very accurately shaped glass vessels. Many clay moulds were also found on the site. A contemporary glasshouse at Sussita on Lake Tiberias yielded a large quantity of glass vessels and wasters (Forbes, 1966). The thinnest and most beautiful glass was produced at Tiberias.

The blown glass of this period is referred to as Sidonian (a term comparable to the much later *façon de Venise*), since it was a tradition of blown glass shapes and techniques used by Syrians and Jews, which were handed from father to son, a training which was encouraged in the fourth century by exemption from taxes. The ancestors of the Jewish glassmakers may have learned something of glass manufacture and glass painting during the Babylonian Exile (seventh to fourth centuries BC).

Sidonian (Syrian and Jewish) glassmakers exploited the glass-blowing technique, migrating west and northwards and establishing glasshouses abroad. Mould-blown glass was being made in Italy by the first century AD, and in the Alpine provinces and north-western Europe by AD 40–50. Glasshouses were founded in the first century AD in Cologne, while the north Gallic and Belgic glasshouses were probably in full production by the second century. Their free- and mould-blown products were of a style directly related to the products of the central and eastern Roman Empire. The Egyptian workers based at Alexandria continued to specialize in cutting glass and in producing fine-coloured wares such as mosaic bowls, and did not adopt the glass-blowing technique until some time after the second century AD.

Glass-blowing techniques

The invention of glass-blowing brought about a complete revolution in the manufacture of glass artefacts. Glass ceased to be a luxury material since scores of vessels could be blown in a day in contrast with the use of the laborious core-forming process. Another great advantage was the possibility of making articles thinner and lighter and thus more acceptable for domestic purposes than was generally possible using the earlier glassmaking processes. There was also a great increase in the variety, shape and number of small hollow articles, and for the first time larger containers and window-panes could be produced.

From the very beginning, many of the vessels have the appearance of having been ripped off the blow iron as fast as they were produced. Handles and ornamentation also have the appearance of having been trailed on quickly. Speed of production gave early blown glass a pace and spontaneity which had previously been unknown. The shapes quickly grew more composite and within a few centuries glassware stood on the tables of ordinary citizens. At Karanis in Egypt a house dating from this period was excavated and yielded no less than eight oval glass dishes, sixteen bowls, five conical lamps, two drinking cups, two jars, two flasks and two jugs. At first blown-glass flasks were, like their forerunners, used for perfumes and other such luxury items and, like the earlier glass vessels, were transported to southern Russia, Gaul or Germany packed in plaited straw covers like the modern chianti bottles. Bottles in this type of packing are shown in a mosaic at El Djem (Tunisia).

The modern process of glass-blowing is described below but it is likely that the ancient process differed little from this, except that the blowpipe may have been simpler, and the furnace would have been far less sophisticated.

The glassworker's blowpipe is a steel tube about 1.5 m long, tapered to a mouthpiece at one end. The gathering head is made by welding on a 100 mm length of thick-walled tube, made of wrought iron (or other alloy resistant to oxidation) having a diameter from 25 to 80 mm, the wider tubes being used for making the heavier ware. Several pipes are used by each chair or shop (a team of workers working from one pot, producing hand-blown glassware) so that a clean pipe at the right temperature will always be ready for the gatherer who starts the cycle of operations (*Figure 3.21*).

Molten glass will wet an iron rod which is hot enough to prevent the formation of a skin when it touches the glass, and hence the gatherer can collect from the pot a quantity of glass (the gather) whose size depends on the diameter of the pipe head, the temperature of the glass and the number of turns given to the pipe. Before blowing starts, it is necessary to form a skin of chilled glass (or the gather will perforate at the hottest point) and to make sure the glass is distributed evenly around the pipe. This is carried out by marvering, or rolling the glass on a hard, smooth surface, probably of stone (and in later times iron).

Large gathers, especially those made by double gathering, are shaped by blocking or turning the gather in a shaped block of wet wood (usually pear wood); the steam produces an air-cushion which prevents the wood from burning. The gatherer will now puff or blow lightly down the pipe to form a small bubble of air and produce an internal viscous skin; the still molten glass between the two skins can now be manipulated to produce the desired distribution of glass needed in the final article. After puffing down the pipe, a thumb is immediately placed over the orifice and the air is allowed to expand until the correct size bubble (Fr. *paraison* or *parison*) is produced.

Figure 3.21 The interior of the cone at the Aston Flint Glass Works, Birmingham. Cones were spacious and provided good working conditions for the glass blowers, working around the central furnace. Such furnaces normally held between eight and twelve pots. The furnace for pre-heating pots (the 'pot arch') can be seen in the background on the right, and the annealing tunnel on the left.

Many glass articles are produced off-hand, that is, without the use of moulds. The blower (gaffer) sits at a glassworker's chair, a special seat invented in the mid-sixteenth century, which has long arms on which the blowpipe is rolled whilst the glass is being shaped (see *Figure 3.21*). The term chair has been extended to describe the team for which the chair is the centre of operations (Charleston, 1962).

Manipulation of the glass was a natural development of glassmaking once a bubble had been blown. By reheating and blowing alternately, and by holding the blowpipe above or below his head, the glassworker could control the shape and thickness of the blown vessel. If the glass-blower was trying to make a vessel to a preconceived design it required a much greater degree of skill to achieve it by free blowing than by the use of a mould carved to the desired shape of the artefact. However, free blowing allowed spontaneity of design and it was perhaps for that reason that its use continued throughout the history of glassmaking up to and including the present day.

In the blowing of exceptionally large vessels a subterfuge could be used. Having blown a bulb, the worker took a mouthful of water and ejected it down the blowpipe quickly putting his thumb over the mouth-piece. The steam generated inside the glass bulb then continued the blowing process until it was released.

By successively reheating the article in a glory hole (a small furnace or an opening which leads to the hot interior of the furnace) a gaffer could manipulate the body of the vessel into a variety of shapes before the metal cooled; adding extra small gathers (brought to him by a servitor) to form stems, handles, bases etc., using basic tools (see *Figure 3.22*).

The marvering surface itself could incorporate shaped hollows in order to produce definite patterns, or the glass could be shaped with the aid of a battledore (Fr. *palette*), a flat wooden board or even with a wad of wet newspaper. Tongs could be used to produce raised ridges and knobs by pinching out portions of the vessel's walls, or the pointed end of a reamer (a flat-bladed tool with a pointed end) could be used to produce ribs and furrows in the glass. It seems probable that the earliest decorative marks were made on glass at this stage, that is, before the molten glass had completely hardened.

When the main body of the article had been completed a solid iron rod, the punty (originally pontil), which had been heated and lightly coated with glass, was attached to the centre of its base. The blower then wetted the glass near the end of the blowpipe or touched it with cold metal so that the glass vessel broke away from the blowpipe and was supported only on the punty iron. The open top was then softened in the glory hole, cut off at the desired height with shears and, if

Figure 3.22 The tools of the glassmaker, taken from *De Arte Vitraria*, Neri–Merrett. First Latin edition, Amsterdam, 1662.

required, further opened or reduced with tongs (Ital. *pucella*). The vessel was then cracked off the punty iron and carried away for annealing. Subsequently, when cold, the scar from the punty (the punty or pontil mark) may be largely or even entirely ground away and polished. (Glass which has been made off-hand has a fire-finished surface which is initially more durable than the surface formed against a mould because the surface becomes alkali-deficient when exposed to the flames of the glory hole; Bruce, 1979.)

Wine bottles were most commonly made by blowing a bulb, marvering it into shape, and then pushing in the closed end to produce the characteristic dimple foot, so carefully reproduced in the modern machine-made bottles. The bases of the bottles were substantially thicker than their necks. In blown glass generally there is a tendency for the material to be thicker at the furthest point from the blow iron.

Mould-blowing

The technique of blowing glass into moulds probably developed simultaneously with the discovery of glass-blowing. Once a gather of glass had been taken from the furnace on the end of a blow-iron, it was marvered, blown into a small, elongated bulb and introduced into a two-piece mould, then blown to fill it. Until modern times the moulds would have been made of clay or wood (the latter was kept wet during use to prevent the wood from burning) (*Figure 3.23*).

Pattern moulding

When glass was blown into a mould with a pattern carved on its interior surface, the pattern was impressed in reverse on the glass (see *Figure 3.23*). Designs on a pattern-moulded vessel could be varied once the vessel had been removed from the mould by blowing or by twisting or swinging the viscous glass on the end of the blow-iron. For example, designs such as ribbing on the sides of a blown vessel were produced by blowing the glass into a ribbed mould. If the mould-blown vessel was removed from the mould and then gently reblown after reheating, the thicker glass between the ribs, being hotter than that forming the ribs, expanded so that the ribs were pushed to the interior surface of

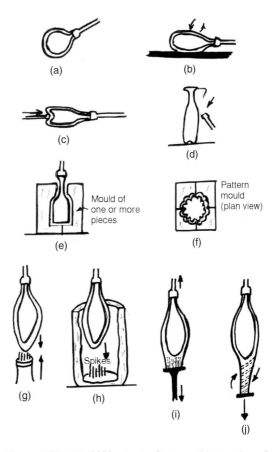

Figure 3.23 Mould-blowing techniques. (a) A gather of glass. (b) Free-blown and shaped by marvering. (c) The base indented. (d) The spout and handle formed. (e) Blowing into a two-part mould. (f) Blowing into a pattern mould. (g) Introducing air twist into a stem by pressing spikes into the base of a blown gather, or (h) dipping it into a mould containing spikes. (i) Drawing the gather off the spikes. (j) Twisting the stem.

the vessel instead of remaining on the outer surface. Glass which has been mould-blown and then additionally blown to increase the size of the object or to soften or modify the lines of the pattern by blowing into a plain mould is sometimes now referred to as having been optic blown.

The process of moulding glass lends itself to considerable variation, including the production of highly decorative effects such as the inclusion of rows of internal air bubbles in various patterns such as spirals (see *Figure 3.24*), and the incorporation of white and coloured threads of glass.

Air bubbles and air-twists

A highly decorative effect was produced in the stems of British drinking glasses by twisting a rod of glass in which were embedded threads or tapes of opaque white or coloured glass (as described above), or air bubbles and air-twists. The technique of deliberately incorporating air in glass stems dates from *circa* 1735, and was popular from the 1740s until the 1760s. It has been stated that there are over 150 varieties in different forms and combinations. Numerous examples are illustrated by Bickerton (1971).

Air-twists were produced by two basic methods: by making slots in a rod of glass, then drawing the rod until it became thin and twisting it to make the columns of air spiral; or by moulding a pattern of circular holes or flat slits in the top of a glass rod, covering them with molten glass, and then drawing and twisting the rod to make a spiral pattern of air (used to make multiple series twists). A quarter twist in a four-column stem would appear to produce a complete twist of 360°. In the early examples the twist was irregularly formed and spaced, but later the threading was uniform; it was sometimes carried down from the bowl of a two-piece glass. Another process involved placing several rods containing elongated tears into a cylindrical mould with grooves on its interior surface, then covering them with molten glass and, after withdrawing the mass on the punty, attaching another punty and twisting until the desired pattern was produced. In some examples one twist is concentrically within another (made by repeating the process with the mould, thus twice twisting the inner rod into a tighter twist); these are termed double series air-twist or even triple series air-twist. Occasionally an air-twist stem includes one or more knops, and the twist continues unbroken (but sometimes slightly distorted) through the knops (*Figure 3.24*).

Paperweights or other solid glass objects decorated with a pattern of regularly spaced air bubbles, were made in a spot-mould. The mould was sectional with small spikes protruding in the interior. When the *paraison* (sometimes already having an interior decorative motif) was introduced, the sectional parts of the mould were tightened around it forcing the spikes into the glass. In this way small cavities were formed so that when the piece

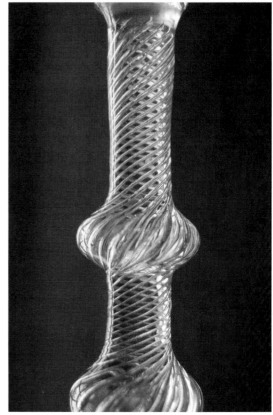

Figure 3.24 Detail of an air twist in a wineglass stem.

was cased, air bubbles were trapped thus forming a pattern (Newman, 1977).

Casing and cupping

Cased glassware is made of two or more layers of differently coloured glass. To achieve this the glassblower either dipped a partially inflated mass of glass (*paraison*) into a crucible containing glass of a different colour, thus gathering it over the top (casing), or formed a cup of glass into which the second glass was blown (cupping). Having cased (or cupped), for example, a blue glass with a white glass, the body of the vessel would be brought to the required size and shape by further blowing and by rolling on a metal marver. (In making flashed window glass, the coloured glass is usually gathered first, termed the post and then the colourless glass is gathered over the top of it.) When the glass had been annealed, the outer layer of glass would be carefully abraded away to form a design in which the underlying glass was exposed or seen in varying degrees through the outer layer. An early example of cased glass dating from the first century AD is the Portland Vase (see *Figure 3.19*).

Technological features of the Portland Vase have attracted much attention since it was first discovered (probably in 1582). For instance, there is a complication in its supposed manufacture by blowing since the opal white glass casing only extends part way up the translucent blue glass vessel; and there are two substantial blue glass handles added over the white layer. The coefficients of expansion of the blue and white glasses apparently matched each other so perfectly that there is no evidence of strain in the vase (Bimson and Freestone, 1983).

Filigrana

Filigrana (Ital. *vetro filigranato*) is the Italian term which has been applied to glass artefacts, originally made in Murano *circa* 1527–1529, of clear glass with various styles of decoration produced by embedding threads of solid opaque white-glass (*lattimo*) forming *latticino* (or *latticinio*); or of coloured glass (or even occasionally a single white thread). It is now used to refer to all styles of decoration on clear glass made by a pattern formed by embedding threads of glass, including *vetro a fili* (threaded glass), *vetro a reticello* (glass with a small network formerly termed *a redexelo* and *a redexin* in Murano) (Ger. *Netzglas*), and *vetro a retorti* (or *retortoli*), originally made in Murano but now termed *zanfirico* or *sanfirico* in Venice and Murano. *Vetro de trina* (lace-glass) is a term which has been used loosely to describe various types of filigrana glass, and is now considered to be superfluous and of no historical significance. Modern Venetian glassworkers find it hard to achieve the accuracy and lightness of design in filigrana of their predecessors.

In *vetro a fili* the opaque white and/or coloured glass threads are embedded in clear glass in continuous lines without any crossing of the threads, the lines being in a spiral or helix pattern (e.g. on plates) or in a spiral or volute pattern (e.g. on vases). In *vetro a reticello*, the threads are embedded in clear glass in the form of criss-cross diagonal threads forming an overall diamond lattice network. There are three separate varieties, depending on whether the pattern is made with fine threads, coarse threads, or fine and coarse threads running in opposite directions. As the threads protrude slightly, tiny air bubbles (sometimes microscopic) are entrapped within each criss-cross diamond, the size depending on the process of production. On a few rare examples there are, instead of the air bubbles, thin wavy lines running in only one direction between the rows of white threads. The style has been used on vases, bowls, jugs etc. and also on plates (where the network often becomes distorted towards the centre or the edge of the plate). Several processes have been documented, and in Murano, according to local glassmakers, several methods have been used (*Figure 3.25*); the first two methods detailed below are the most authoritatively stated:

(i) A bulb (or cylinder) of blown glass in a mould, on which have been picked up on a gather parallel threads of glass (almost always *lattimo*) running diagonally in one direction (resulting from twisting the paraison after gathering the threads) and which is then blown into another similar bulb (or cylinder) with threads running in the opposite direction; the two bulbs (or cylinders) become fused together. The difficulty arises from the necessity of having the threads on each bulb exactly equidistant so that they will form equal and similar diamonds (except for distortions toward the extremities of the glass).

(ii) A bulb of glass is made, as described above, with diagonal threads, and then half of the bulb is bent into the other half and fused, thus making the criss-cross threads. This method assures equal spacing, but is a difficult process.

(iii) A bulb of glass is made, as described above, with diagonal threads, and then the glassblower sucks on the tube and collapses the further half of the bulb into the nearer half making a double wall with criss-cross threads.

(iv) A bulb of glass is made, as described above, with diagonal threads, then it is cut and twirled to make, by centrifugal force,

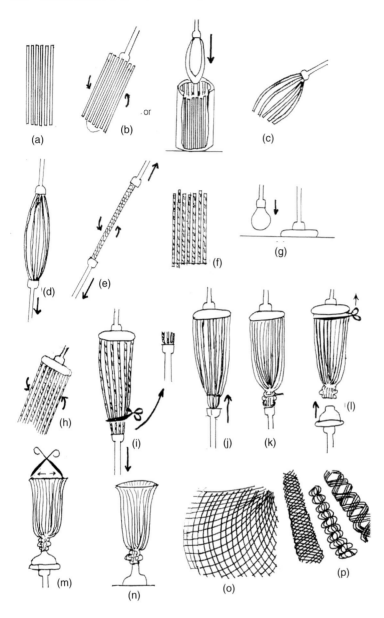

Figure 3.25 Stages in forming a *filigrana* vessel, and (o–p) details of the *filigrana* patterns. (a) Row of coloured glass canes, (b) picked up on a gather of glass or arranged around the sides of a mould and (c) picked up on a gather of glass. (d) The free ends gathered in onto an iron, and (e) drawn out and twisted. (f) Rows of twisted, coloured glass canes picked up on (g) a flattened gather of glass. (h) The free ends attached to an iron and drawn out. (i) The bottom cut off with shears. (j) After the base of the bowl has been shaped, the glass forming the knop is attached and (k) shaped. (l) A clear glass foot is attached, and the top of the vessel is sheared off. (m) The mouth of the vessel is widened and rounded off. (n) The completed vessel is detached from the iron and annealed. (o) Detail of *Vetro a retorti* showing parallel canes with twisted designs. (p) Detail of *Vetro a reticello* showing crossed opaque white glass threads and entrapped air bubbles.

a flat open plate; another such plate is made with threads running in the opposite direction, and then the two plates are fused together by heating. This method also presents the difficulty of obtaining equal spacing of the threads on both plates.

In all these methods there develop, within the interstitial spaces made by the crossed threads, small (sometimes microscopic) bubbles, but occasionally they are elongated into thin wavy lines, and the enclosed areas sometimes have unequal sides. After the piece of glass with the crossed threads is made it is reheated, then blown and manipulated into various forms such as vases, plates and jugs.

Vetro a retorti is the Italian term applied to a style of decoration with parallel adjacent canes (vertical or spiral) of glass having embedded threads in various intricate patterns (as in the stems of some British wine glasses) and made by flattening the canes and fusing them together. It includes decoration made with opaque white or coloured glass threads or both embedded in the fused canes. The style has been used for plates, bowls, vases and, occasionally, for paperweights (Newman, 1977).

Sand-moulding

Sand-moulding invented in 1870 is a special form of moulding used to make glass liners for silver vessels. A wooden block is carved to fit exactly into the metal vessel, then removed and forced into a bed of damp sand. It is carefully withdrawn so that its exact impression remains in the sand. A gather of glass is then blown into the impression to form the glass liner. When cool it is abraded and polished.

Lamp-working (at the lamp; at the flame)

Lamp-working is the technique of manipulating glass at the lamp by heating it with a small flame (*Figure 3.26*); and was probably discovered in the Roman era. Examples of pieces produced in this way range from small figures and objects to large composite three-dimensional scenic groups.

The technique of Verre de Nevers is closely allied to lamp-work. Small figures made of

Figure 3.26 Lamp-worked figures in the tradition of Jaroslav Brychta. Made by Jaroslav Janus, Želený Brod, Czech Republic.

opaque fusible glass, were produced at Nevers and elsewhere in France, in the late sixteenth and early seventeenth centuries. Examples vary from 25 to 150 mm in height and are very detailed. Single figures often have stands of trailed glass threads; a figure without such a stand has usually been broken from a grotto (tableau). Some animals are mould-blown, with applied thin glass threads (Fr. *verre frisée*).

Occasionally large groups were made, such as a crucifixion scene or several figures with animals. They were made with portions of glass rods softened at the lamp and then manipulated with pincers or other instruments, and often fastened on an armature of copper wire. The names of some artists are known, including Jean Prestereau (1595) and his son Léon.

Such ware, being made of white opaque material, might be mistaken for porcelain or faience. Most examples display coloured details. Similar figures were made in Venice, Germany, England and Spain in the seventeenth century and later; they are not readily distinguishable or dateable.

Decoration of glass artefacts

Since glass production began, glassmakers and decoratori have sought to improve simple glass shapes. The numerous techniques used can thus be divided broadly into two groups: those produced by the glassmaker whilst the glass was still hot; and those produced by the decorator on cold glass.

Glassmaking techniques of decoration include colouring (and decolourizing), free blowing and shaping, including special effects produced by tooling and marvering, and by pattern moulding. Embellishments produced by the glass decorator include cutting, engraving, cold painting, gilding and lustre and enamel painting. Lustre and enamel painting and some forms of gilding, however, require the use of a kiln to complete the process.

Glassmaking techniques

Colouring, free blowing and blowing into patterned moulds have already been discussed under methods of glass vessel production.

Figure 3.27 Examples of hot-worked (tooled) glass: leaves and canes.

Tooling the glass

It seems probable that tooling hot glass was one of the earliest forms of decoration. Some early Islamic glass bowls and saucers bear patterns such as bulls eye circlets, rosettes etc. which were impressed on their sides by means of patterned tongs whilst the glass was still hot. Cylindrical bowls of the same period bear other designs such as lozenges and small birds impressed in the hot glass by shaped pincers (Harden, 1971). Pincering was a fairly general technique (*Figure 3.27*)

Addition of glass blobs and trails

The addition of glass blobs and trails has been used since the late second millennium BC for decorating core-formed vessels with lines, dots, rings and hieroglyphic inscriptions (Harden, 1968). After trailing on the design of hot glass, probably from a metal rod, the trails were marvered flush with the surface, although in some areas which would be difficult to marver such as the foot or neck, the trails remained in relief. The Romans were particularly fond of trailing in relief. Threads marvered into the glass body could be combed by dragging a pointed tool across them before the trails cooled.

Newman (1977) refers to a rare type of decoration (underglaze) where the coloured trails have themselves been covered with transparent glass, as in the case of the hollow fish-shaped container dating from the Eighteenth Dynasty (1567–1320 BC) and now in the Brooklyn Museum, New York. Trailing

was especially popular in the sixteenth and seventeenth centuries AD and is still carried out in modern glassmaking. Allied to trailing is the intricate stem work so popular with Venetian and *façon de Venise* glassmakers in the seventeenth century, though in these cases the trails are mostly free-standing.

Another relatively simple form of applied decoration is the use of blobs and prunts on glass vessels. Sometimes while still hot the blobs were stamped into designs such as raspberry or strawberry prunts with a metal die. The addition of prunts to a vessel besides being decorative also helped it to be held more easily in the absence of a handle. A further development was the application of hot blobs of glass to a vessel while it was still on the blowpipe. The vessel was then reblown so that the hot blobs blew out further than the cooler walls of the body. These were then drawn out with pincers, and blown at the same time to keep them hollow, then reattached lower down the vessel (Harden *et al.*, 1968).

The earliest prunted beaker seems to be the dolphin beaker of the fourth century, but they became common in Saxon times (claw beakers) (Harden, 1971), and particularly so in the fifteenth century (Harden, 1971; Tait, 1968). In the *daumenglaser* from Germany this technique has been put into reverse. After the blobs were applied to the heated body of the vessel, the glassmaker sucked through the blowing iron so that the blobs were made to extend into the interior of the vessel, forming hollow finger-grips on the outside (Newman, 1977).

Other forms of applied decoration owe more to the skill of the artist trained in other media than to the skill of the glassmaker.

Special effects produced by marvering

A variety of special effects can be produced by spreading various materials (such as chopped coloured glass rod, glass powder, chalk etc.) on the marver. The first gather is formed, marvered so that the powdered material is incorporated in the surface, and then a second gather is made. The chopped coloured rod spreads out like coloured worms, and the powdered chalk decomposes to produce particles of lime and copious bubbles of carbon dioxide. Shapes resembling petals can be

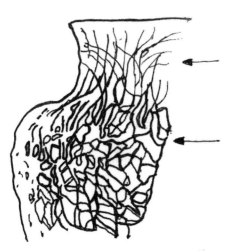

Fine shallow cracks, where the surface has not been very stretched

Deep cracks in a rough surface where the glass has been greatly stretched by blowing

Figure 3.28 Detail of Venetian frosted or ice glass, created by plunging the hot glass into water for a moment and immediately reheating. The roughened surface, resembling ice, became popular in Venice in the sixteenth century and spread to Northern Europe, where it remained in vogue into the seventeenth century.

produced by making several gathers, spreading chalk on the top of each, and pressing in a spike so that all the layers are depressed and trumpet-like shapes are produced (Newman, 1977).

Ice-glass

Ice-glass (cracked glass, Italian, *vetro a ghiaccio*), which has a rough irregular outer surface resembling cracked ice, was first produced in Venice in the sixteenth century, by two processes: plunging the partially blown gathering of hot glass momentarily into cold water and immediately reheating lightly so as not to close the cracks caused by the sudden cooling, and then fully blowing to enlarge the spaces in the labyrinth of small fissures (*Figure 3.28*); or rolling the hot glass on an iron marver covered with small glass splinters (sometimes covered) which adhered to the surface and became fused when lightly heated, a process which also removed the sharp edges.

Ice-glass was produced in Liège, Belgium, and in Spain in the seventeenth century. It was revived in England in about 1850 by Apsley Pellat, who called it 'Anglo Venetian glass'. In nineteenth-century France the first method described above produced a glass called *verre craquelé*, and the second method an effect called *broc à glaces*. A third method developed in modern times by Venini involves the use of hydrofluoric acid and produces *vetro corroso*. Ice-glass has been produced in the United

States since the nineteenth century, where it is termed overshot glass.

Davenport's Patent glass

This was decorated with the intention of imitating engraving or etching although it resembled neither. The process was patented in 1806, by John Davenport of Longport, Stoke-on-Trent, an English potter and glassmaker. The process involved covering the outer surface of the glassware with a paste containing powdered glass, then removing the surface paste so as to leave the intended design and quickly firing at a low temperature to fuse the glass powder onto the surface without melting it. The designs were often heraldic insignia and sporting scenes. Such glassware was usually inscribed Patent on a label made and affixed by the same method.

Decorating the surface of cold glass

Enamelling

Enamelling is the process of decorating the surface of glassware by the application of a vitreous material, coloured with metallic oxides, to the surface, after which the enamel is fixed by low temperature firing in a muffle kiln. Enamel decoration is in the form of scenes, figures, inscriptions and heraldry.

Enamel colours are metallic oxides mixed with a glass frit of finely powdered glass suspended in an oily medium (formerly honey)

for ease of application with a brush. The colours are applied to the surface of the glass artefact and fixed by low temperature firing, in the range 700–900°C, in a muffle kiln, during which the medium burns out. A flux mixed with the enamel colours lowers the firing point to below that of the glass to which they have been applied. Enamel colours differ from cold colours in that they are fixed to the glass surface and are therefore not so readily affected by wear; the firing results in a smooth surface only slightly palpable to the fingers; and the final colours of the enamels are not often apparent upon application but only after firing.

In gilt enamelling the decoration was first outlined with pen and brush and fixed in the kiln. Then the colours were spread on the outlying areas and the vessel fired a second time at a lower temperature. The vitreous colours are opaque and cover the surface in a thick coating. The numerous gilt designs were enclosed in red enamel lines for added emphasis. The colours used for enamelling modern glass tableware are usually based on glasses that contain substantial amounts of lead oxide, in order to reduce the fluxing temperature (e.g. 590°C) to below that of the softening point of the glass, and to produce a glossy finish on the fired enamel.

Enamelling was used extensively in Venice from the fifteenth century and elsewhere in Europe from the sixteenth century onwards. The technique was used in China in the eighteenth century.

The process of enamelling glass is a technique that can be dated back to the fifteenth century BC: a small Egyptian jug bearing the name of. Tuthmosis III (*c.* 1504–1450 BC) was decorated with powdered glass fired to the body of the vessel (see *Figure 2.1*). Some Roman glassware was decorated with enamel painting, which was carried out both in the East and in Italy in the first century AD (Harden, 1969a). Vessels decorated in Egypt tended to feature human, animal and plant motifs; whereas those depicting wild beasts in the arena or in gladiatorial combat seem to have been made in the Rhineland. Italian glassware from the sixth to seventh centuries returned to trailed decoration (Harden, 1971) or had marvered splashes and blobs of white, yellow, or red glass all over their surfaces.

Islamic enamelling, consisting of opaque vitreous enamelling (with gilding) as decoration on glassware was made between 1170 and 1402, when Tamerlane (Timur) sacked Damascus and the local glass industry was moved to Samarkand, and some glassware associated with Fustat (Egypt) said to date from about 1270 to 1340. It is of five tentatively identifiable groups based on the criteria of style and date rather than any proven connection with the places of production identified with the groups, that is Raqqa, Syro-Frankish, Aleppo, Damascus, Chinese-Islamic and Syrian glassware (see *Figure 2.11*).

In the third quarter of the fifteenth century there was a phase in Venice when gorgeously decorated ware was made (Harden, 1971). Enamelling was executed at Murano on clear coloured glass and on opaque white glass. From the late fifteenth century enamelling was carried out in a manner similar to that of Islamic glassware of the thirteenth and fourteenth centuries, the technique being said to have been re-invented by Anzolo Barovier. It was first used on sapphire blue glassware and other coloured transparent glassware, but in Venice, towards the end of the fifteenth century, coloured glass tended to be superseded for this purpose by colourless glass. By the end of the sixteenth century enamelling was little used there except on opaque white glass, which again became popular in the eighteenth century.

The earliest German enamelling on glass was in the second half of the sixteenth century, copying the Venetian enamelled armorial glasses that had previously been imported. The German enamelling is found on the typical German *humpen* and *stangenglas*, where the style evolved to cover almost the entire surface with painting subordinating the glass itself. Bright colours created the decorative effects, but the painting was not of superior quality. The early motifs were coats of arms, followed by a great variety of subjects, for example, painting of a religious, allegorical, historical or scenic nature, or showing artisan or guild activities, or satirical or family scenes, usually with dates or long datable inscriptions added. The place of production is usually unidentifiable, except in some special types such as the *Ochsenkopfglas* (Franconia), *Hallorenglas* (Halle) and

Figure 3.29 The Beilby family, working in Newcastle upon Tyne, were responsible for much of the enamelled glass made in England from the 1760s. William Beilby had trained as an enameller in Birmingham. (© V&A Picture Library).

Hofkellereiglas (Saxony or Thuringia). In the seventeenth century enamelling became more restrained and skilfully executed, with the artists usually signing the pieces. A new style of enamelled decoration, *Schwarzlot*, was introduced by Johann Schaper and his followers, Johann Ludwig Faber, Abraham Helmback and Hermann Benckertt. The use of opaque enamel was superseded by transparent enamel, introduced in about 1810 by Samuel Mohn and also used by his son Gottlob Samuel Mohn and Franz Anton Siebel. In the 1750s some enamelling was carried out on opaque white glass.

The earliest mention of enamelling on glassware in England is a notice by a Mr Grillet in 1696, but no examples are extant. Enamelling was introduced by artists from Germany and the Low Countries, and was of the type known as thin or wash enamel, more suitable for the softer English lead glass, and was executed within outlines previously etched on the glass. Later dense enamel became the usual medium, first with designs of festoons and flowers, but later landscapes, figure subjects and coats of

arms. It was in this period that the members of the Beilby family, William and his younger sister Mary, produced their remarkable enamelled ware. They always worked as a pair (in the period 1762–1778) and their association has been claimed as one of the greatest in the history of artistic glass, their fame bringing commissions from many noble families in England. William and Mary Beilby, and possibly Michael Edkins, were the leading enamellers of the eighteenth century; they decorated on clear glass and opaque white glass, respectively (*Figure 3.29*). Some ware was enamelled by glasshouses in Stourbridge in the nineteenth century, and possibly by London jewellers and silversmiths doing work on glass boxes and scent bottles, as well as by artists who decorated porcelain in imitation of Sèvres porcelain and who did similar work on glassware in the mid-nineteenth century (Charleston, 1972). (See Painted and stained glass windows.)

Cold painting

Cold painting (Ger. *Kaltmalerei*; Ital. *di pinto freddo*) of glass dates back to the Roman

Figure 3.30   The Daphne Ewer, cold-painted and gilded. H 222 mm. *Circa* late second or early third century. Roman Empire, possibly Syria. (Corning Museum of Glass).

Figure 3.31   Artist copying a European print on glass. Water-colour on paper. China (Canton). *Circa* 1770. 34.1 × 41.5 cm. (© V&A Picture Library).

period but, lacking the durability of fired enamels and therefore being easily rubbed off, it is a poorer form of coloured decoration (*Figure 3.30*). In this process lacquer colours or oil paint were applied to the surface of glassware. Cold painting is particularly effective when applied to the back of the surface through which it is to be viewed, and protected by a layer of varnish, metal foil, or by another sheet of glass (Ger. *Hinterglasmalerei*). The process was sometimes used on *humpen* and other large glasses of *waldglas*. This was possibly because the glasses were too large to be enamelled and fired in a muffle kiln; because the glass was not sufficiently durable to withstand firing; or because the painting was carried out by peasants, without access to a furnace.

In the nineteenth century there was a great interest in the leisure-art of painting scenes in reverse on the backs of glass plates, sheets of glass, mirrors etc. so that the design was protected by the glass when viewed from the front (*Figure 3.31*). There was a bright luminosity in such paintings since there was no air gap between the paint and the glass (Stahl, 1915; Newman, 1977; Bretz in Lanz and Seelig, 2000). The development of reverse painting on glass is given in Chapter 2.

Lustre painting

Lustre painting is the term given to the process of applying metallic oxide pigments to the glass surface and firing under reducing conditions to produce a metallic iridescent effect (a lustre) (Lamm, 1941; Newman, 1977). The process could be used to produce a ground completely covering the surface, or simply to produce a design. Oxides of gold, copper or silver (and, in modern times, platinum and bismuth) were dissolved in acid and, after being mixed with an oily medium, were painted on the glass. Firing in a reduced atmosphere, smoky and rich in carbon monoxide, caused the metal to fuse into a thin film, producing a non-palpable, evenly distributed metallic flashing. Gold and copper yielded a ruby colour and silver a straw yellow colour. This style of decoration appears on Islamic glass from the ninth to the eleventh centuries; most specimens having been found in and attributed to Egypt, where the technique is thought to have originated. Examples of lustre-painted glass in Egypt are dateable to the sixth if not the fifth century (Harden, 1971). The technique continued to be practised until the late twelfth century (Pinder-Wilson, 1968).

Iridescence

Ancient glasses may become iridescent as a result of the weathering process having produced layers of silica at their surfaces, which are interspersed with air spaces within which light can cause optical interference phenomena; and as a result of deposition of metallic oxide ions on the surface. However, glass can be deliberately made iridescent by spraying on a solution of stannic chloride followed by firing in a reduced atmosphere to produce a transparent layer of stannic oxide, which is thick enough to produce optical interference colours. Decorative yellow, orange or red effects can be produced on glass by firing on compounds of silver and copper, and then refiring.

Gilding

The technique of gilding is the process of decorating glassware on the surface, or on the back of the glass, by the use of gold leaf, gold paint, or gold dust. The history and technique of gilding have been comprehensively described by Charleston (1972). Early examples of the application of gold sheet to glass are Tutankhamun's head-rest (Cairo Museum), and the plain gold bands on a lidded eye-paint container (1457–1425 BC) in the British Museum.

In the process of fired gilding, gold was applied to the outer surface of a glass by using gold leaf pulverized in honey, or powdered gold, and affixed by low temperature firing to assure reasonable permanency. The resulting appearance was dull with a rich and sumptuous effect but the gold could be burnished to brightness. Gold could be more permanently fixed to a glass surface by brushing on an amalgam of gold and mercury. Low-temperature firing caused the mercury to vaporize, leaving a gold deposit forming the design, which could then be burnished to brightness. Mercuric gold has a thin, metallic, brassy appearance quite unlike the dull rich colour of honey gilding; it is much cheaper and easier to fix.

Some German diamond-point engraving is supplemented with gilding. By the seventeenth century, decoration on the surface of glass was carried out by firing gold leaf, using one of several methods (see above), or, especially in Venice, Hall-in-Tyrol, Austria, and the Netherlands by unfired gold painting. Such methods of decoration were for gold borders on engraved glassware, and in Germany on some Court glassware with gilt in relief. Gilding on the surface of English glassware in the eighteenth and nineteenth centuries was carried out by Lazarus Jacobs, William and Mary Beilby, Michael Edkins and James Giles. In Spain gilding was applied to wheel-engraved glassware at La Granja de San Ildefonso in the eighteenth century, and similar work was produced in Germany.

The process of unfired gilding involved applying gold, in a medium, to the outer surface of glass, resulting in a lack of permanency. It was a primitive method by which a preparation of linseed oil was applied to the glass with a brush after which the gold leaf was laid on and the oil allowed to dry. As it was unfired the gold readily rubbed off and, of course, it could not be burnished. This method was used in Britain on some opaque white glass and on countrymarket glass of the nineteenth century. It was also used on some German, Bohemian and Spanish glass, which has lasted better than that done in England, perhaps due to the fixative employed. Where such gilding has been rubbed off, the design may still be observed by the pattern on the glass left by the fixative. This method of gilding is also called cold-, oil-, size-, lacquer-, or varnish-gilding and is similar to applying cold colours.

Acid gilding has been used more recently, usually to produce decorative borders. A design, or ground, is etched on the glass with hydrofluoric acid, gold leaf is then applied overall. After being burnished, the polished raised areas contrast with the matt etched areas.

Sandwiched gold leaf

Gold leaf, with engraved designs, could be sandwiched between layers of glass. Some of the earliest sandwich gold glasses are the Hellenistic bowls found at Canosa in Apulia, Italy, dating to the third century BC, and now in the British Museum London (*Figure 3.32*).

Heraclius described the manufacture of gold-decorated glass bowls of the Canosa type (Forbes, 1966):

> I obtained several bowls of high sparkling glass
> These I painted with a brush dipped in a resin called gum
> Then onto the golden bowls I
> Began to put leaves of gold, and when I found them dried
> I engraved little birds, and men, flowers and lions According to my desire. Then I coated the bowls
> With thin layers of glass for protection, blown at the fire
> And when this glass had enjoyed the even heat
> It enclosed the bowls perfectly in a thin layer.

The outer bowl, which reaches just below the rim of the inner one, has not been fused or adhered to the inner bowl but the two layers hold together simply because they match each other perfectly. Sandwiching gold between two layers of glass protected the gold leaf, but there was always the disadvantage that air bubbles might get between the two layers and disfigure the design. Later examples, where the gold leaf lay under only parts of the surface, to which it was fused with a layer of glass (*fondi d'oro*, see *Figure 2.7*), were found in the catacombs in Rome and in the Rhineland in the fourth century AD (Painter, in Harden *et al.*, 1968). Examples of gold leaf protected between two layers of glass are known from the Parthian or Sassanian periods in Persia, perhaps the second to fourth centuries AD, and from Egypt and Syria, when a piece of glass was gilded and engraved on its reverse and then fused to a layer of clear glass. A leaf of gold, or silver, fixed to the back of a sheet of

Figure 3.32 Detail of a gold-glass bowl from Canosa, Italy, showing its fine decoration of a floral design in gold leaf, sandwiched between two layers of colourless glass. In this early period, the layers were not fused together, as in late Roman and Renaissance sandwich gold glass. (© Copyright The British Museum).

colourless glass and formed into a pattern or scene, is known as *verre eglomisé* (see Chapter 7). Highlights are produced by scraping away the foil to reveal the glass beneath it.

Some Roman glass gilding was done by applying gold leaf to a hot bubble of glass which, when blown, would break the leaf into speckles. Another method used on Roman glass and later on Venetian glass, was sprinkling granular gold dust on to molten glass. Islamic glass in the twelfth to fourteenth centuries was very rarely decorated only with gilding, applied by the use of colloidal gold and then fired; but mainly such glass combined gilding with enamelling, for example mosque lamps. Some Venetian glassware of the sixteenth century has gilding as the sole decoration, but normally enamelling was combined with it. The history and techniques of gilding glass have been comprehensively described by Charleston (1972); and the production of gold *tesserae* is discussed below under Architectural Glass.

In Bohemia a technique of sandwiching gold between two layers of glass was developed in the 1730s to decorate a type of drinking glass (Ger. *Zwischengoldglas*). The vessels were decorated with gold leaf by a process whereby the outer surface of one glass was coated with gold leaf, the design engraved through it, and then a bottomless glass was sealed over the top (using a colourless resin) to protect the design. The inner glass had been ground down with great exactness for almost its whole height so as to permit the outer glass to be fitted precisely over it. On early rare Bohemian examples the joint showed at the top of the rim, but on later ones the rim of the inner glass was of double thickness for a distance of about 10 mm, so that a projecting flange fitted over the outer glass. The outer glass projected slightly at the bottom, and the space below, in the case of a beaker, was filled with a glass disc with similar gold engraving and sealed by transparent colourless resin. The outer surface of the double-walled glass was sometimes further decorated by cutting 12–18 narrow vertical facets or flutes. Silver leaf was sometimes used instead of gold. A frequent form of this type of vessel was a small straight-sided beaker, and popular decorations were hunting scenes, views of monasteries, Bohemian saints and armorial bearings, all very delicately engraved. The best examples date from the 1730s, but others were made until about 1755. Such decoration was also used on beakers, goblets and other double-walled vessels, sometimes combined with cold painting on coloured glass or with enamelling. Such ware is sometimes termed double glass. Johann Josef Mildner revived and elaborated the technique in 1787 (Newman, 1977).

Nineteenth- and twentieth-century industrial glassmaking: a summary

The nineteenth century was a period of great change (yet the rate of change was certainly eclipsed in the twentieth century), and only a few highlights can be recorded here. Great improvements in melting efficiency became possible when the Siemens regenerative furnace was introduced in 1861 (Douglas and Frank, 1972), to be followed by the tank furnace. There were 126 bottle-houses in Britain in 1833, but the number rose to its peak of 240 in 1874 (Meigh, 1972), thereafter declining as the tank furnaces became larger and more efficient. The first semi-automatic machinery for making jars (Arbogast) was introduced in America in 1882, and the first for making narrow-neck bottles was invented by Ashley in Britain in 1886.

The construction of the Crystal Palace in 1851 was an extraordinary achievement for which nearly one million square feet of glass was required (Hollister, 1974). The first safety glass was invented in 1874 and shown at the Motor Show of 1906. The first electric lamp bulbs were made at Lemington (near Newcastle-upon-Tyne) for Sir Joseph Swan in 1860; to be followed by the Corning Glassworks in America who supplied Edison in 1881 (Douglas and Frank, 1972). Optical glasses were first studied seriously by Dollond in 1758, but the materials were of poor quality (Douglas and Frank, 1972). In 1798, Guinand discovered how to make glass homogeneous by stirring it during melting (the only effective means of obtaining homogeneity), but commercially satisfactory optical glass was not made until 1848, when Bontemps (1868) joined Chance Brothers in Birmingham. The firm's leadership in this field was not maintained, however, but passed to Germany when, in 1846, Carl Zeiss opened a workshop. Zeiss was later (1875) joined in the venture by a physicist, Abbé. Between them Zeiss and Abbé made a spectacular range of glasses during the 1880s. These had new optical properties which enabled great advances to be made in the design of lenses for cameras, microscopes and telescopes.

Even more remarkable advances were made in glassmaking in the twentieth century, Douglas and Frank (1972). The first half of the century could be said to have been dominated by engineering-type developments whereas the post-1950 period has seen quite extraordinary changes in the compositions of glasses, especially in the fields of non-silicate glasses.

In making flat glass, the first Lubbers cylinder machine was introduced in 1903, but the Fourcault machine for sheet glass was developed in 1913 and the mammoth machine for the continuous grinding and polishing of plate glass (it was about 400 m long) was invented by Pilkington Brothers in the 1930s (Douglas and Frank, 1972). This process was replacing all previous methods of making plate glass when, in 1959, the announcement of the float glass process, in which a perfectly smooth and brilliant fire-polished glass is floated from a bath of molten tin, secured for Pilkington Brothers the world lead in flat glass technology. The automatic machinery for making bottles and jars also developed greatly during the first half of the century.

The Owens *suction machine* was first successful in 1903 and it rapidly dominated the glass container-making industry all over the world, partly because of its technical efficiency but partly because a cartel was set up regarding its use which excluded all others. Gradually, however, between the First and Second World Wars, various types of *gob-fed* machine overtook the cumbersome Owens machines and displaced them. The numbers of bottles and jars increased from 2.9 thousand million per annum in the United States in 1918 (and 0.5 in the United Kingdom) to 15.3 (3.1 in the United Kingdom) in 1950 to 44.3 (6.9 United Kingdom) in 1977; the 1977 total for the United Kingdom and the United States represented 14.3 million metric tons of glass.

The understanding of the chemical constitution of glasses, and the relationship between it and the physical properties has increased greatly: Pyrex glass was developed in 1915 (Society of Glass Technology, 1951); the delicate colouring produced by rare-earth oxides was discovered in 1927; top-of-the-stove ware was introduced in 1935; and glass fibre was first produced on a commercial basis in 1938. Remarkable improvements were made in optical glasses in which entirely new types of glass were made: the fluoroborates, phosphates, germanates, and all-fluoride glasses possess different combinations of refractive index and dispersion, which had never been anticipated in the previous century (Douglas and Frank, 1972). Special ultra-pure high-transmission glasses have been developed for lasers and optical communication systems and a range of glass-ceramics has been produced which have a zero coefficient of expansion. The photosensitive silver-containing glasses, which were first introduced in 1950, have been developed for special purposes, such as sun-glasses which adjust their absorption coefficient according to the light intensity, and polychromatic glasses which can develop any colour in the spectrum according to the extent to which they are exposed to ultra-violet light and a subsequent heat treatment.

Enamels

Enamels are coloured vitreous powders, applied and fused at relatively low temperatures between 500 and 700°C in a muffle kiln, to glass, ceramics or metal substrates to form decorative designs. Enamel colours when applied to glass and ceramic objects and to window glass, are referred to as enamelling or enamelled decoration. Enamel objects are formed when dry vitreous powders are applied to a metal substrate, normally of gold, silver, copper, bronze or iron (Maryon, 1971).

Most early enamels failed because the highly fusible frit never actually fused to the metallic substrates. Enamels must be formulated so as to have a co-efficient of contraction roughly equivalent to that of the metal base; and its melting point must be approximate to, but lower than that of the metal, to ensure fusion occurs. For these reasons, enamels are composed of soda or potash glass with or without the addition of colourants and opacifiers. On thin or extensive areas of metalwork, the contraction of the enamel on cooling might be sufficient to cause the metal to warp. To counteract this, the reverse of the object might also be enamelled, a process known as enamel backing or counter enamelling.

Enamel is generally a comparatively soft glass; a compound of flint or sand, red lead and soda or potash, melted together to produce an almost clear glass with a bluish or greenish tinge known as flux or frit. It is made in different degrees of 'hardness', that is, the more lead and potash it contains the more brilliant but softer it is. The clear flux or frit is the base from which coloured enamels are made by the addition of metallic oxides. The inclusion of 2–3 per cent of an oxide to the molten flux is generally sufficient to produce colour. The enamel, after being thoroughly stirred, is poured out onto a slab in cakes about 110 mm in diameter. For use it is broken up, ground in a mortar to a fine powder, thoroughly washed, dried and applied to the metal. The work is placed in a furnace until the powdered enamel fuses and adheres to its metal base. Soft enamels require less heat to fire them and are therefore more convenient to use, but not so durable. In creating a design, the hardest colours are applied and fired first, and successively softer ones fused during subsequent firings, at lower temperatures. Thus an object such as a plaque, may be fired a dozen or more times, depending upon the number of colours to be applied.

Opaque enamel usually required a lower firing temperature (Fr. *petit feu*) than translucent enamel, about 300°C. Higher temperature firing was known as grand feu. Translucent enamelling involves the firing of transparent layers of enamel, onto a metal guilloche surface, engraved by hand or engine turned. There may be as many as five or six layers of enamel each of which had to be fired separately at successively lower temperatures. Sometimes gold leaf patterns or paillons or painted decoration or scenes were incorporated in the design. This effect was achieved by applying and firing the gold leaf or enamel onto an already fired enamel surface, before being sealed with a top layer of enamel, which was then fired. The completed enamel then required careful polishing with a wooden wheel and fine abrasives, to smooth down any irregularities in the surface, and then finishing with a buff.

Enamel objects are classified according to the relationship of the frit to, and the structure of, the metal base (*Figure 3.33*). *Dipped enamelling*, by which a heated metal core was dipped into and coated with molten glass and shaped to the desired form, was introduced into Hellenistic jewellery in the third century BC. The technique was used mainly to produce pendants for ear-rings. However, the enamel was usually applied in such a way as to form a level surface with the surrounding metal, by forming compartments into which the frit was fired. This was achieved by soldering thin metal wires or bands (Fr. *cloisons*) onto the metal to form cells, a technique known as

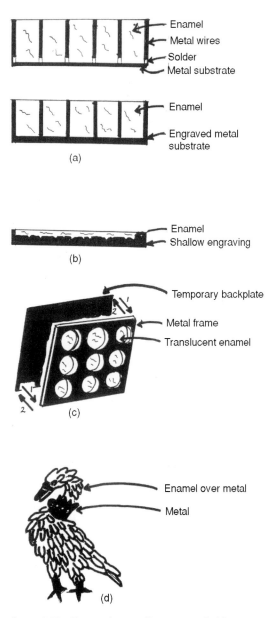

Figure 3.33 Types of enamelling on metal: (a) *cloisonné*, (b) *champlevé*, (c) *plique à jour*, (d) *en ronde bosse*.

cloisonné, or by providing for sunken areas in the original metal casting, a technique known as *champlevé* (Fr. for 'raised field'), or *en taille d'epergne* (Fr. for 'economic cut'). Another group of enamels did not rely upon having metal boundaries, but on knowledge of colours and firing temperatures. These include *painted* and *encrusted* (Fr. *en ronde bosse* or 'in the round') enamels.

Cloisonné is the most primitive form of enamel. Each mass of powdered glass was placed in a separate compartment formed from strips of metal wire to which, and to the background if it had one, the enamel is fused by heating in a kiln (*Figure 3.34*). On very thin metalwork the contraction of the enamel on cooling might be sufficient to cause the metal to warp, and to counteract this the reverse face of the object might also be enamelled, a process known as counter-enamelling or enamel backing. In 1453 *cloisonné* enamelling virtually ended with the fall of the Byzantine Empire, but it continued in the form of *filigree* enamelling. In this process, thin twisted wires of copper or silver were enclosed the enamel in the *cloisonné*

manner. The technique is thought to have originated near Venice in the second half of the fourteenth century, and is best known for fifteenth century Hungarian examples.

Enamels could also be made without a permanent backing, being held to the metal only at the edges – *plique à jour* (Fr. for 'against the light' (*Figure 3.35*). The areas to contain the enamel were fretted and given a temporary backing of sheet mica or some similar material to which the enamel would not adhere. Once the enamel had been fused into the framework by heating, the backing was removed leaving translucent enamel like a painted glass window, the lead lines of a window being replaced by the metal cloisons of the enamel. This type of work is fragile and not suitable for objects that are subject to rough handling.

In the second group, known as *champlevé*, or *en taille d'epargne*, the powdered enamel was fused into cells, cut with chasing tools, carved, stamped or cast into the metal base-plate. To ensure a good grip for the enamels, it was customary to leave the floor of the recesses rough. The metal base was normally thick, and so did not require counter-enamelling to prevent its distortion. In the earliest examples only lines of design were incised into the base plate, but over time,

Figure 3.34 Detail of *cloisonné* enamel on a vase, in which the strips of metal defining the design can be clearly seen. (Courtesy of S. Dove).

Figure 3.35 *Plique à jour* enamel cross. The empty ring on the right shows that the enamel (now missing) had no backing.

Figure 3.36 Tie-pin decorated in *champlevé* enamel with symbols of the four playing card suites.

more of the base was cut away, leaving only thin partitions, resembling the earlier *cloisonné* work in appearance. Beautiful examples of this work are known from Celtic and Anglo-Saxon Britain. Another centre from which great quantities of *champlevé* work came was the town of Limoges in central France, from where in the twelfth, thirteenth and later centuries thousands of reliquaries, crosses, altar vessels and other works were sent to all parts of Europe. In most of the early work from Limoges each decorated space was filled with broken opaque colours, often blues and greens touched with creamy white. The

ground was generally gilded, and the head of figures often made by *repoussé* work in fairly high relief from a separate piece of copper or bronze, rivetted on and gilded prior to being enamelled.

A sub division of this group is known as *bassetaille* (Fr. for 'shallow cut') enamel. In this process, a layer of translucent enamel was fused over a design cut in low relief, chased or engraved on a metal base-plate. Sometimes a panel produced primarily by chasing was sharpened by a certain amount of engraving. Considerable traces of such work can be seen on the Royal Gold Cup (British Museum, London) (*Figure 3.37*), although the major portion of the work was executed by chasing. The cup was made *circa* AD 1530, probably in Burgundy or Paris, and decorated with scenes from the life of St Agnes. In many medieval works executed in the *bassetaille* technique, the enamel extended right across the panel, with no metal surface left exposed. The colours were prevented from running into one another by mixing a little gum of tragacanth with them, and by allowing each colour to dry before the next was added alongside it. In panels with figures, even the flesh was covered with a layer of clear enamel, which allowed the modelling of the face and hands to show through. In the case of the Royal Gold Cup, the whole of each figure, tree, scroll or piece of furniture represented is covered from side to side with enamels, which

Figure 3.37 The Royal Gold Cup, detail of the *bassetaille* enamel, showing a scene from the story of St Agnes. H 236 mm. 1380–1. France. (© Copyright The British Museum).

extend as a level surface right across them. Each is thus shown in silhouette against the gold background. The detailed modelling of the faces, hands, the folds of the robes, and other objects are seen through the enamel, the deeper depressions appear richer in tone than their shallower neighbours.

The process of *en resille sur verre* entailed packing the enamel frit into gold-lined incisions engraved on a medallion of blue or green glass, to which it fused on firing. This difficult technique was only adopted during the second quarter of the seventeenth century in France, where it was mainly used to decorate miniature cases.

A rich technique of covering figures or decorative devices formed in the round, with opaque enamel, *en ronde bosse* (Fr. for 'in rounded relief'), was used in Paris at the beginning of the fifteenth century on large reliquaries; and in England, where it was known as encrusted enamelling, and was used to decorate irregular surfaces, for example, the shoulders of finger rings, to ornament the mounts of cups or a figure in high relief formed by *repoussé* work and chasing. The Dunstable Swan in the British Museum, London is a fine example of this process. From the sixteenth century, goldsmiths enriched their work with touches of coloured enamel. One of the principal problems arising from the use of enamel in this way concerns the manner in which the object can be supported during firing. An elaborately constructed finger ring may have a number of soldered joints, which would melt if exposed to the heat of the furnace. Such joints must be protected, by painting them with rouge or whiting before the enamel is fired. A pendant jewel built up from a number of separately formed pieces held together by solder, may have enamelled decorations on surfaces inclined at many angles. During the firing process, the solder can be protected with plaster-of-Paris.

Enamels of the third group come under the general classification of painted enamels, although as with colours on a canvas, the material was sometimes applied with a palette knife. The process was invented in Limoges, France in the fifteenth century. Painted enamels have a plain foundation of a sheet of metal, generally slightly domed, and as a rule the whole surface on both sides of the metal

Figure 3.38 Detail of a Chinese painted enamel dish. (Courtesy of J. McConnell).

is covered with enamel (*Figure 3.38*). The technique relied upon a more sophisticated knowledge of enamel compositions and firing temperatures. With each colour having to be fired at successively lower temperatures, in order not to destroy the previous work, the technique is painstakingly slow and prone to irreparable flaws.

Cloisonné and *champlevé* enamels had been made for many centuries before it was discovered that the metal outlines between the different colours were not essential to the permanence of the work, valuable though they were from the decorative point of view. Towards the end of the fifteenth century the craftsmen at Limoges in France began, in the enamelled pictures which they fitted into the work, to leave out the metal divisions altogether. The way in which they worked has been followed, with little variation, by enamellers ever since.

Wetted finely ground enamel frit mixed with oil for ease of application was painted over a design scratched in a metal base-plate and each colour allowed to dry before the next was applied. The object, such as a plaque or box, was first covered with a layer of white opaque enamel and fired. The design and/or instructions were applied in different colours, and fired in a low temperature muffle kiln (approx. 500–700°C). The medium burned out during firing. Different firings at successively lower temperatures were required to fuse different colours of the same hardness, in order to prevent them running into one another.

If a copper plaque were given a coat of flux

before enamelling, the enamels would show much more brilliantly. Copper, with a coating of clear flux, appeared a bright golden or a pink coppery colour according to the composition of the flux used and to the temperature at which it was fired. Silver seen through clear flux resembled white satin; whereas the colour of gold hardly changed at all. Any design on the metal, whether scratched in with a steel point, or drawn with a lead pencil, showed clearly through the flux. The surface of the flux could, however, be roughened, then washed over with hydrofluoric acid to avoid milkiness in the colour, and the design transferred to it. The coloured enamels were then applied where required. The colours could be modified, shading if necessary, gold or silver foil added to make a more brilliant patch, parts of the design outlined, or touches of gold added.

Gold leaf or foil may be employed in various ways in enamel work: it may be used to cover part of the background, such as figure as in some primitive Italian and other paintings. For such work a foundation of translucent yellow enamel was provided over which the gold could be laid. Before laying the gold, the surface was moistened and kept moist by breathing gently on the film of gold while it was applied. A temperature just high enough to fuse the enamel was sufficient to fix the gold. If any defects appeared, the gold was brushed with a glass brush, another layer of gold placed over the first to cover the gaps, and refired. It was not necessary to cover the gold with enamel.

In the technique of *Swiss enamelling*, a neutral-coloured enamel was fused over a gold panel to form a matt surface. A picture was then painted, fired and given a translucent covering. Examples are found on nineteenth-century plaques decorated with pictures of Swiss girls wearing typical cantonal peasant dress.

Stars, fleurs-de-lys, rosettes or other devices could be stamped out in low relief in gold foil and laid on a foundation layer of enamel to form a diaper or other patterns. They were overlaid with a coating of translucent enamel, and the work fired. Translucent colours looked brighter when fired on a background of gold or silver than on copper or on the black or dark blue background employed by many medieval enamellers (Maryon, 1971).

Apart from the use of plain coloured enamels, a number of techniques for enamel decoration were employed which were very similar to those used on glass, such as mosaic and *millefiore*.

Architectural glass

By far the most widespread use of glass in the architectural context was in the form of painted window glass, from medieval times onwards. However, in Roman times, glass in the form of mosaics and *opus sectile* had been used to decorate the interiors of buildings (see *Figure 3.39*) and glass with a greenish tint had been used for small window-panes (see *Figure 7.28f*).

Mosaics

The architectural process of embedding small pieces of roughly squared glass (*tesserae*) in cement on walls or floors to form a picture was first developed by the Greeks, and then used extensively in the Roman and Byzantine periods. Roman mosaics were generally composed of stones, but there are early examples made of glass in Rome; and seventh century AD examples occur in Ravenna and Torcello, Italy. According to Theophilus (trans. Hawthorne and Stanley Smith, 1979), the Greeks made sheets of glass a finger (20 mm) thick and split them with a hot iron into tiny square pieces and covered them on one side with gold leaf, coating them with clear ground glass 'as a solder glass before firing in a kiln to fuse the gold leaf in place; Glass of this kind, interspersed in mosaic work, embellishes it very beautifully'. Vasari (1511–1571) gives a description of the preparation of mosaic cubes. First, the glass is made opaque by the addition of tin oxide and/or coloured by the addition of metallic oxides. When the glass was sufficiently melted and fused it was ladled out in small quantities onto a metal table and pressed into circular cakes about 20 cm in diameter and from 1.0 to 1.25 cm thick. The solidified glass was then annealed, cooled and cracked into *tesserae*. The fractured surface was generally used to form the upper surface of the mosaic since it had a more pleasing

Figure 3.39   Mosaic panel of Roman glass. 160 mm. 100 BC to AD 100. (© V&A Picture Library).

Figure 3.40   Fragment of *opus sectile* wall revetment. Cast and mosaic glass set in resin. Roman Empire. Late first or early second century AD. L 7.5 cm. (Corning Museum of Glass).

surface and richness of colour. The thickness of the glass cake therefore regulated the texture.

Gilded *tesserae* were produced by hermetically sealing gold leaf between two sheets of glass (*Figure 3.39*). The technique of producing the *fondi d'oro* or glass vessels adorned with designs in gold and found in the Roman catacombs, was of the same nature (see *Figure 2.7*). According to Vasari a glass disc was damped with gum-water and gold leaf applied to it. The gold-covered disc was then placed on an iron shovel in the mouth of the furnace. The glass covering was either made of a glass bubble or from broken glass bottles (cullet) so that one piece covered the entire disc. The disc was then held in the furnace until it almost reached red heat when it was quickly drawn out and cooled. In order to set the *tesserae* on walls or ceilings, a cartoon (drawing) was first pounced (pricked through) portion by portion on soft cement. Sometimes the resulting outline was coloured as a guide before the application of a thick cement and setting of the *tesserae*. The stucco cement remained soft for two to four days depending upon the weather. It was made of lime cement mixed with water, that is travertine, lime, pounded brick, gum-tragacanth and white of egg, and once made was kept moist with damp cloths while the *tesserae* were set (Maclehose, 1907).

Opus sectile

During the excavations at Kenchreai, the eastern port of Corinth (Greece), during the 1960s, over 100 panels of *opus sectile* worked

in glass were found, stacked on the floor of a building in the harbour area. The building and others associated with it were in the process of being remodelled or redecorated, when they were submerged during a seismic disturbance in AD 375. Other examples of *opus sectile* are known (*Figure 3.40*), but the Kenchreai panels are the most extensive.

The panels can properly be regarded as a stage in the historic evolution of the use of richly coloured glasses fitted or fused together to form ornamental designs. The origins of this tradition lie in the early glass of Egypt, and develop through the Nimrud ivory inlays and the fused mosaic glass vessels like those from Hasanlu and Marlik. But the most immediate technological precursors of the Kenchreai panels are the whole array of objects from the world of ribbon glass and *millefiori*, including miniature fused mosaic plaques. The Kenchreai panels might be considered to be just a slightly different version of other *opus sectile* work, such as those at Ostia (Italy), except that they were executed in glass instead of stone. But the separate units in many of the details and highlights of the panels are themselves polychrome pieces of glass. These details were not formed by simply arranging separate, tiny units of differently coloured monochrome glasses. They were made by a series of intricate processes in which carefully shaped bits of monochrome glasses were fitted, fused together by heating, and while still softened, manipulated in various ways into complicated polychrome design components like the details of fish scales and bird feathers. This characteristic puts the work squarely into the *millefiori* tradition. It is a technique that could only have been executed in glass and should not be construed as purely an inlay or mosaic technique, which could have been executed, for example, with shaped, polished, coloured stones. The Kenchreai panels are a product of the pyrotechnological arts, and not simply the lapidary art (Scranton, 1967; Ibrahim *et al.*, 1976).

The panels may not only be a stage in this tradition, but could conceivably be regarded as its culmination; for it does not appear to continue. In the West a few inlays in caskets and jewellery occur later and eventually the *cloisonné* technique evolves. In the Byzantine world mosaics flourished on a grander scale than ever before, but still as a part of their own mosaic tradition: one colour for each cube, and only cube after cube, with few other geometrical shapes being utilized. With the decline of the Roman world, the centre of glassmaking moved eastwards, and along with the other chemical arts, glassmaking flowered in the Islamic world. But by then glass artists had become totally preoccupied with glass-blowing, three-dimensional forms and transparency.

The panels were of various sizes and shapes – squares and oblongs – among which the smallest dimension would be around 0.3 cm, and the largest almost 2.0 cm. According to one hypothesis, a surface of appropriate size and shape was prepared first on a table, or a tray with raised edges. On this was then laid a kind of pavement of large potsherds cut from coarse amphorae, approximately rectangular in shape. Over these potsherds, and impressed into the interstices, was laid a thick coat, perhaps 20 mm over the potsherds, of a kind of plaster of which the chief ingredients were pine resin and finely pulverized marble. This was brought to a smooth surface. On this surface were laid pieces of glass of various colours, cut to various shapes (about 2 mm thick), in order to create the desired pattern, and these were glued down with more resin. According to a second hypothesis, the pieces of glass would be laid face down on the tray, and covered with the coat of resin plaster into which the potsherds would be impressed.

When found, some of the glass was firm and hard, some had disintegrated to a powder, and some was preserved in one of a variety of states in between. Although the panels were colourful when found, the colours presented were apparently not the same as the original colours, in most cases at least. Thus the characteristics of the various kinds of glass at the time when they were applied to the panels can only be inferred. However, it would seem that some kinds, notably those used for human flesh and for the masonry of buildings, were cut from large thin sheets. Of other kinds, notably the neutral backgrounds, it has been suspected that they were trowelled into place while in a more or less pasty state, though this is not certain. Some thin dividing lines, and especially the curved stems of flowers, may have been set in place as still-soft rods, or conceivably even as an extruded paste. More complex forms such as the seed-pods of lotus plants or the bodies of certain fish or birds give the appearance of having been made in a kind of *millefiori* and fused-glass mosaic techniques, externally moulded so that in cross-section the block would have the intended inner markings. Some particular shapes, such as the heads of birds or animals, may have been built up plastically in separate moulds, with certain details engraved or impressed on the face intended to be visible.

Mosaic and *opus sectile* techniques were revived in the eighteenth century in the United Kingdom (*Figures 3.41* and *3.42*).

Manufacture of window glass

Mould-cast glass panes

In Roman times, small panes of glass were produced by casting molten glass into shallow trays and spreading it out manually as it cooled. There is no contemporary reference to this process, but a number of mould-cast glass pane fragments have been excavated, for example, at Pompeii in Italy, and on several Romano-British villa sites. There is a fragment of Roman window glass from Caerleon in Wales (Boon, 1966), which seems to have been cast on wet wood judging from the impressions of wood grain on one side of it, although this has been disputed. Fragments of an almost complete pane of window glass dating from the second century AD were excavated in 1974 in a bath-house complex at the Romano-British iron-working settlement at Garden Hill, Hartfield in East Sussex (Money,

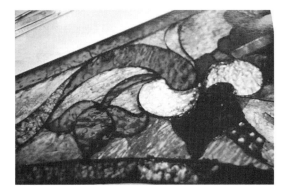

Figure 3.41 Detail of nineteenth century glass *opus sectile* in the Crown Liquor Saloon, Belfast, Northern Ireland. (Courtesy of The National Trust).

Figure 3.42 Detail of a nineteenth-century panel made of glass mosaic and glass frit *opus sectile*. St George's Church, Crowhurst, Kent (UK).

1976). The pane (see *Figure 7.28f*) measured 235 mm × 255 mm and is now in the British Museum. It has one flat side on which there are marks, which suggest that it was cast on a bed of sand. Two edges are rounded while the others are grozed. The one remaining original rounded corner bears a mark made by pushing the molten glass into the mould with a pointed instrument. There may have been other panes in the bath complex; and they were certainly used elsewhere on the site since fragments representing several panes were unearthed in several locations. Fragments of window glass excavated at Stonea, Cambridgeshire in 1981 bear marks of wood grain on one side, and one bears evidence of having been manipulated to fill the mould.

Cylinder glass

The most prevalent and long-lived methods of producing early Roman window glass, however, were the spinning process, which produced crown glass; and the cylinder process, which produced cylinder glass (also known as hroad, sheet, spread or muff glass, later Lorraine glass or German sheet) (*Figure 3.43*). Cylinder glass tended to be irregular in thickness between the ninth and thirteenth centuries, and it lacked flatness, although it was glossy on both sides, unlike the Roman cylinder glass with one matt and one glossy side, probably because the kilns were not as hot as the Roman type. Chambon (1963) gives a very detailed account of the developments in making cylinder glass.

Cylinder glassmaking seems to have been the earlier invention, but cylinder and crown glassmaking repeatedly replaced each other during the fourth to the nineteenth centuries depending on the fashion; for example, Tudor leaded windows had crown glass, after which the methods were superseded by mechanical methods of sheet glass production. Cylinder glass was certainly used in Roman buildings in Britain, Italy and Greece (at Corinth) before crown glass became the fashion.

The cylinder process enabled larger and more even sheets of glass to be made than those produced by the mould-cast method. A gathering of glass was first blown into a broad bulb up to 1.5 m in length, and then given a cylindrical shape by swinging it back and forth (to lengthen it) and marvering (to keep it cylindrical). The ends were then cut off and the cylinder split longitudinally by a hot iron, and then reheated on the flat bed of a kiln. When it was hot enough, the glass could be flattened into a sheet with iron tongs and a smooth piece of iron or wood called a rake, croppie or flattener (see *Figure 3.44*). This description is simplified in its essentials because the exact method of production varied from era to era. For example, Theophilus states (Dodwell, 1961; Hawthorne and Smith, 1963) that, after the bulb was blown, the end was pierced (by blowing it out after heating the end in a glory hole), the hole was widened to equal the bulb's widest diameter, and then pinched together so that the pontil could be attached. At other times

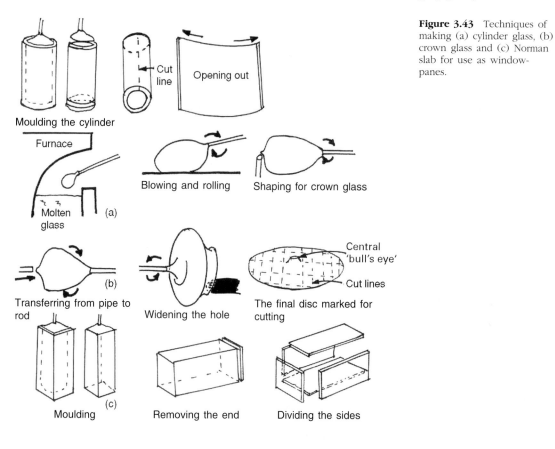

Figure 3.43 Techniques of making (a) cylinder glass, (b) crown glass and (c) Norman slab for use as window-panes.

the cylinder was cut with shears while still hot; there is evidence that this was the method used in Roman times (Harden, 1959). Cylinder-made glass can be identified by the shape of the air bubbles (seed) which it contains because they become elongated in straight parallel lines consistent with the elongated shape of the glass bulb. The edges of a sheet may also identify it as being made by the cylinder process since the top and bottom of the cylinder (the long sides of the resultant sheet) were rounded in the flame and hence become slightly thickened to produce a thumb edge (Harden, 1961). The longitudinal split made in the cylinder (the edges of which are the short sides of the sheet) may show shear marks, or may be quite sharp. Much Roman cylinder glass is of the one matt, one glossy sided type because the cylinder was opened, and then pressed down by the croppie onto the sanded floor of the kiln. Green (1979) considered that the earliest type, which had a very flat and matt

lower surface, and an undulating upper surface, was opened in a too-hot kiln. Later the glassmakers' increased skill resulted in the lower edge not being roughened, and eventually panes were produced which remained glossy on both sides. In 1973 Harden examined Romano-British glass excavated at Shakenoke Farm near Oxford and concluded that equal quantities of matt/glossy sided and double glossy sided window glass were used concurrently during the third and fourth centuries.

Harden (1961) describes some large panes of Roman glass, one measuring 395mm × 260 mm, and another, an almost complete pane of cylinder glass measuring 535mm × 305 mm. Two pieces, excavated in 1972 at Hartfield, Sussex, were 255mm × 235mm and 275 mm by more than 215 mm, and they varied in thickness from 2 to 5 mm (Harden, 1974). Other large pieces from Italy, also listed, were 330mm × 270 mm and 267 mm × 267 mm (Harden, 1961).

facing page 448   Plate CXV

Grinding and Pollishing of PLATE GLASS

Figure 3.44 Production of early flat glass. Uneven and scarred glass was evened and polished in a grinding shop. Large sheets of glass were fixed to the spokes of a wheel (B). Emery and wet sand (A) were spread on the surfaces, which then ground each other smooth. Finally the glass had to be polished with felt buffers affixed to jointed ribs which maintained a constant pressure (C). Plate from Diderot's *Encyclopédie*.

It seems likely that northern Gaul and the Rhineland exported glass to Britain during the first seven centuries of the millennium, but there was certainly some local production, at least from the late seventh century. In AD 675 Benedict Biscop imported workmen from Gaul to help in constructing the monastery at Monkwearmouth in Sunderland (UK), 'in the Roman manner', and glaziers to glaze the windows of the church, porticus and refectory.

That these glaziers melted glass on the site has been confirmed by Cramp's excavations; and the glass all seems to have been made by the cylinder process. The glassmaking technique seems not to have become firmly established, for in AD 758, another appeal was made by Cuthbert for glassmakers to be sent to Britain. Glass with similar characteristics to that found at Monkwearmouth was excavated by Hunter (1977) at Escomb near Durham, Repton near Derby, Brixworth near Northampton and Hamwic (the Saxon settlement in Southampton). The fragments of Saxon glass were all quite small, the largest being only about 65 mm long.

In the fourteenth century there was a noticeable improvement in the quality of cylinder glass which probably first took place in Bohemia. The knowledge of its production was taken to Lorraine by four known glassmaking families, and thus cylinder glass became known as Lorraine glass (Fr. *verre façon de Lorraine* or *verre en table*). Also in the fourteenth century, the Venetians used the cylinder process to make glass for mirrors in lieu of the wasteful crown glass method. In the eighteenth century a device was introduced to help maintain the shape of the cylinder during working. This was a wet wooden mould 'shaped like half a cannon', and an improved surface finish was achieved by opening the cylinder out and flattening it out on a sheet of clean glass. The hand cylinder technique continued in use until the nineteenth century when it was replaced by machine drawn cylinder glass (Lubbers process).

Crown glass

The first examples of crown glass date from the fourth century AD, both in the East (from Jerash, Samaria) (Harden, 1959, 1961) and in the West (from Chichester, Sussex) (Charlesworth, 1977). These early crowns were quite small, being some 150–200 mm in diameter, and (at least in the East) they were mounted in pairs in plaster frames. It was not until a much later date that larger crowns were cut into panes (quarries).

The flat panes of glass (crowns) were produced by blowing a gather of glass into a globular shape, transferring it from the blowing iron to the pontil, cutting it open and then after reheating in the glory hole, the pontil would be spun rapidly so that by centrifugal force the glass assumed the shape of a flat disc up to 1.2 cm in diameter. The glass was then annealed, either used whole or cut into rectangular- or diamond-shaped panes.

Pieces of crown glass can be identified by the curved lines in which the seed lie (with the pontil at the centre) and by the curved ripples in the surface (see *Figure 3.43*). The complete crown has a much thicker centre, called a boss, bullion or bull's eye with the rough circular mark in the centre where it was broken from the pontil when cold; the pieces cut from near the boss are thicker than those cut from near the edge.

Harden (1971) drew attention to the sixth century crown glass window panes found at the church of San Vitale in Ravenna in such a position that they almost certainly came from the windows of the apse. They are mostly monochrome panes, 170 to 260 mm in diameter, although one fragmentary piece bears an outline drawing of Christ nimbed and enthroned and this may be a distant precursor of painted glass windows. Bovini (1964) and Harden (1971) suggest that these small crowns form a link between the fourth-century ones made in the East and the Normandy mode crowns of the fourteenth century. In Britain, however, cylinder blown glass continued to be used in the tenth century, as shown by a sample from Thetford, Essex (Harden, 1961).

The surfaces of crown glass were always bright and shiny because they had been heated in a glory hole and had not touched a sanded surface such as that which impaired the lower surface of cylinder glass. Thus a brighter and more transparent window glass could be made by the crown process, than was possible by the cylinder process (at least in antiquity), and the relative competition between the two processes depended on the fashion at the time. Thus a demand for large windows could only be met by the cylinder process whereas leaded light windows could be made better with crown glass. The crown glass process was later termed the Normandy method, its invention having been uncertainly attributed to Philippe de Caqueray of Normandy who established a glassworks in

Normandy in 1330 where crowns of 500–600 mm diameters were produced; despite the fact that crown glass had been in use for many centuries.

In the sixteenth century Dutch crowns had an even better reputation than those from Normandy and the discs became larger so that, by 1700, the diameter was 800–850 mm. In 1724 an *Arrêt du Conseil d'Etat* obliged even the Normands to make discs which were 38 pouces (about 1010 mm) in diameter (Chambon, 1963), but this was evidently quite difficult to do because few were made that size, being generally only 30 to 36 pouces (800–960 mm) in diameter. The manufacture of large crowns was more complicated than shown in *Figure 3.44*; Chambon (1963, Plate II) illustrates 16 different operations.

Chance Brothers continued to make crown glass at least until 1832. Chance (1919) commented that 'Crown glass excels in brilliance and transparency, but yields in other respects to plate and sheet ... [the centre lump] and the circular form of the tables, prevent the cutting of large rectangular panes from them, and there is much waste... And, as the tables have a slight convexity the panes, unless flattened, show a distinct curvature and distortion of vision. ... Owing to ... the British public [being] habituated to the small bright panes, it survived there for many years longer than on the Continent.

Norman slab

A simple technique for making window glass involves blowing a square-sided glass bottle into a mould, and then cutting it into the four side panels and the base panel (see *Figure 3.43*). It was not possible to make large areas of glass in this manner; the largest square Roman bottles would have provided panels that were only some 200 mm × 100 mm.

The technique is now called Norman slab although its origin is unknown (Harden, 1961). When whole panels survive they can be recognized by their thin edges, because it is not easy to blow glass into the corners of a square mould and maintain the same thickness as in the rest of the bottle. The edges may also show some curvature if the cut does not run exactly down the edge of the bottle; but pieces cut from the panel may not be recognizable as such. Nevertheless, the bubbles will not be elongated in parallel rows as is often the case with cylinder glass, and observations that some of the Jarrow glass had rounded bubbles could support a suggestion that the Norman slab technique might have been used (Cramp, 1975).

Flat glass sheets

Plate or cast glass, run out onto a flat metal table, had to be quite thick, to allow for the grinding and polishing processes which were necessary to render the glass clear enough to be transparent. The hardened glass had a rough, dull surface, which had to be ground and polished with abrasives in order to achieve the brilliance required for its use as windows and mirrors (*Figure 3.44*). Around 1845 Frederick Masson and J. Conqueror invented a machine for squeezing molten glass between two rollers, opening the way for the development of many different processes for the making of sheet glass. However there was still little advancement in the size or flatness of the panes produced. From this time, polished sheet glass became widely available, and resulted in the production of expansive windows, reaching from floor to cornice, and usually reserved for grand buildings. The main producer of rolled glass in Britain during the nineteenth century was the company of James Hartley of Sunderland, whose products can still be seen in many Victorian railway stations.

During the eighteenth and nineteenth centuries, glass sheet introduced to Britain by Chance with the aid of Bontemps was termed *German sheet*. (The sheets were in fact large cylinders, also known as *patent plate* and *improved cylinder glass*.) Following the development of German sheet, drawn cylinder glass was produced about 1923. The continuous flow process was introduced in 1921 on the continent (1923 in Britain), but the glass still had to be polished. In 1933 the first vertical drawn float glass was produced. In 1923, Pilkingtons (UK) invented the first continuous on-line grinding and polishing process, followed by the development of the twin grinding and polishing process in 1937. The resulting high quality, thick glass is used for large display windows, mirrors, table-tops etc. In 1959, Pilkingtons (UK) introduced the *float glass* method of producing sheet glass, in

which a continuous ribbon of molten glass, up to 3.30 metres wide, moved out of a melting furnace and floated along the surface of a molten bath of tin. The controlled atmosphere and temperature prevent irregularities from forming in the glass, and the resulting flat glass can be produced to a thickness ranging between 2.5 and 25 mm. The glass is fire-polished and annealed without the need for grinding and polishing. The electro-float process, developed in 1967, enables the glass to be tinted as it passes over the float bath.

Painted and stained window glass

A number of decorative techniques were used to embellish glass windows, especially those in ecclesiastical buildings. During manufacture the glass could be coloured, or clear glass could be flashed with a thin coating of

Figure 3.45 Detail of a medieval stained glass window showing the design formed of leaded stained and painted pieces of glass.

coloured glass on one side. The panes themselves could be painted, enamelled, stained, etched or engraved (*Figure 3.45*).

Throughout the Middle Ages decorative windows were composed of pieces of white and coloured glass, cut to fit the basic design (cartoon), and held together in a frame-work of leads. With the exception of black enamel painting and silver–yellow stain, the colour in medieval window glass came from the glass itself, the pot-metal having been coloured so that the colour ran through the entire thickness of the pane and was as permanent as the glass itself. Certain colours, however, particularly ruby, were so dense in tone that they would not transmit light sufficiently. In the twelfth and thirteenth centuries, therefore, the translucent red colour was produced by making multi-layered glasses. It is not known exactly how such glasses came to be made but there are so many very thin layers, perhaps as many as fifty, which bend back on each other in the manner of hairpins, that it seems likely that they were not made by a process of repeated gathering alternatively from colourless and red glass pots. One suggestion regarding the method of manufacture of multi-layered glasses was that red glass was stirred into a pot of colourless glass, and the gather for the cylinder was made before proper mixing of the glass had taken place. However, the conditions necessary for producing the ruby colour exist in a suitably non-homogeneous manner when the colour is prepared in a very dilute form, and thus the layering may at first have been an accidental consequence which was later deliberately exploited (Cable, personal communications, 1979). Apparently it is much easier to produce a homogeneous red colour when enough copper has been incorporated to produce a red glass, which would be too dense to use in the thickness of 5 mm required for a window.

There are, in addition, some twelfth-century glasses which are multilayered in about half their thickness, the other half being of greenish glass. It is possible that the greenish part is a copper-containing glass, which failed to strike during the essential reheating process, or it may be an early attempt at producing a flashed glass. The multi-layered part is, however, so thick that glasses of this type should not, strictly speaking, be described as flashed glass.

The difficulty of producing transparent red glass was finally overcome in the fourteenth century by the production of flashed glass. The manufacturing process is relatively simple: a first small gather (the post) was taken from the pot containing the glass batch which, although colourless in appearance, had been so formulated as to strike a red colour during an essential reheating process. A second, much heavier gather of colourless glass was then taken over the top of the first. The glass was blown to form a cylinder, which was then cut, opened out and flattened. (Crown glass could also be flashed.) Finally, the flashed glass pane was subjected to a controlled reheating process to strike the colour. The original necessity of flashing dense colours was frequently turned to advantage by the medieval glazier. By abrading the thin layer of coloured flashing, both white and colour could be obtained on one sheet of glass. For example, if a figure had a ruby tunic trimmed with white cuffs, the glazier abraded the area of the cuff from a piece of flashed ruby instead of having to cut and lead on extra pieces of white glass. In heraldry, with intricate charges on coloured grounds, this technique was particularly useful, especially as all the gold charges could also be obtained by painting the white abraded areas with yellow stain.

Applying enamels and yellow stain

In the initial stages of painting, the glass is laid over the drawing, the line work then being traced in glass paint on the surface of the glass. Using a sable-haired 'rigger' or tracing brush the painter gathers sufficient paint to produce a firm black line. Too little paint on the brush will produce a streaky or washy line, too much produces a blob, which is difficult to control. Alternatively, a piece of glass may be coated overall with an opaque layer of paint, the design, be it lettering or diaper, then being scratched out of the black background by means of a sharp stick, needle or dart. Lettering on most twelfth- and thirteenth-century glass was carried out in this way.

With one or two exceptions the methods of glass painting have changed little since the eleventh century. Since that time two colouring agents have been used to decorate windows in association with clear and coloured glass panes. The first of these was the opaque black or dark brown enamel which was used for painting all the main outlines or trace lines, the washed tones and the shading on the glass; the second colouring agent was a silver–yellow stain. The enamel was originally made from a highly fusible green lead glass mixed with copper or iron oxide, a binding medium such as gum arabic (sugar, treacle or vegetable oil) and a flux. The use of copper and iron oxides varied at different periods, which explains the changes in colour from a full black to a somewhat reddish-brown. The ingredients were mixed together cold, as opposed to being mixed under heat, as were the later translucent enamels. The binding medium had the effect of enabling the enamel to flow and to adhere to the glass, and also hardened the paint, thus making it more resistant to accidental damage before firing. The addition of a flux was necessary to lower the softening point of the enamel below that of the substrate glass. After the painting was completed, the pieces of glass were fired, the flux of lead glass melting and fusing the enamel onto the substrate (Lee *et al.*, 1982). The effect of coloured jewels in a painted glass window, for example, on the hem of a robe, can easily be produced by employing spots of different enamel colours; but at earlier periods four other processes were used.

Theophilus (trans. Dodwell, 1961; Hawthorne and Smith, 1963), described a technique in which the jewels were cut from a piece of coloured glass, and fixed to the substrate glass with a thick ring of (black) enamel paint which was then fired. If the jewel subsequently fell off, the thick ring of paint remained to show where it had been. A Romanesque example of this type of jewel survives on the Jesse Tree window (1225–1230) at Regensburg Cathedral, west Germany; and fifteenth-century examples are known from the St Cuthbert window in York Minster, and St Michael's Church, Spurriergate, York (UK). A second technique for producing jewels is somewhat similar to that described above. Because the glass is reheated, the technique is misleadingly referred to by art historians as 'annealing'. In this method, the two glasses (i.e. the jewel and the substrate glass) were sealed together by applying a layer of ground green glass (perhaps a lead glass) between them before refiring. The powdered glass melts and acts as a solder. Examples of such jewels do not seem to be known. The third technique was to insert circular jewels into the substrate glass. Holes were drilled, somewhat larger than the jewels to be inserted, and the jewels were then leaded into the holes. There are examples of this technique in the UK in St John's Church, Stamford, in Brown's Hospital, Stamford, in Canterbury Cathedral and elsewhere. The fourth technique, occasionally confused with the third approach, was to lead-in small pieces of coloured glass using ordinary glazing techniques, as can be seen in York Minster, for example the northernmost window of the east wall of the North Transept.

During the sixteenth century a type of translucent enamel was developed. The enamels were made by mixing a flux of highly fusible lead glass with various metallic oxide colourants. With this type of enamel the oxide was dissolved in the flux by strong heat producing the required colour. The enamel was therefore merely a highly fusible coloured glass ground to a fine powder, which, mixed with a suitable medium, could be applied to the window pane as a paint. On being fired onto the pane of clear glass it regained the transparency it had partially lost through being powdered, and became a thin coat of transparent coloured glass upon the surface to which it had been applied. It is an anomaly that some of the earliest surviving window glass has perfectly preserved paint while, from the fifteenth century onwards, an irregular but steady decline in condition of the paint persisted until some of the worst is found in the first half of the nineteenth century. Although some of this is attributable to the addition of borax to the paint, some is certainly due to inconsistency of firing, as testified by variations within the bounds of a single window. The firing was carried out in a muffle kiln (Fr. *petit feu*) at temperatures that did not cause the substrate to melt. While the temperature for fusing pigment into glass is between 600 and 620°C, much depends on the time that the glass is held at a given temperature. In the case of medieval firing, the temperature was gradually built up in the clay furnace, and the fire extinguished, or withdrawn, when the temperature was judged to be correct. The heat was thus retained by the clay walls, and the resultant slow cooling gave a good period of annealing.

The application of silver nitrate (or silver sulphide) to the back of the glass to produce a yellow colour when fired was introduced early in the fourteenth century and revolutionized painted glass design by providing the ability to incorporate more than one colour on a single piece of glass, for instance, golden hair or crown on the head of the Virgin.

The medieval practice of preparing silver stain appears to have been to cut some silver metal into small pieces or to use it in thin sheets, and to burn it with sulphur in a crucible, which converted it into a sulphide. This was finely ground and mixed with an earthy vehicle such as pipe-clay which made the stain easier to apply. Yellow stain in medieval glass was usually painted on clear glass and was chiefly used to heighten details of figure or canopy work or *grisaille* ground patterns, but in later times it was painted on coloured glass in order to change the tint of the piece, or part of a piece. For instance, using blue glass and yellow stain, a green hill and the sky could be painted on one piece of glass. In figure painting, both hair and face could be painted on one piece of glass; and decorated borders to white robes were frequently stained yellow. Broadly speaking, fourteenth-century stain was golden in colour and some deepening came about until the red stain of the sixteenth century, and its associated lighter tints, brought about the high point of the stainer's art, at the time when availability and variety of pot metal colours was severely limited.

While at first confined to the yellow-on-white combination, it was extended within the next century to produce a green tint by applying the stain to blue. It was also realized that, by abrading away the coloured surface of flashed glass and staining the resulting white areas yellow, the interpretation of heraldry into glass became much simpler and enabled such charges as golden lions on a ruby ground to be carried out without complex leading.

The effect of silver stain depends on the amount of stain applied and the number of applications, the temperature at which it is fired and the chemical composition of the glass. The finest staining on glass is known as kelp, its alkali content being said to be derived from seaweed, although it probably contained additional metallic oxides such as tin. It was extensively used from the sixteenth to the twentieth centuries and could produce a stain which was almost a true red and which maintained a clarity equal to that of pot metal yellow or red glass. It was used by Peckitt in York Minster (UK).

The first use of enamels had been on a small-scale for transferring complex heraldic charges on to glass, and for colouring the fruit and flowers of garlands, but subsequently it was used for the flesh tones of figures and ultimately it superseded most of the pot metal colours. However, at no time were the colours as transparent as those of silver-stained glass, or of coloured pot metal, nor did the enamels have a durability comparable to that of the coloured glass.

Mirrors

In the manufacture of seventeenth-century mirrors on plate glass a piece of tin foil, approximately a tenth of a millimetre thick, was laid on a perfectly flat piece of marble. The protective layer of tin oxide was removed from its surface by rubbing mercury over the foil until the surface was shiny. Next a layer of mercury was poured over the foil to a depth of 3–5 mm (this was the quantity of mercury which could lie on a horizontal tin plate, and corresponded to *circa* 50 kg of mercury per square metre of glass). A scum of tin oxide accumulated on the surface of the mercury and was removed with a glass edge. Meanwhile, the glass sheet had been thoroughly cleaned by rubbing it with washed ash and polishing it with a linen cloth. In a single movement, the glass sheet was slid over the mercury with the leading edge dipped into the mercury and without scraping the tin. In the case of small mirrors, a thin sheet of paper was laid on the mercury, the glass then laid on top and gently pressed down whilst the paper was drawn out. The glass was then pressed down to make good contact with the tin foil. A great deal of mercury ran out, but excess was removed, by weighting the glass,

Pl . I .

Figure 3.46 Glass mirror manufacture in the mid eighteenth century. A flat piece of glass which will form the base of a mirror. The uneven surface is ground and polished. The glass is slid onto a sheet of tin foil coated with mercury, and weighted with rocks. A rim around the table prevents the liquid from running off. When the excess mercury has been squeezed out, the finished products are stacked upright to drain further and to harden.

and then tilting the marble support. The amalgam process began the moment the mercury came into contact with the metal foil. Complete conversion of the tin to tin–mercury compound occurred within 24 hours. The weights were then removed and the mirror lifted off the marble support. However the amalgam was still very soft and mobile so that the mirror had to immediately be laid flat, glass side down, and then tilted very slowly, first toward one side and then to the corner, so that enough of the liquid phase could flow and evaporate away to leave a solid, stable amalgam layer. The hardening process took up to a month, depending on the size of the mirror (*Figure 3.46*).

The tin–mercury amalgam mirror is a two-phase reflective coating, the mercury having reacted with the tin to form a layer of crystals containing about 19 wt per cent of mercury alloyed with the tin. The voids between the crystals are filled with a fluid containing about 0.5 per cent tin in mercury. The production of amalgam mirrors was technically difficult, dangerous and time-consuming and therefore costly. The glass itself had to be colourless,

free of bubbles and of uniform thickness, before being ground and polished on both sides. Application of the amalgam involved the use of a large quantity of mercury, which resulted in the workers suffering from mercury poisoning.

The technique of producing amalgam mirrors remained largely the same, with only minor developments. An eighteenth-century English account of mirror-making mentions the mixing of lead, tin and marcasite (probably antimony or bismuth) with the mercury in order that 'the glass may dry sooner'. Several later sources mention that the tin foil can contain up to 2 per cent copper, which results in a better adhesion to the glass. However such additions were probably uncommon.

There were two methods of making curved mirrors. A free-flowing liquid amalgam was formed by melting bismuth, lead and tin together and then mixing them with mercury. Whilst still warm, the mixture could be poured into concave glass or into hollow glass balls, and then poured out again, leaving a thin film on the glass which hardened on cooling to produce a convex mirror. Concave mirrors were formed by pouring the same amalgam into a gap between curved glass and a varnished plaster of Paris mould. Pure tin amalgam could also be used to make curved mirrors by first pressing tin foil into a plaster mould taken from the curved glass. Mercury was then poured into the foil to produce a concave mirror or into the curved glass, after which the foil was pressed into place, to form a convex mirror. The glass and the foil-covered mould were then pressed together. During each process, the glass had to lie uppermost during the amalgam maturing process to allow the tin alloy crystals to float upwards in the heavy mercury to form the mirrored surface against the glass.

In the middle of the nineteenth century the technique of depositing a thin layer of silver on glass by adding an aldehyde to a silver nitrate solution was discovered. This method was quick and relatively safe; however the first silver mirrors were not durable, and so did not compete effectively with tin amalgam mirrors until around 1900. Tin amalgam mirrors continued to be made in the first decades of the twentieth century (Schweig, 1973; Child, 1990).

Tin amalgam and silver mirrors differ from one another in colour and reflectivity; tin amalgam has a bluish tint and reflects significantly much less light than silver mirrors, which appear slightly yellow. The glass itself also contributes to the difference in appearance since the older glass is generally darker (more grey). However, it must be remembered that both types of mirror become darker and foggier with the onset of corrosion. Hadsund (1993) suggests that it is sometimes possible to differentiate between the two types of mirror by viewing them through a piece of thin (tracing) paper, when the silver mirror will appear brighter. Amalgam mirrors were very seldom painted at the time of manufacture, normally only when they were for use in damp rooms or at sea. Sometimes mirrors are found which have been painted on the reverse in an attempt at preservation of the mirrored surface. The reverse side of silvered mirrors was always protected by several layers of paint, based on red lead. Modern silvered mirrors are copper plated before being painted in order to provide greater protection.

Part 2: Furnaces and melting techniques

Mesopotamian glassmaking

The earliest records of glass technology, in the form of cuneiform tablets, were found in Mesopotamia. The earliest text giving a recipe for glaze was found near Tell 'Umar (Seleucia) on the River Tigris. The tablet dates from the seventeenth century BC but presumes a well-established glassmaking tradition. Amongst the many thousands of Assyrian cuneiform tablets excavated from the site of the library of Ashurbanipal (668–627 BC), a small number record information concerning the manufacture of coloured glass and glazes. These tablets were evidently copies of originals produced in the last centuries of the second millennium BC, showing that the essential principles of glassmaking were understood in about 1700 BC. An important philological aspect of the cuneiform glassmaking texts is that the seventh-century copies contain the earlier Sumerian words and their later Akkadian translations; moreover, the former are related to words used in Ur III texts and the latter are related to words used by glassmakers on the Phoenician coast in Roman times. Thus the glassmaking tradition seems to have been an extremely conservative one, the same terms (and no doubt the same tried and tested formulae) being handed down for more than two millennia.

Comparatively few glass artefacts have been excavated in Mesopotamia, but this may well be due to the moisture content of the soil, and to the rise of the water-table in historic times, causing the destruction of much of the early glass which was inherently unstable in its chemical composition (and therefore slowly soluble in water) (Oppenheim, 1973). There is also the fact that glassmaking would have only been carried out on a small scale, and that wasters would have been reused as cullet.

The cuneiform texts with specific references to glass have been translated at various times, notably by Thompson (1925), Oppenheim *et al.* (1970) and Brill (1970b,c). However, translation is notably difficult. The earlier translations contain many errors, based on a lack of understanding of glassmaking techniques. The philologist needs the help of a glass technologist to interpret the methods and materials described; the glass technologist who advised Thompson was not aware of the composition of the plant ash used, and its profound effect on the composition of the glass. Thompson erroneously referred to the use of human embryos 'born before their time' as a constituent of Babylonian glass. In Oppenheim's translation, however, the relevant word is *kubu* (images); images were in fact set up as part of the ritual for building a furnace. Thompson also referred to the use of arsenic and antimony in glassmaking, but Turner (1956a) pointed out that the arsenic is only a trace element in Babylonian or Assyrian glasses, and Brill (1970b,c) concluded that since there was no description of ingredients containing antimony in cuneiform texts, there was no reason to believe that the Assyrians knew of antimony as such. Similarly, it seems that Douglas and Frank (1972) were misled into believing that lime was specified as an ingredient of Assyrian glass. Despite their technical content, the texts were not technical instructions, but, 'They have to be considered, strange as it may seem, as literary creations within a complex literary tradition ... [were] subject to certain stylistic requirements; their wording and their literary forms were historically conditioned ...' (Oppenheim *et al.*, 1970).

In Mesopotamia there were many words used for glass, glass intermediates and glass-like substances (Oppenheim *et al.*, 1970). A coherent interpretation of the cuneiform texts was made by Brill (1970b,c). As a result of investigation, it seems that the naga plant may well have been *Salsola kali* or a similar plant; and that *ahussu*, the plant ash prepared from it, probably contained about 55 per cent Na_2CO_3, 8 per cent KCl, 8 per cent MgO, 4 per cent NaCl, 5 per cent $CaSO_4$ etc. *Immanakku* was ground quartzite pebbles from a river bed, probably containing 95 per cent SiO_2, 2.5 per cent Al_2O_3 etc.; and *zukû* was an intermediate reaction product (a frit)

obtained by heating the silica with plant ash at 'a heat which has the colour of the red of red grapes', that is, probably less than 850°C. After fritting was complete, the cold *zukû* was ground up and the colouring agents were added (see below); the mixture was then heated to 'a heat which is yellow' (probably about 1000°C) to produce the final glass.

Chief among the materials added at this second stage of glass melting were *urudu.hi.a* (slow copper) and *sipparuarhu* (fast bronze). These materials have not yet been identified with any certainty but it is possible that slow copper was copper oxide (CuO) and that fast bronze was a (metallic) alloy of copper, tin and lead which would melt, form a layer below the glass, and confer a blue colour to it (Brill, 1970b).

Having established the probable nature of the ingredients of *zukû*, Brill (1970c) then heated them together for 10 hours at 920°C to obtain a frit, which was cooled, pulverized and then heated for 16 hours at 1100°C to produce a well-melted homogeneous piece of pale bluish glass of very good quality. The resultant *zukû* glass contains 56.0 per cent SiO_2, 23.8 per cent Na_2O, 6.6 per cent CaO, 5.6 per cent MgO, 3.8 per cent K_2O, 2.2 per cent Al_2O_3 and various minor ingredients. Thus the glass was not unlike typical Mesopotamian glasses; and from its composition it would be expected to have a reasonable durability.

Mesopotamian furnaces and melting procedures

The religio-magic preparations associated with the setting up of a furnace, described in translation by Oppenheim (1973), reflect the limits of the Mesopotamian glassmakers' technical knowledge, which was essentially empirical in nature.

According to Thorpe (1938) it would seem as though there were three types of furnace described in the cuneiform texts. The glasshouse (the *bît kûri* or house of the furnaces) contained the *kûri sa abni* or furnace for the pot metal in which the glass batch was formed. The *kûri ša siknat ênâit-pel-ša* (furnace with a floor of eyes) was the founding furnace ('that where the workmen work'). A much later usage of the term 'eye' in this context is that of the Italian *occhio* or *lumella*, that is the circular opening between the siege (middle or founding) storey of the three-storey furnace and the upper (annealing or tower) storey. The Mesopotamian furnace could probably achieve temperatures as high as 1000–1100°C. Finally the *kuri sa takkanni* (furnace of the arch) appears to have been a door (*bab kûri*) through which the finished articles were introduced. This corresponds to a lehr or annealing furnace.

The fire was made of logs from poplar trees, found growing along the River Euphrates, and the duration of the found was, in certain cases, as long as seven days, during which it must have been difficult to maintain the high temperatures required. However, there is no doubt that by the seventh century BC, Mesopotamian glass furnaces had developed enough for this to be possible. Although no description exists of furnaces constructed specifically for glassmaking, and no furnaces have been excavated, Forbes (1966) suggested that the reverbatory furnace (a precondition for glass-blowing), may have originated in Mesopotamia.

The texts make no distinction between the batch of unmelted materials and the frit, both *billu* and *abnu* (stone) being used to describe the mix. The glass pot or crucible (*taptu zakatu*) had to be clean and it was stilted (*nimedu*, stilt or support) so that it did not touch the furnace ceiling. Several types of mould appear to have been used (open and closed), the moulding processes possibly having been derived from bronze-working. The cuneiform texts also mention the hook or rake (*mutirru*, Syr. *mattara*, Lat. *rutabulum*), and a ladle (*su'lu*) for moving molten glass from large glass pots to smaller ones and for skimming the batch. When producing the frit, the instructions were:

When the glass assumes the colour of ripe (red) grapes, you keep it boiling (for a time) [this is probably the evolution of carbon dioxide from the reaction between the sodium carbonate and the silica]. [Then] you pour it [the glass] on a kiln-fired brick ... You put [it] into a kiln which has four fire openings and place it on a stand ... You keep a good and smokeless fire burning [so that the flames come out of the openings] ... Not until the glass glows red do you close the

door of the kiln and stir it once 'towards you' [with a rake] until it becomes yellow [hot]. After it has become yellow [hot], you observe some drops [forming at the tip of the rake]. If the glass is homogeneous [without bubbles] you pour it [inside the kiln] into a new *dabtu-pan* ... (Oppenheim *et al.*, 1970)

The constructional differences between the fritting furnace and the fusion furnace have been noted by Oppenheim *et al.* (1970). There are a number of technologically important observations to be made here: the use of a red heat (less than 850°C) for the first fritting and a yellow heat (1100°C) for the second firing, and also the use of a smokeless fire, so that reducing conditions were avoided. By experiment, these conditions can now be seen to be important for the success of the operation. Nevertheless, the variability in composition of the plant ash must have been a frequent source of failures. Analyses of plant ash from bushes, bracken and seaweed showed that the soda content could vary widely, from 14.2 to 42.5 per cent. Each complete glassmaking operation might have produced about 3500 cm³ of *zuku* frit and 800 cm³ (about 2 kg) of the copper-containing red glass (Brill, 1970b,c).

Mesopotamian glass

Transparent glasses

In view of such limited knowledge, it is unlikely that the glassmakers could make the slight deliberate additions of antimony or manganese which, it has been suggested, were required to decolourize the glass (Sayre, 1963). Such additions were probably accidental as impurities in the raw materials forming the glass batch (Newton, 1985b).

Analytical results for Mesopotamian transparent glasses are quoted by Turner (1954b) and by Brill (1970c). The glasses would be expected to be reasonably durable. Two samples quoted by Turner (1954b) showed weathering, equivalent to losses of substance of 0.18 mm per century (sample A) and 0.04 mm per century (sample B). However, all the non-red glasses from this era have much the same composition, and Turner (1954b) commented that it is a remarkable fact that glass from Nimrud, from Eighteenth Dynasty

Egypt, and from Knossos in Crete have so much resemblance in composition despite the fact that they are spread over 700 years and a distance of 1700 km. This could be explained by the possibility that all the glassmaking was carried out in Syria, and only glass-melting was performed in the other centres. A dark blue ingot found at Eridu (about 175 km WNW of Basra) and dated to about 2000 BC (Brill, 1970b,c), seems to have been an ingot for remelting and this aspect of glassworking occurs repeatedly in the history of glass – that is, that the secret of making good quality glass was by no means known to all glassworkers and many of them, perhaps even most, had to obtain their best glass from other sources (Forbes, 1966, 1961; Brill, 1970c), and this still applied almost four thousand years later (Charleston, 1963, 1967; Oppenheim *et al.*, 1970; Newton, 1971b,c).

The possibility that the raw glass (cullet) was all made in Upper Syria, and that it was based on a traditional recipe, with manufacturing processes that were well-guarded secrets, may be a more feasible explanation of this uniformity in composition than the alternative hypothesis that different glassmakers experimented with different local raw materials, even though they might be following a traditional recipe. (However, it has to be borne in mind that any glass having a distinctly different composition from those surviving may have had such a poor durability that it may have entirely perished during the intervening millennium.)

Opal glasses

There are two kinds of Mesopotamian glass which deserve special mention: the green and yellow opals which contain yellow lead antimonate ($Pb_2Sb_2O_7$) and the copper-containing sealing wax red glasses which had to be used in a special manner (in this early period they do not contain much lead, in contrast to the high-lead sealing wax red of the seventh century BC). The use of lead antimonate is particularly interesting because it seems that the Assyrians had no direct knowledge of antimony as such.

Brill (1970d) points out that the yellow $Pb_2Sb_2O_7$ was added to the blue transparent glass (*tersītu*) to form a greenish-coloured

artificial lapis lazuli, and hence the lead antimonate is likely to be either *anzahhu* or *būsu*. It also seems that *anzahhu* was prepared by craftsmen other than the glassmakers and that it had been known over a period of fifteen centuries; it could therefore have been an article of trade and its use by the Assyrians need not imply a knowledge of the properties of antimony, either as an opacifier or as a decolourizer. The sealing wax red glasses are of even greater interest; their colour is due to the presence of colloidal cuprous oxide (Cu_2O) and its manufacture has its difficulties even today. It must be prepared under suitable reducing conditions, or the Cu_2O will be oxidized to give a transparent blue glass (Brill, 1970d), and the cuneiform texts specify that closed containers and long firing times should be used, and that the glass should be cooled within the kiln.

Cable (personal communication, 1979) melted some of these glasses and points out that the cast slabs all have a black tarnished metallic lustre. If the surface film of metallic oxide was ground away, and the pieces reheated, the surface blackened again within 2 mm at 550°C, at which temperature the glass is still quite solid, and thus such a glass could not have been hot-worked, as was the case with the other glasses. Turner (1954b) stated that, in 1952, the archaeologist Mallowan discovered traces of furnaces at Nimrud, and nearby cakes of sealing wax red glass had fragments of charcoal on them (which would have helped to maintain the necessary reducing conditions until the glass was cold). Secondly, that from such cakes of opaque glass Egyptian craftsmen cut thin plates, which were ground and polished to use as inlays on funerary furniture. It thus seems likely that the sealing wax glasses were used only for lapidary purposes and not for hot-working. Brill (1970c) also remarked on the dark surface of the glass.

Egyptian furnaces and melting procedures

Due to lack of archaeological evidence before the late twentieth century, it had been generally held that the Egyptians had failed to learn the secret of glassmaking, despite the fact that they were skilled craftsmen in general, and included glassmakers, i.e. makers of artefacts from glass cullet, imported from Upper Syria (Turner, 1954a). However, work carried out in Egypt in 1993 and 1994, which included the construction and firing of a glassmaking kiln (see below), has demonstrated that the ancient Egyptians did in fact have the technology to produce glass from its raw materials (Nicholson, 1997). Reuren *et al.* (1998) published details of a glass colouring works within a copper-centred Bronze Age industrial complex at Qantir in the Nile Delta.

Oppenheim (1973) gives evidence for stating that 'The craftsmen who produced the magnificent glass objects for the Egyptian Court depended for their basic raw materials, or for the essential ingredient thereof, on imports from Asia'. It is evident, from the urgency of the appeals from the Kings of Egypt for *ehlipakku* and *mekku* (both words for raw glass, the former of Hurrian origin and the latter West Semitic) that the Egyptians had initially failed to learn the secret of the Assyrian fritting technique. Communication between Egypt and Mesopotamia would have been infrequent, and of course the Mesopotamians would have guarded their glass production recipes, thus maintaining the status quo.

In the light of the foregoing, it is perhaps suprising that the earliest Egyptian glassworking complex known, at Tell el-Amarna (excavated by Flinders-Petrie in 1891), is dated over 100 years later than the discovery of glassworking in Egypt. Tell-el-Amarna, the new capital of Akhenaton, required a large amount of decorative work, with the result that factories sprang up to supply the materials. Glazes and glass were the two principal manufactures, in which a variety and brilliancy was achieved that was never reached in earlier or later times in Egypt. So far as the use of glazes is possible, this period shows the highest degree of success, and the greatest variety of application.

The sites of three or four glass factories, and two large glazing works were discovered; and although the actual workrooms had almost vanished, the waste heaps were full of fragments which showed the types of product and their method of manufacture. Frits made in Egypt from the Twelfth Dynasty onward were composed of silica, lime, alkaline carbonates and copper carbonate varying from 3 per cent in delicate greenish blue, up to 20 per cent in rich purple blue. The green tints were always produced when iron was present, which was usually the case when sand was the source of silica.

One of the first requisites therefore was to obtain raw materials free from iron. The question of how this was achieved was answered with the discovery of a piece of a pan of frit, which had been broken in the furnace and rejected before the frit had completely combined. This contained chips of white silica throughout the mass, which were clearly the result of using crushed quartz pebbles as a source of silica instead of sand. The lime, alkali and copper had already combined, and the silica was in the course of solution and combination with the alkali and lime. The carbonic acid in the alkali and lime had been partly liberated by the dissolved silica, and had raised the mass into a spongy paste. With longer continued heating the silica in other samples had entirely disappeared, and formed a mixture of more or less fusible silicates. These made a pasty mass when kept at the temperature required to produce the fine colours. The mass was then moulded into pats, and heated in the furnace until the desired tint was reached. On being cooled, a soft, crystalline, porous friable cake of colour was produced.

Amongst the furnace waste were many white quartz pebbles. These had been laid as a cobble floor in the furnace, and served as a clean space on which to roast the pats of colour, scraps of which were found adhering to the cobbles. The floor also served to lay objects on for glazing; superfluous glaze had spread over the pebbles in a thin green wash. Doubtless this use of the pebbles was two-fold; they provided a clean furnace floor, and they became disintegrated by the repeated heating so that they were the more readily crushed for mixture in the frits afterwards.

The half-pan of uncombined frit shows the size and form of the fritting pans: about 254 mm across and 76 mm deep. Among the furnace waste were also many pieces of cylindrical jars, about 178 mm across and 127 mm high. These jars almost always bore runs of glaze on the outside from the base to the rim; the glaze, being of various colours, blue, green, white, black etc., evidently leaked from the pans, hence the jars must have stood mouth downward in the furnace to support the fritting pans and glass crucibles above the fire.

Of the furnaces used for glass-melting, there was no certain example; but a furnace discovered near the great mould and glaze factory contained a great quantity of charcoal, but no trace of pans, jars or glass. The furnace was an irregular square varying from 1092 mm to 1448 mm at the sides. It was originally about 889 mm high, but the roof had been destroyed. The northern door was 737 mm high and 381 mm wide, to admit the north wind and to serve for tending the furnace on the windward side. The south or exit door was 406 mm high and 330 mm wide to allow gases to escape. Probably the glazing furnaces were based on the same principle, and perhaps even the same furnace would be used for varying purposes.

Of the stages of production of the glass there is ample evidence. The crucibles in which it was melted were deeper than the fritting pans, being about 58 and 76 mm in depth and diameter. Their form was known from the shape of unused pieces of glass showing the section of the vessels in which they cooled. Many such pieces of glass were found retaining the rough surface, and even chips of crucible adhering to them, while the ancient top surface shows the smooth melted face, with edges drawn up by capillary action.

The upper part of the glass was often frothy and useless. The presence of the froth (of carbonic acid expelled by the melting reaction) suggests that the glass was fused in the pans. The manner in which the crucible had been chipped off the lump of solidified glass in every case shows that the glass was left to cool in the crucible so as to allow the scum gradually to rise and the sediment to sink. If the glass had been poured out these features would not have been found, on the contrary masses of cast glass should have been in evidence. While the glass was being made samples were taken out by means of pincers, to test the colour and quality, and many of these samplings were found showing the impression of the round-tipped pincers.

Analysis of the crucibles showed that they were not made of clay in the true sense but seemed to consist of mud and sand mixed together. Heating trials showed that the crucibles would have begun to vitrify at a temperature of 1100°C and that they fused to a black mass after 1 hour at 1150°C. It seems likely that the highest temperature for prolonged heating would be lower than 1100°C, and since no really high temperature could have been attained therefore, the glass was probably worked in a pasty state, mainly by drawing out threads and constantly marvering them on a flat slab. This supposition seems to be borne out by the excavated evidence (Petrie, 1894).

Petrie's excavations have since been supplemented by those of the Egypt Exploration Society (Nicholson, 1995; Nicholson and

Figure 3.47 Kilns excavated at Tell el-Amarna, in Egypt, site 045.1. Kiln 3 (left) and kiln 2 (right) are believed to have been used for melting glass. An extensive layer of vitrified clay can be seen on the right side of kiln 3. The scale rods are 2 metres long. (Courtesy of P.T. Nicholson, Egypt Exploration Society).

Jackson, 1997). Jackson *et al.* (1998) believed that the long-held contention that all raw glass had to be imported from Syria might be incorrect; and remarked that neither Petrie nor his colleague Howard Carter had given the exact locations for the glazing factories, which had been discovered in the 1890s. A proton magnotometer survey was undertaken in an area believed to be near one of Petrie's excavations. This identified an area thought worthy of excavation; preliminary work was undertaken in 1993 and was followed up the following year (Nicholson, 1997).

During the 1994 excavations, two large furnaces were revealed (*Figure 3.47*), roughly circular, with a 1.5 m internal diameter, and formed of three layers of brickwork. The furnaces contained vitrified material (known locally as *khorfush*), which proved to be the remains of vitrified brick and of a 'sacrificial render' (lining material), making it clear that the furnaces had not been used for smelting metal. In order to determine whether such large furnaces could have reached and maintained the high temperatures required for glassmaking, a replica was constructed, using local materials as representative as possible of those used in ancient times, and glass made in it. The raw materials used were plant ash prepared from seaweed from Penarth (South Wales, UK), local sand and modern cullet in the form of crushed green bottle glass, and the fuel was wood. After five hours' firing, temperatures of 1100–1150°C were achieved, and a satisfactory glass obtained. The experiment thus demonstrated that glassmaking could have been in existence in Egypt by *circa* 1350 BC.

Glassmaking during the Roman Empire

In contrast with the considerable amount of glass surviving from the Roman period, there is a dearth of evidence regarding the actual glassworking operations (Strong and Brown, 1976). Remains of a Roman furnace site at Trier excavated in 1922 helped to identify the type of crucible used. Iron tubes excavated at Badajoz (Spain), may have been glassblowing pipes (Lang and Price, 1975).

Unlike Roman pottery kilns, which were sunk in the ground, glass furnaces were built

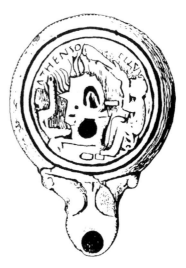

Figure 3.48 A scene on the discus of a lamp showing two glassworkers at a glass furnace. First century AD. Asseria, Dalmatia.

at ground level or even raised above it. The glass furnaces mentioned by Pliny (AD 77) were probably small beehive-shaped hearth furnaces with one or two compartments for annealing the glass. The earliest contemporary evidence of Roman glassworking would seem to be a representation on a clay lamp, attributable to the first century AD, of what may reasonably be taken to be two glassworkers at a furnace. The details are far from clear, but it seems that the furnace was in two tiers at least; presumably a stoke-hole below (represented by the filling hole in the lamp itself) and a chamber above (*Figure 3.48*).

During the latter half of the twentieth century, excavations in many countries formerly under Roman occupation, have revealed the remains of glassworking operations (Jackson *et al.*, 1991; Seibel, 2000; Nenna, in Kordas, 2002; Skordara *et al.*, in Kordas, 2002). However, the degree to which glassworking of chunk glass imported from Mediterranean glassmaking sites was carried out, and actual manufacture of glass from its raw materials in the north is still under consideration.

Glassmaking had spread to Gaul (France) and the Rhineland (Germany) by at least 50 AD. The structural remains of Roman glass

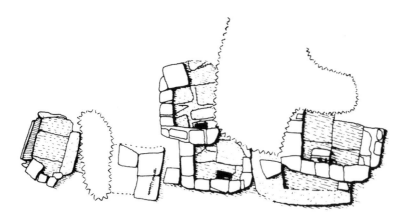

Figure 3.49 Plan of the furnaces excavated at Eigelstein near Cologne, Germany, showing successive rebuildings of the furnaces on the same site. Overall measurements: *c.* 4.9 m.

furnaces had been excavated at Eigelstein near Cologne before the Second World War (*Figure 3.49*). Although the excavation plans of the site were destroyed during the war, it is known that the remains represented the lower courses of both circular and rectangular structures, somewhat separate from each other, but without any clear indication of their relationship. The excavations showed that the furnaces had been rebuilt, each rebuilding being carried out over the previous furnaces, which had been razed to their foundations. Between the layers fragments of completely colourless glass were found (Doppelfeld, 1965).

Five glassworking sites excavated in the Hambacher forest area of the Rhineland revealed two types of furnace, the one circular and the other semi-circular, along with refractories and glass articles. The raw material may have been chunk glass, possibly imported from the Mediterranean (Hadera, Israel) (Seibel, 2000).

In Britain, the excavation of putative Roman glass sites found at Wilderspool and Middlewich in Cheshire, Mancetter in Warwickshire, Wroxeter in Shropshire and Caistor St Edmund in Norfolk have revealed little structural detail. Five workshops were found at Wilderspool; the furnaces were described as small oval ovens with outlets and flues. Work in 1964–5 and 1969–71 on a Roman glass site at Mancetter revealed a small, almost circular (880 mm × 770 mm) furnace (Hurst Vose, 1980). It is presumed that the glass made in this furnace was melted from cullet.

Brill (1963) carried out melting experiments using a gradient furnace, and concluded that a typical silica–soda–lime Roman glass would require a final melting temperature (i.e. when ground up and remixed after the fritting operation) of 1100°C; and that the glass would have had to be held at a temperature of at least 1080°C for satisfactory glass-blowing operations to be performed.

Near Eastern glassmaking

Surviving *in situ* in a cave in the ancient Jewish necropolis of Bet She'arim, Israel, is a massive glass slab, measuring approximately 3.40 × 1.95 × 0.45 metres, and which is estimated to weigh about nine tonnes. It was extensively investigated by Brill and Wosinski (1965), and was originally dated to the fourth century AD. The date now assigned to the slab is early ninth century AD. The glass was obviously melted in a tank furnace in site, however the process failed due to the composition of the glass, which contained far too much lime so that it either did not melt fully or devitrified extensively upon cooling.

Although the slab is the only one intact and *in situ*, it is not unique in the ancient glassmaking world. A group of seventeen tank furnaces, each of which produced large slabs of glass has been excavated at Bet Eli'ezer near Hadera (Israel) (*Figure 3.50*). On the basis of associated finds, the group is dated to the sixth to seventh centuries AD (Perrot, 1971; Freestone and Gorin-Rosen, 1999). The furnaces seem to be connected to the produc-

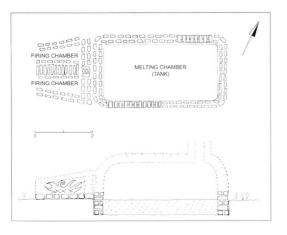

Figure 3.50 Schematic plan and reconstructed section of a sixth- to seventh-century AD furnace at Bet Eli'ezer, Hadera, Israel (Drawing: Michael Miles). (Corning Museum of Glass).

tion of primary unformed glass from local sources of sand and alkali, and their situation to be a consequence of the nearby source of fine sand, with a long proven used for glass-making, at the mouth of the River Belus.

Evidence for primary glassmaking is also found on a large scale in the region of Alexandria and the Wadi el-Natrun in Egypt. It seems likely that in the late Byzantine period (sixth to seventh centuries AD, and perhaps earlier), raw glass was manufactured near the source of raw materials and then exported for fabrication into glass objects at other sites.

The analysis of chunk glass from Bet Eli'ezer, Dor and Apollonia, all dated to the sixth and seventh centuries, and later Islamic glass from Barias (eleventh to thirteenth centuries), and a group of glass vessels from Ramla (eighth to eleventh centuries) showed them all to be silica–soda–lime glasses; but that the levels of potash and manganese were much higher in the later Islamic glass from Barias than in the Byzantine glass. The transition from the lower manganese/high potash composition to the high manganese/low potash composition had been observed by Sayre and Smith in 1961, and is generally considered to reflect a change of raw materials.

Throughout the Roman and Byzantine periods, glasses produced in the Mediterranean area were based on the use of natron, a relatively pure mineral soda, as a flux. However, in the Islamic period, a plant ash containing potash, magnesia and lime in addition to soda, was introduced (Henderson, 1985). Plant ash had been used to make glass in Mesopotamia in the Parthian and Sassanian periods (Smith, 1963a,b; Sayre, 1965), so this change in the source of alkali does not represent an entirely new glass technology. In Egypt, the changeover from natron based, low magnesium glass to a high magnesium plant ash has been dated to the middle of the ninth century AD, based on the analysis of glass weights inscribed with the names of officials, and therefore datable (Sayre and Smith, 1974; Gratuze and Barrandon, 1990). The two types of glass have been found together in eighth- to ninth-century dumps at Raqqa in Syria (Henderson, 1995); and glass samples from Ramla indicate that the new high magnesium composition was introduced in the eighth and ninth centuries with some overlap in the use of natron-based glass (Freestone, 2001).

The major change in glass composition, which occurred in the Near East during the eighth and ninth centuries, had an impact as far away as northwestern Europe, where a change from natron-based silica-soda–lime glass to a potash-rich forest glass composition was taking place about the same time (Hunter, 1981; Henderson, 1991, 1993a).

Paradoxically, it is only with the Dark Ages that evidence becomes available to indicate what early glassmaking furnaces were like. Under the unifying influence of the Roman Empire, glassmaking practices in different parts of the Empire remained much the same. Around the time of the collapse of the Empire, however, a marked cleavage in glass technology occurred, the origins of which are still not completely certain. Different styles of glassmaking furnace developed north and south of the Alps and it has been suggested that this was the result of the supply of maritime plants having become scarce at a time when there was a great demand for coloured glass in northern Europe. This caused the glassmakers to migrate to forested areas where a supply of alkali could be obtained in the form of plant ash. The distribution of glassmaking sites north of the Alps closely corresponds to the distribution of beech woods (Barrelet, 1953; Newton, 1985b). Newton (1985b) has suggested that the northern type of furnace (which had a good draught) was adapted for using beechwood, whereas the southern type of furnace (in areas deficient of beech forests) were able to continue using traditional sources of alkali, and continued to be of the traditional furnace design.

The southern European type of glassmaking furnace

The first reasonably full description of a southern type of furnace is given in a Syrian manuscript (in the British Museum), which apparently cannot be dated earlier than the ninth century AD:

> The furnace of the glassmakers should have six compartments, of which three are disposed in storeys one above the other ... the lower compartment should be deep, in it is the fire; that of the middle storey has an opening in front of the central chambers, these last should be equal, disposed on the sides and not in the center[?], so that the fire from below may rise towards the central region where the glass is and heat and melt the materials. The upper compartment, which is vaulted, is arranged so as uniformly to roof over the middle storey; it is used to cool the vessels after their manufacture.

Not all the details of this account are clear, but the essentials are that the furnace was in three storeys, with a fire chamber at the bottom, a central chamber into which the heat rises to melt the glass, and a vaulted upper compartment in which the glass may cool.

This arrangement may be seen in the earliest certain representation of a glass furnace (*Figure 3.51*) in a manuscript dating from 1023 in the library at Monte Cassino, a text of the work *De Universo* by Hrabanus Maurus (Archbishop of Mainz *c.* 776–856). Again the details are not unequivocally clear, but the artist appears to have attempted to represent a cylindrical structure, although the roof is shown as a simple tent shape. The manuscript may have been a copy of an earlier one dating

from the fourth or fifth century AD. The main body of the furnace has been interpreted as being rectangular in plan, but this seems unlikely from the elliptical rendering of the glory holes, which would certainly not in any case be made at the corners of a rectangular structure; furthermore, the tent-like upper storey is carefully depicted as being adapted to the curved structure below. The essential features, however, are these: a single stoke-hole at the bottom, a middle chamber with multiple glory holes giving access to glass pots, and an upper compartment in which a glass may be seen annealing. If indeed the furnace represented was cylindrical or round in section, the illumination provides a most useful link, for on the one hand the later furnaces of this type were almost always circular, while on the other hand the remains of a seventh/eighth-century glassmaking complex on the Venetian island of Torcello, excavated in 1961/2 (Gasparetto, 1965, 1967; Tabaczynska, 1968), include the foundations of a circular structure which may have been a fritting furnace. However, it seems far more likely to have been the main (founding) furnace since it stood in the middle of the complex, as would be natural for the working furnace to which all surrounding structures are

Figure 3.51   The earliest illustration of a glass furnace three tiers high. The craftsman on the three-legged stool is blowing a vessel, another vessel can be seen undergoing the annealing process in the top compartment of the kiln. Illustrated miniature from the manuscript of Hrabanus Maurus, *De Universo*, datable to 1023 AD. Abbey of Monte Cassino. (Codex 132).

ancillary. A study of the site shows that temperatures of 1270°C had been reached in the melting furnace.

The glass mosaics used for decorating the Basilica of Santa Maria Assunta on Torcello started in AD 639 were probably made in the furnaces described above, but the glassworks was so close to the church (only about 35 m to the west of its walls) that it seems likely that it was dismantled when the basilica was completed. The spread of broken pots, glass waste etc. on the site was probably the result of clearance and disturbance at the time of demolition.

On a glass site at Corinth in Greece (Weinberg, 1975) (Agora, South Centre site) however, dating from the eleventh/twelfth century, the foundations of a square furnace were unearthed which, from the absence of any ancillary furnace, were reasonably taken by the excavators to have been the lowest storey of a three-tiered arrangement (Weinberg, 1975). The original conclusions have been modified by later finds, notably some limestone blocks covered with glass drippings which seem to suggest that either small rectangular tanks (320 mm × 270 mm) or square containers were used in the glassmaking process. Finds of refractory pots with glass adhering, however, found in association with the Agora north-east glassmaking complex (if such it is) suggest the more normal method of founding the metal. Fragments of glass found in the Agora South Centre have been reinterpreted as pontil wads and suggest that (unless they were cullet, which seems somewhat unlikely) glass was actually worked in the vicinity of this furnace (i.e. that it was not merely a fritting or annealing furnace). The fact that there was so little space surrounding the furnace structure (barely 500 mm on three sides) is the strongest counter-indication.

A furnace excavated at Monte Lecco in the Apennines about 30 km from Genoa, and probably dating from the late fourteenth or early fifteenth century clearly revealed a circular structure, with a central fire trench running between two roughly segmented solid sieges (banks on which the glass pots stood). The fire trench was dug down into an ash pit in the ground at the front, and had an outlet at the bank, presumably for the clearance of ashes. The furnace has been tentatively reconstructed as a three-tiered structure on the basis of a picture, perhaps dating from *circa* 1590, in the Oratorio of St Rocco at Altare. The absence of any structures in the immediate vicinity of the furnace suggests that all the processes were carried out in the one furnace, and that this was therefore likely to have been a three-tiered structure.

As the finds at Torcello suggest, the circular furnace (perhaps in three storeys) was probably of the first type used by the Venetian glassmakers who, from the mid-fifteenth century at the latest, began to dominate the world markets with their superior crystal glass. Two illuminations in manuscripts in the Vatican library portray glassmakers at work (Charleston, 1978). The cruder of the two shows two glassblowers sitting on three-legged stools, while another man attends to the stoke-hole. On the furnace is written unequivocally *fornax vitr* (glass furnace). It is represented clearly as three storeys, the upper two set slightly back, and this detail is repeated in the second miniature. Here, however, four out of the six ribs are visible, rising from the broader ledge just below the level of the *bocca*. This ledge no doubt provided space for a marver. The *bocca* is shown as a round-topped arched opening, and the glassblower to the right holds his iron with his right hand in the circular *boccarella* (or little mouth). In front there is a circular aperture through which perhaps the tiseur could check the condition of the fire: alternatively, it may indicate in false perspective the central opening of the furnace. From the sixteenth century there survives an eyewitness account of an Italian furnace. In 1508, Peder Månsson, a Swedish priest living in Rome, interested himself closely in the glass industry, then unknown in Scandinavia, and compiled an account of it (Månsson, 1520). Månsson described the furnace as follows:

> The second furnace, in which the glass is to be founded, is more difficult to build. It must be entirely built and walled up with damp clay capable of resisting the fiercest heat, and must be in the middle of a wide, roomy house. You lay the foundation wall round in a circle, with a diameter of 3.8 m (12 ½ ft). At the point where the furnace mouth is to be beneath the ground, you lay no wall

foundation. This furnace must have three arches, one above the other. The first and lowest arch must occupy the whole interior right up to the walls, and not be higher than 760 mm (2 ½ ft) from the floor and 508 mm (1 ft 8 in) in diameter. [This must mean 'in width'. Vault would perhaps give a clearer idea of the construction than arch.] On this arch must be set the pots in which the glass frit is put. Then you arrange the wall outside so that it has six thin ribs, and between each set of ribs you reserve an opening, through which the glass mass is drawn out, worked, inserted and handled. Directly in front of each opening a pot must be set in the furnace with the batch in such a way that the height exactly suits the opening. The second arch is made 1.27 m (4 ft 2 in) high above the first, extending over the whole furnace, except for a round opening, 250–380 mm (10–15 in) in diameter in the middle of the arch. Round the top of the opening there must be a ledge, so that the glasses, when put there to cool, may not fall down into the furnace. The third and top arch extends over the whole furnace, and there must be 1.0 m (3 ft 4 in) between it and the second arch, and three openings 250 mm (10 in) broad, through which the smoke discharges and the glasses are put in to cool. The furnace mouth below in the earth should be 510 mm (1 ft 8 in) broad. You stoke it with dry wood, the length of which corresponds to the inner breadth of the furnace; and for this purpose one digs out the earth in front of the furnace mouth ...

This suggests that there may have been a fire trench in the furnace, and this detail together with the mention of digging out the earth in front of the furnace, strongly recalls the furnace at Monte Lecco. A woodcut illustrating a glass furnace of this type appears in *De la Pirotechnia* (Biringuccio, 1540) (*Figure 3.52*). This shows a hive-shaped furnace with six external ribs, the stoke-hole to the front, the tiseur carrying an armful of faggots with which to replenish it. The glassblowers sit on either side on three-legged stools. In front of each (seen better on the right-hand side of the woodcut) is a screen to protect the blower from the glare of the glory hole, through which the glass pots are reached. Projecting from the side of the furnace below is a marble

Figure 3.52 Woodcut depicting glassworkers at a furnace, illustrating Vannoccio Biringuccio, *De La Pirotechnia*, Venice, 1540.

shelf supported on an arch, the rudimentary form of the modern marver, on which the glass drawn from the pot is rolled to smooth it as a preliminary to blowing.

Biringuccio describes the furnace as follows:

Now in order to complete the purification, a round furnace is built of rough bricks from a clay that does not melt or calcine from the fire. Its vault has a diameter of about four *braccia* (550 mm) and a height of six *bracchia* (3.32 m). It is arranged in this way. First a passage for the fire is made which leads the flames into the middle of the furnace; around the circle at the bottom a shelf ¾ *braccio* wide (100 mm) is made on which are to be placed the pots that hold the glass, and this must be about one *bracchio* (140 mm) above the ground. Around this five or six well-made little arches are built as supports for the vault, and under these are made the little openings which allow one to look inside and to take out the glass for working at will. Then the vault is continued to cover the glass, and only in the middle is a little opening of a *palmo* (280 mm) or less left. Above this vault another vault is made which seals up and covers the whole; this is two *braccia* (280 mm) high above the first so that it completes the reverbatory furnace. This is the cooling chamber for the works when they have been made, for if they did not receive a certain tempering of air in this, all the vessels would break as soon as they were finished when they felt the cold.

By a curious convention, the illustrator of Biringuccio's work, in representing the top storey, or annealing chamber of the furnace, has shown the holes through which the glasses were inserted to anneal as seen from the outside, but has cut away the central panel of the furnace wall to reveal on the inside the hole through which the heat ascends from the founding chamber to the annealing chamber above. This cut is defective in many ways. It does not for example illustrate the arches made above the siege to accommodate the working openings. These arches were structurally necessary to support the vault above them when the glass pots were changed, as was necessary when an old pot cracked or otherwise became defective, and a new, preheated pot had to be substituted quickly with the minimum disturbance to the general working of the furnace. Biringuccio (1540) gave some indication of how this was achieved:

> After six or eight months from the time they were made, when you wish to put them [the glass pots] in the furnace in order to begin work, that place which you left open under the arches is a quarter closed with a wall and only enough space is left to allow one of the said vessels to enter ...

The aperture was then closed with clay, making two small holes from one large one so that the worker can take out the glass with his tube from whichever vessel he wishes in order to work it. In the other opening he keeps another iron tube so that it will be hot. Outside in front of these openings there is a support made of a marble shelf placed on an arch. Above this shelf and in front of the opening for the glass a screen is made to serve as a protection for the eyes of the workers and to carry an iron support which holds up the tube ...

These hooks (*halsinelle*) or supports for the blowing iron and pontil are not shown in Biringuccio's woodcut. Probably at a quite early date it was found convenient to incorporate the working opening in a slab of fire clay, which could be removed and replaced when the pots were changed. Fragments of such slabs were found on the early seventeenth-century glassmaking site at Jamestown in Virginia, USA (Harrington, 1952) and have been reported from glassmaking sites in

474   DE RE METALLICA

Sed qui carent prima fornace, hi, cùm munus diurnũ perfecerint, uesperi materiã in ollas inijciũt: quæ noctu cocta liquescit & in uitrũ abit. Duo aũt pueri

Figure 3.53 Woodcut illustrating G. Agricola, *Die Re Metallica*, Basle, 1556, showing the three-tier 'second glass furnace', i.e. annealing furnace.

Denmark. The structure of these arched openings, not shown in Biringuccio's woodcut, is illustrated in the woodcuts to what is perhaps the most systematic account of glassmaking surviving from the sixteenth century, the twelfth chapter of Georgius Agricola's *De Re Metallica* (1556) (*Figures 3.53* and *3.54*).

In many particulars Agricola was obviously dependent on Biringuccio as a source of information, but the situation on glassmaking which he described was far more complex, probably because in Agricola's time, in Saxony and elsewhere in Germany, the indigenous

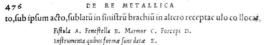

to,ſub ipſum acto,ſublatū in ſiniſtrū brachiū in altero receptaculo collocat.

Fiſtula A, Feneſtella B, Marmor C, Forceps D,
Inſtrumenta quibus formæ ſunt datæ E.

Vitrarij

Figure 3.54 Woodcut illustrating G. Agricola, *De Re Metallica*, Basle, 1556, depicting a southern glass furnace of the sixteenth century. The furnace has three sections, the lower one for the fire, the middle one for the glass pots, and the upper one for annealing the glass. The glass blowers are working around the furnace and the vessels are packed in the large box seen in the bottom right-hand corner. In the background the sale of the glass is being discussed, and a pedlar carries away the vessels. In the sixteenth century the customer either ordered his glass direct from the maker or bought it from the travelling hawker.

'northern' tradition was being penetrated by the Venetian tradition. The detailed woodcuts in *De Re Metallica* show a three-tiered furnace. In *Figure 3.54* the arched openings to the siege storey of the furnace can be seen (but with a square *bocca* and no *boccarella*), and

in the sectional rendering there is an indication of the vault supporting the siege itself, the central holes allowing the passage of the heat (the upper one square instead of circular), and the arched opening allowing access to the annealing chamber. In his text Agricola refers to 'six arched openings' but the illustration would suggest that there were at least eight. A similar discrepancy appears in his description of the two-storey 'second furnace' which is said to be strengthened on the outside with five ribs whereas 'in the wall of the upper chamber between the ribs there should be eight windows ...'. The illustration suggests that there would have been at least eight ribs.

These illustrations were interpreted in a sixteenth-century wall-painting by G.M. Butteri which decorates the *studiolo* of Francesco I de' Medici in the Palazzo Vecchio in Florence. It shows the Grand Duke's glasshouse, which is known to have been of the Venetian type, and which seems to have begun operating about 1568/9. In the background of the wall-painting can be seen the great glowing furnace, the gaffers seated on their three-legged stools before the glory holes, from the glare of which they are protected by the fire-clay screen described by Biringuccio, whilst to one side and slightly lower down are the boccarelle accommodating three or more irons. The master to the left warms-in his glass at the glory hole, resting the iron on the lowest of the *balsinelle*. Above the masters' heads glow the apertures leading to the annealing chamber, through one of which a servitor (to the left of the picture) is placing a finished glass to cool. To the right of the seated gaffer, with his back to the onlooker, can be seen the stoke-hole, toward which the *tiseuer*, apparently stripped to the waist, brings a fresh bundle of faggots. Above the furnace is a framework of beams on which the wood for fuel was set to dry, with a resultant very grave risk of fire. (When the Crutched Friars glasshouse in London burned down in 1575 it had 'within it neere fortie thousand billits of wood'; Thorpe, 1961.)

The furnace in Butteri's painting appears to be a developed form of that illustrated by Biringuccio or Agricola. The ribs of the furnace delineated as rather thin in Biringuccio and Agricola here have become of considerable depth, at least at the base, thus providing a much wider working surface for the gaffer. This detail is seen again in seventeenth-century representations of Italian-type furnaces.

One curious feature of the Florence furnace is its asymmetrical form at the right-hand side, where the vault appears to project in an overhang. It seems possible that this may be the beginning of what later became the tunnel lehr. This development may be found in Biringuccio. The text is not easy to follow, but the French translation by Jacques Vincent offers an easier interpretation. Vincent (1556) writes, 'this cooling-off is effected by a certain opening made on the left-hand side', Biringuccio says 'at the back, and this channel is shaped like a trumpet; from it all the cooled vessels are skillfully drawn by means of a long iron, one after the other, in three or four goes, until they reach the mouth and are taken outside'. This 'trumpet-shaped opening' is perhaps the beginning of the lehr, and the man standing on the right of Biringuccio's woodcut is no doubt performing the office of moving the glasses along from hotter to cooler positions.

Merrett (1662), in a translation of Neri (1612) *Dell'Arte Vetraria* (The Art of Glass) (see Turner, 1962, 1963), wrote:

'The Leer (made by Agricola, the third furnace, to anneal and cool the vessels, made as the second was to melt the Metall, and to keep it in fusion) comprehends two parts, the tower and leer. The tower is that part which lies directly above the melting furnace with a partition betwixt them, a foot [300 mm] thick, in the midst whereof, and in the same perpendicular with that of the second furnace, there's a round hole [*Imperat.* and Agricola make it square and small] through which the flame and heat passeth into the tower; this hole is called *Occhio* or *Lumella*, having an Iron ring encircling it called the *Cavalet* or Crown; on the floor or bottom of this tower the vessels fashioned by the Mrs [masters] are set to anneal; it hath 2. Boccas or mouths, one opposite to the other, to put the Glasses in as soon as made, taken with a Fork by the Servitors, and set on the floor of the tower, & after some time these Glasses are put into Iron pans, Agricola makes them of clay call'd Fraches, which by degrees are

drawn by the Sarole man all along the Leer, which is five or six yards [4.5–5.5 mm] long, that all the Glasses may cool *radatim*, for when they are drawn to the end of the Leer they become cold. This leer is continued to the tower, and arched all along about four foot [1.2 m] wide and high within. The mouth thereof enters into a room, where the Glasses are taken out and set. This room they call the Sarosel.

This structure may be seen on the frontispiece of the 1669 Latin edition of Neri, published in Amsterdam (*Figure 3.55*), and a similar

Figure 3.55 Frontispiece to the 1669 Latin translation of A. Neri, *L'Arte Vetraria*.

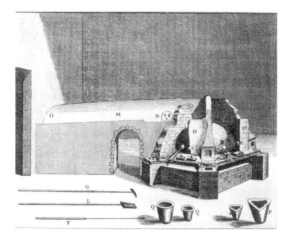

Figure 3.56 Plate IV from the French translation of A. Neri's *L'Arte Vetraria* (*Art de La Verrerie*, Paris, 1752) showing the 'Amsterdam' furnace.

Figure 3.57 Plate from Diderot, *Encyclopédie* showing '*Verrerie en Bois, Coupe et Plans d'une petite Verrerie a pivette: et Coupe de La Cave it braise*' (pl. vol. X. pl. 3) showing the grille composed of very short bars to span the firing channel.

engraving illustrates the 1752 French edition of the same work (*Figure 3.56*). In these furnaces, however, the glasses appear to have been put directly into the lehr through small doors (N in *Figure 3.56*). The same feature appears in Diderot and D'Alembert's *Encyclopédie* (1772) (*Figure 3.57*). The same volume also gives a vivid view of the interior of the lehr seen from the Sarosel room, with the *fraches* moving in two lines down the tunnel (*Figure 3.58*). An improved version of tunnel lehr was invented by George Ensell, at Coalbrook in the British Stourbridge glass-making district, about 1780, but it is not absolutely certain what the improvement was. It may well have been the provision of a separately heated lehr, perhaps one with two tunnels, for large and small objects respectively, such as became standard in British glasshouses in the nineteenth century. (By the mid-nineteenth century the pans were moved along the lehr mechanically and the double lehr had become a quadruple one.)

An illustration of an Italian furnace of the mid-eighteenth century appeared as the frontispiece of *Due Lettere di Fisica al Signor Marchese Scipione Maffei* by Gian-Lodovico Bianconi, published in Venice in 1746 (*Figure 3.59*). Although it is difficult to envisage just how this furnace worked (it seems to have derived some of its features from Kunckel although its basic principles are different, and it

seems to have one storey too many), the nature of its long lehr, with central archway, is unmistakable. A second piece of evidence concerning mid-eighteenth century furnaces is a tin-glazed pottery (*maiolica*) model of a furnace in the Science Museum, London. In this model, the long tunnel lehr is clearly in evidence, with the glass visible in the tower, apparently heated by the updraft from the founding furnace conveyed through a chimney, which does not connect directly with the floor of the lehr.

Figure 3.58 Plate from Diderot, *Encyclopédie* showing '*Verrerie en Bois, l'operation de retirer les Feraces et les transporter au Magasin*' (pl. vol. X, pl. 22).

Figure 3.59 Frontispiece to G.L. Bianconi, *Due Lettere di Fisica*, Venice, 1746. (Corning Museum of Glass).

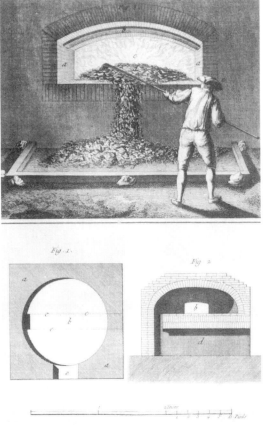

Figure 3.60 Plate from Diderot, *Encyclopédie* showing *'Verrerie en Bois, Plan et coupe de la Calcaisse, et l'Operation de retirer la fritte cuite'* (pl. vol. X. pl. 15).

The Venetian-style glasshouse had one further subsidiary furnace. This was used for the preliminary roasting (fritting) of the silica and ash. Biringuccio described this process as follows:

> Then put all these things [that is, silica, soda, and manganese for decolourizing] mixed together into the reverbatory furnace made for this purpose, three braccia long, two wide, and one high, and apply enough of the strong flames of a wood fire by means of the reverberator, so that the composition is melted well and is converted all into one mass.

Månsson confirms this general picture, adding the detail: 'The mixture is often stirred and turned around with an iron hook'. No really explicit representation, however, is available until the publication of the *Encyclopédie* (Diderot and D'Alembert, 1772) which contains an engraving showing the furnace in plan and section, and an illustration of the furnace-man at work raking the frit from the mouth of the furnace (*Figure 3.60*). Agricola's illustration of a fritting furnace also shows a round construction, although the text seems to indicate an oblong structure ('Their first furnace should be arched over and resemble an oven. In its upper compartment, six feet long, four broad, and two high, the frit is cooked ...'). The *Encyclopédie* version is square on plan although the internal shape is circular. It has the advantage that it is fired at

the side, for the greater convenience of the worker stirring the frit (Charleston, 1978).

The northern European type of glassmaking furnace

There is no evidence to throw light on the northern type of furnace as early as that available for the southern type. The earliest source is a chapter in a twelfth century manuscript, *Schedula Diversarum Artium* (Treatise on Diverse Arts), by Theophilus Presbyter (translated by Dodwell, 1961 and by Hawthorne and Smith, 1963). It is thought that Theophilus was the Benedictine monk Roger of Helmarshausen, and that the manuscript was compiled between AD 1110 and 1140. If the identification is correct, the author was a practising metal-worker who was personally able to carry out most of the techniques he described and who would certainly have described the glassmaking process with the insight of a craftsman:

> If you have the intention of making glass, first cut many beech wood logs and dry them out. Then burn them all together in a clean place and carefully collect the ashes, taking care that you do not mix any earth or stones with them. When the ashes have been well mixed for a long time, take them up with the iron shovel and put them in the smaller part of the kiln over the top of the hearth to roast [i.e. to frit]. When they begin to get hot, immediately stir them with the same shovel so they do not melt with the heat of the fire and run together. Continue this throughout a night and a day. (Dodwell, 1961; Hawthorne and Smith, 1963)

Theophilus also gives precise instructions for making crucibles out of clay, and for making glass articles, but the important point to note here is that the frit must not be allowed to melt (and, by implication, the small part of the furnace must not be allowed to get too hot) so that the solid-state reactions can continue for a long time (a night and a day) without any molten glass being formed that would trap the released carbon dioxide as bubbles in the melt.

> After this build a furnace of stones and clay fifteen feet [4.5 m] long and ten feet [3 m] wide in this way. First, lay down foundations on each long side one foot [300 mm] thick, and in between them make a firm, smooth, flat hearth with stones and clay. Mark off three equal parts and build a cross-wall separating one-third from the other two. Then make a hole in each of the short sides through which fire and wood can be put in, and building the encircling wall up to a height of almost four feet [1.2 m], again make a firm, smooth, flat hearth over the whole area, and let the dividing wall rise a little above it. After this, in the larger section, make four holes through the hearth along one of the long sides, and four along the other. The work pots are to be placed in these. Then

make two openings in the centre through which the flame can rise. Now, as you build the encircling wall, make two separate windows on each side, a span long and wide, one opposite [each] of the flame openings, through which the work pots and whatever is placed in them can be put in and taken out. In the smaller section also make an opening [for the flame] through the hearth close to the cross-wall, and a window, a span in size, near the short wall, through which whatever is necessary for the work can be put in and taken out.

> When you have arranged everything like this, enclose the interior with an outer wall, so that the inside is the shape of an arched vault, rising a little more than half a foot [150 mm], and the top is made into a smooth, flat hearth, with a threefinger-high lip all around it, so that whatever work or instruments are laid on top cannot fall off. This furnace is called the work furnace ... Now build another furnace ten feet [3 m] long, eight feet [2.5 m] wide, and four feet [1.2 m] high. Then make a hole in one of the faces for putting in and taking out whatever is necessary. Inside, make firm, smooth, flat hearth. This furnace is called the annealing furnace. ... Now build a third furnace, six feet [1.8 m] long, four feet [1.2 m] wide, and three feet [900 mm] high, with a [fire] hole, a window and a hearth as above. This furnace is called the furnace for spreading out and flattening. The implements needed for this work are an iron [blow] pipe, two cubits long and as thick as your thumb, two pairs of tongs each hammered out of a single piece of iron, two long-handled iron ladles, and such other wooden and iron tools as you want. (Smedley *et al.*, 1998)

The illustration of the model of Theophilus' furnace made at the Science Museum, London is probably incorrect in showing four working holes per side instead of two. The feature of the holes made in the siege to take pots is unique, and one is tempted to wonder whether Theophilus was not misled, by seeing in a furnace the ring of glass left on the siege when a broken pot was removed. The reconstructions (Theobald, 1933) have always been made very trim and square; the furnaces were probably always somewhat more rough and ready in practice. It should be noted that in this instance the small furnace was used for fritting, and a separate furnace for annealing. These procedures were often reversed, and sometimes the subsidiary furnace was used for both fritting and annealing. For the units of measurements used see Hawthorne and Smith (1963).

The treatise entitled *De Coloribus et Artibus Romanorum* (*On the Colours and Arts of the Romans*), attributed to a certain Eraclius (pre AD 1000), contains chapters on glassmaking which have been added, probably in the twelfth or thirteenth century, to an existing manuscript. These describe a tripartite furnace of which the largest section is in the centre and is the founding and working furnace. This has one glory hole on either side, apparently with two pots to each, perhaps in the same manner as the Theophilus furnace. To the left of this should be a smaller furnace used for fritting and pot arching, and to the right a still smaller compartment presumably for annealing. The actual ground plan of these furnaces is not prescribed, and they may not necessarily have been rectangular. (For the text, see Merrifield, 1949.) The fire trench down the middle of the whole furnace is clearly indicated, and it may be assumed that there were solid sieges to either side of it, rather than the improbably flimsy structure reproduced by Maurach.

That rectangularity was by no means the rule in practice seems to be shown by the evidence of a glass furnace at Glastonbury (UK). This appears to date from late Saxon times (between the eighth and the eleventh centuries AD). Although not enough of the structure has survived to permit an exact reconstruction, the ground plan appears to have been oval. Similarly, four furnaces attributed to the ninth century AD excavated at Nitra in Slovakia had oval ground plans. This has been interpreted to suggest that the Bohemian furnace was of a type 'entirely different from the well-known description' in Theophilus (Hejdová, 1965). It may well be, however, that the essential element in the northern tradition was not so much the rectangularity of the ground plan as the fact that the main and subsidiary furnaces (or at least one of them) were on the same level and shared their heat either by having the same fire trench running the length of the

composite furnace (as in Theophilus) or by transmitting the heat laterally from the main furnace to the subsidiary one, or by both. An arrangement of this kind can be seen in the famous illustration to Mandeville's *Travels* in a manuscript in the British Museum, London (*Plate 1*). This manuscript is thought to have been compiled in Bohemia in about 1420. There is no description accompanying the original manuscript, but that given by Kenyon (1967) seems to be the most interesting and the following is adapted from it.

All round there is forest, with a man carrying fuel in a basket, two others carrying ash in sacks, one man digging sand from a hill in a clearing in the forest with a stream at its foot, and another carrying the sand to the glasshouse in a shoulder hod. The glasshouse has a rough shingle-roofed open shed with its stoke-hole entrance sheltered by a roof made of wood billets drying on a heavy timber frame. The furnace appears to be rectangular, having rounded and domed corners with a circular flue on top. Part of the roof is missing, perhaps to allow the furnace gases to escape. The furnace may have had four crucibles, two each side, and the annealing furnace is built on at the end. Vessel glass is being made and the master, in a hat, inspects a jug with a handle; a workman is taking a vessel out to finish its annealing in a large storage jar. Two glassmakers, wearing sweat rags on their brows, are shown; one is gathering glass from a crucible with his blowing iron. The boy stoker is attending to the fire. The stream in the background suggests a need for water, for washing the sand, mixing the ash, and perhaps preparing the crucible clay.

The whole lively scene, with its emphasis on the temporary woodland shack is representative of a northern glasshouse. The artist's rendering of the crown of the furnace would suggest an oval ground plan.

An actual furnace of about this period excavated at Skenarice (in the Semily district of the present day Czech Republic) revealed an oval ground plan extended by two parallel lines of masonry, perhaps the original fire trench. Another structure close by and apparently of rectangular form has been interpreted as being the fritting furnace. Yet another furnace of this general type has been excavated in the Czech Republic at Ververi

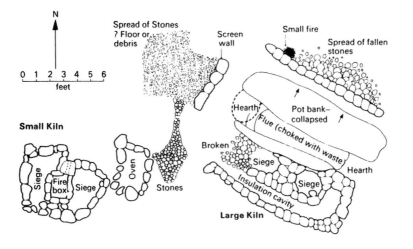

Figure 3.61 Plan of the medieval glasshouse at Blunden's Wood, Hambledon, Surrey. (After Wood, 1965).

Bityska. That the Bohemian furnace was not always oval, however, is suggested by the excavation of a late fifteenth/early sixteenth century at Pocatky (in the district of Pelhrimov, Czech Republic). Here three walls of a furnace were preserved to a height of 400 mm and revealed a rectangular ground plan. A further complex of three rectangular furnaces, dating from some time later in the sixteenth century was excavated at Rejdice. The same pattern was confirmed by finds at the nearby contemporary glassworks at Syriste (founded 1558). Whether the variation between oval and rectangular furnaces in Bohemia is a question of date or of function, it is difficult to say in the light of current available evidence.

In Britain, the rectangular furnace appears to have been the rule from, at the latest, the fourteenth century onward. At Blunden's Wood, Hambledon (Surrey), a roughly rectangular furnace dating roughly from about 1330 (*Figure 3.61*) had a central fire trench roughly 3.2 m long by probably originally 610 mm wide, with a hearth at either end; to each side of this was a siege for two pots, 2.6 m long by 690 mm wide and 610 mm high (*Figure 3.62*). This showed the unusual feature of (apparently) a cavity between the siege and the outside wall, either for insulation purposes or possibly as a means of constructing the vaulted roof. This main furnace was accompanied by two subsidiary structures, presumably for the operations of the fritting, ably for the operations of the fritting,

pot-arching and annealing (Wood, 1965) (*Figure 3.63*).

A similar furnace, brick-built and almost 6.4 m long and 770 mm wide, with clearly marked firing chambers at either end, was found well-preserved at Fernfold, Sussex, on a site connected with Jean Carré, founder of the 'modern' glass industry in Britain in 1567. A comparable furnace of early sixteenth-century date, 3.7 m long, built of brick and stone and with sieges for three pots each side, was discovered at Bagot's Park, near Abbots Bromley, Staffordshire, and one ancillary furnace was excavated in the vicinity. Almost 300 kg of cullet was found on the site. A rectangular furnace site 3.7 m long by 1.2 m wide was found at St Weonards, Herefordshire

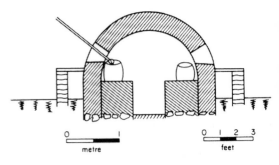

Figure 3.62 Reconstructed section of the glasshouse at Blunden's Wood, Hambledon, Surrey (see *Figure 3.58*). (After Wood, 1965).

Figure 3.63 Reconstruction by James Gardner of a medieval glasshouse, based largely on Blunden's Wood. A = main working furnace with hearth at each end; B = apertures for pots; C = hearth; D = small furnaces for annealing and pre-heating pots; E = fuel (billets of beechwood); F = cullet (broken glass); G = raw material (sand etc.); H = new pots ready for furnace (pots not made at this site); I = marver on which glass was rolled and smoothed; J = water trough for cooling; L = bed of charcoal and sand on which to rest finished crown of glass; M = finished crowns of window glass; N = blowpipe and other tools.

in 1961. It was probably built of brick and stone, a square of large stones in the centre of a burned area probably representing the foundations of the founding chamber. Further rectangular furnaces, dating from the mid-sixteenth century, with three pots per siege, were excavated at Knightons, Alfold, Surrey, in 1973 (*Figure 3.64*). Associated with these furnaces was a pair of smaller rectangular furnaces, perhaps for spreading window glass (Kenyon, 1967).

The picture at Blunden's Wood is repeated in essence at a late sixteenth- to early seventeenth-century glasshouse site at Blore Park, in Eccleshall, northwest Staffordshire. Here a fairly well preserved stone furnace foundation was found and excavated, revealing a more or less square furnace with a long fire

trench running east and west, and a siege on either side 300 mm high, 420 mm wide and 860 mm in length, accommodating two pots on each side. This furnace appeared to be complete in itself, and no other structure was excavated, although traces were found in neighbouring mounds. There is therefore no means of knowing how the ancillary processes were carried out at this site (Pape, 1933). At the more or less contemporary site of Vann, near Chiddingfold, Sussex, however, the foundations of a larger, brick-built structure were excavated, the main furnace being an oblong (3.7 m × 1.7 m) at the corners of which were four diagonally projecting, fan-shaped wings (*Figure 3.65*). These were no doubt originally used for annealing, fritting and pot-arching. There was a great concentration of medieval glasshouses in

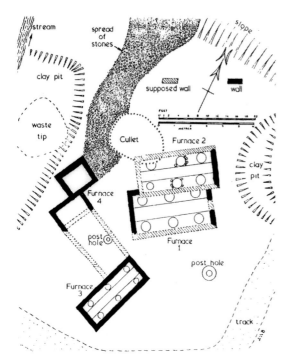

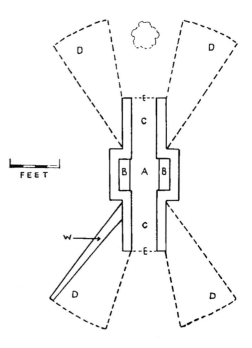

Figure 3.64 Plan of the glass furnace at Knightons, Alfold, Surrey. *Circa* 1550. Note the three six-pot furnaces, furnace 2 overlying furnace 1, and the two-chamber annealing furnace 4. (After Wood, 1965).

Figure 3.65 Plan of the Vann Copse furnace at Hambledon, Surrey, showing four 'wing' furnaces attached to the main furnace. A = fire chamber; B = sieges; C = hearth; D = (?) annealing chambers; E = hearth lip (tease hole); W = taper wing wall. (Based on a rough sketch by S.E. Winbolt, modified by A.D.R. Caroe).

the Chiddingfold area; at least 36 sites have been positively identified. (There are however by comparison 186 known medieval glass furnaces in France.) An interesting feature of the medieval forest glasshouses is that upon excavation they were found to contain very little broken glass; and it would seem that all the cullet was carefully collected when the glassmakers abandoned each site (perhaps because the furnace collapsed or because the supply of wood was exhausted in the vicinity) for use at the next.

The only excavated British glass furnace which does not fall into the general pattern of a rectangular ground plan, with or without wings, is that at Woodchester in Gloucestershire, excavated around 1904. The circular structure was apparently 4.9 m in diameter with an internal diameter of 3 m, making the walls 900 mm thick, a feature

which must arouse some doubt. The firing hole was 1 m wide on the outside and 910 mm on the inside, exceptionally wide. If any feature still remains, a new excavation would be highly desirable. An adjacent rectangular structure 2.7 m by 2.1 m was interpreted as an annealing furnace. It has been suggested that the round furnace at Woodchester may be explained by the presence there of Flemish glassmakers. All these glasshouses made green forest glass, and their structure was described by Merrett in 1662:

The Green Glass furnaces are made square, having at each angle an arch to anneal their Glasses ... For green Glass on two opposite sides they work their Metall, and on the other sides they have their Calcars, into which linnet holes are made for the fire to come from the furnace, to bake and to prepare their

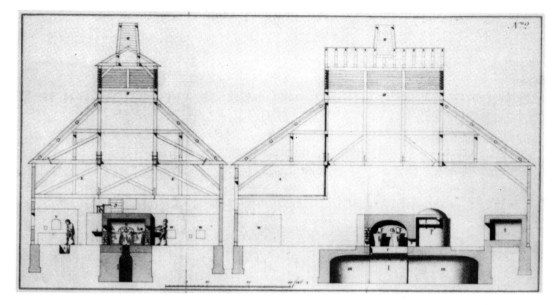

Figure 3.66   View of a bottle-house in Gravel Lane, Southwark, London. *Circa* 1777. c represents the grill.
(Drawing by C.W. Carlberg).

Frit, and also for the discharge of the smoke. But they make fires in the arches, to anneal their vessels, so that they make all their processes in one furnace onely.

This general layout of furnace survived in Britain and France until at least the 1770s, although the adapted Venetian-type furnace was by now well established in both countries. Its characteristic of heating subsidiary furnaces through linnet holes recalls the two-chamber furnaces of Theophilus and the Mandeville illumination (*Plate 1*). This plan appears to have survived in Germany until at least the end of the seventeenth century.

A four-pot bottle furnace with two (circular) wings was in operation from at least 1777 in Gravel Lane, Southwark, London (*Figures 3.66 and 3.67*). Here one wing was used for fritting, the other for heating bottle cullet before its transference to the pots. Annealing was carried out in seven independent subsidiary furnaces (oo and ww on the plan), and pot arching in another (t on plan). The origins of this type of furnace are at present uncertain. A furnace with a ground plan of this type excavated at Heindert (Canton d'Arlon,

Luxembourg) is supposed to date from at least Carolingian times. In Britain, apart from Vann (see above), three-winged furnaces have been excavated at Hutton and Rosedale in Yorkshire (Crossley and Aberg, 1972) and at Kimmeridge in Dorset in 1980/81.

At Hutton, an earlier furnace of plain fire-trench type, was overlaid by a second furnace with two fan-shaped wings to north-east and south-west, these being incorporated with a third overlying two-pot furnace. A second furnace, standing apart, may have been an annealing furnace for the first phase. The last phase of the furnace was dated to the late sixteenth century by thermo-remnant magnetism. At Rosedale (*Figure 3.68*) a two-pot furnace of similar date had four fan-shaped wings.

Both furnaces were built of stone and clay (Frank, 1982). Excavations at Kimmeridge in 1980/81 revealed the foundations of an early seventeenth-century glasshouse having four fan-shaped wings (*Figure 3.69*). The sieges were badly eroded so that it was not possible to be certain how many crucibles had been set in the furnace, but there appeared to be ample space for four pots. Underground air

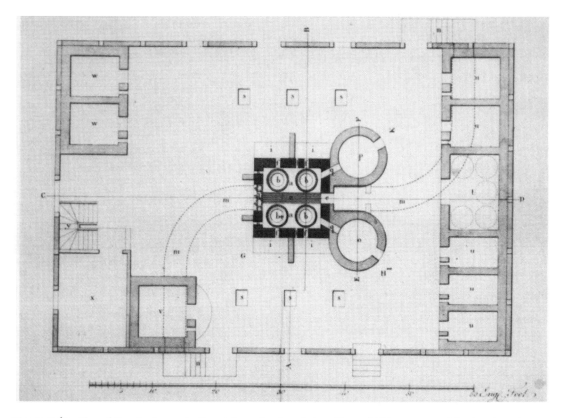

Figure 3.67 Plan of the glasshouse in Gravel Lane, Southwark (see Figure 3.66). qq are explained as 'openings into the vaults of these two furnaces, through which the heat is communicated from the founding-furnace'; uu are annealing furnaces, the largest, accommodating 800 bottles, is a pot-arching furnace; v is a furnace for chemical apparatus and other large pieces, the annealing furnace for which is at ww.

passages were necessary to provide draught for the local oil-shale, which was used as a source of fuel. The floors of the air passages were slabbed with stone and beneath them a drain channelled water towards the sea. Stone steps at the ends of the air passages farthest from the furnace gave access for raking out ash. The furnace was contained within a rectangular cover building with a shale-tile roof supported on timber on a stone foundation wall. This building protected the furnace and the working areas located on either side of it between the wings, which were presumably used for ancillary processes.

From a previous era of archaeology there is a record of a furnace excavated at Buckholt near Salisbury in Wiltshire, which appears to have had a winged construction. The Buckholt

glassmakers seem to have been, with one possible exception, French by origin; and the Vann glasshouse appears to have produced green glasses of the normal Wealden 'Lorraine' type.

The two Yorkshire glasshouses also produced characteristic green vessels of the same type, but it seems that higher temperatures had been employed than in the glasshouses of the Chiddingfold (Weald) area of southern Britain (Cable and Smedley, 1987). On the whole, it seems likely that the winged furnace was of French origin. That it enjoyed a wider diffusion at a later date is shown by the British examples quoted above and by the following: a stone-built furnace in a glasshouse at Karlova Hut, in the Czech Republic, founded in 1758; and a furnace in the Amelung factory at New Bremen, Maryland, USA (*Figure 3.70*),

ROSEDALE

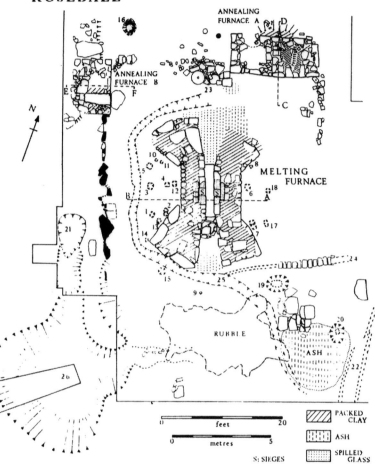

built after 1774 (and probably after 1784) (Hume, 1976). Both these furnaces appear to have had a plain firing trench, without a grill, no doubt reflecting the use of wood rather than coal as a fuel. Amelung had begun his career at Grünenplan south of Hanover in Germany, and in Maryland took over a factory that had previously been run by Germans. Therefore it may reasonably be concluded that the winged furnace was also established in the German-speaking countries by, at the latest, the middle of the eighteenth century. It seems likely that the six-pot furnace with two annexed annealing furnaces was used at the Notsjö factory in Finland in 1799 (Seela, 1974).

Kunckel illustrated a German furnace (*Ars Experimentalis*, or *Experiments in the Art of Glass*, 1679) (*Figures 3.71* and *3.72*). Here the working furnace and the fritting or annealing furnace are simply two chambers of the same structure, with the fire chamber running through their combined length (see *Figure 3.72*). It is not clear from the engravings whether there was also a linnet-hole connecting the upper chamber (that is, the working storey of the main furnace and the actual annealing chamber of the subsidiary one), and Kunckel provided no explanatory text. However, the illustrations were reproduced with explanatory text in the 1752 French edition of Neri (1612):

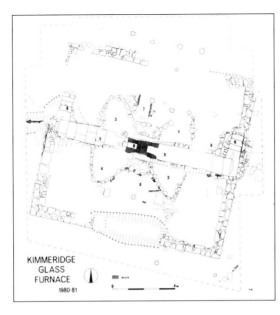

Figure 3.69 Plan of the early seventeenth-century glasshouse at Kimmeridge, Dorset, based on the 1980/1981 excavations. Features: 1–4, wings; 5, air passages; 6, steps giving access to air passages; 7–8, working areas; 9, fire-box; 10, robbing pit; 11, wall footing. (Courtesy of D.W. Crossley).

Figure 3.70 Aerial view of part of the Amelung glasshouse, USA, excavated in 1963, showing the western melting furnace with its four wings, which are believed to have housed small fritting ovens. Beyond these foundations, to the right, can be seen the remains of a pair of annealing ovens, while in the top left corner stands the east melting furnace. The modern metal roof in the background covers the pair of fritting ovens excavated in 1962. (From Schwartz, 1974.) (Corning Museum of Glass).

It is important to note that the subsidiary furnace was used for annealing as well as for fritting; the opening marked × on the plan is described as an opening for placing the glass to anneal. This type of furnace was clearly domesticated in France about as early as the winged furnace was established in Germany/Bohemia, for among the supplementary plates of Diderot (1751–1771) is a series of engravings illustrating this double type of furnace, entitled 'Round furnace or French furnace'. There are changes of detail, notably a square plan for the subsidiary furnace and four ribs to the beehive-shaped founding furnace.

That the type of furnace represented in the French edition of Neri was continuously in use up to the date of Kunckel's book is indicated by the results of an excavation carried out on the site of a glasshouse at Trestenhult, in Sweden, dating from about 1630. That it was essentially a German-type furnace is confirmed

by the fact that this factory was under the leadership of a certain Påvel Gaukunkel, probably one of a West German family of glassmakers, and that it made green glass of the German *waldglas* type. This furnace had an octagonal founding furnace with four pots, and a stoke-hole running throughout the length of the entire structure, which included an annealing furnace of circular plan, set slightly askew to the axis of the main furnace, with the result that the square hole permitting the passage of heat from the fire chamber to the annealing chamber is off-centre (*Figure 3.73*). The two furnaces are interconnected at first floor level by a linnet-hole (K on the drawing, *Figure 3.73*) (Roosma, 1969).

A furnace of the same basic type was already known to Agricola (*Figure 3.74*) in the sixteenth century, although in his illustration the annealing furnace is rectangular in plan, perhaps a throwback to the earlier traditions of Eraclius and Theophilus. Agricola described the furnace in the following terms:

Figure 3.71 View of Kunckel's furnace (from the 1752 French translation of A. Neri, *L'Arte Vetraria*).

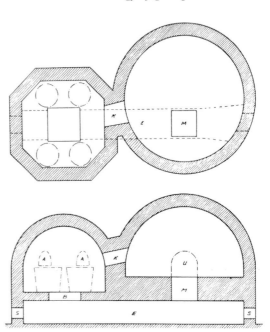

Figure 3.73 Reconstructed section of a green glass furnace found at Trestenhult, Sweden, *circa* 1630.

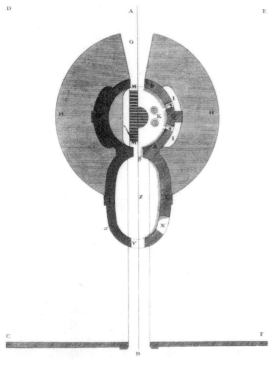

Figure 3.72 Plan of Kunckel's furnace, shown in Figure 3.71.

The second furnace is rounded, ten feet [3 m] broad and eight feet [2.5 m] high, and strengthened on the outside with five ribs [460 mm thick]. This again consists of two chambers, the roof of the lower being [460 mm thick]. This lower chamber has in front a narrow opening for stoking the logs on the ground-level hearth; and in the middle of its roof is a big round aperture opening into the upper compartment so that the flames may penetrate into it. But in the wall of the upper chamber between the ribs there should be eight windows so large that through them the bellied pots may be put on the floor round the big aperture. ... At the back of the furnace is a square opening, in height and breadth 1 palm, through which the heat may penetrate into the third furnace, adjoining. This is oblong eight feet [2.5 m] by six feet [1.8 m] broad, similarly consisting of two chambers, of which the lower has an opening in front for stoking the hearth ...' (Winbolt, 1933).

This is in all essentials the Trestenhult furnace, except for the ground plan and for the fact that apparently each furnace here has its own firebox, one set at right-angles to the other. But

Figure 3.74 Woodcut illustrating G. Agricola, *De Re Metallica*, Basle, 1556, showing a 'second furnace' with conjoined annealing furnace. H shows the clay 'tunnels' in which the glasses were annealed.

the express mention of interconnection at the first floor level is a vital point and such a feature may have also existed in the furnace of Mandeville's illustration (see *Plate 1*). Evidence for further furnaces of this type is to be found in the German-speaking areas of Central Europe:

(i) A *humpen* attributed to Christian Preussler, with a view of the Zeilberg glasshouse, Bohemia 1680 (Museum of Applied Arts, Prague).

(ii) A second Preussler family *humpen* of 1727, showing a virtually identical furnace (*Figure 3.75*). To the right may be seen the subsidiary furnace with something stretched across the access door, as in the case of the 1680 *humpen*, which seems to show pot arching in progress. To the left is a separate secondary furnace (for fritting?).

(iii) A glasshouse at Reichenau (probably that on the Buquoy estates at Gratzen on the Austrian side of the South Bohemian border), shown in *Figure 3.76*. The house clearly made both window and vessel glass (the latter by the muff process), with the circular furnace for vessel, the structure to its left being designated by the key as the annealing furnace, and that to the extreme left as the *Taffel Offen*, presumably the furnace for window glass. The structural connection, if any, between these two last is unclear from the engraving, but the lehr is clearly connected with the circular vessel-glass furnace, although it seems to be in use for annealing (and perhaps spreading?) muffs. Probably this should be regarded as a bastardized version of the German-type furnace.

(iv) The illustration from the *Augsburg Bible* of 1730, showing all the features of the Kunckel engraving, and perhaps derived directly from it.

Figure 3.75 Humpen of the Preussler family, depicting a glasshouse. Bohemia, 1727. (After Partsch, *Der Preusslerhumpen*, 1928).

Figure 3.76 Engraving showing the glasshouse at Reichenau, from a drawing by Clemens Benttler. Middle seventeenth century.

(v) Excavations of the Junkernfelde furnace.

Three sites excavated in Denmark seem to suggest that the German-type furnace was also in use there:

(i) Hyttekaer in Tem Glarbo, in the general area of Arhus, Jutland. Here six furnaces were discovered, not all necessarily of the same period, of which two appeared to have a common fire trench, one being circular, the other an oblong structure. Two further furnaces were apparently circular on plan, but although close to each other, their fire trenches were aligned roughly at right angles. Of the remaining furnaces apparently only the fire trenches survived, without any indication of their external shape.

(ii) Tinsholt, south of Aalborg in Jutland. At least one furnace (or two contiguous furnaces) here apparently correspond to the main Hyttekaer furnace, although the published details are somewhat unclear.

(iii) Stenhule in Tem Glarbo (see above). Three furnaces were found (discounting an apparently earlier circular foundation), of which the founding furnace, probably for six pots, may have been almost square, 3.4 m × 2.7 m, with chamfered corners. Its very long firebox, projecting on the west side, may have heated a long, narrow subsidiary (annealing?) furnace, which would have resembled that at Reichenau.

The two remaining furnaces, apparently circular and oval on plan respectively, were possibly for fritting and spreading of window glass. However, the site at Nejsum in Vendsyssel north of Aalborg, the plan of which seems clearer than some of those mentioned, reveals a central fire trench projecting a long way out at either side of an almost circular furnace plan – very much as at Fernfold in the Weald, except that the furnace there was rectangular. The Stenhule furnace could well be reconstructed in the same sense. It should be noted that all the glassmakers associated with these Jutland sites were Germans, some specifically from Hesse.

A glasshouse at Henrikstorp in Skane, Sweden, had a ground plan suggesting an exceptionally long fire trench, and may have been a structure resembling that at Reichenau. Its reconstruction with four pots on one side of an offset fire channel, and with a circular annealing furnace, seems very improbable. Finally, a glasshouse dating from about 1530 excavated at Junkersfelde, in eastern West-phalia, revealed a four-pot furnace rectangular in plan, with chamfered angles (as at Trestenhult and Stenhule), apparently leading to an annexed annealing furnace.

Development of coal firing and the chimney furnace

With the exception of the glasshouse at Kimmeridge in Dorset, all the furnaces hitherto

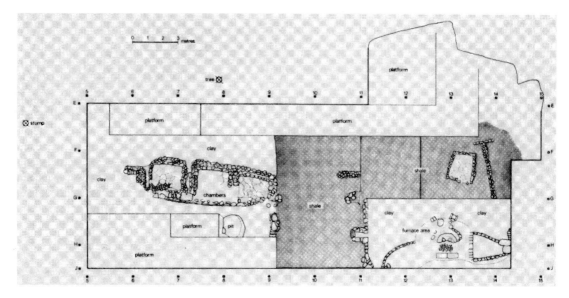

Figure 3.77   Plan of the seventeenth-century glasshouse at Haughton Green, Denton (near Manchester). The main furnace lies to the bottom right, with (?) annealing chambers to the left. (From Hurst-Vose, 1980).

described were fired by wood. It fell to Britain in the sixteenth century, with the increasing competition among wood-using industries for the output of coppiced woodlands, to develop the use of coal for this purpose. The late sixteenth and early seventeenth centuries were filled with the clamour of rival patentees claiming monopolies for their particular systems of using coal for this and that industrial process. In glassmaking, sufficient progress had been made by 1615 to enable the government of the day to issue a 'Proclamation touching Glass', forbidding the burning of wood in the glass industry (Crossley, 1998).

The essential feature of the coal-burning furnace was the use of a grill of iron bars on which the coals could be laid and raked periodically, the ashes falling into a pit below. In general, the furnace at Kimmeridge, operational between 1615 and 1623, resembled the wood-burning furnaces that have been excavated on both sides of the English Channel (see *Figure 3.69*). There was a central passage between sieges on which the crucibles had been set. At each corner was a triangular wing. The wings had formed the bases of four subsidiary structures in which the preparation of raw materials, and the working and annealing of the glass, could be

carried out. They may also have been used for the prefiring of crucibles. Outside the sieges, between each pair of wings, there were platforms on which lay fragments of stone floors. The main difference between Kimmeridge and the woodburning furnaces of the Lorraine tradition were the size of the firebox and the long vaulted passages used to supply air. When burning wood, it was possible to lay fires between the wings and to allow the flames to travel into the arched structure in which the pots were set. However, a coal fire gave a shorter flame, and therefore had to be placed in the centre of a furnace. At Kimmeridge a central block of brickwork lay between the sieges in a stone-lined channel approximately 1.4 m deep and 1 cm wide. The 'coal' (bituminous shale) was placed upon the central block, or above it on fire-bars, of which no trace survived at the time of excavation (1981). Another example of an early seventeenth-century four-pot furnace with an ash-pit below the sieges, and an apparently vaulted firing chamber, was excavated by Hurst-Vose (1980) and Burke at Haughton Green, Denton near Manchester (*Figure 3.77*).

The development of air passages is to be expected at this time. The account by Merrett (1662) of furnace procedure described air

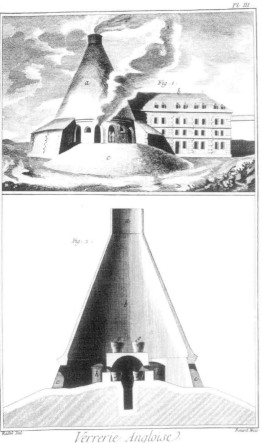

Pl. III

Fig. 1

Fig. 2

Verrerie Angloise.
Vue extérieure de la Verrerie, et Coupe sur la largeur.

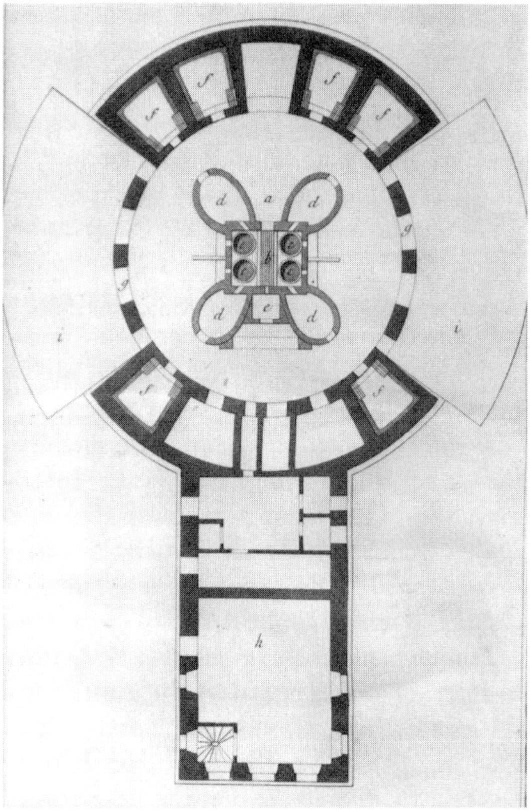

Figure 3.79 Plan of the glasshouse shown in Figure 3.78 (pl. 1); b in Fig. 2 is the grill. The 'linnet-holes' to the 'wing' furnaces are visible in the engraving.

Figure 3.78 Plate from Diderot, *Encyclopédie* showing '*Verrerie Angloise, Vue et Coupe sur la Longueur de la Verrerie*' (pl. vol. N. pl. 2 of article '*Verrerie Angloise*').

passages, and the use of fire-bars, 'Sleepers are the great Iron bars crossing smaller ones which hinder the passing of the coals, but give passage to the descent of the ashes'. This appears to be the earliest reference to this device, but it is clearly shown in the drawing of a London glasshouse made by a Swedish architect visiting England in 1777–8 (see *Figure 3.67*). The grill system seems to have been adopted on the Continent. It is shown in an illustration by Kunckel in 1679 (see *Figures 3.71* and *3.72*) and is clearly seen in the illustrations by Diderot and D'Alembert in their *Encyclopédie* of 1772. The provision of an ash chamber added, as it were, an extra storey to the furnace.

Clearly the provision of an adequate draft was of critical importance in the firing of a coal furnace, and it was inevitably in this field that the British made a further important contribution to glass technology. The principle was to have a cone-shaped building to house the furnace, capable of having all its outlets closed. Underground flues, no doubt arranged with regard to the prevalent wind, led to the furnace itself. By closing the cone doors and opening the flues, a tremendous through-draft was created, the great cone acting as a chimney. Glassworks cones were built only in Britain and the Hanover region of Germany (which at that time had strong royal connections with Britain), but not in France or Belgium. Bontemps (1868) in a *Guide de Verrier* (Guide to Glass) states, 'It is generally known that the English glasshouses are huge cones which surround the furnace. The English furnaces are thus situated under big chimneys which encourage energetic combustion in a way that is impossible in our French furnaces, which have a louvered opening above the furnace for the combustion products' (*Figures 3.78* and *3.79*).

The advantages of this system were described in Diderot and D'Alembert's *Encyclopédie* (1772). The writer of the article *Verrerie* stressed the importance of the single upward movement of air facilitated by the cone superstructure, all the outward exits of which were shut during founding, allowing the air to enter the building only through three broad ducts laid in the foundations under the furnace. This increased the efficiency of the British furnace enormously in comparison with that of the French type, the former being able, all other things being equal, to make in 12 days the same number of bottles as a French factory made in 15 days.

The same points are chosen for comment by a Danish visitor to London in 1727:

> It is known that the English glass is of high quality, and this is ascribed to the intense heat of the coal which is used for this purpose; I therefore also visited two of their glass furnaces, which stand on an eminence, and in the ground there is an open passage from both sides to a very large iron grill, which is in the middle, and the coals on and about it; by means of this passage the coals receive the air they need and one can stir them with appropriate instruments.

Gunther (1961b) pointed out that the cones served a dual purpose, being both a glass factory (i.e. a manufacturing area) and a waste gas extraction system. Gunther was particularly interested in their technical performance and quotes the general height as being 15–25 m; the volume of masonry as being 1100 m³ (the cone at Obernkirchen weighing 2800 tonne); the (diluted) waste gas temperature as 400°C; the exit velocity as 1 ms⁻¹, concluding that, at any time, the cones enable coal to be burnt more efficiently than in any other manner for

achieving melting temperatures, and gave a more equable environment for the workmen. However, the cones no longer had this advantage in fuel efficiency once the Siemens regenerative furnace had been introduced (Gunther, 1961a).

It is not certain exactly when the glass cone was first devised. Godfrey (1975) has an interesting discussion of the development of the cone furnace, including some eyewitness descriptions of the Winchester House furnace, probably from as early as 1610. There is, however, some misunderstanding of the functions of the glass cone, which is quite different from a chimney leading from the furnace. The point is that the heat should be drawn over the glass pots and not out of the crown of the furnace. The cone and the underground passages simply augment the draft, which follows this course, emerging at the working holes of the furnace.

Captain Philip Roche was building a cone in Dublin as early as 1696 but this was probably preceded by a period of experiment. In 1702 *The London Gazette* reports the existence of a glass cone, '94 Foot high and 60 Foot broad' (28.7 m × 18.3 m). The 10.7 m (35 ft) high building constructed in 1621 at Ballnegery was evidently a normal frame and shingle glasshouse with presumably no effect on the draft. *The Belfast News Letter* for 19 August 1785 referred to a new glasshouse 31.1 m (120 ft) high 'being the largest of any in Great Britain or Ireland'. In 1823 a cone 32.0 m (150 ft) high was recorded in the same city. In 1784, a prohibition was promulgated in Dublin against any glasshouse chimney less than 15.2 m (50 ft) in height.

Possibly the great heat reported by Merrett (above) was due to this device as early as 1662. More probably the cone was invented between this date and the end of the century. A few cones still survive although they are no longer in use (Ashurst, 1970; Lewis, 1973). In Britain they are now preserved as Ancient Monuments and can be seen at Alloa (Scotland), Lemington (near Newcastle-upon-Tyne), Stourbridge (near Birmingham) and at Catcliffe and Gawber in Yorkshire. The cone glasshouse at Gawber was probably constructed in the eighteenth century and is known to have been in ruins by 1823 (*Figure 3.80*). It illustrates the use of underground flues to induce the draft under the

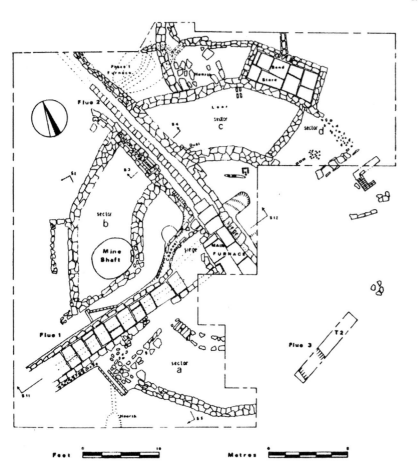

Figure 3.80 Plan of the cone glass-house at Gawber, South Yorkshire, showing three flues or air intakes, feeding air from the exterior to the central furnace. Sl-Sj2 refer to sections drawn during excavations. Site of the earlier (Phase I) furnace is shown in the top left-hand area. T2 (Trench 2) confirmed that Flue 2 continued into Flue 3. Flue 1 was added at a later date. Sector 'a' seemed to be a smith's hearth for maintenance of glassworkers' equipment. Sector 'b' contained a mine-shaft, which antedates the main cone structure. Sector 'c' was probably the 'lehr' or annealing area, with a sand store adjoining the exterior wall. (Denis Ashurst).

furnace. On the site of the main furnace were found lengths of fire bar, 2–3 ft (600–900 mm) long by 1¼ in (30 mm) square section, and a sandstone block carved with a slot into which a fire bar exactly fitted, to form the detachable fire grate. This seems to be the only archaeological record of the dimensions of fire bars. In Germany there are examples of glassworks cones at Obernkirchen and Steinkrug (near Hanover) and at Gernheim (near Minden).

The difference between the heat needed for making drinking glasses and that for window glass is made explicit in an entry in the diary of Sir James Hope in 1647 concerning the Wemyss (Scotland) glasshouse:

That window glasses and drinking glasses cannot be made in one fornace because those requyre a great deall stronger heatt than these: That the fornace for those is yrfore long vaulted; and for these round bot however yt could not make window glass, nather possiblie could find workmen who have skill of both ...

These observations were based on the experience of an Italian glassmaker, Christopher Visitella. The great heat reached in the green-glass furnaces is emphasized by Merrett: 'The heat of those furnaces, is the greatest that ever I felt ... The workmen say tis twice as strong as that in the other Glass-furnaces ...'

One further British invention resulted from the use of coal for firing. This was the covered glass pot. That open pots continued to be used in circumstances where the fumes of the coal made little difference (e.g. in bottle making) is proved by the details of the interiors of British bottle houses given by Carlberg in 1777–78 (see *Figure 3.68* and *3.69*) and by the illustrator of the *Encyelopédie* in 1772. Here the old type of pot is clearly visible. It seems more likely, therefore, that the development of the covered pot was associated with the evolution of lead crystal, for this is irreparably damaged by the sulphur compounds which result from the combustion of coal. Curiously enough the earliest mention of it appears to come from Norway. In 1756 at the Nostetangen factory there were prepared '16 English covered pots'. The earliest pictorial representation would appear to date from as late as 1802 (Newton, 1988).

The theory that there was a southern tradition of furnace building (in which the founding furnace was normally circular and incorporated a third storey for annealing); and a northern tradition in which the founding furnace was normally rectangular or oblong on plan and the annealing furnace often on a level with it and interconnecting by means of a common fore channel, and usually also by linnet holes, seems in general to have been borne out by archaeological discoveries. The differences are discussed by Newton (1985b) in terms of the availability of beech trees. The northern tradition clearly bifurcated at some point, probably in the sixteenth century, into those furnaces that were built with wings for subsidiary firing processes on the one hand and, on the other, two-chamber furnaces of the type represented in the Mandeville manuscript and Kunckel's engravings. These general developments must be viewed in the context of all the variables imposed in particular cases by site, available building materials etc.

Twentieth- and twenty-first-century glass-making furnaces, which are outside the scope of this discussion of ancient and historic technologies of glassmaking, are of sophisticated design: the Siemens regenerative furnace, cold top electric furnace and float glass furnace make use of gas, oil or electricity as sources of fuel.

4

Deterioration of glass

Thousands of ancient glass artefacts have survived exposure to burial environments. However it is reasonable to suppose that these represent only the more durable (stable) of the glasses manufactured in the past, and those that were buried in conditions which were favourable for their survival (and which since their recovery have been stored in conditions ideal for their preservation). Historic glasses that have never been buried, and European medieval glass windows (buried and *in situ*) have also survived in great number.

Much of the investigation into the mechanisms of glass deterioration has centred around the decay of European medieval window glass (Newton, 1982b; 1985a). Very little has been written concerning the deterioration of archaeological glass (Geilmann, 1956, 1960; Shaw, 1965; Knight, 1999; Freestone, 2001); and the understanding of the processes of its deterioration is limited. There is, however, a substantial body of literature concerning investigation and experimental research relating to the chemical principles controlling the weathering (or durability) of container glasses (e.g. Hench, 1975b; Paul, 1977). Whilst the same scientific principles control the interaction of archaeological and historic glasses to their environments, the purely scientific approach to glass deterioration does not translate easily to archaeology/conservation; and the results contained therein cannot be used to predict the nature of actual deterioration products which will be formed on complex glasses over centuries or millennia, except in the most general terms.

In 1936, Harden stated that

The term weathering is applied to any change for the worse on the surface ... of glass that is caused, during the passage of time, by contact with outside influences ... the term covers, therefore, a wide range of phenomena ... it is quite impossible to foresee what type or degree of weathering will be produced on a piece of glass after preservation for a fixed time under seemingly fixed circumstances ... even a very slight change in environment may produce a markedly different kind or degree of weathering on two parts of the same vessel ... No strict rules can therefore be formulated. The causes and effects of weathering are as manifold as they are elusive.

This statement is still true, despite the fact that it has been scientifically proven that deterioration is related to the chemical composition of glass and its environment (Cox *et al.*, 1979; Newton and Fuchs, 1988, Freestone, 2001).

In order to be clear about the processes, deterioration will be used to describe the decay of buried or submerged glass, weathering, to describe decay to due atmospheric influences, and corrosion avoided, since this term refers essentially to deterioration of metals.

There are three main aspects to the deterioration of glass artefacts. Subject to their environment, they may deteriorate (i) as a result of physical damage, (ii) from superficial disfigurement, and (iii) from chemical deterioration.

Physical damage

The fragility of glass renders it susceptible to physical damage by mechanical shock. The causes of physical damage to glass can result

Figure 4.1 A stone in glass, which has subsequently caused the glass to crack.

Figure 4.2 Large wine cooler broke into three pieces (see Figures 7.25a–b).

from (i) manufacturing defects; (ii) impact damage; (iii) thermal shock damage; (iv) abrasion; and (v) previous treatment.

(i) Glasses may break if they were poorly crafted, or were of an impractical design; there were weaknesses in the glass (striations, seed, stone, see *Figure 4.1*) or the batch recipe was poorly formulated (leading to chemical instability, discussed below). Thin, blown objects may spring out of shape due to release of tension in the glass. Some objects are particularly susceptible to impact damage: those made of more than one piece, figures with projecting limbs, tall, top heavy objects; and those with rounded bases.

(ii) Impact damage is the most common form of physical deterioration to objects held in collections and which are otherwise in good condition, resulting from accident, careless handling or packing, or vandalism (*Figure 4.2*). The glass breaks when it comes into contact with a harder material or by falling, cracking and breaking. Objects suffer some disruption in the form of scratches, cracks, chips and complete breakage, which may lead to loss of fragments. Vibration from pedestrian movement and all forms of traffic can cause objects to fall over, or move along and off shelves.

(iii) Damage by thermal shock occurs when sudden warming or cooling of the glass causes uneven rates of expansion or contraction. The resulting stress causes the glass to crack or break. This type of damage most often occurs when glass is washed in hot water, or when candles are allowed to burn too close to the glass (*Figure 4.3*). Glass should never be dried in direct sunlight or by artificial sources of heat (Bimson and Werner, 1964a). It is not always possible to tell how glass will behave under heat stress. Even if heated to 90°C over 8 hours, glass may crizzle to the extent of becoming opaque. Enamelled decoration may alter in appearance or spring off and gilding become dulled. Glass subjected to fire will crizzle or shatter. In extreme heat where temperatures may rise above the original firing temperature of the glass, glass will melt. Lead glass, for example, may be reduced to black molten lumps. Tar and carbon deposits may be difficult or even impossible to remove, especially from deteriorated surfaces and within cracks.

(iv) Abrasion of glass occurs as (a) a result of use during its lifetime (e.g. scratches from eating utensils); (b) the use of harsh cleaning methods; (c) previous conservation/ restoration (removal of materials used for repair and filling), and scratches made by scalpels, abrasives (sandpaper) and metal tools (*Figure 4.4*). (It has to be borne in mind that conservation techniques have the potential to harm glass at the time of

Figure 4.3 Glass cracked by the heat of a candle, which had been allowed to burn too close to it.

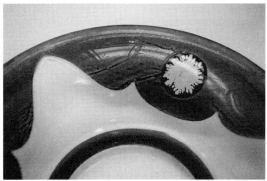

Figure 4.5 A gilded design, which has almost disappeared as a result of abrasion.

Figure 4.4 Fragments of glass deliberately scratched by filing during a damaging attempt at repair.

application or in the future). Generally any surface decoration, which was unfired (cold painting and gilding) or was fired at low temperatures, e.g. gilding, lustre and enamel decoration, tends to be susceptible to abrasion (*Figure 4.5*). (In addition to physical damage, irreversible chemical damage is caused by the improper use of commercial cleaning agents, acids and alkalis etc., discussed below.)

Superficial disfigurement

Foreign material, from a number of sources, may accumulate on the surface of glass (and inside hollow vessels). These derive from (i) use; (ii) encrustations during burial; (iii) stains

from metal corrosion products or from metal ties or rivets; (iv) excess use of conservation materials; and (v) atmospheric pollution.

(i) Stains and residues resulting from use may be required to be kept as archaeological/ historical evidence, e.g. remains of cremation, food, drink, medicines, ink etc. These may have become trapped inside closed forms such as bottles, or held within flaws in the glass, such as cracks, chips, pin holes and crizzled surfaces (in the latter case alkali salts can become trapped). Limescale can form on the interior of containers such as vases (*Figure 4.6*).

(ii) Glass is normally recovered from excavation covered by soil (see *Figure 6.1*). Thick calcium deposits of organic origin may form during burial (especially in a marine environment), or black sulphide during burial in anaerobic deposits (*Figure 4.7*). Encrustations of carbonates, sulphates and silicates may form to obliterate the surface of buried glass in climates where there is sufficient precipitation to dissolve these compounds (which are nevertheless regarded as insoluble, since they are poorly soluble in water), but where there is also sufficient evaporation to permit them to be deposited again (*Figure 4.8*). Being the least soluble in water, silicates are the least common, but where they exist in the soil in great quantity, as in the Near East, a silicate crust may form on the surface of glass, or

Figure 4.6 Limescale deposits inside a glass vessel.

Figure 4.8 A deposit of insoluble salts, blending with the weathering crusts and obscuring the surface of the glass.

Figure 4.9
Iron corrosion products deposited on a glass flask, during prolonged burial next to an iron object.

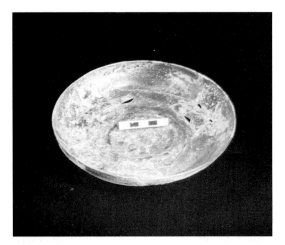

Figure 4.7 A Roman silica–soda–lime glass after conservation, which has a thin opaque blackened surface, thought to have resulted from its burial in anaerobic conditions, where hydrogen sulphide became deposited with the leached surface. (Courtesy of S.M. Smith).

from mortar (if the glass has been embedded in a wall for instance). Glass incorporated into a building structure may be covered with mortar.

(iii) Metal deposits can result from burial of glass in close proximity to deteriorating metal objects (*Figure 4.9*), or from metal rivets, ties and dowels used to repair historic glass objects (*Figure 4.10*).

(iv) Excess use of materials for repair/restoration such as pressure-sensitive tapes (*Figure 4.11*), adhesives and filling materials can leave deposits, or become trapped

Figure 4.10 Rivets used to repair the foot of a wineglass, which have subsequently corroded.

Figure 4.11 Gilding removed from the surface of a glass vessel, on Sellotape used to tape fragments together.

Figure 4.12 Damage to the base of a wineglass caused by prolonged contact with a gummed paper label. (Victoria and Albert Museum, London).

in a deteriorated glass surface. Adhesive labels can accentuate the deterioration of glass, presumably by holding moisture in contact with the glass (*Figure 4.12*).

(v) Atmospheric pollution in the form of water- or wind-borne chemicals, and accumulating particulate matter, cause deterioration of glass (*Figure 4.13*). The type and concentration of polluting agencies will depend on location. These may include incomplete fuel combustion associated with traffic and industry, building materials, and skin and clothing particles introduced by visitors.

Chemical deterioration

Factors affecting chemical deterioration

The chemical processes associated with the deterioration of ancient and historic glasses arise as the result of the internal composition

Figure 4.13 Medieval glass which has formed an encrustation due to prolonged exposure to the atmosphere. Part of the crust has fallen away, exposing the blue glass beneath. (Courtesy of S. Strobl).

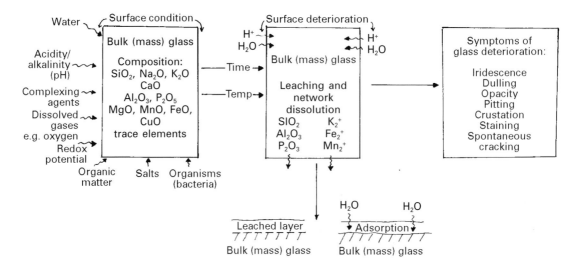

Figure 4.14   Processes of glass deterioration.

of the glass being attacked on a molecular level by external forces, principally involving water (*Figure 4.14*). In simple terms, when a glass reacts with water, or with an aqueous solution, chemical changes occur at the glass surface, which then progress into the body. Two mechanisms are involved: de-alkalization (commonly referred to as leaching), and network dissolution.

Besides the presence of water, other inter-dependent factors affecting the decomposition of glass, fall into two main categories: (i) those relating to the glass itself, and (ii) those relating to the environment. Those relating to the glass are the nature of its surface, composition of the bulk glass, phase separation or other inhomogeneities in the glass, and the firing process. Those relating to the burial, aqueous or atmospheric environment, are the amount of water or water vapour present, the nature of the attacking solution, i.e. the pH, the particular ions present and their concentration, the presence of complexing agents and salts, the time of exposure to attack, temperature, organisms, and to some extent pressure, in the case of burial at depth on land or beneath the sea (see *Figure 4.14*). Glass in collections, and to a much greater extent, medieval window glass *in situ*, is affected by atmospheric pollution, condensation, humidity and solarization.

The presence of water and, above all, accumulated moisture, is the most important

factor initiating and sustaining forms of glass decomposition. Without water, glass can remain in excellent condition for centuries, little, if any, attack occurring in dry conditions. Water is essential for the replacement by protons of the diffusing alkali ions (leaching) and the subsequent hydration and dissolution of the silica network. It also removes the soluble salts formed from such reactions. Even damage caused by dehydration is the consequence of previous attack by water. Literary references to the leached glass layer refer to it in different terms, such as being alkali-deficient, silica-rich, or as hydrogen glass, or the gel-layer.

The damaging effect of water on glass was appreciated as early as the sixteenth century. In a letter dated 1595, concerning glass imported from Venice, the instructions from the importer stated that the glass should be 'carefullij packt up and with thorou drij weeds, for if the weeds be not well drijed or doe take anij wett after theij be packt theij staijne and spoijle the glasses' (Charleston, 1967).

The fact that water is the primary agent of the environment for causing the deterioration of glass, was established by Lavoisier as early as 1770. The earliest scientific examination of weathered glass was that undertaken by Brewster (1863), on iridescent glasses from Nineveh; which demonstrated that the play of colours on the glass surface resulted from the interference between rays of light reflected from thin alternating layers of air and weathered glass crusts. If the gaps were injected with water the iridescence disappeared, only to return when the water evaporated. Brewster (1855, 1863) and Loubengager (1931) found that deterioration of the glass surface by water proceeded downwards faster than it did sideways; a fact subsequently verified in experiments undertaken during the twenty-first century.

De-alkalization (ion exchange)

In Chapter 1 it was shown that the negatively charged alkali and metal cations are free to move around within the glass network, from one space to another. In a damp or wet environment, they are extracted from the glass by water, to form a sodium or potassium hydroxide solution. However, since the electrical neutrality of the glass must be maintained, hydronium ions (H_3O^+) from the water exchange positively charged hydrogen ions (protons) for the alkali ions leaching from the glass network. This process results in a hydrated silica-rich surface layer, sometimes referred to as a gel layer. Water molecules react with the non-bridging ions in the glass to produce hydroxyl ions, which migrate out of the glass with the alkali cations. The water thus contains an excess of hydrogen ions, which increases its alkalinity and potential for attacking glass.

$$H_3O^+ + \equiv Si-O^--Na^+ \quad \equiv Si-OH + H_2O + Na \quad (4.1)$$

Since the hydrogen protons are much smaller than the sodium or potassium ions they replace, the alkali-depleted surface layer will have a smaller volume than the underlying glass. Furthermore, the hydrogen ions have a strong covalent bond with oxygen, which results in a contraction and weakening of the glass network (Ernsberger, 1980).

Potash glasses have about half the durability of soda glasses because the potassium ions, are larger than those of sodium ions, and take up more space in the glass network. Thus, when potassium ions are leached out of the glass, they allow a greater number of water molecules in. The resulting reduction in volume of the leached layer causes shrinkage

to occur, and further shrinkage takes place if a hydrated alkali-deficient (hence silica-rich) layer then loses water, e.g. upon excavation. Thus dehydration of glass, often thought of as a cause of deterioration, merely highlights the deterioration which has already occurred. The decrease in volume can lead to microporosity of the surface layer and this may be the cause of the many-layered effects found in the surface crusts of some medieval glasses (Scholze *et al.*, 1975).

If, however, the alkali-deficient surface layer remains undamaged, at least for a time, it may cause the alkali diffusion rate to decrease, since the ions must diffuse through it in order to reach the unaltered glass. Therefore the rate of extraction, which initially decreased with the square root of time, becomes slower, and linear with time. (Thus a false impression can be given that the glass has become more durable as time progresses; Hench, 1975a,b; Hench and Sanders, 1974; Clark *et al.*, 1979.)

The nature of the leached surface layer on glass is of fundamental importance in understanding glass deterioration/durability. Unless the leach solution is frequently renewed by water, the accumulation of alkali ions in the water leads to an increase in the pH value. The speed at which the critical value of pH 9 is reached (at which point more rapid de-alkalization occurs), depends on many parameters, two of these being the surface area of the glass (SA) and the volume (V) of water involved.

Network dissolution

The water of the attacking solution will usually be either slightly acidic or alkaline depending on the soil or the atmospheric conditions. As mentioned above, under alkaline conditions, the oxygen bridges of the glass network itself may be broken down and the silica dissolve:

$$\equiv Si-O-Si + \equiv OH^- \quad \equiv Si-OH + \equiv Si-O^- \quad (4.2)$$

This reaction is strongly pH-dependent (e.g. Adams, 1984). In general, the rate of alkali extraction from glass in a buffered system at a pH of less than 9 is constant and independent of pH. There are exceptions to this, for example in a soda–lime–silica glass where the lime content is greater than 10 mol per cent there is a rapid increase in the rate of extraction when the pH drops below 3. The increased extraction is due to the increased solubility of lime, whose extraction was otherwise negligible. In contrast to alkali extraction, silica extraction is almost non-existent below pH 9, but increases noticeably above this. At the critical point of pH9, both the silica and the divalent network modifiers (calcium, magnesium, lead etc.) can be leached out of glass, and eventually total dissolution of the surface will occur, opening up the glass beneath to further attack.

In effect, the processes of glass deterioration, i.e. ion exchange and network dissolution, are in competition. If leaching of alkali proceeds more rapidly than dissolution of the network, the glass surface will develop a leached layer composed of hydrated silica. If, however, network dissolution is the predominant mechanism, a hydrated silica layer will not form and the glass will be gradually dissolved away. Since most ground water is of intermediate pH, ion exchange appears to be the dominant mechanism, so that a hydrated silica-rich layer is formed on many buried archaeological glasses. Network dissolution appears to be a more progressive phenomena in glasses above ground, for example windows. Whereas in the ground alkalis leached from the glass are washed away, in the atmosphere they tend to remain as salts on the glass surface, creating alkaline conditions, which favour breakdown of the network (Freestone, 2001).

The glass

The nature of the glass surface

The surface of a glass is highly influential in the effects of the deterioration processes that occur on it since the amount of constituents released during decomposition is proportional to the exposed surface area (SA/V). The surface is a defect in itself, because all surface ions are in a state of incomplete coordination. This asymmetry of the surface produces abnormal interatomic distances and hence the space occupied by the surface ions is greater than usual, enabling replacement by ions of a larger or smaller radius to occur. Thus, the subsurface glass layer is porous on a microscopic scale, and this enables surface reaction with molecules of water, sulphur dioxide, oxygen and hydrochloric acid etc. to take place to a considerable depth.

As the ratio of surface area to volume (SA/V) of the leaching solution increases, there is an increase in the extraction of silica. However, this can be attributed to the accompanying increase in pH of the solution on release of the alkali. In contrast, the quantity of alkali extracted does not vary with changing SA/V. It would be expected that the increase of pH would suppress further release of alkali from the glass, but this possibility is counteracted by the release of silica from the network as the pH increases (Newton and Seddon, 1992). This dissolution of the silica network causes alkali to pass into solution, and reduces the thickness of the surface gel (leached layer).

The original glass surface would rarely have been homogeneous, even though it may have originally had a slightly protective surface on completion of manufacture. The surface would have been physically altered by internal or external stress, for example by cold working (Pilosi in Kordas, 2002), or accidental damage. On the other hand, a slightly protective surface could be formed, at least in the initial stages of surface alteration (see above). In either case, the surface would have begun to be chemically altered (leached by moisture) from the moment it was made. As a result of these interferences, the glass surface would be microscopically uneven, or macroscopically rough, thus presenting a greater surface area to the attacking solution (SA/V). In other words, the glass would have sites of damage, which would be more prone to deterioration than others.

The composition of the bulk (mass) glass

The composition of glasses, i.e. the ratio of silica, alkali (soda, potash or less commonly lead) and calcium oxide (lime), additives such as metallic oxides and opacifiers and the inclusion of trace elements, all have a part in determining their durability. The majority of ancient and historic glasses are of soda–lime–silicate composition: a network of silica and other metallic oxides in the roles of glass *formers*, *modifiers* and *intermediates* (see *Figures 1.4 and 1.5*). *Network formers* are limited to those oxides which have high bond strengths, the most common being silicon oxide (silica). Theoretically, fused silica would form a highly durable glass, but such high temperatures would be required to melt it that, for practical reasons, modifiers always had to be added to act as *fluxes*, which lower the melting temperature. The concentration of silica is a crucial factor in determining decomposition of glass. Experimentally, it has been shown that below 62–66 mol per cent, the silicon atoms in the glass become associated with a *modifier*, sodium, calcium etc., as their second neighbours. Consequently, there is always an interconnecting path of neighbouring silicon oxide (Si–O) groups, which provide suitable sites for the movement of interchanging ions between the solution and the glass. The decaying glass has a tendency to form a surface crust. Above 66 mol per cent of silica, the SiO_2 groups are isolated by Si–O–Si groups, which suppress the movement of ions involved in the leaching process (Bettembourg, 1976; Collongues, 1977; Cox *et al.*, 1979; Perez-y-Jorba *et al.*, 1975; Schreiner, 1987; Newton and Fuchs, 1988).

As mentioned above, *modifiers* break up the silica network, bonding ionically with the glassy network and altering properties such as viscosity, thermal expansion and durability. They have relatively low bond strengths and fall into two main groups: *fluxes and stabilizers*. *Fluxes*, materials with the chemical composition R_2O, the oxides of sodium (Na_2O), potassium (K_2O), present in about 15 per cent, which reduce the viscosity of the batch. It is largely the presence, type and quantity of the modifiers which impair the highly durable nature of a pure silica network.

Alkaline earth oxides with the chemical composition RO, usually lime or calcium (CaO) and magnesium (MgO), are referred to as *stabilizers*. Present in about 10 per cent of the batch, they prevent crystallization from occurring as the batch cools, and improves the chemical stability of the glass, making it less soluble in water. If lime (CaO) is added to the glass in increasing amounts up to 10 mol per cent, there is a rapid decline in soda extraction, owing to the increasing stability of the surface (gel) layer. The stability is due to the

presence of CaO increasing the coupling of the vibrational modes of the silica non-bridging oxygen modifier bonds to the bridging of the Si–O–Si network. It would be expected that the replacement of one Ca^{2+} ion by two protons (H+) would have the same effect as replacing two ions from the network, but in the latter case a much more porous layer is formed. If the lime content is increased above 15 mol per cent, the resistance to deterioration starts being drastically reduced. Lime was not specified as a constituent of pre-seventeenth-century glasses, and hence stable (durable) glasses were prepared more or less accidentally either from calcareous sands (in ancient times) or from high-lime wood ash (in medieval times); thus it is not surprising that there was a period when the addition of extra lime was regarded as being positively harmful (Turner, 1956a).

Some minor components in glass such as alumina (Al_2O_3), phosphorous (P_2O) and iron (Fe_2O_3), are *intermediates* present in glass in a forming or modifying position. They derive from (i) trace elements in the raw materials, (ii) extractions in the clay crucibles or pots in which the glass was melted, or (iii) have entered the glass network from the surrounding environment. The intermediate oxides all have a low solubility (intermediate bond strengths), and therefore their presence within a glass surface may increase its resistance to dissolution, by immobilizing the alkali ions, so that they are no longer free to move through the silicate network.

As mentioned above, the greater the percentage of silica, the less tendency there is for it to be extracted from the glass, whereas in the case of alkali, the greater the percentage, the greater its potential to be extracted. In general the greater proportion of glass modifier, such as calcium, to the alkali sodium or potassium, the more stable the glass. However, if a glass containing large amounts of alkali does deteriorate, the calcium will be leached out along with it. The remaining silica may be so small a proportion as to be unable to maintain the internal bonds, thus the glass will disintegrate.

It was formerly believed that, because differently coloured glasses decay in different manners, the colour *per se* influenced the weathering of medieval window glass. This arose from the mistaken impression that all glass made for the same window (and hence made at the same time by the same glass-maker) would have essentially the same composition (Newton, 1978). In fact, there was little control over raw materials in medieval times, and the sources of colouring oxides might be highly contaminated by, for example, clay or lime, both of which would profoundly affect the weathering of glass made with it. In addition, the concentration of colourant ions is low, usually less than 1 per cent, and is therefore not significant. It is the bulk composition of the coloured glass which is different, and which explains the difference in durability. For example, in 1972, attention was drawn to a late twelfth-century border panel from the nave clerestory of York Minster in which all the pink glass had resisted weathering, and had shiny surfaces, whereas the green glass had rough crusted surfaces. Partial analyses of the glasses revealed that the green pieces contained relatively more lime, compared with potash, than did the pink pieces and it was this difference in composition, rather than the colour *per se*, which was responsible for the differences in weathering (Hedges and Newton, 1974). In some cases coloured medieval glass is found to be better preserved than colourless glass.

In view of the above discussion concerning the effects of composition, it can be appreciated that the rate of deterioration of ancient/historical glasses is greatly influenced by production technology, governed in turn by cultural and geological factors (see Chapters 2 and 3). The difference in composition of glass, for instance, is the reason for the difference in deterioration between relatively stable Mediterranean soda–lime–silica glass and poorly durable medieval glass, made from plant and beechwood ash, and containing too much potash and sand lime to ensure its stability. The hydrated layer on much Roman glass with a typical composition of 15–20 per cent Na_2O, 5–10 per cent CaO, 2–3 per cent Al_2O_3 and circa 70 per cent SiO_2, is negligible, only a few tens of micrometres thick depending upon its burial environment. On the other hand, medieval European forest glass, which is low in silica, high in alkali (potash) and alkaline earths, is notoriously susceptible to deterioration, and typically develops substantial

hydrated layers, even after a few centuries. For example, such a glass might contain 15 per cent potassium monoxide (K_2O), 15 per cent calcium oxide (CaO_3) and 55 per cent silicon dioxide (SiO_2), plus small quantities (*circa* 1 per cent) of other oxides, e.g. iron and manganese, derived from the use of impure sand, but mainly from the wood ash.

Soda–lime–silica glasses produced from plant ash in the Near East also differ from the glasses described above, in that they have a reduced silica content, lower aluminium and higher alkaline earths (calcium and magnesium). This results in their being less stable than Roman soda–lime–silica glass. For example, glass found in Mesopotamia, dating from the Sassanian period (fourth century AD), can be excavated with opaque surface crusts several millimetres thick, alongside Roman glass having a thin iridescent skin. Glass of this type may be recovered in an extremely good state of preservation from the Egyptian desert because of the very low ambient humidity. There is little data concerning the deterioration of lead–silica glasses. However, the lead-rich opaque red enamels on medieval Celtic metalwork are often extremely heavily deteriorated in comparison with other (low lead) colours. Chinese glasses produced during the Han dynasty (206 BC to 220 AD) of barium–lead–silica composition (see Chapter 2), frequently developed a thick deteriorated surface layer during burial.

Colourless *cristallo* glass was made in Venice from the fifteenth century, by purifying plant ash by the solution and precipitation of the alkalis. Since the stabilizing alkaline earths were also removed during the process, the resulting low-lime glass was inherently unstable and susceptible to attack by atmospheric moisture. Such glass is said to be suffering from glass disease, or to be sick or weeping (see *Figure 4.15*). As mentioned above, the optimum lime content is about 10 mol per cent of CaO in the final glass, but some glasses were made in the middle of the seventeenth century by Ravenscroft (particularly in the period 1674–76), and in Venice at the beginning of the fifteenth century, which now have crizzled or weeping surfaces (Freestone, 2001). Since the early stages of glass deterioration occur at a molecular level, they may go unnoticed. Later the glass object may appear

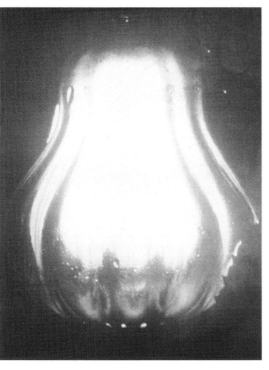

Figure 4.15 Close-up view of a weeping glass vessel, showing the drops of alkaline moisture, which form on the surface. (© Copyright The British Museum, London).

Figure 4.16 Deposits of alkali salts on the interior of a weeping glass ewer. (© Copyright The British Museum).

dull or misty as deterioration products accumulate on the surface. In humid conditions, these attract moisture to the surface, which may then exhibit drops of moisture or a general slipperiness (*Figure 4.15*). If the atmosphere becomes drier, alkali salts are deposited on the surface of the glass (*Figure 4.16*). As the process continues, a network of minute fractures (crizzles) develops in the surface layers of the glass, a stage known as incipient crizzling. Under magnification, and later with the naked eye, a network of very fine cracks can be seen (*Figure 4.17*). If the process continues unchecked, the network of cracks extends deeper into the glass surface, causing small flakes to spall away. The glass becomes entirely crizzled and exhibits an overall cloudiness and lack of transparency. In extreme cases, the glass may lose its mechanical strength and collapse, disintegrating

entirely. The term crizzling has been used to describe such deteriorated glass since at least the sixteenth century. Although these are the classic examples, many other examples are found in glass from other countries and centuries. These glasses are characterized by lime contents which are usually less than 5 mol per cent CaO (and sometimes less than 1 per cent) and their situation is frequently made worse because they contain potash as the alkali instead of soda. It was formerly believed that pink glasses had a greater tendency to crizzle than clear glass. However Brill (1975) showed that the pink colour of crizzled glass is confined to the surface of otherwise colourless glass. The phenomena of weeping and crizzling may also occur on enamelled metal objects. Chemically unstable glass has been investigated by Bakardjiev (1977a,b), Scholze (1978), Ryan *et al.* (1993, 1996), Hogg *et al.*

Figure 4.17 A crizzled posset pot, on which the network of fine surface cracks can be seen. (© Copyright The British Museum).

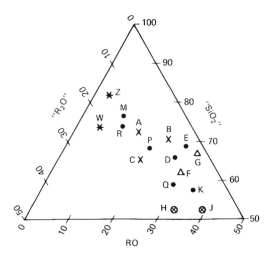

Figure 4.18 A triangular representation of glass compositions in which highly durable glasses (A, M, R) are placed near the centre, and the least durable glasses (H, J, K) fall at the bottom and to the right; glasses of the composition W and Z may even decay in some museum atmospheres. A = modern float glass; B = window glass (1710) from Gawber, Yorkshire; C = sheet glass (1855) from St Helens, Lancashire; D = uncrusted glass (1535) from Bagot's Park, Staffordshire; E = glass from Rosedale; F = crusted glass from Bagot's Park; G = crusted glass from Hutton, Yorkshire, all sixteenth century; H = badly decayed, heavily crusted medieval Austrian window glass; J = badly decayed, heavily crusted glass medieval glass from the Lady Chapel, Ely Cathedral; K = medieval glass from Weobley Castle; M = durable Saxon glass from Monkwearmouth; R = Roman glass; P, Q = pink and green twelfth-century glass from York Minster; W = 'weeping glass'; Z = 'crizzled glass'. (Iliffe and Newton, 1976).

(1998, 1999) (other articles are published in the Proc. of the 18th Int. Congr. on Glass, San Francisco, 1998, CD ROM).

The triangular diagram

In 1975 a triangular diagram (*Figure 4.18*) was formulated, on which the compositions of glasses were plotted, as an aid to understanding the relative weathering behaviour of different glasses, (Newton, 1975; Iliffe and Newton, 1976). The diagram remains a good general guide to which chemical compositions of glass are more durable than others.

The compositions of the glasses are obtained by analysis, and converted to molecular percentages of the constituent oxides. These are then grouped into three categories, the network formers, the alkaline earth network modifiers and the effective alkali content. However, the fact that most of the glasses lie on the line Z to J in *Figure 4.18*, means that, in the majority of cases, it is necessary only to know the molar proportion of network formers in order to establish approximately where the glass will lie in the diagram. Thus, as a first approximation, the problems of analysis and calculation can be reduced by determining only the silica content.

The constituents of the glass exercise their effect on the weathering of that glass by virtue of the numbers of their molecules, in association with each other, and not by the weight of those molecules (which is the convention usually adopted, in reporting the results of analyses of glasses). The difference between the numbers of molecules and the weight of the molecules would not be significant if all the molecules had similar weights, but this is by no means the case. The two main alkalis differ considerably, the molecule of potash (K_2O) being 52 per cent heavier than the molecule of soda (Na_2O). A molecule of lime (CaO) is 39 per cent heavier than the molecule of magnesia (MgO), and lead oxide is 550 per cent heavier than MgO. To obtain the relative numbers of molecules, the weight percentages are divided by the factors in *Table 4.1* (which

Plate 1 A miniature depicting numerous activities relating to a late medieval forest glasshouse, which has a lehr built alongside the furnace. Painted to accompany a copy of the medieval manuscript, *Sir John Mandeville's Travels*. Probably Bohemia, 1420–50. (© Copyright The British Museum).

Plate 2 A damaged Egyptian faience object showing the white core covered with a copper-coloured outer layer.

Plate 4 The Lycurgus cup, a cage cup (*diatreta*), made of dichroic glass. The decoration depicts the story of Lycurgus, the ill-fated Thracian king strangled by vines after taunting the god Dionysus. Viewed by transmitted light appears deep red, often described as magenta, and amethystine purple on the body of Lycurgus. Viewed by reflected light, the glass appears opaque olive green. The silver gilt rim mount, stem and foot were added probably in the late seventeenth or eighteenth century. Perhaps made in the Rhineland, fourth century AD. H 16.5 cm. (© Copyright The British Museum).

Plate 5 A fragment of glass displaying an iridescent surface, the result of decomposition.

Plate 3 Squares of glass mosaic decorating an object of copper alloy, and partly obscured by copper corrosion products. (Courtesy of J.M. Cronyn).

Plate 6 Nubian beads of glass or faience, with traces of the woollen thread on which they were originally strung. The deteriorated, enamel-like surface layer has fallen away from some beads, revealing the turquoise colour of the glass beneath.

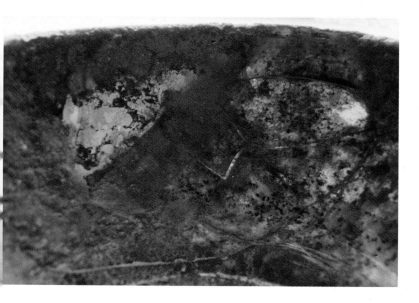

Plate 7 A detail of fake restoration. A fragment of a turquoise bowl has been inserted in a deep blue glass bowl of identical design. The area was then covered over with mud and flakes of iridescence.

Plate 8 A batch of coloured polyester resin, from which small amounts are measured out and catalysed as required.

Plate 9 Colour-matching resin to the glass object to be restored. (Courtesy of K. van Lookeren Campagne).

Plate 10 A glass *epergne* (table centre to hold cut flowers) after restoration with coloured polyester resin. (Courtesy of K. van Lookeren Campagne).

Table 4.1 Factors for converting weight percentages into relative molar percentages, for frequently occurring glass-making oxides

Oxide	Factor	Oxide	Factor	Oxide	Factor
SiO_2	0.601	PbO	2.232	Al_2O_3	1.020
K_2O	0.942	CuO	0.796	Fe_2O_3	1.597
Na_2O	0.620	MnO	0.710	Sb_2O_3	2.915
Li_2O	0.299	ZnO	0.814	As_2O_3	1.979
CaO	0.561	CoO	0.749	B_2O_3	0.696
MgO	0.403	TiO_2	0.799	P_2O_5	1.420
BaO	1.534	SnO_2	0507	SO_3	0.801

Table 4.2 Worked example, converting weight percentages to molar percentages

Oxide	Weight percentage	Factor	Relative molar proportions	Molar percentage
SiO_2	64.3	0.601	107.0	65.9
K_2O	16.7	0.942	17.7	10.9
Na_2O	0.7	0.620	1.1	0.7
CaO	10.0	0.561	17.8	11.0
MgO	7.1	0.403	17.6	10.8
Al_2O_3	1.2	1.019	1.2	0.7
	100.0		162.4	100.0

are each one-hundredth of the corresponding molecular weight), and then the results are adjusted so that their total is 100 per cent. The method of calculation is shown in the worked example given in *Table 4.2*. The first column is the composition of the glass in terms of its constituent oxides; the second column is the usual weight percentage distribution of these oxides; and the third column gives the factors, taken from *Table 4.1*, by which the weight percentages are divided. The fourth column gives the relative molar proportions, and their total is 162.4, so that each has to be divided by 1.624 in order to obtain the molar percentages given in the fifth column. It should be noted that the weight percentages of MgO, CaO and K_2O are quite different, but the molar percentages are almost the same.

These molar proportions of oxides (Table 4.2) are combined according to the following rules: the alkaline earth component, RO, is obtained by adding together all the oxides with this formula, i.e. CaO + MgO + MnO + CuO + PbO etc. In this example it is CaO + MgO, or 11.0 + 10.8 = 21.8 per cent.

The network formers are almost entirely silica (SiO_2) but forest-type glasses often contain as much as 5 per cent P_2O_5 and this must be added to the SiO2, as well as any TiO_2, ZrO_2, SnO_2 etc. In addition, it was shown in Chapter 1 that Al_2O_3 occupies a special place, each molecule being able to immobilize an alkali ion, and it can also be incorporated into the network. Thus the total of the network oxides has to be increased by twice the Al_2O_3 (and similar oxides, such as Fe_2O_2, Cr_2O_3 etc.). In the example, the total of network-forming oxides (called 'SiO2' because it is mainly SiO_2) is given by $SiO_2 + 2(Al_2O_3)$ = 65.9 + 1.4 = 67.3 per cent.

The remaining component in the triangular diagram is the alkali oxide, called 'R_2O' because it represents only the *available* alkali, and not the total alkali, some of the alkali being immobilized by the alumina. Thus 'R_2O' = K_2O + Na_2O–Al_2O_3 = 10.9 + 0.7 – 0.7 = 10.9 per cent.

The total of 'RO' + 'SiO$_2$' + 'R_2O' = 21.8 + 67.3 + 10.9 = 100 per cent. When the three values are plotted in the triangular diagram (*Figure 4.18*), it should be noted that in each case, the coordinate lines run parallel to the side which becomes the base when the triangle is turned so that the numbers can be read in a horizontal manner.

In *Figure 4.18*, the upper, central area indicates the range of durable glasses. The four points D to G confirm the fact that glass durability decreases when the silica content is less than 66.7 mol per cent, the line separating D and F being at 65 mol per cent of network formers. The glasses in the bottom right-hand corner are poorly durable. The two remaining points, the stars at W and Z, indicate, respectively, weeping and crizzling glasses. Thus it can be seen that the durability of glass decreases very markedly as soon as the composition of the glass moves a little to the left of the group A, M, R. The importance of the RO (lime) content can now be seen by considering the glasses Z, M, A, P, D, F, J; they all have about 15 mol per cent of available alkali but the RO varies from less than 5 mol per cent in Z to nearly 40 mol per cent in J and the durable glasses lie in a narrow band between 10 and 20 per cent RO.

Whilst the triangular diagram is a convenient method of displaying the effects of differences in glass composition, it does have limitations. For example, it does not discriminate between soda and potash, yet the soda glasses have about twice the durability of the potash glasses, or between the effects of lime and magnesia. Neither does it discriminate between different types of glass surface. It is even probable that there is a central plateau of very highly durable glass, and that the durability will fall off, suddenly and precipitously, especially as the composition moves to the left but also as one moves towards the bottom right-hand corner; if so, it could have a bearing on the existence of highly durable pre-first century AD glasses and complete absence (through deterioration) of glasses with less durable compositions.

The environment

Environmental factors affecting decomposition are: (i) water in the context of damp to waterlogged wetland sites, or underwater burial sites; or in the atmosphere both inside and outside buildings (precipitation, humidity, condensation); (ii) pollution of the atmosphere by gases which combine with water to produce acid solutions and/or form deposits on the glass. The effects of these agencies are linked to time and temperature. In the case of deep land or underwater burials the effects of pressure may also have to be considered (see *Figure 4.17*). Other environmental factors to be considered in connection with the deterioration of glass are those of temperature and temperature fluctuations, solarization, microorganisms, and, more recently, vibrations caused by road, rail and air traffic.

Burial

Physical aspects

Physical damage can occur as the result of animal or root action, ploughing, soil pressure, or land movement. Buried glass may also have been broken accidentally or deliberately before burial (e.g. glassmaking chunk glass, cullet, wasters, ritual etc.). Physical disintegration of glass may also occur as the result of repeated dissolution and crystallization of soluble salts within it, particularly on exposure to the air (Vandiver, 1992; Freestone, 2001).

Chemical aspects

Since water is the primary agent of corrosion, glass buried in a dry environment might be expected to survive indefinitely. However, even in desert areas, water tables can rise due to annual river flooding, irrigation, habitation, dam construction and earth movement. In a damp or wetland environment, where glass is continually exposed to water, its constituents will be leached out, particularly if the attacking solution is alkaline in nature. Glass is hardly affected by weak acid pollutants.

Newton and Seddon (1999) discuss various conditions where water could become saturated with ions and thus have a reduced leaching effect on glass (e.g. within stagnant waterlogged sites such as the bottom of disused wells). In soils, especially in peat or other humic horizons, there are numerous chelating or complexing agents, such as amines, citrates and acetates, many of which can have a detrimental effect on the durability of buried glass.

In Western Europe, the burial environment below *circa* 30 cm is much more stable than above ground. The RH is rarely less than 98 per cent, and the temperature is low and fairly constant. Above ground the RH varies widely and the temperature can change by several degrees within minutes. However, despite the high RH, the soil is not waterlogged; rather, each particle of soil is surrounded by a thin layer of water, so that the soil atmosphere (the space between the particles) is in close contact with water, and almost saturated. Consequently glass that on excavation appears dry, may in fact be hydrated and suffer a rapid and irreversible change in appearance, as the water evaporates.

Visible symptoms of deterioration

In general, glasses of a soda–lime–silica composition are more stable, and therefore survive burial better than those of a silica–potash–lime composition. The main visual varieties of glass surface alteration are dulling, iridescence and the formation of lamellar or enamel-like crusts, which may have become blackened. Deteriorated surfaces may also exhibit cracking, flaking and the formation of pits. Glass may also be recovered from burial in an apparently undeteriorated condition, appearing shiny, transparent and reflective. Rapid, irreversible changes in the appearance of heavily deteriorated glass can occur on exposure to the atmosphere (i.e. upon excavation). It may lose up to 23 per cent water by weight, becoming opaque and fragmentary.

Dulling
Dulling describes the condition of glass which has lost its original clarity and transparency, and become translucent (*Figure 4.19*). It is easily distinguished from dulling that is due to scratches, abrasion or stains.

Iridescence
Iridescence describes a variegated coloration of the surface of glass, sometimes occurring alone (*Plate 5*), and sometimes associated with other types of weathering. The thickness of the surface layers containing a concentration of metal oxides (in the order of hundreds of nanometres) causes light interference, resulting in the vivid iridescent colours, such as gold, purple and pink. When found alone, it is first

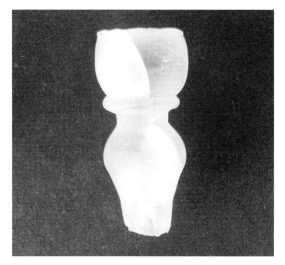

Figure 4.19 Dulling, the simplest type of weathering, in which glass loses its original clarity and transparency. (Courtesy of J.M. Cronyn).

visible in filmy patches, and it may then become abraded in powdery form. If undisturbed, the iridescence may develop into a thick layer, which may flake away. Thick layers of glass flaking away may eventually weaken the glass so severely that it collapses entirely.

Spontaneous cracking
Spontaneous cracking of glass occurs as the result of deterioration processes.

(i) The formation of a thick hydrated surface layer, which then undergoes dehydration with extensive loss of silica and thus a decrease in volume. The resulting strain on the surface is relieved by the formation of fractures. The process is likely to be the cause of a surface being covered with a network of tiny cracks similar in appearance to frost on windows (termed frosting). The cracks may be confined to the surface layers, or penetrate deeper (*Figure 4.20*), allowing ingress of attacking solutions, and may eventually lead to the total collapse of the glass (Wiederhorn, 1967). In such cases, moisture within the cracks and layers of decomposed glass, may be all that holds the object together, so that it disintegrates on drying (see also crizzling, below).

Figure 4.20 Spontaneous cracking of glass during burial, termed frosting, since the overall effect, resembles frost on windows.

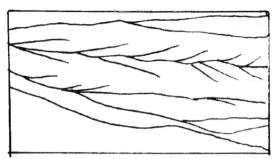

Figure 4.21 Spontaneous cracking, in the form of 'feather-type' cracks.

subsidiary branches. After some one thousand eight hundred years' burial the central cracks are some 1.5–2.5 mm deep and the side branches are 0.3–0.7 mm deep.' Cramp (1975) also reported this type of spontaneous cracking on glass from the Monastery at Jarrow (UK), but incorrectly described the phenomenon as a feather pattern incised on the surface.

(iv) A relatively slight scratch in the surface of the glass may subsequently lead to the formation of shell fractures on one side of the crack. These characteristic fractures grow in a curved manner and reach the surface of the glass again so that a small lenticular fragment can leave the surface. A pit remains, which is usually elliptical in shape, except where it abuts the scratch that initiated it, and is shallow, the sides bearing conchoidal fracture marks. Scratches in the surface may penetrate a soluble surface layer and thus lead to greatly accelerated corrosion beneath the scratch.

Milky or enamel-like surfaces

As the name suggests, milky or enamel-like deterioration products are usually opaque white, but they may also be light brown or mottled brownish-black in colour. In its incipient stage, when visible merely as small spots or streaks of white, it has been termed milky weathering, and may sometimes be confused with stone inclusions. The spots, which represent sites of deterioration, gradually progress into the body of the glass. It may flake away in small crystals, leaving pits in the glass.

(ii) The outer layers of hydrated silica are no different from silica gel (and are referred to by glass scientists as the gel layer). Being hygroscopic, they behave in the same manner in response to changes in atmospheric water (relative humidity) or liquid water. The layers absorb and desorb water (vapour) at the same time expanding and contracting, which leads to the formation of microscopic surface cracks. These allow agents of destruction to penetrate deeper into the glass.

(iii) Spontaneous cracking following the physical scratching of glass (on a fragment of Roman window glass from Great Casterton, Leicestershire) was reported by Harden (1959) (see *Figure 4.21*): 'The original scratches (of unknown depth and date) have subsequently developed

Figure 4.22 The surface of a glass torso of Aphrodite, covered by a thick milky-white weathering surface, which in some areas has flaked away to reveal an iridescent layer beneath. H 95 mm. *Circa* first to second century AD. Near East or Italy. (Corning Museum of Glass).

Figure 4.23 Section through a fragment of deteriorated glass, showing the invasion of the interior. (Courtesy of J.M. Cronyn).

On the other hand, the patches of milky weathering may remain and develop over the glass surface, forming layers ranging in thickness from a few micrometres to millimetres. The most developed form, enamel-like weathering, appears as a thick coating varying in colour from white to brownish-black, over a large part of the entire surface of an object (*Figure 4.22*). This too has a tendency to chip off, exposing highly iridescent pits and thin lamellae. When highly deteriorated, with little or no recognizable glassy core remaining, an object may collapse (*Figures 4.23* and *4.24*). A deteriorated glass surface may actually consist of many layers, usually sub-parallel to the original surface. (It has formerly been suggested that these layers may have offered a method of dating glass, since it was observed that the number of bands on some glasses was close to their calendar ages in years. However, this is not the case, see Chapter 6.) The layers may represent variations in the hydrated silica concentration, since

Figure 4.24 A fragment of glass with a thick blackened enamel-like surface. The glass has become so weakened through deterioration that pieces are falling away. (Courtesy of J.M. Cronyn).

in many decay products these are virtually the only components present, with only small concentrations of sodium or potassium and of calcium. In addition to leaching of the alkali, less soluble chemical components of the glass may be concentrated in the surface layers. For example, where lead is present, even in low concentrations, lead salts (carbonates, phosphates, sulphates) may be precipitated as the result of lead leaching out and anionic components leaching in. Similarly iron, aluminium, manganese, tin and antimony oxides, all of which commonly occurred in ancient glasses, may be enriched in the deterioration layers.

Black discoloration

Excavated glass may have an opaque blackened layer on the surface (see *Figures 4.8* and *4.24*). The darkening or blackening may be due to (i) oxidation of iron and manganese ions present in the glass (see below) (Shaw, 1965, Knight, 1999); (ii) the action of sulphur-reducing bacteria actively producing hydrogen sulphide in anaerobic conditions; or (iii), rarely, due to the formation of lead sulphide. This only occurs in glasses having a high lead content (not usual in medieval glass), buried in anaerobic conditions where sulphate-reducing bacteria are actively producing hydrogen sulphide (HS) (Smithsonian Institution, 1969).

Potash glass used to make much medieval glass in northern Europe has a tendency to develop dark spots (pits) and an opaque lamellar crust during burial, which is often dark brown or black in colour in contrast with the featureless fissured and pale colour of the atmospheric corrosion product found on medieval glass windows. The darkening effect is due to the oxidation of iron (II) and manganese (II) ions present in the original glass, derived from sand and beechwood ash used in its manufacture. In their reduced states the $Fe(II)$ and $Mn(II)$ cause the pale green colour of most glass, but during the leaching process, the ions are hydrated and oxidized. Pale pink hydrated $Mn(II)$ ions and pale green $Fe(II)$ ions are converted into dark brown $MnOOH$ and $FeOOH$. The result is a dark amorphous precipitate of hydrated iron (III) and manganese (III) oxides held in the pores of the leached hydrated silica layer. The oxidation process is most rapid in the highly alkaline conditions at the leached layer/bulk glass interface. In section, under magnification, a brownish-black dendritic invasion of the interior of the glass may also be observed,

Figure 4.25 Magnified section through a fragment of glass, showing deterioration proceeding from the surface to the interior, presumably following the lines of cracks. (Courtesy of J.M. Cronyn).

apparently following the lines of cracks into the glass (*Figures 4.24* and *4.25*). The staining appears to have diffused into the glass on either side of the cracks. (X-ray diffraction gives only a very weak pattern for quartz.) It has been stated formerly that iron and manganese diffuses into the glass from the surrounding soil. This is not the case, however, since iron and manganese oxides are only soluble at very low pH and are completely insoluble at pH 8 or 9, which is the level present at the glass surface as a consequence of the leaching of the alkali cations.

Freshwater

Ancient and historic glass artefacts may be recovered from freshwater environments such as the bottoms of rivers and lakes, where they will have been subject to physical damage, insoluble salt deposition and chemical deterioration. Depending on the purity or pollution of the water, the glass may or may not be affected by salts (Singley, 1988).

Seawater

A study of the effects of the marine environment on inorganic artefacts has been published by Weier (1973). Ancient and historic glass artefacts may be recovered from shipwrecks, where the presence of the glass ranges from cullet used as ballast, cargo and

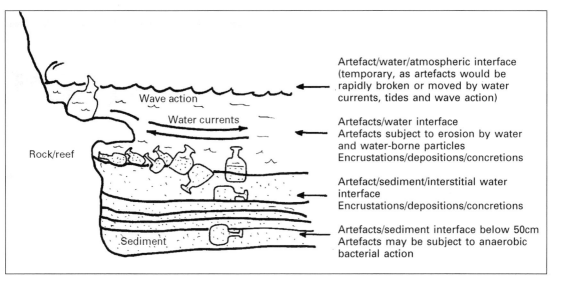

Wave action

Water currents

Rock/reef

Sediment

Artefact/water/atmospheric interface
(temporary, as artefacts would be
rapidly broken or moved by water
currents, tides and wave action)

Artefacts/water interface
Artefacts subject to erosion by water
and water-borne particles
Encrustations/depositions/concretions

Artefact/sediment/interstitial water
interface
Encrustations/depositions/concretions

Artefacts/sediment interface below 50cm
Artefacts may be subject to anaerobic
bacterial action

Figure 4.26   Deterioration of glass in a marine environment.

glass artefacts for the use of crew and passengers. In 1969, 120 panels of glass *opus sectile* were recovered from an ancient warehouse in Kenchreai, the ancient port of Corinth in Greece (see *Figures 7.7a–e*). Apart from a few known fragments of *opus sectile*, these panels are unique, and continue to be the subject of much investigation (Koob *et al.*, 1996, Moraitou in Kordas, 2002).

The wrecks at Ulu Burun and Kaş off the southern coast of Turkey (Bass, 1979, 1980, 1984) and that at Sadana Island (Ward, 1998) have been excavated by the American Institute of Nautical Archaeology, in Turkey and Egypt respectively. Conservation of the glass from these sites has been reported by Pannell (1990). In 1969 a wreck dating from *circa* 80 BC was discovered off the Greek island of Kythera south of the Peleponnese. The ship was found to have been carrying a cargo of glass amongst which were polychrome and gold glass vessels. Roman glass has been recovered from Baia near Naples (Branda *et al.*, 1999). Cox and Ford (1989) investigated glass excavated from the wrecks of *The Amsterdam* (Hastings, UK) and the *Drottengina af Sverige* (Lerwick Harbour, Shetland Islands, UK). Over many years, a series of shipwreck sites has been investigated and partly excavated by teams of maritime archaeologists and conservators from the Western Australian Museum in Freemantle (Pearson, 1975; MacLeod and Davies, 1987; Corvaia *et al.*, 1996; MacLeod and Beng, 1998). The glass recovered from the wrecks has undergone investigation and analysis.

Physical aspects

The condition in which glass artefacts are recovered from a marine environment will have been determined by the physical and chemical aspects of the seawater and the bottom sediments in which it has lain (Weier, 1973) (*Figure 4.26*). Dramatic physical damage can occur on objects recovered from a marine environment (or salt laden land site) by the action of soluble salts upon drying. Soluble salts dissolved in water within the object will, upon evaporation, crystallize within or upon the surface, causing disruption. If the relative humidity of the air increases, the salts will dissolve, only to reform when the relative humidity falls. If this action is repeated continuously, the object will be severely damaged or destroyed (*Figure 4.26*).

Seawater is a physiologically balanced, dilute salt solution containing the known elements, some dissolved gases and traces of many organic compounds. Apart from a few constituents produced or consumed by biological activity, the composition of unpolluted seawater is relatively constant. Seawater with

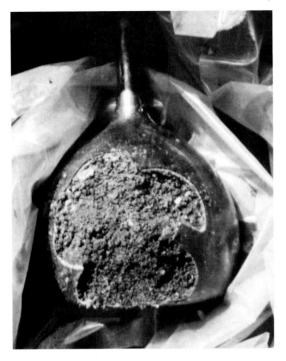

Figure 4.27 Marine concretion inside a glass flask, which has hardened on drying. Soluble salt crystals have formed on the surface of the concretion. (Courtesy of the Institute of Nautical Archaeology, Texas).

Figure 4.28 Marine encrustation on a bottle. (Courtesy of A. Alonso Olvera).

a salinity of 34.325 per ml is considered standard. The dissolved oxygen content of seawater is determined by temperature, pressure, salinity and biological activity. The solubility of oxygen increases with decreasing temperature and decreasing salinity.

The physical aspects of light, temperature and water movement determine the kind of marine life that will inhabit the sea, and in turn will affect the number of organisms, the oxygen concentration and the pH of the water (seawater is only slightly alkaline, pH 7.8 to 8.2). Light and temperature will effect diurnal or seasonal cycles. Pollution by domestic sewage or organic wastes greatly increases the concentration of organic derivatives such as nitrogen compounds and phosphates, and may result in a marked deficiency in the oxygen concentration. Archaeological objects found on the seabed may have been in an environment with little or no oxygen depending on pollution, organic decay and microbiological activity. Sulphur-reducing bacteria have been known to blacken glass objects, both in the sediments and under concretions.

The sea-bed is predominantly rock, sand, silt or clay. Objects deriving from a ship wrecked in a rocky area may be physically destroyed, or be washed into cracks and crevices in the rock, where they may lie protected and become covered over with sand. Objects lying on sand overlying bedrock or on a sandy bottom swept by currents can be rapidly destroyed. Silt, being of smaller grain size, does not settle where there are strong currents and therefore artefacts deposited in it will probably not be subject to water movement and may be protected by the silt. Clay binds tightly to any object buried in it as a consequence of its colloidal properties and small grain size. However it is more likely that artefacts will be deposited on the clay surface having an overlay of fine silt, and therefore be subject to physical damage. Hollow or broken glass objects will become filled with debris, which may harden on exposure to the air (*Figure 4.27*).

Because of their fragility, glass artefacts are unlikely to survive if they are exposed on the seabed. However, if they are initially protected in a wreck or other shelter, other than by burial, they may become covered by marine fouling organisms, which leave behind their mud homes, or calcareous shells or skeletons (see *Figure 4.28*). These take a number of forms:

- Semi-motile fouling organisms: (i) sea anemones and allied forms; (ii) worms which build more or less temporary, loosely adherent tubes of mud and sand for protection. These organisms frequently abandon their tubes – often 20 cm (8 in) or more in length – and move to another location; (iii) certain crustacea, e.g. corophium, build small temporary sand and mud tubes which they cement to material submerged in salt water; (iv) various molluscs, e.g. mussels, attach themselves to objects by means of a mat of very strong chitinous hairs (a complex organic material), and this remains firmly attached to the artefact after the mussels have died.
- Sessile organisms: organisms that build hard calcareous or chitinous shells, and which cannot survive without becoming firmly attached to a suitable base: (i) annelids, which form coiled or twisted tubes; (ii) barnacles, which construct cone-shaped shells built up of laminated plates; (iii) encrusting bryozoa, colonial animals which form flat, spreading, multi-cellular, coral like patches; (iv) molluscs of several species, e.g. oysters and mussels; (v) corals, of which there are many forms. Organisms without hard shells: (i) marine algae: green, brown or red filament growths; (ii) filamentous byozoa – fern- or tree-like growths; (iii) coelenterates (hydroids), such as tubularia, with stalk-like or branching growths, each branch terminating in an expanded tip; (iv) tunicates (sea squids) – soft spongy masses; (v) calcareous and siliceous sponges.

Fouling usually begins with the arrival of marine bacteria or other unicellular marine organisms. They form a thin film on the artefact, which then provides a favourable foothold for macro-organisms. These themselves are commonly in the minute larval or undeveloped juvenile form and secure a foothold in a manner characteristic to their particular group. A hard, smooth surface such as glass provides a firmer footing than a soft material. They help to protect the glass by slowing down the diffusion of ions, and therefore it is possible that glass artefacts may suffer little damage despite the fact that it is in a slightly alkaline medium of seawater. Most concretions on objects recovered from the sea are porous (those on iron being the most porous because of the rapidity with which they were formed).

Chemical aspects

Seawater is a buffered, very slightly alkaline solution, with a pH ranging from 7.5 to 8.5. When in equilibrium with the carbon dioxide of the atmosphere, the pH of seawater ranges from 8.1 to 8.3. The removal of carbon dioxide by photosynthetic processes of marine plants increases the pH; the decomposition of organic matter removed from the influence of the atmosphere decreases the pH. Certain generalizations can be made concerning the pH of marine sediments: the pore-size of the sediment can sometimes be an indication of the oxidation state, sandy bottoms allowing for the movement of water containing air (resulting in a higher pH); while a finer grained silt generally promotes reducing anaerobic conditions by the prevention of water circulation (resulting in a lower pH). The colour of a sediment is also an indication: highly oxidized sediments are usually brown, whilst the reduced acidic sediments vary from grey to green to black. The colour is affected by the amount of marine humus and the amount of hydrogen sulphide produced by bacterial activity. The greatest bacterial activity might be expected to occur in coastal areas receiving land drainage. However, as a result of sedimentation, by which bacteria are carried to the sea bottom by sediment particles, greater bacterial concentrations are found within the sediment.

Carbonate precipitation

Most of the dissolved carbonate in the sea (derived from atmospheric carbon dioxide) is in the form of hydrogen carbonate (HCO_3). The CO_2 content decreases as the pH increases, there being no free CO_2 in solution in seawater more alkaline than 7.5, most of it occurring in combination as bicarbonates and carbonates. If the temperature, salinity or pH of the seawater increase, carbonates will be precipitated, usually as calcium, magnesium and/or strontium carbonate. Carbonate concretions covering inorganic materials recovered from the sea can be formed in four ways, but only the first two are relevant to glass: (i) physically (by the growth of organisms, see above); (ii) biochemically (by various microbiological activities which ultimately lower the pH); (iii) physio-chemically (by the solution and re-precipitation of carbonates, especially stone); (iv) electrochemically (by precipitation on the cathodic and anodic areas, especially metals). The sulphate reducing bacteria play an important role in carbonate precipitation because they release H_2S into the environment, which rapidly lowers the pH. Concretions formed in the sea are often heavily stained by iron salts, and it has been established that the hydrogen sulphide released by the sulphate-reducing bacteria reacts with the ferrous irons in the water or sediment to form iron sulphide which precipitates with the calcium carbonate.

The atmosphere

Chemical effects of air pollution

Examination of European medieval window glass has provided evidence of glass decay occurring as the result of atmospheric environments (Newton, 1982b; Römich, 1999a). Glasses held in collections for many decades may also have been affected by atmospheric pollution, humidity, incorrect storage conditions (Ryan *et al.*, 1993, 1996) or previous attempts at conservation and restoration.

It had long been supposed that air pollution, and in particular sulphur dioxide (SO_2), had been responsible for the deterioration of medieval window glass (Fitz *et al.*, 1984). Nevertheless, there seems to be no direct evidence that sulphur dioxide actually attacks the glass, although it accounts for the presence of the sulphates always found on the surface. Similarly, carbon dioxide (CO_2) does not attack glass directly, but combines with water, and

converts the hydroxides produced by the attack of water on glass, to carbonates; it accounts for the calcite frequently found as part of the weathering crust. The damaging effect of so-called acid rain is the result of atmospheric CO_2 and SO_2 being dissolved by rainwater, thus forming weak acids which attack the glass. (Carbonic acid may also help in the formation of alkali carbonates, which, being hygroscopic, will attract water to the glass.)

Three stages are involved: first, an attack of the glass by water to produce hydroxides; then the subsequent conversion of hydroxides to carbonates by the carbon dioxide in the atmosphere; and finally conversion of carbonates to sulphates (Newton, 1979, 1987). Sulphites may play a role in the chain of events. It is also likely that other industrial pollutants such as hydrogen fluoride may account for damage to medieval window glass. The durability of medieval glass windows has been reviewed by Newton (1982b).

The weathering crusts found on medieval window glass *in situ* are a form of enamel-like weathering. The crust may be more than 1 mm thick, and the window rendered quite opaque, thus no longer fulfilling its original function of allowing light into a building (see Figure 4.13). The crust may be very soft and powdery, or hard and flinty. It may appear white, brownish or even blackish, and a great deal of gypsum (calcium sulphate) is usually present. Scott (1932) seems to have been the first to demonstrate that the weathering products (on fourteenth-century painted window glass from Wells Cathedral, Somerset, UK), consist largely of sulphates. This is accounted for by SO_2 in the air, arising from natural sources (Newton, 1982b). The most informative studies of weathering crusts on medieval window glass have been carried out by Collongues (1974, 1977; Collongues and Perez-y-Jorba, 1973; Collongues *et al.*, 1976; Perez-y-Jorba *et al.*, 1975, 1978, 1980) and Cox *et al.* (1979).

Visible symptoms of deterioration

Formation of surface pits and crusts

Pits and crusts form on the surface of glass during burial, immersion or in the atmosphere, but have been studied mainly in the context of medieval window glass. The deterioration of glass resulting from the formation of surface pits and crusts was originally regarded as being essentially two different phenomena. Bimson and Werner (1971) suggested that pits only formed in potash glasses, and that crusts only formed on soda glasses, but in fact this is not the case. It seems likely that the formation of surface crusts is actually preceded by the formation of pits in the glass surface. Cox *et al.* (1979) demonstrated that undeteriorated glass from York Minster (UK) generally had a SiO_2 content greater than 60 mol per cent; that crusted glasses usually contained less than 60 mol per cent SiO_2; and that pitted glasses generally lay in the range 57 to 63 mol per cent SiO_2.

It has been noted on fragments of medieval window glass from more than one source, that, at least in the early stages, (i) pits have a distinctive cylindrical shape; (ii) they seem to be uniform in size on any given piece of glass; (iii) the size of pits varies from one piece of glass to another; and (iv) pits form in some glasses but not in others. The reasons for these phenomena have not been fully explained. However, it is thought that the size, depth and distribution of pits are related to the size and distribution of the water droplets on the glass surface (see solution marks and condensation); and that defects in the glass surface may also play a part in promoting their formation, by holding water in specific sites by surface tension. The formation of crusts on glass, or in the pits which contain white deposits, may sometimes have a protective action, by preventing aggressive agents from reaching the glass; or conversely, by retaining water and alkali in close contact with the glass, may have an accelerating action on its deterioration. Fissures in deteriorated glass would enable water to enter pits where it would be held by surface tension and accelerate the attack. This may also account for the fact that pits develop downwards, i.e. into the glass, and for their distinctive cylindrical shape (Cox and Khooli, 1992).

Humidity

Atmospheric moisture in the form of humidity (water vapour) and condensation can cause the deterioration of glass objects, Egyptian faience and enamels held in collections, glass stored in damp conditions, and to medieval glass *in situ*. It is a particular problem in countries having a climate of high temperatures and humidity (Walters and Adams, 1975).

In the case of opaque glass objects having what appears to be a stable surface, any heterogeneity in the interior, which may be affected by humidity, will be concealed as long as the outer shell remains intact. Such a condition existed in the case of a large Egyptian scarab of the Eighteenth Dynasty, which had been on exhibition at the British Museum (London) for many decades. There had been no reason to regard it as being abnormal in any respect, when it was reported as having suddenly developed cracks. On examination it was found to be so hygroscopic that it would not remain dry for 2 minutes at a time. The glass scarab fell to pieces; from an examination of its interior, it became obvious that the condition was different from that of the exterior.

A white salt efflorescence formed on parts of the fractured surface but no such crystallization occurred on the exterior. It had only required a micro-crack to form in the surface of the object for moisture to have access to the hygroscopic material inside. The mobilized salts then crystallized and caused the disintegration of the scarab. A similar example is shown in *Figure 7.54*.

Chemically unstable glass, which is described as sick, weeping, sweating or crizzling, repeatedly generates droplets of moisture on its surface, if exposed to conditions of high humidity. This is the result of alkali being leached out of the glass by the atmospheric moisture (see discussion of weeping and crizzled glass in the earlier section on chemical deterioration, and *Figures 4.15–4.17*).

During the Second World War (1939–45), a great deal of European medieval window glass was placed in protective storage. Unfortunately this was often in damp cellars. Exposure to 100 per cent RH, and probably also surface moisture, for 5 years or more seems to have developed a hydrated surface layer on the glass. This was subsequently prone to rapid deterioration, probably due to the opening up of fissures in the hydrated layer as it dried out when the windows were reinstalled. (Thus the glass could have seemed to be in good condition when it was removed from storage, and to have decayed more rapidly during the following time period.)

Condensation

Studies of the effect of condensation have suggested both that glass decays more rapidly when exposed to cycles of condensation or drying than it does when exposed to a continuous level of high humidity (Simpson, 1953), and that the reverse is also true (Newton and Bettembourg, 1976). This apparent contradiction may be explained by the extent to which condensed water has run off the glass surface. If the condensation was so heavy that the droplets merged into a film which was thick enough to run off the glass, leached alkali would also be removed. If, however, the condensation occurred in minute discrete droplets, which then dried out, leached alkali would remain on the surface, to form nuclei around which droplets formed during the next phase of condensation would accumulate (Adlerborn, 1971). Solutions of high pH would then form at each site, furthering the attack on the glass. It seems also that deterioration is more rapid at a liquid/air/glass boundary (Weyl and Marboe, 1967). It seems reasonable to conclude that the formation of pits in a glass surface may be the result of water and leached alkali accumulating in droplets.

The effect of enamel colours, yellow staining and leading

Enamel paint, and/or the yellow stain, fired on to stained glass can either play a protective role, or promote localized deterioration of the underlying glass (Newton, 1976b). Their effects have been investigated in connection with medieval window glass, but are also known on vessel glass (*Figure 4.29*). The paint is generally more durable than the glass so that, after weathering has occurred, the painted line-work may be raised above the rest of the surface of the glass. Less frequently it can have the reverse effect, and marked deterioration has occurred where the glass had been painted. In the case of the yellow stain, Knowles (1959) stated, incorrectly, that 'The yellow stain which is applied always to the back of the glass (i.e. facing the outside of the building) invariably protects it from corrosion.'

Various hypotheses have been forwarded in an attempt to explain the phenomena; for

Figure 4.29 Detail of a medieval glass beaker, showing the effect of the loss of enamelled decoration.

example, the paint could encourage corrosion if it had too high an alkali content, and it might protect the glass if it lost much of its alkali content to the atmosphere during firing. Similarly, the protective effect of silver stain could readily be explained on the grounds that the sodium ions in the surface have been replaced by silver ions, and leaching of the silver would not make the solution alkaline in the way that sodium ions would. Also, the silver compounds were applied in a medium or slurry of various binders. However, none of these plausible hypotheses has yet been put to the test.

It was formerly believed that the enamel on the interior surface of medieval window glass seemed to extract material from the glass, and render it more liable to deterioration on the exterior, a phenomenon termed back-matching corrosion (Knowles, 1959). It has now been shown (Newton, 1976b) that the corrosion on the outside is restricted to areas where the original artist, in a wish to strengthen the design on the inside, had applied matting (smeared or stippled paint) on the outside to match (or supplement) the paintwork on the inside. The matting, being porous, retained water, thus encouraging deterioration to occur.

Another phenomenon associated with the deterioration of glass in connection with painted decoration is the existence of ghost images of the design. These have been shown to be caused by the volatilization of alkali from the paint on another piece of glass from the same panel when both were fired, one on top of the other, in the same kiln (Newton, 1976b). The volatilized alkali had left the glass more prone to deterioration, and over eight centuries it had lost 0.2 mm in thickness.

The leading on window glass has also been reported as having an effect on the durability of the glass. In some cases the corrosion appears to be enhanced along the sides of the leading, perhaps by virtue of moisture containing dissolved atmospheric pollutants being retained under the lip of the leads if the cement had fallen out. Since lead is a better conductor of heat than glass, there is greater tendency for dew to form along the leads. What are more difficult to understand are the many cases where the middle part of a piece of glass has corroded but the corrosion is absent in a band within about 20 mm of the leading. If the leads have been cemented well, the original thickness of weathered glass can be estimated by measuring the part which had been protected; the original thickness could not have been greater than the width of the 'heart' of the leading.

Physical effects

Solarization

In 1825 Faraday produced a scientific report on the effect on glass of solarization. Glass, which had originally been colourless, has been known to develop a marked purple tint when exposed to sunlight for a long time. This phenomenon, known as solarization, was first shown to have been produced by the interaction of Fe_2O_3 and MnO, leading to the formation of Mn_2O_3 and Fe_2O_3 (Pelouze, 1867) (compare Equation 1.3 in Chapter 1). The effect is particularly noticeable in examples of nineteenth-century house windows, which have assumed a marked purple hue in the course of time. This effect can be seen, for example, in the windows of old houses along Beacon Street in Boston, Massachusetts, USA (Brill, 1963). Examples can also be seen in Antwerp in Belgium, and most restorers of nineteenth-century window glass will have encountered it.

Micro-organisms

Organic growths may be found on glass stored in damp conditions, and on neglected medieval church windows, and may be associated with glass deterioration. Obviously the most difficult problems associated with organic growths on glass are found in hot, humid countries. Micro-organisms such as mosses, lichens, liverworts and algae, do not attack clean glass. While they do not require any nutrients since they obtain food by photosynthesis, they require dirt, grease or pitting as a substrate to provide a foothold on the glass. Lichenous growths probably do not attack glass directly but promote corrosion by trapping moisture next to the glass and thus help to accelerate decomposition. The most common types of lichen found on church windows are *Diploica lanescens Ach.*, *Pertusaria leucosora Nyl.* and *Lepraria flava Ach.*, all frequently being found on smooth glass. Most have a crust-like growth and are best adapted to growth on an exposed substratum because the whole of their undersurface is attached to the support. Most lichens are found on the outer side of the glass, particularly on north-, west- and east-facing windows, where there is good air circulation, a certain intensity of light and some humidity; but wind and hot sun-rays are inhibiting. It seems that water is retained between the glass and the lichen by capillary action. The water contains CO_2 from respiration of the lichen. As the *hyphae* become more or less turgid due to growth and water availability, so the glass is subjected to pressure and chemical attack. Fungi may also be found on glass. They require an organic source of nutrient, which seems to be available from CO_2 in the atmosphere (Tennent, 1981).

It has been suggested that 'silicophage' bacteria may attack buried glass, but no details appear to have been published (Winter, 1965, Newton, 1982b). Examination of a batch of blackened water-logged glass from the marine underwater archaeological site *HMS Sapphire* (1696) at Bay of Bulls, Newfoundland, by Florian (1979), showed that the blackening was due to the deposition of ferrous sulphide, and that much of the deterioration of such glass is associated with microbiological organisms – bacteria being present on all surfaces examined (the samples had been stored in fresh water for nearly a year prior to examination).

Previous treatments

The use of chemicals to 'clean' glass or to remove encrustations, causes irreversible damage. Chemicals may be difficult to remove entirely, even by washing, and should only be used when absolutely necessary, for example use of acid to reduce thick marine concretion to a thickness that can be removed mechanically. (If acid reaches exposed areas of glass it will damage it.) The results of treatment with chemicals, adhesives, consolidants, moulding and gap-filling materials should be known, and as far as possible, be reversible without damage to the artefact under treatment. The use of commercial cleaning agents of unknown or uncertain composition (and which may contain chelating or complexing agents), the over-use of acids, alkalis etc. or their non-removal after treatment does irreversible damage to glass.

Ancient glass artefacts are unlikely to be placed in a dishwasher, but incredibly cases are known of historic glass collections being

Figure 4.30 Permanent bloom (cloudiness) on a wineglass, the result of being cleaned in a household dishwashing machine.

cleaned in this way. Chemicals in the detergent or finishing powders can do irreversible damage, particularly to lead glasses, on which a white bloom forms (*Figure 4.30*).

EDTA (ethylenediaminetetra-acetic acid) has been recommended for removing weathering crusts and other stubborn surface encrustation, particularly in relation to the cleaning of medieval window glass (Bettembourg, 1973; Bettembourg and Burck, 1974). However, since EDTA also attacks glass (Paul and Youssefi, 1978), cleaning has to be very carefully controlled, and the EDTA washed off as soon as glass becomes exposed.

EDTA favours rapid lead extraction in potash lead silicate glasses, and as a consequence increases the extraction of potash. This is not due to the formation of complex K^+ salts, as potassium does not form a stable complex, but to the removal of the blocking effect of the lead from the hydrated silica surface. As the concentration of EDTA increases, the K_2O/PbO extracted ratio decreases. Barham (1999) used selected chelating agents to remove obscuring deposits, thus revealing the painted decoration on medieval window glass.

Some complexing agents can decrease the rate of corrosion, as is the case with ethanol, which is adsorbed onto the surface of the hydrated silica and forms insoluble ethyl silicate, which acts as a protective layer, retarding leaching.

Glass science

Investigations related to the chemical durability of commercial and industrially produced glasses were included in the discussion of the deterioration of ancient and historic glasses by Newton in Newton and Davison (1989). However, the distinction between the results obtained and the natural deterioration products found on ancient and historic glass was not made. Most of the studies of chemical durability have been carried out on glasses of simple (binary, i.e. silica and alkali) composition, whereas ancient glasses are complex, by virtue of impurities in the raw materials used, and the fact that their manufacture was based on empirical knowledge.

As previously mentioned, the parameters governing the deterioration of glass are inter-dependent and complex. Experiments have been helpful in understanding the fundamental principles of glass deterioration, but cannot be used as an indicator to the actual deterioration products which will have occurred on complex archaeological glasses that will have been subjected to uncontrolled, natural environments over long periods of time. The research may prove helpful in predicting the response of archaeological, and more likely, historical glasses to various storage and display conditions. This would be of particular significance in countries having a moderate to high rainfall and/or a high variable humidity.

Understanding the altered surfaces of deteriorating glass

As mentioned above, the surface of a glass is highly influential on the effects of the deterioration processes that occur on it. However, there are a limited number of possible permutations of fresh glass-leached layer-precipitated phase formation. As the results of experiment, Hench (1977, 1982) and Hench and Clark (1978) described these in terms of six generic types of glass surface formed as a result of exposure to an aqueous solution. These are shown in *Figure 4.31*. The six types of glass surface do not of course describe the many different compound surfaces which form on the surfaces of archaeological glass. Only three of them (Types II, IV and V) would seem to be relevant to the deterioration of ancient/historical glass.

The Type I surface has an extremely thin (less than 5 nm) hydrated layer and no significant change in surface composition, either by loss of alkali or of the silica network. It represents an extremely durable glass (such as vitreous silica) exposed to a solution with a neutral pH. It is therefore unlikely that there are any ancient glasses with a Type I surface.

The Type II surface possesses a silica-rich protective film, where the alkali has been lost but the silica network has not been damaged. The glass is very durable; it has a low alkali content and the pH of the leaching solution (for one reason or another) does not rise above 9.0. However, if flat glass having a Type II surface is stacked closely together in moist conditions, a large surface area (*SA*) is exposed to a small volume of water (*V*) trapped between the layers of glass, where it gradually

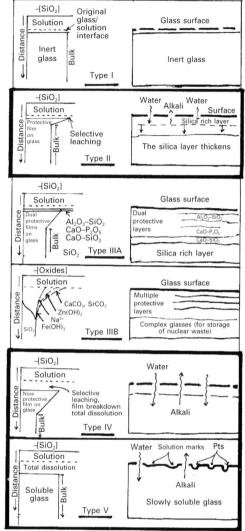

Figure 4.31 Six types of glass surface defined by Hench (1982), interpreted in archaeological/conservation terms, by the author. (a) Type I, an extremely thin hydrated surface (5 nm) with no significant change to surface composition; an extremely durable glass surface, which would not occur in antiquity. (b) Type II, a silica-rich protective film with loss of alkali, but no further changes to the silica network. Ancient and historic glasses may develop this type of surface. (c) Type IIIA, a double protective film consisting of aluminium silicate or of calcium phosphate, deliberately formed on modern glasses in laboratory experiments. (d) Type IIIB, multiple protective layers deliberately formed on glasses used for the storage of radioactive waste. (e) Type IV, a silica-rich film, which however is not thick enough to prevent loss of alkali or destruction of the silica network. Ancient and historic glasses may develop this type of surface. (f) Type V, a glass surface which is slowly soluble in water, and may therefore develop solution marks and corrosion pits. Ancient and historic glasses may develop this type of surface.

becomes highly alkaline. As a result of this, the surface loses its durability. This effect can be observed, for instance, on poorly stored lantern slides, or panels of window glass.

Glasses with Type II or Type IIIA surfaces appear quite glossy and unmarked, and undeteriorated, with any original surface blemishes easily visible. Nevertheless, the surfaces would be largely leached of alkali.

The Type III layer is a double protective surface film of aluminium silicate or calcium phosphate, and can exist in two versions, IIIA and IIIB. The addition of aluminium oxide or phosphorus oxide to the glass results in the formation of an aluminium silicate – or a calcium phosphate-rich glass on top of a silica-rich layer. These protective films can be produced by adding the oxides mentioned above to the glass batch, by alkali extraction from a glass containing the oxides, or by precipitating the alumina or phosphate from solution. The addition of sufficient Al^{3+} ions to the water, for example, as aluminium chloride ($AlCl_3$) at a concentration of more than 25 ppm of Al^{3+}, can greatly reduce the leaching of alkali and destruction of the glass network in both acid and alkaline conditions, due to the formation of a Type IIIA surface. At first (for example, in the first few hours, depending on the Al_2O_3 content of the glass), the attack on such a glass can be relatively rapid, a Type V surface being formed, but within a day or two the situation becomes reversed due to the precipitation of an alumina-silicate complex on the surface (Hench and Clark, 1978).

Archaeological glass may contain traces of alumina and phosphorus, but it is unlikely that the amounts would be sufficient to have a significant effect on its deterioration/preservation, especially since there are more dominant parameters at play. Many medieval window glasses contain substantial amounts of both Al_2O_3 and P_2O and the formation of Type IIIA surfaces must be considered as part of the general situation regarding their complex weathering behaviour. (The Type IIIB surface, added by Hench (1982), is characterized by the formation of multiple protective layers composed of oxides, hydroxides and hydrated silicates. It is found on complex glasses for the storage of nuclear waste.)

The Type IV surface is also a silica-rich film, but the silica concentration is insufficient to protect the glass from migration of alkali or destruction of the network. Many medieval window glasses may be considered to fall into this category because of their low silica content.

The Type V surface is slowly soluble in the leaching solution. There is extensive loss of alkali accompanied by loss of silica, but because the attack on the glass is uniform, the surface composition remains the same as that of the bulk glass, and thus it superficially resembles that of the durable surface Type I. However, as the glass is attacked, solution marks develop on the surface. These are particularly noticeable on transparent samples viewed in oblique illumination (Newton, 1982a). The Type V surface also has a marked ability to form corrosion pits, because the local concentration of alkali in surface defects (solution spots) can exceed pH 9.0, the critical point at which attack on the glass becomes progressive. This mechanism, and the manner in which it was investigated, is described in detail by Sanders and Hench (1973). Type V surfaces are extremely susceptible to scratching and abrasion when the scratches are deeper than 0.2 μm. The scratch produces a small trough in which the extracted alkali can collect and progressive degradation of the network then occurs at that point. Scanning electron micrographs in Sanders and Hench (1973) show very fine scratches produced by 600-grit silicon carbide, which have developed into relatively deep (perhaps 0.4 μm) troughs by exposure to a small amount of water for 216 hours (this glass had a very low durability). When 120-grit silicon carbide was used as the abrasive, the resultant troughs are perhaps 1 μm deep.

Experimental research into chemical durability of glass

Accelerated ageing tests

In order to obtain an idea of the deterioration processes associated with glass, within a short period of time, accelerated ageing tests are undertaken in laboratory conditions. These include increasing the surface area of the glass to the volume of the attacking solution, raising the temperature, cyclical increase and decrease of the relative humidity and exposure of glass to acid or alkaline environments. As a result of such experiments, there is a large body of literature concerned with the durability of glass (e.g. Hench, 1975b; Paul, 1977). Whilst the results of accelerated ageing tests can give an indication of the natural weathering processes, which might be expected to occur over time, it cannot be assumed that the two processes correlate exactly.

Increasing the surface area of glass to the attacking solution

Many accelerated ageing tests involve increasing the ratio of glass surface area to the attacking solution volume (SA/V), often by using the glass in crushed form. This procedure may yield valid information on the properties of the bulk of the glass, but these are likely to be very different from the properties of the ancient glass surface, where other parameters come into play (Ethridge *et al.*, 1979).

Raising the temperature

Raising the temperature of its environment, increases the rate of attack on glass by aggressive agents.

Thermodynamics

Attempts have been made to predict the deterioration of glasses from their composition by thermodynamic approaches, first proposed by Paul (1977) and developed by Jantzen and Plodinec (1984). Thermodynamics relate the loss from glass as a result of deterioration with a calculated free energy of hydration for the glass composition concerned.

Paul (1977) states that, for most silicate glasses, the quantity leached in a given time is doubled for every 8–15°C rise in temperature, depending upon the composition of the glass and the type of alkali ion in question. Bacon (1968) gives the following formula:

$$\log t1 = \log t2 + (T2 - T1)/23.4 \qquad (4.3)$$

where $t1$ and $t2$ are the times for leaching at temperature $T1$ and $T2$ in °C. This produces a doubling in the rate of leaching for a rise of 7°C. There is the possibility that reactions will occur at higher temperatures, which hardly occur at all at ambient temperatures (Hench and Clark, 1978). In addition, the thickness of the protective high-silica surface layer formed on heating is far less than that formed at ambient temperatures.

In terms of thermodynamics, there is a good correlation where compositional differences between glasses is high, for example between volcanic obsidian glass and soda–lime–silica glass. However, in terms of differentiating between compositionally similar archaeological glasses, the method is less useful. As an example, Cox and Ford (1993) calculate similar free energies of hydration for Roman glasses excavated from Wroxeter, (Shropshire, UK), which show apparent deterioration rates (derived from the thickness of the hydrated layers) differing by factors approaching an order of magnitude. Freestone (2001) expressed the opinion that a difference in correlation rate of this order is crucial, in that it can determine whether a thin glass vessel, of 1–2 mm wall thickness, has a thin layer of deterioration or is totally destroyed. Thus minor differences in glass composition and local environmental factors are likely to be of greater significance than free energies of hydration, calculated using present models, in determining the relative rates of decay of archaeological glasses (Freestone, 2001).

Cyclical humidity

A test that may yield results similar to those obtained, particularly on historic glass and on medieval window glass *in situ*, is the cyclic increase and decrease of humidity (Simpson, 1953; Bacon and Calcamuggio, 1967; Römich in Kordas, 2002).

The effect of acids on glass

Experimentally, El-Shamy *et al.* (1972) studied the effect of acids on glass, down to pH 1.0, and showed that the pH was not significant unless there was some 20 mol per cent of CaO in the glass. In that case, the extraction of NaO and CaO increased greatly as the pH was reduced below 4. Such high-lime glasses are readily soluble in mineral acids (El-Shamy *et al.*, 1975). El-Shamy (1973) conducted experiments involving glasses made to medieval compositions, and showed that the extraction of CaO by 0.5 mol HCl (hydrochloric acid) was greatly increased when the CaO or MgO content of the glass was as much as 15 mol per cent. When the CaO and the MgO were both present at 15 mol per cent, the extraction of both was more than doubled. Neither of these papers discusses what happens to medieval-type glasses exposed to weak acids, such as carbonic acid (a solution of CO_2 in water) or sulphurous acid (a solution of SO_2 in water), when the pH value is between 6 and 7, corresponding to rainwater or even polluted rainwater. Ferrazzini (1977) applied 1 mol HCl on a medieval glass sample, and produced an ion-exchanged layer 1 mm thick in one hour.

Burial experiments

Short-term burial experiments have been carried out by Römich (Römich *et al.*, 1998; Römich, 1999a,b; Römich in Kordas, 2002) on a number of potassium-rich model glasses. These were buried in garden soil saturated with water at varying ranges of pH 7.8, 3.5 and 8.9, at room temperature and for periods of between six weeks and seven months. After nine months, the following results were obtained: (i) at pH 3.5, a single deterioration layer, cracks and local deterioration had occurred; (ii) at pH 7.8 approximately 50 per cent of the glass had deteriorated; (iii) at pH 7.8, a layered structure had formed over the entire glass surface and deep cracks had formed in the glass. The samples were analysed by light microscopy, scanning electron microscopy on cross sections and infrared spectroscopy.

In 1970, a long-term glass burial experiment was begun at Ballidon (Derbyshire, UK), with the intention of recovering samples at different times until the year 2482. Nine types of glass were buried in a mound, at ground level and mid-mound level. In 1986, 28 samples were removed for examination and 46 commercial samples of glass were buried. Not all the original samples were found. Of those exhumed, six of the nine types showed no significantly visible signs of deterioration and thus would seem to have been of a too durable nature to reveal the intended information. The six types were: no. 1, a simulated Roman glass; no. 4, polished plate glass; no. 5, 'as produced' plate glass; no. 7 Pyrex ovenware; no. 8 high-quality soda–lime–silica glass; and no. 9, a high lead optical glass. The worst signs of deterioration were slight iridescence on sample no. 8 and the emphasis on a few old scratches on samples nos. 5, 7 and 8. The three types of glass which did show appreciable signs of deterioration were no. 6E, glass marbles, which had developed wing fractures at impact points where the marbles had rolled against one another after manufacture. No. 2, a simulated medieval glass, displayed a surface iridescence which tended to run in lines, perhaps following otherwise imperceptible differences in homogeneity. The only type which showed obvious deterioration was no. 13, a simulated Saxon type of glass, which had developed an extensively crazed surface layer about 260 µm thick which could easily be removed (Newton, 1992).

5

Materials used for glass conservation

The materials used in the processes of conservation and restoration fall into several categories: solvents and reagents, adhesives and consolidants, surface coatings, modelling, moulding and casting materials, pigments and dyes. In addition, there are those used to construct supports to facilitate the safe display of fragile pieces, and those used for safe storage and packaging.

It is important to bear in mind that all chemicals are potentially dangerous, and care is required wherever they are stored, used or discarded. Manufacturers' data sheets should be obtained, and safety instructions contained within them heeded. Whenever appropriate, safety goggles, fume or dust extraction masks and protective gloves and clothing should be worn, and fume extraction facilities used. Solvent hazards fall into three categories: flammability, toxicity and corrosiveness. All chemicals should be clearly marked with the appropriate hazard labels. Detailed information on materials used for conservation is given by Horie (1987).

Cleaning agents

The materials chosen to clean a particular piece of glass will depend on the condition of the glass and any applied surface decoration, and upon the substances to be removed. Extraneous matter can range from mud, calcareous or iron deposits or other accretion found on glass recovered from land, water or marine sites, to previous repair or restoration materials. In addition, products formed during the decomposition of glass may have to be removed. A wide range of materials may therefore be required for cleaning glass: water, detergents, chelating (sequestering) agents, acids, organic solvents and biocides. It must be remembered that these materials, especially those which are formulated commercially, may have deleterious effects on glass if used injudiciously. Their uses are described in Chapter 7, but their important properties in relation to use on glass, and dangers to the conservator, will be discussed in this chapter. Mechanical methods of cleaning and the use of cleaning agents both have advantages and disadvantages, which should be evaluated before work begins.

Water

Despite the fact that water is the primary agent for causing glass to deteriorate, it is also the most commonly used solvent for cleaning glass. The reason for this apparent contradiction is that if glass and any decorative surface are sound, short exposure to water does not harm it. Water will, however, remove poorly adhering paint or gilding and loose glass flakes from the surface of deteriorated glass (during burial or conservation cleaning). Prolonged exposure, e.g. during burial or submersion, will cause dissolution of alkali from the glass. Water may be used in several forms, e.g. sea water (gradually replaced with tap water), tap-water, or de-ionized or distilled water which have been treated to remove dissolved salts. Tap water usually contains calcium and magnesium hydrogen carbonates, chlorides and sulphates. The amounts vary with the district; in hard-water areas the amount of salts can be more than 170 mg per litre. The hydrogen carbonates which cause temporary hardness are stable in solution only when the water is acidified with dissolved carbon dioxide. These salts can therefore be precipitated from ground or atmospheric water by boiling. The sulphates and chlorides cannot be removed by boiling and cause permanent hardness.

When droplets of water evaporate on a glass surface, tiny deposits of salts may be visible, e.g. calcium, sulphates and magnesium (also potassium or sodium hydroxides (or carbonates) in the case of unstable glass). Such deposits are commonly erroneously referred to as water stains. Very visible deposits of calcium carbonate can sometimes be formed in vessels such as flower vases that have constantly contained water. In order to prevent such deposition therefore, purified water (which has had the salts removed) should be used when treating glass objects. Impurities in water can be removed by two methods: distillation (to produce distilled water); and treatment by ion-exchange resins (producing de-ionized water). Washing of glass with water should be kept to a minimum; glass should not be left to soak, if possible (obviously this cannot apply to glass from wet environments, stored in water).

Detergents

The term detergent is applied both to the chemical compounds (surfactants) and the commercial products (formulae) that act in a solvent to aid the removal of soiling and contaminants. Surface active materials for use in water can be divided into three groups: anionic, cationic and non-ionic. The terms refer to the nature of the polar, hydrophilic, group in the molecular structure of the surfactant. Surface-active compounds have a two-fold nature, since each molecule has a polar and a non-polar end. One end is compatible with the solvent used and the other will interact with the soiling substances. The most commonly used non-ionic detergents used in conservation were the nonylphenol ethoxylates (NPEs), examples being Lissapol, Synperonic and Triton brands. Their use is being phased out as a European Community Directive (EC PARCOM Directive 92/8), (although still available in Canada and the USA), because their degradation products mimic oestrogen, and when discharged into the environment, affect marine life. A number

of surfactants is being tested to ascertain their suitability for use in conservation (Fields, 2000). The manufacturer of the Synperonic range of surfactants has introduced Synperonic A7, an alcohol ethoxylate which is readily biodegradable, and conforms to EEC directive 82/242. Glass is most commonly washed with an inert detergent dissolved in distilled water, although detergents have been developed with the increased use of non-aqueous (i.e. dry-cleaning) solvents.

A commercial detergent formula is a mixture of chemicals each of which plays a role in the cleaning operation. A typical formulation for washing powder contains alkali, surface-active chemicals, chelating agents, suspension and thickening agents. Many of these ingredients can damage glass or other surfaces. The use of commercial products cannot be recommended because their ingredients are unknown in detail and thus the effects of their ingredients on ancient glasses cannot be foreseen.

It is unlikely that the commonly used detergents have any serious toxicity if used sensibly. However, long immersion of the hands in detergent solutions will extract the oily protective chemicals from the skin and leave it open to invasion by infection; since the use of barrier creams may contaminate an object, it is preferable that conservators with a sensitive skin should wear protective gloves (Davidsohn and Milwidsky, 1978).

Chelating (sequestering) agents

Many metal ions are stable in water solutions only when the pH is in the correct range, or when appropriate anions are present. Chelating agents can stabilize metal ions over a wide range of solvent conditions. A chelating agent has a strong reaction with the metal ion, enclosing it in a protective complex (Richey, 1975), for example, ethylenediaminetetra acetic acid (EDTA):

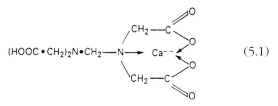

$$(HOOC \bullet CH_2)_2 N \bullet CH_2 - N \longrightarrow Ca^{--} \eqno(5.1)$$

The characteristic of chelating agents is the formation of stable, multiple bonds between the chelating agent and the metal ion. The materials that usually have to be removed from glass with chelating agents are weathering crusts that consist of calcium carbonates and sulphates in combination with silica. The metal ions that have to be removed are the same as those that make up the glass, and it is therefore difficult to apply any solution to the weathering crust that will not penetrate and react with the glass beneath, or react with the glass as soon as the crust has been removed. For this reason the use of chelating agents must be assumed to affect the underlying glass and it is the conservator's job to minimize the contact of these reagents with the glass surface (Ferrazzini, 1977). The use of pastes made up with a thickening agent such as Sepiolite (magnesium trisilicate) or carboxymethylcellulose sodium salt may confine the action of the solution to the surface to which it is applied. However, chelating agents will extract the more accessible atoms first and it is therefore possible that the weathering crust may be weakened before any significant attack on the underlying glass takes place. The weakened crust may then be removed by gentle mechanical means (Bauer, 1976), but the removal of crusts from glass is a drastic treatment that needs careful consideration. Chelating agents can conveniently be divided into three groups: polyphosphates, aminocarboxylic acids and hydroxycarboxylic acids. Their use has been largely in the field of medieval stained glass conservation, however, a few references to this work are given here, as there may be a need to consider their use, as a last resort, to clean other types of glass.

Polyphosphates

Polyphosphates were introduced as water softeners in the 1930s to chelate and keep in solution calcium and magnesium ions. They are still widely used in commercial detergents; Calgon, for instance, is a polyphosphate where the value of n (below) is about 12 (Albright and Wilson, 1978). They can therefore be used to dissolve calcium and magnesium salts from hard crusts.

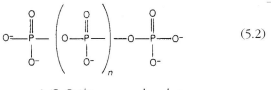

$$(5.2)$$

$n = 0$ $(P_2O_7)^{4-}$ pyrophosphate
$n = 1$ $(P_3O_{10})^{5-}$ tripolyphosphate

Other phosphates are:

PO_4^{3-} orthophosphate
$(PO_3^-)_n$ metaphosphate (a ring structure)

Bettembourg (1972, 1973) used a solution (solution A) consisting of an aqueous solution of 10 per cent sodium thiosulphate (NaSO .5HO) and 5 per cent sodium pyrophosphate (NaPO.10HO) to clean medieval window glass. The reported effects of these polyphosphates on glass seem contradictory, and it is possible that much may depend on the nature of the actual piece of medieval glass being cleaned. Frenzel (1970) recommended the use of Calgon, but Frodl-Kraft (1967) used it only with caution, provided the solution process was halted before the actual surface of the glass was reached. Four years later, however, Frodl-Kraft discontinued the use of Calgon because it was found to creep along the glass surface, under the painted decoration, and loosen it (Frodl-Kraft, 1970, 1971). Ferrazzini (1977, Figures 2 and 3) has published illustrations showing how Calgon produced cracks and other types of damage on glass surfaces, which become apparent on drying or aging.

Polyphosphates tend to hydrolyse in solution to the orthophosphate anion, which forms insoluble salts with alkaline earths, and should therefore not be used on glass.

Aminocarboxylic acids

The most commonly used chelating agent of this class is EDTA:

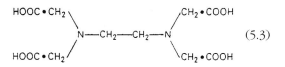

$$(5.3)$$

The tetra acid can be partly or totally reacted with sodium hydroxide, and various

EDTA products with different proportions of sodium are available (Richey, 1975, Table 1). EDTA can be used to hold calcium and magnesium ions over a wide range of pH values between pH 7 and pH 11, and it will chelate lead from a lead-containing glass (Paul and Youssefi, 1978; Olsen *et al.*, 1969). There is a large number of other aminocarboxylic acids which are similar to EDTA but provide a range of potentially useful properties. An example is N, N-*bis* (2-hydroxyethyl) glycine, HOOC-CH2N(CH2 CH2 OH)2. This does not chelate calcium and magnesium ions but does hold other metal ions in solution (Davidsohn and Milwidsky, 1978). Solution B used by Bettembourg (1972a, 1973) is an aqueous solution of the sodium salt of EDTA, 30 gl⁻¹ buffered with 30 gl⁻¹ ammonium hydrogen carbonate (NH4.HCO3). At first the solution would seem to have been used without any other caution, soaking entire glass panels (still in their leading) in baths of EDTA solution for 2–3 hours, or until the required degree of cleaning had been achieved. However, in 1975, Bettembourg and Perrot (1976) changed the procedure to three successive applications of the solution on cotton wool swabs. Bauer (1976) claimed that EDTA does not harm the surface of glass, whereas Ferrazzini (1977) has illustrated damage caused by EDTA to poorly durable glass surfaces. No doubt, like the experience with Calgon, much depends upon the type of glass which is being treated, but there is sufficient evidence of the deleterious effects of EDTA on glass to show that great caution must be exercised in its use.

Hydroxycarboxylic acids

Hydroxycarboxylic acids act in two different ways at different pH values. Below pH 11 these acids form only weak complexes with alkaline earths, and a large excess of the chelating agent is necessary to ensure the dissolution of calcium ions. Above pH 11 they are more effective than EDTA or polyphosphates as chelating agents for calcium. Hydroxycarboxylic acids chelate iron and other multivalent ions over the whole pH range.

At pH 7, therefore, gluconic acid might be used to extract copper or iron staining from glass with relatively little effect on the alkaline modifiers of the glass. Citric acid is well

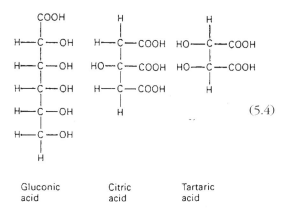

$$(5.4)$$

| Gluconic acid | Citric acid | Tartaric acid |

known for the damaging effect that it can have on glass surfaces (Bacon and Raggon, 1959). As previously discussed, chelating agents are non-specific in their action and will attack glass, especially at high pH values, causing damage by complete removal of the surface, or by selective leaching of the alkaline earth modifiers (Paul, 1978). Glass surfaces that have been treated with chelating agents are therefore made more liable to deterioration (Ferrazzini, 1977). The solutions must therefore be applied locally. As yet there is no chemical treatment for safely removing the iron staining from glass surfaces; improvements to chelating agents may, however, produce reagents that are more ion-specific. A review of chelating agents by Richey (1975) outlines the toxic hazards and main points of interest in their use.

Hydrogen peroxide

Aqueous hydrogen peroxide solutions can be used to bleach out organic stains on glass surfaces (Moncrieff, 1975). Hydrogen peroxide breaks down in solution to evoke an active form of oxygen $H_2O_2 \quad H_2O + [O]$ that can react with and decolourize organic material. A preservative, typically parts per million of phosphates, is added to solutions to slow down the spontaneous production of oxygen, and alkali can be added to increase the rate of oxidation. Hydrogen peroxide is purchased as a solution in water. The concentration of the solution is normally indicated by the volume of oxygen gas which one unit volume of solution will produce. For example, 100 vol. hydrogen peroxide is a 30 per cent solution.

The solution should be diluted to a 10 vol. solution for use on glass.

As oxygen can be evolved in large amounts, which rise as bubbles to the surface, hydrogen peroxide should not be used or stored near highly inflammable substances such as solvents. Hydrogen peroxide can oxidize organic material such as skin or clothing and it should be used with care, especially when in concentrated solution.

Mineral acids

Before the deleterious effects of applying acids to glass were fully understood, the mineral acids – hydrochloric, nitric and hydrofluoric – were used to remove surface deposits. All of these can attack poorly durable ancient glasses, especially when the lime content is high; and should not normally be used on glass artefacts (despite the customary use of nitric and chromic acids for cleaning laboratory glassware). Alternative, less invasive treatments are now available.

Mineral acids are supplied in the form of concentrated solutions: hydrochloric acid (HCl) 30 per cent; nitric acid (HNO_3) 75 or 90 per cent; sulphuric acid (H_2SO_4) 98 per cent; hydrofluoric acid (HF) 40 per cent. All of these, but especially sulphuric acid, become very hot when added to water. For this reason acid should always be added to water, never the other way around. This will reduce the danger of concentrated acid boiling and spitting when it comes into contact with water.

Mineral acids can cause burns on the skin, and hence protective clothing (gloves, eye-shields and aprons) is needed, and scrupulous cleanliness is important. Dilute solutions splashed on clothing, or on the bench, will evaporate, become more concentrated and be likely to cause burns hours after the acid bottles have been put away in a safe place.

Hydrofluoric acid is particularly dangerous because it differs from other acids in the way it attacks living tissue. The concentrated acid can attack the surface of the skin, as do other acids, but the fluoride ion diffuses through healthy skin and fingernails to precipitate calcium in the tissues beneath, thus causing intense pain which can occur some hours after contact with dilute fluoride solutions has ceased. Although still used commercially for etching glass, hydrofluoric acid should not normally be used for conservation work. However, should its use ever become necessary, it is of the utmost importance that advice be sought upon the stringent safety precautions to be taken and the specific First Aid treatment required in the event of an accident occurring. Antidotes for poisoning with hydrofluoric acid are calcium gluconate gel in the United Kingdom and zephiran chloride (a benzalkonium chloride) in the United States.

Organic solvents

Organic solvents are used for three purposes in conservation: for removing greasy dirt, for applying or diluting polymers in solution, and for removing polymers. The term solvent is usually assumed, as here, to mean a mobile organic liquid, but it can be extended to cover solids, such as those polymers that can dissolve dyes etc. by absorption. Polymer-solvent interactions are important, and it is therefore necessary to understand those properties (Horie, 1987).

As previously mentioned, all solvents are potentially dangerous to those using them, and to the environment, in terms of their toxicity and flammability, and care is required whenever they are used. Fume extraction facilities should be used wherever possible. It is sometimes possible to exchange a dangerous solvent for a less hazardous one, yet still retain suitable solvent properties, and this should always be done.

All organic solvents, except the highly halogenated ones, are flammable. Any fire must start in an air/vapour mixture, and hence the more volatile the solvent, the more readily it is ignited. A good indication is the closed cup flash point, which is the lowest temperature at which a spark above the liquid will cause the vapour to ignite. The lower the flash point, the greater the hazard, and the vapours can travel some distance from an open vessel containing the solvent. Hence naked flames, cigarettes, electric switches and other sources of sparks must not be used when solvents are employed. Even the non-flammable chlorinated solvents such as trichloroethylene can be dangerous when exposed to naked flames or cigarettes because they can be converted to the poisonous gas phosgene.

All solvents are toxic to some extent. Perhaps the most common and insidious damage is caused by breathing solvent vapour over extended periods of time; for this reason the effects and relative dangers of solvent vapour have been extensively studied (see below). However, liquid solvents can be absorbed through the skin and they dissolve the protective chemicals from the skin, thereby allowing ease of entry for infection.

There are two different kinds of vapour toxicity, both of which may occur with the same solvent:

- narcotic effects, causing drunkenness or poisoning, which wear off as the solvent is eliminated from the body (e.g. ethanol); and chronic effects, which persist long after the solvent was initially absorbed (e.g. methanol). The cancers induced by some solvents fall into the category of chronic damage.

The type of toxicity caused by two chemically similar solvents, such as ethanol and methanol, is not necessarily the same. Ethanol in moderate doses causes drunkenness and even unconsciousness, but the effects wear off as the ethanol is eliminated from the body. Methanol, on the other hand, is metabolized into products that cause permanent damage to the nervous system and may lead to blindness.

The danger of breathing solvent vapours is assessed in each country by its relevant authority, which should be consulted before using a material. In the United Kingdom the risk is summarized in the Occupational Exposure Limit (OEL), and in the United States of America in the Threshold Limit Value (TLV). In both cases, these specify the maximum concentration of the solvent vapour in the air that can be tolerated by a worker, without significant health risk. The measurement of the concentration of a solvent vapour has been made much easier in recent years by the development of simple and relatively inexpensive instruments. For example, the Draeger system works by drawing a known amount of air through a tube of chemicals, which indicate the concentration of vapour in the air by changing colour.

The OEL (HSE 2000) and TLV (ACGIH 2000) listings are updated annually and are part of a wider assessment of risk, also published by these and other similar authorities.

Biocides

Micro-organisms can cause difficulties during the conservation of glass. Archaeological glass excavated from waterlogged conditions is frequently dirty and hence can support fungal and bacterial growths; stained glass can act as a support for the growth of mosses and lichens.

When archaeological glass from wet sites is stored, biocides should be added to prevent spoilage of the excavated material. Alkaline sodium salts should not be used because it is likely that they will cause corrosion during storage, and the quaternary ammo-compounds can form a hydrophobic layer (see above). 2-Hydroxybiphenyl is the only appropriate material that seems to have been investigated (for conservation use on wood). A saturated stock solution in water (0.07 per cent) can be added to packaged material awaiting stabilization. The weight of solution should be approximately equal to the weight of preserved material, thus producing a 0.035 per cent solution, which is sufficient to kill fungi. Too low a concentration of 2-hydroxybiphenyl should not be used because it may not immediately kill the organisms and they may become resistant to the biocide. Algae may be more troublesome to control, but they rely on light for photosynthesis to occur and hence the treated packages of glass should be stored in cool dark locations. Any package that has been treated with a biocide should be marked with the name of the material used, the amount added and the date.

Adhesives, consolidants and lacquers

Before the advent of synthetic polymers, the materials used for the consolidation, repair and restoration of ancient glasses were animal glues, natural waxes and resins, notably beeswax and shellac (Davison, 1984; Horie, 1987), and plaster of Paris. Their only advantage was that they held the fragments together, at least for a limited period. All had serious disadvantages compared with modern materials: glue shrinks, wax flows and attracts dirt, natural resins are brittle and plaster of Paris is opaque. These traditional materials are still used in some countries, and may be found on ancient glasses from collections.

Animal glues are composed of polyamides derived from the protein connective tissue (collagen) derived from bones and skin. The various types of glue (hide, bone or fish) are prepared by boiling the raw material in water with hydrolysing catalysts, which break down the collagen structure. The glues range from pale to dark brown in colour. They are applied in a warm liquid state and gel on cooling. As the gel dries, it shrinks through loss of water and this may cause sufficient tension to detach the surface of fragile glass objects. Animal glues and consolidants can be removed by the use of warm water applied either on cotton wool swabs, or, if the condition of the glass will allow it, by immersion.

Shellac is the alcohol-soluble portion of the exudate of the lac insect *Tacchardia lacca*. It is a polyester in which 20–40 per cent of the resin is aleuric acid; other components of the resin include aldehydes, hydroxyls, other carboxylic acids and unsaturated groups. It is dark brown in colour and is therefore unsightly. Shellac is initially soluble in ethanol and other solvents, but on ageing, polymerizes (cross-links) into a virtually insoluble mass. This mass is often difficult if not impossible to remove from fragile glass.

In contrast to animal glues and shellac, Canada balsam, the resinous component of the exudate from the pine *Abies balsama*, has a refractive index of 1.52, which is close to that of colourless soda glass. It has therefore been widely used for the cementing of optical elements in lenses, but apparently not for the repair of glass antiquities.

Adhesives based on dextrin have been used both to repair glass and as gum on labels to mark glass. Dextrins are polysaccharides produced by breaking down starches to form more soluble products; and they suffer the same form of degradation as cellulose. Moreover, the low molecular weight of dextrin makes the product hygroscopic and therefore unsuitable for the conservation of glass.

During and after the Second World War there were considerable advances in commercial and industrial polymer chemistry, one result of which was to make available many new materials, and further developments have tended to create a particular product for the intended end-use. But it is also necessary to evaluate the materials for permanence of their properties. In practice, however, it is usually necessary to make a compromise by selecting the material that has the least number of disadvantages with regard to the particular conservation task in hand. It has often been the case that, once a polymer has been found that satisfies enough of the requirements, it tends to be widely recommended until it is superseded by a new material. However, the formulation may be changed by the manufacturer without notice and this may affect the result when it is used in conservation.

At present the materials used in conservation, and discussed in this chapter, are: cellulose derivatives, epoxy, polyester and acrylic resins (including cyanoacrylates and photoactivated or ultraviolet curing adhesives), vinyl polymers, polyurethanes and silicones. Where possible, the chemical composition of materials should be known, also their toxicity before and during curing, and/or their potential as a cause of skin ailments such as dermatitis. The use of a fume-cupboard, extraction fan, goggles or protective gloves may be necessary. In general, products should be easily available at a reasonable cost, and preferably in small amounts, to reduce wastage due to expiry of shelf-life. The shelf-life of unmixed components should be known. Horie (1987) reviews of the use of polymers in conservation.

Theory of adhesion

In order for materials to fulfil their roles as adhesives, consolidants or gap-fillers, it is obvious that they must have a reasonable adhesion to glass. In order for this to be so, materials used to conserve and restore glass must have a strong attraction for glass surfaces; thus, when applied, they will flow and cover the glass so wetting it. They must then set (cure) to prevent movement of the fragments or vessels being treated. They must be able to adjust to strains set up during and after setting, should not put undue strain on the glass, and be as unobtrusive as possible. It is also desirable that adhesives, consolidants and gap-fillers should remain soluble over considerable periods of time.

Glass has a high-energy surface and, when clean and dry, will be readily wetted by any adhesive or contaminant. It is therefore essential that the surfaces to be adhered should be thoroughly cleaned to remove grease and dirt. However, the surface of glass is very hygroscopic and in normal humidities has many molecular thicknesses of water lying on it. The non-hydrogen bonding organic liquids do not spread spontaneously on the water-bearing glass surfaces. The area of contact between organic liquids and glass can be increased by lowering the level of relative humidity. It is therefore likely that poor initial wetting of the glass surface by the adhesive will result from the use of adhesives that cannot displace the water from the glass surface. Having once formed the adhesive bond, an adhesive (or gap-filler) may gradually be displaced from the surface by the attraction of glass for water. This displacement may be further induced by the deterioration reactions that occur at glass surfaces exposed to water; alkali ions in the glass migrate to the surface to produce their soluble hydroxides.

All polymers are permeable to water to a greater or lesser extent. All adhesives therefore allow the penetration of water through their films, and on to the glass surface. The water molecules can react in the pores of the glass surface that have not been coated with polymer and also at the interface of the glass under the coating. The alkaline solution formed in the pores and at the interface will absorb more water by osmosis, which will gradually generate a hydrostatic pressure confined by the adhesive. This pressure will put a stress on the polymer–glass adhesion and promote further loss of adhesion. The hydrolysis reactions take place faster on highly alkaline glasses than on the more stable modern glasses.

Silane treatment

It has been suggested that the problem of adhesion might be solved by pre-treating the glass surface with a coupling agent before application of an adhesive (Errett *et al.*, 1984). Such pre-treatment may be particularly useful in the field of medieval stained glass, where the glass is to remain *in situ*, but its use of glass in museums is not normally necessary

and would render repairs irreversible by means that would not damage the glass. However, it is worth discussing the use of silanes in order to elucidate on the above statement. There are various families of coupling agents, including phosphate and chromate, but the silane family has the most widespread use, and has already shown promising results in the field of stone-restoration.

Silane coupling agents are a class of monomers in which both the silicon group and the organic radicals contain reactive groups. They are of the general form R-Si(Y)$_3$, Y being commonly –OCH$_3$ methoxy or –OC$_2$H$_5$ ethoxy, and R is a reactive organic group. The Y groups hydrolyse with water to form reactive silanol R-Si(OH)$_3$ groups which can then react with themselves and with the surfaces to which they are applied. The R group can be chosen to react with a polymer which is subsequently applied to the surface; for example, unsaturated R groups are chosen to improve adhesion of vinyl-reacting polymers such as polyesters, and amine-containing R groups can be chosen for epoxies.

A typical silane coupling agent is amino-propyltrimethoxysilane: H$_2$N-CH$_2$–CH$_2$–CH$_2$–Si (OCH$_3$)$_3$. This is used to promote glass–epoxy adhesion, but many other silanes, with different organo-functional groups, are available.

The silane, applied in a dilute solution, reacts with water, on the glass surface and in the air, to form silantriols by eliminating the hydrolysable groups:

$$R - Si(OC_2H_5)_3 + 3H_2O$$
$$\rightarrow R - Si(OH)_3 + 3C_2H_5OH \text{ (ethanol)}$$

$$(5.5)$$

The silantriols react with hydroxyl groups on the surface, and with themselves, to form a tightly cross-linked three-dimensional layer attached to the surface with strong covalent bonds.

A polymer system that will react with the organo-functional groups can then be applied, the amino groups on the silane reacting with epoxy groups and bonding chemically to the adhesive. Coupling agents considerably

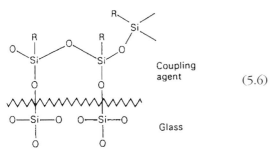

Coupling
agent   (5.6)

Glass

Table 5.1   Coefficients of expansion of polymers and glasses

Material	Coefficient of linear expansion (cm °C^{-1} × 10^{-6})	Tensile modulus (10^8 Pa)
Epoxy resins	45–90	24
Polystyrene	60–80	28–41
Silicones	200–400	0.6
Medieval window glass	8–15	–
Modern window glass	8	–

improve the adhesion of polymers to glass, both initially and on prolonged exposure to water. The silane groups immobilize the silicon atoms to which they are attached and reduce the adsorption and reaction of water thus delaying failure of an adhesive bond. However, coupling agents will not be able to prevent the diffusion of water molecules into the pores and onto the surface completely. The use of coupling agents can therefore increase the initial strength and life expectancy of an adhesive join considerably, but the bond will eventually fail due to water penetration and glass decay. However, their use on glass artefacts in the relatively dry atmosphere in museums may ensure that adhesive bonds will be effectively non-reversible.

Strain

Stress and strain on glass can result during and after curing of polymers, which invariably shrink on gelation due to loss of solvent, or to a polymerization reaction. This shrinkage sets up stresses at the interface between the polymer and the glass surface that makes the bond susceptible to both mechanical and chemical attack, for example, by the absorption of water, and the glass may deteriorate in special ways (Newton *et al.*, 1981). The effects of such stress will depend upon the force (elastic modulus) necessary to maintain the adhesive stretched over the non-yielding surface of the glass. A large shrinkage of the adhesive will cause only slight stress when the elastic modulus of the polymer is low. If, however, the elastic modulus is high, such as in the case of epoxy resins, then large stresses are created even though there is only a small shrinkage of the resin during curing.

Strains may also arise from the mismatch of thermal expansion coefficient between the glass and the polymer (see *Table 5.1*). The amount of strain produced at the interface will depend on the temperature change and the force necessary to compress the polymer when it tends to expand more than the glass. Strain may remain locked in the polymer system and thus remain a potential source of weakness in the bond; or cause cracking of the glass, in the polymer, or along the adhesive interface. Alternatively the polymer may slowly flow to relieve the strain.

Refractive index

Reflections result from light striking an interface between two materials with different refractive indices, for example air and glass, or polymer and glass. The larger the difference in refractive indices, the greater the degree of reflectance. Theoretically, the refractive index of an adhesive should match that of the glass exactly in order to avoid reflections from the surfaces of breaks, etc. (*Figure 5.1*).

For purposes such as joining the glass elements in an optical instrument, the refractive index of the adhesive need only match that of the glass to ±0.02. In optical elements, however, the light strikes the glass/adhesive interface nearly at right angles, but as the angle becomes more glancing the reflection increases. Light strikes a repaired glass object from all angles and hence cracks and joins will be rendered visible by glancing reflections from the crack surfaces, unless the refractive indices match by ±0.01 (Tennent and Townsend, 1984a).

The refractive index of a material varies with the wavelength, that is, the colour of the light. The value usually stated for a material is the refractive index found using sodium (yellow) light (this is the nD value). A slight mismatch of refractive index may lead to the formation of colours within cracks in the glass (Tennent and Townsend, 1984a,b). An added difficulty in matching the indices is the change of refractive index that occurs at a glass surface when weathering takes place.

However, there are other sources of reflection; when glass vessels break, they tend to spring out of shape, releasing the stresses in the glass, and a reconstruction is likely to leave slight misalignment between fragments which create thin lines of reflective surfaces across the vessel. Excess adhesive is frequently removed from a join before it hardens, by using solvents, or mechanically after setting. If too much adhesive is removed, reflections will arise from the dry edges left uncovered.

Deterioration of polymers

The polymers used for glass conservation are to a large extent derived from organic molecules and, therefore, like other organic materials, they are susceptible to oxidation and deterioration. The main environmental influences acting on polymers used in conservation are light (Tennent and Townsend, 1984a,b; Horie, 1987), oxygen and water; heat only rarely causes problems.

The mechanisms of deterioration are characteristic for each polymer and they are frequently difficult to unravel, but some general remarks can be made. Any or all of the following reactions can be caused by light, oxygen, water, or other impurities in the polymer film: cross-linking of chains; breaking of the chains (chain scission); formation of chromophores (groups which absorb light) leading to yellowing of the polymer. The cross-linking reaction in thermoplastics will convert a soluble film into an insoluble one.

Chain-breaking reactions cut the polymer chain, thus reducing the molecular weight. (It is this reaction that causes shortening of the cellulose chains in paper, thus weakening it rapidly when exposed to light and/or air.) Those polymers containing ester groups along the chain, such as polyester resins and polyurethanes, can be hydrolysed. They can, therefore, be slowly weakened by chain scission when exposed to water.

Yellowing of resins is caused by the absorption of blue or ultraviolet light by the chromophores. In most of the cases studied, the chromophores arise from loss or alteration of side groups to form conjugated double bonds and carbonyl groups along the chain. These chromophores are reactive and will absorb more energy from the light, causing further deterioration. The energy contained in light, especially ultraviolet radiation, is sufficiently powerful to break chemical bonds in polymers; it frequently initiates deterioration, and is a common cause of failure in polymers. All the forms of deterioration described above are caused by chemical changes in the molecular structure, but the physical state of the polymer can change in response to the environment. If the temperature rises above its glass transition temperature (Tg) a polymer has sufficient mobility in its molecules to be able to flow. For this reason even very tough thermoplastics, such as Nylon, cannot be used where a constant force is applied. Creep under stress (cold flow) results in the stretching of joins made with polyvinyl acetate. Movement of the polymer chains can also occur on a smaller scale and a particle of dust or dirt lying on the surface of a polymer above its Tg can be slowly incorporated and become fixed in the polymer film; this effect can be seen in emulsion paints where the Tg is less than 4°C, and in polyethylene bags (Tg = −20°C), both of which attract and hold dirt, even after washing. In addition, water will dissolve in a polymer film, causing slight swelling which may create stresses between the glass and the polymer.

The majority of polymer properties can be altered by adding another material. For example, polyvinyl chloride has mechanical properties which are similar to polymethyl methacrylate but the addition of softening agents (plasticizers) makes the PVC polymer flexible. The plasticizers are liquids that act as non-volatile solvents, but they can slowly migrate or evaporate, causing the polymer to become brittle.

Reversibility

The deterioration of polymers may or may not make their removal convenient. In any event, products used for conservation should have clearly established methods of removal (US: redissolubility), which avoids damage to the glass at any time in the future. The concept of reversibility, that is, that of taking the object back to its state before treatment, is basic to the whole of conservation, nevertheless it must be honestly stated that many conservation processes are not reversible. Everything, from drying the article to removal of weathering crusts, transforms the object in some way, and hence some information about the original state of the object may be lost during its treatment. However, the condition of some objects is so poor that action must be urgently taken to stop them disintegrating (Oddy and Carroll, 1999).

Reversibility must be seen on two levels: whether the gross treatment of an object, coating, adhesive, etc., can be removed without harm to the object; and whether the treatment, even after it has been reversed, distorted the information that could have been obtained from the original state of the object, for example by chemical analysis. Studies of the traces of adhesive left after self-adhesive tapes were stripped from glass plates have shown that minute quantities of adhesive remain, and can be detected, on an apparently clean, smooth surface. The same may well be true of the polymers alleged to have been completely extracted from the pitted and porous surfaces encountered in conservation. Therefore the treatment of an object with any polymer cannot be considered completely reversible because of the likelihood of traces remaining, but the treatment used must be recorded for future reference.

In practice, however, reversibility must be considered on a less rigorous basis, and polymers have been placed in two categories: permanently soluble polymers and polymers that form cross-links. It must always be borne in mind that it is the particular use of the polymer (the process) that determines whether the treatment is reversible, not the potential solubility of the polymer. For example, the majority of cross-linking resins will swell considerably when soaked in solvents, and this swelling will usually disrupt any edge-to-edge join, or surface coating, sufficiently to permit mechanical removal of the bulk of the resin. This use of cross-linking resins is therefore reversible when the surfaces of the object are smooth and non-porous, even though the polymer is not soluble.

Swelling of a polymer, whether cross-linked or not, will put stress on the object to which it is attached. Therefore, it is better to remove as much adhesive or coating as possible by mechanical means before swelling, in order to reduce the final stress on the object. The stress is likely to be low when the polymer is free to expand in at least one direction, for example, when used as a coating. However, when the polymer has penetrated into pores or between fragments of an object, the swelling of the polymer will tend to push the fragments of the object apart.

The process of consolidation uses the polymer to penetrate, harden and thereby bind fragments of an object together. It is in such a situation that removal of the consolidant will do most harm because the swelling will tend to disrupt the consolidated part of the object. Unfortunately the swelling of the polymer will tend to put the object into tension, the kind of force that most friable structures are least able to withstand. Thus any process involving the partial or complete consolidation of a porous object with any polymer should be considered to be irreversible.

As conservation methods improve, treatments that were considered to be irreversible may be able to be reversed. For example, the possibility of removing organic materials by the use of oxidizing plasmas has been demonstrated. This technique may permit the removal of so-called insoluble coatings.

The polymer selected to fulfil a particular role will depend upon the influences that the bond is expected to resist. A glass vessel standing in a museum case has less need for a water-stable adhesive than glass in a window which is frequently wetted, and which is inaccessible to further conservation work. Although it would be undesirable, the vessel could be restored every few years, but painted glass in a window must be expected to remain in place for more than one hundred years.

It is unlikely that an adhesive joint can combine reversibility with durability. The achievement of durability in the glass–polymer bond seems to require chemical reaction between the polymer and the glass surface. The durable bond will degrade in time, with the loss of some part of the glass surface. The reversible glass–polymer bond will operate by physical attraction and so it can be displaced

Table 5.2   Comparative table of optically clear epoxy resins used for glass conservation (manufacturers' data)

Trade/chemical name	Mixing proportions		Pot life @ 25°C	Viscosity of mixed resin	Curing time @ 25°C	RI	Comments
	Wt.	Vol.					
Ablebond 342-1 (Ablestick Lab. California USA)			8 hours	200 cps	48 hours	1.565	Resin crystallized at room temperature. No longer manufactured
Bisphenol A diglycidyl ether	10	10					
Polyoxypropylene diamine	3	4.6					
Araldite AY103/HY956 (Vantico)			1.5–2 hours	140 cps	24 hours	No data	Especially formulated for use on glass
Bisphenol A diglycidyl ether	10	10					
Modified aliphatic polyamine	1.6–1.8	1.8–2.0					
Araldite 2020 (formerly XW396/XW 397) (Vantico)			8 hours	130 cps	16 hours	1.553	Resin crystallizes at room temperature. Designed for optical filters
Bisphenol A diglycidyl ether	10	10					
Aliphatic polyamine	3	3.5					
Epotek 301-2 (Epoxy Technology Inc. USA)			1 hour	100 cps	24 hours	1.564	Resin crystallizes at room temperature
Bisphenol A diglycidyl ether	10						
Aliphatic amine	3.5						
Fynebond (Fyne Conservation Services, UK)			8 hours	No data	36–48 hours	1.565	Formulated for glass by Dr N. Tennent Expensive in UK Best ageing performance
Bisphenol A, epichlorohydrin	10	10					
Polyoxypropylene diamine	3.2	4.1					
HXTAL-NYL-1 (Conservators' Emporium, USA)			15 hours	No data	7 days	1.549	Formulated for glass by Herbert Hillary
Hydrogenated Bisphenol A, diglycidal ether	3						
Polyoxypropylene triamine	1						

physically by water in the environment; thus it is less durable.

To create the most durable chemical bonds between most polymers and glass, a coupling agent should be used. The improvement in adhesion will be gained only when both the polymer and the glass react with the coupling agent. This implies the use of one of the reactive, cross-linking, polymers as adhesives, consolidants or lacquers.

Types of synthetic polymer

Cellulose derivatives
Cellulose derivatives have been used for the adhesion and consolidation of antiquities for many years, and their properties are well understood. Cellulose nitrate (sometimes incorrectly referred to as nitrocellulose) was the first major plastic in commercial use, having been derived from natural cellulose in 1838, and produced industrially as early as 1845. Plasticized with camphor, cellulose nitrate was patented in Britain in 1864, and was discovered independently in America in 1869, where it was marketed as Celluloid. Cellulose nitrate is formed by the reaction of nitric acid with cellulose under carefully controlled conditions, and externally plasticized, commonly with dibutyl phthalate. Plasticized cellulose nitrate has a refractive index of 1.45–1.50. References to the early use of cellulose nitrate on decayed glass relate to a product called Zapon (Pazaurek,1903), and another marketed as Durofix (Plenderleith and Werner, 1976) In the form of HMG, Durofix and Duco Cement (US), cellulose nitrate is still in common use (Koob, 1982). In the form of the lacquer Frigiline, it was suggested for use as a consolidant for decayed enamels. A more suitable polymer would be Paraloid B-72 (US: Acryloid B-72, an ethyl methacrylate/methyl acrylate copolymer).

However, cellulose nitrate is known to have poor ageing qualities (Hedvall *et al.*, 1951; Koob, 1982). Despite the fact that attention has been drawn to the long-term instability of cellulose nitrate, it still remains a most useful adhesive for the restoration of glass, because of its comparative lack of colour, ease of application from a tube, and reversibility in acetone. As the product HMG as it is widely used for the repair of archaeological glass in Britain.

Soluble nylon
Before the use of the chemically stable product Paraloid B-72 (methyl methacrylate copolymer) as a consolidant in many areas of conservation, a product known as, Soluble nylon (N-methoxymethyl nylon) was widely used in the 1950s and 1960s. Marketed as Calaton CA and CB and Maranyl C109/P, it was usually made into a 3 per cent w/v solution in industrial methylated spirits. Its use on flaking glass surfaces has been mentioned by Dowman (1970), and Melucco (1971), who added that soluble nylon acted as a holding treatment, not prejudicing future treatments of the glass. The problem of cross-linking together with the fact that soluble nylon attracts dust onto the surface of objects on which it has been used, has resulted in the strong discouragement of its use (Sease, 1981).

Undeteriorated glass is almost impermeable to solvent vapour, and hence resins that require solvents to evaporate in order to effect their cure are inconvenient for use in repair, consolidation or restoration. For this reason, resins that polymerize *in situ*, and do not require access to the air for evaporation of solvent, are more suitable. In addition, the shrinkage of a polymerizing polymer is considerably less than a solvent-deposited polymer and hence strains are less likely to be exerted upon the glass.

Epoxy resins
Epoxy resins used in conservation are typically composed of two parts, a di-epoxy component and a polyamine cross-linking agent, both of which are compounded with diluents and catalysts (*Table 5.2*).

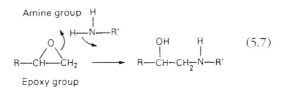

(5.7)

The hydroxyl groups formed in this reaction can take part in and contribute to further reaction with epoxy groups.

The epoxy resin shown in (5.8) is commonly used, and is a bisphenol A and epichlorohydrin condensate. The value of *n*

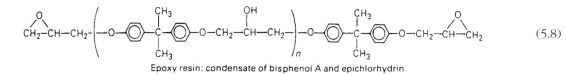

$$(5.8)$$

Epoxy resin: condensate of bisphenol A and epichlorhydrin

usually should be less than two in order to maintain the epoxy as an easily worked liquid. There is a wide range of amines available for use; many of the low viscosity amines are skin sensitizers and have a dangerously high volatility. For domestic use less unpleasant liquid polyamides are used with a catalyst. The polyfunctional epoxies and amines ensure a cross-linked polymer of high strength. The advantages of epoxy adhesives and gap-fillers are their relatively high adhesion and low shrinkage on curing. However, there is always some shrinkage in the polymerization of monomers. The shrinkage of an epoxy resin occurs at two stages, the first during the liquid state, and the second (greater amount) after gelation. A disadvantage of the bisphenol A/amine adhesives is their tendency to yellow with time and light exposure, owing to the formation of chromophores arising from the benzine rings that react with amine breakdown products. Bisphenol A epoxies, when cured with anhydride cross-linking agents at 80°C, form stable, non-yellowing polymers. Slight discoloration of the resin may be noticeable in time, when it is used on optically clear glass.

A disadvantage of aliphatic epoxies is their greater sensitivity to moisture. The use of epoxy resin has been suggested for consolidation of archaeological glass on site (Wihr, 1977), but the resin yellows, is difficult to remove from the glass surface, and is irremovable from porous materials such as decayed glass. In general, epoxy resins should not be considered for use as glass consolidants, particularly as there are more suitable products available, such as Paraloid B-72.

An American epoxy resin, Ablebond 342-1, was formerly widely used in the UK and the United States in the 1970s and 1980s for glass bonding, but is no longer available. A disadvantage of this product was that the hardener tended to crystallize at room temperature so that, on being measured for use, the hardener had to be warmed to liquidize it, before

mixing it with the resin. Other resins used are Araldite AY103/HY956 and Araldite 2020 (formerly known as XW396/XW397 in its experimental stage), the latter specifically designed for bonding glass.

At present excellent results in the repair and restoration of glass artefacts are being obtained by the use of a number of optically clear epoxy resins: Araldite 2020, HXTAL NYL-1 and EPO-TEK 301-2 (both US products) and Fynebond (UK). Unlike other optically clear epoxy resins, the chemicals in HXTAL NYL-1 and Fynebond, whilst not being specially synthesized, are optimized for conservation use. HXTAL NYL 1 is very expensive to import to the UK, and takes a week to cure fully. The resin component of Fynebond tends to crystallize at room temperature and so has to be melted before being mixed with its hardener.

When testing resins for bonding glass, it should be noted that their specification can be within the manufacturer's tolerance but not up to the standard required for conservation. This accounts for the colour differences that occur from batch to batch and for the fact that tests carried out on the products by conservation scientists may be meaningless if the batch tested is at the high end of the manufacturer's tolerance, but a batch used by a conservator is at the lower end. Other factors such as the age of the resin when tested will render comparative tests on epoxy resins (and other materials) meaningless. Many factors affect the discoloration of epoxy resins, not all of which are fully understood. However it is known that (i) the hardeners are not exactly the same for each type of epoxy resin, and may cause long term instability, (ii) some resins contain additives (e.g. dibutyl phthalate plasticizers) which can increase their tendency to yellow, and (iii) the purity of both components is important as even minor impurities may decrease the stability of a resin. Down (1986) has reported on the yellowing of epoxy resins. Messenger and Lansbury (1989) and Augerson and Messenger (1993) have reported on the

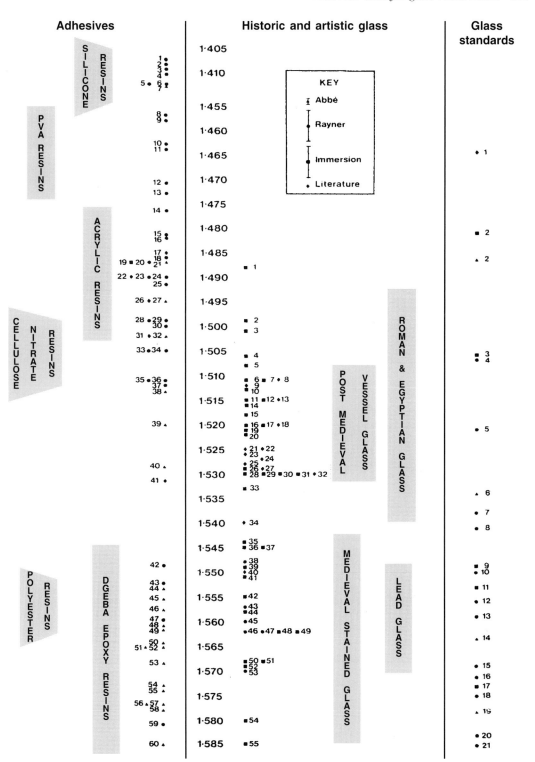

Figure 5.1 The results of RI measurements on a variety of adhesives, and historic glasses, compared with glass standard.

ADHESIVES

1 Arbosil Aquarium Sealant (*silicone*). Adshead Rateliffe & Co. Ltd, Belper, Derbyshire DE5 1WJ, UK

2 Eccosil 2 CN (*silicone*). Emerson & Cuming (UK) Ltd, 1 South Park Road, Scunthorpe, South Humberside DN17 2BY, UK

3 Silastic 732 RTV (*silicone*) ⎫ Dow Corning Ltd,
4 Dow Corning 3140 RTV (*silicone*) ⎪ Reading Bridge
5 Dow Corning 3144 RTV (*silicone*) ⎬ House, Reading, Berks
7 Sylgard 184 (*silicone*) ⎭ RG1 8PW, UK

6 Loctite Clear Silicone Sealant ⎫ Loctite UK, Loctite
   (*silicone*) ⎪ Holdings Ltd,
30 Loctite 357 (*UV curing, urethane* ⎪ Watchmead, Welwyn
   acrylic) ⎬ Garden City, Herts
33 Loctite 350 (*UV curing acrylic*) ⎪ AL7 1JB, UK
38 Loctite 'Glass Bond' (*UV curing* ⎭
   system)

8 ⎱ Rhodopas M (*PVA*): after casting ⎫ Rhodia (UK) Ltd,
10 ⎰ from solution (8), as supplied (10) ⎬ 14 Essex St, London
                                        ⎭ WC2R 3AA, UK

9 Vinalac 5254 (*PVA*). Vinyl Products Ltd, Mill Lane, Carshalton, Surrey, UK

11 UHU 'All-purpose' (*PVA*). Beecham UHU, Brentford, Middlesex, UK

12 Evostik 'Resin W' (*PVA*) ⎫ Evode Ltd, Common
35 Evostik 'Clear' (*cellulose nitrate*) ⎬ Road, Stafford, UK

13 Berol 'Merlin' (*PVA*). Berol Ltd, Oldmedow Road, King's Lynn, Norfolk, UK

14 Paraloid F10 (*acrylic*) ⎫
15 ⎱ Paraloid B72 (*acrylic*): after ⎪
19 ⎰ casting from solution (15), ⎬ Rohm & Haas (UK)
   as supplied (19) ⎪ Ltd, Lennig House,
16 Paraloid B82 (*acrylic*) ⎪ 2 Mason's Avenue,
18 Paraloid B67 (*acrylic*) ⎪ Croydon CR9 3NB,
20 Paraloid B66 (*acrylic*) ⎪ UK
23 Paraloid A30 (*acrylic*) ⎪
25 Paraloid B44 (*acrylic*) ⎭

17 ⎱ Butvar B76, B79 (*polyvinyl* ⎫
   butyral, PVB) ⎪ Monsanto Ltd,
22 ⎱ Butvar B72, B74, B90. B98 ⎪ Monsanto House,
   (*PVB*) ⎬ 10–18 Victoria Street,
26 ⎱ Formar 12/85 (*polyvinyl formal*, ⎪ London SW1 0NQ,
   PVF) ⎪ UK. (Manufacturer's
31 ⎱ Formar 5/95E, 6/95E, 15/95E ⎪ data)
   (*PVF*) ⎭

21 Plastogen G (*acrylic*) ⎫
28 Durafix (*cellulose nitrate*) ⎪ Frank W. Joel Ltd,
34 HMG (*cellulose nitrate*) ⎪ Oldmeadow Road,
36 Frigilene (*cellulose nitrate*) ⎬ Hardwick Industrial
37 Ercalene (*cellulose nitrate*) ⎪ Estate, King's Lynn,
40 Rutapox 1200 (*epoxy*) ⎪ Norfolk PE30 4HH,
44 Plastogen EP (*epoxy*) ⎪ UK
57 Rutapox 1210 (*epoxy*) ⎭

24 Lascaux Acrylglasur 40X (*acrylic*). Alois K. Diethelm Farbenfabrik, CH-8306 Brüttisellen, Switzerland

27 Technovit 4004A (*acrylic*). Rubert & Co. Ltd, Dennings Road, Cheadle, Cheshire, UK

29 Bostik 5293 adhesive (*cellulose nitrate*). Bostik Ltd, Ulverscroft Road, Leicester LE4 6BW, UK

32 L.R. White Resin (*acrylic*). London Resin Co., PO Box 24, Basingstoke, Hants RG22 5AS, UK

39 HXTAL NYL-1 (*epoxy*) ⎫ Conservation Materials
50 Ablebond 342-1 (*epoxy*) ⎪ Ltd, 340 Freeport
51 Devcon '2-ton' (*epoxy*) ⎬ Blvd, Sparks, NV
52 Devcon '5-minute' (*epoxy*) ⎭ 89431, USA

41 Opticon UV-57 (*UV-curing system*). Opticon Chemical, PO Box 2445, Palos Verdes Peninsula, CA 90274, USA [6]

42 Norland Optical Adhesive 63 ⎫
   (*UV-curing system*) ⎪ Leader House, 117–120
47 Norland Optical Adhesive 61 ⎬ Snargate Street, Dover,
   (*UV-curing system*) ⎪ Kent CT17 9DB, UK
59 Vitralit DAC ⎪
   (*UV-curing system*) ⎭

43 Tiranti Embedding Resin (*polyester*). A. Tiranti Ltd, 20 Goodge Place, London W1, UK

45 Epotek 301 (*epoxy*). Epoxy Technology Inc., 65 Grove Street, Watertown, MA 02172, USA

46 ⎱ Metset Resin SW (*polyester*): first batch (46), second batch
48 ⎰ (48). Metallurgical Services Laboratories Ltd, Reliant Works, Brockham, Betchworth, Surrey RH3 7HW, UK

49 Araldite MY790/X83-19/DY040 ⎫ Ciba-Geigy Plastics
   (*epoxy*) ⎪ and Additives Co.,
55 ⎱ Araldite AY103/HY951 (*epoxy*): ⎬ Plastics Division,
58 ⎰ first batch (55), second batch (58) ⎪ Duxford, Cambridge
60 Araldite AY1OS/HY951 (*epoxy*) ⎭ CB2 4QA, UK

53 Epofix (*epoxy*). Struers, Copenhagen, Denmark

54 CXL (*epoxy*). Resin Coatings Ltd, Colebrand House. 20 Warwick Street, Regent Street, London W1R 6BE, UK

56 Permabond E27 (*epoxy*). Permabond Adhesives Ltd, Woodside Road, Eastleigh. Hants S05 4EX, UK

HISTORIC AND ARTISTIC GLASS*

1 GMAG/DA/96.38a. *Cristallo* (greenish) Venetian Tazza, 16th century

2 NHT. Clear (2) and violet (3) glass from Alexandrine

3 *Zwischengoldglas* fragment, 1st century AD

4 GMAG/BC/17.64. Dark blue transparent glass from Roman bottle, early centuries AD

5 R/NM10754.248. Bohemian glass, wheel-engraved, mid-18th century

6 GMAG/DA/97S0bv. Spanish (Catalonia) jug, clear glass,

28 18th century: vessel glass (6), ornament glass (28)

7 NHT. Clear glass from Islamic lamp fragment, 13th/14th century AD

8 Egyptian vessel stamp, 8th century AD [19, Table 1]

9 Eleven Egyptian vessel stamps, coin weights, etc., 8th century AD [19, Table 1]

10 NHT. Clear glass from Islamic lamp fragment, 13th/14th century AD

11 R/NM10754.270 Russian (?) covered beaker, wheel-engraved, mid-18th century

12 GMAG/A/03.185gp. Cypriot glass flask, early centuries AD

13 Egyptian beads: one pale green from Tell Asmar, 2700–2500 BC [15, p.10, specimen no. 7]; two blue from Qau, 7525 [16]

14 ⎱ NHT. Transparent amber (14) and blue (16) glass from
16 ⎰ Alexandrine lozenge-shaped decorative glass, *c.* 1st century AD

15 R/NM8326. Bohemian glass, wheel-engraved, 1725–1750 AD

17 GMAG/A/03.185iz. Cypriot glass dish, early centuries AD

18 Egyptian blue bead from Tell el-Amarna, XVIII Dynasty [16]

19 GMAG/DA/97.50cq. Southern Spanish bull-shaped ornament, green glass, 19th century?

* Explanation of registration codes: GMAG/DA, GMAG/BC, GMAG/A = Glasgow Museums and Art Galleries, Department of Decorative Art, Burrell Collection, Department of Archaeology, respectively; NHT = N.H. Tennent's collection; R = Rijksmuseum, Amsterdam.

20 GMAG/DA/97.50bu. Spanish (Catalonia) jug, clear glass, 16th century?

21 Three Egyptian red beads from Armant, 1200A [16], XII Dynasty

22 Egyptian vessel stamp, early-middle 8th century AD [19, Table 1]

23 Egyptian ring weight, 8th century AD [19, Table 1]

24 Egyptian green glass bead from Qau, 612 [15, p. 14, specimen no. 1], XI Dynasty [16]

25 Egyptian coin weight, early 9th century AD [19, Table 1].

26 GMAG/DA/96.38c. Venetian wine glass, late 16th century

27 Egyptian coin weight, late 8th/early 9th century AD [19 Table 1]

29 ⎫ GMAG/DA/93.93w. Blue (29) and opal (54) glass from
54 ⎭ Venetian wine glass, 16th/17th century

30 NHT. Transparent dark blue vessel glass fragment, Tell el-Amarna, XVIII Dynasty

31 GMAG/BC/17.49. Pale green glass from Roman jar, early centuries AD

32 Arabic bead from Assint, probably 14th–18th century AD [16]

33 NHT. Transparent turquoise vessel glass fragment, Tell el-Amarna, XVIII Dynasty

34 Transparent pink bead from Armant, 1200A [16]

35 ⎫
36 ⎬ Excavated medieval stained glass from St Andrews
37 ⎪ Cathedral (35; StA1) and Elgin Cathedral (36; EC4. 37;
55 ⎭ EC5, 55; EC1). See [17] for analytical data.

38 GMAG/BC/45.470. Clear glass from Flemish roundel, early 16th century

39 GMAG/DA/97.50bo. Spanish (Andalusia) vase, green glass, 17th century

40 Clear dark blue bead from Armant, 1213D [16]

41 GMAG/DA/27.90e.3. Water-glass, Scottish (John Baird Glassworks), *c.* 1881

42 GMAG/BC/45.484. Clear, blue and green glass from German (Nuremburg) stained glass panel, *c.* 1470–1480

43 GMAG/BC/45.462. Clear glass from Flemish roundel, 16th century

44 ⎫ GMAG/DA/88.65a. Clear (44) and yellow (49) glass from
49 ⎭ ruby glass goblet, Rhine Glass Works Co., *c.* 1888

45 GMAG/BC/45.17. Clear glass border dated 1577 (enclosing a 14th century roundel)

46 GMAG/BC/45551. Clear glass from Dutch panel, dated 1686

47 GMAG/BC/45.499. Clear glass from Swiss panel, late 16th century

48 GMAG/BC/Inv 151. Wine glass. Dutch/British, mid-18th century

50 R/NM10754.78. Wine glass, stipple engraved. Dutch, late-18th century

51 R/NM4015. Wine glass, diamond engraved, English, 1725–1750

52 R/RBK 1966.61. Wine glass, wheel-engraved in Holland, English, *c.* 1750

53 GMAG/45.32. Clear glass from English panel, 14th century

GLASS STANDARDS

1	Glass FK3: Schott Glaswerke, Hattenbergstrasse 10, D-6500 Mainz, W Germany	
2,2'	Glass Standard No. 4	⎫ Society of Glass Technology,
3	Glass Standard No. 5	⎬ 20 Hallam Gate Road,
11	Glass Standard No. 3	⎭ Sheffield S10 5BT, UK
4	Zinc Crown, ZC 508612	
5	Hard Crown, HC 524592	
7	Extra Light Flint, ELF 541472	⎫ Pilkington Brothers plc,
8	Extra Light Flint, ELF 548456	⎬ Research & Development Laboratories, Ormskirk, Lancashire L40 5UF, UK
15	Light Flint, LF 567428	
19	Light Flint, LF 579411	⎭
6	Glass Standard B	⎫ Standards prepared for the Corning Museum to
9	Glass Standard D	⎬ simulate the composition of ancient glasses [21]
10	Standard 76-C-151	⎫ Series of synthetic
12	Standard 76-C-158	⎪ medieval stained glass
13	Standard 76-C-149	⎪ compositions prepared by
14	Standard 76-C-144	⎬ Pilkington Brothers for
16	Standard 76-C-150	⎪ Professor R.G. Newton
17	Standard 77-C-33	⎪ [22]
18	Standard 76-C-145	
20	Standard 76-C-147	
21	Standard 76-C-148	⎭

control of the refractive index of the epoxy resins Ablebond 342-1 and HXTAL NYL-1. In *Figure 5.1* a comparison is made between various optically clear epoxy resins that have been used for glass repair.

Polyester resins

Polyester casting resins are widely used for joining glass elements in optical instruments, but there are few recommendations for their use as adhesives in the conservation of glass antiquities. However, those incorporating an ultraviolet light absorbant are extremely useful as gap-fillers, and will be discussed in more detail in the section on casting materials.

Casting and laminating polyesters are solutions of unsaturated polyesters in an unsaturated reactive monomer. Typical polyesters are made from propylene glycol, maleic anhydride and phthalic anhydride, and have a short molecule (molecular weight 2000), of the general formula shown in (5.9).

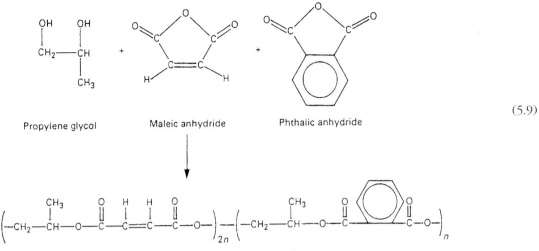

(5.9)

Propylene glycol   Maleic anhydride   Phthalic anhydride

Components of a typical polyester resin, n 4

This represents a highly unsaturated polymer. Styrene is usually chosen as the reactive monomer because of its low cost and ease of use. Methyl methacrylate can replace some of the styrene when resistance to light is required. The cross-linking between the chains is achieved by copolymerizing the styrene with the unsaturated bonds in the chain by using a peroxide initiator. This results in a cross-linked polymer that is both hard and rigid. The properties of the cross-linked, cured resin can be varied, by altering any of the several components that make up the formulation. All polymerization reactions result in shrinkage, and polyester formulation is no exception. A typical value for the shrinkage is 8 per cent by volume, most of which occurs after gelation. Heat generated during polymerization can lead to charring and cracking when large masses of polyester resins are being cast. (Large amounts of resin are not commonly used in the conservation of glass.) The refractive index of stabilized polyester resins is typically 1.54–1.56.

Acrylic resins

The monomers from which acrylic polymers are made fall into two groups, acrylates and methacrylates. The methacrylates were one of the first synthetic resins used to coat glass (Hedvall *et al.*, 1951), and as consolidants they are still amongst the most popular. Acrylates and methacrylates are nominally derived from acrylic and methacrylic acids, respectively. These acids can be esterified with alcohol to produce a wide range of monomers:

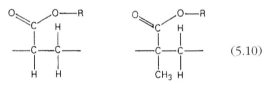

(5.10)

Poly (alkyl acrylate)   Poly (alkyl methacrylate)

Acrylic polymers, monomer units. The alkyl (—R) group can be chosen to produce a range of polymers

The polymers made from the acrylates tend to have lower Tg points than the equivalent methacrylates. For example, a polymethyl methacrylate such as Perspex has a Tg of 105°C, whereas polymethyl acrylate has a Tg of 3°C. Polymethyl methacrylate sheet does not yellow on ageing and typifies the major advantage of acrylics; that is, their lack of colour change and resistance to oxidation. However, both the polyacrylates and the higher polymethacrylates will cross-link under the influence of ultraviolet light and will eventually become insoluble. Polymethyl methacrylate is the most stable of the acrylic polymers, reacting only very slowly to ultraviolet light. The presence of methyl methacrylate in copolymers increases the resistance to deterioration by light disproportionately to its concentration in the polymer. For this reason methyl methacrylate is much used in both acrylic and other polymers.

As polymethyl methacrylate has too high a T_g for many adhesive and coating uses, softer acrylic polymers, which still retain colour stability, are prepared. Poly(butyl methacrylate), which has frequently been used in the past, has been shown to cross-link in ultraviolet light (Feller, 1972), and hence suggestions for its use, often under the trade-name of Bedacryl 122X (now Synocryl 9122X) should be reconsidered. Wihr (1977) used a solution of Plexigum 24, a polybutyl methacrylate, and stated that it did not yellow and adhered well to the glass. However, this material could be expected to cross-link in time. Paraloid B-72 is now being widely used in conservation as a consolidant both on vessels and painted window glass. Paraloid B-72 is a very stable resin with a T_g of 40°C and a refractive index of 1.49. Poly(alkyl methacrylates) with longer side chains have lower T_g values and may be useful for conservation purposes. Copolymers of the methacrylates with acrylates such as ethyl- or 2-ethylbexylacrylate are used to achieve softer products with good colour stability. The relatively good stability of acrylic polymers over other polymers has resulted in a large number of speciality adhesives and coatings designed for use where degradation is a problem.

Cyanoacrylate resins

Cyanoacrylate resins have been recommended for use in repairing glass (Moncrieff, 1975; André, 1976) because of their ease of application. Cyanoacrylates polymerize *in situ* in a few seconds at room temperature without the addition of a catalyst, the reaction being promoted by the presence of moisture or weak bases present on the glass surface.

The cured products are high molecular weight polymers that can be dissolved in organic solvents. The dilute alkali solutions on the glass surface cause deterioration of the polymer; thus cyanoacrylate adhesives are generally unsuitable for glass restoration except for effecting temporary repairs, for example when pressure-sensitive tape cannot

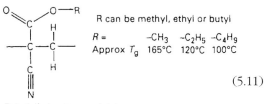

$$R \text{ can be methyl, ethyl or butyl}$$

$$R = \quad -CH_3 \quad -C_2H_5 \quad -C_4H_9$$
$$\text{Approx } T_g \quad 165°C \quad 120°C \quad 100°C$$

(5.11)

Poly (alkyl cyanoacrylate)

Cyanacrylate monomer unit. The alkyl (—R) group can be varied to modify the polymer properties

be used on a delicate surface. Care should be taken in their use since cyanoacrylate resins bond very readily with skin tissue. In order to prolong their shelf-life the resins should be stored at a temperature of −20°C.

Ultraviolet curing (photosensitive) acrylic resins

Acrylic resin formulations that cure on exposure to ultraviolet (UV) light have been specially developed for joining glass to glass and other substrates. The curing reaction results in a highly cross-linked polymer:

$$A-(HN-CO-O-R_2-CO-CH{=}CH_2)n$$
$$\vert$$
$$R_1$$

(5.12)

$R_1 = HCH_3$

$R_2 = -C_2H_4-, -C_2H_4 (CH_3)-$

A = poly(isocyanate), e.g. diphenylmethane 4,4-diisocyanate

The only brand of UV curing acrylate which has been tested for use in conservation and published (Madsen, 1972) is the American product Opticon UV57 which was found by Moncrieff (1975) to have poor physical properties both in the uncured and cured states. A second American UV curing adhesive, Norland Optical Adhesive 61, has been used for tacking small fragments of glass, which are difficult to tape. The use of UV curing adhesives should normally be considered to be non-reversible especially on porous glass surfaces where it is likely that mechanical keying will hold the polymer in the pores of the glass thereby making the bond virtually impossible to separate. The bond may only be considered to be reversible if it has been made between two smooth surfaces, which can be cleaned mechanically after the join has been disrupted by soaking in solvents such as acetone or dichloromethane. Alternatively, prolonged soaking in water can destroy the adhesive bond (but not dissolve the adhesive) if no coupling agent has been used.

An unexpected danger has been noticed when exposing glass to UV light. A test-piece, which was joined with a UV curing adhesive, crizzled during the exposure to UV radiation.

Polyurethane resins

Polyurethane resins adhere well to polar surfaces because the isocyanate groups react with adsorbed water and hydroxyl groups; the tightly cross-linked network is fairly resistant to swelling by solvents. They are not recommended for direct contact with glass, but polyurethane foams are useful for block lifting fragile objects and structures (see Lifting Materials, below).

Silicones and silanes

The term silicone is used as a loose description for the many compounds formed from silicon and organic radicals, and it therefore covers a series of compounds analogous to carbon compounds, but containing silicon in the main chain.

Silicon materials used in conservation (Horie, 1987) may be divided between the silanes and the silicones. The silanes are fairly simple molecules that are formulated to react strongly and irreversibly. These alkoxysilanes penetrate well and are used primarily (as coupling agents) to increase adhesion between a surface and a polymer, though they may also add to consolidation and reinforcement (Errett *et al.*, 1984). Silicone rubbers (US: silastomers) are used where a flexible, stable rubber is required for joining fragments, as mastic, or as a moulding material, and are of the room temperature vulcanizing (RTV) type. They have the general formula:

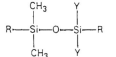

(5.13)

The rubbers start as viscous liquids (composed of large silicone molecules plus fillers etc.) that then react to form a cross-linked rubbery solid, more or less rigid depending on the formulation. The large molecules have reactive end groups that cross-link through small reactive molecules (silanes). Traces of water and metal catalysts are normally required. The liquid pre-polymers are available as two-part formulations where the catalyst is added, or as one-part formulations where water is excluded until they are used. All the formulations contain a proportion of un-reacted silicone oil that, because it has a low surface tension, can migrate away from the rubber to cause staining of porous materials, and may act as a release agent.

The rubber products made from silanes are inherently water white and have exceptional weathering stability. They change hardly at all with exposure to light and water, but they have little strength compared with other elastomers. The two-part (RTV) silicones do not have much adhesion to surfaces such as metal, but have sufficient adhesion to glass to need a separating agent when silicone rubber moulds are made. The one-part curing silicones can have appreciable adhesion, depending on their cross-linking functional groups, although they may require coupling agents for maximum adhesion. Silicones are insoluble in solvents but they will swell considerably in aliphatic, aromatic and chlorinated hydrocarbons.

Clear silicone rubbers with a refractive index of 1.43 are used commercially to repair damaged plate glass windows. However, since they have a very low Tg of $-123°C$ they attract dirt and within a few weeks the lines of silicone rubber become grey and then blackened as a result of dirt held on, and eventually in, the polymer. The products are not suitable for repairing archaeological and historic glasses.

Silane coupling agents were discussed in the section on adhesion, and silicone moulding materials will be discussed under moulding materials.

Vinyl resins

Polyvinyl acetate (PVAC) has been used in conservation for many years, including the consolidation of glass, but has largely been superseded by the use of Paraloid B-72 (Dowman, 1970; Brill, 1971a; Majewski, 1973; Hutchinson, 1981). PVAC is stable, has a refractive index of 1.46 (similar to that of glass), a good resistance to yellowing and it is available in a wide range of molecular weights. The molecular weight is related to the viscosity of the solution and is important for achieving adequate penetration, for example, a PVAC molecule with a molecular weight (MW) of 51 000, equivalent to 600 monomer units per chain (the degree of polymerization, DP), would have a minimum diameter of 13 nm, and thus it could not penetrate pores as small as that. However, it has a low Tg (28°C) and is therefore prone to cold flow, and to attracting and absorbing dirt, when the MW is low (<57 000). In order to inhibit this tendency to attract dirt, a top coat of a compatible polymer with a higher T should be applied. PVAC appears to be a useful consolidant for dehydrated glass, as a 25 per cent solution in toluene, or as more dilute solutions in alcohol.

Polyvinyl chloride (PVC) solutions (Derm-O-Plast SC, ArcheoDerm) have been recommended for consolidating degraded glass (Wihr, 1977). Unfortunately, PVC is one of the most unstable polymers in commercial production and should therefore not be used in direct contact with antiquities; it will degrade, discolour, release hydrochloric acid and probably become insoluble with time.

Polyvinyl butyral (PVB) has a refractive index of 1.49 (and is used as the interlayer of laminated windscreens for motor vehicles); it has good adhesion to glass and a fairly satisfactory Tg of 62–68°C, but it cross-links on prolonged exposure to light and should therefore be considered to be insoluble in the long term. Of the grades of PVB that have been recommended for glass conservation are those with lower molecular weights, for example, Butvar B-98 (Monsanto) and Mowital B20H (Hoechst). PVB has been used by Vos-Davidse (1969).

Vinyl polymers that are polymerized in emulsion can be significantly different from those polymerized by other techniques because surfactants and other emulsifiers become inextricably incorporated in the polymer. The advantage of emulsions is that water (inexpensive and non-toxic) is used as

the diluent, and the absence of hazardous solvents has encouraged the use of emulsions where large open areas of liquid are required, such as in the conservation of textiles and paper.

A polymer emulsion has a very high solids content with a low viscosity. The viscosity of the emulsion is often deliberately increased by the manufacturer, to make handling easier. The high content of solids permits thicker films to be deposited, with less shrinkage than is the case with films applied from solvents. Up to 10 per cent of the solids content of an emulsion consists of the emulsifiers and stabilizers. When the emulsion dries to form a film, the emulsifiers in the polymer film are known to cause sensitivity to water and a lowering of clarity. Many of the emulsifiers cause yellowing of the film, for example, films of PVAC cast from emulsions turn yellow far more rapidly than those cast from solution. Further problems arise when polymeric emulsifiers such as polyvinyl alcohol (PVAL) or polyacrylic acid have been incorporated into the film. Both can undergo cross-linking reactions and thus reduce the solubility of the polymer to which they are attached.

Emulsifiers usually work best with a proper balance of ionic materials in the solution. There are three categories of emulsifiers: anionic, non-ionic and cationic. The cationic emulsifiers are rarely used. Anionic emulsifiers require acid conditions, while non-ionic emulsifiers can withstand a wider pH range. Before using any emulsion on glass, conservators should ensure that it has a pH at which that glass is stable. The films formed from emulsions are frequently soft, with Tg below room temperature. As the water evaporates from an emulsion, the polymer particles are forced closer together. These particles must coalesce if a coherent film is to form and therefore the particles must be soft enough to flow into one another. In general the polymer particles must be above their Tg for coalescence to occur and thus the polymer film is usually above its Tg when set. Films formed at room temperature will therefore have a Tg below room temperature and will absorb dirt. Volatile solvents may be added to the emulsion in order to soften the polymer temporarily. Only small quantities can be added before the solvents destabilize the emulsion. Emulsions are usually formulated by manufacturers to meet a particular need. From the conservation point of view, many of the detrimental effects of commercially available emulsions could be reduced by changes in product formulation.

Modelling materials

Missing areas of glass may be modelled up *in situ* prior to moulding, using one of several commercially produced modelling materials. Those most commonly used are potters' clay and Plasticine, a putty composed of petroleum jelly, fatty acids and whiting. The oily substances enable the Plasticine to be worked to a smooth surface; however, it does not adhere very well to glass, and will contaminate the surface. Plasticine residues should be removed with cotton wool swabs moistened with a degreasing solvent such as acetone or toluene before adhesives are applied to the glass. Aloplast is a modelling material similar to Plasticine in texture, but formulated especially for use against polyester resins. The use of the buff-coloured version is to be preferred, since colour from the dark blue version may discolour the resin.

Damp potters' clay adheres very well to glass and is easily worked to a smooth surface with a spatula dipped in water. In addition, any fragments of glass that can be positioned accurately but do not actually join to the body of a vessel (i.e. floating fragments) may be held in position by placing them *in situ* on a clay former. The disadvantage of using clay is that moisture contained within it separates any adhesive used in the repair from the glass. Backing joins with tape, rubber latex or thin sheets of wax does not prevent this from occurring. In fact, adhesive on Sellotape and masking tape breaks down with moisture to form a messy substance, removal of the wax sometimes causes the joins to fail, and latex flows into tiny cracks and chips and is difficult to remove without dismantling the glass.

Moulding materials

Materials used for taking moulds from glass artefacts should have the following properties:

They should not harm the object physically by adhering too strongly to the surface, by pulling off glass projections, or by heat generation. They should not harm the glass chemically by contaminating or reacting with it. Moulding materials should reproduce all the fine details of the original without distortion. The viscosity and thixotropic properties should be sufficiently variable by the manufacturer or conservator to allow the materials to be adapted to meet different requirements. They should preferably be available at reasonable cost and have an adequate shelf-life. Moulds must be able to withstand heat of polymerization of the proposed casting material and must not react with that material. For moulding glass the most suitable materials are toughened dental wax and silicone rubber (US: silastomer), which is available in several grades of thixotropicity. Large silicone rubber moulds are sometimes given added strength by the addition of an outer case or mother-mould, constructed of plaster of Paris, or of polyester resin incorporating glass-fibre matting.

Dental waxes

Dental waxes are composed of a number of different waxes and are often supplied as sheets measuring 180 mm × 82 mm × 1.5 mm. Dental waxes are available in various grades of hardness, in sheet sizes up to 305 mm × 203 mm, and in thicknesses of 0.4 to 3.0 mm. For making moulds, the sheets or parts of them can be softened by gentle heating in water or warm air before shaping them over the glass object. Before casting, the wax mould must be coated with polyvinyl alcohol (PVAL) (which is difficult because it tends to run into pools) as a release agent between the wax and the resin to be cast against it. The PVAL tends to crawl back from the wax surface into pools. This can be alleviated, by adding a drop of non-ionic detergent to the PVAL to break the surface tension, and if necessary by continuously gently brushing the release agent until it has almost set. It may be necessary to apply a second coat when the first has dried; this must be done carefully in order not to disrupt the first layer, which will have dried to form an easily disruptable skin over the wax surface.

Silicone rubber (US: elastomer)

The majority of silicone rubber products used for moulding cure by catalytic elimination of alcohol to form cross-links between the chains. When the alcohol evaporates, the rubber shrinks but the amount of shrinkage is small (less than 1 per cent) and occurs over a period of a few days. However, shrinkage of 2.2 per cent has been observed to occur over a number of years. Silicones are insoluble in solvents but can be swelled considerably by the use of aliphatic, aromatic and chlorinated hydrocarbons. Wihr (1977) has suggested swelling silicone rubber back to size by exposing it to organic solvents, but this would seem to be an unreliable method. In the majority of cases silicone rubber requires no release agent between it and the glass surface, although instances of silicone rubber adhering to glass and porcelain have been known (Morgos *et al.*, 1984), and therefore preliminary tests must be undertaken. A release agent such as petroleum jelly or an organic lacquer must be used if silicone rubber is to be cast against a cured section of silicone rubber, or the two will adhere. Thin layers of silicone rubber may tear when peeled off an object, but thick layers are hard-wearing and the moulds are reusable. If necessary, it may be over-catalysed to shorten its setting time, for instance, when silicone rubber is being used to reattach a silicone rubber mould to glass.

Inert fillers such as kaolin, talc or aerosol silica may be added to thicken mobile grades of silicone rubber. Unfortunately, many cured silicone rubbers are prone to tearing and must be applied in thick section and often with a rigid case mould for support. Rubber latex shrinks too much to be of use in moulding such a precise material as glass; a small shrinkage will mean that details such as trailed threads on the glass will not match up with those on the cast. A mould must remain stable for several days or weeks whilst restoration is in progress.

Hot-melt preparations

Hot-melt preparations such as gelatine, Formalose and Vinamold (PVC) should be avoided for direct use on glass since the heat may cause damage. However, Formalose, a gelatine material containing glycerine to keep it flexible (Wihr, 1977), is useful for reproducing the interior shape of an object with a narrow neck where plaster or rubber cannot be introduced. The Formalose can be poured hot into a plaster mould and, on cooling, it sets and begins to shrink uniformly. A watch must be kept and when there is a gap between the Formalose and the plaster, representing the thickness of the glass vessel to be reproduced, resin can be cast into the gap. The Formalose core must be supported away from the plaster walls. The method is described by Petermann (1969).

Plaster of Paris

Plaster of Paris (calcium sulphate) is prepared by heating gypsum ($CaSO_4.2H_2O$) to drive off some of the combined water, forming $2CaSO_4.H_2O$. On adding more water, the calcium sulphate rehydrates, forming interlocking crystals, which set to a rock-like mass with very slight expansion, typically 0.5 per cent. Various grades of plaster are available with different setting times, expansions and particle fineness. Dental plasters are available which set to form very hard solids with minimal expansion. The material is cheap and is a useful product for the construction of case-moulds over silicone rubber. However, it requires release agents between plaster-to-plaster surfaces and plaster-to-resin ones. It is rigid and hence any undercuts on the glass must be moulded separately, preferably in silicone rubber. If incorrectly placed, it is difficult to remove without causing damage.

Release agents

Release agents must prevent adhesion between objects, moulds and casts; the agent chosen will depend upon the materials being used. As previously mentioned, silicone rubber only requires the use of a release agent such as petroleum jelly or organic lacquer when it is being cast against a section of cured silicone rubber. The surface of plaster of Paris mould pieces, however, must be sealed as each is made to prevent it adhering to the adjacent pieces; and release agents must be applied to facilitate removal of resin if it is cast directly into a plaster mould.

Shellac in a solution of industrial methylated spirit (IMS; US: grain alcohol), or a solution of PVAL, can be used to seal the surface of dry plaster of Paris mould-pieces, after which the surface is coated with soft soap, Vaseline, detergent, petroleum jelly or a wax emulsion. If the resin is to be cast directly into plaster moulds, a specially formulated release agent such as Scopas (PVAL) (supplied by Tiranti) must be applied to the plaster surface. Release agents may be supplied as colourless or coloured, in order that it can be seen when all the surfaces have been covered adequately. However, traces of colour may remain on the cast. It is preferable therefore to use a colourless release agent and to take care in its application.

Silicone release agents are available as liquids or in spray cans, but are not recommended for use in glass conservation since traces of silicone oils will remain on the cast, and if they are not removed completely they can prevent paint or adhesives bonding properly to the surface. The same is true for polytetrafluoroethane (PTFE) dispersions in aerosol cans.

Casting materials

The requirements for casting materials for use with glass are very severe. It should be possible to pour the material into moulds; it should set with minimal shrinkage to form a hard solid; and it should be crystal clear and remain colourless indefinitely. No materials meet this specification completely, although some come close to it.

Polyester resins

Many clear polyester embedding resins are available, but it is obviously outside the scope of this book to discuss them all. Suffice it to say that before restoration work begins, the resin to be used should be tested by mixing and casting it into a mould of the same material to be used in the final reconstruction. This will ensure that the resin's shelf-life has not expired and its performance is as expected (i.e. the formula of the product has not been altered by the manufacturer since it was last ordered). Because of their high mobility,

polyester resins are normally cast into closed moulds. Small quantities of resins may be accurately weighed on a digital balance, or dispensed from a graduated disposable syringe (minus the needle), provided that care is taken not to introduce air bubbles with the resin.

Where polyester resin is applied as a flat surface against a one-sided mould, it must be applied in thin layers, each layer being allowed to gel in turn. However, subsequent layers of resin should be applied before each has fully cured, in order to prevent the formation of visible interfaces in the cast. If the gap to be cast is very thin, the cast may be strengthened, by incorporating a layer of fine glass-fibre surfacing tissue in the resin as it is cast. However, the fibre filaments will remain slightly visible within the resin (see Figure 7.31). Clear polyester resins may be coloured without noticeably altering their transparency by the addition of minute quantities of translucent polyester pigments.

Disadvantages in the use of polyester resins are the shrinkage of 8 per cent during curing (though this can partly be compensated for by topping up the mould as the resin polymerizes), the emission of styrene for some considerable time after curing, and the fact that the resin surface often remains tacky for some time. Reasons for this latter phenomenon are interference from atmospheric moisture causing the cessation of chain-building mechanisms during polymerization, ageing of the hardener, or, if the resin and hardener are stored under refrigeration, their use before having reached room temperature, thus inhibiting a complete chemical reaction from occurring. Hardening of the surface may be aided by polymerizing the cast in a dry atmosphere, for example, in a sealed cabinet containing trays of silica gel. Warming the cast in an oven is not recommended since it may cause premature discoloration of the resin. Polyester embedding resins abrade and polish easily.

Polymethyl methacrylate resins

Plastogen G with Lumopal hardener, used by Wihr (1963) and Errett (1972) is transparent and mobile and is therefore normally cast into closed moulds (see above). The liquid resin is mixed with 0.25–0.5 per cent hardener (powder) that is difficult to assess in small quantities, and the addition of too much hardener may cause premature discoloration of the resin. Plastogen G has a 15-minute pot-life but cannot be worked during that time because a skin quickly forms over the surface; it also has an extremely powerful, unpleasant smell. After mixing, and if necessary colouring, the resin should be covered and left to stand whilst air bubbles escape.

The methacrylate Technovit 4004A is translucent and therefore can only be used as a gap-filler on opaque glass. The polymer (powder) is mixed with the liquid monomer in the ratio of five parts to three, but the proportions are not critical and the setting-time may be varied, by changing the amount of powder. When mixed in the recommended proportions, Technovit 4004A sets at room temperature in 10–15 mm, but can be worked with a spatula during this time. This product is guaranteed by the manufacturer not to shrink or expand on curing. It emits heat if cast in large amounts. Technovit adheres well to glass, is relatively hard and can be abraded and polished. This particular grade of Technovit is no longer manufactured (Koob, 2000), but other grades are available.

Epoxy resins

Epoxy resins can be used to gap-fill losses in glass. They can be pigmented with pre-mixed colours in epoxy paste (although these are usually opaque), or with dyes. In general, epoxy resins do not respond well to polishing after abrasion. For large areas of restoration, polyester resins are a cheaper alternative.

Colouring materials

Materials used for colouring fall into two categories: those used for mixing in with resin and those applied to the resin after it has cured. Colours for mixing in with the resin may be transparent or opaque depending upon the desired effect; enough coloured resin must be produced to complete the restoration and allowance must be made for areas which may have to be cast more than once, or may have to be made good. This is important since a colour can rarely be exactly matched a

second or third time. Hardener is then added to small amounts of the coloured resin as required for use, and the resin is allowed to stand before use to enable air bubbles to escape before being introduced into a mould. Casts can be made colourless and then coloured by hand or by air-brushing with pigments and media. This may have the advantage of being able to remove and re-apply colour, provided that the retouching materials can be removed from the cast without spoiling its surface.

Most glass on display in museum cases is exposed to high levels of illumination and hence light-resistant pigments are needed in any restored portions. Improvements in pigment technology have provided the conservator with a fairly wide palette of colours. A list of light-resistant pigments is given by Thomson (1998). Other pigments are used by Wihr (1963), Errett (1972) and Staude (1972), and Davison (1998). Occasionally, pigments can produce adverse effects with some reactive polymers and hence it is then more satisfactory to purchase ready-mixed colours. There are colours for polyesters, silicones and for epoxies; their light stability must be checked before use. Transparent epoxy and polyester resins used as adhesive and casting materials often require the use of dyes rather than pigments to colour them, in order to retain their transparency. The range of light-stable dyes available for use in polymers is limited (Horie, 1987).

Retouching lacquers

The lacquers usually employed for retouching the restored portions of glass objects are frequently those used in the restoration of ceramics, porcelain in particular. Transparency and retention of colour are important. In the UK, Rustin's Clearglaze (a urea-formaldehyde/ melamine-formaldehyde mixture catalysed with butanol normal/sulphuric acid) is used for this purpose. It forms a hard clear coating when catalysed, and has reasonable colour retention. However, this type of polymer is almost unaffected by solvents (except dichloromethane), and it would be most difficult to remove from a glass surface, or even from a resin cast without spoiling it.

Enamelled decoration may be copied on resin casts using any pigments and media used for ceramic restoration, provided that they adhere to the cast and the solvent does not damage it. Gold decoration may be copied in leaf gold applied on a size, or as liquid metallic paints, though the latter will probably discolour on aging.

Lifting materials

Materials for the removal of artefacts from archaeological sites are discussed by Watkinson and Neal (1998). See also polyurethane foam below.

Polyethylene glycol

Polyethylene glycols (PEG) are widely recommended for providing reinforcement and bulking during removal of objects such as wood from the ground. Various grades are available, but it is the harder, higher molecular weight polymers (4000 and 6000) that are used for this purpose. PEG will shrink slightly on freezing, and also on cooling to room temperature. PEG can be removed by remelting it, or cleaning the artefact in solvents such as water, alcohols, trichloroethane or toluene. There is only one reference to the impregnation of archaeological glass with PEG, where it was used to provide mechanical strength to the remains of severely deteriorated medieval potash glass alembics (Bimson and Werner, 1971; see Chapter 7).

Polyvinyl chloride

Vinyl polymers have already been discussed, but the use of polyvinyl chloride in the field should be mentioned here. A polyvinyl chloride solution, Derm-O-Plast SG, has been used during excavation, for consolidating both the soil and fragile objects (Wihr, 1977). Such treatment should be considered irreversible, and may have a long-term deleterious effect on the consolidated object. The product has now been discontinued but a new product (Archaeo-Derm), presumably of the same type, has been substituted (Filoform). PVC is one of the most unstable polymers in commercial production and should not be used in contact with artefacts. Small traces remaining after cleaning will degrade, discolour, release hydrochloric acid and probably become insoluble (Watkinson and Neal, 1998).

Flexible polyurethane foam

Flexible polyurethane foams are relatively expensive, but may be convenient materials to use, for lifting and for packaging excavated artefacts and fragile structural remains (e.g. glass kilns, Price, 1992), owing to their lightness. Polyurethane foams are formed by mixing an isocyanate (generally toluene diisocyanate), with a polyhydroxyl component (a polyester or a polyether), each of which is available in a range of formulations. This in turn creates a range of products of varying properties, for example, flexibility and stability. The greatest variability is the polyol component, which may be polyester or polyether. Various catalysts such as amines and tin compounds are incorporated in the components; these may increase the degradation of the foam and its effects on objects. The foaming action itself is frequently achieved by adding small amounts of water, which react with the isocyanate to produce carbon dioxide. The adhesion of foamed polyurethanes is similar to that of the polyurethanes used for coatings; their resistance to solvents is greater, but they are less stable on ageing (Moncrieff, 1971; Watkinson and Leigh, 1978).

(5.14)

On mixing, the components expand to form foam within 3 minutes, the exact time being dependent upon the prevailing temperature. All the isocyanates are very toxic but the smaller and more volatile compounds are the most dangerous because of the ease of breathing in the vapour. For example, toxic fumes (TLV, 0.02 ppm) are given off by the isocyanate component in polyurethane foam and this can survive unchanged in the completed foam. Thus extreme care must be taken when using products based on polyurethane. The flexible foams are resilient open cell structures. In general, the polyether-derived foam is preferred for packaging, having better cushioning properties and being less likely to degrade. However, both polyester and polyether foams will gradually deteriorate on ageing, especially when exposed to light; polyester foams in particular can disintegrate, forming a sticky powder.

Packaging materials

Flexible food-wrapping films are often suggested for keeping objects wet during storage. Such products as Clingfilm (US: Saranwrap) are polyvinyl chloride films heavily plasticized with a material such as dioctyladipate, and are prone to degradation especially if exposed to light. Polyvinyl chloride films will retain water to a certain extent, but the rate of water diffusion through them is greater than through polyethylene sheeting of the same thickness. For storage periods longer than a few days therefore, heavy gauge polyethylene sheeting, heat-sealed around the edges, would provide better protection for objects.

Self-adhesive (pressure-sensitive) tapes are widely used in conservation for packaging purposes and do not present any problems. Where greater strength is required, plastic tape or string may be used. However, certain difficulties may be encountered in the use of self-adhesive tapes for temporarily holding fragments of glass in place whilst adhesives cure. The tapes are coated with a tacky substance, which is in reality an extremely viscous liquid. In warm conditions this can flow into the pores of an object, and may increase the adhesion of the tape to the surface of objects if the tapes are left in position for longer than necessary. Thus on removal the tapes may lift fragments of glass with it and traces of the adhesive may remain in the object. Tape alone should never be used for supporting fragments of glass during storage, since it will degrade to a brittle or sticky mass with some resulting damage to objects. If there is any risk of endangering the

object, solvents should be used to soften the adhesive before attempting to remove the tape. The tapes use a natural rubber, or similar, contact adhesive, which can degrade more or less rapidly to form an intractable brown mass. As it may well be impossible to remove the last traces of the adhesive from this type of self-adhesive tape, it would be wise to use only those tapes which use a more stable adhesive, such as an acrylic, which have been introduced in recent years.

Nevertheless, efforts should always be made, by using solvents, to remove the last traces of any adhesive which remain after stripping the tape from the object. A useful mixture for removing self-adhesive tape from antiquities is made up as follows: 5 ml toluene, 5 ml. 1,1,1-trichloroethane, 1 ml concentrated ammonia and 10 ml industrial methylated spirits. Fragile objects will need to be packed in acid-free tissue (never cotton wool) and/or inert foam inside strong cardboard boxes. Paper used for storage must be long-lasting, and as such will normally consist of highly purified cellulose, perhaps buffered to ensure that the paper is acid-free. The term acid-free means only that the paper is currently non-acidic, and is no guarantee that deterioration will not produce acids or other harmful emissions. However, for the majority of chemically insensitive materials higher specification than acid-free is unnecessary.

Plastazote and Ethazote are chemically inert polyethylene foams composed of polyethylene (sometimes copolymerized with vinyl acetate), which has been blown into foamed sheets. The foam is made of closed cells, which result in increased stiffness and resistance to compression. It is available in a range of thicknesses, split or laminated from the standard sheet size; and is easily cut with a sharp knife.

Cardboard boxes are made of compressed paper pulp (usually recycled), which is made into board of various thicknesses by building up layers of thinner plies, and frequently faced with brown paper. The boards commonly used range from 1.0 to 2.2 mm thick. The board is bent to shape and fixed by staples (stitches), brass being preferable to stainless steel. On ageing, fibre-board oxidizes and weakens, a process which is accelerated in damp conditions since it is permeable and absorbs water vapour. The lifespan of a good fibre-board box in good storage conditions seems to be in excess of twenty years. In poorer conditions and over longer periods there is increased danger of the box collapsing. Correx board, a white, ethylene propylene copolymer extrusion, can be used to form mounts and boxes to store and display glass objects. It is similar in appearance to corrugated cardboard, but unlike card, is chemically inert (Navarro, 1999; Lindsey, 2000).

6

Examination of glass, recording and documentation

One of the most crucial stages of the conservation process is the initial examination of an object. Only after examination will it be possible to determine the condition of an object, to suggest whether conservation is actually necessary, and if so, the most appropriate approach. The processes of observing and documenting observations and actions, should, in theory, be commenced at the same time.

Recording and documentation

The primary purpose of making records is to ensure that the information gained from examination and during the processes of conservation is not lost. The information will be valuable to the interpretation of the object, will provide data against which the condition of the object can be monitored, and will be available for reference if the object has to be re-treated at a future date.

Condition/conservation reports should contain the following information:

(i) The condition of the object (appearance and strength of the surface and body; number and type of breaks and condition of the break edges; presence of soluble or insoluble salts; stains and concretions; and the effects of any previous treatment).

(ii) Archaeological evidence (type of glass, provenance and approximate date of manufacture; ancient repair; function/evidence of use, and possibly contents).

(iii) Technical evidence (method of manufacture and decoration; evidence of the use of tools, moulds etc.; inclusions such as air bubbles).

(iv) Diagnosis of condition and suggested conservation treatment.

(v) Factors other than condition which may affect the choice of treatment. (What the object is needed for; level of conservation, e.g. for stabilization to display; future reversibility of the treatment if possible; different approaches to the conservation/restoration.)

(vi) Further evidence which may become apparent during the course of treatment, and which may cause the treatment to be modified.

(vii) Measured drawings and sketches; photographs; X-radiographs; analysis results where appropriate.

For larger institutions, the future of documentation lies with information technology and computerization, but such an approach may be inappropriate for small conservation laboratories or some countries. Notebooks (sometimes referred to as Day Books) can be used for noting brief observations, reminders and drawings, which can then be transferred to a standard condition or conservation report form which allows a more systematic approach to recording to take place. The forms could be enclosed in an envelope, which would bear the basic details on the outside. This approach would enable reports, photographs, X-radiographs and small samples to be kept together.

In order to extend the lifespan of record forms or cards, they should be made of archival quality paper and inks, particularly in hot and humid climates, and filled in by the conservator using permanent ink, also of archival quality. The format should include a section for standard information which describes, identifies and locates the object.

The majority of the record document will contain a description of the conservation processes, and should include information about the techniques and materials used, giving both the proprietary names (trade names) and chemical names of materials, e.g. Araldite 2020 (epoxy) resin. Whilst drawings may help to give more information, photography has the potential to be more accurate. Ideally, several photographs should be taken, before, during and after conservation. The choice of whether to use black and white or colour photography or transparencies is determined by personal preference, cost or organization policy. A scale of measurement (in millimetres/centimetres) and an identification should normally be included in every photograph. Some glass objects will need to be photographed by transmitted light in addition to reflected light, or in a raking light which will highlight surface details.

During work on the site of an archaeological excavation, any first aid or emergency treatment given to preserve objects should be accurately documented. The records will provide clear information for conservators carrying out future treatments in a laboratory.

Condition surveys of collections will require specially formulated record forms, which in addition to recording the condition of objects, can be used to accompany loans of objects for exhibitions.

Basic examination techniques

The majority of objects a glass conservator will encounter routinely will not require more specialized techniques or equipment than those described in the following section.

Visual examination

Visual examination is the first stage in examining an object when it arrives in a conservation laboratory; and in order to be reliable it should be carried out in good lighting conditions. A raking light (light directed at the surface at an angle almost parallel to the surface plane) will highlight surface irregularities and textures. Placing transparent glass on a light box will reveal irregularities within the glass itself. Besides observing the nature of any damage or deterioration, visual examination may identify the type and colour of the glass and any surface decoration. These physical characteristics relate to the nature of the glass, and will affect the choice of treatment.

Simple magnification

A simple hand-held magnifier can extend the powers of the naked eye up to ten times, depending on the magnification of the individual lens. Other useful aids are a magnifier, which fits against the eye, or a jeweller's loop, which attaches to spectacles.

Optical microscopy

It is possible to obtain more detailed information by viewing an object through a microscope. Microscopes range from the simple binocular types, which produce a stereoscopic (3-dimensional image), which can be used at the bench, to much more sophisticated instruments with zoom facilities, fibre-optic lighting and attachments for cameras.

The examination process

The glass surface and the nature of obscuring deposits

As is the case with much excavated material, glass will normally be found covered in a layer of obscuring deposits (*Figure 6.1*). These are normally removed mechanically or with distilled water. If the deposits are resistant, it will be necessary to identify them in order to determine the appropriate treatment for their removal (see, for example, the tests for determining insoluble salts below). Where possible, a small sample is removed for testing. Before its removal, material adhering to the glass should be examined as it may reveal the presence of other materials in association with the glass. For example, in the case of glass beads, there may be traces of fibres from the cords on which they were threaded (see *Plate 8*), or of metal rods on which they were wound during manufacture. The presence of metal corrosion products on glass (or enamel)

Figure 6.1   Obscuring mass of soil adhering to excavated glass.

will indicate that it had been had been set into a metal base, or that it had been buried adjacent to metal artefacts.

As the deposits are cleared away, a search must be made for any applied decoration, such as gilding or painting, to avoid its removal. As work progresses, more will be revealed of the decoration (if present) and state of deterioration of the glass. Finally, the shape and colour of the object will be revealed, and details of its method of manufacture sought. If, at any stage, an item of interest is uncovered, it should be photographed. The dimensions of sherds and thicknesses of vessel walls should be measured, immediately in the case of heavily decayed glass, in case it flakes or crumbles without warning. Bearing in mind that it may be necessary to analyse soil found within a hollow glass object, to determine whether there are traces of original contents present, soil samples should be taken for further examination or analysis.

The glass body

By viewing glass by transmitted light (e.g. on a photographic light box), it will be seen to be either translucent or opaque, clear or coloured. If the glass is opaque, it should be determined whether this was the original condition, or whether it is the result of deterioration. If the glass is transparent, it may be clear and homogeneous, or it may contain inhomogeneities such as air bubbles (seed) (*Figure 6.2*), *striae* and cords (streaks in the glass which have a different refractive index from the body of the glass), or opaque inclusions (stones) (see *Figure 4.1*). Viewing the object by means of transmitted light may be helpful in distinguishing between glass and hard gemstones, e.g. if air bubbles are seen to be present). The glass may be coloured throughout (colour having been added to the batch during manufacture) or flashed (a thin application of coloured glass to clear glass, sometimes found in window glass) or cased (a thick application of one or more coloured glass gathered over another, which when cold, were carved to varying depths to produce a design).

If the furnace temperature had been insufficient to melt all the quartz grains (sand) into glass, microscopic examination of the material would reveal anisotropic quartz grains embedded in an isotropic base (i.e. crystals in amorphous glass). When viewed in a polariscope, quartz grains are pleiochroic, i.e. display different colours according to the angles in which they are viewed.

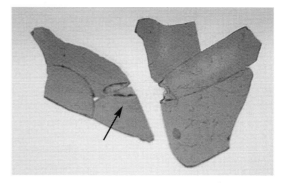

Figure 6.2   Inhomogeneities in glass seen by transmitted light from a photographic light box: air bubbles which cross the breaks in glass fragments, and which can be an aid to confirming the accuracy of joins during conservation.

Indications of fabrication techniques

Close examination of a glass artefact will often reveal details of its manufacture. There are many types of information which may be revealed during examination and initial cleaning; archaeologists and conservators must be continually aware of the possibilities. Examples of the evidence to look for are: order of manufacture, for example, handles etc. added after blowing, flash lines (seam marks) resulting from mould blowing or pressing; jagged broken marks on the bases of vessels, left by a punty iron (punty mark); and circular grinding marks on vessels ground from a casting or from a solid block of glass, especially on the interior, where less trouble would be taken to polish the marks away. If the article was cast, or pressed into a mould, there may be flow lines where the glass flowed into projections of the mould (such as a rimmed base) or into a corner. These flow lines can be identified by the lines of seed, or the elongated shape of the air bubbles, or lines of *striae*, which follow them (Bimson and Werner, 1964b). If seed are present, they may be spherical (showing that the glass was undisturbed as it cooled), or elongated (showing that they were stretched as the glass flowed while it was being manipulated when hot to form the artefact). If the air bubbles are large and distort the glass surface, they are called blisters; and if broken, weathering of the glass may have taken place inside them. Flat bubbles can also occur between the layers of successive gathers. *Striae* and cords can be observed by holding the glass against a brightly lit area with a dark edge (such as a light box), and moving it back and forth across the edge, or by using a cord-detector.

Differentiating glass from other transparent materials

Beads made of crystalline quartz, calcite or fluorite are often mistaken for glass beads even though they have quite a different chemical composition and can be distinguished from a true glass (for other materials which can be mistaken for glass beads, see Chapter 7). Quartz is harder than glass and twice as refractive; calcite, although also twice as refractive, is much softer and has a hardness of only three, compared with glass at six; fluorite has a hardness of four but, unlike quartz and calcite, is isotropic. There are also differences in specific gravity but these tests should be used only as a rough guide, and the exact composition of a particular glass is not easy to determine.

Evidence of previous repair and restoration

Archaeological glass that has not come directly from an excavation may have undergone previous repair or restoration. There may have been attempts to disguise the work by the application of adhesive, mud and glass flakes; or an outright attempt at forgery (see Chapter 7).

Historical glass is even more likely to have undergone repair and restoration. If the work has not been carried out by a conservator, there are not usually any records of the work. One of the advantages of glass being transparent is that the application of restoration materials is normally visible. However, as this cannot be taken for granted, the glass must be carefully examined.

Use of a hand-held metal detector (such as those used by electricians to detect hidden wiring), can assist in revealing metal components such as wire, rivets and dowels, which may have been incorporated in previous restorations. This may be especially useful when examining previously restored archaeological glass, which has been heavily covered with mud and glass flakes in an attempt to disguise the restoration, and heavily over-restored historical glass.

Ultraviolet (UV) light

Ultraviolet (UV) light provided by a hand-held lamp in a dark room can reveal synthetic materials used to restore glass and enamels, and forgeries, since different materials fluoresce slightly differently (Goldstein, 1977; Bly, 1986). A trained eye may be required to determine the differences in fluorescence, particularly if it is being used to determine or compare glass compositions (Brain, 1999).

X-radiography (X-rays)

X-rays can be useful for detecting metal components in previous restorations, the marrying together of pieces from different objects or other types of fakes and forgeries. Air bubbles, striations, inclusions, stress points may become visible and assist in determining manufacturing techniques. Although X-radiography is normally outside the scope of small laboratories, conservators may make arrangements with extra mural sources having X-ray facilities, such as a museum, university or hospital.

Infra-red (IR) photography

Infra-red photography can be useful for revealing indistinct surface decoration such as gilding or unfired paint, obscured by overlying material which is difficult to remove without causing damage; or gold decoration which has virtually disappeared (leaving a ghost of a pattern on the glass surface).

Universal indicator papers

Universal indicator papers can be used to determine the pH (alkalinity or acidity) of the surface of a glass, its immediate environment (e.g. soil) or of a liquid, which it is proposed to use in the conservation process. For example, some fungicides are highly alkaline. Electrically operated pH meters are available, but the use of universal indicator papers is simple and adequate for conservation purposes.

Strongly alkaline solutions (those with a pH value of 9.0 or greater) will eventually cause the breakdown of most glasses and certainly all ancient glasses. Similarly, acid solutions (those with a pH value of 5.0 or less) will attack the high-lime medieval glasses such as H and J in *Figure 4.18*. It is therefore useful to have a simple test with which to measure the pH. If an historic glass is found to have a damp, greasy surface, it is in a sweating or weeping condition, and the pH (alkalinity) of the surface liquid can be tested.

Universal indicator papers are available in three types: the full-range paper, where pH 1 shows as a red colour, through shades of orange to pH 7 (a greenish yellow) to a deep blue colour at pH 14; the narrow-range paper for acid solutions, where pH 4.0 is yellow and pH 5 is blue; and the narrow-range paper for alkaline solutions where pH 7.0 is green and pH 9.0 is dark blue. A small piece of indicator paper is torn off, moistened with the liquid to be tested, and laid on a white tile; after 30 seconds the colour is compared with the colour chart supplied with the indicator paper.

Methods of examination for research

Measurement of density

A simple test for identifying lead-containing glasses is to measure the density. Lead oxide has a pronounced effect on the density of glass (see *Figure 1.8*, which shows how density is related to lead content). Lead glasses made by Ravenscroft, have a density of about 3150 kg m^3, compared with 2460 kg m^3 for soda–lime–silica glass, 3580 kg m^3 for opaque Bristol blue glass; but some lead glass beads can have a density of 6000 kg m^3. The density of an object can be determined, by weighing it first in air and then in water. The loss of weight of the glass in water (weight in air – weight in water) is approximately equal to the volume of the glass in ml and hence the density = weight in air (g) divided by the volume (ml). Further accuracy can be maintained by making corrections for the density of the air and the temperature of the water, but this is rarely worthwhile for ancient glasses. The presence of an air-twist stem, a tear stem, a hollow stem, or even many seed in the glass, will invalidate the result (the apparent density will be less than the true one owing to the presence of the air inside the glass). If the glass is in small pieces, or if a fragment can be obtained, the most accurate determinations are made by the sink–float method (Scholze, 1977).

Some Chinese glasses contain substantial amounts of barium, which has a marked effect on their density. Care must be taken to distinguish between lead- and barium-containing glass.

Measurement of refractive index (RI)

The refractive index (RI) and the density of glass are closely correlated, but different relationships apply to different types of glass. The RI. and density of the glass can be calculated by various empirical formulae, from the analysed composition of the glass. However, the simplest procedure is to refer to the graph in *Figure 1.11*, in which it can be seen that the lead crystal glasses (with potash as the alkali), lie on a line at the right-hand side of the graph, the average value of C being 0.19. The weight percentage of PbO is indicated on the line.

Soda–lime–silica glasses lie on a much steeper line to the left of the diagram, with an average value of C = 0.21, and it connects the point for fused silica (at the bottom) with a glass containing 60 per cent SiO_2, 20 per cent CaO and 10 per cent Na_2O (at the top), intermediate values of CaO being spaced, more or less equidistantly, on the line. (C is a constant and differs for each type (composition) of glass; Huggins and Sun, 1946).

Ancient glasses lie between the two lines; Roman glass lies at the point R (70 per cent SiO_2, 10 per cent CaO, 20 per cent Na_2O), but medieval glasses fall within the shaded area, because the MgO, Al_2O_3 and P_2O_3 which they contain have more effect on the density than on the RI. It is interesting to note that quartz, which has the same chemical composition as fused silica, falls in quite a different position on the graph (at Q) because the crystalline material is more dense, and has a much higher RI than the amorphous (fused) silica. The RI of a glass object is of importance when choosing materials for conserving glass (Tennent and Townsend, 1984a,b) (see *Figure 5.1*).

Examination by immersion in liquids

It is often difficult to see details inside a piece of glass, even when the glass is transparent, because (i) the surface may be scratched, abraded, etched or sand-blasted, (ii) may be curved so that it acts as a lens and distorts the detail, or (iii) there may be reflections from surface features such as cut glass designs. The visual effects of such surface features can be removed, by immersing the glass object in a liquid that has the same or close RI. If the RI match is exact, the surface of the glass seems to disappear, and its internal features, such as seed, striae and stones become easily visible.

The RI of soda–lime–silica glasses lies in the range 1.51–1.52, whereas full-lead crystal glass has an RI of 1.565 (see *Figure 1.11*). The RI of a glass of known composition can be calculated (Gilard and Dubrul, 1937) and it can be seen that high-lime glasses will also have a high RI. The poorly durable medieval glasses at the bottom of the triangular diagram in *Figure 4.18* are glasses of that type, and those having a composition of 50 per cent SiO_2, 15 per cent K_2O and 35 per cent CaO, would have an RI of 1.59 and a density of 3.1, that is, at point H in *Figure 1.11*.

Convenient immersion liquids, and their RI values, are: xylene (1.490), chlorobenzene (1.525), nitrobenzene (1.553), aniline (NB a carcinogen) (1.586) and quinoline (1.624). Bimson and Werner (1964b) used the immersion technique to prove that one of the minute heads on the Tara Brooch (found in County Wexford, Ireland) was in fact glass rather than a carved gemstone. Immersion in toluene (RI = 1.496) revealed the presence of air bubbles, and characteristic markings showed that the heads had been made by casting the glass into moulds. The detection of *striae* is greatly affected by the orientation of the sample. For example, none may be seen when looking through a piece of window glass, yet they are quite obvious when looking through the edge of the glass.

Detection of strain

If glass contains numerous cords and *striae*, or has been badly annealed, it will exhibit signs of strain, which can be detected by means of a strain-viewer (Werner *et al.*, 1975). Badly annealed ancient glass will not usually be encountered since it is unlikely to have survived, but there may be occasion to look for the presence of strain-producing inhomogeneities. Glass subjected to strain (bending or stretching) becomes bi-refringent, that is, it acquires two different refractive indices. Thus a single ray of light entering the glass will emerge as two separate rays. This phenomenon can be used to detect, and to measure, the frozen strains resulting from unsatisfactory annealing. Briefly, when plane polarized light passes through a material of a bi-refringent nature, it becomes elliptically polarized, and hence strain-viewers make use of polarized light produced either by reflection from a polished metal surface, or by the use of Polaroid filters. There are various commercial instruments available; or a strain-viewer can be made, in which the polarization of light is produced by two pieces of black plate glass, placed at Brewster's angle (56.50).

Fracture analysis

Fracture analysis is a technique that enables the origin of a fracture in glass to be identified by showing the directions in which the fracture propagated itself. The technique may be useful in the study of well-preserved glass. Fractures which occur at speed (experimentally) are easy to study, but those which occur perhaps as slowly as a few millimetres per century are more difficult to understand. In the great majority of cases the break starts at a single point and the fractures spread out from this point of origin. If the glass is broken into a number of fragments the smallest ones are closest to the point of origin. A fracture arises from a tensile stress in the glass and hence it starts at right angles to the stress which produced it. However, if the stress is great the crack, once started, may fork so that there is an acute angle between the two new branches. Cracks rarely join up and hence these acute-angled forks point towards the origin of the cracks.

At the actual origin of the crack the broken edge bears a characteristic mirror area which (see *Figure 1.13*) is surrounded by grey areas, hackle marks and, finally, rib marks which may extend a long distance from the origin and indicate the direction in which the fracture travelled. The rib marks are places where the fracture has hesitated briefly before continuing its start–stop advance, and they represent the leading edge of the fracture at successive moments. The rib marks are always curved and present their convex face to the direction in which they were formed. They are thus important for determining the direction in which the crack was growing. The investigator simply follows the reverse direction to the point at which the rib marks point the other way. When glass breaks due to excessive local heating, the rib marks are spaced well apart on the cold side and they crowd together on the hot side. The origin of the fracture is always at the surface of the glass and the rib marks generally face the same side as the origin of the fracture. If the outside of a vessel has been given a sharp blow, the area which receives the blow may be crushed (causing a bruise consisting of powdered glass), with a surrounding stressed ring from which a family of cracks start. This ring of cracks forms an impact cone, which may separate from the glass in the form of a plug (see *Figures 1.12* and *1.13*).

Another feature of the fractured surface is the size of the mirror area. The energy of a fracture is directly related to the diameter of the mirror area; for example, a mirror diameter of 0.1 mm corresponds to a stress of about 200 MNm^{-2} (30000 psi), whereas one of 2.5 mm corresponds to only some 40 MNm^{-2} (6000 psi). Discussions of fracture analysis can be found in Ernsberger (1977) and Scholze (1977).

Instrumental methods of analysing glass for scientific research

In addition to physical and chemical methods of examination, a large and ever increasing number of instrumental methods used in other areas of scientific analysis is being applied to the examination of the surface and bulk compositions of ancient and historic glass objects. The composition of a weathered glass surface and the body of a glass differ substantially as a result of the leaching processes, which have occurred over time, and therefore it will be necessary to remove surface material in order to obtain a true sample of the glass body. Through the application of instrumental methods of analysis, information can be obtained concerning condition, provenance and fabrication technology. Analysis determines (i) the reduced composition of the glasses, i.e. the main elements which characterize them: the oxides of silicon, sodium, potassium, calcium, iron, magnesium and aluminium; (ii) the additives, i.e. opacifiers and colourants: the metallic oxides; and (iii) the trace elements which indicate differences in raw materials from different sources: oxides of boron, titanium, manganese, antimony and sulphur.

A brief introduction to the instrumental methods of analysis is given below, stating the purposes which they serve. They can be conveniently grouped as (i) electron beam methods, (ii) X-ray methods, optical spectrometric methods, (iii) mass spectrometric methods, and (iv) oxidation state methods. Full details can be found in Mass (1999). Before scientific methods of analysis can be used with confidence, it must be certain that the results of analyses in one laboratory will be essentially the same as those from the same glass from another laboratory. Otherwise, observed differences in composition etc. could be due either to true compositional differences, or to those inherent in the particular analytical procedures of the laboratories concerned, the accuracy of which will depend very much upon the expertise of the scientist undertaking the work. It is for this reason that analyses of glasses have not been included in this volume.

The establishment of standard reference glasses is therefore important in order to achieve any meaningful results (particularly as glasses have such a complex nature).

A conservator will normally be party to the identification of a need for analysis, and may supply the samples for analysis. This is particularly the case if glass is fragmentary, otherwise a conservation scientist may prepare the sample. (Note that many of the instrumental methods of analysis are destructive, in that they require a sample, albeit minute, to be taken from the glass.) Very few conservation laboratories will contain the specialized equipment for scientific examination and analysis, but it is often possible to work in collaboration with a research laboratory in a museum or university.

Figure 6.3   Scanning electron micrograph of deterioration layers on glass (×700).

Electron beam methods

Electron beam methods of analysis involve measuring the signals generated by a beam of high energy electrons impinging on a (glass) sample. The SEM (scanning electron microscope) can be used to image the surface of ancient glasses; SEM-EDS or energy dispersive X-ray analysis, AES or auger emission spectrometry, and EPMA or electron probe X-ray microanalysis, are all used for the compositional analysis of ancient glass surfaces. The SEM can be used in conjunction with electron microprobe analysis to provide a micro chemical analysis of the area in the field of view of the SEM.

Scanning electron microscopy (SEM)

Scanning electron microscopy is a technique used to image the surface of a (glass) sample and reveal features that are less than 0.4 μm or 400 nm in diameter). The SEM is usually operated at magnifications between 5000× to 100 000×, and it has an extraordinary depth of field. Three-dimensional views, which can be photographed, can be obtained by tilting the sample under magnification. The only (slight) disadvantage of the use of an SEM is the need to apply a thin and invisible electrically conductive coating such as carbon or gold to the glass sample, in order to prevent the build-up and release of electrical charges

which would appear as bright streaks across the image (Adlerborn, 1971).

SEM has been extensively used to study the surfaces and microstructures of ancient and historic glasses: SEM has been used to detect faked weathering surfaces (Gairola, 1960; Werner *et al.*, 1975); opacifiers and colourants in glasses (Brundle *et al.*, 1992; Freestone, 1993; Henderson, 1993a; Verita, 1995; Freestone and Bimson, 1995; Freestone and Stapleton, 1998; Mass, 1999). Krawczyk-Barsch *et al.*, (1998) used SEM and ion-beam slope-cutting to study the thickness of weathering on glass. Hogg *et al.*, (1999) drew attention to the possible changes in the surface of a specimen, due to the inevitable dehydration of the surface which occurs when a specimen is placed in the high vacuum. The use of an environmental SEM (e-SEM) may overcome these problems.

Energy dispersive X-ray spectrometry (EDS)

SEM-EDS has been widely used to study the composition of ancient and historic glass: second millennium BC Mesopotamian glass (Vandiver, 1982); pre-Malkata Egyptian glass (Lilyquist and Brill, 1993); thirteenth- to sixteenth-century glass and glass waste in Guildford Museum, Surrey (UK) (Mortimer, 1993); early Venetian enamels (Freestone and Bimson, 1995); glass recovered from an eighteenth-century shipwreck (Corvaia *et al.*, 1996).

Electron probe microanalysis (EPMA), also known as wavelength dispersive X-ray analysis (SEM-WDS) or electron microprobe analysis

The electron microprobe can either be used with the SEM (as above) or separately. The principle is similar to that of X-ray fluorescence (XRF) except that electrons are used as the exciting radiation instead of X-rays. EMPA is widely used for the chemical analysis of glass samples as it requires very small samples, and can be applied to broken surfaces, or cut sections of glass (Brill, 1968; Verita, 1985; Henderson, 1988, 1991; Barrera and Velde, 1989; Mortimer, 1995; Hartmann *et al.*, 1997; Wedepohl *et al.*, 1997).

It is of great value in interpreting complex chemical situations such as the contents of pits in a glass surface. It can be seen that air pollution does not attack painted glass because sulphur-containing compounds are found only at the surface of a pit, and not at the bottom where corrosion reactions are occurring. The disadvantages are that it analyses the surface layer only; lighter elements are harder to measure than the heavier ones, and alkali elements can be forced deeper into the glass by the charge on the electron beam.

Verita *et al.* (1994) compared two related tests, using wavelength dispersive systems (WDS) or EMPA and energy dispersive systems (EDS). It was concluded that both methods were poorly sensitive to elements lighter than sodium; and that EDS could be inaccurately interpreted due to peak overlap. The disadvantage of WDS is that unless precautions are taken, the higher energy used with it can cause sodium ions to migrate away from the test area, resulting in a lower result for the element, unless the microprobe beam is defocused. EDS with its limited account rate capability is regarded as being less accurate, but is more readily available than WDS (see also Mass, 1999).

Auger electron spectrometry (AES); auger microprobe analysis

In analysis by AES, the surface of the glass sample is bombarded in such a way as to cause the emission of Auger electrons from its surface, by means of which elements within the glass can be identified (Mass, 1999). The results are limited to the first few atomic layers of the surface, so that AES was used to investigate the durability of medieval window glass (Dawson *et al.*, 1978) and by Pollard (1979).

X-ray methods

X-ray methods of analysis are all non-destructive, i.e. do not require a sample to be taken from the (glass) objects. The techniques of analysis produce signals which result from the interaction of the atoms in a (glass) sample with incident X-rays: diffracted X-ray beams (XRD or X-ray diffraction); outer shell electron ejection energies (XPS or X-ray photoelectron spectrometry, also known as ESCA, electron spectrometry for chemical analysis): and fluorescent X-rays (XRF or X-ray fluorescence). XRD is used to identify crystalline phases in glass; XRF and XPS determine the surface compositions of glass. XPS will also identify the oxidation states of surface atoms in glass.

X-ray diffraction (XRD)

X-ray diffraction is frequently used in the study of ancient glass to identify undissolved raw materials, opacifying agents, devitrification products and undissolved raw materials (Newton and Davison, 1989). When a beam of diffracted X-rays is passed through powdered crystalline material, diffraction patterns are formed which can be detected photographically as a series of curved lines that can be interpreted as having come from the particular material.

Since it determines crystalline phases, the technique can also be used to differentiate between glass and semi-precious stones, Egyptian faience or metallurgical slags. XRD has been used by Dandrige and Wypyski (1992), to identify crystalline opacifying agents present in medieval enamels; by Hoffman (1994) in the study of crystalline colourant/opacifiers in Merovingian beads from German grave deposits; and McRay *et al.* (1995) in the identification of the lead arsenate crystals responsible for the colouring of Venetian *girasole* glass.

X-ray diffraction can be useful in determining whether a glass object has been repaired, especially if the repair has been obliterated by the application of weathering products from elsewhere (*Plate 7*).

Goldstein (1977) illustrated two examples of repairs detected by X-rays; a large amphora with a tip reconstructed from a modern dropper tube, and an ewer to which a plastics handle had been added (see *Figure 7.49*). The possibility of darkening of lead glass by the use of X-rays must be considered.

X-ray fluorescence (XRF)

XRF is a non-destructive technique which is widely used for the chemical analysis of materials because it is rapid and accurate, and can be carried out on equipment that is available commercially (Brill and Moll, 1961). A suitably prepared test piece (hence not truly non-destructive) is irradiated with suitable primary X-rays, and the sample then emits secondary X-rays that are characteristic of the elements that make up the sample. The secondary X-rays can be detected in two ways: the earlier technique measured their wavelengths (Hall *et al.*, 1964; Hall and Schweizer, 1973); energy-dispersive XRF tests measure their energies, which appear as peaks on a video monitor; the positions of the peaks indicate the chemical elements, and the heights of the peaks measure their concentrations. A computer program assists in the interpretations and makes allowance for the mutual interferences of certain elements. The sample can be affected by the test; Brill (1968) mentions damage by radiation burns, and lead-containing glasses can be darkened unless suitable precautions are taken. Cox and Pollard (1977) showed that older weathered glasses possessed an ion-exchange layer from which alkali ions had been removed so that the surface layer (even though it looked quite unaltered) had a composition different from that of the interior; they found it necessary to grind part of the surface away to a depth of 0.5 mm and then polish it smooth. Pollard (1979) used the technique extensively in his thesis, and many other workers have found it invaluable.

X-ray photo-electron spectrometry (XPS), also known as electron spectrometry for chemical analysis (ESCA)

This method analyses the surface of glass by means of photoelectrons emitted from the surface when it is bombarded by suitable X-rays. XPS has not been widely used in the study of ancient glass. Hench (1975a) used it to follow the early stages of weathering processes which occur in ancient glass; Lambert *et al.* (1978) used XPS to identify the copper oxidation states responsible for the blue colour of ancient Egyptian glass.

Secondary ion mass spectroscopy (SIMS)

This is highly specialized, but it has the advantage that any element or isotope (including hydrogen) can be analysed, and the alkali ions are not driven further into the glass, which is the case with EMPA (Hench, 1975a).

Infrared reflection spectroscopy (IRRS)

This again is restricted to the study of glass surfaces, and it has been used by Hench *et al.* (1979) to characterize the weathering of medieval glasses, and for predicting the weathering behaviour of others.

Particle methods

In these techniques of analysis, a (glass) sample is placed into a beam or flux of particles and the characteristic radiation resulting from the sample–particle interaction is measured. NAA (neutron activation analysis) and PIXE (particle induced X-ray emission, using protons instead of neutrons) are used to measure the major, minor and trace element compositions of bulk glass samples and their surfaces respectively.

Particle induced X-ray emission (PIXE)

Conservation scientists have frequently used PIXE to study ancient glasses: Fleming and Swann (1994) studied the production formulae and colourants used in the manufacture of Roman onyx glass; McGovern *et al.* (1991) studied glass beads from mid-second millennium BC sites in Iran; Swann *et al.* (1990) and Vandiver *et al.* (1991) studied glass workshop debris from Tell el-Amarna in Egypt; Germain-Bonne *et al.* (1996) investigated the compositions and deterioration of fifteenth- and sixteenth-century painted enamels; and Borbely-Kiss *et al.* (1994) classified late Roman glass seals.

Neutron activation analysis (NAA)

NAA is a valuable technique for determining the bulk chemical composition of a glass, and it is particularly suitable for detecting minor and trace elements, but it has two disadvantages; it is restricted to the availability of a nuclear reactor and, although it is described as being non-destructive, some samples, for example those that contain much antimony or cobalt, are rendered so radioactive that it may be many years before they are safe to return to the owner.

NAA has been frequently applied to the elemental analysis of ancient glass to study its provenance, colourants and opacifying agents. For example, the technique has been used to identify the origins of the dichroic colour of the Roman Lycurgus cup (British Museum, London); and in the study of medieval window glass (Brill, 1965; Olin *et al.*, 1972). Hancock *et al.* (1994) and Kenyon *et al.* (1995) applied non destructive NAA to the study of the colourants and opacifying agents in European glass trade beads, by developing a system of short irradiations which allowed the beads to be returned to their collections after two weeks.

Optical methods

Optical methods of analysis include ICP–OES (inductively coupled plasma-optical emission spectrometry), and AAS (atomic absorption spectrometry), which have been routinely used to determine major, minor and trace elements in the compositions of ancient glass. They are based on the measurement of bands of UV-VIS radiation resulting from electronic transitions, which have been excited in inorganic samples (in this instance glass) at high temperatures.

Inductively coupled plasma-optical emission spectrometry (ICP-OES)

ICP–OES is a destructive form of analysis requiring a sample of 0.1–0.5 g. It has been used in the study of many ancient and historic glasses: medieval Hungarian glass (El-Nady *et al.*, 1985); glass bead fragments from Hungarian graves of the great migration period and glass fragments from the king's palace at Buda Castle (Zimmer, 1988); Saxon glass from Southampton and Winchester (UK) (Heyworth *et al.*, 1989); and Roman glass from Augusta, Praetoria (Mirti *et al.*, 1993): compositions of Venetian *girasole* glass (McCray *et al.*, 1995); compositional variations among Romano-British glass from Colchester, Essex (UK) (Baxter *et al.*, 1995).

Atomic absorption spectrometry (AAS)

Atomic absorption spectometry is a destructive method of analysis requiring a sample of 0.05–0.50 g., and is used in the study of elements used to determine the concentration of metal ions in solution. The greatest limitation to AAS is that the measurement for all the elements must be made serially because the light source has to be changed for each element. Consequently this technique is more appropriate for the study of groups of elements already known to be present in a glass sample, than for the study of entirely unknown glass compositions. However, AAS has been extensively used in the study of ancient glass compositions: ancient Egyptian glass (Brill, 1973); early American glass from the New Bremen glass manufactory (Brill and Hanson, 1976): Renaissance Venetian glass (Brill and Barnes, 1988); and early Islamic glass (Brill, 1995); characterization of medieval Scottish cathedral glass (Tennent *et al.*, 1984b); and the identification of a modern forgery of early Roman or late Hellenistic glass from the Ashmolean Museum, Oxford (UK) (Newton and Brill, 1983). Salem *et al.* (1994) used AAS in conjunction with atomic emission spectrometry to measure the concentration of alkali and alkali earth ions in acidic solutions, which had been applied to medieval-type glass.

Mass spectrometry methods

These methods of analysis include ICPMS (inductively coupled plasma mass spectrometry), SIMS (secondary ion mass spectrometry) and lead isotope ratio determination, and are used to determine the major, minor and trace element compositions of ancient glasses as well as their isotopic compositions. They all require destructive sampling of the object to be studied.

Inductively coupled plasma mass spectrometry (ICPMS)

The advantage of IPCMS is that many elements can be analysed simultaneously; the disadvantages are that the technique is costly and requires destructive sampling to obtain 100–250 g of glass.

Secondary ion mass spectrometry (SIMS)

SIMS is a bulk analytical technique used to determine the major, minor and trace elements (from hydrogen to uranium) in a (glass) sample (which should be less than 2.5 cm in diameter and 1.0 cm thick), by bombarding it with the heavy primary ions (such as oxygen or caesium). It will detect elements in the surface of the glass in the parts-per-million range. Since its range is limited to a depth of 50–100 A, SIMS is a valuable aid to the study of weathering phenomena on ancient glass surfaces, such as medieval window glass (Schreiner *et al.*, 1984). It has been used to study the deterioration of ancient glass in museum environments (Ryan *et al.*, 1996), the deterioration of weeping Venetian glass (Rogers *et al.*, 1993) and Hogg *et al.*, 1999).

Isotope ratio analysis

Lead and oxygen isotope ratio analysis requires destructive sampling of the object to be studied. There are four stable isotopes of lead, created by radioactivity. Three of these, (206Pb, 207Pb and 208Pb) are produced by the decay of 238U, 235U and 232Th respectively. Thus the ratios of the four lead isotopes in a lead ore deposit will depend upon the geological age of the deposition of the ore. Theoretically then, the lead isotope ratios in a lead-containing glass will have the potential to provide information about the particular lead deposit exploited for its manufacture (Brill, 1967a,b, 1968, 1970a,b; Brill *et al.*, 1970; Barnes *et al.*, 1978). For example, lead from Derbyshire (UK) has 206 Pb/204 Pb = 18.6 and 208 Pb/207 Pb = 2.46, whereas lead of Italian origin has values of 18.8 and 2.48, respectively. Although these pairs differ only by about 1 per cent they are nevertheless statistically significant. However, since several lead sources can have the same geological age, lead isotope ratios alone can only be used to eliminate potential lead sources, not to assign the provenance of an object. Ore deposits containing lead isotope ratios different from those of an object can be disregarded as potential sources of lead for the object; conversely, ore deposits with lead isotope ratios similar to those of an object can be considered as potential sources of lead for the object.

Unlike the concentrations of trace and minor elements, lead isotope ratios will not be affected by the chemical and pyrotechnological transformations that raw materials undergo during their conversion to glass. However the interpretation of lead isotope ratios is made difficult by the long-range trade of materials containing lead, which can result in the use of lead from several sources in one object; and by the frequent practice in antiquity of melting-down and re-using glass (and metal) objects.

This technique of analysis has been frequently applied to the study of coloured opaque ancient glasses with high lead contents, such as red and yellow opaque glasses, primarily to identify the sources of lead used, or for identification of groups of glass which were prepared from the same source of lead ore: Egyptian (Brill *et al.*, 1970, 1974), Japanese and Chinese glasses (Brill *et al.*, 1991), third millennium BC glass bead from Nippur (Vandiver *et al.*, 1995).

In a similar manner, the proportion of the oxygen isotope 18O can be characteristic of glasses made from different sources of raw material (Brill, 1968, 1970a, 1988).

Radiation monitoring of potash glass

Radiation monitoring of potash glass can be of use in determining whether painted window glass is medieval or a later replacement. The former will contain potash, derived from the beechwood ash from which it was made, and therefore contain the natural radioactive isotope of potash (40K), the B radiation from which can be detected with a standard radiation monitoring badge shown as a darkening of the badge over a period of approximately two months. Glass made later (certainly after the sixteenth century) will have been made from an alkali, which was predominantly soda. Potassium contains a naturally occurring, weakly radioactive isotope (40K), and hence medieval glass will slowly cause darkening of a radiation-monitoring badge over a period of about two months (Hudson and Newton, 1976).

Oxidation state methods

Oxidation state methods of analysis include ESR (electron spin resonance) and UV–VIS (ultraviolet and visible spectroscopy), which in the study of ancient glasses are used primarily for the determination of the oxidation states of the glass colourants and clarifying agents.

Electron spin resonance (ESR), also known as electron paramagnetic resonance (EPR)

ESR requires destructive sampling to obtain a 15–20 mg sample of glass. Sellner (1977) and Sellner *et al.* (1979) used ESR to measure the states of oxidation of iron and manganese in medieval glasses from two sites, and thus show that a wide range of colours could be obtained by using beechwood ash as the source of alkali and varying the state of oxidation of the glass.

Ultraviolet and visible spectroscopy (UV–VIS)

UV–VIS can be used to identify transition metal ions present in glass, and their state of oxidation. UV–VIS has been used to study the colours produced by iron and sulphur in late Roman glass (Schreurs and Brill, 1984); iron oxidation states in medieval stained glass (Longworth *et al.*, 1982); in the study of Roman and of post medieval glass (Green and Hart, 1987); and identification of the colourants used to prepare the red and yellow stained glass windows of Toledo Cathedral (Spain) (Fernandez Navarro and La Iglesia, 1994).

Rarely used and out-dated analysis techniques

Chemical analysis

The chemical analyses of glasses by traditional methods have largely fallen into disuse. The reasons for this are that chemical analyses are extremely time consuming, require highly trained analysts, need substantial amounts of glass as samples, and require preliminary dissolution of the glass with hydrofluoric acid, or by fusion with sodium carbonate. (See Chapter 5 for the dangers of using hydrofluoric acid.) Nevertheless, in competent hands, excellent results can be obtained by chemical analysis of very small glass samples, and would still be used as a reference before the introduction of a new instrumental method of analysis.

Emission spectroscopy (spectrography)

The analysis of glass by emission spectrography, which required the use of a massive amount of equipment, has now been superseded by other methods. This destructive technique of analysis required a tiny fragment of glass to be totally destroyed (volatilized in an electric arc discharge), so that individual elements, seen as a visible spectrum, could be identified. It will analyse for almost any element in a semi-quantitative manner, can be used over a wide range of concentrations, and was the classical technique of analysis used in the early part of the twentieth century. Sayre and Smith (1974) used it for their study of glass from the New Kingdom to early Islam. Newton and Renfrew (1970) made use of results which had been obtained a generation before to study the origins of British faience beads. Emission spectroscopy has been replaced by XRF.

Counting the weathering layers

Glasses, which have weathered in conditions where the alkali has leached out in an unusual manner, may develop a thick crust on the surface. The crust may be 4 mm thick and, when a section is examined under a microscope, it can be seen to consist of a multitude of very thin layers (see *Figure 6.1*). Brewster (1855) found twenty or thirty layers in one-fiftieth of an inch; the layering phenomena was recorded by Fowler (1881), Raw (1955) and Geilmann (1960). Brill and Hood (1961) noted that, in eleven out of about two hundred samples examined, the number of layers in the crust was approximately the same as the number of years that they had been buried, or immersed in fresh- or seawater. Despite the fact that eleven samples out of two hundred cannot be considered to be statistically significant, it was hypothesized that the layers represented an annual phenomenon which could be used for dating the glasses (in the same way that annual growth rings are used to date trees). Newton (1966, 1969, 1971a) concluded that there were too many inconsistencies in the technique to enable it to be reliable. These include the effect of temperature (ten layers were produced in four hours in an autoclave); and evidence that layers could merge into each other (Newton, 1972). Douglas (in Newton, 1971a, p. 7) suggested that the layers were in fact the result of the alternation of two weathering processes, which accidentally took about a year to complete a cycle. Shaw (1965) used EMPA to show that the silicon and calcium contents of the crust alternately rose and fell with a periodicity of 6–8 µm, the same as that of the visible layers in the crust. Newton and Shaw (1988) illustrate a case in which the weathering layers are at an angle to one another other. It would seem that the formation of surface lamellae does not correspond to yearly cycles, but form as a result of minute changes in the composition of the glass.

Hydration rind dating

Lanford (1977, 1986) found that the alkali-deficient layer on the surface of weathered glass were thickest on the oldest glass samples, and suggested that measurement of the weathered layer could be used for dating samples. However, it proved difficult to substantiate this hypothesis, and the research was abandoned.

Fission track dating

Fission track dating depends on the assessment of damage done to glass over a considerable length of time, by the tracks from nuclear fission, caused by the spontaneous disintegration of uranium atoms that it contains (Nishimura, 1971). However, man-made glasses rarely contain uranium, and are not old enough for sufficient fission tracks to have formed (Brill *et al.*, 1964

Radiocarbon (14C) dating

Radiocarbon dating is used to date carbon-containing materials such as wood. However there have been two instances where the technique has been indirectly useful in dating glass. Glass from the great slab at Bet She'arim was found to contain 3 per cent of dissolved carbon dioxide; Brill (1968) stated that radiocarbon dating had been carried out on a sample of the glass, but the results seem not to have been published. Fiorentini-Roncuzzi (1970) dated Byzantine mosaics at Ravenna to AD 345–695, by radiocarbon dating the straw binder in the original mortar in which the glass *tesserae* had been embedded.

Thermoluminescence (TL)

TL is used to date ancient pottery by releasing energy (as thermoluminescence) stored from the time the pottery was fired. (Any subsequent application of heat will have negated the result, i.e. in effect having become

the last firing; Brain, 1999.) A modification of the technique, radioactively induced TL, has been used for characterizing obsidian (Huntley and Bailey, 1978).

Beta-ray backscattering

Beta-ray backscattering has been used to determine the lead content of glasses by irradiating the surface with electrons, and then measuring those which are scattered back again by the atoms of lead. Emeleus (1960) used it to study numerous samples of the first glasses made by George Ravenscroft in the seventeenth century (see Chapter 2). Asahina *et al.* (1973) used it to determine the lead content of a Japanese blue glass bowl.

Use of a profilometer

At one time it was thought that the chemical composition of a glass could be deduced by making sufficient well-chosen measurements of physical properties but that is now considered to be unlikely.

A profilometer can be used to measure the smoothness of the surface of a glass; this has been of value in considering how any roughness affects the strength of glass. The British version of the profilometer (the Talysurf), can measure the roughness in 25 nm. When enamel paint is fired on to glass, it creates depressions in the glass (i.e. an image), less than one wavelength of visible light, but which can be measured by means of a profilometer. Newton (1974b) used the technique to detect the image left by painted decoration on medieval window glass, which had been removed by inappropriate cleaning. There are also optical methods of studying surfaces, such as the Schmaltz light cut (Vickers Projection Microscope Handbook).

Infra-red reflection spectroscopy (IRRS)

IRRS has been used to characterize the weathered surface of medieval glasses (Hench *et al.*, 1979; Schreiner *et al.*, 1999). The technique depends upon observing the changes that occur in the vibrations of the 'silicon-bridging oxygen stretching', and 'silicon non-bridging oxygen bond' in a molecule.

Ion beam spectrochemical analysis (IBSCA)

IBSCA is an extremely sensitive technique of analysis, which, for example, permits studies to be made of the relative durabilities of different areas of any piece of glass (Hench *et al.*, 1979; Rauch, 1985; Lanford, 1986).

Techniques of the future

Techniques of analysis are continually evolving. Those which may become applicable to the study of glass are laser-induced breakdown spectroscopy (LIBS) (Mansfield *et al.*, 1998), atomic force microscopy (Techmer and Rädlein, 1998), Brillouin light scattering (Cavaillé *et al.*, 1998), voltammetry of immobilized microparticles (Perez-Arantegui *et al.*, 2000) and X-ray tomography (mCT) (Römich and Lopez, in Kordas, 2002).

7

Conservation and restoration of glass

Conservation has two aspects: first, the control of the environment to minimize the decay of artefacts and materials (*passive conservation*); and secondly, treatment to arrest decay and to stabilize them where possible, against further deterioration (*active conservation*). It has become increasingly common for environmental control to be allowed for in the financial budget to refurbish or construct museum galleries. However, environmental control is by no means universal, either within museums or storage areas. In relation to glass, special storage conditions are required for damp or wet archaeological glass, and for storing/ displaying historical weeping glasses, Egyptian faience and enamels. Restoration is the extension of conservation, by which part or all of incomplete objects are reinstated without falsification, using synthetic materials. This may be done to render an object safe for storage or display, or to aid in its interpretation.

In considering conservation and restoration of objects, the ethics of conservation need to be continually borne in mind. Briefly stated, these are: the assessment of risks to the object associated with conservation (Ashley-Smith, 1999); that all treatment should be adequately documented, and that there should be no structural and decorative falsification of objects. In addition, it is generally agreed that: all conservation/restoration processes should, as far as is practicable, be fully reversible, even after a number of years; that where possible decayed parts of objects should be conserved *in situ*, and where this is not possible, loose fragments should be carefully labelled, packaged and placed in storage; and that the natural consequences of ageing of

the original material (iridescence and flakes in the case of glass) should not normally be disguised or removed.

Glass is a difficult material to conserve, especially when it retains its transparency or translucency. It can be perfectly clear, coloured in an almost infinite range, or be opaque. It is always fragile and in some cases, its composition results in it being chemically unstable.

Different approaches are taken in the way in which conservators deal with archaeological, i.e. excavated, ancient glass, and historical glass. In the case of archaeological glass, a policy of minimum intervention is generally followed. Removal of weathering layers solely for the purpose of enhancing the glass is considered unethical. However, in rare instances, it may be necessary to remove some or all of mud-encrusted deterioration products in order to identify the object or its true colour. Missing areas of a glass artefact should only be filled where necessary to add support or aid interpretation, and where possible, the gap-fills made away from the object. Glass fragments can be mounted on a Perspex (US Plexiglas) frame or stand, or adhered to a former made of resin or glass. It is difficult to blow glass to the shape of an ancient glass of inexact measurements, and therefore this can be a time-consuming and consequently expensive option.

Before the advent of synthetic resins, the only was of achieving a transparent fill in glass, was to cut and insert a piece of glass from a similar object. Although this practice is still carried out in some countries, it is generally considered to be unethical. In the case of decayed archaeological glass and enamel, it is not necessary to match the refractive indices of conservation materials to the glass, whereas in the case of uncoloured, transparent historical glasses, matching the refractive index can result in repair and restoration being less visible. Repairs to ancient glasses are not expected to be invisible. However, those to historical glass, which may, for example, be high art objects representative of the culture in which they were produced, presentation pieces, or simply of aesthetic or sentimental value, need to be as unobtrusive as possible, since the emphasis is on viewing the glass as an art object. In order to restore missing areas of glass, moulds are often taken directly off a corresponding area of the object, sealed in place over the missing area, and a synthetic resin poured into the mould *in situ*. For this to be done, the glass and any surface decoration must be sound and firmly attached to one another.

The case histories used in this chapter to illustrate conservation procedures are intended to be taken as treatments that have been devised to meet specific problems, and which can be adapted and modified.

Part 1: Excavated glass

The first stage of conservation takes place before an excavation begins: in theory there should be no excavation without prior consideration being given to conservation of the finds, although in practice, the budget for post-excavation work is often very limited. Liaison between the excavator, conservator and the curator of the museum or store in which the finds will ultimately be deposited, should determine the amount of time, money, space and administration available to deal with any glass that may be retrieved from excavation. On-site conservation consists of correct lifting, labelling, packaging, storage and transport, processes which are well documented (Dowman, 1970; Sease, 1988; Cronyn, 1992). However some preliminary preservation work, such as de-salting and cleaning, may be carried out if time permits. In the laboratory, more detailed and therefore time-consuming conservation can be undertaken.

During archaeological excavations, glass may be found in the form of whole, broken or completely shattered artefacts, pieces being either more or less in their original positions, or disturbed and scattered over a wide area. The most common glass artefacts encountered are vessels, window panes, manufacturing waste, wall or floor mosaics, or small objects such as bracelets and beads, the latter sometimes attached to textiles and ethnographical materials. Glass may also be found as a minor constituent of objects (*Plate 3*), such as inlay in furniture and jewellery (Bimson, 1975; Cronyn *et al.*, in Bacon and Knight, 1987). The greatest quantity of excavated glass, however, consists of individual fragments from any of these sources. Nevertheless, shapes, profiles and other information such as details of the technology can be retrieved from fragmentary evidence. As archaeology and its associated techniques continue to develop, new questions will be asked of the evidence, and therefore all excavated glass should be retained for future examination (Wihr, 1968, 1977; Eshøj, 1988; Newton and Davison, 1989).

Water content

One of the major uses of glass vessels is for the storage of liquids, which would tend to suggest that glass is impervious to water. However, this is not strictly true, as alkali is leached out of the glass during prolonged contact with water. The mechanisms involved in the deterioration of glass are discussed in Chapter 4. The water content of deteriorated buried glass can vary from *saturation* of material excavated from marine or water-logged land environments, though *damp* in glass from the majority of sites in cool, temperate climates, to *dry* from sites in warmer seasons or climates. In hot seasons or semi-arid climates, the glass may be *partially desiccated* (free from surface water). In arid environments, such as desert tombs or caves, the glass can be *totally desiccated* although, in a physical sense, there will always be some free water. Surviving archaeological glass represents only the best formulated glass of a much larger output.

During its burial, glass will have reacted with its particular environment and may even have achieved a state of equilibrium with it. Assessing and dealing with the water content of excavated glass is crucial to its survival. Upon excavation, glass is suddenly exposed to a new set of environmental conditions, perhaps after hundreds of years; thus it cannot be considered surprising if it immediately reacts to the change in environment. Glass which may seem to be in good condition upon excavation, may form iridescent layers within a few minutes or hours. The change in appearance is not a result of a rapid increase in the rate of deterioration of the glass, but is simply a revelation, as a result of dehydration, of the deterioration that has already taken place. The free water, which is present in newly excavated glass, maintains the transparency and also holds weathered layers together by virtue of surface tension. Hence drying may cause the glass to crumble or flake. Once the free water has evaporated, allowing air to enter the weathering crust, it is extremely difficult (if not impossible) to render the glass translucent again. The free water will also contain dissolved salts, derived either from the environment or from the decaying glass itself. On drying, these salts will crystallize out, disrupting the weathering crust and (if allowed to remain) ultimately destroying it by the oscillation of their volumes as the ambient humidity changes. Consequently, the glass must be photographed immediately on exposure, being kept damp between shots, by covering it over with damp tissue and Polythene sheeting. (If a large amount of glass is involved, it may be advisable to lift the glass and place it immediately into a controlled environment pending photography.) An important aspect of on-site conservation, therefore, is the provision of first-aid treatment, with adequate packaging incorporating basic environmental control, in order to preserve glass in the condition in which it was found. Correct treatment and regular monitoring can delay the further deterioration of glass after excavation for a considerable period of time. Ideally, packaging should be devised to cover the short period between excavation and laboratory conservation. In practice, however, as mentioned above, this period of non-treatment often becomes permanent due to lack of funds, and this fact must be taken into consideration when planning the work.

Removal of glass from the ground

Conservation time (and therefore money) can be saved if the glass can be correctly lifted by the archaeologists. If, however, conservators are on site, they will be required to work as quickly as practicable without unduly disrupting the progress of the excavation. Conservators should check that the area in which they are working has been recorded, especially if the earth has to be removed to any depth in order to recover artefacts. Lifting methods will vary with the state of the glass and the nature of the surrounding soil.

The total extent of glass deterioration may or may not be immediately visible, depending on its state of preservation, and its degree of saturation with water. Glass from damp deposits must therefore initially be kept damp after exposure. After recording and photography, it may be convenient to allow a small, representative sherd to dry out slowly away from direct heat. If no appreciable deterioration occurs, the glass may be allowed to dry out. If deterioration of the sample occurs, the bulk of the glass must be packed in damp acid-free tissue or Plastazote in self-seal Polythene bags (*Figure 7.1*) or polypropylene

Figure 7.1 Wet glass fragments stored in a self-seal Polythene bag.

boxes and stored or sent for laboratory treatment.

Depending upon their structural strength, glass objects or fragments may be simply lifted out of the ground. However, where there are signs of flaking or of gilding or painting, a layer of soil must be allowed to remain attached to the glass to prevent the surface layer becoming detached. Complete vessels must be totally uncovered before removal to prevent damage from occurring as they are lifted. In the case of fragmented glass, the recording of the spatial relationship of the pieces may be essential to aid later reconstruction, or in the case of window glass, interpretation of the iconography. Thus, before these are removed individually, they must be plotted, drawn and photographed.

For economic and other reasons, full conservation of all excavated material may not be possible or desirable. A selection process may have to be adopted, following discussions between the archaeologist, conservator and site director or museum curator, to ensure that all the relevant criteria are considered for gaining the maximum information. The most important is the archaeological significance of the glass, not only in relation to the discipline as a whole, but also to its own particular context. Selected glass may be simply recorded in terms of amount; or cleaned and drawn for study or publication. Other glass may be conserved and repaired. Subsequent full reconstruction (and restoration or mounting) may be restricted to those objects required for display.

Certain categories of glass may best be removed from site immobilized in a block of soil: glass fragments or objects which are so thin or degraded that they are in danger of disintegrating; an extensive spread of fragments in dry or damp deposits; or objects that will not support their own weight (especially if filled with debris). The aim of the lifting technique is (i) to preserve the glass in the condition in which it was excavated; and (ii) to render the glass itself immobile; or (iii) to render the soil around the glass immobile so that it will support the glass during its removal, storage and/or transport to a laboratory. Methods that may prejudice future conservation treatments should not be used, and all methods should follow the conservation ethic of minimal intervention.

Immobilization of the glass alone

It is difficult to immobilize glass by consolidation when it is still in the ground, and it may be premature to do so for several reasons. First, because the glass cannot usually be cleaned thoroughly, dirt inevitably becomes consolidated on the surface. It is not always possible to remove either the dirt or consolidant at a later stage without damage to a flaking glass surface. Secondly, the consolidant is unlikely to penetrate throughout the weathering crust, so that spalling may occur at a later date. Thirdly, damp or wet glass would have to be dried before consolidation (which may cause damage), or a water-miscible consolidation system must be used. In order to overcome the problems posed by working in damp conditions, Bimson and Werner (1971) suggested adapting a technique using Carbowax 6000 (polyethylene glycol) for use in the field. An extremely dilute solution would have to be used in order to ensure good penetration and hygroscopicity of the wax may cause difficulties in moist storage conditions. However the consolidant would be resoluble in water. Wihr (1977) and Ypey (1960–61, 1965) advocated the use of Dermoplast SC Normaal (polyvinyl chloride) in a ketone hydrocarbon solution for consolidating glass *in situ*. However, polyvinyl chloride is unstable and will cause future conservation problems. Emulsions such as those of polyvinyl acetate may be useful in damp conditions, but they may not penetrate fully, and are difficult to remove at a later date. Another approach used in the past was to dehydrate the glass first and then to apply a resin. Wihr (1977) described such a method in which Araldite AYIO3/HY956 (epoxy) was applied to a glass vessel in the ground after the vessel had been dehydrated by filling it with two changes of acetone. Apart from causing damage to the glass by dehydration, potentially dangerous, grinding and abrading techniques had to be used to remove excess resin. Impregnation of glass in this way, still carried out in some countries, has the advantage of restoring translucency in some cases, but the long-term effects are likely to be deleterious. More suitable methods of lifting glass untreated, are described below.

(a)

(b)

(c)

(d)

(e)

Figure 7.2 The removal of archaeological glass from the site by isolating the soil in which it lies, with a plaster of Paris case. (a) Glass within a block of earth, protected by aluminium foil, over which the plaster case is applied. (b) Sides wrapped with gauze bandage dipped in plaster of Paris, and a metal sheet slid beneath to facilitate its removal. (c) Block inverted and the base protected by foil prior to applying plaster of Paris. (d) Completed case secured with plaster bandage and removed from site. (e) Removal of the case at a later date.

Immobilization of a soil block

The simplest and quickest method of providing support is to isolate the glass on a platform of soil, and then to push a thin metal sheet or spade into the soil well below the glass. The soil platform may be strengthened, by covering it with aluminium foil, held in place by and wrapping the block with gauze

bandages dipped in plaster of Paris (*Figure 7.2 a–e*). Such a system should only be considered as a temporary measure in order to remove the glass from its burial place; it is not strong enough to support the glass during transport to a museum. Another temporary support of this nature was used by Garlake (1969) in the dry climate of South Africa:

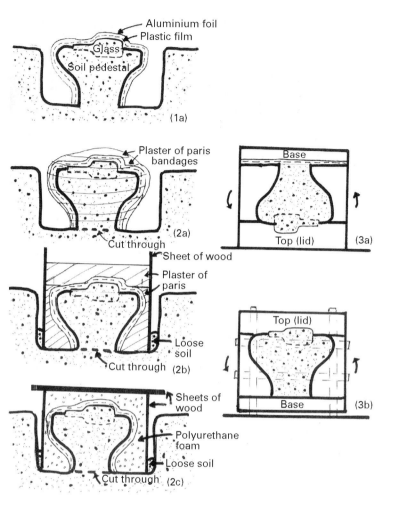

Figure 7.3 Removing archaeological glass from site by isolating the surrounding soil, in a plaster of Paris or foamed polyurethane casing. (1a) Glass on a pedestal of earth and protected by foil or vinyl wrapping. (2a) Assembly strengthened by wrapping it with cotton bandage dipped in liquid plaster of Paris, forming a cocoon. (2b) Surrounded by a collar of corrugated cardboard, and commencement of application of foaming polyurethane. (2c) Flat sheet of wood placed on the foam to produce a flat surface. (3a) Inverted block after inversion and application of more foam to complete the casing. (3b) The casing secured with straps. Alternatively a case could be made of six plaster sides, applying a release agent between the pieces as they were made.

polyvinyl acetate was painted around the edges of the soil platform. Consolidating the *soil* in this way, with a moisture-curing resin such as Quentglaze (polyurethane), has also been suggested (Dowman, 1970), but as such a resin is not re-soluble it must not be allowed to come into contact with the glass itself.

Another method for immobilizing the soil block is to freeze it with dry ice (frozen carbon dioxide). This method has been used in Sweden (Arrhenius, 1973) for lifting archaeological materials on site, and it is conceivable that this technique might occasionally be of use in temperate climates, if there was immediate access to freezer storage.

A more sophisticated method for immobilizing a soil block is the construction of a protective casing with plaster of Paris or polyurethane foam (see *Figure 7.3*). In this method, both the glass and the surrounding soil are rendered immobile by enclosing them in a rigid casing. Great care must be taken to prevent the materials of which the casing is constructed from coming into contact with the glass itself. The block is isolated with damp paper tissue, followed by aluminium foil or thin vinyl plastic film (e.g. Clingfilm; US: Saranwrap).

Plaster of Paris is cheap but also heavy, so that for the construction of large casings it may be preferable to use polyurethane foam, which although expensive, is light, rigid and easily cut with a knife for removal at a later date. The foam is formed when two components are mixed together, setting hard in about 5–10 minutes. The foaming reaction is exothermic.

If there is any risk of the heat affecting the decayed glass, an insulating layer of closely packed sand or earth or of Plastazote could be placed over the isolating film before the foam is applied; or the foam could be applied in several thin layers. It may not cure in cold or damp conditions, and there is a potential health hazard in its use since one of the components is isocyanate-based and can cause severe irritation of mucous membranes and of the skin. Great care must therefore be taken not to allow it to come into contact with the skin or be inhaled when it is being mixed, or when the foam is cut at a later date (Moncrieff, 1971; Escritt and Greenacre, 1972; ICI, 1977; Watkinson and Leigh, 1978). Protective gloves and a face-mask must be worn (and fume or dust extraction utilized if the foam is mixed or cut indoors).

The procedure for making a casing around a small glass object is shown in *Figure 7.3*, and described below. The measurements quoted can be adjusted according to the size of the object to be lifted. The object is isolated on a platform of soil some 25 mm larger than itself. This platform is then undercut as far as possible leaving the object on a pedestal about 50 mm high. Any undercuts in the object are filled with soft soil or tissue. A collar of corrugated cardboard, rigid plastic, wood or metal, is placed around the pedestal, allowing a gap of 20–30 mm between it and the collar and allowing the collar to stand 20 mm proud of the uppermost surface of the object. Soil is heaped around the outside of the collar, blocking any gaps and holding it down. To prevent the foam coming into contact with the glass, the object and pedestal are then covered with a piece of clear vinyl plastic film, thin Polythene sheeting or aluminium foil. A small quantity of foam is applied from an aerosol can, or is mixed according to the manufacturer's instructions, and poured into the collar, ensuring that it runs beneath the pedestal. This process is repeated until the foam nears the top of the collar, when a piece of wood is placed over it and light pressure exerted to produce a flat surface. The surface should be marked with the site-name, year, orientation and details of its position on site, also with the word 'TOP'. The pedestal and collar are then undercut by inserting a thin metal sheet, and the whole case is inverted. The surface

thus exposed is isolated as described above and a layer of foam applied. The complete case is then re-inverted so that it stands on its original base. The case should be wrapped in Polythene sheeting and stored in cool conditions until it is transported to a conservation laboratory.

Glass that can only be removed by using the lifting methods described above may already show considerable signs of deterioration in the ground. If it has been lifted simply in a block of soil, the moisture content of the burial environment should be maintained as far as possible in packaging. Thus, blocks of soil and glass should be placed in well-sealed Polythene bags or boxes, stored in cool surroundings, and treated in a laboratory as soon as possible. If soil blocks are allowed to dry out, the glass will become dehydrated, and the soil block may crumble within the casing, causing the destruction of the glass within. Therefore the casing should only be left in position temporarily, and should be opened and its contents fully excavated and treated as soon as possible.

Occasionally entire glass kilns are removed from site, either in sections (Hurst-Vose, 1980), or as a block lift (Price, 1992).

Glass from waterlogged land sites

Glass found in waterlogged land sites should be kept wet before lifting by covering it with wet paper, saturated plastic sponge and sheets of Polythene. After lifting, the glass must be kept *wet*, but not necessarily *immersed* in water, unless the presence of large quantities of salts is suspected, or long-term storage envisaged. For a short period it can be placed in self-seal or heat-sealed, water-tight Polythene bags together with a few millilitres of distilled water. Since such bags are never totally water-tight, they should be placed in plastic boxes with tightly fitting lids, which can be carefully stacked on top of one another, separated by padding, such as shredded Polythene sheeting or plastic sponge. To prevent the growth of fungus or bacteria, a neutral biocide can be added, no tissue or other organic packing or labelling materials should be included, and the glass should be kept cool or refrigerated. In such waterlogged conditions, hydrolytic breakdown of the glass

Figure 7.4 Storage of a large quantity of objects from a marine site, in a tank of water. The tank is constructed of concrete, and has metal roll-top covers (right), which are operated by ropes tied to their handles.

can continue, especially when the pH within the bags rises. Thus this type of storage should not be needlessly prolonged. However, long-term storage is sometimes inevitable.

The possibility of deep-freezing glass at a temperature of −20°C has been suggested (Arrhenius, 1973; Nylén, 1975). However, further work on freeze-drying excavated glass is essential before such a method can be recommended unreservedly. Another possibility during prolonged periods of storage is to begin the process of consolidation, by replacing the water with an inert solvent, which allows the glass to be de-watered, but which prevents air entering the weathering crust. The wet glass should be immersed in a 50 per cent mixture of ethanol and water and, after approximately an hour, moved into increasingly solvent-rich mixtures until the glass can be stored in a pure solvent. The experiences of rescuing damaged glass objects, following a disastrous flood in the Corning Museum of Glass (New York State), have been documented by Martin (1977).

Removal of glass from marine or freshwater sites

Glass fragments or objects are recovered from rivers, lakes (Singley, 1998) and the sea, most notably from submerged buildings, or shipwrecks, when glass was being carried or traded in the form of complete objects or as cullet, which also acted as ship's ballast (Pearson, 1975, 1987). Depending upon their condition, individual objects or fragments of glass may be lifted from their burial sites, with or without the aid of supports, and kept wet until treated (*Figure 7.4*).

The support and lifting of a fragile glass bottle from the sea is described by Turner (in Piercy, 1978). A case bottle retrieved from a shipwreck off Mombasa was found virtually complete, but the glass itself had begun to exfoliate, was badly cracked and only held together by the compacted clay inside. Since removal of the clay would cause disintegration of the bottle it was decided to trim down the mud to leave a 5 mm lining, by excavating it through a hole in one side of the bottle from which glass had been lost during burial. It was then proposed to reinforce the mud lining with netting and resin. To support the glass while the mud was being removed, the bottle was faced with netting held in place with PVAC (polyvinyl acetate), but because of the fragile condition of the glass the facing could only be applied while the bottle was still supported in water. The level of the water was reduced to expose the upper face alone, which was dried thoroughly by swabbing with IMS and acetone. The surface was consolidated with PVAC and a synthetic net facing applied. The facing was secure enough to withstand soaking in water while the other sides were faced. The mud was then removed to leave a thin layer on the inside of the bottle. At this stage the bottle could be taken out of the water and dried, after which a netting support was applied to the inside layer of mud with 5 per cent Paraloid B-72 (in acetone), an acrylic resin which is not soluble in IMS. The PVAC and net outer facing could be safely removed with this solvent with no risk of weakening the lining. Finally, the surfaces were cleaned and given a final consolidating coat of PVAC. If the conservator had access to a museum laboratory (and time), an attempt may have been made to remove the last vestiges of mud from the case bottle.

In some instances, however, solidified marine concretion, inside glass vessels, which have subsequently become partially or totally destroyed, may represent the original shape and form of the artefacts. It is advisable to determine the state of preservation of the artefacts, and to group the objects accordingly. This will aid in packaging, and in alerting the laboratory conservator to the conditions of the objects before they are unpacked. Ideally, there should be no attempt to clean the glass on site since evidence of manufacture, original design and shape preserved in the weathering crust may be removed. If glass from a marine site is allowed to dry immediately upon recovery, salts will crystallize in the weathering crust and disrupt it (Pearson, 1975), and concretions will harden to a cement-like state (see *Figure 4.27*). Salts must therefore be removed as quickly as is practicable (Macleod and Davies, 1987).

Desalination

Desalination is accomplished by slowly reducing the salt content of the water in which the glass was found, followed by immersion in changes of fresh water. The salt level of the water used for desalination should be known. The glass should not be placed directly into fresh (tap or distilled) water in case an osmotic pressure develops between the salt-laden glass and the wash water, causing the water to force entry into the decayed weathering crust and disrupt it. Desalination in water can be carried out by one of three methods (*Figure 7.5*):

(i) A static immersion process in which the objects are placed in a sealed container of water, which is then changed at regular intervals. For the first day the water should be changed twice, e.g. morning and evening, then once a day at the same time of day. In cases where the amount of objects being desalinated is too large or fragile to be moved, samples of the wash water can be syphoned off for testing. The process is very slow, as pockets of salts (registering a relatively high conductivity) will accumulate in the solution, reducing the efficiency of salt removal, by reducing the osmotic pressure difference between the salt in the object(s) and that in the solution. It is, however, probably the best method for use on extremely fragile glass, although the lack of water movement has to be balanced against the amount of time the glass needs to remain immersed.

(ii) Gentle agitation of the wash solution will prevent pockets of high salt concentration from occurring, thus an optimum osmotic pressure differential is maintained thereby increasing the efficiency of the desalting process. Stirrers or pumps can be used to agitate the water gently. Olive and Pearson (1975) suggest the conversion of old washing machines with a cyclic one hour on and one hour off washing process, by which the desalting process was increased by a factor of four times that of the static immersion process.

(iii) A flow through immersion process is more efficient but requires a constant supply first of tap- and then of distilled water. The pressure or movement of the water should not be allowed to disrupt the weathering crust from the glass surface and, if possible, the object should not be lifted in and out of the bath, as spontaneous drying will affect the deteriorated glass.

Where there is a high salt content, the initial desalination may be carried out using tap water provided it, itself, does not have a high salt content (or even diluted sea water for objects recovered from marine excavations). The tap water may be allowed to run through a bath containing the objects, or changed several times a day. When conductivity

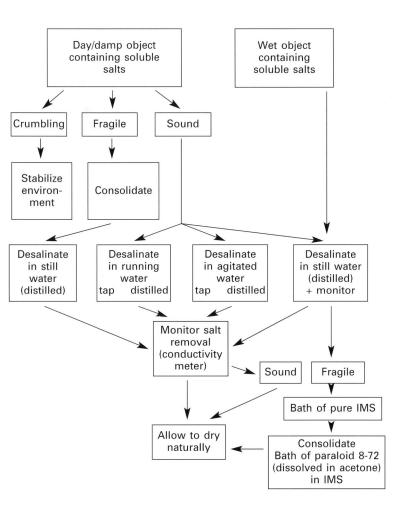

Figure 7.5 Options for desalinating porous objects.

readings on the wash water indicate that the salt level of tap water has been reached, distilled or de-ionized water is used to complete the washing. When tap water is used, the tap is turned off at night and the wash water left to stand overnight before a sample is drawn off and tested.

Monitoring the salt content of the wash water

The treatment progress can be monitored by using a conductivity meter to measure the electrical conductivity of the wash water. The readings are a measure of the amount of dissolved salts in the water, *not* of which salts are present. (A specific chloride conductivity bridge is manufactured, but it is important to remember that chlorides are not the only destructive soluble salt. The specific test for

the presence of chloride ions, with silver nitrate, is given below.) The meter measures the *concentration* of salts in the wash water by measuring the current passing through, the two being in proportion to each other. The conductivity cell is dipped into the wash water, and stirred gently to ensure that it is not in a salt-free or salt-laden pocket, and the reading taken (*Figure 7.6*). After each reading the wash water is changed. The volume of the wash water in every bath should be the same.

Conductivity readings on the wash water are taken at regular intervals, e.g. morning, afternoon and evening. The regularity of the testing will to some extent depend upon the quantity of material under treatment, and upon the conservator's general workload. Provided that the glass will withstand continuous washing, treatment should continue until

Figure 7.6 Use of a conductivity meter to monitor the desalination process.

conductivity readings taken at regular intervals remain constant over a period of a few days. It is not necessary to remove every trace of soluble salts from objects (and they will be reintroduced to some extent through handling).

Once the desalination is complete, the glass should not be allowed to dry out since the apparent state of preservation in the wet state is no real indication of what the object may look like once it has dehydrated. The glass should be kept wet temporarily (bearing in mind that prolonged contact with water promotes its deterioration). Following desalination, wet glass may need to be consolidated (see section on consolidation, later in the chapter).

Chemical tests for identifying soluble and insoluble salts

Soluble salts
The wash water used for desalinating objects containing soluble salts can be electronically monitored to detect the presence of the salts: chlorides and nitrates (see above). Alternatively, it may be possible to remove a sample of salt crystals from an object prior to desalination, dissolve the sample in distilled water, and test the water.

Chlorides
1   The sample is dissolved in distilled water.
2   Ten millilitres of the solution is placed in a clean test-tube which has been rinsed with distilled water.

3   Three drops of dilute nitric acid are added to remove any carbonate ions, which would confuse the test result.
4   Three drops of molar silver nitrate solution are added. The formation of a cloudy white precipitate indicates that chlorides are present. This is an extremely sensitive test which will detect a few parts per million of chloride.

Nitrates
1   The sample is dissolved in distilled water.
2   A few drops of sulphuric acid are added to acidify the solution.
3   Ten millilitres of the solution is placed in a clean test tube, which has been rinsed with distilled water.
4   A few crystals of fresh ferrous sulphate are added and dissolved.
5   The test tube is tilted, and a few millilitres of concentrated sulphuric acid are trickled down the side of the test tube into the solution. The formation of a brown ring of ferrous nitrate indicates that nitrates are present.

Insoluble salts
Deposits of insoluble salts are usually carbonates, sulphates, or silicates, either combined or on their own. When a small drop of dilute acid is placed on a sample of the deposit, a strong effervescence will suggest that it is composed of carbonates, whilst a less vigorous reaction would indicate the presence of sulphates. Silicates do not react with most acids, and if necessary would have to be removed from an object mechanically.

Sulphates
1   A sample is placed in 10 ml of distilled water in a clean test tube, which has been rinsed with distilled water.
2   A few drops of hydrochloric acid are added to remove any carbonate ions.
3   A few drops of barium chloride solution are added. The formation of a white precipitate indicates that sulphates are present.

If samples of the objects are to be taken for biological or analytical study, either in the field or at some later date, the glass should be stored in 70 per cent ethanol. This will prevent further biological attack from solutions not experienced by the object during burial, and will preserve the micro-organisms present on the glass. If possible, soil and water samples from the region of retrieval should be taken for study purposes. The glass, stored in ethanol or fresh water and fungicide, should be packed in heat-sealed Polythene bags and the fragments separated from each other by wads of polyester foam or bubble packing. The objects should be coded so that the more fragile glass is placed near the top of the container and thus more easily retrieved for conservation.

Investigation of glass deterioration resulting from storage systems for waterlogged archaeological glass, have been undertaken by Earl (1999). These included the commonly recommended immersion and high humidity environments; low temperature and ethanol/water mixtures; and novel approaches, based on research for the glass industry, with the potential for improved stabilization, notably solutions containing phosphate, aluminium, calcium and silicate ions and pH buffers. At intervals throughout the study, Fourier transform infrared microscopy was used to examine the glass surfaces. The position and relative intensity of the bands, due to the stretching mode of Si–O–Si (bridging oxygen and Si–X (non-bridging oxygen), change according to the nature and extent of deterioration. Some of the storage environments were also evaluated using scanning electron microscope and energy dispersive X-ray analysis to examine the glass surfaces. The development of surface effects such as crystal growth and highly localized depletion of alkali and alkaline earth metal ions was noted. As a result of the findings, the relative efficacy of the environments was assessed. It was concluded that the high humidity systems and those containing ions that affect the surface chemistry of the glass should be avoided in the conservation of archaeological glass, and that ethanol/water mixtures at low temperatures are worthy of further investigation. The best of these was storage at temperatures below 0°C in a 50/50 vol/vol ethanol water mixture.

Glass opus sectile panels from Kenchreai, Greece

During excavations between 1965 and 1968 of the submerged site of Kenchreai, one of the two ancient ports of Corinth in Greece (Ibrahim *et al.*, 1976), a cache of over one hundred *opus sectile* glass panels was recovered from the sea (Koob, Brill and Thimme, 1996) (*Figures 7.7a–c*). The panels had been in temporary storage still in their shipping crates, leaning against the walls at an angle fairly close to the vertical with one long side resting on the floor. There were four to ten crates in each of nine stacks (*Figure 7.7a*). As a result of an earthquake, which destroyed the port in antiquity, the entire building was submerged, and tilted, so that the floors sloped downward towards the south. It must be assumed that the panels themselves were disturbed by the shock. Most important, they were waterlogged, so that the plaster slab on which the glass was affixed lost its cohesion and the panels were no longer solid or rigid; they could not be moved without crumbling to pieces. Presumably other damage was caused by the fact that the edges of the crate resting on the floor would have been dislodged as they slid away from the walls, allowing the panels to sag and warp.

The building and its contents were subsequently abandoned, filled in with debris and built over. During one thousand six hundred years of submerged burial, continuous reaction of the glass with chemicals in the sea water and with decaying animal and vegetable life, resulted in extensive decomposition of much of the glass. The parts of most crates highest above the floor were eroded by wave action or by subsequent despoiling of the walls to obtain building material.

Clearance of the site began in 1965, and excavation began in 1968, when large storage/desalination tanks were constructed on the shore. During excavation, work had to be carried out in shallow water, in order to prevent the building from drying out, although pumps constantly lowered the water level temporarily. Various lifting techniques were used to remove the stacks of *opus sectile*; in 1968, two entire stacks were block-lifted and transferred to the freshwater storage tanks on shore. The water was replaced daily over a period of one month, and readings of the salinity of the water taken at the end of each day. The results (unpublished) seemed to show that by the end of the period of immersion, the salts had been removed. The panels

(a)

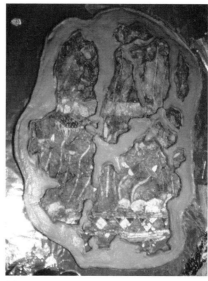

(c)

(b)

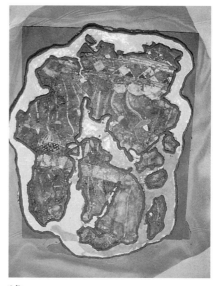

(d)

Figure 7.7 (a) Stacks containing panels of *opus sectile* with preserved end-pieces of the crates *in situ*, after preliminary cleaning. Kenchreai, Greece. (b) Cleaned and consolidated fragment of *opus sectile* (panel number 2 layer B), fixed to a sheet of fibre-glass screening. (c) Part of a panel with potters' clay isolating the glass fragments and filling the voids. (d) The voids filled (over the clay) with Vel-Mix. (e) Restored section of a panel, similar to that shown in (a–d), on display in Nauplion, Greece. (Courtesy of T.K. Lord).

(e)

in these stacks were the only panels to be fully desalinated. The crates were then taken to Nauplion (Greece) with the intention of dissecting and conserving them, as time permitted. The panels had been packed face-to-face, two to a crate, and had through the processes of deterioration become fused to one another. Keeping part of the stack in its accustomed state of saturation with water, whilst spending an indefinite amount of time conserving the exposed panel, was impracticable, because the moisture from the wet part of the stack would move continuously toward the dry part. Therefore, the glass panels could not, excepting in two or three instances, be fully dissected, cleaned and consolidated. Although there has been extensive loss, what has survived is of such a nature that it has preserved a disproportionately large amount of evidence.

Although very few records were kept, it seems certain that the majority of panels received only minimal treatment. A thick coating of polyvinyl acetate (PVA) resin 'dissolved in a mixture of different solvents' (Ibrahim *et al.*, 1976) was applied to the back of some of the panels. The majority of the panels were backed with bandage/cotton gauze impregnated with PVA, and they were then wrapped in yellow flannel cloth for protection and supported on sheets of Masonite.

In 1971, seven fragments of the *opus sectile* panels were sent to the Corning Museum of Glass (USA) to undergo conservation research and restoration. It was hoped to be able to devise a method of conservation which would stabilize the fragments, and which could be used at a later date on the remaining panels in Greece. The treated panels were eventually returned mounted for display in the Isthmia Museum in 1976.

Upon arrival at Corning, the panel fragments were examined visually and by radiography, before being stored in their original packing until conservation experiments could begin. Unfortunately, Corning Museum itself was inundated by a flood during 1972, and it was nearly three weeks before the panels were retrieved. The glass was covered with mud, a layer of mould-growth developed on the flannel, and the Masonite supports had warped. The flood waters had softened the original background material of the panels, and the consolidant, so that the gauze and the flannel cloth adhered to and in some areas had become partially embedded in the panel surfaces. The panels were cleaned superficially and set aside, worked on when time permitted.

Conservation experiments began in 1974. A new set of X-radiographs was made in order to achieve a better understanding of exactly which areas of each panel were of glass, and which were of matrix material. With a few exceptions the glasses were heavily weathered and had little resemblance to their original colours. The shapes which stood out most clearly in the radiographs were the areas of red, yellow and green glass, owing to the lead, tin and copper in their compositions (known from chemical analysis of similar glass in other panels). The materials used in making the panels were the glasses themselves, the plaster (an adhesive mix of resin and crushed marble), the pottery backing tiles which provided support and the wooden slats of the crates in which the panels had been shipped in antiquity.

Preliminary experiments were carried out on the fragments, as a result of which a treatment for the cleaning, consolidation and mounting of the panels was devised and applied to one of the smaller panels. The treatment consisted of removing the gauze backing from the surfaces of the panel with ethanol, and then covering the surfaces with polyester gauze. The fragment and its polyester support was then placed on a wooden stretcher and further cleaned by soaking it in ethanol baths, which removed any foreign matter and any resinous deposits on the surface of the glass. After these baths, cotton wool swabs moistened with ethanol were used to remove the final traces of dirt. The fragment was then placed on a fibre-glass support and immersed in dilute baths of ethanol and 15 per cent AYAF, polyvinyl acetate, in order to consolidate it. On removal from the final bath, excess consolidant was removed with ethanol, and a second frame was placed over the panel to complete the consolidating and mounting procedures. From this and a number of other experiments, it was clear that care would have to be taken not to saturate the panels with water, alcohol, acetone or any other solvent, since after prolonged contact the fragments became weak and sticky.

The specific aims of the conservation procedures were defined as follows. To clean and consolidate the panels as thoroughly as possible, and to provide sufficient rigidity to allow them to be exhibited; to protect the glass from further deterioration; and where possible, to clean individual glass pieces so as to expose the original colour and shape of the undeteriorated glass.

Initially it was necessary to decide if an attempt should be made to separate each pair of panels (they had been crated two panels to a crate, placed face to face). Over the centuries, the complex of materials supporting the panels had coalesced so that each pair had in effect become one. Thus when they had been excavated only the reverse side of each panel was visible. It soon became evident that it would be virtually impossible to separate the pairs of panels since such an operation would completely destroy the integrity of both faces. Thus it was decided to expose and treat one (reverse) face only, and as far as possible, to leave the (reverse) face of the second panel visible for examination.

Previous attempts at removing weathering crusts from the glasses had consisted of mechanically scraping the surfaces with small tools. However, this was not only tedious and time-consuming, but damaged the glass. It was therefore decided to clean the glass fragments with the aid of an Airbrasive unit, using microscopic glass beads and crushed glass as the abrasives.

Once the panels had been superficially cleaned, they were fumigated in order to kill micro-organisms which might have been present as a consequence of the flooding and wet storage. This was carried out by placing the panels in a sealed fumigation chamber containing two dishes of water to cultivate the micro-organisms under a vacuum of 28 psi. Oxyfume 12, a fumigant–sterilant gas, was then introduced for a period of 15 hours. Following this treatment, the panels were removed from the chamber, the Masonite supports removed, and the panels placed on sheets of cardboard. They were then ready to undergo the cleaning techniques which had been formulated.

First, the flannel wrapping was lightly moistened with water and cut away from the top surface of the panel. Alcohol and acetone were applied on cotton wool swabs to loosen the layers of gauze, which had become fixed to the upper side of the glass fragments. The gauze was then cut away with scissors and scalpels. The sticky resinous substance, which coated many surface areas, was removed with acetone. The panel was turned over and the cleaning procedures repeated. A sheet of fibreglass screen was laid on the glass and adhered with a 12 per cent solution of AYAF, polyvinyl acetate, in alcohol; the solution also acted as a consolidant to some extent (*Figure 7.7b*).

The panel was left overnight so that the alcohol could evaporate. The panel was then turned over in order that the other side could be cleaned mechanically and with acetone to remove gauze and other foreign matter from the surface. The surface was then carefully cleaned in the Airbrasive unit using crushed glass as the abrasive, using a pressure of approximately 60 psi with a powder flow of 2.5–3.0. For stubborn areas the pressure was increased to 80 psi with a powder flow of 3.0–4.0. Residual powder was blown off the glass by attaching a quick release 3 mm high pressure air nozzle to the air compressor, followed by further cleaning with alcohol on swabs where necessary.

In general, the Airbrasive unit proved to be an excellent method for cleaning the *opus sectile* fragments. The principal disadvantage was the possibility of working right through the glass if the abrasive was concentrated on one spot for too long. However, within a few seconds of beginning the cleaning of a corner or edge, it became apparent as to whether or not there was any glass remaining beneath the deteriorated layer. If there was no glass present the treatment was stopped immediately. Another problem was the tendency of the abrasive powder to adhere to the background material, from which it was difficult to remove. Some of the powder was removed with compressed air after which the remainder was removed with cotton wool swabs moistened with alcohol, taking care that a minimum amount of solvent came into contact with the glass. When the cleaning had been completed, a more thorough consolidation process was carried out, after which the panels were mounted for exhibition.

A wall of potters' clay was laid around the edge of each fragment a few centimetres from it, and also around the edges of any voids in the interior. The wall was of the same height as the fragments, so that the material used to gap-fill missing areas would not have to be filed down with the risk of damage to original material. The panel, still on its layer of fibre-glass screen, was then placed on a sheet of aluminium foil. Kerr Vel-Mix stone coloured with Liquitex acrylic pigments and textured with sand was used to fill the missing areas and to form a surrounding support. Vel-Mix is similar to dental plaster but is harder and much more durable. The mixing proportions are 22–25 ml water to 100 g of powder (approximately 1 part water to 4 parts powder by volume). The powder was added to the water and mixed for about 1 minute. It was then poured into the areas to be filled where it settled out forming a smooth surface, and set in approximately 10 minutes. On setting, the texture was improved by working the Vel-Mix with wooden tools (*Figure 7.7c*).

Where necessary, the filler was reduced with sanding discs attached to a flexible drill. The fibre-glass screening which extended beyond the newly formed border, was then trimmed. The panel was turned over and a layer of filling material poured around the edges and into the voids to raise the level to that of the fragments. The majority of this side was left exposed so that future study of the glass is still possible. The Vel-Mix was then coloured with Liquitex pigments, and a thin layer of Liquitex Matte Varnish applied to the restored areas in order to reduce the glossy appearance of the paint.

To protect the edges of the panel, which were vulnerable to chipping, it was edged with lead came secured with a layer of Dow Corning Clear Seal (mastic). Where necessary the lead cames were cut and soldered to fit the panel, soldered areas being smoothed with steel wool. To restore a glassy appearance to the surfaces of the cleaned glass, each piece was coated with Paraloid B-72 in acetone; Paraloid B-72 was not, however, applied to the opaque surface crusts.

Upon their return to Greece in 1976, the *opus sectile* panels from Kenchreai were in a stable condition. The panels had been cleaned as thoroughly as possible, so that either the original colours were visible, or a clear understanding of the form and design of the fragments were apparent. Any extraneous foreign material had been removed, either mechanically or chemically, and the panels had been treated so that any further deterioration would be retarded (Corning, 1976). Mounting the panels on screens of fibre-glass enabled them to be framed for display (*Figure 7.7e*), or more readily handled for study purposes (Rothaus, Brill and Moraitou *et al.*, in Kordas, 2002).

Cleaning and repair on site

Ideally, first-aid treatment should begin immediately glass is exposed, not after it has been lying in a 'finds tray' for several hours or days. Cleaning of glass finds on site should normally be kept to the minimum required to define them, since they should be thoroughly examined both before and during cleaning and this is difficult and too time-consuming to achieve during an excavation. Exceptions to this rule may be the cleaning of large quantities of glass waste (cullet) from glass-making sites or shipwrecks; and cleaning of important glass finds prior to marking. Where cleaning has to be carried out on site, laboratory methods should be used, adapting them to suit local conditions. Deposits are usually much easier to clean off the glass when they are damp as they will be softer; if allowed to dry out, the soil or other deposit may contract and damage the delicate glass surface.

For example, large quantities of a variety of ancient glass have been recovered by the Institute of Nautical Archaeology in Turkey, from a Late Bronze Age shipwreck (*c.*1350 BC) lying in 44–51 metres of water off the cape of Ulu Burun near Kaş in Turkey; and of medieval glass from a wreck lying in 36 metres of water, within the rocky confines of Serçe Liman, a natural harbour on the southern Turkish coast opposite the Greek island of Rhodes (Bass, 1978, 1979, 1980, 1984). The glass from the shipwrecks was mechanically cleaned by hand, using small brushes and scalpels (*Figure 7.8*). Occasionally the careful use of a hammer and small chisel was necessary to separate large masses of glass from the surrounding concretion (*Figure 7.9*). During

Figure 7.8 Retrieving glass beads from an amphora found on the Bronze Age shipwreck at Ulu Burun, Turkey. (Courtesy of Institute of Nautical Archaeology, Texas).

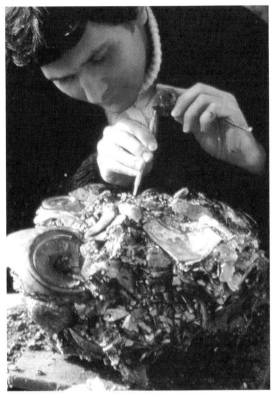

Figure 7.9 Glass objects found in the shipwreck at Serçe Liman, Turkey, being removed from a mass of concretion by the careful use of a small hammer and chisel. (Courtesy of the Institute of Nautical Archaeology, Texas).

this process the glass was kept wet and desalted from sea to tap water. The glass was found to be in good condition, and after desalting could be dried naturally and repaired (Pannell, 1990).

In considering the repair and/or reconstruction of broken glass artefacts, i.e. the physical joining together of fragments, there are three important factors to consider. The condition of the glass itself, the type of adhesive to be used, and the method of supporting the vessel whilst the adhesive sets. On-site repair of glass may have to be undertaken if this is the only treatment it will have, and/or the glass is required for the purposes of study, drawing for publication, display, or to maintain the continuity of several sherds, which join together. A point to remember is that the glass will take up more storage space as partially or fully repaired objects, than it will as fragments, and may be more likely to become further damaged, than a properly stored group of sherds.

In attempting to join decayed glass, penetration of the deteriorated layer along the edges to be joined, and strong bonding with the remaining glass core by the adhesive, are essential, otherwise the weathered layer will simply pull away from the glass at a later date. Thus the chosen resin must act both as an adhesive and as a consolidant. Filling gaps in iridescent or consolidated glass is extremely difficult and should be attempted only where this is absolutely necessary for the safety of the object. In choosing treatments for individual conservation problems, the conservator must be aware of the condition of the glass, and understand the effects of the processes and materials used.

Marking glass

Marking glass on site is difficult, and time-consuming, if glass is present in large quantities. Dry glass which is neither crumbling nor flaking, but which has a porous surface, can be marked by first creating a writing surface on a small area of the artefact. This is achieved by applying a coat of lacquer or consolidant to the area to receive the marking. When dry, the data is applied using black waterproof, fibre-tipped pen, or ink applied using a fine-pointed wooden stick as an applicator in order not to scratch the glass (*Figure 7.10*). A

Figure 7.11 Stem of an excavated wine glass packed in polyethylene foam and a strong cardboard box. (Courtesy of O. Theofanopolou).

Figure 7.10 Marking glass with its site identification.

second layer of lacquer is applied over the ink. It is probable that most excavated glass will be unsuitable for direct marking without such surface treatment. (Glass with a sound surface, particularly historical vessels etc. which have not been buried, may be marked as described above, but without the application of a lacquer to the surface.) If the glass is damp or wet, the data should be recorded on a waterproof label (using a waterproof pen) placed in the Polythene bag containing the glass, and repeated on the exterior of the bag.

Storage of dry and treated glass

Consideration must be given to the question of long-term storage of glass fragments or objects, which should be such that even untreated glass will be protected from further damage. A small proportion of glass from each

site should, where possible, be conserved simply by correct packing and storage, without any intervention in terms of cleaning or introduction of synthetic resins, in order to provide a source for future analysis of uncontaminated material, should this be required.

Glass from dry deposits should be maintained in dry conditions. The fragments should be placed in self-seal Polythene bags and laid horizontally in strong cardboard boxes padded with Plastazote inert polyester foam or pads of acid-free tissue paper. Cotton wool (US: surgical cotton or cotton batting) must be avoided in direct contact with the glass as its threads can be difficult to remove from delicate artefacts. Entire vessels should be well padded with acid-free tissue and polyethylene foam and placed in strong boxes with well fitting lids (*Figure 7.11*). To prevent further dehydration, excavated glass should never be stored in less than 42 per cent relative humidity (RH), even if the glass appears to be well preserved.

It is conceivable that glass may be recovered from conditions of low humidity, which have caused it to become permeated with a network of fine cracks (see Chapter 4), though none has been reported at the time of excavation. Such cracks may also result from stresses set up by the weight of soil. In some cases it may well be that all that holds the glass together is a small amount of chemically combined water or surrounding soil, so that the glass may disintegrate on lifting.

Treated excavated glass, although robust, should never be stored in either excessively dry or wet conditions because further dehydration or hydrolysis can occur through a layer of consolidant. The glass should be kept cool because consolidants and adhesives may begin to creep as the temperature rises, or become tacky and pick up dirt, or adhere to packing materials. To avoid this last problem, consolidated glass could be covered with acid-free tissue or silicone paper.

Sherds should be stored horizontally in perforated Polythene bags. Vessels must be stored in dust-free cases or boxes with adequate padding of inert foam or acid-free tissue paper (never newspaper or cotton wool). Where glass is patinated or iridescent, handling must be kept to a minimum to prevent further damage to the surface. The humidity should be regularly monitored by the installation of a thermometer and a hygrometer. It is normally sufficient to note the readings of these instruments at regular intervals, perhaps twice a day. However a continuous record can be provided by installing a thermo-hygrograph, which records both temperature and relative humidity on a paper chart. Such instruments require re-calibrating every month. The environment for storage and display of artefacts is discussed in detail by Thomson (1998).

Problems of storage may arise when glass is found in association with some other materials, such as metals, (e.g. enamels) or ethnographic material (Lougheed and Shaw, 1986). Recommendations for packaging and storage can be found in Watkinson and Neal (1998), Sease (1988) and Cronyn (1990).

Laboratory treatments

The conservation treatments carried out in a laboratory may include any or all of the following processes: excavation, examination and report writing (including photography), cleaning, consolidation, repair, and possibly also restoration with synthetic resins or glass replacements (Fisher and Norman, 1987; Newton and Davison, 1989; Hogan, 1993; Koob, 2000).

Examination

Visual examination is one of the fundamental principles of archaeological conservation.

Before and during cleaning, the conservator should look for clues as to the technology, decoration, use, type of burial deposit and associated material, as well as the actual shape and state of deterioration of the artefact. Records must be kept at the time of any features noted. A good light source and the aid of a ×4 magnifying lens or a binocular reflecting-light microscope are essential (see Chapter 6).

Cleaning

As previously mentioned, cleaning of excavated glass involves the removal of obscuring soluble and insoluble deposits to reveal the shape, decoration and original surface of the glass. It may be virtually impossible to remove disfiguring deposits from fragile glass even if the glass is consolidated prior to or during the cleaning process (see *Figure 4.7*). Routine cleaning of glass in collections may also be necessary, or the removal of old restoration materials prior to treatment. The parameters governing these cleaning methods are relatively clear compared with those concerning the removal or non-removal of a decayed weathering crust.

When glass deteriorates in the ground, it does not increase in volume and thus the original surface and dimensions of the glass will be represented by the deteriorated surface. It follows therefore that if the whole crust is removed, or if part of a thick crust is removed in order to create a smooth patina, the dimensions of the artefact are irretrievably altered. Even though it may not be immediately apparent, the deterioration may have proceeded right through the glass and removal of the crust in such a case could lead to complete destruction of the object (see *Figure 4.23*). In the case of cuprous red glass, which has become superficially green, there may be an argument for removing some or all of the surface, in order to reveal the original colour. Such treatment was carried out on escutcheons on Anglo-Saxon hanging bowls from Sutton Hoo in Suffolk (UK) (Bruce-Mitford, 1975). In the case of a hanging bowl from Lincoln where a similar problem of discoloration was encountered, the original surface was retained (Foley and Hunter, in Bacon and Knight, 1987). It is possible that a green crust need not be removed completely in order to reveal its true colour, since the last traces could be rendered transparent by consolidation with a resin, a test first being made with toluene to ascertain if enough crust has been removed. However, removal of any or all of the crust will destroy the flush finish of the glass in its setting, and this discrepancy in level *may* have to be made up with a suitable resin to maintain the coherency of the design. Thus removal of weathering crusts on enamels is not to be recommended in general. Hughes (in Bacon and Knight, 1987) has shown that important archaeometric data can be retrieved from the weathering crusts of enamels.

Nevertheless, since the weathering crusts on glass are often iridescent, opaque or black, and hence the original colour and transparency cannot be seen, removal of crusts has often been advocated on aesthetic grounds. Although this cannot necessarily be condoned, it may be that the removal of light opaque powdery deposits, which do not form a substantial surface of the original glass, may be justified. Should removal of deterioration crusts become necessary it is probably best carried out mechanically, as this treatment can be confined to small areas, by using scalpels, wooden picks and soft paint brushes.

Removal of soluble or removable deposits

The removal of soluble salts from glass from wet land sites or marine excavations was described earlier as a treatment that could be undertaken during a period of temporary storage. However, if salt removal has not already been achieved in the field, it must be carried out in the laboratory as soon as possible.

If glass has been lifted from an excavation inside a protective casing, its micro-excavation is carried out in the laboratory. If the glass is particularly badly deteriorated, then only small areas at a time are exposed. These are cleaned and consolidated before the next is uncovered. Where it has been necessary to consolidate glass prior to cleaning, the overlying deposits may be softened by placing the artefact in a vapour of the solvent in which the consolidant was dissolved, for a short period of time. The deposits can then be removed mechanically with a soft sable brush, a scalpel and solvent on cotton wool swabs.

Glass bearing unfired pigments, or flaking paint or gilding must be treated with the greatest of care, and must not be washed. It may be desirable to consolidate the decoration, and to re-affix flaking paint or gilding, with a consolidant, bearing in mind that such treatment would be irreversible.

By careful cleaning of a small area it should be ascertained whether or not decayed glass is actually being held together by dirt or calcium concretions. These may fall off unaided, but may be encouraged to do so by using small wooden toothpicks and soft brushes. Barely damp cotton wool swabs of distilled water, propan-2-ol, or industrial methylated spirits (IMS) can be used to remove the last of the dirt but care must then be taken not to use excess amounts of IMS or blanching of the glass may occur (Dowman, 1970). Lal (1962–63) suggests binding flaking glass with cotton thread before it is cleaned in order to keep any loose fragments in place. However, this is likely to cause physical damage to the glass. In general, dirt should be left on the glass rather than risk the removal of a flaking surface (see *Figure 4.7*). Sound archaeological glass may be washed in water, preferably distilled or de-ionized. Artefacts from muddy deposits, especially urban excavation, are often covered in a film of grease, which should be removed from the glass using water or other solvents before it is dried, consolidated or repaired. In rare cases, a 25 per cent aqueous solution of hydrogen peroxide may be used to loosen stains and dirt held in cracks on this type of glass. Metal deposits may be removed by mechanical methods, or by the controlled use of chemicals. However they may be so bound up in the decayed glass surface, that they are best left untreated. The Roman glass flask shown in *Figure 7.12* was cleaned using a wooden pick. It had been covered with a deposit of iron (see *Figure 4.9*), and the ease with which the deposit fell away, exposing an undeteriorated glass surface, raises a question of its authenticity.

It is sometimes possible to remove mud trapped inside hollow parts of an undecorated broken vessel, by flushing it out with jets of water from a pipette. Alternatively if the glass surface appears to be sound, the object may be immersed in water in an ultrasonic tank for a few seconds at a time, in order to flush out

Figure 7.12 The Roman glass flask shown in Figure 4.9, after removal of iron deposits.

the cavities. Ultrasonic transducers generate high-frequency (non-audible) sound waves, typically 20–50 kHz, which interact in a liquid to produce minute bubbles. These bubbles expand and contract violently and it is the shock waves produced by this action which speed up the loosening of dirt. This effect, combined with the vibration induced by the ultrasonic waves in friable materials, can cause rapid disintegration of the structure of the material. For this reason it is most useful for removing mud and porous encrustation, but can also cause severe damage to friable substrates. It is essential that the progress of cleaning should be constantly monitored.

Ultrasonic cleaning has been successfully and safely used on medieval window glass in good condition (Gibson and Newton, 1974), but damage has been shown to be severe on medieval painted window glass, and there is always the potential danger of promoting cracks. In particular it should be noted that the aqueous cleaning solutions recommended by suppliers of ultrasonic equipment are frequently harmful to glass. Only mild cleaning agents should be used, especially when such a powerful cleaning method is employed. Occasionally encrustations have been removed from glass objects using the Airbrasive technique.

Dilute concentrations of acids have been used in attempts to remove carbonate, and

even iron and manganese, from within the weathering crusts, in order to produce brightened silica surfaces. However, the resulting effervescence tended to disrupt the fragile weathering crusts, and the blackening seemed little improved.

The only method attested for the removal of lead sulphide (PbS) was carried out at the Conservation Analytical Laboratory of the Smithsonian Institution (Smithsonian Institution, 1969). A blackened, nineteenth-century goblet was lightened by immersion in dilute hydrochloric acid for one minute; this was said to convert the PbS to yellow sulphur, much of which could be removed with a soft brush. Any sulphur caught within the weathered layer was dissolved by immersion in carbon disulphide (CS_2) for 24 hours, leaving the glass colourless but hazy because the weathering had been made visible (note that CS_2 is very toxic, with a TLV of 20 ppm).

Dilute mineral acids have been used to remove weathering crusts entirely; however, even dilute acids may affect the remaining glass and will penetrate deep into the glass through cracks and flaws endangering the whole object.

Lībiete (1998) reported two methods of cleaning glass beads dating from between the third and seventeenth centuries, which had been excavated from the Daugmale Castle mound in Latvia. The first method involved soaking the beads in a warm solution (40–50°C) of acetic acid, and then rinsing them in distilled water. In the second, the beads were boiled for 5 minutes in alternate solutions of acetic and alkaline solutions (3 per cent acetic acid and 3 per cent potassium hydroxide, after which they were boiled in changes of distilled water to remove residual chemicals. The beads were dried by immersing them in ethyl alcohol for approximately one hour, removed and left to dry in air. Bead fragments were repaired with acrylic adhesive. The beads were coated with a 7 per cent solution of polyvinyl butyral (C_2H_5OH) to prevent further decay.

Subsequent examination confirmed the effectiveness of the methods, and that the deterioration process was halted without changing the glass structure. However, this may only be short term, and such drastic intervention is not to be recommended. It is possible that sequestering

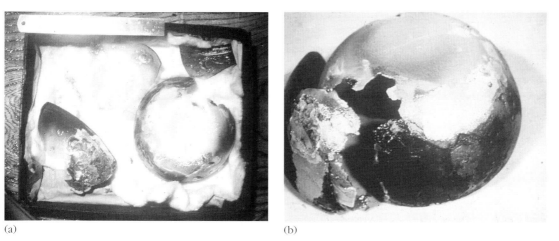

(a)   (b)

Figure 7.13   (a) A fragile and flaking glass bowl, (b) repaired piece by piece, with cellulose nitrate adhesive.

agents in the form of pastes could be used either to remove weathering crusts or selective ions within them. For example Catechol, 1,2-dihydroxtbenzene, $C_6H_4(OH)_2$, sequesters silica, and tetrasodium ethylenediaminetetra-acetic acid (EDTA), $(HOOC.CH_2)2N.CH_2$, sequesters calcium and magnesium, but these have both been shown to attack glass at high pH values, even though the damage may not be visible at first. It should be remembered that sequestering agents will also affect enamelling and gilding, and hence if employed, they must be used with the greatest of caution.

Repair

Repairs to archaeological glass may follow the same general procedures as those described for decorative and utilitarian glass (see below). However, it is unlikely that epoxy resin can be used to repair the majority of fragile archaeological glasses since it is too strong, and difficult to remove at a later date, without causing damage. Repairs are generally made using a cellulose nitrate based adhesive, e.g. HMG (UK), Duco cement (US), or polymethyl methacrylate, e.g. Paraloid B-72 (Acryloid B-72- US) *(Figure 7.13a,b)*.

Consolidation

Consolidation of deteriorated glass or fragile surface decoration with a resin may be under-taken when the glass is liable to crumble or flake upon drying or handling. It has also been used to re-introduce a measure of transparency to thin surface crusts. The treatment should be considered to be irreversible, even when resins that are normally re-soluble, are used. This is because resins swell during solvation and the glass is unlikely to survive both this swelling and the prolonged immersion required to remove a consolidant. It is also unlikely that all traces of a resin could be removed if required at a later date. Consolidation should therefore only be carried out where it is absolutely necessary for the survival of the artefact. The question of whether to consolidate before or after cleaning is problematic. Pre-consolidation may make subsequent removal of surface dirt from a fragile artefact more difficult. On the other hand, it may not be possible to clean fragile glass before it has been consolidated. Therefore each case must be judged on its own merit.

It is not only necessary to consider the glass crust as the substrate; there may also be a solid glass core to which the consolidant must adhere. The surface of the core is normally associated with water molecules, but (the amorphous silica of the weathering crust being hydrophilic) it is usually highly hydrated. Thus, to obtain enhanced penetration and adhesion, a consolidation system which displaces or incorporates this water must be

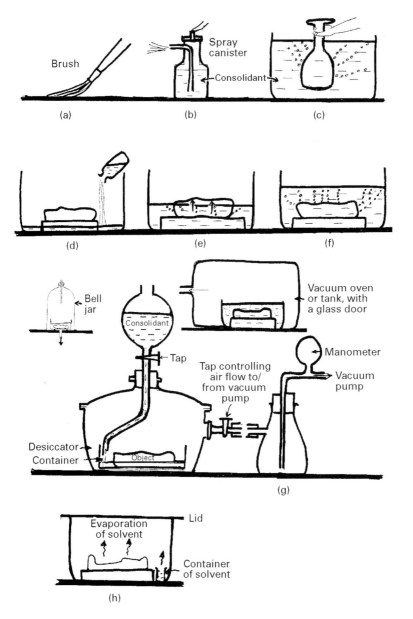

Figure 7.14 Options for consolidation of porous glass objects. (a) Brushing; (b) spraying; (c) dipping; (d) adding a consolidation system beside an object; (e) partial immersion; (f) total immersion; (g) vacuum impregnation; (h) drying an object after consolidation.

employed. Preliminary drying out of a crust, especially by heat or vacuum, must be avoided since this would lead to shrinkage and disruption. In general, the approach to the consolidation of extensively weathered glass has been either that of preliminary de-watering with solvents, or that of using a water-miscible consolidation system, and of choosing a consolidation system which combines low viscosity with a high deposition of solids on setting.

The term *consolidant* is used to define a resin used for the purposes of consolidation, and *consolidation system* to define the liquid phase in which the consolidant is applied, whether it be molten, in solution, or as a polymer pre-treatment. When choosing a consolidation system, the conservator must bear in mind the nature and properties of the resins and solvents to be used (see Chapter 5), the condition of the decayed glass to be treated, and the manner in which the consolidation system is applied (*Figure 7.14a–h*).

Systems that are too viscous fail to penetrate the glass, resulting in the formation of skins which spall off, whilst those with too low a solids content fail to fill the interstices. Viscosity varies with consolidant, and with concentration of the consolidation system. Thus, for example, Paraloid B-72 in a 20 per cent solution of toluene at 21°C has a viscosity of only 29×10^{-3} Nsm^{-2}. Polyvinyl acetate (of approximately 520 degrees of polymerization) in a 20 per cent solution has a viscosity of 40×10^{-3} Nsm^{-2}. Reduction of viscosity can be achieved by a number of means, most commonly by altering the concentrations of the consolidation system. Another method would be the application of heat, but temperatures in excess of 60°C must be stringently avoided in order to safeguard the glass; and consideration must be given to the vapour pressure and flash point of the solvent in use.

If the glass in question is not completely waterlogged, that is, the decayed surface layers contain air, then the consolidation system may be best applied under conditions of reduced pressure. The glass can either be immersed in a consolidant and the pressure reduced, or the pressure can be reduced and the solution dripped beside the glass, until it is covered. The former method may give better support to a whole, fragile vessel but greater disruption is likely when the pressure is reduced. If the dripping method is used, for example, in cases where the glass is liable to lose flakes in solution, sufficient consolidant to cover the fragment should be dripped into the consolidation chamber before the vacuum is released.

Reduced pressure is used primarily to remove air from the pores and capillaries of decayed glass, which would otherwise impede the penetration of the consolidation system. Also, to introduce a low pressure into the pores so that, when the assembly is returned to atmospheric pressure, more of the consolidation system is forced into them due to the pressure differential. This lowest practical pressure will depend in part on the apparatus and pump available, and in part on the vapour pressure of the liquid at the given temperature (because a liquid boils when the ambient pressure reaches its vapour pressure); solvents with high vapour pressures will evaporate even when the pressure is only slightly reduced. However, it should be remembered that the vapour pressure of a solution is lower than that of a pure solvent. Reduced pressure will therefore tend to concentrate the solution and, if taken to excess, it could cause the consolidant to solidify. An excessively low pressure should, however, be avoided because there is a danger that any sealed bubbles (seed) which are very close to the surface of the solid glass might burst.

The atmospheric pressure should be reduced only slowly in order to prevent air rushing from the glass and causing it to disintegrate and to allow time for the pressure in partially sealed pores to come to equilibrium. This is especially true when the glass is immersed in a liquid before the pressure is reduced, because the viscosity of the liquid retards the process. Again, the reduced pressure should only be slowly increased in order to avoid air rushing into cavities where the solution has not fully penetrated. The equipment for consolidating glass under reduced pressure is shown in *Figure 7.14*).

After consolidation by immersion, the glass is removed from the consolidation system with a pair of plastic tweezers, and dipped briefly in solvent to dilute surplus consolidant of the surface of the object. The glass is placed on silicone (US: glassine) paper and excess consolidant allowed to drain off the surface. This process may be aided by the use of cotton swabs soaked in solvent or simply by absorbing solvent with tissue. It is then advisable to replace the object in a solvent atmosphere whilst it dries out, either in a glass receptacle or, if in the ground, by covering the glass with a Polythene bag (Garlake, 1969). Drying the glass in this way will slow the rate of evaporation so that the resin remaining on the surface will be more thinly dispersed and therefore appear matt. Covering the glass also prevents dust from adhering to the consolidant (see *Figure 7.14b*).

Generally speaking, a matt surface will render surface details, such as engraving or paint, more readily visible on an uneven weathered surface. Hedvall *et al.* (1951) achieved such a finish by gently heating the consolidant bath, but this is an unnecessary procedure, adding the potential risk of damage to the glass, or of causing a fire.

Spraying, dripping or painting the consolidant solution on the glass are far less efficacious than the methods described above but

Figure 7.15 Application of a consolidant (10 per cent Paraloid B-72 in toluene) to flaking glass by brush.

they might have to be used on individual fragments or objects on site; or in the case of large or very delicate objects (*Figures 7.14a–c* and *7.15*). In these cases, the first applications must have a low viscosity in order to achieve deep penetration, and hence several dilute coats are much more helpful than one thick one. A pipette or syringe may be useful for impregnating areas of an object that are difficult to reach with a brush.

Silane as a pre-treatment has been successfully used as a coupling agent for the bond between hydrated glass, weathering crusts and the acrylic consolidant Paraloid B-72 on extensively weathered glass by Errett *et al.* (1984). The long-term stability of the technique is unknown, and it is unlikely to have a wide application on archaeological glass, being more suited to the conservation of window glass *in situ*.

A method of consolidating fully decayed glass was developed by Bimson and Werner (1971) for the treatment of a fragile potash glass alembic head dating from the fourteenth or fifteenth century AD. The alembic head had· been successfully excavated, along with several other fragments of medieval distilling apparatus, but had been subsequently severely damaged by poor storage. More than half the object had been crushed to tiny flakes and the remainder was in an extremely fragile condition and could not be safely handled. The problem was not only to consolidate those fragments so that they could be safely

handled, but also to use a consolidant that would serve as a gap-filler, because most of the fragments were joined only at one or two points. Glass and amorphous silica are hydrophilic, and therefore Carbowax 6000, a polyethylene glycol wax which is also hydrophilic, was chosen as the consolidant.

The procedure used was as follows. Each fragment of glass was supported on a raft of aluminium foil. This was laid on the surface of the molten Carbowax 6000 in a dish, placed in an oven at a temperature of about 80°C. It was feared that the Carbowax 6000, having a relatively high viscosity, might disintegrate the glass further, but this did not occur. After 2 hours the raft with its fragment of glass had sunk to the bottom of the molten wax and all the bubbles of displaced air had separated from the glass surface. The fragments were then gently removed from the wax bath by lifting the corners of the raft, and replaced in the oven on a pile of absorbent tissues. When excess molten wax had run off, the aluminium raft was carefully removed, and any remaining wax blotted away with paper tissues. The alembic fragments were allowed to cool to room temperature, when it was found that they had sufficient mechanical strength to be handled safely, and their appearance showed remarkably little change.

In order to join treated fragments, the wax on their edges was melted using a Microweld torch, which restricted the heating area to a few square millimetres. This enabled wax in any given area, to be melted without softening joins already made, and badly fitting joins to be strengthened by melting small lumps of the wax to fill gaps. Whilst the treated glass was not in a strong physical condition, several years later it was possible to handle it in order to fit mounts for display.

The following method for temporary storage and consolidation of wet excavated medieval window glass was developed by Hutchinson (abstract No. 416 in Newton, 1982b) in the English Heritage conservation laboratory in London (formerly the Historic Buildings and Monuments Commission for England). On excavation, the glass was kept wet and packed in single layers between sheets of polyester foam, of a grade that retained water well. The glass was then placed in two self-seal Polythene bags, one inside the other, and labelled both on the outside and on a water-proof label inside the outer bag. The glass was kept in a cool place. (If a refrigerator is used to store the wet glass there must be no possibility of the water freezing.) During temporary wet storage the water surrounding the glass should not be changed; it was found that the pH of the solution does not rise above 8.0.

Once in the laboratory, the glass was unpacked and whilst being kept wet as much mud and loose encrustation as possible was removed mechanically. The fragments were then consolidated with a mixture of PEG 4000 (polyethylene glycol) and Vinamul 6815, a polyvinyl acetate emulsion. This acted as a bulk filler and consolidant. The mixture was prepared as follows: the required amount of Vinamul 6815 was diluted with an equal amount of distilled water and the required amount of PEG 4000 was dissolved in water in the proportion 500 g to 1 litre of water. The consolidation system itself was composed of four parts diluted polyvinyl acetate emulsion, two parts distilled water, and two parts polyethylene glycol solution, all parts being measured by volume.

The glass fragments were laid flat on coarse Nylon netting in a shallow container. The netting ensured that the consolidant completely surrounded the glass. It was allowed to overhang the sides of the container for ease of lifting the delicate fragments after treatment. Several layers of net and glass could be placed in one container. The consolidant was then slowly added to the dish, ensuring that the fragments did not float (they did not if waterlogged), until there was at least 10 mm of liquid above the glass. The top of the container, clearly labelled with its contents, was covered with plastic film to prevent evaporation, and left for approximately 2 months. After this time, the fragments were removed from the consolidation system, and excess wax removed with paper tissues. There were some loose flakes of glass, which could not be re-attached. The glass was then placed on silicone paper and allowed to dry. Repairs were carried out at this stage, using a cellulose nitrate adhesive (HMG). Finally all the surfaces of the glass (including the edges) were painted with a 30 per cent solution of polyvinyl-acetate in toluene. Since toluene is less volatile than, for example, acetone, the

solution did not form into brush lines on the surface while drying. Lacquering the glass in this way altered the optical appearance of the surface, thus enabling the painted design to be seen through the thin layers of dirt and decayed glass remaining. Glass treated by this method has been found to be in good condition several years later; favourable storage conditions will be a major contributing factor to this. Experiments with the method are continuing; however, it may be that the use of Paraloid B-72 and aqueous solutions of acrylic emulsions described below will prove to be more widely accepted.

Koob (1981) began experimenting with acrylic colloidal dispersions as a consolidant for newly excavated archaeological bone. Since the smaller particle size and low viscosity of the colloidal dispersion system permitted better penetration at higher concentrations, it was concluded that they were the most suitable consolidant in a water-based system for the consolidation of fragile materials, especially bone and other organic materials because of their near neutral pH. Furthermore, resistance to high temperatures, and characteristically good working properties, are assured by the glass transition temperature, and the minimum film temperature respectively. In addition, the relatively high moisture barrier, due to an acrylic film's low water permeability and absorption, protected objects against climatic fluctuation. After drying, the acrylic resin film was hard and durable.

In 1983 an aqueous solution of Primal WS-24 acrylic emulsion was used to consolidate fragments of excavated glass beads and painted window glass in Denmark (Roberts, 1984). The glass beads, dated to between AD 400 and 700, arrived for treatment packed in a self-seal Polythene bag. Since condensation had formed on the inside of the bag, it was at first difficult to determine their exact quantity and condition (*Figure 7.16a*). However, it could be seen that the fragments were in an extremely friable condition (due in part to improper lifting and packaging), and that they would require consolidation before being cleaned. To this end, a number of tests were carried using 20, 50 and 100 per cent solutions of Primal WS-12, WS-24 and WS-50 acrylic emulsions on silica gel lying on damp soil to represent the beads. A 50 per cent aqueous solution of Primal WS-24 was chosen as the solution with which to consolidate the glass under moist conditions.

The bag containing the bead fragments was then placed on a glass plate for support and cut open to reveal the contents to be one glass bead and one bead fragment. The exposed surfaces of the beads were consolidated with a few drops of 100 per cent Primal WS-24 (i.e. as supplied). While the earth was still moist from condensation and the Primal solution, it was removed from the intact glass bead, using soft brushes and distilled water. Cleaning in this manner was terminated if the glass began to split, and consolidation was renewed with a 50 per cent aqueous solution of Primal WS-24. The consolidation medium was applied drop by drop, until the glass was saturated, and excess was removed with cotton wool swabs. In order to slow down the evaporation rate of the water, the bead was placed in an open plastic bag under a slightly raised glass beaker. After an hour the bead was transferred to silicon release paper (US: glassine paper) and was further consolidated with a 50 per cent aqueous solution of Primal WS-24. When excess was apparent, consolidation was terminated. The glass bead was allowed to dry overnight (*Figure 7.16b*).

Final cleaning was accomplished by dissolving the consolidant on the surface, with toluene, and cleaning the bead with a soft brush. The cleaned surface was then re-consolidated with an 8 per cent solution of Paraloid B-72 in toluene glass (*Figure 7.16c*). After treatment, the glass bead could be seen to be turquoise in colour with a marvered design of bands of white and orange-red.

A method of consolidating excavated glass with Primal WS-24 and Paraloid B-72 was also used to conserve a fragment of a painted glass roundel (*kabinettscheibe*) from Slagelse in Denmark (Roberts, 1984). The roundel had a diameter of 72 mm and was decorated with a fired enamel design and script on the front, and with evidence of a silver stain on the reverse. The fragment was received for treatment in a waterlogged condition, but had subsequently been allowed to dry out. Upon drying, the glass surface and consequently the paint layer began flaking and cupping on both sides of the fragment (*Figure 7.17a*). Treatment was begun using a 3 per cent

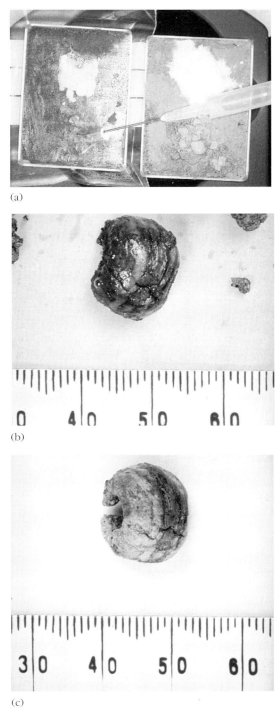

(a)

(b)

(c)

Figure 7.16 (a) Excavated wet glass bead fragments in a self-seal Polythene bag, obscured by gravel. Light cleaning being undertaken with a sable brush. (b) Glass bead after consolidation with 50 per cent Primal WS-24. (c) Glass bead after removal of excess solvent.

(a)

(b)

Figure 7.17 (a) Flaking and cupping of a fragment of painted glass roundel (*kabinettscheibe*). (b) The same fragment after consolidation with a 20 per cent aqueous solution of Primal WS-24, and surface treatment with 5 per cent Paraloid B-72 in toluene.

solution of Paraloid B-72 in toluene applied to selected areas and allowed to penetrate the surface layers by capillary action. Since it was observed that moisture relaxed the flaking surfaces of both the glass and the paint layer, a water-soluble acrylic consolidant, Primal WS-24 (as a 20 per cent solution in water), was introduced with a brush. Capillary action distributed the consolidant. After drying, the surface of the glass was brushed with a solution of 8 per cent Paraloid B-72 in toluene. In areas of heavy flaking, such as the painted script, the surfaces of both the glass and paint were gently warmed with a heated spatula (temperature controlled at 25°C), in order to aid the flattening and relaying of the paint.

During this process, some of the flakes broke. The results can be seen in *Figure 7.17b*.

The use of an electrically heated spatula, applied to the glass and/or paint usually over a small piece of Melinex sheet, in conjunction with small amounts of solvent and/or consolidant to relax the surfaces, is often successful in relaxing and relaying flaking designs painted on glass (see also *hinterglasmalerei* at the end of this chapter).

Surface treatments

Other methods have been used to reveal surface detail. A thick layer of polyvinyl acetate was applied to the surface of the blackened sherds of medieval window glass to reveal paint (Hutchinson, 1981; Newton, 1982b entry No. 416); and the application of a glossy resin (Plexigum P24) over the primary treatment, a fluoro-silicate, Durol-Polier-Fluat SD (Karl, 1970). However, none of these methods can be recommended for reasons previously discussed.

In order to adhere flaking glass surfaces and cracked enamels, solutions of various resins, such as polyvinyl acetate or the methacrylate copolymer Paraloid B-72, have been applied as a surface treatment (Wihr, 1977; Dove, 1981). Improved transparency of decayed glass crusts on small glass objects has been variously achieved by surface treatment with Paraloid B-72 after solvent de-watering, or with epoxy resin after air-drying. The success of such an operation depends upon the condition of the glass undergoing treatment. Whilst such treatment may also reduce the visual effect of iridescence, neither it nor the consolidation systems previously discussed can restore transparency to a thin weathering crust completely, and are not recommended for general use.

The use of organic lacquers has been suggested as a protective film for weeping glass; and Hedvall *et al.* (1951) have described a technique in which such a glass was impregnated with a polymethyl methacrylate under vacuum. Lacquering may appear to delay further deterioration, but all organic lacquers are permeable to water vapour, and the chemical reaction of disintegration will continue. Thus the reaction products will be trapped at the interface, and their build-up may eventually cause the total collapse of the glass object. The latest approach to conserving unstable (weeping and crizzling) glass by alkali ion replacement is discussed later in the chapter.

Corvaia *et al.* (1996) describe the treatment of an exfoliant surface layer on several green glass bottles recovered from the wreck of the *Zuytdorp* (1712) in 1988. The bottles were extremely weathered and stained. Scanning electron microscope/energy dispersive X-ray analysis (SEM/EDXRA) and thermal analysis showed that the hydrated outer layer of glass had suffered a calcium loss of approximately 21 per cent and that water represented 41 per cent of the total mass of the glass. Treatment of the surface layer with calcium acetate solution was successful in re-depositing calcium ions into the weathered layer. Exfoliation of the degraded layer was prevented by treatment combining the calcium acetate solution and an emulsion of Primal AC-235 (copolymer polybutylacrylate/polymethyl methacrylate). The addition of Primal AC-21 slowed down the rate of calcium diffusion into the glass, but resulted in allowing the glass to be air-dried without exfoliation of the surface glass. (See also relaying of paint on *hinterglasmalerei*, at the end of the chapter.)

Consolidation of wet glass

Experiments are continuing into the preservation of glass from waterlogged environments; it seems that consolidation with acrylic emulsion, or with Paraloid B-72 after dewatering through solvents, will produce the most satisfactory results.

Allowing damp or waterlogged glass to dehydrate normally results in loss of transparency, surface flaking, or even total collapse of the glass. Therefore, water in the surface layers and core of the glass must be displaced by a solvent. This in its turn will be replaced by or incorporated in the consolidation system, e.g. Paraloid B-72 in acetone. Hydrophilic solvents, such as ethanol, propan-2-ol, acetone or butanone, are suitable. Without allowing the glass to dry, it is first placed in a 50:50 mixture of water and solvent. Every few hours, it is passed through a succession of baths of increasing concentration of the solvent in which the consolidant is dissolved. Finally the glass can be transferred to the consolidation system itself.

Reisman and Lucas (preliminary report, undated) carried out experimental research into retrieval and consolidation of glass from underwater environments in 1978. The method of consolidation was as follows. The object was weighed on removal from its last water bath, and then immersed in a bath of ethanol (anhydrous ethanol). The ethanol bath was changed every few days to ensure that the water was being replaced. After a few changes, the specific gravity of the ethanol bath was tested to ensure that it was water-free. When the ethanol exchange was complete, the glass object was re-weighed. It was then submerged in the consolidating material, PVA-AYAA 5 per cent in 95 per cent ethanol. The object was left in the consolidant for 15 minutes, after which a vacuum was drawn to 5 in Hg and held for 15–20 minutes. The percentage concentration of the solution was increased to 7 per cent by adding more PVA–AYAA, the vacuum drawn to 5 in Hg, and after 15 minutes, to 7 in. After a further 15 minutes, the percentage of PVA-AYAA was increased to 10 per cent, the vacuum applied and if possible the percentage of the PVA–AYAA further increased. The highest concentration of consolidant possible consistent with impregnation should be achieved, especially if the glass surface is insecure.

The object was then removed from the vacuum and placed in a chamber over ethanol vapour for several hours to force the PVA-AYAA into the surface of the crust even further and to prevent the surface from drying with a glossy appearance. During this time the object was observed to note any shrinkage, delamination or spalling, of which there was none. The object was then removed from the desiccator and allowed to dry at ambient temperature.

Reinforcing

It is possible that heavily decayed glass may not be strong enough to handle even after consolidation, and that a support in the form of a backing material will be required. Working on very decayed glass from Sardis in Turkey, Majewski (1973) used Japanese mulberry tissue with polyvinyl acetate (PVAC), the resin which had already been used for consolidating the glass. It would have been preferable to have chosen a resin that would not dissolve in the same solvent as the consolidant in case the backing material needed to be removed at a later date. Artal-Isbrand (1998) filled losses in a fragile, opaque Roman glass with Japanese tissue paper coloured with water-colour paints, and secured to the glass with Paraloid B-72 (see also *Figure 7.31*).

Restoration

Gap-filling missing areas in archaeological glass is best undertaken by reinforcing the glass as described above, if the glass is particularly fragile. Where a glass vessel has large areas missing but does not warrant total reconstruction because, for example, it will remain in storage, it may be partially restored for safe handling, e.g. during study, photography or drawing for publication. Strips of fine glass-fibre tissue cut to size and impregnated with cellulose nitrate adhesive or epoxy or polyester resins are used to bridge gaps in the glass and to hold floating fragments in their correct positions. Total reconstruction of small vessels is also possible by this method, with the results shown in *Figure 7.31*. It is not aesthetically pleasing but may be useful as a temporary measure (Newton and Davison, 1989). Artal-Isbrand (1998) used Japanese tissue paper as a gap-filling material (see above). Where the condition of the glass allows, gap-filling may be undertaken by the moulding and casting techniques described for historical glass (Wihr, 1963, 1968, 1977; Davison, 1998; Newton and Davison, 1989).

Part 2: Historic and decorative glass

Cleaning

Glass is an immensely versatile material, which, as discussed in Chapters 2 and 3, can be formed and decorated with infinite variety. For at least a thousand years, glass has been used to form items for storing and serving food and drink. Other liquids stored in glass have ranged from perfume, paint, ink and chemicals. In use for lighting, glass was formed into candlesticks, candelabra, tapersticks, wall lights, sconces, lanterns, lamps and chandeliers. It was used to form decorative inlays and panels on furniture (Davison, 1992). Other decorative uses were for armorial, masonic and commemorative wares, animals and figures, friggers, centre-pieces, such as *epergnes*, *nefs* and domes, paperweights and sculptures. For personal use, glass was used to form looking-glasses, and jewellery in the form of beads, bracelets and rings, ear-rings, inlays and mosaic, and paste in imitation of precious and semi-precious stones. Thoresen (1998) discusses the use of glass in the production of classical intaglios. Glass panes were used as substrates in the production of plaques and panels, mirrors, paintings executed in reverse, mirror pictures, *verre églomisé* and photographic images. Glass also has many varied uses scientifically, commercially and industrially.

As in every other field of conservation, certain generalities concerning repair and restoration can be laid down. There are, however, certain glass objects, which, because of their shape, require specialist treatment. Yet others, such as paintings in reverse on glass, mirrors and chandeliers, require the assistance of other specialist conservators or companies. In these instances only general guidance will be given, indicating the range of treatments available.

Removal of previous repair and restoration materials

In the case of glass artefacts which have been in a collection for a number of years, there may be evidence of previous repair and restoration. This often consists of the use of adhesives ranging from animal glues to epoxy- and rubber-based compositions, with wax or plaster of Paris as the replacement for missing areas of glass, coloured with a variety of paints (Wihr, 1963), as shown in (*Figures 7.18* and *7.43*).

Figure 7.18 Old, unsightly restoration on a wing-handled cup, gap-filled with plaster of Paris and painted silver. From Canosa, Italy. (© Copyright The British Museum).

It may not always be possible for the conservator to know which materials have been used. Provided they can be removed without damage to the glass, a sample of the material can be removed and tested in order that the correct solvent may be chosen. Otherwise, the usual practice is to begin removal of previously applied materials, with the least toxic solvent, i.e. cold water, and if this has no effect to try warm water, followed by acetone, industrial methylated spirits (IMS), white spirit, xylene and dichloromethane. The object may either be exposed to solvent vapour in a closed container, or the solvent may be applied directly by means of a small sable paint brush, pipette, or cotton wool swabs laid along the joins (*Figure 7.19a–f*). Once softened, the material may be

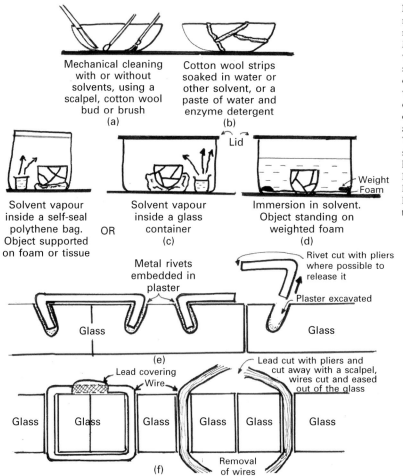

Mechanical cleaning with or without solvents, using a scalpel, cotton wool bud or brush
(a)

Cotton wool strips soaked in water or other solvent, or a paste of water and enzyme detergent
(b)

Lid

Solvent vapour inside a self-seal polythene bag. Object supported on foam or tissue

OR

Solvent vapour inside a glass container
(c)

Immersion in solvent. Object standing on weighted foam
(d)

Weight
Foam

Metal rivets embedded in plaster

Rivet cut with pliers where possible to release it

Plaster excavated

Glass

Glass

(e)

Lead covering
Wire

Lead cut with pliers and cut away with a scalpel, wires cut and eased out of the glass

Glass   Glass   Glass

Glass   Glass   Glass

Removal of wires
(f)

Figure 7.19 Options for removal of materials used for repair and restoration. (a) Mechanical cleaning with or without solvents, using a scalpel, cotton wool brush or cotton wool swab. (b) Cotton wool rolls soaked in solvent, or a paste of water and enzyme detergent, placed along previous joins. (c) Vapour solvent inside a self-seal Polythene bag, or a lidded container. (d) Immersion in solvent. (e) Removal of metal rivets. (f) Removal of lead-covered wire ties.

completely removed using a sable paint brush or small cotton wool swabs and solvent, or by careful use of a scalpel. Force should never be applied since fragile glass may break before a strong adhesive is dislodged.

Williams (1989) described the dismantling of the Portland Vase prior to its subsequent repair. The interior of the vase was lined with three layers of damp blotting paper, held in place by a thin layer of plaster of Paris. Three layers of damp blotting paper were applied to the exterior, followed by a number of flexible plastic *tourniquets* to give support. The vase was then placed inside a glass dessicator over a bowl of warm water. After three days, the old adhesive (animal glue) had softened, and as the blotting paper was rolled away, the glass fragments, 189 in all, could be removed in a controlled manner (*Figure 7.20*).

Figure 7.20 Damp blotting paper applied to the surface of the Portland Vase in order to facilitate its dismantling. The cameo-glass amphora known as the Portland Vase, after its former owners, of cobalt-blue glass cased with opaque white, in which a mythological scene is cut cameo-fashion in relief. H 245–248 mm, GD 177 mm, T (at bottom of broken edge of blue glass) 3 mm. Perhaps from Rome where it was probably made in the early first century AD. (© Copyright The British Museum).

Washing sound glass

Prior to washing, glass objects (excavated or otherwise) that have been in collections for some years should be carefully examined for signs of previous restoration, as this may not be immediately apparent. If the glass has not been repaired or restored and is otherwise sound, it can be washed in tepid water (*never hot*) in a plastic bowl (to prevent breakage should the vessel slip). A few drops of a non-ionic detergent may be added to the water (if too much is used the glass will not be visible through the suds) and only one object should be placed in the bowl at a time. Care must be taken not to exert pressure on the glass during cleaning, especially on fragile areas such as a rim or stem of a drinking vessel. When clean, the glass is laid on paper towelling to drain. The towelling will absorb water and also prevent the glass from sliding on a wet surface. Breaks may occur on the slightest impact and therefore the working surfaces should not be overcrowded, especially as it is sometimes difficult to judge how much space there is between transparent objects. Drinking glasses should not be held by the stem whilst being dried, in case they snap under pressure, but should be supported by cupping the hand under the bowl. A soft, lint-free cloth, or paper towelling, is used to dry the glass, taking care not to exert any pressure. Drying should be carried out over a bench spread with a thick layer of towelling, in case the glass should slip. The glass should be free from surface moisture before being displayed or stored.

Decanters

The most commonly encountered problems with decanters are:

(i) part of the bowl having split off due to the vessel having been filled with hot water;
(ii) so-called water-marks around the bowl;
(iii) a white 'bloom', especially on lead glass;
(iv) small holes at the corners of the base of square-shaped decanters;
(v) the decanter stopper having become jammed in the neck, after which attempts to remove it may have caused the stopper to have broken, leaving the lower part fixed in position, or the decanter neck to have broken.

A broken bowl may be repaired in the usual way; however, the owner would be well advised not to put the decanter to everyday use since if it contains liquid all the time the bond may eventually fail without warning due to the penetration of liquid between the glass and adhesive.

There are many home remedies recorded for the removal of 'water-marks' around the bowls of decanters. These include filling the bowl with water and newspaper (thereby forming a weak acid solution); the use of tablets marketed for cleaning dentures, for sterilizing babies' or wine bottles or for de-scaling kettles; use of weak or concentrated organic acids; and scouring the inside with materials ranging from sand to lead shot. Some of these remedies work some of the time, but are not recommended for use, because of the risk of damaging the object. Sometimes the mark may seem to disappear whilst the glass is wet, only to re-appear when the surface dries out. It is of course important to realize that the mark may be a deposit of lime-scale (calcium) or other insoluble salt, or may simply be a mark formed when wine has been allowed to evaporate. However the surface of the glass itself may have deteriorated, especially in the case of old glass which has been in long term use.

If the use of a weak concentration of hydrochloric acid does not remove a deposit, it is probably best left alone. The interior of the decanter can be commercially abraded/polished with mild abrasives, or a thin layer of glass removed by swilling the interior with hydrofluoric acid (HF). This is an extremely dangerous acid and must only be used by specialist companies competent to deal with it (see Chapter 5). Pinkish stains, the remains of wine, port etc., can be removed by filling the decanter with a weak, tepid aqueous solution of an enzyme detergent for a few hours. If necessary a Nylon bottle-brush (wrapping the end of the metal holder with plastic tape, so that it does not scratch the glass) can be used.

A white 'bloom' may form on the surface of glass, especially lead glass, which has been put through a dishwashing machine. This is the result of a reaction between the glass and chemicals in the finishing agent, and is irreversible (see *Figure 4.30*).

There are also home remedies for the release of stoppers that have become wedged in the neck of their decanters. Some of these may also work some of the time, and to some extent whether they do or not will depend upon how long the stopper has been in place and what attempts have previously been made to free it. It is sometimes the habit of people replacing a stopper after pouring wine etc. to give the stopper a final pat, and this may cause it to become wedged in place. The most obvious solution is to place the decanter in warm to hand hot water (gradually increasing the warmth) and, whilst the stopper is immersed gently trying to pull it free. If this does not work, the introduction of liquid soap or thin lubricating oil may suffice. However, if these are not thoroughly removed, they may dry out and act as adhesives. Another remedy may be to warm the decanter itself in water (thereby slightly expanding the glass), whilst applying ice to the stopper (preventing it from expanding), so that just enough discrepancy is achieved to free the stopper. Tapping the stopper gently all round may loosen it, but if extreme care is not taken this approach may break the neck, as will forceful twisting of the stopper. A stopper may remain firmly stuck and there may be nothing to be done.

In the case of stoppers that have broken off in the neck, these may be dislodged by adhering a wooden handle to the stump, after which any of the methods described above, may be applied. If the stump is removed, the adhesive securing the 'handle' is dissolved and the stump adhered to the rest of the stopper if this is present. As a final resort, it may be possible for the remains of a stopper to be commercially ground out. It is not advisable to effect a repair to a stopper, part of which has become wedged *in situ*, as there is little guarantee that adhesive will not run inside the neck and thus compound the problem.

Laser cleaning

Laser beams have been successfully used to remove (ablate) defined areas of dirt deposits in other fields of conservation such as stone (Cooper, 1998). Ablation is the term used to describe the removal of surface dirt layer by layer. As early as 1975, Asmus advocated the use of laser beams for cleaning glass.

However, the equipment is extremely expensive, and much research on the technique is still needed. The Fraunhofer Institut für Silicatforshung in Germany is undertaking a research project aimed at examining the advantages and limitations of laser cleaning heavily corroded medieval window glass by the application of KrF excimer laser beams (wavelength 248 nm) to model glasses (Römich in Kordas, 2002). It has been shown that it is impossible to remove corrosion crusts on model glasses without significant damage to the sensitive gel layer (the softened layer beneath the corrosion). Further experiments are necessary to determine the appropriate laser parameters for cleaning heavily corroded glass with an uneven surface before original glass can be laser cleaned, and the effect of laser irradiation on the corrosion crust itself. The influence of the colour and composition on the laser treatment has to be investigated. Laser treatment may not be applicable to object glass conservation except perhaps for cleaning large quantities of marine encrusted or fire-blackened deteriorated glass. Glass 'jewels' on the Albert Memorial in London were successfully cleaned by the use of Nd-Yag lasers.

Repair

Decorative glass, more specifically glass vessels, form one of the most difficult groups of antiquities to repair for a number of reasons. The edges of un-decayed glass are normally smooth and therefore do not provide a key for good adhesion; the surfaces of glass objects are covered with many molecular layers of adsorbed water, thus reducing the bond strengths of adhesives; and since most glasses are transparent, the repair or restoration is more visible than it would be on other materials. In comparison with other materials therefore, relatively little early work has been published in the field of glass object conservation, the majority having been concerned with painted European medieval glass windows *in situ*. However, this situation has greatly improved in the past four decades, as the discipline of glass conservation has expanded. The choice of resins suitable for repairing and restoring glass is continually

changing, allowing ever more complicated procedures to be undertaken (Petermann, 1969; Errett, 1972; Wihr, 1963, 1968, 1977; Staude, 1972; Fiorentino and Borelli, 1975; Martin, 1977; Davison, 1988, 1998; Jackson, 1982a, 1983; Fisher, 1998; Newton and Davison, 1989; Brain, 1992; Depassiot, 1997).

Glass restoration can entail complicated and time-consuming operations, which although resulting in results acceptable for museum or historic house display, may not be aesthetically pleasing enough for a private collector. Even skilled restorers are limited by the materials available.

Choice of materials

The choice of adhesives for repairing glass is discussed in Chapter 5, with easily reversible adhesives such as those based on cellulose nitrate and methyl methacrylate copolymers being the most suitable for the repair of decayed archaeological glass. Glass which is badly deteriorated, can lose up to 75 per cent of its weight, and glass which has lost its surface through time or misadventure can be very thin and delicate. In this condition glass may be joined by adhesives that set by loss of solvent because the solvent can to some extent evaporate through decayed glass whereas it does not do so through un-deteriorated glass. Furthermore, adhesion of decayed glass will be facilitated by the keying of adhesive into the surface of micro-cracks. If the glass has been consolidated, the characteristics of the adhesive must match those of the consolidant, remembering that the solvent used to apply the adhesive will probably cause the consolidant to swell. A similar problem is encountered when attempts are made to remove the adhesive.

Cellulose nitrate, marketed in Britain as HMG and Durofix (and in the US as Duco cement), has been used successfully for joining decayed glass and it is convenient to use. Its long-term instability has been mentioned (Koob, 1982) and this should be taken into account. No long-term tests have been carried out on the stability of the joint when cellulose nitrate has been used on consolidated glass. Polyvinyl acetate has also been used as an adhesive but it has a tendency to plastic flow if kept in a warm environment. Paraloid B-72 formulated as an adhesive can also be used to repair fragile glass (Taylor, 1984). However it tends to become stringy very quickly and to contain air bubbles, due to rapid evaporation of the acetone solvent, and is therefore not as convenient for use as cellulose nitrate. The major disadvantage of weaker adhesives is that a restored object may eventually fall apart causing further damage, not only to the object itself, but possibly to others nearby. However, epoxy resins have continued to be used for repairing and even consolidating decayed glass in some countries.

Once such resins penetrate and consolidate the weathering layers they must be considered as irreversible. Fiorentino and Borrelli (1975) suggest that this irreversibility can be circumvented by the use of a stable soluble resin such as Paraloid B-72 as a primer underneath the epoxy, but several hours of immersion in a solvent are still required to break down such joins. However, in the absence of satisfactory alternatives to provide strong joints for vessels or display pieces such a system might be useful. For much archaeological glass, strong adhesives are neither necessary nor advisable.

In the publications cited above the materials used for glass vessel restoration are epoxy, polyester and polymethacrylate resins whose trade names, compositions and properties will to some extent vary with the country of origin.

Literature references to the use of epoxy resins for the repair of glass include Araldite AY103/HY956 and Araldite 2020 (formerly known as Araldite XW956/XW957 in its experimental stage), Fynebond (UK), and EPOTEK-1, Ablebond 342-1 and HXTAL-NYL-1 (Fisher, 1992) (the last three manufactured in the US). Fynebond and HXTAL-NYL-1 are specially formulated for conservation use. Details can be found in Chapter 5. Williams (1989) used HXTAL-NYL-1 for the reconstruction of the Portland Vase, in combination with ultra-violet curing adhesive by which the fragments were held in position during application and curing of the epoxy resin.

It has been reported that on ageing, epoxy resins may exert enough force on the glass to pull flakes from the surface (Bimson and Werner, 1971; Moncrieff, 1975), however no recent cases of this occurring are known. Epoxy- and polyester resins cannot be

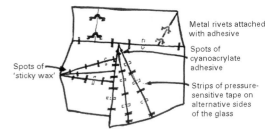

Figure 7.21 Supporting glass fragments during repair with adhesive, with strips of pressure-sensitive tape, spots of cyanoacrylate adhesive or 'Sticky Wax', or metal 'bridges' secured with adhesive.

dissolved, only softened and swelled by the use of solvents.

Supporting glass fragments during repair

While adhesive is setting, glass fragments can be supported in a number of ways depending upon their size and weight (*Figures 7.21* and *7.22a–e*). Glass having a sound surface may be supported by strips of pressure-sensitive tape, ensuring that the tape is of a type that can easily be peeled from the glass without damaging it, e.g. Scotch Magic Tape 810, and/or partially immersing it in a tray filled with glass beads, rice, dried pulses or sand, placing a paper barrier between the glass and the sand (*Figure 7.22a*). Small plastic clamps can be used if necessary.

In many cases the objects are self-supporting, provided that the fragments to be joined are correctly balanced, and the adhesive in one crack is allowed to set before the next fragment is added. However, it may be necessary to use drops of faster-setting adhesives such as cyanoacrylate on surfaces that are delicate or decorated and therefore difficult to tape without causing damage to the glass. A dental product useful for the temporary support of glass fragments is 'Sticky Wax' (beeswax, cerecine wax and gum dammar mix). Supplied in pencil-thick sticks, small drops of the wax can be melted with an electrically heated spatula and dropped across cracks and joins between fragments. The wax becomes sticky when heated, but it hardens quickly on cooling (see *Figure 7.22b*). Once the glass fragments have been secured with adhesive,

(a)

(b)

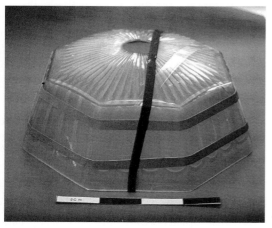

(c)

(d)

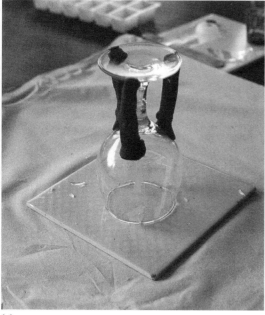

(e)

Figure 7.22 Supporting objects during repair: (a) a sand-tray with a paper barrier; (b) with 'Sticky Wax' and thin strips of pressure-sensitive tape; (c) a large, heavy object supported by wide elastic bands; (d) a clamp stand; (e) stumps of Plasticine.

the wax is easily removed from the glass by slight pressure from a fingernail or blunt scalpel blade.

A method of supporting sound glass fragments by the use of metal bridges (termed staples) originated in Germany (Augustin-Jeutter, 1997; Depassiot, 1997) (see *Figure 7.21*). The bridges were easily made from brass wires of different diameters by bending them with small pliers. Although time-consuming to make in any number, they could be re-used. The size of the bridges depended on the size, weight and number of glass fragments to be supported. The bridges were secured to the glass surface at angles across the joins with cyanoacrylate adhesive. However as this adhesive does not make a strong bond with the glass, drops of 5-minute curing epoxy resin were applied to each end of the bridges with a cocktail stick. Epoxy resin was then applied to the breaks in order to repair the glass. Once this had cured the small metal bridges were removed using a scalpel. The larger ones were easier to remove using a rotating rubber disc on a flexible drill. The rotating disc was applied to the top of the metal, and the heat produced by friction softened the adhesive in a few seconds. Whilst the metal is still hot it could be removed with a pair of pliers, or with a scalpel. Adhesive remains were removed with a scalpel and/or acetone on cotton wool swabs. This method of supporting ancient or historic glass fragments cannot be recommended for general use, because of the amount of interference with the glass surface, the possibility that not all the adhesive used to affix the bridges will be removed, and the potential risk of damage when removing the bridges. It could, however, prove useful for supporting fragments of heavy glass objects such as sculptures.

Increasingly, heavy glass figures, especially those made in Venice, are requiring repair and restoration. Some are extremely large and consequently heavy, and pose particular conservation problems. Apart from the difficulties of supporting heavy, awkward shapes, there is also the question of how to bond broken fragments. In general, the glass shatters and chips easily, and it is therefore inadvisable to attempt to insert dowels. The broken edges may be keyed by scratching them deeply with a diamond point. Epoxy resin is

the adhesive most likely to hold the glass. If the glass is opaque, missing chips of glass surrounding the breaks can be filled using a thick paste composed of colourless epoxy resin, fumed silica and dry artists' pigments (see *Figure 7.29*). Over a long period of time, epoxy resin can separate as a sheet, from the smooth surfaces of heavy glass items.

Procedure

First, the glass fragments should be sorted, for example rim fragments from pieces of the body and base, and laid out as nearly as possible in their correct positions (*Figure 7.23*). Secondly, the broken surfaces are cleaned with acetone on tightly wound cotton wool swabs (US: cotton buds) to remove grease from handling. (Uniform wetting by the acetone often indicates that the adhesive will disperse uniformly.) If the glass is to be repaired with a cellulose nitrate adhesive such as HMG, repair begins by working from the heaviest section, normally the base or rim, and allowing the adhesive on each piece to set before applying the next, or supporting the fragments as described above.

Adhesives which are not available in tube form may be conveniently applied with syringe, cocktail stick or fine paint brush. Tiny fragments of glass can be manipulated with hand-held or vacuum tweezers. André (1976) suggests manipulating fragments by attaching them to a small ball of clay on the end of a stick, but this cannot be recommended since

Figure 7.23 Fragments of glass laid out in order, prior to repair.

Figure 7.24 The last fragment inserted into a closed glass vessel, using a cocktail stick adhered with water-soluble adhesive, as a temporary handle.

the clay may adhere to loosely adhering decoration or flakes of glass, and detach them.

Fragments can be manipulated with hand-held- or vacuum tweezers. Those which fit into a hole can be manoeuvred by attaching a cocktail stick to act as a handle, using water-soluble adhesive (*Figure 7.24*). Fragments of glass which cannot be located should be put in labelled containers and kept with the object. They may be of use for analysis at a later date. Care must be taken not to apply an excessive amount of adhesive to weathered or flaking glass since it will be difficult to remove from the surface. Excess adhesive may be removed with cotton swabs moistened with acetone.

If the glass is sound, and the vessel does not bear vulnerable decoration such as gilding or unfired painting, epoxy resins may be used for its reconstruction. Glass that can be repaired in this way will also need to be able to withstand future removal of the resins by softening and swelling them with commercial paint strippers. These have been traditionally based on dichloromethane, e.g. Nitromors water or solvent miscible systems, or Desolv 292, but are now being phased out of the market in the UK for health and safety reasons, and being replaced with Nitromors Superstrip (based on dimethoxysulphide).

If the glass is to be reconstructed with an epoxy resin, work again proceeds from the heaviest section, using narrow strips of self-adhesive tape placed on alternate sides of the glass to support the fragments, as shown in *Figure 7.21* (assuming that the interior of the

vessel is accessible). Spots of cyanoacrylate resin or of Sticky Wax placed at each end of every break (*Figure 7.21*) will provide temporary support, especially where the interior of the vessel cannot be reached after repair, or when the humidity of the surrounding air is such that it causes tape to peel away from the surface of the glass.

No epoxy resin is applied at this stage and it can thus be ensured that all the fragments fit together accurately, there being no build-up of adhesive to distort the shape. The components of the adhesive to be used are mixed together using a wooden stick (a metal spatula may affect the hardening or the colour of the adhesive). To ensure that the resin hardening has begun before the adhesive is applied to the glass, the mixture is allowed to stand for a few minutes, covering the container to prevent dust from settling in it. The adhesive is then applied along the joins in the assembly with the wooden stick (*Figure 7.25a–c*). Being highly mobile, it seeps into the cracks and by capillary action is drawn along, even behind the thin strips of tape, completely filling the voids.

After about an hour, any excess resin that may have run down the surface of the glass may be removed with cotton wool swabs moistened with acetone. However, over-cleaning with solvent at this stage will weaken the adhesive or even prevent it from setting. It is therefore better to apply the resin sparingly, and to leave the excess to set overnight, before removing small excesses with a scalpel and cotton wool swabs moistened with acetone. In some cases, such as cone-shaped or narrow-necked vessels, where both sides of the vessel are not accessible, it may be necessary to reconstruct the vessel in two halves with tape on both sides. The two halves can then be married together to ensure that they will fit, then separated and epoxy resin applied to the cracks in each half. When this has set, the tape can be removed from the inside and the two halves joined with tape on the outside and secured with adhesive (see *Figures 7.45a,b*).

The effect of heat on glass and glazes generated from, for example, too rapid drying in direct sunlight, or conservation techniques, is unpredictable. For several reasons, notably dehydration of the glass, which may lead to

(a)

(b)

(c)

Figure 7.25 (a) Introducing epoxy resin into breaks in a glass vessel (see Figure 4.2), by capillary action. (b) The two parallel lines across the centre represent each glass surface, the area in between having been filled with epoxy resin, whose refractive index closely matches that of the glass itself. (c) The cracks are only visible as hair-lines.

visible crizzling (Brill, 1975, 1978), or even surface damage (Bimson and Werner, 1964b), any repair using direct heat from a desk lamp or infra-red lamp is not to be recommended. Despite the danger, several techniques for the treatment of glass which involve heating at some stage have been described in the past (Schroder and Kaufman, 1959; Staude, 1972; Wihr, 1968, 1977). It would, however, be acceptable to warm an adhesive before applying it to the glass (but this might cause premature discoloration of the adhesive).

Springing
When thin blown glass breaks, the object may 'spring', i.e. move slightly out of its original shape (see Glass domes below). This is caused by the release of tension created either when the glass was made (particularly in the area of a bowl where the glass has been stretched by blowing, and the tension not removed by annealing) or by hydration of the surface. The result is that the glass fragments do not fit together correctly when reconstructed. Because glass is fragile it may not be possible to make a successful repair using strips of tape, or a tourniquet, to close the gap after the adhesive has been applied, as is sometimes the case with ceramics.

Cracks
Broken glass may be found in a damaged condition in which cracks do not run right through the glass (so-called *running* or *travelling* cracks). Although these may have no effect upon the joining of other fragments unless the glass has sprung out of shape, their presence in a glass artefact is potentially dangerous. As breaks in the glass surface, cracks are points of weakness from which damage may propagate if the artefact is subjected to mechanical or thermal stress. As cracks constitute glass/air/glass interfaces, they present a plane for reflection of light, which is a distraction to the eye and thus detracts from the aesthetic qualities of the object.

Historically, the lengthening of cracks was sometimes arrested by inserting rivets, or by drilling through the glass at a point just beyond their closed end. This action is not recommended for ethical reasons, and because it may result in further damage and in any case results in an unsightly repair similar in

Figure 7.26 An unsightly repair on a heavy cut glass bowl, in which lead-covered wire ties have been used to secure a fragment.

appearance to the repairs shown in *Figures 4.10* and *7.26*.

In order to prevent cracks from lengthening, it is usually possible to introduce a highly mobile epoxy resin into them by capillary action, by applying resin along the cracks with a cocktail stick (see *Figure 7.25a–c*). Bearing in mind the dangers of heating glass mentioned above, it may help the resin to penetrate cracks if the glass is warm. On modern glass, this action can be made more effective if the object is alternately gently heated with a warm air blower and then allowed to cool several times. Of course if cracks can be gently eased open it will be easier to introduce the resin, but this action may cause cracks to lengthen dramatically!

For the repair of cracked, optically clear glass, a close match of refractive indices (RI) is desirable (Tennent and Townsend, 1984a) (see *Figure 5.1* and *Table 5.2*). This might be difficult to obtain for the following reasons: the RI of glass changes with composition; the surface RI of glass changes on weathering and the RI value of a recent crack could be different from that of an old one in the same object. It may be possible to formulate a range of adhesives of different RI values, so that the adhesives could be matched to the glass. However, since adhesives are expected to yellow with age, thus disclosing the area of repair, exact matching may not be important, except in special cases, although Tennent and Townsend (1984a) point out that yellowing of

a crack may not be important when the crack is to be viewed endwise. There is also the ethical consideration of whether cracks should be concealed.

Dowelling

In the case of broken wine glasses or glass figures, it may be necessary to insert an acrylic or glass dowel to strengthen a repair (*Figure 7.27a–e*). This is a potentially dangerous operation since it necessitates the drilling of small holes in the glass, which may cause the glass to fracture. Dowelling cannot therefore be recommended as a general procedure.

Larney (1975) refers to a dowelling technique which involves drilling a hole free-hand into each half of the wine glass stem, and inserting a piece of glass-rod ground down to fit. A problem encountered in using this technique is the difficulty of locating the exact centre of the glass stem, particularly on an uneven surface. Unless the centre point of each half of the broken stem is accurately determined, the dowel cannot be inserted. This can be achieved by placing a small dot of easily removable ink or paint on one side of the stem, and by touching it accurately against the other half, marking it. It is also difficult to ensure that the holes are drilled vertically into the stem. Alternatively, it may be possible to drill oversized holes in the glass stems, to allow some leeway in inserting the dowel. However this risks causing further damage. The minimum thickness of glass rod available is 3.0 mm and in practice this would have to be considerably ground down to be used as a dowel, unless the glass can be heated and drawn out by a glassworker.

The problems associated with this technique were overcome by producing a metal collar on a lathe, which fitted over the stem of the wine glass and through which a central dowel hole could be drilled into the glass (Jackson, 1982a) (*Figure 7.27b*). The size of the hole was reduced by using a 1.0 mm Perspex rod (methyl methacrylate) (US: Plexiglas) as the dowel. Having measured the diameter of the wine glass (the greatest diameter if the stem is not truly round) with a micrometer, (a) a short length of mild steel rod, with a diameter sufficient to enable it to fit over the glass stem to form a sleeve with an adequate radial thickness (*Figure 7.27c*) was placed in a lathe

(a)

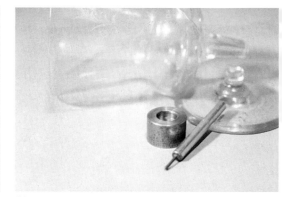

(b)

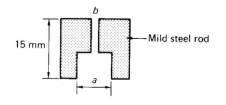

(c)

(e)

(d)

Figure 7.27   (a) A broken stem of a wine glass, which requires the insertion of a dowel to strengthen the repair. (b) A metal collar used to centre the drill on the break edges of the wine glass stem. (c) Section through the metal collar. (d) The use of a diamond-tipped drill to form a dowel-hole in each section of the wine glass stem. (e) The repaired wine glass stem incorporating a Perspex dowel secured with epoxy resin. (Courtesy of P.R. Jackson).

(a)

(c)

(b)

(d)

Figure 7.28 Mounting glass fragments for display or storage. (a) A blown glass form supporting an Islamic bottle. (b) A slumped glass form, shown with the plaster of Paris mould taken from the original glass dish. (c) A Perspex form supporting an Islamic glass lamp. (d) A three-part Perspex mount for enclosing a pane of moulded green window glass from a Roman villa at Garden Hill, Hartfield, East Sussex (after restoration). Upper and right-hand sides grozed. H 255 mm, D 235 mm. (e) A resin cast (mount) on which fragile glass is displayed. (© Copyright The British Museum).

(e)

and faced. The centre point was marked, with a centre bit, and a hole, of a diameter accommodating a 1.0 mm glass drill bit (b), drilled to a depth in excess of 15 mm. This was followed by a drill with the same diameter as the stem (a) and drilled to a depth of 10 mm. The rod was cut to a length of 15 mm, reversed in the lathe and faced. The metal collar was placed over the section of broken stem attached to the foot of the glass. Using a 1.0 mm MM Glazemaster diamond-tipped glass-drill, a hole was drilled into the stem (*Figure 7.27d*). The broken stem attached to the bowl was drilled in the same way. A Perspex rod was cut to the correct length to form a dowel and secured in the holes with epoxy resin, thus bringing the base and bowl of the wine glass together (*Figure 7.27e*). The use of a metal collar as a jig to hold the drill bit in place produced very accurate results. The dowel holes were only 1.0 mm in diameter and were correctly centred, aligned and vertical (Jackson, 1982a).

Mounting fragmentary objects

Objects that are too fragmentary to enable them to be interpreted can be mounted for storage or display. The most aesthetically pleasing mounts are those made from blown glass, acrylic sheets and rod or resin formers (*Figures 7.28a–f*).

Restoration

Restoration (replacement of missing areas with a synthetic resin) may be undertaken to improve the stability of an object such as a glass vessel, to aid in its interpretation, or to improve its appearance for display purposes. If a great deal of the vessel is missing it may not be worth restoring in terms of the time taken to carry out the work, unless the glass is historically important or is of particular value to a collection.

There are a number of factors to be taken into account when considering the restoration of incomplete glass artefacts:

(i)   whether the condition of the glass will permit the work to be undertaken;
(ii) whether such a procedure is desirable on ethical grounds; and
(iii) whether restoration is feasible.

Feasibility is usually determined by the percentage of the object remaining, the shape and thickness of the glass, the condition and type of any applied decoration present (Davison, 1998), and the materials available.

Restoration, as opposed to reconstruction from existing fragments, is essentially a moulding and casting operation. Moulds may be taken from the glass itself or from a modelled clay or Plasticine (US: Plastilina) former representing the missing glass. The moulds are then secured over the area to be replaced and a clear resin is cast into them. The choice of materials is governed by the effect desired from the restoration, cost, availability and properties in relation to the job in hand (Jackson, 1982b, 1984; Davison, 1988, 1998).

Restoration techniques can be conveniently classified as shown below. The techniques are described and illustrated with diagrams and actual case histories: however, it is part of a conservator's task to adapt restoration techniques as required, since each restoration is an individual undertaking.

- Filling losses in opaque glass
- Filling tiny losses
- Partial restoration
- Detachable gap-fills
- Gap-filling with casts from moulds taken from the original glass
- Gap-filling with casts from a mould taken from a clay model or a previous restoration
- Gap-filling where the interior of a vessel is inaccessible for working

Filling losses in opaque glass

Losses in opaque glass can be filled with paste made by mixing optically clear epoxy resin with fumed silica and dry artists' pigments (*Figure 7.29*), or with epoxy putty such as Milliput (UK) coloured with epoxy- or acrylic colours (*Figures 7.30a,b*).

Filling tiny losses

Pressure-sensitive tape can be used as a backing behind tiny areas of loss, such as holes or chips, in order to fill them. A strip of pressure-sensitive tape is fixed across the loss on one side, and a drop of resin applied. When the resin has cured, the tape is removed. Small losses on flat or gently curved glass can be filled by sealing a piece of wax coated with polyvinyl alcohol to the exterior of the glass in such a way as to cover the loss. The object is then supported in a sand tray, so that the area to be filled lies in a horizontal plane, in order that resin can be poured into the gap and find its own level. If the glass is thick-walled, the resin can be poured in one or two thin layers, provided that each layer is only allowed to set, not fully cure, or the layers may not bond to each other.

Partial restoration

Where a glass vessel has large areas missing but does not warrant total reconstruction, for example because of the time involved, or because the object is destined for storage or occasional study, it may be partially restored for safe handling. Strips of glass fibre surfacing tissue cut to size and impregnated with cellulose nitrate adhesive, Paraloid B-72, epoxy- or polyester resins, are used to bridge gaps in the glass and to hold floating fragments in their correct positions. Total reconstruction of small vessels is also possible by this method, with the results shown in *Figure 7.31*. It is not aesthetically pleasing but

Figure 7.29 An opaque glass sculpture restored with coloured epoxy paste.

(a)

(b)

Figure 7.30 An opaque mosaic glass bowl restored with coloured epoxy putty.

Figure 7.31 An Anglo-Saxon claw beaker partially restored with polyester resin and glass-fibre surfacing tissue. (© Copyright The British Museum).

Figure 7.32 A mould made of silicone dental impression compound, and an epoxy resin cast used to replace a missing glass knob on a lid.

may be useful as a temporary measure for study or drawing purposes.

Gap-filling with casts from moulds taken from the original glass

Silicone rubber dental impression compound
Small three-dimensional features on glass, such as knobs, handles and applied decoration such as prunts, can be reproduced by taking a mould with a rapid-setting dental silicone impression compound such as Amsil (UK) from another identical object. The mould is peeled off, or slit, to enable it to be removed, supported in a sand tray and filled with resin. Once the resin has cured, the cast is removed and the ends trimmed to fit the broken glass, to which it is attached with epoxy resin (*Figure 7.32*). The cast usually has a matt finish and can be given a coat of epoxy resin to restore its clarity.

Casting resin into wax or silicone rubber moulds

For replacing all but the smallest missing areas of glass, and glass with surface detail, resin must be cast into a closed mould, made from sheets of dental wax (which is cheap, but does not reproduce very fine detail), or silicone rubber (which is expensive but reproduces fine detail). The moulds are then filled with a synthetic resin to form casts, which replace the missing areas of glass. Once the resin has cured, it can be sanded and polished if necessary, although it can rarely be brought to absolute clarity. Casts can be made of clear resin and be left unpainted, although this

approach may result in their being visually distracting. Alternatively, the casts can be painted by hand, or by airbrush if the glass can be safely masked off, or the resin can be pigmented before being cast.

The manufacturers of epoxy- and polyester resins produce pigmented pastes for colouring the resin. Only a few of these are transparent, and are polyester-based. The colours are intermixable and their brightness can be toned down by the minute addition of black opaque polyester pigment. The coloured pastes are so strong that very little is needed to colour the resin. Consequently, whilst it is not generally recommended to mix resins, it is possible to mix tiny amounts of epoxy pigmented paste with polyester resins, without impairing its curing.

Where coloured resin gap-fills are to be made, it is recommended that a batch of coloured resin be prepared in advance (*Plate 8*). As each cast is made, a small amount of coloured resin is measured out and catalysed. The batch will ensure that exactly the same colour is used for each cast, and that extra resin is available should a cast have to be made more than once. In general it is better to tint the resin to match the original glass as seen by transmitted light, the reasons for this being that the cast will absorb colour from the surrounding glass (especially if original glass is also behind the cast glass, e.g. in the case of a bottle). Also if the cast is made to match the colour of glass seen by reflected light, it will appear too dense (*Plate 9*).

Wax moulds

Where the gap to be filled is the edge of a rim or foot of an object, a two-part wax mould, open at the edge, is made from small pieces of dental wax (*Figures 7.33* and *7.34a–j*). Without touching the flat surfaces of the wax sheets, so as not to mark them, two pieces of wax, slightly larger than the area to be gap-filled, are cut, and slightly softened with a hot air blower (or in warm water). It is then gently pressed over an existing area of glass – one on the inside and one on the outside of the vessel – which conforms to the same shape as the missing area (i.e. is on the same horizontal plane) (*Figures 7.34* and *7.35a*). If the wax is over-heated so that its surface becomes tacky, it will adhere to the

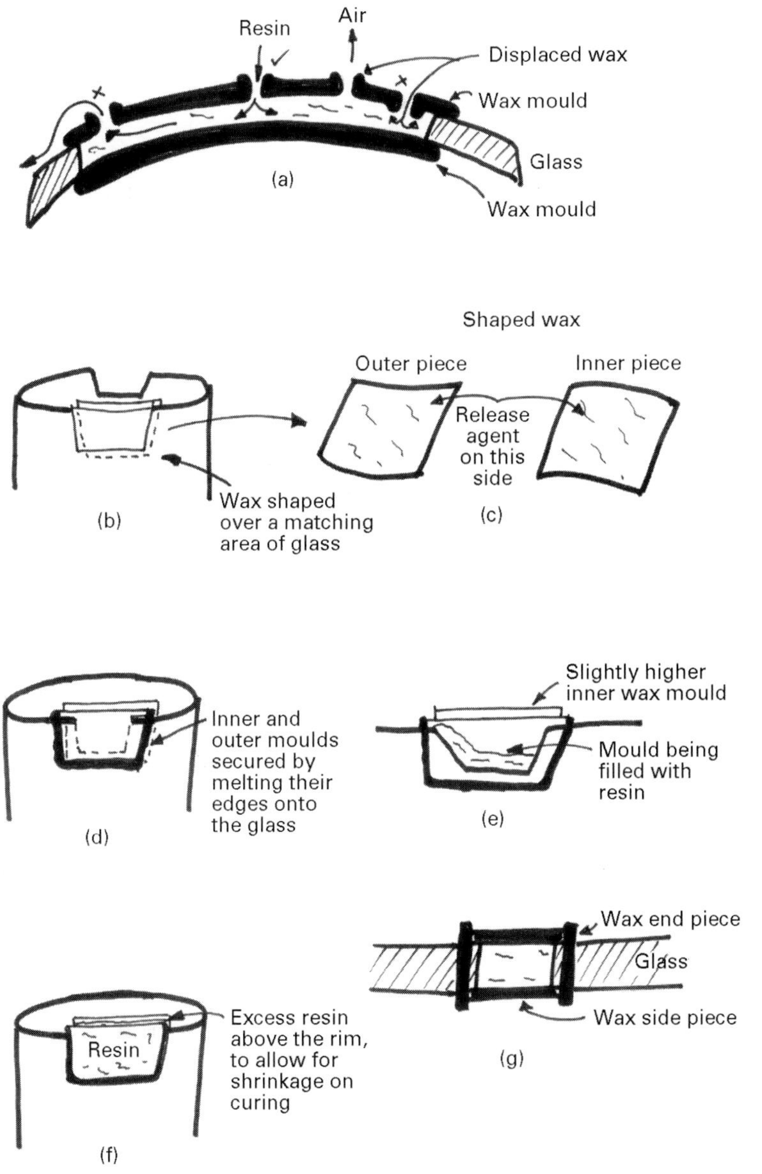

Figure 7.33 Stages in constructing a wax mould. (a) A section through a two-part wax mould. (b) Shaping wax over matching areas of glass. (c) Coating the wax with release agent. (d) The edges of the wax melted with a heated spatula, to seal it to the glass surface. (e) Resin introduced to the mould. (f) Excess resin above the rim of the glass to allow for shrinkage. (g) Plan view of a wax mould made on a thick glass object, which requires ends, to form a dam to contain resin.

glass and tear when removed. The sides of the wax, which will be in contact with the resin, are brushed with a solution of polyvinyl alcohol, to which has been added one or two drops of a non-ionic detergent to break its surface tension. (Otherwise the separating agent has a tendency to collect in pools on the wax – *Figure 7.34c.*) The application of the separating agent facilitates easier removal of the wax after the resin has cured, but also prevents colour from the pink or red wax being absorbed by the resin.

When this has dried, the wax piece forming the inside of the mould is fixed in position by running the point of a small electrically heated spatula around its edges (*Figure 7.34d*). The closeness of the fit of the wax against the glass can be checked at this point and, if necessary, improved by slightly warming the wax and pressing it against the glass. Care must be

(a)

(b)

(c)

(d)

(e)

(f)

Figure 7.34 The neck of a whisky dispenser restored by casting resin into a wax mould. (a) A missing section of rim. (b) Two pieces of wax cut to shape, warmed and shaped by pressing it onto the glass, one piece on either side. (c) The sides of the wax which will be next to the resin, coated with release agent. (d) Wax sheet secured to the interior of the glass. (e) Wax sheet being sealed to the exterior of the glass, by melting the edge with a heated spatula. (f) Mould being filled with resin. (g) Removing the exterior sheet of wax. (h) Removing the interior sheet of wax. (i) The resin cast before final cleaning with white spirit. (j) The completed restoration.

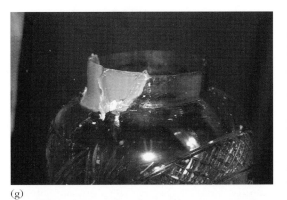

(g)

(h)

(i)

(j)

taken not to distort the wax by pressing it where it is unsupported by the glass. The wax forming the outside of the mould is then fixed in position with the heated spatula (*Figure 7.34e*). It is difficult but important to ensure that the wax fits tightly against the glass, or the resin, when introduced, will seep over the glass leaving a large amount to be cleaned off after the mould is removed. The resin is poured into the mould, through which it can be seen (*Figure 7.34f*). Once the resin has set, the wax is carefully removed (*Figure 7.34g,h*), by releasing the edges with the tip of a metal spatula, and then peeling it off.

Wax remaining on the glass and cast should be removed with the spatula or fingernail taking care not to scratch the surface. The surface can then be wiped with swabs of cotton wool and white spirit (US: Stoddart solvent) to remove the last vestiges of wax (*Figure 7.34i*). Any polyvinyl alcohol which has remained on the cast can be removed with water. The top of the resin cast is then

trimmed and if necessary abraded and polished (*Figure 7.34j*) (Staude, 1972; Davison, 1998).

Generally speaking, if the cast is found to be too thick, resulting in a step around the edges, it is better to remove the cast and start again. If the step is on the inside of a vessel made of dark glass, or with a narrow neck, where it will not be seen, there is no need to remove the cast. Although it is possible to abrade a resin cast as described below, it requires a great deal of time and the cast can never be brought to the clarity of unworked resin. Excesses of resin above the rim or foot can be removed by the careful use of a dental drill and burs, and if necessary, lightly filed and sanded, though care must be taken not to crack the cast or separate it from the glass by applying too great a pressure. If the cast should become separated from the glass, it can be reattached with adhesive, provided that the adhesive is not allowed to spread onto and mark the surface of the cast.

After sanding with progressively finer grades of abrasive such as Micromesh, the surface may be polished using a fine abrasive paste such as Solvol Autosol, on a small buffing wheel held in the drill-head. (However, care must be taken in the use of abrasive pastes, since they may become irremovably trapped in small deficiencies in the cast such as air bubbles, or at the junction between the cast and original glass.) During any operation involving the use of a dental drill, it is wise to step down the current with a rheostat in order to prevent friction from melting the surface of the resin, and to prevent the restored object from being accidentally spun out of the conservator's hands.

In cases where the area to be filled lies within the main body of the glass, a different method of filling the mould has to be adopted. The wax moulds are shaped as described above and the piece of wax which will form the inner side of the mould, coated with polyvinyl alcohol and secured to the glass by melting its edges. Before applying release agent to the piece of wax which will form the outer side of the mould, small airhole(s) and a slightly larger pour-hole are made through the wax, at the highest point of its curve. The holes are made by pushing a small metal prong through the wax, from the concave side, which ensures that the displaced wax from the holes is on the outside of the mould (see *Figure 7.35*). The pour-hole is then carefully enlarged with a scalpel, and the wax

forming the outside of the mould is fixed in position with a heated spatula.

The mould is filled with resin dripped into the pour-hole from a wooden cocktail stick or metal spatula. If the area to be filled is complex, with several undercuts, the mould may take time to fill. It may be helpful to attach a small funnel made of aluminium foil to the edge of the pour-hole with a heated spatula. The glass is supported with the funnel uppermost in the sand-tray, and the resin poured into the funnel (or directly into the mould), until it begins to seep out of the airholes. At this point the funnel may be broken off so that excess resin does not continue to flow out over the surface of the glass. (It may sometimes be possible to use a medical syringe without the needle to introduce resin into the mould, but it is not easy to control the flow of the resin, or to prevent the introduction of air bubbles.) Once the resin has fully cured, the wax mould is carefully removed, taking care not to mark the cast. The cast is then cleaned and if necessary trimmed and polished (see *Figure 7.34j*; see also *Plate 5*).

Domes

Glass domes were made from the eighteenth century onwards in France to encase glass figurines (such as those made at Nevers and elsewhere), and in other parts of Europe to protect clocks from dust and grime, thereby helping to ensure accurate timekeeping. In

Figure 7.35 A hole in a globular glass lampshade, restored by dripping resin through a small hole in the outer side of a two-piece wax mould.

Figure 7.36 Missing section of a glass dome restored by casting resin into a mould made of a double thickness of dental wax.

nineteenth-century England, numerous large domes (or shades) were made to protect ornamental displays of wax fruits, artificial flowers, flowers made of shells, stuffed birds and animals, glass ships and elaborate 'bird fountains'.

Domes were made by the broad (cylinder) glass process. A bubble of glass was worked into a rounded cylindrical shape, one end of which was cut and the other left dome-shaped, the whole being given a smooth finish by re-heating it before the final annealing process. Domes continue to be made, but usually on a smaller scale, and tend to be circular in shape.

Antique glass domes are difficult to repair and restore. Some are very large and their general shape, flat on two sides, with curved ends and a domed top, make them difficult to handle and to support whilst undergoing repair. In addition the glass tends to be thin and brittle, and to spring out of shape when broken. Glass domes can be repaired with epoxy resin, and missing areas restored with polyester embedding resin cast between sheets of wax, coated on one side with a separating agent. If the restoration is being carried out on a curved part of the dome, it may be necessary to construct the mould using two sheets of glass on either side. This has the effect of strengthening the mould, and thus preventing the wax sheets from being sucked together as the resin cures (*Figure 7.36*). It is sometimes possible to obtain replacement domes from a specialist company, which keeps a stock of antique domes or the original moulds.

Silicone rubber moulds

Wax is generally unsuitable for moulding surfaces with intricate detail, those which are two-dimensional, e.g. deeply cut glass, or which curve sharply both from top to bottom and from side to side. In these instances, and where the area of loss is larger than dental wax sheets, silicone rubber can be used to make the moulds (*Figure 7.37a–b*). Where the loss is at the glass rim or the edge of a foot, a thin coating of catalysed silicone rubber is poured over the rim and both sides of an intact section of the glass vessel, covering an area slightly larger than that which is to be replaced (*Figure 7.38a–e*). The rubber will run very thin at the glass edge so that the glass

can be seen through it, nevertheless it will have coated the surface.

When this has cured, a second layer of silicone rubber, mixed to a stiff consistency with an inert filler such as silicone matting agent (e.g. Santocel), is applied over the first layer to strengthen it and to prevent the rubber from tearing when it is eventually removed. However, the silicone rubber layer should not be so thick as to prevent it from being slightly flexible. When the silicone rubber has cured, a slit is made in the mould along the rim with a scalpel. The slit can be as wide and as long as possible provided that the mould will remain intact at either end. The sealed ends will locate the mould on the glass rim on either side of the area of loss. Opening up the mould in this way will prevent air bubbles from being trapped in the cast. The slit is made at this stage, for if it were made after the mould was in position over the gap, the mould might be inadvertently cut below the level of the glass rim, or loose pieces of rubber might fall into the cavity.

The mould is then removed from the glass by loosening it on both sides and slowly peeling it off, and is secured over the missing area as follows, using silicone rubber as an 'adhesive'. A small amount of catalysed silicone rubber is applied around both sides of the missing area of glass and over the edge, taking care that the amount of rubber and its proximity to the gap does not result in rubber running onto the break edges when the moulds are replaced (*Figure 7.38b*). When the rubber 'adhesive' has cured, more silicone rubber, mixed to a stiff consistency with fumed silica, can be applied around the edges of the mould, as a secondary line of defence against resin escaping from the mould. Resin is then dripped or poured through the slit into the mould, which is occasionally slowly and gently squeezed to expel the air (taking care not to introduce air). The process is repeated until the mould is full. It may be necessary to add a little more resin, just before it gels, to compensate for a small amount of shrinkage. The resin is then allowed to set, after which the mould is removed and any necessary finishing work carried out to the cast (*Figure 7.38c,d*).

Where a missing area is a hole in the main body of the glass vessel, a comparable area of

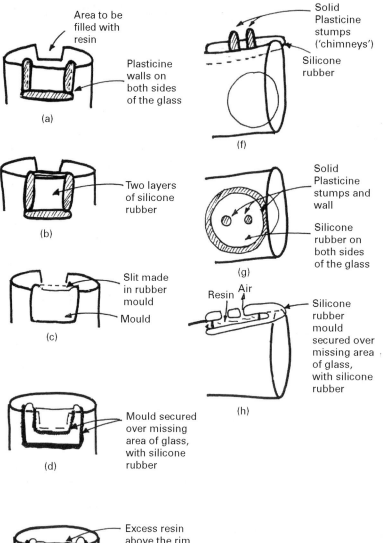

Figure 7.37 Stages in the construction of a silicone rubber mould. (a) An area of glass outlined with a Plasticine wall. (b) Application of a thin layer of silicone rubber, followed by a thick second layer. (c) Plasticine removed, and a slit made in the top of the mould. (d) Mould peeled off the glass and secured over the area to be filled. (e) Resin poured into the mould. (f) Similar process where the missing area is in the body of the vessel. (g) Stumps of Plasticine, which will form (h) pour- and airholes through the mould.

the vessel will have to be moulded both inside and out with silicone rubber. The moulds are then peeled off and attached over the missing area, using uncured silicone rubber. A hole is made with a scalpel through the silicone rubber on one side of the vessel (normally that on the outside for ease of working), and the resin is introduced as described above. Alternatively, two thin clay stumps, or chimneys formed from paper or plastic drinking straws, can be attached to the glass before the mould is made. These when eventually removed will have formed holes through the silicone rubber mould. A similar approach can be taken in the case of an uneven rim, in order to form pour-and airholes in a mould (*Figures 7.39a,b*). Rigid materials such as Perspex should not be used in this way, as they will prove difficult to remove from the silicone rubber.

(a)

(b)

(c)

(d)

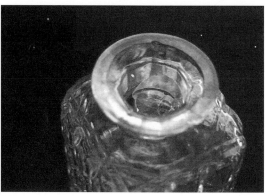

(e)

Figure 7.38 Restoration of the rim of a decanter. (a) Silicone rubber used to form a mould over an area of glass similar to that to be replaced. (b) A thin strip of silicone rubber trailed close to the broken edge, on both sides of the glass, in order to secure the silicone rubber mould. (c) The silicone rubber mould secured over the area to be filled. Note the slit in the rim, through which the mould will be filled with resin, and through which air will escape. (d) The polyester resin cast after finishing and polishing. (e) Close-up view of the restored rim.

(a)   (b)

Figure 7.39   (a) Clay chimneys placed on the edge of the existing glass form pour- and airholes through the silicone wax mould. (b) The completed restoration using polyester resin to replace the missing area of glass.

A more complicated version of the silicone rubber moulding technique had to be devised in order to restore the Auldjo Jug, a cameo glass on display in the British Museum (*Figures 7.40a–l*). This vessel has a narrow neck and therefore access to the interior for moulding purposes was severely restricted (Jackson, 1985). The jug had been broken at some time in its past and a considerable amount of the body was missing. It had previously been repaired, probably with animal glue, and gap-filled with plaster of Paris coloured dark blue to match the remaining glass. The plaster restoration had become damaged and unsightly and it was therefore decided to remove the plaster in order to effect a more accurate, light-weight and aesthetically pleasing restoration. In order to achieve this it was necessary to produce two silicone rubber moulds, which conformed to the inner and outer profiles of the jug. Since the plaster was actually dimensionally correct, it was repaired, and a silicone rubber mould made over it. The positions of funnels through which to introduce resin into the area at present occupied by the plaster was decided upon. To form them, plastic drinking straws were attached to the plaster with small lumps of Aloplast (a modelling compound similar to Plasticine, but especially formulated for use with polyester resins).

The globular shape of the Auldjo Jug determined that the outer silicone rubber mould would have to be made in two sections in order to facilitate its removal from the vessel. To contain the uncured rubber, a wall of Aloplast was laid over the glass surface so that it divided the jug into two sections. A thin strip of lead wire was embedded in one side of the wall to form a key in order to reposition the mould accurately prior to casting the resin (*Figure 7.40a*). The jug was then laid on its side and a thin layer of silicone rubber was brushed over the uppermost side thus covering the previous restoration and remaining glass fragments. When the silicone rubber had cured it was reinforced with glass fibre woven matting and a second layer of silicone rubber. The jug was then turned over and supported with the opposite side uppermost. The

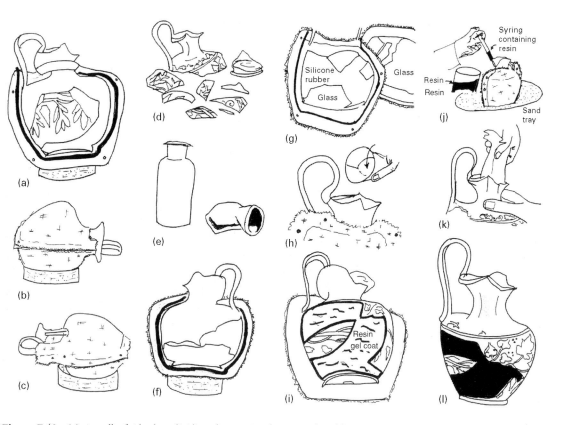

Figure 7.40 (a) A wall of Aloplast dividing the previously restored Auldjo Jug into two sections; and incorporating a thin lead strip to form a key. The thin wooden sticks will form holes through the mould into which small nuts and bolts will be inserted to secure the mould pieces during the casting process. (b) The completed silicone rubber mould. (c) Completed glass fibre mother-mould secured by nuts and bolts; and incorporating plastic straws to form pour- and airholes. (d) Fragments of the Auldjo Jug after removal of the old restoration. (e) Comparison of different types of silicone rubber, from which an inner mould is to be made: Silicoset 105 (left) and Rhodorsil 11504A (right). (f) Fragments of the Auldjo Jug repositioned in one half of the outer mould, showing the extent of the missing areas of glass. (g) Missing areas of glass filled with Aloplast. (h) Forming the inner mould with silicone rubber. (i) Coloured polyester rigid laminating resin coating the inner silicone rubber mould to prevent the next layer of resin from seeping between the mould and the glass. (j) Introducing the coloured polyester embedding resin from a syringe. (k) Removal of the silicone rubber mould. (l) Completed restoration of the Auldjo Jug after polishing the resin cast.

Aloplast wall was removed and polyvinyl alcohol painted along the exposed edge of silicone rubber to act as a separating agent between it and the second part of the mould which was made as previously described (*Figure 7.40b*). A two-piece mother mould was then made over the silicone rubber using rigid polyester laminating resin strengthened with heavy grade glass fibre matting. Small holes were made through the flanges of the mould pieces where they joined each other in order to incorporate nuts and bolts, which would secure the mould during the casting process (*Figure 7.40c*). This completed the construction of the outer mould, which was then carefully dismantled and removed from the jug. The adhesive and plaster used in the previous restoration was easily removed from the glass fragments by soaking the jug in warm water (*Figure 7.40d*).

Since access to the interior was restricted it was not possible to make or to remove a mould of the interior profile in the same manner as the outer moulds. Therefore a different method had to be devised. The completed mould would have to be thin and flexible enough to be pulled out through the narrow neck after the restoration was complete; firm enough to support the weight of the glass neck and handle of the jug during restoration; and capable of adhering to the inner surface of the glass fragments in order to prevent resin from flowing behind them. In order to choose a moulding material that would fulfil these criteria, a number of experiments were carried out using a narrow-necked laboratory jug to represent the Auldjo Jug. After several attempts at filling a toy balloon with air, sand or water, it was found to be impossible to fit the balloon closely against the sides of the bottle.

A method was then devised to produce a rubber skin similar to the balloon, but which conformed closely to the inner surface of the bottle. For this purpose several different grades of silicone rubber and rubber latex were tested. Each rubber moulding material was poured into a bottle, which was then slowly rotated so that a thin skin formed over the interior, before the excess rubber was poured out through the neck. The rubber was then left to cure and the resulting mould pulled out of the bottle, thus testing the tear strength of the rubber. Other observations made were the extent to which the material had coated the inside of the bottle, and the ease with which the rubber could be removed. As a result of these tests, two brands of silicone rubber were selected for further testing: Silcoset 105 and Rhodorsil 11504A, although neither product possessed all the required qualities (*Figure 7.40e*). Silcoset 105 was extremely fluid, coated the glass surface well and was self-supporting. However, when cured it was rather rigid and thus proved difficult to remove from the bottle. The addition of silicone oil as a thinner produced a less rigid mould but considerably reduced the tear strength of the Silcoset 105. Rhodorsil 11504A produced a very thin, flexible mould which was easily removed from the bottle but which was not self-supporting. Various attempts were made to support the mould in situ by filling the bottle with sand, water or vermiculite granules, of which the latter proved to be the most successful. Vermiculite had the advantages of being dry,

extremely light, easy to use, and, although the granules tended to compress slightly, easy to remove. Rhodorsil 11504A supported by vermiculite granules were therefore chosen as the materials from which to make the interior mould.

The fragments of the Auldjo Jug were coated with polyvinyl alcohol to prevent excess resin from adhering to them during the casting, and were reconstructed using Ablebond 342-1 (epoxy resin, no longer available), and laid in one half of the outer mould (*Figure 7.40f*). Areas of the jug from which the glass was missing were then filled with Aloplast which was modelled and smoothed to represent the thickness of the original glass (*Figure 7.40g*). Fragments of glass which overlapped the edge of the mould, (i.e. which overlapped into the other half of the mould) were carefully removed without disturbing the Aloplast model. These and other remaining fragments were laid in the second half of the outer mould and the areas of missing glass filled with Aloplast as previously described. The two sections of the silicone rubber mould and the glass fibre outer mould were then brought together and located in their correct positions by means of the keys incorporated in their adjoining edges, and secured with small nuts and bolts. The interior of the jug was then inspected with the aid of a small dental mirror to ensure that the glass fragments and Aloplast had remained undisturbed. The seam-line between the modelling compound in the two halves of the mould was smoothed down on the inside using a Perspex tool made especially for the purpose.

Rhodorsil 11504A was then poured into the jug through the neck opening and the vessel slowly rotated so that the rubber flowed over the interior completely covering the glass and Aloplast (*Figure 7.40h*). Excess rubber was then allowed to drain out by inverting the mould. When the Rhodorsil 11504A had cured the interior of the vessel was again inspected to ensure that the rubber had completely covered it, after which the jug was packed with vermiculite granules to support the mould during the casting process. At this stage the jug with its missing sections temporarily replaced with Aloplast was totally enclosed between two moulds. The next step was to remove the Aloplast and to replace it with polyester resin. In order for this to be achieved, one half of the outer mould was carefully dismantled so that the Aloplast could be removed carefully with a spatula thus exposing the inner rubber mould surface. This was cleaned with acetone, and a thin layer of polyester gel coat (a thixotropic paste), which had been coloured with blue polyester pigment paste was brushed over the mould and over the broken edges of the glass (*Figure 7.40i*). The outer mould was then replaced and the process repeated on the other half of the jug. The two sections of the mould were then again bolted together. This procedure ensured that the gel coat resin was in close contact with the inner mould and the edges of the glass fragments, and that the casting resin would be less able to flow behind the remaining glass.

A batch of clear polyester resin was coloured with opaque blue polyester pigment to match the glass. The bulk of the resin was catalysed and introduced to the mould from a syringe through the plastic straws incorporated in the outer mould to form funnels for this purpose (*Figure 7.40j*). A small amount of the coloured resin was kept un-catalysed in order to effect any necessary repairs to the cast. Air bubbles in the resin were encouraged to rise and to escape through other straws forming airholes by gently tapping the mould. The resin was then allowed to cure for three days before removing the exterior mould. The vermiculite granules were poured out of the jug and the inner rubber mould removed in one piece (*Figure 7.40k*).

Excess resin on the outer surface of the cast in the form of seam-lines and stumps which had formed in the pour- and airholes was removed with a small metal grinding wheel attached to a flexible drive drill. Tiny faults in the cast in the form of holes caused by trapped air bubbles were filled using coloured resin applied with a syringe. When the resin had fully cured the restored areas were polished to a glossy finish using a felt polishing buff attached to the dental drill, and Solvol Autosol, a mild abrasive paste (*Figure 7.40l*). In the case of simple globular shapes, it may be possible to use a toy balloon to form an inner mould.

Replacement by casts from a mould taken from a clay model or a previous restoration

Clay models
In the case of glass vessels having extensive, or more complex, missing areas, or where a raised design must be copied, a former is constructed of modelling clay on to which the remaining fragments are placed. The missing part of the design is modelled in the clay, and the entire assembly is then moulded, after which the clay is removed in order that resin may be cast into the areas of missing glass (*Figures 7.41 and 7.42a–d*). *Figure 7.41* shows the restoration of a missing section of applied decoration on a Saxon cone beaker. *Figure 7.42a* shows a group of Roman glass vessels, which were restored by modelling the missing areas in clay and then moulding and casting them.

The first step is to make any joins in the original glass. For this a cellulose nitrate adhesive such as HMG will suffice, because the various processes that follow will cause the fragments to part, and the adhesive will be easy to remove. The fragments are then placed over a former of clay, which may be turned or modelled up by hand, on a sheet of plate glass on a turn-table (*Figure 7.42b*). The area of plate glass around the model is coated

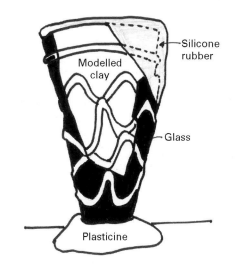

Figure 7.41 The missing section of an Anglo-Saxon cone vessel, modelled in clay, prior to being moulded.

(a)

(b)

(c)

(d)

Figure 7.42   (a) A group of Roman glass vessels restored by modelling their missing sections in clay, making silicone rubber moulds and casting in the missing areas with resin. (b) Remaining fragments mounted on a clay former. (c) After moulding the exterior, the assembly is inverted, and the clay removed. (d) A thin layer of clay replacing the missing glass.

with Vaseline or liquid soap to ease the eventual removal of the mould. It is usually better to invert the glass vessel so that the even rim rests on the plate glass and the vessel does not bear the weight of the clay. Where fragments are missing, the clay is built up to the outer surface of the glass and any modelling of the design is carried out, loose fragments being floated into the design. If necessary, two clay stumps are attached at the highest point of the clay model, which will eventually form pour- and airholes through the mould.

A mould of the entire structure is then made. Silicone rubber is poured over the whole assembly, to form a thin layer, ensuring that it entirely covers the glass and clay.

A wall of clay can be laid around the glass, about 20 mm from it, to contain the flow of rubber. When the rubber has cured, a second layer, mixed to a stiff consistency with an inert filler, is applied over the first layer to strengthen it and to prevent the rubber from tearing when it is eventually removed, but ensuring that the mould remains slightly flexible (*Figure 7.42f*). (If the object being restored is relatively small, with no great curvature, the silicone rubber layer may suffice, so that a supporting plaster of Paris or resin mother-mould will not be needed.) When the silicone rubber has cured, the mould is carefully peeled off the plate glass and inverted. Taking care not to disturb the glass fragments attached to the interior of the mould, the clay

(e) Moulding the interior. (f) Removal of the interior mould. (g) Interior mould secured with silicone rubber, and resin introduced through a gap at the front edge. (h) The completed restoration.

is removed from the interior, except for a thin layer, which fills the missing areas of the vessel *(Figure 7.42d,e)*. The top edges of the rubber mould are coated with a release agent such as Vaseline, and a silicone rubber mould made of the interior of the vessel, as described above *(Figure 7.42f)*.

When the rubber has cured, the mould is removed, followed by the remaining clay, again not disturbing the glass fragments. Water on cotton wool swabs is used to remove final traces of clay from the glass edges. Fragments that do become dislodged can be replaced using a small amount of silicone rubber as an 'adhesive'. Faults in the mould can be made good by filling them with clay and sealing them with polyvinyl alcohol release agent

(Figure 7.42g). The surface of the glass is coated with polyvinyl release agent, following which the interior mould is replaced and sealed to the outer mould with silicone rubber. This will prevent the mould from floating when the resin is introduced *(Figure 7.42h)*. Once the resin has cured, the moulds are removed and any finishing of the cast carried out *(Figure 7.42i)*.

Moulds made around large or heavy clay models and glass objects *(Figure 7.43a)* may require the addition of a plaster of Paris mother-mould *(Figure 7.43b–d)*, about 40 mm thick, constructed with a flat top, so that it will stand safely when inverted. (Note that a spherical shape cannot be moulded in plaster of Paris in fewer than three pieces since the

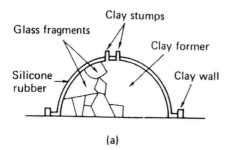

(a)

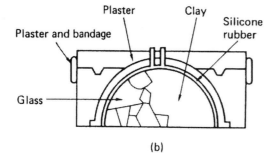

(b)

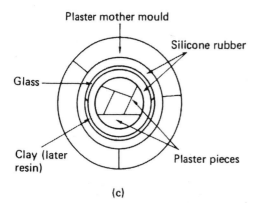

(c)

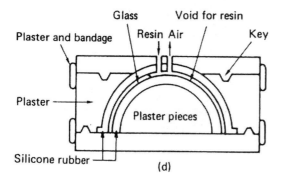

(d)

curvature would prevent its removal – *Figure 7.43b.*) No release agents are required either between the glass and the silicone rubber or between the silicone rubber and the plaster, but a release agent such as Vaseline or liquid soap is required between the plaster pieces, and between them and the plate-glass. The plaster pieces should be numbered in order of manufacture since they will be removed in reverse order, and, on completion, the plaster pieces are secured to one another with cotton bandage or scrim dipped in plaster of a creamy consistency. When the plaster has set, the whole assemblage is inverted on to its flat top (which thus becomes the base). The silicone rubber flange is trimmed back to the inner edge of the plaster, and the bulk of the clay former removed with a spatula, taking care not to dislodge any of the glass fragments now supported in the silicone rubber mould. If any fragments are loosened, they should be reattached with silicone rubber (see below). Clay is left in the areas of missing glass and smoothed with a spatula until it is level with the inner surface of the vessel, i.e. representing the missing glass. Vaseline is applied to the top edge of the silicone rubber mould and a thin layer of silicone rubber poured over the interior. When this has set, a second thickened layer is applied as before, and a 10 mm wide flange modelled up at the rim.

The interior of the vessel is filled with a plaster piece-mould in order to support the silicone rubber, and on which to key a plaster lid on which the mould will stand during casting. *Figure 7.43c* demonstrates the way in which the plaster pieces should be constructed, chamfering the edges of each piece so that they do not overlap one another. To ensure that these plaster pieces can eventually be removed easily, each one should be removed after it has set, sealed with shellac,

Figure 7.43 Diagrams showing (a) a silicone rubber mould over a missing area of glass which has been modelled in clay; (b) the construction of a plaster of Paris mother-mould over the silicone rubber mould; (c) the construction of a plaster of Paris piece-mould over the silicone rubber inside the vessel; and (d) the completed plaster of Paris mother-mould.

and Vaseline (white petroleum jelly) applied as a release agent before casting the next piece against it. The tops of the pieces must be flush with the top edge of the rubber and the outer mother-mould, except for the centre piece which should project for ease of removal. (This being the last piece made, will be the first to be removed.) The top edges of the interior plaster piece-mould, and the mother-mould, are given a coat of shellac and Vaseline. Plaster of a creamy consistency is then applied over the top area in order to form the lid about 40 mm thick.

When the plaster has set, the lid is removed, followed by the inner piece-mould, the inner rubber mould (which may have to be slit with a scalpel and later resealed with silicone rubber), and the clay. On no account should the mother-mould be disturbed. Every trace of clay must be removed with moist swabs of cotton wool, and any loose fragments of glass rejoined with HMG.

It is very likely that floating fragments of glass may become loose at this stage. The only satisfactory method of replacing them is to use silicone rubber as an adhesive (for this purpose it may be overcatalysed to save time) and to wait for this to set before proceeding with the restoration. When all the fragments are secure in the mould, a 5 mm wide, normal mixture of silicone rubber is painted around the areas of the missing glass, leaving a 25 mm gap between the silicone rubber and the edges. The inner silicone rubber mould is then replaced before the silicone rubber sets and the strip of silicone rubber seals it to the glass surface (the 25 mm gap from the edge of the break is to allow for the liquid rubber to spread out during replacement of the mould). This prevents resin seeping into the gap created by removing the mould and breaking the suction between it and the glass. This is extremely important since the resin finds its way into the smallest gap.

Next, the upper edges of the silicone rubber moulds are degreased with a tissue and sealed together with a normal mixture of silicone rubber; this again is to prevent resin seepage. When the silicone rubber has set the plaster pieces are replaced, followed by the lid, which is sealed to the mother-mould with plaster and bandage as previously described. The whole assemblage is then inverted and catalysed

resin is poured into the mould through one hole until it appears in the other, indicating that the mould is full (*Figure 7.43d*). When this occurs, the resin is left to cure, after which the mould can be dismantled and the glass and cast removed together. Any joins that come apart are remade with HMG or, if the condition of the glass allows, it may be reconstructed using epoxy resin.

Previous restoration

If a previous restoration needs replacement for aesthetic reasons, but is dimensionally accurate, a mould may be taken from it before it is removed (see restoration of the Auldjo Jug, described above). This will dispense with the need to model-up the missing area in clay or Plasticine. *Figure 7.44* illustrates such a case, in which only the base, and half the circumference, had remained of a blue glass pyx. The earlier restoration had consisted of filling the remains with plaster of Paris, shaping it to the original dimensions and colouring it blue to match the glass. The restoration was heavy and obscured the interior of the jar, and therefore it was decided to remove the plaster and to replace it with a more aesthetically pleasing polyester resin. However, since the restoration was dimensionally correct, a mould was taken from the plaster prior to its removal.

Figure 7.44 Small blue glass pyx restored by filling it with plaster of Paris, painted to match the colour of the remaining glass.

The pyx was inverted on a piece of plate glass, and thickened silicone rubber poured over it to a thickness of 15 mm. Once the silicone rubber had cured, it was slit down one side, using a sharp scalpel, to allow the glass to be released. The slit was carefully cut against the original glass so that when the slit was later joined using silicone rubber as 'adhesive', a seam mark would not be left in the cast. Meanwhile, the plaster of Paris was removed from the glass by soaking in water, followed by the use of a scalpel. Once the glass fragments were clean and dry, joins were made with a cellulose nitrate adhesive. The glass was then replaced in the mould in its correct position and the missing area of glass filled with pieces of toughened dental wax, cut to shape and melted together where necessary using a heated spatula. (The wax happened to be exactly the same thickness as the walls of the vessel.) A short length of acrylic rod (Perspex; US: Plexiglas) was fixed at each end of the wax (by softening the wax) to form holes through to the interior mould which was to be constructed. (Plastic drinking straws or wax stumps would have been a better choice, as the rigid Perspex rods proved extremely difficult to release from the silicone rubber.) The top edge of the silicone rubber was greased with Vaseline to act as a separating agent, and thickened silicone rubber applied to the interior to a thickness of 15 mm. The relative positions of the two mould pieces were marked, by drawing lines across the joint with a felt-tip pen.

Once the silicone rubber had set, it was removed, followed by the acrylic rods and dental wax. At this stage several of the joins made in the original glass broke down and had to be remade with HMG. The glass was again inserted in the outer mould and the inner mould placed in position. The two moulds were sealed using catalysed silicone rubber around their junction to prevent resin escaping. Tiranti's clear polyester embedding resin, coloured with blue translucent pigment, was then poured into the mould through one hole until it began to appear at the other, thus indicating that the mould was full. After a few minutes the resin had settled in the mould and it was topped up. When the resin had set, the joint between the two moulds was slit with a scalpel, and the inner mould was released.

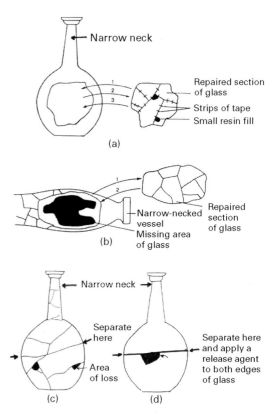

Figure 7.45   Repair of glass objects with narrow necks, where the interior is inaccessible. (a) A section of glass pieced together *in situ*, taped and bonded, then removed and gap-filled, replaced and bonded. (b) A repaired section of glass removed from the side of a vessel, in order to gain access to the opposite side, which requires gap-filling. (c) A repaired object separated above an area of loss, to enable gap-filling to be carried out. (d) A repaired object separated along the edge of a missing area, to enable gap-filling to be carried out.

The two resin stumps, left in the pour- and airholes, were abraded away with a drill and the circles left in the resin were polished until they were hardly visible.

By leaving the glass and cast in the outer mould during these operations it was hoped to prevent vibration causing separation of the cast from the glass fragments, but once the outer mould was slit open, the glass and cast separated from one another as they were removed. This was turned to advantage because a thin layer of resin had seeped behind the glass in the mould. This was easily

(a)

(b)

Figure 7.46 (a) Broken Roman glass flask with a narrow neck, which makes the interior inaccessible for working purposes. (b) Completed restoration of the vessel. (c) Closer view of the restored area of the vessel.

(c)

released from the glass using a scalpel, and could be detached from the now separate cast, which could be polished before joining it to the original glass, with epoxy resin.

Gap-filling where the interior of the vessel is inaccessible for working

If the vessel to be restored has a narrow neck, so that the interior cannot be reached, it will be necessary to adopt special methods of restoration (*see Figure 7.45a–d and 7.46a–c*). If the vessel is damaged only in the body, that is, the neck has not become detached, the fragments must be taped in position and epoxy resin introduced to all the cracks except those around the perimeter of the damaged area. Care has to taken to ensure that the resin does not flow to the perimeter, which can be

given a coat of PVA release agent, to ensure that the two parts of the object can be separated after the resin has cured.

Once the resin has set, the damaged area can be removed as one piece, missing areas within it backed with tape, wax or silicone rubber, depending upon their size, and filled with resin. When the resin has hardened and any necessary cleaning has been carried out, the repaired section may be taped in position on the vessel, and the perimeter cracks sealed (*Figure 7.45a and 7.46a–c*).

If, however, the vessel is much damaged, and has a large area of glass missing from the body, it may still be possible to reconstruct it with epoxy resin as described above, leaving a large area unglued around the edges so that it can be removed (*Figure 7.45b*). This allows access to the interior of the vessel for ease of working. When gap-filling of the missing glass is complete, the glass can be replaced and the perimeter cracks sealed. In the case of a tall glass amphora, a sheet of dental wax was shaped over the outside of the glass, coated with polyvinyl alcohol, and then transferred to cover the missing area and fixed there by running a warm spatula around its edges. A large area of glass was removed from the opposite side of the vessel to enable work to continue in the interior. A piece of glass-fibre surfacing tissue was cut to the shape of the gap to be filled, laid in it and covered with a thin layer of polyester resin. When this had set a second layer of resin was introduced and, when this had hardened, the wax mould was cut away, the polyvinyl alcohol removed with water, and the resin cleaned and polished. (See also restoration of the Auldjo Jug, described above.)

Another approach is to reconstruct a broken object in two parts, and separate it along joins which do not run through an area that needs to be filled (*Figure 7.45c*). Restoration of missing areas is carried out, after which the two parts are joined together. If the separation has to be made along a line adjoining a missing area (*Figure 7.45d*), the procedure is as for *Figure 7.45c*, except that the resin cast will have to be carefully abraded along its free edge in order that the two parts of the glass will fit together.

Small holes, especially those in the corners of decanters, can only be filled with some difficulty, and the owners should be advised not to put the vessel to everyday use. First, a wax mould is taken from a complete corner and its inner surface coated with separating agent. The mould is then sealed over the hole on the outside, by melting its edges onto the glass using an electrically heated spatula. The decanter is then positioned on an angle so that the corner is at its lowest point. Epoxy resin is then carefully introduced to the mould, a drop at a time, through the neck off the tip of a long bamboo satay stick. Great care must be taken not to introduce more resin than is required to fill the hole, since of course it will not be possible to smooth its surface once the resin has cured. Similarly, any resin, which is dropped on the side of the glass must be removed before curing, using swabs of cotton

wool lightly moistened with acetone. Once the resin has cured, the mould can be removed and any excess wax cleaned away with swabs and white spirit.

Detachable resin fills
Detachable resin gap-fills for the restoration of missing glass rim, feet and handles are easier to make than those for replacing losses within the body of a glass (see restoration of the *oinochoe* described below). This technique has the advantages over casting the resin *in situ* of not creating undue stress on weak joins or glass during moulding and casting of the resin, and of minimizing contact with the surface of the glass during the finishing processes (sanding and polishing) (Koob, 2000).

Thermosoftening resins
An alternative method of replacing missing areas of glass was to cut the shapes from pre-formed acrylic sheets (Perspex; US: Plexiglas), bend them to the required curve after softening with a hot air blower, and attach them to the glass with adhesive. However, this is a lengthy process requiring accuracy in cutting and filing, and the finished result is in no way as aesthetically pleasing as casting in the missing fragments with a clear resin; it is therefore not recommended for general use.

An alternative approach makes use of the fact that methacrylates are thermoplastic, softening at temperatures around 600°C. Once cured, they can be softened by heat and reshaped by hand. The thermosoftening property of Technovit 4004a (a grade of polymethyl methacrylate, no longer available) was exploited by Errett (1972) to reshape small casts and thus dispense with the need to make complicated moulds. The technique was also used by Jackson (1983) to restore a blue glass, core-formed Italic *oinochoe* (jug) with prunts, dating from the sixth or fifth century BC (*Figures 7.47a–f*).

The *oinochoe* was about 80 mm in height and the glass itself was in fairly good condition (*Figure 7.47a*). There was some surface weathering but no actual flaking occurring. The neck, spout and handle were missing but the foot and prunts had previously been restored with wax. It was decided to leave the previous restorations intact since they were dimensionally and aesthetically stable,

(a)

(e)

(b)

(f)

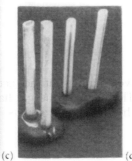

(c)   (d)

Figure 7.47 Restoration of the neck, spout and handle of a glass *oinochoe* (jug). (a) The remaining glass; (b) the neck and spout modelled in clay, prior to moulding; (c) neck and spout cast in Technovit 4004a. The cast was produced in a silicone rubber mould made over the model shown in (b). (d) The handle was made by casting resin into a drinking straw. (e) Spout and handle shaped and attached to the glass. (f) The completed restoration coloured to tone with the original glass.

and to reconstruct the neck, spout and handle, which could be copied from a photograph of a similar *oinochoe*. From the illustration it can be seen that in order to produce a one-piece cast, the mould required would be both difficult and time-consuming to produce. In particular, the thin, curved flange forming the spout would present problems in the moulding process. Experiments were undertaken in heating and reshaping simple resin casts to form complicated shapes. As a preliminary to the project, several discs of a size and thickness similar to those of the spout were cast in Vosschemie (polyester) resin and Technovit 4004a. When cured, the discs were heated in various ways (i.e. warm air, warm water and boiling water) until they became pliable enough to fold into shape. The folded discs were then held in cold water until they hardened. It was found that the polyester resin disc softened at a much lower temperature than the methacrylate disc, which had in fact to be placed in boiling water for a few minutes until it could be shaped easily. The polyester resin disc softened easily in warm air, but in warm water it became opaque. The discs of resin were left overnight under a desk lamp (approximately 27°C) to determine whether they would distort under display conditions. The polyester discs flattened considerably whereas the shape of the methacrylate disc did not alter at all.

The neck and spout of the *oinochoe* were modelled *in situ* in fine-quality potters' clay (*Figure 7.47b*). The curved flange of the spout was not actually modelled to shape but was left as a flat disc and the neck was modelled without a hole through the middle. Once the clay was leather hard (after 4 hours) the model was removed from the *oinochoe* and moulded with Dow Corning Silastic E RTV (silicone rubber). After curing, the rubber mould was removed from the clay and the mould cleaned with water. The mould was filled from the top with Technovit 4004a, which was allowed to cure. The rubber was then cut away revealing the cast (*Figure 7.47c*). Using the appropriate sized drill bit, a vertical hole was drilled through the centre of the resin cast. Holding the piece by the neck with tongs, the flat resin cast was placed in boiling water until it had softened, removed and the edges of the disc

bent up by hand to form the flange shown in *Figure 7.47e*. When the required shape had been achieved the resin was immediately held in cold water until it hardened. The surface was then finished with fine glass paper. The moulded neck and spout were then attached to the broken neck of the *oinochoe* with Araldite AY103/HY956 (epoxy resin) and gaps between the glass and the cast filled with Technovit 4004a.

The handle was produced by a similar but more direct method (*Figure 7.47d*). A rod of Technovit 4004a was cast using a glass tube as a mould. The tube was filled with resin; when this was hard (approximately 30 mm) the glass was broken away. As shown in the photograph, plastic straws could have been used as moulds, but in this particular case the glass tube happened to be of exactly the right diameter. The resin rod was subsequently cut to the length of the original handle, heating in boiling water, bent to shape and hardened in cold water. The handle was attached to the *oinochoe* with Araldite AY103/HY956 (*Figure 7.47d*). Deka glass colours (fabric dyes) were used to colour the reconstruction to match the glass (*Figure 7.47f*).

For this particular object the method used proved to be very successful. The working time was substantially reduced, first because it was not necessary to make a complicated piece-mould from a clay model; and secondly because the methacrylate resin used cured in 30 mm whereas polyester resin would have taken 24 hours. Furthermore, there were no problems with mould relocation on the *oinochoe* or removal of flash-lines left on the cast by use of a piece-mould. As the Technovit 4004a could be softened and reshaped after it had been cast into a basic form it was very easy to make minor adjustments to the curves of the spout and handle. Thus the method proved to be both much more flexible and less time-consuming than casting alone and should be considered whenever a complicated shape is to be copied and water-white clarity of the restoration is not a priority.

Thermohardening resins

A method of filling gaps in glass with preformed casts of epoxy resin was devised by Hogan (1993), in order to enable a badly damaged green glass bottle to be exhibited.

The vessel, approximately 25 cm high, had an unusually thin base (*c.* 1 mm.) in comparison to its thicker, heavier, neck and rim (*c.* 3 mm.). About a third of the original vessel was missing. The bottle was reconstructed in two parts, the main body and the neck and shoulders, using a UV curing acrylic (Loctite 350 engineering adhesive).

The joins between the top and bottom of the vessel were not substantial and some filling was necessary to give support. A method of support with minimum use of strategically placed resin infills was devised. Detachable resin fills were constructed away from the object and adhered to the glass after curing. Sheets of epoxy resin AY103/HY956 were cast, to correspond to the varying thickness of the glass vessel in simple hexagonal moulds, made from sheets of dental wax. When the cured resin was removed from the mould a thin film of wax remained on its surface, and was removed with a spatula, followed by cleaning with white spirit. A sheet of dental wax was placed across the gaps in the glass that were to be filled, and the outline of the gap scribed onto the wax. The shapes were then cut out of the wax and placed *in situ* in the vessel, to ensure that they fitted well, and secured there with strips of pressure-sensitive tape (Sellotape). Each wax shape was removed in turn, using acetone to release the Sellotape, and laid on a resin sheet of the required thickness. Its outline was scribed onto the resin. The resin was then gently heated with a hot air blower to make it pliable enough for the shape to be cut out with scissors. The edges of the resin sherds were filed where necessary with fine metal needle files to ensure close contact with the glass. Where appropriate the resin sherds were reheated and the curvature was modified to comply with the contour of the glass vessel. The finished pieces were placed in position and secured with HMG (cellulose nitrate) adhesive. The restored areas were then painted with one coat of Rustin's Clear Plastic Coating (urea formaldehyde) coloured with Maimeri Restoration colours to match the colour of the glass.

As this method of gap-filling proved successful, variations upon the technique using different resins were used to restore other glass vessels. A clear Anglo Saxon glass was gap-filled using the same method but using clear HXTAL NYL-1 epoxy resin to form the cast. The resin was heated gently by immersing the pieces in warm water, before being shaped and bonded in position with HMG. Another small, delicate flask needed support to its neck in order to connect it to the body and base. A mould was made of the interior of the neck, by forming a cylinder of dental wax. A sheet of Araldite 2020 (epoxy resin) was cast in a wax mould as previously described. Before it had completely cured, the resin was removed from the mould, and while still flexible, it was formed around the plaster core using Cling Film plastic food wrapping as a barrier, and left to cure fully. Once the resin had cured, the plaster core was removed by splitting the resin with a scalpel blade. The resin backing, now in two sections, was inserted in the neck of the flask, and adjustments made to secure a good fit. It was then bonded with HMG, giving full support to the neck. It is essential that the HXTAL NYL-1 and Araldite 2020 resin casts have fully cured before being bonded in position with HMG to prevent discoloration of the epoxy resin.

The method proved to be extremely effective, both in terms of the final appearance of the glass vessels, and in the support provided. Being able to work on the resin fills away from the glass surface, avoiding the need for individual moulding and casting of sherds, makes this a quick and safe method of filling fragile glass. The fact that the resin pieces are bonded in position with cellulose nitrate makes future removal easy and safe for archaeological glass. Disadvantages may be in the heating of the resin, which could accelerate discoloration. However, no immediate yellowing of the HXTAL NYL-1 or Araldite 2020 was observed. In the case of the Araldite AY103 used on the green glass, this aspect may not present a problem. A previous case of heating HXTAL NYL-1 epoxy with a hot air blower caused yellowing of the resin. In view of this the use of warm water to soften the resin is preferred. This method could, in theory, be used to complete the gap-filling of an entire vessel, depending on the intricacy of the missing shapes. Detachable fills for restoring ancient glass are also discussed by Koob (2000).

Commercial 'restoration'

There are companies who quite legitimately use glassmaking techniques to reproduce copies of ancient and historic glass objects (see below), and replacement parts for chandeliers, and objects such as silver salts and sugar bowls, requiring blue glass liners. Others grind and polish chips on the edge of glass items such as wine glasses, and 'polish' the interior of vases and decanters (by removing the surface with fine abrasive or hydrofluoric acid). However, there are others who specialize in cutting and modifying glass, and even marrying parts of similar objects together for the glass antique trade. Glasses can be expertly cut in such a way that joins made with adhesive between two or more pieces can be concealed. Sometimes silver mounts are transferred from one glass object to another, or added to conceal joins.

Replicas and fakes

From the foregoing section it will be realized that the conservator is not only able to carry out repair and restoration to great effect, but that it is also possible for replicas of glass objects to be made (von Saldern, 1970). Wihr (1963, 1968) made copies of a whole series of Roman glass vessels, and illustrates three of them: a dish engraved with a design of Abraham and Isaac, an extremely delicate *diatreta* glass, and a Portland vase (Wihr, 1963). Methods of glass reproduction are also given by Petermann (1969).

Replicas of glass vessels may be produced for loan to institutions and/or for study purposes where the original is too valuable or fragile to be handled (Goldstein, 1977). With the synthetic materials now available, the transparency and colouring of the replica can be so good that, visually, it can be very difficult to distinguish between the original and the copy (Mehlman, 1982). However, differences both in the weight and feel of the synthetic material, compared with the glass, will usually enable one to distinguish between the two. The ability to produce copies of glass vessels raises the possibility of replicas being passed off as original, but this would be unusual for the reasons mentioned above. It would, however, be easier for a broken vessel with a heavy weathering crust to be heavily restored and presented as being complete.

It is also possible to copy glass vessels in modern glass and, if necessary, create a patina by chemical treatment. In the last quarter of the nineteenth century archaeological excavations, the development of museum collections, exhibitions of famous glass collections and publications such as *The Stones of Venice* (Ruskin, 1852) and pattern books full of designs, created a fashion for historical reproduction of glass in glass, throughout Europe. Bly (1986) records the types of glassware which have been reproduced or faked, and gives indications as how to identify them.

A more serious possibility of faking would be that of modern decoration of an ancient glass vessel, for instance by engraving a design on the surface; or by artificial ageing (perhaps by etching with hydrofluoric acid) to increase its monetary value. Pilosi and Wypyski (1998) describe two ancient glass vessels with modern decoration in the Metropolitan Museum of Art. No doubt further such examples will continue to be exposed in other collections. Glass is still being made, altered or 'restored' with the intention of deceiving the buyer. Ancient glass is particularly easily faked, as the modern glass can be artificially aged with chemicals, or disguised by applying flakes of iridescence and mud, sometimes bound in an adhesive, to its surface. Parts of similar objects may be cut and married together beneath a muddy or fake iridescent surface (*Plate 7*). Modern sources of forgeries are Israeli, Turkish and Egyptian glassblowers, working in primitive conditions. Knowledge of glass style and technology usually enables a conservator to identify fakes: for example, the visual appearance of the surface, mould flash lines where there should not be any, drilled holes in what should be hollow core-formed vessels (*Figure 7.48a*), incorrect patterns and colours (*Figure 7.48b*). By the use of a binocular microscope or a scanning electron microscope, it may be seen that detail such as engraving continues unbroken over a damaged surface, or that the 'engraving' is in reality etched, so that the edges of the lines are polished, not cut (Werner *et al.*, 1975). Examination under ultraviolet light may enable areas of restoration to be identified, if they fluoresce differently from the original glass.

(a)

(b)

Figure 7.48 A fake Egyptian core-formed vessel. (a) The pattern is incorrect, the object is heavy, and when viewed from the top (b) it can be seen that the vessel is not hollow, but has been drilled.

In the 1970s a number of glass figures of bulls, purporting to be ancient, appeared for sale at much the same time in several countries, a fact which in itself raised suspicion. The figures were exposed as forgeries by Werner *et al.* (1975). It was discovered that the legs had been added by lamp-working techniques, rather than having been drawn out of the softened body of glass with pincers. Their flaky, iridescent covering contained apatite, showing that the finished articles had been exposed to the vapour of hydrofluoric acid (discovered in 1770). Newton and Brill (1983) identified a 'Roman' weeping glass bowl as a forgery or hoax. Chemical analysis of the glass showed it to be free from trace elements and to contain only 0.33 per cent CaO and 0.01 per cent MgO. The lack of modifying oxides seemed to indicate that the bowl had been made either by a modern inexperienced glassworker or had been made from laboratory glass. X-radiography can also prove useful in detecting fakes, especially if metal components have been incorporated, or parts of more than one object have been fitted together beneath a convincing deterioration layer or restoration (*Figure 7.49*).

Figure 7.49 Radiograph of a glass ewer in which can be seen the addition of a ribbed ewer spout and neck to a pincer-decorated bottle. (The addition of a snake-like handle of plastic, seen as a faint shadow on the right of the radiograph, is not visible in the illustration.) Note that there are several non-joining pincer-decorated rosettes and concentric circles 'floating' in the body of the vessel. H 146 mm. (Corning Museum of Glass).

Storage and display

Materials used for display and storage of glass – wood, adhesives, varnishes, paints and textiles – can become carbonyl pollutants by emitting acetic, formic, formaldehyde and acetaldehyde acids. Unstable glass is particularly vulnerable to attack from these acids, resulting in the formation of white crystalline salts on the surface and within hollow parts of vessels. Ideally display cabinets should be constructed from metal and glass; this has the added advantage of glass objects being highly visible. Glass objects should not be allowed to touch each other, and unless by deliberate design, shelves should not be overcrowded. Vessels that have more than one component need special care; lids and stoppers should either be stored separately (and identified), or tied in place with lightweight Nylon fishing line, knotted at the ends, so that they cannot fall when the vessel is lifted. Smaller items of glass should be placed at the fronts of the shelves so that they are easily seen. If mould growth is noticed, for instance on animal glue restoration, it must be removed with a dilute solution of a disinfectant such as Panacide on swabs. It may be necessary to dismantle and restore such a vessel, using a more suitable adhesive.

Display cases and the shelves within them should be stable and level so that glass exhibits cannot move due to vibrations caused by visitor-movement, passing vehicles, trains, underground railways or aeroplanes etc. If necessary, glass objects can be supported by acrylic mounts; and mirrors may be used to reflect light upward on to details of decoration so that the objects need not be placed immediately over light bulbs. Ideally, lighting should be external and properly situated so as not to cause a heat build-up, and infra-red absorbing filters should be used. The effects of heat build-up can be very serious on certain types of glass, for example glass with incipient crizzling, painted surfaces or weathering products (Brill, 1975, 1978), because it lowers the relative humidity of the air. The deleterious effects of spotlighting glass vessels for dramatic exhibition are appreciated by conservators but not by all curators or collectors.

Enamels should be kept in a constant temperature so that the differential expansion between the glass and the metal does not lead to disruption of the object. Those enamels in which it has not been possible to stabilize the metal, must be kept in an atmosphere that is neither too damp to allow the metal to corrode, nor too dry to desiccate the glass. In the case of copper alloys this would be about 35 per cent RH. Brill (1978) has discussed a

Figure 7.50 Storage of weeping and crizzling glass and enamels in a relatively air-tight case incorporating a dehumidifier which maintains the atmosphere inside at a constant relative humidity. (© Copyright The British Museum).

method of controlling humidity in museum cases. Special storage conditions are required for unstable glass and enamels (see below); it may be necessary to install a de-humidifier in storage cases containing large numbers of unstable glasses/enamels (*Figure 7.50*).

Navarro (1999) describes and illustrates the mounting of some 1,500 small glass items for display in the glass gallery of the Victoria and Albert Museum, which opened in 1994 (Oakley, 1999). The majority of the pieces are fragments, but also include complete items, such as beads, cameos, medallions, cutlery, bowls and bottles and glass tiles all between 1 cm and 20 cm in size. The methods by which the fragments were secured, were

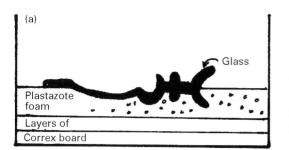

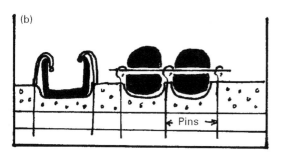

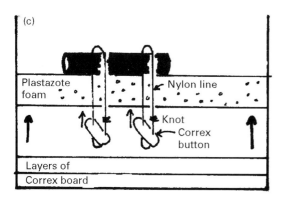

Figure 7.51 Securing glass fragments and small objects to a substrate for storage. (a) Part of a wine glass stem embedded in Plastazote (see also *Figure 7.11*). (b) Pinning; a fragment and threaded hollow beads pinned to a substrate. (c) Sewing: a heavy object secured with Nylon fishing line; the buttons made from Correx, prevent the Plastazote from buckling. (After Navarro, 1999).

embedding, pinning or sewing onto Plastazote LD 45 (a cross-linked, closed-cell, chemically inert polyethylene foam), used singly or in combination depending upon the requirements of each piece of glass (*Figure 7.51a–c*).

They were mounted in two chests of eight drawers each, and constructed in metal, glass and plastic. The drawers incorporate a complex braking system designed to reduce impact when the drawers are closed, and their design is such that no two drawers can be opened simultaneously. Each drawer contains three white plastic trays and is sealed with a sheet of clear laminated glass. The trays were lined with two 4 mm layers of white Correx boards (ethylene propylene copolymer extrusion) and one 9 mm layer of white Plastazote. The glass fragments were mounted as follows: each tray was lined with paper, and the objects arranged for display. An accurate pencil line was then drawn around each piece of glass, and then as each was transferred to a lined drawer, its accession number written beside the outline in order to identify it. The plan served as a permanent reference, and was filed with other related documentation.

The glass fragments were then secured to the Plastazote by the methods mentioned above. The most common of these was to cut the shape of the object out of the Plastazote using a scalpel blade, thus forming a hollow in which to house the object. It was then pinned into the Plastazote with headless or Nylon-headed stainless steel pins varying in thickness between 0.3 mm and 0.6 mm, the heads of which had been coated with Paraloid B-48N (methyl methacrylate copolymer) to prevent them from scratching the objects, and to provide a good hold. The pins, were cut, bent and shaped to match the requirements of each object. They were long enough to penetrate through the Correx board. Where the pins were in contact with break edges of with large areas of glass, they were covered with heat-shrinkable polyethylene tubing (HST). Pinning was not suitable for attaching heavy objects (and would not be suitable for attaching heavy objects in drawers without a braking system). Some glass objects were sewn onto the Plastazote using Nylon fishing line (10 lb or 20 lb breaking strength). A pared down piece of Correx board placed beneath the foam acted as an anchor and minimized distortion of the foam and movement of the objects. Where sewing was used to secure objects with a particularly fragile surface, the fishing line was covered with HST. Some medallions were too small to pin or sew in place and were placed in cut out shapes in the foam and secured with a dot of Paraloid

B-72 (methyl methacrylate copolymer) applied to their reverse side, and avoiding the accession numbers.

Handling

Glass, being light, is easily knocked over, and in the case of clear, transparent glass, is easily damaged by misjudging distances when setting it down. Some objects are particularly prone to damage, e.g. figures with projecting limbs, tall top-heavy objects that can topple, objects made in two or more parts or having weak original joints such as handles, and objects with rounded bases. When items have to be moved out of the way in order to reach an object, they should be placed on another adjacent surface and not merely pushed to one side, especially if the shelf is crowded. On no account should one reach over glass vessels to move others at the back of a shelf.

Before moving a glass, a check should be made that it does not consist of more than one piece, or that any previous restoration is not failing. Glass objects should never be picked up by the rim, but the bowl should be cupped in one hand and the base supported in the other in order to cradle the glass against knocks. Vessels should be carried one at a time unless a carrying basket or tray is being used, in which case the trays should be lined with cotton wool covered with neutral tissue paper, and the objects separated from one another by twists of tissue paper.

One should never turn to talk to anyone while setting a piece of glass down, since the distance between the base of the object and the table-top will almost certainly be misjudged and the glass may be broken. The base of a glass should be set down flat and not heavily at an angle. Glass objects should never he left near the edge of a table as they could easily be brushed against and knocked over, particularly as they can be difficult to see. Adherence to these simple rules will help to prevent accidents.

Packing

Temporary packing of glass vessels for transit within a building has been dealt with above. Before objects are sent on loan, detailed condition reports, which include photographs

of any damage, should be made. On arrival at their destination, and again on their return, the objects can be checked against the original photographs.

For transport to other institutions at home or abroad, glass vessels should be extremely well packed in sturdy wooden boxes filled with sheets of solid polyester or polyethylene foam such as Plastazote (*Figure 7.52*). The packing operation should be planned so that, if possible, glass is separated from other materials, and that in any event, heavier objects are placed at the bottom of the container. Enough squares of 50 mm thick foam should be cut to fill the box being used to transport the glass. (Other materials which can be used are Kempac, Bubble-Wrap and thick wads of twisted acid-free tissue paper: Wakefield, 1963; Lindsey, 2000.) The vessels should be placed on a sheet of foam (on their sides if they are tall), their shapes being first marked on the sheet and then cut out using a sharp knife, through enough layers of foam to encompass their depth. There should be at least 50 mm of solid foam between two objects. The vessels should then be wrapped in acid-free tissue paper, and the foam cut-outs trimmed down and fitted inside the glass. They are thus fully supported inside and out, and cushioned from shock. Should an accident occur, or a repair break down in transit, all the fragments will be retained in the tissue paper in their relevant positions.

The lids of boxes are best secured with a hook-lock, which can be easily opened for

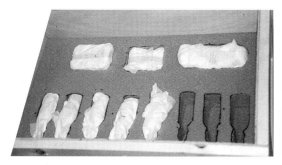

Figure 7.52 Glass objects packed for transport outside a building. Each object is wrapped in acid-free tissue paper and set into a shape cut out of dense Plastazote foam, laid in a strong wooden crate, secured with metal clasps.

Customs inspection if necessary, and which will enable the box to be re-used. If boxes with screwed-on lids are re-used the screw-holes eventually become enlarged and there is a possibility of the lid becoming loose during transit. Securing the box with string is not to be recommended since string can easily become chafed or cut. Metal handles may be screwed on to the box. The box should be clearly labelled 'Fragile' (using the international glass symbol) and with its origin and destination. Loans should always be accompanied by a member of the staff from the lending institution, preferably by whoever has checked the condition of the objects, packed them and will place them on exhibition at their destination. This will ensure that the glass does not undergo rough handling.

Glass requiring specialized conservation treatment

Objects made of Egyptian faience and of enamel will require different treatments to those commonly applied to glass conservation and restoration. In addition, there are several types of glass objects, such as those which are unstable (weeping or crizzling), which themselves will require specialized treatment; and yet others which will involve experts in a particular field of conservation or other conservation disciplines. This last group will include glass found in association with other materials, such as metals, textiles and ethnographical materials, chandeliers, mirrors, and paintings on or composed of glass.

Deterioration and conservation of Egyptian faience

The friability of Egyptian faience (*Figure 7.53*) can be attributed to its manufacture (Smith, 1996). It is subject to the leaching out of its alkali content, in the same way as true glass, to crumbling of the friable core material, and to damage caused by the action of soluble salts. Leaching of the alkali content may lead to an overall whitening of the glaze, and deterioration of the metallic salts may result in a change of glaze colour. The strength of the quartz core depends upon the amount of interstitial glass present. Where interstitial glass

Figure 7.53 An Egyptian faience *ushabti* figure, broken as the result of having an unstable mount.

content is low, the body is brittle. Only in Harappan faience (2300–1800 BC) and later 'glassy' faience, where frit was intentionally added to the quartz in order to produce a homogenous glassy phase throughout the object, is the body strong enough to withstand abrasion once the surface glaze has been lost.

Soluble salts can be present in Egyptian faience either as a result of the manufacturing process, or as a result of burial in a salt-laden environment. Their action can result in the disruption and loss of the glaze surface, or the total disintegration of an object. If the outer glaze layer rather than any interstitial glass is holding the majority of the quartz grains forming the body in place, the introduction of water to remove soluble salts may cause the disintegration of the core and total collapse of the object. Where soluble salts are crystallizing from an intact glaze, it may be possible to desalinate without causing loss of material from the core. The danger is that as the core of the faience takes up water during salt removal, pressure can build up within the object, which may cause cracking or total disintegration. If salts cannot be removed, Egyptian faience objects should be stored with silica gel (*Figure 7.54*) or kept in a constant relative humidity.

If the surface permits, any necessary conservation work is limited to dry cleaning methods and repair with a relatively weak and readily re-dissolvable adhesive such as Paraloid B-72 (methyl methacrylate copolymer) or HMG (cellulose nitrate). Repair may have to be preceded by local consolidation of the crumbling edges; it should be remembered

Figure 7.54 A repaired Egyptian faience scarab, which had split due to the action of atmospheric moisture on the hygroscopic interior, shown after repair and storage with silica gel in a (lidded) box. (© Copyright The British Museum, London).

that the consolidation can trap soluble salts in the faience body and that the solvents can mobilize them, resulting in internal disruption and damage to the objects. This risk can be minimized by using dried distilled solvents, which contain less water than standard laboratory solvents. The consolidation will result in some colour change and will be irreversible. Thus a system with proven long-term ageing properties must be used, such as Paraloid B-72, B-67 and B-99. All have good adhesive properties, but the system chosen will have to be decided by local climatic conditions, since their glass transition temperatures vary. Dismantling adhesive repairs also poses a risk of damage. If this should become necessary, the safest option may be to soften the joins by placing the object in a solvent vapour during the day when a conservator can be present to dismantle the joins as soon as the adhesive softens. Should gap-filling be required, Smith (1996) suggests using a stiff paste composed of glass micro-balloons in a 30 per cent solution of Paraloid B-72 in 50:50 acetone/IMS applied directly onto the consolidated core. The filling material is strong but lightweight, and on drying forms a textured surface compatible with the faience. (If necessary, the filling can be easily removed with acetone.) Fine-ground dry pigments in an acrylic gloss medium can be used for colouring the restored areas. It is probably best not to attempt the conservation of faience unless, by doing nothing, the object will be lost.

Chemically unstable (weeping or crizzling glass)

Some of the past attempts to preserve chemically unstable glass have severely interfered with the glass itself. An investigation by Bohm (1998) into the treatment of crizzled glass in Swedish collections revealed a number of early attempts to stabilize the glass. Heribert Seitz, an art historian, conducted conservation experiments when curator of the Nordiska Museet (National Museum of Cultural History), Stockholm. The work, dating from 1935, 1938 and 1942, was documented on the object record cards. Protective coatings of Zapon lacquer (cellulose nitrate) thinned with acetone or Zapon lacquer thinner were applied to some glasses. Others were coated with chlorinated rubber thinned with xylene, which discoloured to a dark brown colour within a few years. It was removed and replaced with Zapon lacquer. Seitz recommended storage of the glass at 40 per cent RH using air-tight cases containing silica gel, or a saturated solution of calcium chloride. The elimination of atmospheric carbon dioxide using sodic calcium (soda lime) was also considered.

Hedvall and Olson developed a treatment for weeping glass by impregnating it with polymethyl methacrylate under vacuum. The records of this treatment are scanty. It seems to have been in use in the 1960s, and treated glass is in several Swedish collections. The glass was degreased in carbon tetrachloride and leached alkaline products were removed with 5 per cent nitric acid, followed by thorough rinsing in distilled water and air drying. The glass was then placed in a vacuum chamber and heated to 60–70°C (apparently to lower the vapour pressure in the capillaries of the glass and to improve impregnation with 50 per cent polymethyl methacrylate resin). Excess resin was allowed to drain out of the glass before it was removed from the chamber. In 1956, Bostrom invented an apparatus to preserve a pair of seventeenth-century, deteriorated Venetian glass goblets in Perspex cylinders from which the air was evacuated and replaced with argon gas. The glass was removed from the cylinders in the 1980s, after some 25 years, for aesthetic reasons.

The application of surface coatings as protection for unstable glass has been unsuccessful as they were prone to failure and discoloration and were not entirely impervious to moisture. Water thus penetrated the lacquer or entering the glass where the coating was not continuous, producing a corrosive high pH concentration, and allowing the leaching process to continue with inevitable results. The required level of RH may be achieved by the inclusion, in a well-fitting display case, of trays of silica gel which have been previously equilibrated to the target RH (Brill, 1975, 1978; Thomson, 1998). However, the silica gel has to be changed at regular intervals (i.e. when it has turned from blue to pink due to the absorption of water), and unless it has been equilibrated to the required level prior to use, it may over-dry the atmosphere and cause dehydration of the glass.

More recently, however, experiments to stabilize glass by introducing ions into the network have been undertaken. (This work should not be confused with the application of calcium ions to deteriorated glass from a marine environment: Corvaia *et al.*, 1996.)

Between 1987 and 1990 an in-house survey was made of glass in the collections of the Victoria and Albert Museum, London. Following this survey, research began with Imperial College, London to investigate vessel glass deterioration in a museum environment, and to try to gain a greater understanding of the deterioration process. By using sophisticated analytical techniques to investigate the mechanisms by which glass decays, the research has given an insight into why some glasses are more susceptible than others. In 1992, Ryan investigated the mechanisms of active corrosion (Ryan, 1995; Ryan *et al.*, 1996) and in 1995, Hogg began experimenting with active consolidation techniques. Hogg *et al.* (1998, 1999) treated susceptible glasses with mono-functional organo-silanes in order to inhibit the deterioration process and suggest that, by this process, the lifetime of the glass may be extended by a factor of ten. The protection is probably mostly due to the action of the silane bonding to the glass surface. The replacement of Si–OH groups with Si–O–Si bonds removes the possibility of hydrogen bonding between atmospheric moisture and the glass surface. There is the ethical question of reversibility to consider. Since organo-silanes are only monofunctional and do not cross-link, they exist only as a molecular mono-layer on the surface. (This does not imply reversibility, but then neither is it possible to remove an entire coating of consolidant or lacquer from a fragile glass surface.) The organic groups on the silane are known to be stable, and breakdown of the silane will not produce corrosive by-products. If the coating were to degrade, being only bound to one site on the surface, it would not cause damage over a larger area, as is often the case with lacquers and other surface coatings. The results of the research have enabled conservation scientists to give recommendations for the care and display of unstable glass. The work has also extended to the development of new methods of active surface treatment to arrest deterioration.

Unstable glass (Egyptian faience and enamels) is best stored in a stable relative humidity of 35–40 per cent, with 42 per cent (the point at which potassium carbonate deliquesces) being the upper limit, to prevent alkali being leached by moisture. Periodic cleaning to remove the build-up of alkali on the surface of weeping glass may be advisable. The frequency of this treatment needs to be balanced against the risk of causing further damage and disruption of the surface. De-ionized or distilled water should be used for washing and rinsing the glass, and gloves should be used when handling and washing the glass, to avoid the transfer of salts and acid present on the skin. Such a cleaning process may be complicated by the fact that it may not be advisable to immerse objects, and that the use of cotton wool swabs must be avoided if a glass surface is cracked, as cotton filaments would snag and detach fragments. It may be possible to use a fine spray of water administered from a hand-held spray held at some distance from the object. A few drops of a non-ionic detergent may be added to the water to aid the removal of grease and dirt.

When washing collections of glass, the washing water should be changed frequently. Since the glass surface is slightly acidic, a rinse in de-ionized water should help to neutralize the surface in addition to removing traces of detergent. The objects should be thoroughly dried either by gently blotting with acid-free paper or by placing them in a flow of cool air. No form of heat drying should be used, as this would cause rapid crizzling to occur, sometimes instantaneously. Alcohols are effective at removing grease and dirt, and it has been suggested that their use might be advantageous (Newton and Davison, 1989), in that alcohols displace surface water held in cracks and pores. However, the application of alcohol to the surface of a hydrated silica gel may cause water held in cracks and pores to be replaced to such an extent that the glass is dehydrated.

Washing will help to retard the deterioration of weeping glass for a short time and will also improve its appearance by removing dirt adhering to the slippery surface; it does not, however, offer any long-term protection against recurrence of weeping.

Severely deteriorated (crizzled) glass objects cannot be washed without endangering them, and will require to be stored in carefully controlled environmental conditions. However, if the humidity is too low, the hydrated glass surface may dehydrate: removal of water molecules will generate tensile stresses in the surface layer, which are then relieved by the formation and propagation of surface cracks. The temperature and relative humidity of controlled storage and display cases should be regularly monitored by the installation of a thermometer and a hygrometer, or a recording thermo-hygrograph.

The provision of environmental control and suitable lighting levels in both storage and exhibition conditions is the safest method of slowing down an inevitable worsening of the condition (see *Figure 7.50*). This is usually achieved by means of establishing microclimates in cases rather than by controlling an entire gallery (Weintraub, 1998). In general, and also specifically for unstable glass, the environmental parameters that need to be controlled include temperature, relative humidity and gaseous – and particulate pollutants. Within a showcase there are a variety of passive and active methods which can be used to effect control. Passive conservation in the form of high-grade, air-tight case design is the least expensive option in the long term. In addition to being well-sealed, any materials

used within the interior display areas, such as textiles, wood or paint, must not emit harmful gaseous pollutants. Provisions must be included for the use of passive environmental control materials such as silica gel and pollution scavengers. Specialist advice from a conservation scientist and companies specializing in museum case design will be required. Active systems for environmental control are generally expensive and time-consuming to maintain, especially if applied to a large number of cases. Here again, a conservation scientist will normally be required to give advice on the type and amount of silica gel to use, its method of installation and frequency of its renewal. In reality, temperature control is difficult to achieve without specialist equipment and case design. The use of temperature control equipment raises concerns regarding the safety of collections within a case. However, the heat generated within a case by lighting can be addressed by the use of fibre optic transmitters and fluorescent ballasts, and by isolating lighting systems by the use of diffusers. A passive relative humidity control system in storage or display cases involves the use of conditioned silica gel. This serves as a buffer to offset changes in relative humidity caused by air infiltration or through temperature variations.

Artsorb silica gel equilibrated to 38 per cent RH has been used to condition display cases in the glass gallery of the Victoria and Albert Museum, London since 1993. Its use has proved to be a relatively simple and inexpensive method for protecting a large number of susceptible glass objects. The large-scale renovation of the exhibitions at the Corning Museum of Glass has enabled the design for the galleries and cases to address the special requirements of crizzled glass objects. Methods of stabilizing glasses in various stages of crizzling and of displaying them safely (structural supports, suitable lighting and humidity control) have been investigated (Page, 1998). Similar investigations have been carried out in connection with crizzled glass vessels of the Chinese Qing Dynasty (1644–1911) in the Freer Gallery of Art and Arthur M. Sackler Gallery, Smithsonian Institution (Koob, 2000). The glasses are extremely hygroscopic, having a high potassium content and (presumed) lack of sodium. Both galleries now have environmental control throughout the buildings, maintained at 21°C (70°F) and 50 per cent RH.

Further analysis will identify the exact compositions of the glasses. If the potassium is found to be the most reactive component, a lower humidity (40–42 per cent) would be recommended for storage, to which end it might be necessary to provide a custom-built case with a higher air exchange to ensure greater stability. Koob (2000) describes the conservation treatment of two of the glasses from these galleries, which had previously been repaired. The subsequent re-repair was carried out using Paraloid B-72 adhesive. Schack von Wittenau (1998) describes a collaboration between the Kunstsammlungen der Vest Coburg with the Institute for Material Research of Glass and Ceramics of the University of Erlangen-Nuremberg, to research the problems of crizzled glass, and later with the Fraunhofer Institute for Silicate Research and to formulate a design for environmentally controlled display cases for the Glass Collections of the Veste Coburg in Germany.

There are 22 controlled cases, seven of which are wall cases with fabric-covered wood backing; the others are free-standing. The glass and steel cases are constructed using neutral sealing compounds and appropriate adhesives. The base of each free-standing case is formed of three high-grade stainless steel cupboards, which contain plastic containers filled with a saturated solution of magnesium chloride. The cupboards can be opened from the exterior, which allows for maintenance, as every three months the salt levels have to be checked and replenished, and the surplus salt solution that results from the climate control process, removed. A lattice is fitted across the top of the base and this allows an exchange of gases within the cases. Seven layers of silica gel in the form of absorption strips about 4.0 cm wide are placed in a criss-cross pattern on the lattice, about 4.0 cm apart from one another. These are covered by a perforated panel covered with textile. The absorption layer is conditioned by a saturated solution of magnesium chloride to a relative humidity of 37–42 per cent. Whilst guaranteeing the desired relative humidity, the saturated salt solution reacts very slowly to fluctuations in humidity. This is balanced by the silica gel, which as a fast buffer, cushions the effects of variations in humidity. Ventilation holes in the top of the light box prevent the build-up of heat. Glass dust shields installed between the light fittings and display area are fitted with a PVP ultraviolet filter. Textiles and wooden backings, which do not emit pollutants, were chosen for lining the cases. The condition of the glasses on display will continue to be monitored and recorded, as will the condition of model glasses (glass sensors) composed of sensitive potassium lime silicate glasses, which were placed in four of the cases.

Glass in association with other materials

Metals

Metal is usually found in association with glass in the form of supports:

(i) a wire armature around which glass is shaped when hot to produce figures such as those from Nevers;

(ii) wires used to outline a design made in enamel (*cloisonné*) (see *Figure 3.33*) or *cloisonné* glass (see *Figure 7.68*);

(iii) a flat support to which a vitreous material, glass or enamel, is fused (see *Figures 3.3, 7.57 and 7.58*);

(iv) a support to which glass, glass beads or fragments are adhered as in the case of glass bead pictures and micromosaics;

(v) a structural support for glazing and chandeliers (see *Figure 7.61c*).

The metal oxides of tin and silver have been used in the form of amalgams with mercury, and lead oxide, to form mirrored surfaces on glass. In addition to the glass itself requiring conservation, problems of deterioration may be associated with a metal support, mirrored surface or materials such as adhesives and resins, which have been used to secure the glass.

Archaeological glass may be coated with corrosion products from metal objects buried adjacent to them (*Figure 4.9*), or into which the glass has been set (*Plate 3*) (Dove, 1981; see also above Archaeological glass). Glass can also be associated with metals, in the form of previous restorations, armatures, supports and stands (*Figure 7.55*), mounts and lids and decoration such as electro-plating, and of course in the form of enamel (see *Figures 7.57* and *7.58*). Metal mounts etc. are often secured to the glass with gesso, with or without the addition of threaded metal rods, nuts and bolts. If they have to be removed for any reason, great care should be taken not to exert pressure on the glass or to scratch either the glass or the metal with tools such as pliers. Metal fixings may have corroded and will require careful use of chemicals such as rust removers, and thin penetrating oil to release them. If necessary, a metals conservator should be consulted before work begins.

Small glass figurines such as flowers in vases, were used as table decorations, chandelier trimmings, table altars, hat-pins, cigarette holders and as scientific models (mostly flowers and insects such as beetles).

Glass figures, constructed over wire armatures, may become broken and misshapen. Conservation problems may arise if metals have transferred corrosion products to the glass, or worse, if a metal armature has been exposed to damp, corroded and expanded, causing the glass to split. It will not normally be possible to remove the armature since the glass is fused around it. Where exposed, the metal can be cleaned and stabilized, the glass fragments replaced, and the object kept in a constant temperature and humidity.

The Ware Collection in the Botanical Museum of Harvard University in Boston, Massachusetts, comprises almost 3,000 botanically accurate plant models, made primarily of

Figure 7.55 Cephalopod made by Blaschka, of glass and mixed media. Nineteenth century. Germany. (Zoology Department, The Manchester Museum).

glass. They represent more than 850 species of flowers, fruits and leaves. The models are the sole production of the Dresden glass-workers Leopold Blascka (1822–1895) and his son Rudolph (1857–1939). Leopold Blascka had begun his career making glass eyes and floral jewellery. He then became famous for the production of models of invertebrate marine animals, such as jellyfish, primarily for museum collections (*Figure 7.55*). The models are in fact of mixed media. Many are formed over a wire armature. Sometimes the glass elements are fused to one another, and at other times they are glued together. The early models were made of clear glass, painted with hide glue or isinglas (fish glue obtained from sturgeon). Striving for greater subtleties, Rudolph began to produce coloured glass formulated to melt at differing temperatures. Thus coloured glasses could be ground to a powder and then dusted onto a base glass and fused by firing, without distorting the base. The most remarkable effects can be seen on the 'diseased fruit' series of models, completed in 1929. However, these now exhibit a corrosion 'bloom' which suggests that the glass formulae were not stable. It is hoped that methods of conservation can be devised to ensure the preservation of these unique models (Pantano, Rossi-Wilcox and Lange, 1998). Apart from the difficulties presented by the mixed media, conservation problems result from the glass being very thin, and from the lack of access to the interior of small hollow objects such as the sea creatures. Methods used by the author to support fragments are the application of the dental cement; Sticky Wax melted across joins in the glass; or a backing made of fine glass-fibre tissue impregnated with HMG (cellulose nitrate adhesive of Paraloid B-72 (methyl methacrylate copolymer)).

The Czech sculptor Jaroslav Brychta (1895–1971) took up glassmaking in Želený Brod, where ancient glassmaking technology was being used to produce glass beads and buttons. This formed the basis for Brychta's characteristic glass figurines, fanciful creatures made of beads and glass rods, the first of which were exhibited at Želený Brod in 1921. Brychta designed the figures, produced detailed drawings of them, and researched glass technology, but the figures were actually made by glassmakers. Further techniques were developed, and in 1927 figures of blown glass began to be made.

Thousands of small figurines were produced (Volf, 1977) (*Figure 7.56*). The figurines were extremely fragile. Brychta recommended that they should be given a protective coat of cellulose nitrate lacquer. It is common to find figurines covered with a thick layer of lacquer, which has discoloured to yellow or dark brown. Some of the figurines were formed by applying the molten glass over a wire armature (probably an alloy of iron, chromium, aluminium and cobalt), which had the same coefficient of expansion as the glass. However, the wire is very fragile and is easily broken and its shape distorted. Great care has to be taken when distorted wires are straightened and in relaying it in its original position against the broken glass. Broken wire can be connected with tin solder. Replacing wires is extremely difficult and usually requires an individual approach to each figurine. Thin

Figure 7.56 Small glass lamp-worked figure in the form of a rabbi, in the style of Jaroslav Brychta. Twentieth century. Czech Republic.

brass wire laid onto the glass with clear polyester resin has been used successfully. Repairs are carried out with clear epoxy resin hidden on the reverse side of the figurine. Brass or steel wires were used in the original constructions for mounting beads, i.e. not embedded in the glass. These are not so fragile and can easily be replaced if necessary. If it becomes necessary to remove the lacquer coating, it can be dissolved in acetone, or, if a thick layer has cracked, by soaking the figurine in water for 24 hours. Water seeps between the lacquer and the glass, after which the lacquer is easily peeled away. Some small missing glass parts can be made of clear epoxy resin, others such as horse bridles have to be reproduced in glass and adhered to the original with epoxy resin, cyanoacrylate being used to hold pieces in position temporarily. A small group of the figures is displayed in the museum in Zeleny Brod (Czech Republic).

Glass beads as decorative elements on textiles and ethnographic materials

Glass beads are often found as decoration on a wide variety of objects from most periods and cultures (Plate 6). Their use on textiles and ethnographic material is particularly frequent. They are often applied to costume and may actually form the major part of it. Baskets, bags, boots, shoes and bead-dresses are just some of the other items which can be decorated with beads. They may even be found on decorative or ritual statuary.

Beads have been made from a very broad range of materials, and it is not uncommon to find a mixture of different types of bead on one item. Whilst some of these are easily distinguished from glass, others are not so obvious. Fake pearls could be made from pearlized glass or cellulose acetate and fish scales. Other materials such as metals, plastics, stone (for example obsidian, a naturally occurring form of glass), bone ivory, amber, shell or Egyptian faience may also be mistaken for glass. As beads are small and easily transported, they may be found far from their place of manufacture. Trade beads are a well-known category; made in Europe but exported to America and Africa where they were made into distinctive native artefacts. Glass may also be recycled, at much lower temperatures than that required to melt glass. For example, beads made from melted bottle glass are known from Inuit and African cultures: the Krobo people of West Africa grind glass into a powder which is poured into a mould and fired in a simple furnace which fuses the granules together.

When approaching the conservation of glass beads, it is important to consider the other materials present. Beads may be attached individually to a substrate such as fabric or leather, strung as a necklace or fringe, or be woven into panels using various types of thread. The thread may be made of animal, plant or synthetic fibre, but sinew, leather and wire are also used. Often a mixture of threads is found, especially where an object has undergone repair from the time it was still in use, or previous conservation treatment. Sometimes beads are embedded in resin or wax applied to a surface such as wood.

There may be health and safety implications to be considered when dealing with glass beads. Pearlized finishes on glass beads may contain lead, some trade beads from the mid-nineteenth century contain arsenic. These substances will be released as the glass degrades. In Namibia bead collars have mud and blood incorporated, used to bind the threads attaching the beads, resulting in a possible biohazard. If the beads are attached to an organic substrate then there may be residual pesticides from a previous fumigation.

In many cases the deterioration of beadwork is more dependent on the condition of the threading than of the beads themselves. Glass beads suffering from glass disease (Fenn, 1987) are an obvious exception, which is a phenomenon described elsewhere. Beads made of materials other than glass, particularly plastics, are subject to their own decay mechanisms, some of which may evolve substances damaging to glass and other materials. Open storage of sensitive objects is recommended to allow any noxious gases formed during degradation processes to dissipate, rather then build up to dangerous levels.

Many problems arise from the makers' use of incompatible or poor quality materials. Beads with rough or sharp edges may damage thread and cause bead loss. Thread which is too strong for the beads may cut through them, whilst beads with glass disease may damage their threads and support fabrics. Many beads are heavy and their weight alone

may cause damage to the support, thread or fabric, thus their handling and display must be carefully considered. Beaded dresses, so popular in Europe in the 1920s, often had a base of silk chiffon, which has now become too fragile to support the weight of the beads attached to it. Older African beadwork is usually strung on vegetable fibre, which becomes very brittle with age, particularly if it has been dyed. For this reason water should never be used for cleaning, as the fibre will become weaker and liable to break.

Threads, sinew and leather will act as wicks if liquid comes into contact with them, so damage to the thread or interior of the bead, caused by damp conditions or previous cleaning involving the use of aqueous solutions, may not be immediately determined. In the case of beads attached to skin or leather substrates, the use of leather dressings should be avoided as they can wick along the threading, causing deterioration of the thread and the interior of the beads.

When the original threading has broken, the introduction of a new thread to support the weight of the beads is usually the best option, retaining the original thread as far as possible. Thread used in conservation work should be waxed to prevent the wicking action mentioned above. The thread is treated with an inert paraffin wax rather than beeswax, which can provide food for insects. In cases where original thread fills the hole through the beads, it is often not possible to re-thread the beads, and other methods of supporting the weakened structure are needed. These may involve the use of adhesive to secure individual beads, or the stitching of the beadwork to a support fabric.

A particular problem is encountered where sinew has been used to thread beads which have deteriorated, e.g. as a result of glass disease. It is very reactive to changes in humidity; swelling in a high humidity causes fragile beads to fracture. However, humidity which is low enough to prevent further glass deterioration may result in the sinew becoming brittle and liable to snap. Metal wires are prone to corrosion; corrosion products may cause beads to split. The combination of poor quality cotton thread and chemically unstable glass beads can be particularly difficult to treat. As the beads are often small and their holes tiny, conservation options are very limited. Methods of immobilizing the beadwork, such as securing them to a rigid support, will help to prevent the flexing and abrasion responsible for much of the deterioration of fragile beads and weak thread.

If the support itself is under biological and/or insect attack and requires fumigation, the effect that the treatment will have on the glass beads must be taken into account. Berkouwer (1994) freeze dried nineteenth-century textiles decorated with glass beads. Inspection of the beads under high magnification showed that there appeared to be no change in the condition of the glass. Where beads requiring conservation are encountered in association with textiles and other organic materials, the advice of a textile conservator should be sought (Lougheed and Shaw, 1986; Hosforth and Davison, 1988; Sirois, 1999).

Enamels

Enamels suffer from physical damage due to handling or to corrosion of the underlying metal whose corrosion products may force the enamel to fall away (*Figure 7.57*), or to the breakdown of the vitreous enamel itself. Some enamel objects may exhibit the 'weeping' phenomena seen in unstable glass. The degradation of Limoges enamels, produced between 1480 and 1530, was investigated by Richter (1998). Severe deterioration of the enamels, especially the blue, mauve and violet enamels, has occurred since they were manufactured. A large selection of painted enamels was studied, using specific ion beam analyses for the chemical characterization of the glass with the accelerator AGLAE using PIXE (proton-induced X-ray emission) and PIGME (proton-induced gamma ray emission). The analyses were carried out without sampling the enamels, using two X-ray detectors and one gamma ray detector. In addition, accelerated ageing tests were carried out on synthetic glasses, similar in composition to some antique enamels. The results were compared with the degraded enamels.

If the damage is due to metal corrosion, and the metal itself has become exposed in part, it may be cleaned and stabilized, before the enamel is readhered to its base. Where the metal is not exposed, the only course of action

Figure 7.57 A damaged enamelled candlestick showing loss of the enamel surface and damage to the copper substrate.

will be to keep the enamel in a constant dry environment.

Early restoration of enamels was carried out using coloured waxes, or by organic binders in the form of natural resins such as shellac or animal glue and its derivatives. These were thickened by the edition of a filling material, such as whiting or gypsum, and coloured by a variety of pigments. Such restorations have usually discoloured with age. They may also have shrunk and become brittle, even falling away, so that the enamel is left prone to further damage. Restorations can be undertaken by adapting the methods and materials used for restoring porcelain. For example, opaque fillers such as epoxy resin thickened with an inert filler, or commercially available epoxy putties were used to fill missing areas of enamel (*Figures 7.58a,b*). These, when cured, were abraded to form a smooth surface

(a)   (b)

Figure 7.58   An enamelled clock dial: (a) damaged, with loss of enamel; (b) restored with coloured epoxy paste.

and then painted by hand with glaze and pigment. The risk of damaging the relatively soft enamel, surrounding metalwork and set stones, when abrading small fills is great. Removal of old restorations may be undertaken by careful use of a scalpel. If solvents are necessary to soften fills these must be kept to an absolute minimum, and not be allowed to flow freely onto the metalwork. Great care must be taken not to cause more damage to the edges of the damaged enamel, particularly by filaments of cotton wool from swabs catching jagged edges. The modern approach to the conservation of enamels is outlined by Cronyn *et al.* (1987).

Transparent enamels can be restored with clear epoxy resin containing a tiny amount of dry pigment, which will not impair the transparency of the resin. Some colour will also be reflected from the surrounding enamel. *Plique à jour* enamel can be restored by providing the metal cells with a temporary backing of dental wax lightly adhered to the metalwork, before introduction of the clear coloured resin. Once the resin has fully cured, the dental wax is removed. The resin which has been in contact with the wax will have a dull surface. This is cleaned with white spirit, then water and left to dry, after which a thin layer of epoxy resin can be painted over the surface and left to cure. Translucent enamels can be restored with a paste mixed to varying degrees of translucency by adding different amounts of dry titanium dioxide pigment and thickening it

with fumed silica. Depending upon the size and depth of the areas to be restored, the paste is applied with a spatula, fine sable brush or a needle. In the latter case, the work may have to be carried out beneath a microscope, in order to apply the correct amount of filler, in order that no further work will be required once the resin has cured. Large, flat expanses of enamel are difficult to restore in terms of attaining a perfect flat surface without being able to abrade and polish it without the risk of damage to adjoining metalwork or other decoration such as set stones. Where it is possible to imitate the original enamel with restoration applied as layers of sprayed coloured glaze, adjoining areas must be masked off. Fisher (1991) describes the cleaning and repair of *cloisonné* metalwork, and restoration of the enamel with the epoxy resin HXTAL NYL-1, of a collection of seventeenth-century enamels. Some so-called enamel can in fact turn out to be unfired lacquers or paints, or to have been restored with such materials, which will be damaged if solvents in conservation materials come into contact with them.

Micromosaics

Conservation problems associated with micromosaics are physical damage, and deterioration of one or more of the components, particularly the disintegration of the adhesive to which the glass *tesserae* are secured to the support (see *Figure 2.17*).

Chandeliers

Conservators and restorers are becoming increasingly involved in the work of preparing condition reports on historic chandeliers and other fixtures and fittings in historic buildings. In some cases conservators are responsible for undertaking the work, in conjunction with specialist firms where necessary, e.g. where chandelier frames require rebuilding – especially of the metalwork – re-pinning, or the manufacture of new glass components. There are commercial firms who specialize in cleaning, repairing and restoring chandeliers. The larger companies are aware of conservation issues and adopt a conservation approach to cleaning and refurbishment; others may clean antique and modern chandeliers by identical methods, using proprietary solutions and abrasives, the contents of which are largely unknown.

There are few published articles describing the treatment of historic glass chandeliers (Davison, 1988; Reilly and Mortimer, 1998, Sommer-Larson, 1999). In the past, many chandeliers in private houses were hung and ignored or 'cared for' by staff or handymen, no records being kept of any work carried out. This seems to have comprised dismantling and cleaning, replacing missing metal and glass sections and re-pinning the lustres which form pendants and chains. Pieces were often incorrectly replaced, or replaced with unmatching glass, chains of lustres removed or incorrectly linked together, and the pots of arms, or the holes in the receiving bowl into which they fitted, filed down when arms were wrongly placed.

Most historic chandeliers – some of which may be two hundred or so years old – will require conservation/restoration (*Figure 7.59*). The glass elements themselves might still be in good condition. However, it is often the case that some glass has been broken during handling and cleaning, by undue pressure having been exerted on arms and by careless use of ladders, during replacement of light bulbs or decoration. Many chandeliers have chipped or missing lustres, broken candle nozzles, greasepans, arms, balusters and bowls.

During the life of a chandelier there may have been much rearrangement of its decorative elements, and even an exchange of parts between chandeliers of the same configura-

Figure 7.59 Damaged glass items from a chandelier: a glass arm broken at its junction with the metal pot; broken glass lustres; broken brass pin, alongside a new pin, and small pliers and cutters used to shape it.

tion, (particularly if they were all dismantled for cleaning at the same time). When glass elements were broken they may have been repaired with inappropriate materials, replaced with new or contemporary pieces, which may not be of the correct size, shape or cut. In addition, parts such as the dressings were changed as fashion demanded. Pendants and chains may be entirely missing or altered without regard for their correct configuration. The surface of metal parts will have oxidized, and may also have been affected by the use of chemical cleaning agents. It is also possible that water from cleaning or from burst water pipes may have penetrated the chandelier and caused the formation of corrosion products such as rust on iron elements, though this does not usually cause safety problems unless the electrical wiring is affected. In extreme cases part or all of a chandelier may have been damaged by heat (such as those in the Brighton Pavilion, UK) (Rogers, 1980), or may have fallen down, e.g. due to incorrect hanging or during a fire (such as those at Hampton Court Palace and at Uppark, UK).

Drawn copper wire was used throughout the late eighteenth and most of the nineteenth centuries to form linking pins between glass lustres. Over time, the links stretch, and many will have been repeatedly unbent and re-bent during dismantling for cleaning, actions which often cause them to break. Water and chemicals used to clean chandeliers can cause corrosion and embrittlement of the wire. Fixings such as screws and nuts may have been lost and not replaced, and metal threads may have become stripped. Plaster of Paris or other fixatives such as gutta percha, which secure glass to metal components, may have become weakened and fail.

Since the introduction of electric lighting in the early nineteenth century, many period chandeliers have been electrically wired and fitted with lamp housings to accommodate light bulbs or imitation candles. The introduction of wiring often causes damage to both glass and metal parts; they were often glued, wired, soldered or twisted along the chandelier arms. Occasionally holes were drilled on glass nozzles in order to pass the wire through to the lamp housing. In order to hide the wiring and to be able to introduce it through small spaces not originally intended for wire, small gauge wire was sometimes used, which is below the current electrical code standards. Wires were sometimes forced into spaces too small to accommodate them, causing cracks and breaks in the glass and damage to the sleeve wiring. In general, wiring is often old and worn, not having withstood repeated movement, adjustment, cleaning and handling. Exposed metal wires and wiring which is not correctly insulated can cause electrical shorts and subsequent fire. The safety requirements for the electrical wiring of lighting are very stringent; all wiring should by undertaken by an appropriately qualified electrician.

Examination

Preliminary examination of the condition of hanging chandeliers is normally undertaken from a metal stepladder. Furniture and any other objects beneath or near the chandelier should be removed to a safe distance. This will allow the free movement of a stepladder around the chandelier; and prevent damage in the event of any glass falling down (not an uncommon occurrence in cases where chandeliers have been neglected for many years). A small dictaphone or pad is required for recording notes of the chandelier's condition. From time to time during examination, the stepladder should be moved around the chandelier, rather than rotating the chandelier itself. The method by which the chandelier is secured to the ceiling joists may not be known at this point, and either the fixing or the

shackle, by which the chandelier is suspended, may become unscrewed with disastrous results. In particular, rotating a chandelier in an anticlockwise direction may cause it to unthread itself if the nut which secures the suspension loop to the central support is missing. Particular care must be taken in cases where chandeliers have been electrified and not undergone regular and recent safety checks. Sub-standard or sub-code wiring is common. Wear and use may have loosened electrical connections, resulting in electrical shorts causing shock to the conservator, or fire. Ideally, the electrical supply should have been turned off.

Chandeliers which have been dismantled for storage or transport present different problems. There may be no record of their original configuration, or simply photographs taken as the chandeliers were hanging. These are usually confusing due to the amount of glass present, the distance from which the photographs were taken and/or their poor quality. Photographs showing chandeliers were often taken to show the entire room rather than the chandeliers themselves. The use of a hand-held magnifying glass may aid their interpretation. The arrangement of the glass components may have to be hypothesized, especially if the chandelier is unique; measuring the total length of the stem pieces and comparing their total to the length of the metal support rod will determine whether all the glass pieces are present. Age and style comparisons will help, although it must be remembered that broken pieces may have been replaced with incorrectly shaped components over time. Where there is doubt, a historian of historic lighting should be consulted. The metal frame and all the brass linking pins require to be checked for signs of weakness and/or corrosion, and for the site of missing screws, washers etc. to be noted; this may require that the chandelier has to be dismantled.

In addition to chandeliers that remain essentially intact, it is sometimes the case that all or part of them falls to the ground. This may happen as a result of the failure of the fixing mechanism, failure of part of the metal frame, of old repairs and restorations, or as a result of damage to the room or building which they decorate, such as a fire. In such cases, a

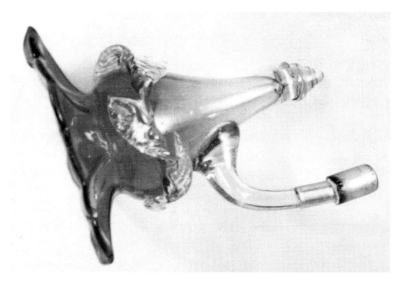

Figure 7.60 A broken glass arm from an *épergne* repaired by extending the metal pot into which it had fitted. The pot extension replaces the missing end of the arm. Similar repairs are carried out on chandelier arms. (Courtesy of K. van Lookeren Campagne).

conservator may be faced with trays of broken glass belonging to one or more chandeliers. A policy decision must then be taken with the owner and insurers, as to how much of the historic glass can be repaired for re-use, or to serve as patterns from which new pieces may be copied (the original remaining in an archive); and how much is beyond economic or practical repair/restoration. Sorting the fragments alone is a time-consuming and therefore costly operation. The first step is to sort the glass fragments by shape, thickness, colour, cut and design into the various components; especially difficult if there are, for example, a number of canopies, which whilst being of a slightly different size to each other, will bear the same cut design. Once the fragments have been sorted into balusters, pendants, greasepans, bowls etc., the glass from the different components can be laid out. Sometimes, as is the case with greasepans, is will be possible to say at this point whether there is sufficient glass to be able to effect a safe and aesthetical repair/restoration. In the case of deeper three-dimensional components such as bowls and balusters, fragments can be taped together, or supported on polystyrene forms.

If there seems to be sufficient glass to effect a repair, the fragments can be adhered with epoxy resin. These shapes are difficult to repair due to the cumulative weight of the glass fragments, and in the case of bowls, the need to align the fragments correctly in curvatures in two directions, i.e. circumference and from rim to base. The glass will usually require a support during the resin curing-time. It is not considered wise to re-hang bowls or canopies if heavy glass pendants will be suspended from the rims. It must be borne in mind that people will walk beneath chandeliers, and that resin repairs such as those just described could fail in time and cause injury or damage furniture below the chandelier. Large broken pieces of glass, such as bowls, if repaired and re-used, must be inspected annually to check the strength of the repairs. In the case of modern chandeliers it is preferable to replace the broken glass, especially if heavy and/or load bearing. Replacing glass sections either with contemporary pieces or with newly made sections can be expensive but may be necessary for reasons of safety. If it is not possible or desirable to use period replacement parts, new ones can be made by taking moulds from original examples, and glass cast or blown and then cut, and metal parts cast and painted or electrotyped. Small glass elements can be reproduced more cheaply using clear polyester or epoxy resins (although these will discolour in time the discoloration is unlikely to be visible from the ground). It may be possible to re-use broken glass arms, depending on the number and position of the breaks in them. Arms broken at the point at which they emerge from their

(a)

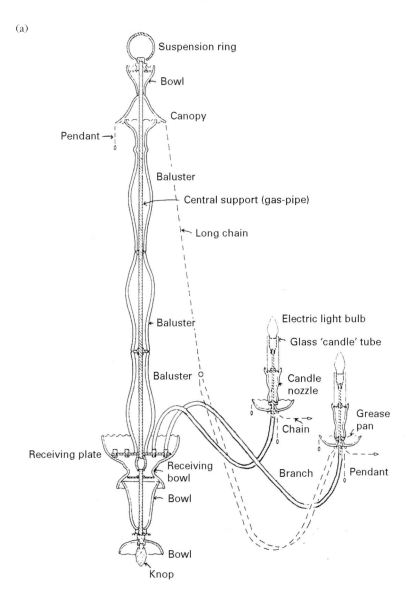

Suspension ring

Bowl

Canopy

Pendant →

Baluster

Central support (gas-pipe)

Long chain

Baluster

Electric light bulb

Glass 'candle' tube

Candle nozzle

Baluster

Chain

Grease pan

Receiving plate

Receiving bowl

Branch

Pendant

Bowl

Bowl

Knop

Figure 7.61 Recording glass chandeliers: (a) section; (b) layout viewed from beneath; (c) dismantled central support; (d) chains and pendants removed from a chandelier and laid out for photography.

metal pot can be repaired and the metal pot extended to cover and support the repair (*Figure 7.60*). Mid-length breaks will need to be repaired, and covered by a metal collar. Old lead and brass collars look unsightly, but white metal, e.g. silver, when polished is not immediately visible, especially if the chandelier is highly decorated. Glass elements should be separated from one another by washers made of chamois leather, or by metal washers, which fit inside the glass.

Dismantling

Before beginning work, it must be ensured that the electricity supply has been turned off. The conservator, accompanying the housekeeper or electrician assigned to do this, should ensure that there is no risk of the power being restored. It is advisable to attach a notice to the fuse board cupboard to the effect that the chandeliers are being worked on and must remain isolated until further notice. The isolation must be confirmed by an electrical test at

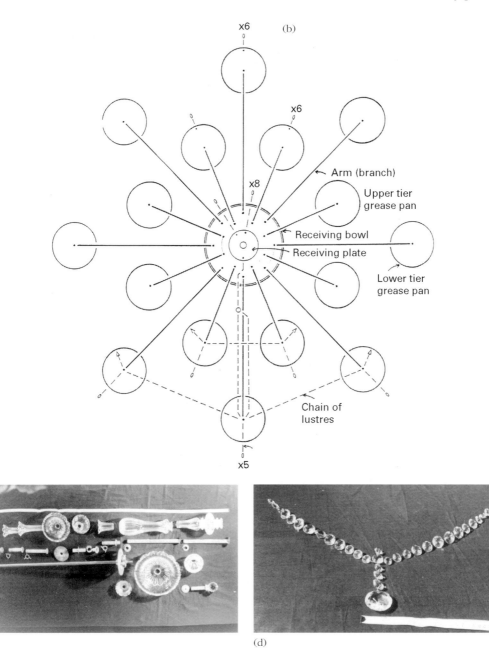

(b)

x6

x6

← Arm (branch)

Upper tier
grease pan

← Receiving bowl

↖ Receiving plate

Lower tier
grease pan

x8

Chain of
lustres

x5

(c)

(d)

each chandelier, i.e. the use of a voltmeter or other indicator to demonstrate the absence of the supply. Adequate space must be cleared beneath and around each chandelier to allow for movement of ladders and/or scaffolding. Soft padding such as decorators' groundsheets should be placed beneath the chandelier to soften the landing of any pieces which might fall. A number of tables also padded will be required nearby for laying out the components as they are dismantled. The components of a chandelier take up a great deal of space when they are laid out. A chandelier can either be dismantled *in situ*, or lowered to a safe working height by means of a block and tackle system attached by snap links to the suspension chain.

Figure 7.62 A receiving plate for chandelier arms. In this example the holes to receive the metal pots into which the glass arms are fitted, are square.

Prior to and during dismantling and cleaning, a photographic and written record is made, by means of notes, sketches, black and white and colour photographs, so that there is a clear record of where each piece of a chandelier belongs in relation to the others (*Figure 7.61a,b*). The amount of glass on a chandelier makes photography difficult. It is easier to photograph the arrangement of chains and pendants by removing one example from the chandelier, and laying it out on a flat surface (*Figure 7.61c*). It is particularly important to note the way in which the branches join the metal receiving plate and the arrangement of electrical wiring (*Figures 7.62*). Other items to note are damaged and repaired glass, missing glass and technological details.

Each chandelier is dismantled in sequence, beginning with the dressings and working from outside inwards and from the bottom upwards (*Figure 7.63a–e*). During this process it is not uncommon for chains to break and for lustres to fall as a result of weak linking pins failing. Although the arrangement of the pendants and chains will require to be recorded, it is not always necessary to note the exact position of every one. Their arrangement should be regular around the chandelier, and the chandelier will have been dismantled and cleaned many times since its installation so that the components are unlikely to be in their original positions. For safety reasons and ease of identification, the pendants and chains are removed in an orderly sequence, placed

in labelled Polythene bags and passed down from the working platform in plastic baskets or trays (*Figure. 7.63a,b*).

Detachable glass nozzles, drip pans, opal glass or cardboard candle tubes (if present) and other ornaments such as spires on threaded mounts should then be removed. The next stage involves the removal of the light bulbs. In order not to put undue strain on the glass arms during this operation, they are supported by placing a hand beneath the greasepan to apply a slight upwards pressure to counteract the slight downward pressure required to release the light bulb, especially from a bayonet fixing (*Figure 7.63c*). It will usually be necessary to remove the lower section of the chandelier next, i.e. up to and including the receiving bowl, which covers the electrical connections joining the arms. The electrical supply already having been isolated, the wiring can be disconnected. If this involves cutting the wires, the arms and/or central stem may have to be rewired before the chandelier is reassembled.

Once the electric wires have been disconnected, the arms themselves can be removed. Glass arms, ending in square or round metal pots, may simply slot into the metal receiving plate; some round pots were locked in position by a locating pin which fitted into a slot in the plate, or secured by a threaded nut below the receiving plate. Gentle upward pressure applied from beneath the receiving plate and controlled sideways pressure is applied to each arm in turn to ascertain whether the arm is loose. If the arm is loose, it can be held firmly at both ends and drawn clear of the plate, taking care not to jerk the arm or to bring it into contact with any nearby glass or metal components. If the arm is not loose, it may be necessary to apply thin lubricating oil around the pot, or even in some cases a small amount of rust remover. The glass branches are removed one at a time, if possible working from alternate sides so that the structure remains hanging evenly, and handed down from the working platform since there would be a danger of them tipping out of a tray (*Figure 7.63d*).

Once all the arms are removed, the metal safety hawser (if present) can be disconnected from below the receiving plate so that the receiving plate and glass and metal sections

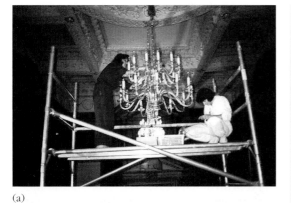

(a)

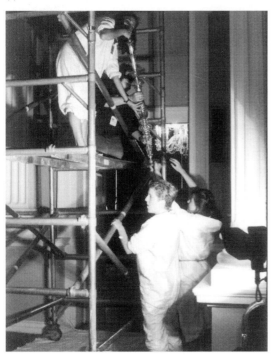

(c)

(b)

(d)

(e)

Figure 7.63 Stages in dismantling a chandelier: (a) removing the dressings (decorative elements); (b) handing pieces down in baskets; (c) supporting the arm whilst removing a light bulb; (d) handing large pieces down to the ground; (e) a fully dismantled chandelier.

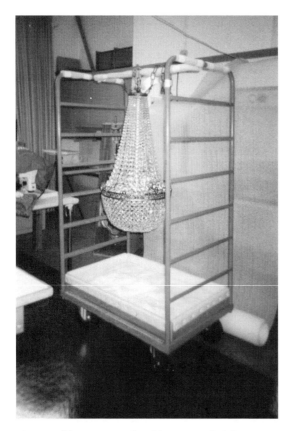

Figure 7.64 Moving a chandelier suspended from a frame on a trolley.

from the upper section of the central support stem can be removed individually. This operation will require two pairs of hands, one to remove the glass a section at a time, and the other to hold the remaining unsecured glass in place. The glass sections are passed down from the working platform in plastic baskets. Lastly, the central support is unhooked from the chain suspending the chandelier from the ceiling. If the chandelier is relatively small and measures no more than about 2 metres in height, it may be considered safer to pass the whole of the central support stem down to the floor in one piece by unhooking it from the suspension chain. Once down, the suspension ring and fittings and/or the circular metal receiving plate are removed, in order to release the glass balusters and bowls and attendant silver metal fittings (tubes, washers and nuts) (*Figure 7.63e*). A sturdy metal or

wooden frame on a rolling base is useful for temporary movement and storage of an assembled shaft of a chandelier (*Figure 7.64*).

If the chandelier is to be transported from site or stored for any length of time, it is preferable to dismantle it fully and pack the components in acid-free tissue and bubblepack in a wooden crate labelled with its fragile contents.

Conservation
Correct installation is the primary factor in preventative conservation. The appropriate weight and type of chain and ceiling hook must be used to suspend the chandelier. The hook itself must be secured into a load-bearing ceiling joist in such a way that complete rotation of the chandelier cannot unscrew the hook or disturb its connection to the ceiling. This is best arranged by a qualified structural engineer, especially in the case of historically important, and extremely heavy chandeliers. The chain from which a chandelier is suspended should be made of closed-link steel or brass. It should be of sufficient strength to bear more than the full weight of the chandelier. It is likely that the chandelier will have to be weighed; easily done by weighing individual or groups of components on a bench balance and adding the total weights. The chandelier itself should hang level and the weight of the stem pieces on the central support rod evenly distributed by the insertion of washers and bushings between them.

Thought must be given as to how the chandelier will be accessed for routine maintenance and cleaning; and how often this will be done. In the case of small chandeliers hung at no great height, this might be managed from a set of stable metal steps or a light scaffolding tower. In the mid-eighteenth century, chandeliers were often hung on counterpoises from a fixed hook. As the chandelier was drawn down, by grasping the finial, compensating counterpoises rose up the chain. Some of these mechanisms remain and, if used, should be checked periodically to ensure that they are in working order. For chandelier installations at great height, purpose-built winches with reduction gear and locking capabilities are desirable. Hand winches are to be preferred to those operated by push buttons, as the latter may jolt to a stop, causing movement and damage to the glass. Glass chandeliers are most prone to damage from mishandling and from knocks by scaffolding or ladders used to enable cleaning or the changing of light bulbs. The risk of damage could be greatly reduced if each chandelier were to be fitted with a rise and fall mechanism, which could incorporate a limiting device restricting the drop of the chandelier. The replacement of light bulbs would be made safer, quicker and easier, thereby reducing maintenance costs after the initial cost of installation.

If the chandelier is electrified it should be examined annually by a qualified electrician. A record of the date when each chandelier is cleaned, dismantled, checked for the safety of the electrical wiring and ceiling connections should be kept by the conservator and by the owner.

The breakage of opal glass 'candle-tubes' often occurs as they are compressed during the insertion of the electric light bulbs. The light fittings are not fixed in the cut glass greasepans or candle nozzles, they therefore rotate whilst the bulbs are being inserted, requiring a certain amount of pressure to be exerted. It should be possible to design a device to prevent this from occurring in the future.

The period of time between each cleaning will need to be determined by conservators and the owners. In deciding the frequency of cleaning, finance will have to be considered and the fact that there is a potential danger in handling and dismantling the chandeliers. If the chandeliers decorate rooms that are in constant use, general cleaning may be necessary at yearly intervals, and in-depth cleaning involving dismantling, perhaps every ten years. If, on the other hand, the chandeliers are in rooms that are closed to the public for part of the year, the amount of dust and dirt that settles on them is reduced if they are protected by large muslin bags.

The glass is cleaned with a 50:50 solution of industrial methylated spirits (IMS) (US: ethanol) and distilled or de-ionised water. Reilly and Mortimer (1998) suggest adding a few drops of ammonia to increase the effectiveness of the cleaning solution; whilst warning against raising the pH above 9.

(Above pH 9 an aqueous alkaline solution potentially dissolves glass, but not in the short time taken to clean a chandelier.) The addition of a few drops of a non-ionic detergent is to be preferred. Care should be taken not to allow the cleaning solution to penetrate the hollow glass branches, or the metal light fittings. The glass is then wiped over with distilled water on a soft cloth and then gently polished with a lint-free, dry cloth to remove smears and finger-prints. Wax deposits can usually be easily dislodged using a chisel-ended bamboo stick, the residue being removed with warm water or white spirit (aliphatic hydrocarbon solvent).

Cleaning using chemicals, if absolutely necessary, should be restricted to the substantial metal parts, and then only to those from which the chemical residues can be safely and conveniently removed. If not removed thoroughly, chemical residues or by-products will remain and eventually attack the glass, metal and metal link pins. The composition of materials used for cleaning should be known, plus the short- and long-term effects on the substrates (and upon the persons undertaking the work). Light deposits of rust (ferric oxide Fe_2O_3) may be removed mechanically using a glass-fibre bristle brush or, if necessary, chemically with a commercial rust remover based on phosphoric acid, which reacts with the ferric oxide to form a protective coating of black iron phosphate, a positive corrosion inhibitor. The use of such a rust remover would also incur the removal of original paint on the iron pipes. Thus it may be necessary to analyse a sample of the paint if any repainting is anticipated.

Light silver tarnish may be removed by immersing the silver in a solution of Goddard's Silver Dip (UK) (active ingredient ammonium thiocyanate). A soft bristle brush is used to clean the silver, alternatively the solution may be applied locally on cotton wool swabs. The bath of solution should be renewed frequently. After cleaning, the silver is rinsed in changes of distilled water. Severe tarnish may necessitate the use of a mild abrasive such as Goddard's Silver Foam, gamma aluminium in alcohol, or precipitated chalk in a distilled water/alcohol mixture. Coarser abrasives would damage the metal surface. Traces of the cleaning agent are removed with copious amounts of warm distilled water and the silver left to air-dry before being polished with a soft cloth impregnated with an anti-tarnishing agent. Lacquering the silver is not recommended since it will easily be scratched off moving parts and thus the silver will tarnish in streaks; often much of the metal is covered by glass and therefore tarnishes very slowly. Lacquer would be time-consuming to remove and renew.

Broken metal parts, which are not structural, can be repaired using a two-part epoxy resin. However, for obvious safety reasons, structural repairs must be carried out by a metal worker, using soldering and brazing techniques. Weak, brittle wire pins should be replaced with new purpose-made chandelier pins. Made of soft brass, they are easily bent to shape, whilst having sufficient strength to support glass lustres and pendants. Care must be taken when cutting away old pins and wiring, as metal wire cutters can easily damage the glass. Reilly and Mortimer (1998) suggest immersing glass dressings having an enormous number of pins in a bathe of dilute nitric acid to dissolve the metal. The acid concentration and length of immersion are not specified, but this course of treatment is not recommended.

During the life of a chandelier, drops, pendants and chains (dressings) will almost certainly have become broken or lost. They may have been replaced at random with any glass lustres to hand irrespective of whether or not they are of the correct size or shape, and dressings incorrectly hooked up to fill a gap. Thus it is important to remember when dismantling the chandelier for cleaning that if pendants and chains are rearranged correctly, the final appearance may be worsened unless new glass lustres can be purchased.

Where individual lustres, pendants and chains have been misplaced, they can be rearranged where possible. However, the reason for misplacement may be that lustres have broken in such a way that there are no longer holes through which to secure the linking pins. New lustres will have to be purchased. If, however, a full restoration is in order, the dressings can be fully dismantled and patterns made up as guides for each set of pendants or chains required. Chains and swags are almost always graded by size, with the larger drops at the bottom (or centre). If

the lustres are pear-shaped, the direction of the lustres changes on either side of the central lustre, which should be oval. The linking pins should be aligned to allow the lustres to hang freely and in plane with the dressing. Correct assembly of dressings for neoclassical chandeliers requires that they should be permanently fixed at their right hand end to a *four-way* (i.e. a glass lustre pierced with four holes), while the left hand end should be provided with a slightly larger eye for attachment to the neighbouring four-way. The vertical chains suspended from swags should remain permanently at the top and bottom of the four-way. These units (a swag, a four-way, a top vertical chain, and a bottom vertical chain) can be removed and replaced as a unit. The vertical drops grade from small to large as they fall. Drops are generally hung with their flat, cut or pressed side to the outside in order to catch and reflect the available light (Reilly and Mortimer, 1998).

Dismantling of old repairs, cleaning, repair and restoration of the glass elements, can be undertaken using the methods described elsewhere in this chapter. On completion of the work, a conservation report is produced which should include instructions on assembly/dismantling, notes of any modifications which may have been made, and safety certificates for suspension hooks, chains, ceiling fixings and the electrical wiring. The conservation of an iron and glass chandelier is described by Sommer-Larson (1999).

Mirrors

Deterioration of the glass itself is discussed in Chapter 4. In addition, deterioration processes will occur in any decoration such as *verre eglomisé* or reverse paintings, within the mirrored surface itself. There may also be problems with the frame (weakened by wood worm or dry rot; the latter also causes blackening of the mirroring); the support (linseed putty drying out) or backboard (which might be flimsy); the backings (such as wool blanketing); and the fixings – pins often with decorative glass heads, either pinned into the frame or secured in place with animal glue and or plaster of Paris. This method of attachment was often used to secure decorative items used to hide joins in the glass plates.

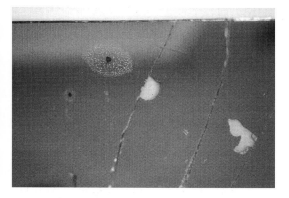

Figure 7.65 Chemical and physical damage of a mirrored glass: deterioration of the amalgam, beginning as dark spots, loss of amalgam, and cracks in the glass.

The first signs of corrosion in a tin–amalgam mirror appears as small dark patches which give the mirror a dark and cloudy appearance (*Figure 7.65*). Massive corrosion shows as a dark grey layer or as concentric coloured bands varying from dark grey to yellow-brown and white. As the amalgam deteriorates, the crystal phase changes, in that the crystals enlarge and cover a larger proportion of the glass surface, whilst the mercury slowly evaporates. In time, tiny voids appear between the glass substrate and the amalgam. The fluid phase also migrates to the bottom of the mirror. Corrosion of the amalgam results in the formation of tin oxide (cassiterite) and tin monoxide (romarchite) and releases liquid mercury from the solid phase. Deteriorating amalgam mirrors contribute a few micrograms of mercury per cubic metre of air in the room in which they are situated, though this level is normally far below the toxic limit of 50 µg. The frames, however, often trap drops of mercury and special precautions are necessary when handling them.

Conservators may be asked to deal with the preservation of mirrors in several different circumstances. Mirrors may be encountered in the form of architectural elements, in glazed doors, recessed alcoves, window bays, wall coverings and even as floor coverings, e.g. the Mirror Room in the Rosenborg Palace in Copenhagen, furnished for King Frederik IV *circa* 1700 and inspired by Louis XIV's palace at Versailles. More commonly, mirrors are framed and fixed to walls, e.g. the pier glasses at Hampton Court Palace (Jackson, 1984, 1987; Quinton, 1998); smaller framed mirrors are hung on nails or other metal fixings. Mirrors are also found as decorative panels on furniture such as side tables and drawer fronts. In the nineteenth century, mirrors combined with paintings on glass, executed in reverse (see Chapter 2), were produced in China for export to Europe. Other types are hand-held mirrors and those produced for scientific use.

Mirrors cannot be considered in isolation from their frame, structure or furniture with which they are associated. It is necessary to agree a level of conservation in order that visual harmony is maintained. As far as possible, the original glass should be preserved; replacing mirror glass in antique furniture would look aesthetically displeasing, and may significantly reduce the value of the piece. Almost all mirrors can be conserved to some degree if the budget allows. Where replacement cannot be avoided, the original should be preserved in an archive. As a general rule glass should be treated *in situ* wherever possible. However, in some cases it will be necessary to remove the glass from its support in order to carry out the conservation. For example, repairs to a mirror frame or furniture may be necessary, whilst the mirror itself may be in good condition. The potential risk of damage to the glass during handling and transport must be considered. It is generally safest for the mirror to be well padded and to travel within the object which it decorates. Depending on the work to be undertaken on frames or furniture, the mirrors may remain *in situ*, but the risk of accidentally scratching the glass with abrasive papers or tools, or of actually breaking it, are considerable.

In addition to such physical damage, there is the possibility of chemical reaction between the amalgam and emissions from wood preservatives, varnishes and paints, adhesives and lacquers. Acetic acid is given off by PVAC adhesives, and by manufactured boards, such as plywood and medium density fibre-board (MDF), which contain adhesive. Materials based on polystyrene resin emit styrene, which blackens tin and silver. Where the glass and furniture are to be treated by different conservators, the object should first be delivered to the glass conservator who will remove the mirrors. Conservation grade materials should be used wherever possible, and wood used to effect replacements chosen with minimal emission of acetic acid.

If mirrors have to be removed from their mounts, it must be ensured that there is adequate room to manoeuvre the glass and to support it in a vertical position without risk of it being broken. This is particularly important in the case of large mirrors, where ideally an area several times larger than the sheet of glass, and several operators, are needed in order to ensure maximum safety. It may, for instance, become necessary to remove mirrors during structural building works or if the support has failed. As with any conservation procedure, it is necessary to balance the risk of leaving the mirror *in situ* against the risks involved in moving it.

Consideration must be given to the size and weight of the glass, its condition, e.g. the presence of cracks or breaks, the strength (thickness), the condition of the mirrored surface and any painted decoration, and the ease of removal of the fixings which secure the glass to the mount. Advance planning should include measures to ensure safe handling, storage and, if necessary, packaging and transport and reinstatement. If the glass is to be removed and laid flat, it should be placed on a surface cushioned with a layer of clean, non-abrasive, non-slip material such as Plastazote (inert polyethylene foam). The mirror glass is unlikely to be completely flat, and undulations must be packed with Plastazote in order to prevent areas of stress concentration. In order to prevent accidental damage, large areas of mirror can be enclosed by a shallow wooden frame; smaller pieces of mirror can be supported in wooden or polypropylene trays lined with Plastazote.

Before and during dismantling the mirror should be fully documented, including photographs. The orientation of the mirror and its backboard should be recorded, and all components, including the fixings, should be labelled and marked on a diagram. When work begins, it is important to ensure that all fixings holding the glass are removed otherwise they might crack or scratch the glass as it is lifted away. The most common fixings are nails, screws, metal clasps or frames, wooden wedges, linseed putty and paper or fabric tape. A soldering iron can be used with care

to soften putty which will have hardened over time and is otherwise difficult to remove. Needless to say, care must be taken not to crack the glass. The glass once, loosened, can be removed and laid on a support, putty side up. Heat can then be applied to any remaining putty in order to peel it away. During and after removal of glass, care must be taken not to damage loose glazing bars or to support frames and support components.

There is no way of preventing the change in structure of a tin–mercury amalgam, and the deterioration is irreversible. Although not possible to predict the outcome accurately, it may be possible to slow the process down by keeping the mirror at a constant low temperature. The amalgam will be adversely affected if the mirror is cooled to the low stability level of 17.5°C or heated to 58°C, at which temperature the crystal phase will change. A relative humidity of about 5 per cent, the lowest tolerated by wooden frames and furniture in which mirrors may be set, is not low enough to prevent corrosion of the amalgam by some hygroscopic salts.

It may be thought logical to cure mirrors with a softening of the amalgam at the lower edge where there is an excess of mercury, by laying them flat horizontally, or even by turning the mirrors onto their sides to redistribute the mercury. However this course of action is to be avoided since it can result in further damage caused by flooding with mercury parts of the mirror which have a tight-packed relatively 'dry' crystalline structure. Excess mercury can be sucked away on tin foil, but removal of too much liquid phase can cause further damage to the two-phase amalgam. Mercury can be collected using mercury salvage kits obtained from chemical suppliers, and disposed of in accordance with current health and safety legislative guidelines.

It is advantageous to remove loose dust and debris such as spiders' webs, although it may be difficult if the amalgam is flaking or liquid. Any attached framework, or surrounding wood should be protected with acid-free tissue. In the case of glass that is undecorated with paint or gilding, loose dust can be removed using small pads made from silk or lint-free cotton (large cloths may snag on delicate elements and should therefore be avoided), and using the absolute minimum of pressure. If it becomes necessary to use wet cleaning methods, solvents such as distilled water with a non-ionic detergent, a 50:50 mixture of distilled water and industrial methylated spirits (IMS), IMS alone, acetone and white spirit (US: Stoddard solvent) may be used on cotton wool swabs. The swabs should be dipped in the solvent and then blotted on paper before use in order to minimize the amount of solvent in use. This is especially important where the mirror remains *in situ*, to prevent solvents leaking beneath frames or beneath the glass. The surround should be protected with Melinex (US: Mylar) sheet, which can often be inserted between the glass and the surround. Wet cleaning treatments should obviously be avoided around cracks, as dirt would be carried into the cracks.

The use of commercial glass cleaning solutions is to be avoided, since their chemical composition is unknown; as is the spray application of solvents, as the spray area is difficult to control. Fine abrasive pastes should not be used to clean glass as the particles may scratch it. A soft cleaning paste can be made up of whiting and containing a drop of ammonia. In the case of mirrors having painted or gilded surfaces, which are well adhered, the surface can be cleaned using a soft sable brush. Paint must be checked to determine whether it is cold (unfired) or fired. Gilding will often have been applied in the form of water gilding, which would be removed by wet treatments.

The amalgam surface of tin–mercury mirrors should not be vacuum cleaned since the mercury will vaporize and be released into the environment. It is particularly important to wear a mask with a mercury filter to prevent the inhalation of vapour, and to wear gloves to prevent mercury from being absorbed by the skin as mercury can cause damage to the nervous system. The wearing of gloves will also prevent acid from the fingers being deposited on the amalgam, to form fingerprints, which eventually penetrate through the amalgam (*Figure 7.66*). Loose debris can be gently removed with a soft sable brush, kept only for use on mirrors and stored in a self-seal plastic bag. In cases where the amalgam is unbroken, a weak rubber-based contact adhesive can be applied in a thin layer, and rolled off after a few minutes as a coherent

Figure 7.66 Fingerprints formed by acid from fingers, in an amalgam surface.

Figure 7.67 Sheet of Scotchtint placed behind a deteriorated mirror, to impart a reflective appearance.

film. If gaps in the amalgam are to be masked by laying metal foil behind it, the new metal must be isolated from the amalgam (e.g. with lacquer) in order to prevent mercury reacting with the metal foil (Hadsund, 1993). The mirror amalgam itself should not be painted or lacquered since it will not be able to remove the coating at a later date, should this become necessary, without risk of damaging the soft amalgam. A better solution used by Jackson is the laying of a reflective coated sheet of Scotchtint Melinex (US: Mylar) behind the damaged glass. This material, developed for use in solar reflective windows, is secured to backboards, *not* to the amalgam surface (*Figure 7.67*).

Consolidation of flaking amalgam or painted/gilded surfaces may be necessary, and should be referred to a conservation specialist. Painted decoration can be particularly problematical since there is a wide variety of materials and techniques (see the section on reverse paintings on glass). Consolidation of flaking amalgam is difficult since the flakes are often brittle so that the traditional method of laying paint flakes by flowing consolidant beneath the flake and then securing it to the substrate by application of a heated spatula, cannot apply. In addition, the amalgam may break down when subjected to heat. In some cases, the application of a small amount of a viscous consolidant, e.g. 50/50 wt/vol solution of Paraloid B-72 (methyl methacrylate copolymer) in acetone, to the thin edge of amalgam flakes may act as a bridge to the glass, thereby keeping it in position. The consolidant should not flow beneath the flake. Any pressure applied to the flake will break or completely shatter it.

The frame and backboard act as a support for the mirror glass and afford protection from dust, dirt and insect nests. The frame and backboard should be reasonably well-fitting, but not trap potentially harmful accumulations of hazardous corrosion products. Suitable backing materials for the glass include conservation grade fabrics, an acid-free card and paper. The backboard can be lined with a sheet of Melinex (US: Mylar). New wood should always be covered with Melinex to protect the mirror from any acid vapours that might be given off. Where possible, the original wedges and nails should be re-used when reinstating a mirror. Hadsund (1993) illustrates a system for mounting and supporting tin–amalgam mirrors, and Dowling (1999) discussed the removal and installation of mirrors in a museum environment.

Conservation of historic chandeliers and mirrors is often undertaken on site, for which considerable forward planning is required (see Appendix I).

Plain glazing

Painted and stained glazing is immediately visually appreciated, and can easily be dated; it has been the subject of much scientific research and conservation/restoration. However, plain quarried, or plain leaded glazing is not so visually attractive or easily dated, and until recent years, broken clear glass windowpanes have simply been replaced. Since the nineteenth century, old glazing has been replaced with hand-made window glass, or worse, with modern machine-made, clear-white glass, without regard for the resulting changes in visual appearance. Old hand-made plain glazings will normally not be entirely flat nor entirely clear, and its light bending properties result in a surface movement. It may have a greyish appearance, or exhibit a huge range of tone, contain air bubbles or exhibit parallel curves (if cut from crowns). In order to date the glass, a study has also to be made of the leading, lead ties, *ferramenta*, timber frames and mortar.

The historical value of original plain and plain leaded glass is beginning to be appreciated. Where it survives it should be recorded, retained, preserved, repaired and re-used where possible. Some specialist glaziers have extensive stocks of original glazing, recovered from old buildings (domestic, public and ecclesiastical). It is important to match the texture and type of replacement glass for missing areas. Hand-made glass is no longer made commercially in Britain, but can be obtained from the Continent.

Features which should be recorded and preserved, either *in situ* or in an archive, are inscriptions on lead, or diamond cut into the glass surface, the survival of pieces of horn, lead ties and the use of pattern-stamped lead grilles glazed in for ventilation. It is important that anyone involved with original glazing in a building, i.e. glazier, architect, should be made aware of its historical value, and of the need to retain as much as possible. Specifications for this should be clear, avoiding such misleading terms as *reglaze, reform, replace,* or *repair as new.* It is possible for an experienced glazier to repair and reconstruct the characteristic irregularities of pre-nineteenth century plain glazing patterns. A lead rubbing is taken of every individual panel before dismantling the glass, then numbering each piece of glass on the glass itself and the rubbing, so that each can be reglazed into its original position. The same width of leading as the original should be used so that the proportional relationship and size of each panel remains the same. Any replacement glass can be cut to size using the lead rubbing as a cartoon (pattern). Nineteenth-century reticulated plain quarry glazing is frequently replaced with modern plain glazing of contemporary design. It should be remembered that plain quarry glazing was so widely used as it was practical, inexpensive and a successful solution to maximizing light and glass because it held together without distortion. When correctly fixed, the interactive network of glass and lead of diamond quarry glazing ensured that the considerable combined weight of the glass and lead in the glazed interspace was carried evenly from top to bottom without stress (Kerr, 1991).

Painted and stained glass

The museum approach to the conservation of painted and stained glass windows, using epoxy resins, is described by Holden (1991). The conservation and restoration of stained glass windows, especially those *in situ*, requires specialist skills (Lee *et al.*, 1982; Newton, 1987; Newton and Davison, 1989; Sloan, 1993).

Resetting excavated window glass

The resetting of fragile, excavated window glass has been undertaken, but ideas are still undeveloped. Much excavated material, even after consolidation, is not strong enough to be releaded, nor stable or transparent enough to be placed in a window opening, due to the presence of opaque surface crusts. However, fragments of the medieval glass found or excavated from churchyards have been releaded and installed as windows, e.g. Kirdford and Chiddingfold in Sussex (UK). A great deal of English medieval church window glass was deliberately destroyed during the Civil War in the seventeenth century. Remains of the medieval glass windows, found buried in the churchyard of St Dunstan's Church, Monks Risborough in Buckinghamshire (UK) were re-leaded in a random fashion, and reinstated in a window in 1807. Undoubtedly this has been done elsewhere, and the work probably involved injudicious cleaning of the

glass itself. Cleaning of discoloured medieval window glass is discussed by Fitz (1981; Fitz *et al.*, 1984). The use of selected chelating agents to reveal painted decoration on excavated medieval glass has been published by Barham (1999).

Fragments of Anglo-Saxon glass excavated from Jarrow Monastery (Northumbria, UK), have been re-leaded for display in Jarrow Museum (Cramp, 1968, 1975). Fragile glass would not withstand incorporation in heavy leading, even for museum display, and therefore, the use of narrow copper foil, fine leads or other materials or devices may have to be explored. For example, a lightweight, rigid synthetic frame could be used, and the window suspended vertically; or the glass could be laid flat, or at a slight angle, and mirrors used to produce a vertical effect. Before resetting, it is essential that details such as grozed edges, which will be hidden by the new cames, or which will be too distant for examination in the new position, are thoroughly recorded.

Cloisonné glass

The manufacture of *cloisonné* glass panels dates from the turn of the nineteenth century. There is little information regarding the manufacturing technique; the following information was taken from publicity material issued by The Cloisonné Glass Company. *Cloisonné* panels were made up, by first outlining the design with thin gilt or silvered metal wire secured with translucent cement (adhesive) to a sheet of clear glass (backplate). The cells thus formed were filled with pot metal coloured glass in granular form (< 1 mm), either globules or squares, and secured in place with adhesive. The panels could be used as an alternative in any situation where stained or leaded glass, mosaic, fresco or tempera would be appropriate.

Deterioration and conservation
The problems most likely to be encountered with this type of glass are damage of the glass covers and to the tinfoil binding. If either is damaged, the glass beads and even the metal may become detached with disastrous results. Another form of damage occurs if water penetrates the interior of the panel, dissolving

(a)

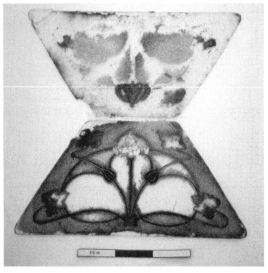

(b)

(c)

Figure 7.68 Restoration of a *cloisonné* glass lampshade. (a) The lampshade after restoration. (b) One of the panels opened up showing details of the *cloisonné* design, and the fact that some of the wires and glass beads have become transferred to the cover glass. (c) Detail of the brass wires forming the *cloisons*, and the coloured glass beads, which form the design.

the adhesive binding the glass beads, and causing the metal strips to corrode. A great deal of restoration of *cloisonné* glass panels has been carried out in Spain. However, the *ballotini* were removed entirely and the panels reformed (Martin, 1985).

The restoration of a lampshade, the sides of which were formed of panels of *cloisonné* stained glass, with a base of transparent rippled green glass, is shown in *Figures 7.68a–c*). The edges of the *cloisonné* panels were bound in lead foil and clipped into a bronze frame. The lampshade was suspended from the ceiling by four metal chains (*Figure 7.68a*). It was in a deteriorated condition as a result of the lead foil, which bound the edges of each panel, being corroded or missing. It was also extremely dirty, and had been immersed in water by its owner, whereupon water had entered between the glass panels, dissolved the animal glue holding the glass *ballotini* in place, and initiated corrosion of the metal bands forming the *cloisons* or cells. One of the panels was so badly damaged, the glass itself being broken and having one corner and parts of the design missing, that it was decided to open the panel up in order to effect the restoration.

The sheet of glass to which the metal *cloisons* had not been originally attached, was carefully lifted, whilst watching for any disruption of the design (*Figure 7.68b*). Metal or glass, which has become detached or which has become transferred to the cover glass, would have to reattached to the base glass, using the tracing of the original design placed beneath the base glass as a guide to enable the metal strips to be correctly positioned. The minute glass beads and fragments (*Figure 7.68c*) were retrieved with tweezers, and, working under magnification, sorted into colours and sizes. In order to secure the glass beads, the surface of the base plate was coated with Arabian glue, which was also used to consolidate the mass. Once the adhesive had dried, the cover plate was replaced, and the edges bound with copper foil strips with an adhesive backing.

Photographic images on glass

Broken glass plates bearing photographic images can be repaired (*Figure 7.69a,b* and

Conservation and restoration of glass 339

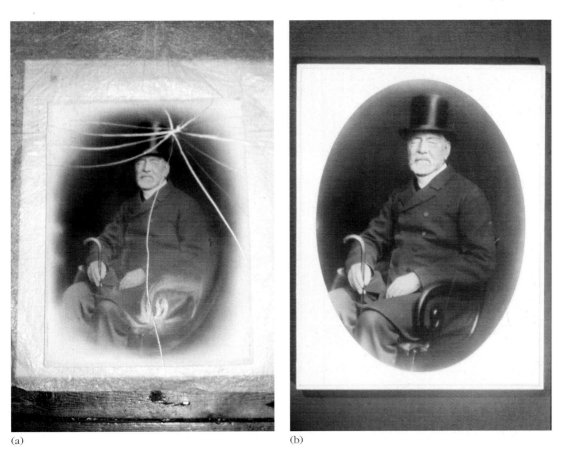

(a)   (b)

Figure 7.69   Photographic image on an opal glass plate, (a) before and (b) after restoration with epoxy resin.

7.70a–c). Great care has to be taken not to allow pressure-sensitive tape, adhesive or solvent to come into contact with the photographic image. The plate is placed, image side down on a clean surface, and the fragments secured by placing narrow strips of pressure-sensitive tapes across the breaks. A small amount of optically clear epoxy resin is applied along the breaks, after which the plate is turned image side up, placed on a sheet of Melinex and the resin left to cure.

Paintings executed in reverse on glass

The causes of damage to paintings on glass can be broadly divided into two categories: (i) those caused as a result of damage to the glass, frame, backboard and other associated materials (*Figure 7.69a–c*; and (ii) those associated with changes to the binding medium and paint layer (*Figure 7.70a,b*).

The most obvious cause of damage to pictures created on glass sheets is the breaking of the glass itself, often as a result of the picture falling to the floor when the cord from which it is suspended rots or frays; or when the picture is undergoing re-framing. The wooden backing and frame may also become weakened by the action of woodworm; or broken, and lead to damage of the glass and/or paint. If the uneven glass is too firmly held in a rigid framework, or a backboard is secured by hammering or pushing in pins, or by firing in staples, the glass cracks or splinters. Wooden supports such as small blocks placed within the frame, directly against the

(a)

(b)

(c)

Figure 7.70   A hand-coloured, photographic image on the reverse side of a sheet of glass. (a) Before repair; (b) after repair and restoration; (c) missing areas of the design, painted in acrylic colours on a sheet of Melinex and placed behind the original glass.

glass, can abrade the paint layer if the glass is loose within the frame, or if they become detached. An applied backing of paper or other material can cause damage, either as a result from adhesive with which it was applied migrating into or beneath the paint layer, or by pulling the paint off the glass if the adhesion between the paper and paint is greater than that between the paint and the glass. The paint layer itself can be damaged in a number of ways.

(i)   Chemical instability of the paint, which can be changed by light etc., so that the original colour can then only be found beneath the edge of the frame, where it was protected from light.

(ii)   Failure of adhesion of the binder with the glass. Loss of the paint layer arises primarily from the glass being broken, or from failure of adhesion between the paint and

the glass or the paint and the transparent priming coat. This occurs due to the effects of oxidation of the paint itself and/or the effects of UV light and heat. These agents can cause powdering, blistering or peeling of the paint, particularly in the case of multi-layered paintings. The paint may even become detached so that fragments are found beneath the frame. The most typical disfigurement occurring to reverse paintings on glass, *amelierung*, *eglomisé* and mezzotints is the distortion caused by the air-pockets (blind cleavage) between the glass and paint layer, which seen from the front appear as a greyish, less saturated areas of paint (*Figure 7.70a*). The gold leaf of gold reverse engravings usually remains in good condition. The cleavage is caused by drying out (oxidation) of the priming coat materials from which the painting was created, and/or the contraction or other movement of any backing materials present. Paint flakes may curl away from the glass or even become detached. Dirt can become trapped under cleaved and lifted paint areas, where it is impossible to remove it without causing further damage.

(iii) Penetration of water/water vapour. Sometimes an osmotic effect can be created between a painting executed in two layers, between a hydrophilic base (of, glue or gum) and a hydrophobic paint layer. The presence of water vapour then causes problems of deterioration. Display or storage environments, where there has been a rising water table or excessive condensation, can cause damage. If hydrophobic material has been painted on the reverse of the painting, micro-organisms can grow.

(iv) Previous attempts at restoration which have proved unsatisfactory, especially if these have been carried out using adhesive tape, gummed paper tape, postage stamps, medical plasters etc.

Conservation and restoration

There are many different types of paintings on glass, and each requires an individual approach to its conservation. Brill *et al.* (1990) published a classification of *zwischengoldglas*, accompanied by a discussion of the conservation problems associated with *zwischengoldglas*.

Where possible, dust and dirt can be carefully removed with a small soft paint brush, or if necessary with a small amount of appropriate solvent. The difficulties of repairing panels of glass bearing reverse glass paintings have been reported by a number of conservators (Wallace, 1976; Davison and Jackson, 1985; Tremain, 1988). All have documented solutions for supporting uneven glass panels following the taping together of fragments and the introduction of a highly mobile form of epoxy resin from the non-painted side (see Figure 7.25a–c). Thornton (1990) describes a light-box apparatus for the repair of flat glass. Great care has to be taken not to allow the resin to flow between the glass and the paint layer where it would cause an irreversible darkening of the painting. Although the procedure is not generally recommended, as the less interference on the painted side the better, coating the original paint on either side of the breaks with water soluble PVA may enable excess resin to be removed without disturbing the paint (Wallace, 1976; Davison and Jackson, 1985). It may, however, be useful in instances where a large number of joins has to be secured at the same time.

In general, the edges of the glass fragments are carefully cleaned to remove dirt, grease or previously used adhesives, mechanically (in the case of adhesives) with small swabs of cotton wool moistened with acetone. The use of solvent has to be severely limited, for fear of disturbing the paint layer. The fragments are then held in place with thin strips of transparent pressure-sensitive tape on the unpainted side only. Occasionally it may be necessary to employ small spots of cyanoacrylate adhesive or Sticky Wax on badly shattered glass. On large panels especially, taping on the one side may pull the entire panel out of alignment, so that it may have to be supported by clamps, in order that it can stand freely on one edge. A short time after application of the adhesive, any excess is removed from the painted side if necessary with dry or slightly acetone-moist cotton wool swabs, discarding each one after use in order not to spread the adhesive over the paint layer. Small flat panels can be laid glass down on a sheet of Melinex placed on a flat surface, in order that excess adhesive drains back onto the glass surface from where it can be removed after curing, with a scalpel blade.

Reattaching the paint layer

Different approaches have been adopted for refixing a paint layer that has become partially detached from the glass substrate. The conservation methods can be broadly grouped into those which employ water-based fixatives, those which use solvent-based techniques and those which use wax, resin or a wax-resin mixture (*Figure 7.71b*, compare to *Figure 7.71a*).

Aqueous consolidation agents were used to secure brittle paint by Schott (1999); Klucel E (hydroxyl-propyl cellulose), Tylose MH 300 (methyl cellulose) and polyvinyl alcohol were found to be elastic enough not to exert stress on the paint layer.

(a)

(b)

Figure 7.71 (a) Detail of flaking paint on a *hinterglasmalerei*; (b) re-laid by the resin-wax method. (Courtesy of S. Bretz).

Solvents have been used by several conservators, to relax and reattach flakes of paint (the Pettenkofer process). These include Paraloid B-72 (methyl methacrylate copolymer) used as a 25 per cent solution in xylene, diluted to 15 per cent with ethylene glycol monoethyl ether (Cellosolve) (Wallace, 1976), or dissolved with xylene alone (Tremain, 1988) or in ethylene glycol monoethyl ether alone (Wallace, 1976; Caldararo, 1997); Paraloid B-67 (Wharton and Oldknow, 1987); Plextol D 466 (dispersion of acrylic resin) (Agnini. 1999) and Plexisol P550 (Caldararo, 1997; Agnini, 1999); PVA-AYAC (polyvinyl acetate) in diacetone alcohol (Graham, 1976); Vinac B-7 in methanol in toluol (Roth in

Caldararo, 1997). The advantages of low-molecular materials, such as hydrocarbon resins, e.g. Regalrez 1094, are their solubility in non-polar solvents, and their light-stability, which can be enhanced by a light-stabilizing additive (HALS – hindered amine light stabilizer) such as Tinuvin 292. Their brittleness can be offset by the addition of plasticizers such as Kraton G1650 (2 per cent), but these can impair the light stability of the resin and may migrate into the paint layer. Paraloid B-72 and Regalrez 1094 were used by Coppieters-Mols (1999). Seidler (1987) suggested impregnating the paint layer with silane (irreversible) and Emery (1991) used Penetrol, a linseed oil dissolved in a slow-drying solvent mixture, but warns against spraying the paint layer with dammar varnish. When resins are flowed under cleaved areas of paint to consolidate them, it is difficult not to trap air bubbles; and further air bubbles can form during evaporation of the solvent. Areas of intact paint film exhibiting blind cleavage cannot have consolidants flowed beneath them without first breaking the paint film. As the paint is generally friable, extensive loss can occur in trying to create an opening through to the glass.

Wallace (1976) describes a method of treatment, in which a 25 per cent solution of Paraloid B-72 (methyl methacrylate copolymer) diluted to 15 per cent with Cellosolve (ethylene glycol monoethyl ether), was used to reattach loose paint on two European portraits and a nineteenth century American picture, all painted in with a thin oleaginous medium. The portraits had an intermediate priming layer of linseed oil; the American painting had no priming layer. The reverse of each fragment was brushed with the Paraloid B-72/Cellosolve mixture and allowed to dry until tacky. The fragments were then placed between four sheets of wet strength paper (two on each side) and placed in a prepared vacuum envelope, exposed to evenly dispersed air-blown heat of *circa* 55°C (130°F). After consolidation, the wet-strength tissues, which had served as isolation during the vacuum and heat treatment, were removed mechanically without difficulty. The panels were repaired, by taping the fragments of glass together on the unpainted side, and introducing an epoxy resin (EPO-TEK 301) to the joins, by capillary action. On one portrait, areas of loss were in-painted directly on the glass using a methacrylate paste using xylene as a diluent; on the other, in-painting was carried out on a rag-board backing, using opaque water colours. Both paintings were sealed between a backing board of 100 per cent rag and a new piece of glass sealed with Scotch Magic Tape 810 pressure-sensitive tape. In-painting from the reverse is extremely difficult both technically and because slight coloration of the glass itself will alter the colours when viewed through it.

Williston and Berrett (1978) describe a method of setting down paint flaking from an American reverse painted glass surrounding a clock face, by relaxation of the paint in a solvent vapour. Caldararo (1997) also reports the Williston and Berrett work in an article which contains an extensive bibliography. Thornton (1981) states that cleavage laid down using solvent-relaxing techniques tends to recur after a period of time, possibly because the dirt and oxidation products at the glass/paint firm interface have not been removed, thus preventing good adhesion of the paint to the glass.

Wax and wax-resin mixtures applied with a heated spatula have been used to secure paint fragments for the past 15 years. Cerowax (micro crystalline hydrocarbon wax with a high proportion of isoparaffin); paraffin wax; and wax–resin mixtures (beeswax with the addition of 5–20 per cent resin) have been used to secure paint fragments. Agnini (1999) used unbleached beeswax as well as low melting point microcrystalline waxes. Schott (1988b, 1999) used a mixture of bleached beeswax with 5 larch-turpentine resin. Coppieters-Mols (1999) used bleached beeswax with Regalrez 1094, but there is a question concerning the possible future separation of the resins. Tremain (1988) and Kleitz (1991) used paraffin wax in petroleum ether in equal proportions. Horton-James (1990) and Agnini (1999) tried using the hot-seal adhesive Beva 371 for conserving paintings.

Thornton (1981) gives a detailed account of a transfer treatment for dealing with cupped paint flakes and blind cleavage and cosmetic compensation for reverse paintings on glass. The process solves many of the problems encountered with previously reported treatments involving solvent relaxation of the paint and/or consolidation with synthetic resins. In the transfer treatment, a severely damaged paint film is transferred off the glass virtually intact, then cleaned and compensated from the front, prior to reattachment with a low viscosity epoxy resin. The process is extremely delicate and time-consuming. Two important considerations are the disturbance of the painting from its original substrate (although this could be likened to the re-lining of a painting on canvas), and the irreversibility of the attachment with epoxy resin in practice. However, the method could be useful in cases where to do nothing may result in the total loss of an entire painting.

Retouching the paint layer

Retouching missing areas of paint on *hinterglasmalerei* is difficult because the thickness

Figure 7.72 Retouching the design on a Chinese painting in reverse on glass, using acrylic pigments.

and colour of the glass can distort the colours when they are viewed through it. This problem can be overcome by setting the painting up in front of or above a mirror; the restoration in progress can be viewed in the mirror. (If the original fixative remains on the glass, it will act as a ground for the new paint.) Alternatively, missing areas can be painted on acid-free paper (Wallace, 1976) or on Melinex sheet, which are then placed behind the original (*Figure 7.70c*). Paints used include Cryla acrylic paints (Davison and Jackson, 1985) (*Figure 7.72*), Aquarel paints, Rebel 2000 in Paraloid B-72 (Coppieter-Mols, 1999)

Storage

Reverse painted glass pictures should remain in their frames during storage with the glass side placed face down on a soft surface such as felt. The pictures should be wrapped in acid-free tissue and placed in an archival quality box resistant to air and water vapour. If a painting is in a poor state of preservation, which does not permit transport, the paint layer should be given a coat of a volatile bonding agent (cyclododecane). The storage environment should be air conditioned, free from air pollution and have a temperature range of 18–20° C, with a relative humidity of 50–55 per cent.

Appendix 1

Materials and equipment for glass conservation and restoration

It would be impractical to attempt to produce a definitive list of materials used for glass conservation throughout the world. The majority are not produced specifically for conservation, but have been tested by conservation scientists, and been proven in use over a number of years.

Generally speaking, it is preferable to obtain materials in the country in which they are to be used, in order to have the possibility of direct communication with manufacturers and suppliers (although communication has been greatly improved by the use of e-mail); and to minimize storage and transport time. It should be remembered that materials that perform well in one part of the world (e.g. in a temperate zone), may not in another (e.g. tropical zone). In many cases, major manufacturers have outlets for their materials in several countries and the addresses can be obtained from the parent company.

Other sources for locating materials and equipment are the conservation sections of museums and other institutions, private restoration studios, manufacturers and suppliers of adhesives, resins, chemicals and suppliers of scientific laboratory equipment.

There are, however, a few specialist suppliers of conservation materials:

- *Conservator's Emporium* (replacing Conservation Materials Ltd), 100 Standing Rock Circle, Reno, Nevada 89511, USA.
- *Conservation Resources International L.L.C.*, 8000-H Forbes Place, Springfield, Virginia 22151, USA.

- *Conservation Resources (UK) Ltd*, Units 1, 2, 4 & 5, Pony Road, Horspath Industrial Estate, Cowley, Oxford OX4 2RD. Conservation Resources' products (which are principally archival) are available from a number of specialist distributors worldwide.
- *Conservation Support Systems*, PO Box 91746, Santa Barbara, California 93190-1746, USA.
- *Stuart R. Stevenson* (Artists' & Gilding Materials), 68 Clerkenwell Road, London EC1M 5QA, UK.

On-site glass conservation/restoration – checklist of materials and equipment

Archaeological excavation

Much of the equipment required is of a general nature, used on archaeological sites (Sease, 1988; Cronyn, 1990). (See also items listed below.) Where the retrieval of glass in large or small quantities is anticipated, special provision will have to be made, especially if the glass is damp or waterlogged. It may, for example, be necessary to construct temporary storage tanks on site.

Packaging materials should include self-seal polythene bags, acid-free polyethylene foam and tissue, pressure-sensitive tapes, labels and marking pens (which may need to be waterproof), rigid plastic boxes with lids, plastic bowls and trays, conservation record forms.

Historic buildings, museum collections etc.

Arrangements to be made in advance of the work commencing:

- A contract stating what the conservator is and is not responsible for.
- Public liability and employer's liability insurance.
- Security clearance, security passes, security arrangements.
- The provision or hiring and erection of scaffolding.
- Sources of electricity, water and means of refuse disposal (including solvents).
- Liaison with a qualified electrician (in the case of lighting e.g. chandeliers).
- Materials, tools and equipment.
- Transport of equipment and personnel to and from site.
- Delivery points and temporary and permanent parking facilities.
- Times of access (particularly any restrictions on working outside normal working hours, or at weekends).
- Facilities for tea-making, eating, location of toilet facilities.
- Use of a telephone for official calls, a list of names and telephone numbers of all personnel involved with the project, including emergency contacts.
- Accommodation (if the site is a considerable distance from base).
- Packaging, transport and secure storage of objects, e.g. dismantled chandeliers, if required.
- Administration costs, including costs of writing and producing condition and conservation reports, and photography.

Tools and equipment

- Adjustable spanners and wrenches, mole wrench, screwdrivers, long-nose pliers and side cutters.
- Light-weight scaffold tower(s), tall stepladder.

- Trestle tables, chairs.
- Torches (large and small).
- Weighing scales – digital platform type (for chandeliers).
- Buckets, bowls, trays, miscellaneous containers.
- Portable vacuum cleaner, dust-pan and brush, broom.
- Hard hats, safety goggles, dust/fume/mercury vapour masks, cotton and disposable vinyl rubber gloves, protective clothing. First-aid kit (especially scissors and plasters).
- Camera(s) and accessories: lights, flash light, film: black and white, colour print, transparencies, batteries, tripod.

Materials

- Soft cloths, paper towelling, cotton wool, satay sticks.
- Non-ionic detergent.
- Clear epoxy resin, rapid cure epoxy resin, cellulose nitrate-based adhesive.
- Paraloid B-72 adhesive and consolidant.
- Acetone, IMS, distilled or de ionized water.
- Fine lubricating oil (spray).
- Rust remover (liquid or gel).
- Silver cleaning solution.
- Melinex sheet.
- Fine abrasives.
- Brass wire and pins.
- Rubbish disposal bags.
- Packaging materials: wooden crates, strong cardboard boxes, Bubblewrap, acid-free tissue, Plastazote (acid-free polyester foam), self-seal Polythene bags; pressure-sensitive tapes (Magic Tape, Sellotape, masking tape, plastic parcel tape); marking pens, stencils for marking crates.

Stationery

Recording/condition report forms, note-pads, paper, pens, pencils, erasers, tie-on and adhesive labels.

Appendix 2

Sources of information

Information concerning all aspects of glass is continually being updated in journals and conservation proceedings, by research projects and in (largely unpublished) university student theses. Information can be found in a number of dictionaries, encyclopaedias and bibliographies. For convenience, a list is given below, with publication details for those works not appearing in the Bibliography of this volume.

Dictionaries, encyclopaedias and bibliographies

ASH, D. (1975) *Dictionary of British Antique Glass.* Pelham Books, London.

BERLYE, M.K. (1963) *The Encyclopaedia of Working with Glass.* Oceana Publications, New York.

BLECK, R.D. (1967–79) *Bibliographie der Archäologisch-Chemischen Literatur* (Nature of Archaeological Materials). Three Volumes.

DIDEROT, D. and D'ALEMBERT, J. le ROND (1751–71) *Dictionnaire Raisonné des Sciences, des Arts, et des Métiers.* Contains entries on eighteenth-century glass-making, window and mirror manufacture. Well illustrated with line drawings.

DUNCAN, G.S. (1960) *Bibliography of Glass* (from the earliest records to 1940).

FLEMING, J. and HONOUR, H. (eds) (1976) *The Penguin Dictionary of Decorative Arts.* Penguin, London. Contains entries on glass and related materials.

HENCH, L.L. and McELDOWNEY, B.A. (1976) *A Bibliography of Ceramics and Glass.* American Ceramics Society International Commission on Glass (1972–1979), *The Chemical Durability of Glass.* Three volumes.

NEWMAN, H. (1977) *An Illustrated Dictionary of Glass.* Glass in general.

NEWTON, R.G. (1973, 1974a, 1982b) Three extensive bibliographies on the conservation of glass; the 1982 revision contains a thirty-page introduction which also serves as an index.

NEWTON, R.G. and DAVISON, S. (1989) *Conservation of Glass.* Butterworth Heinemann, Oxford. Contains an extensive bibliography. Also a section on painted (stained) glass, which is not included in this edition.

TRENCH, L. (ed.) (2000) *Materials and Techniques in the Decorative Arts*, John Murray, London. Contains entries on glass and related materials (by S. Davison).

VANDIVER, P.B. DRUZIK, J.R., WHEELER, G.S. and FREESTONE, I.C. (eds) (1988 and cont.) *Materials Issues in Art and Archaeology.* Materials Research Society Symposium Proceedings, Pittsburgh, PA. In several volumes.

WHITEHOUSE, D. (1993) *A Pocket Dictionary of Terms Commonly Used to Describe Glass and Glassmaking.* New York, The Corning Museum of Glass.

Journals

Glass Engraver, published quarterly by the Guild of Glass Engravers, 8 Rathcoole Ave., London N8 9NA, UK.

Glass News, published by The Association for the History of Glass Ltd, Museum of London, 46 Eagle Wharf Road, London N1 7EE.

Glass Technology, published quarterly by the Society of Glass Technology, Don Valley House, Savile Street East, Sheffield, S4 7UQ. Contains articles in English, comments, information, book reviews and abstracts from a wide range of journals.

Journal of Glass Studies (1959–), published annually by The Corning Museum of Glass, One Museum Way, Corning, NY 14830-2253, USA. Includes an extensive checklist of recently published articles and books on all periods of glass, in its historical, economic and artistic aspects.

Verres, published by the Institut du Verre, 21 Boulevard Pasteur, 75015 Paris, France.

Studies in Conservation (1952–), published quarterly by the International Institute for the Conservation of Historic and Artistic Works, 6 Buckingham St, London WC2N 6BA, UK. Contains occasional articles on conservation of glass and associated materials.

The Conservator (1977–), published annually by the United Kingdom Institute for Conservation of Historic and Artistic Works. Contains occasional articles on conservation of glass and related materials.

Occasional articles on glass matters are published in the conference proceedings of various archaeological, historical association and conservation organizations, e.g. IIC, AIC, UKIC, ICOM–CC, AIHV.

Conservation organizations

IIC – International Institute for the Conservation of Historic and Artistic Works, 6 Buckingham Street, London WC2N 6BA, UK. Details of conservation organizations can be found at: www.iiconservation.org.

Associations related to glass

Association for the History of Glass Ltd, Museum of London, London Wall, London, EC2Y 5HG, UK.

AIHV – Association Internationale pour l'Histoire du Verre, Musee du Verre, quai de Maastricht 13, Liège B-4000, Belgium.

The Glass Association, Broadfield House Glass Museum, Compton Drive, Kingswinford, West Midlands, DY6 9NS, UK. Aims to promote the understanding and appreciation of glass and glassmaking methods.

The Glass Circle, Mrs J.M. Marshall (Hon. Sec.) 2 Downing Court, Grenville Street, London, WC1N 1LX, UK.

The Glass Bead Society of Great Britain, c/o The Horniman Museum, London Road, London, SE23 3PQ, UK. (Trust)

Crafts Council, 44a Pentonville Road, Islington, London, N1 9B, UK. Maintains a register of craftspeople of excellence in the UK.

British National Committee for the Conservation of Stained Glass (Corpus Vitrearum), c/o The British Academy, 20–21 Cornwall Terrace, London, NW1 4QP, UK.

Glass and Glazing Federation, 44–48 Borough High Street, London, SE1 1XB, UK.

British Glass Manufacturers Confederation, (also known as *British Glass*), Northumberland Road, Sheffield, S10 2UA, U.K.

Council for the Care of Churches, 83 London Wall, London, EC2M 5NA, UK.

Society of Glass Technology, Don Valley House, Savile Street East, Sheffield, S4 7UQ, UK.

Selected glass collections

United Kingdom

The British Museum, Great Russell Street, London, WC1B 3DG.

The Victoria and Albert Museum, Cromwell Road, South Kensington, London. SW7 2RL.

The National Glass Centre, Liberty Way, Sunderland, SR6 0GL.

The National Museum of Scotland, Edinburgh, EH1 1JF.

The National Museums and Galleries of Wales, Cardiff, CF11 3NP.

The Fitzwilliam Museum, Cambridge, CB2 1RB.

The Ashmolean Museum, Oxford, OX1 2PH.

Broadfield House Glass Museum, Compton Drive, Kingswinford, West Midlands, DY6 9QA.

Centre for Glass Research, Sir Robert Hadfield Building, Mappin Street, Sheffield, S1 3JD.

The World of Glass (formerly The Pilkington Museum of Glass), Chalon Way East, St Helens, Merseyside, WA10 1BX.

Many other towns and cities have glass collections in museums, galleries and historic houses. Details of these can be found in annual publications (handbooks) produced by The National Trust (for Places of Historic Interest or Natural Beauty), 36 Queen Anne's Gate, London, SW1H 9AS, and English Heritage, 23 Savile Row, London, W1X 1AB; and *in Museums and Galleries in Great Britain and Ireland*, and *Historic Houses, Castles and Gardens*, widely available in libraries and newsagents.

Europe

The National and Applied Art Museums of European countries hold important collections of glass, as do some provincial museums. Only those dedicated specifically to glass are listed below.

Belgium

Musée du Verre, quai de Maastricht 13, Liège B-4000.

Czech Republic

The Glass and Costume Jewellery Museum, Jablonec nad Nisou.

The Glass Museum, Nový Bor.

The Glass Museum, Kamenický Senov.

Finland

Suomen Lasimuseo (The Finnish Glass Museum) (established in a former glasshouse), Tehtaankatu 23, FIN-11910, Riihimaki, Finland. (66 km from Helsinki).

Italy

Musee Vetrario (Museum of Glass), island of Murano, Venice.

United States of America

The Corning Museum of Glass, 1 Museum Way, Corning, NY 14830-2253.

Conservation and restoration departments and studios

The author decided against including a list of conservation departments and studios which undertake the conservation and restoration of archaeological and decorative glass, since the work of some are not known, and others may be inadvertently omitted. Many glass conservation/ restoration departments and studios are attached to museums and other institutions; the addresses of commercial organizations can be found in antique trade and telephone directories.

Bibliography

Abbreviations used to denote institutions

AIC	= American Institute for Conservation
BMP	= British Museum Publications
CCI	= Canadian Conservation Institute
ICOM–CCI–	= International Committee of Museums - Committee for Conservation
IIC	= International Institute for Conservation and Restoration of Historic and Artistic Works of Art
INA	= Institute of Nautical Archaeology
UKIC	= United Kingdom Institute for Conservation

ADAMS, P.B. (1984) Glass corrosion: A record of the past? A predictor of the future? *J. Non-Cryst. Solids,* **67**, 193–205.

ADLERBORN, J. (1971) Investigation of weathered glass surfaces with the scanning microscope. *OECD Report on Science Research on Glass.* Ref: DAS/SPR/71.35.

AGNINI, E. (1999) Hinterglasbilder. Erfahrungen bei der Konservervierung, Restaurierung und Montierung. *Restauro,* **4**, 258–65. Callwey Verlag, Munich.

AGRICOLA (1556) *De re Metallica.* Basle (1556). Translated by H.C. and L.H. Hoover, London (1912).

AIGNER, H. (1992) Die Hinterglasmalerei in Sandl/Buchers. Ein Beitrag zur Sozial- und Wirtschaftgeshicte ds sudböhmisch-österreichischen Raumes (Forschungs- und Dokumentationsprojekt). Hinterglasmuseum Sandl o. J.

ALBRIGHT & WILSON LTD (1978) *The Properties and Application of Calgon.*

ANDRÉ, J.M. (1976) *The Restorer's Handbook of Ceramics and Glass.* Van Nostrand, New York; also *Keramik und Glas,* Berlin.

ARRHENIUS, B. (1973) Teknisk verksamhet. *Kungl. Vitterhets historie och antikvitets akademieus årsbok,* 176–82.

ARTAL-ISBRAND, P. (1998) A minimally intrusive filling and stabilisation solution for very fragile archaeological glass objects. *Proc. ICOM–CC Working Group, Glass Ceramics, and Related Materials,* (A. Paterakis, ed.), EVTEK Institute of Arts & Design, Vantaa, Finland.

ASAHINA, T-I., YAMAZAKI, F., OTSUKA, I., NAMADA, T., SAITO, K. and ODA, S. (1973) On the colorless glass bottle of Tóshódaiji Temple … [b]-ray backscattering. *Sci. Pap. Japn Antiques,* **6**, 14–18. Abstract in *Stud. in Cons.* **I**, 314.

ASHLEY-SMITH, J. (1999) *Risk Assessment for Object Conservation.* Butterworth-Heinemann, Oxford.

ASHURST, D. (1970) Excavations at Gawber Glasshouse, near Barnsley. *Post-Med. Archaeology,* **4**, 135–40.

ASMUS, J.F. (1975) The use of lasers in the conservation of stained glass. In *Preprints of the Contributions to the Stockholm Congress on Conservation in Archaeology and the Applied Arts.* IIC, London (D. Leigh, A. Moncreiff and A. Oddy, eds), pp. 139–42.

ASPINALL, A., WARREN, S.E., CRUMMETT, J.G. and NEWTON, R.G. (1972) Neutron activation analysis of faience beads. *Archaeometry,* **14**, 27–40.

AUGERSON, C.C. and MESSINGER II, J.M. (1993) Controlling the refractive index of epoxy adhesives with acceptable yellowing after ageing. *JAIC,* **32**, 311–14.

BACON, F.R. (1968) The chemical durability of silicate glass. *Glass Ind.,* **49**, 438–9, 442–6, 494–9, 519, 554–9.

BACON, F.R. and CALCAMUGGIO, G.L. (1967) Effect of heat treatment in moist and dry atmospheres on the chemical durability of soda-lime glass bottles. *Bull. Am. Ceram. Soc.,* **46**, 850–5.

BACON, L. and KNIGHT, B. (eds) (1987) *From Pinheads to Hanging Bowls; the Identification, Deterioration and Conservation of Applied Enamel and Glass Decoration on Archaeological Artefacts.* UKIC, London.

BACON, F.R. and RAGGON, F.K. (1959) Promotion of attack on glass and silica by citrate and other anions in neutral solution. *J. Am. Ceram. Soc.,* **42**, 199–205.

BAKARDJIEV, I. (1977a) Korrosionsuntersuchungen an Gläsern des 17. und 18. Jahrhunderts. *DGG Meeting in Frankfurt,* March, 1977 (Abstract No. 274 in *CVMA News Letter* **26**).

BAKARDJIEV, I. (1977b) Stand der Untersuchungen an 'kranken' Gläsern. *Projektgruppe 'Glas' meeting in Würzburg,* 14 September 1977 (Abstract No. 275 in *CVMA News Letter* **26**).

BARHAM, E. (1999) The use of selected chelating agents to reveal the painted decoration on excavated medieval window glass. *Proceedings of Current Research on the History of Glass through Scientific Analysis.* London.

BARNES, I.L., GRAMLICH, J.W., DIAZ, M.G. and BRILL, R.H. (1978) The possible changes of lead isotope ratios in the manufacture of pigments: a fractionation experiment. *Archaeological Chemistry,* **2**. Advances in Chemistry Series 171 (G.F. Carter, ed.), pp. 273–7. American Chemistry Society, New York.

BARRELET, J. (1953) *La Verrerie en France de l'epoque Gallo-Romaine à nos jours.* Larousse, Paris.

BARRERA, J. and VELDE, B. (1989) A study of French medieval glass composition. *Archéologie Médiévale,* **XIX**, 81–130.

BARRERA, W.M. and KIRCH, P.V. (1973) Basaltic glass artefacts from Hawaii: their dating and prehistoric uses. *J. Polynesian Soc.,* **2**, 176–87.

BARRINGTON HAYNES, E. (1959) *Glass Through the Ages.* Pelican Books, Harmondsworth.

BASS, G. (1978) Glass treasure from the Aegean. *National Geographic Magazine.* Washington, DC.

BASS, G. (1979) The shipwreck at Serçe Limani. *Archaeology,* **32** (1).

BASS, G. (1980) The wreck of the Serçe Limani. *INA Newsletter,* **7**, (2/3) 1–6.

BASS, G. (1984) The nature of the Serçe Limani. *Glass: J. Glass Stud.*, **26.**

BAUER, W.P. (1976) Der Einfluss von Reinigungs-methoden auf die Glassoberfläche (Vorläufige Versuche und mikroskopische Untersuchungen). *Verres et Réfract.*, **30,** 62—4. (A longer version, in English, is given in CVMA News Letters, **18,** item 2, and **23,** 12–13.)

BAXTER, M.J., COOL, H.E.M., HEYWORTH, M. and JACKSON, C. (1995) Compositional variability in colour-less Roman vessel glass. *Archaeometry*, **37,** 129–42.

BERKOUWER, M. (1994) Freezing to eradicate insect pests in textiles at Brodsworth Hall. *The Conservator*, **18,** 15–22. UKIC, London.

BESBORODOV, M.A. and ABDURAZAKOV, A..A. (1964) Newly excavated glassworks in the USSR, 3rd-14th centuries AD. *J. Glass Stud.* **6,** 64–9.

BESBORODOV, M.A. and ZADNEPROVSKY, J.R. (1963) The early stages of glassmaking in the USSR. *Advances in Glass Technology., Part 2* (F.R. Matson and G.E. Rindone, eds), pp. 291–2. New York.

BETTEMBOURG, J-M. (1972) Nettoyage par voie chimique et par ultrasons des verres de vitraux. *Compt. Rend. 8e Colloq. CVMA*, York, p. 47.

BETTEMBOURG, J-M. (1973) Cleaning of medieval window glass (A statement of his practice in 1973 is given in *CVMA News Letter* **7**, 3, 1974).

BETTEMBOURG, J-M. (1976) Composition et alteration des verres de vitraux anciens. *Verres et Refract.*, **30,** 36–42.

BETTEMBOURG, J-M. and BURCK, J.J. (1974) Restauration des vitraux anciens. Methodes testées par la Laboratoire de Recherche des Monuments Historiques, 10 pp. typescript; abstracted on pp. 8-9 of *CVMA News Letter* **13**, 1975.

BETTEMBOURG, J-M. and PERROT, F. (1976) La restau-ration des vitraux de la façade occidentale de la cathe-drale de Chartres. *Verres et Réfract.*, **30,** 92–5.

BICKERTON, L.M. (1971) *An Illustrated Guide to Eighteenth Century English Drinking Glasses*. Barrie and Jenkins, London.

BIMSON, M. (1975) Coloured glass and *millefiori* in the Sutton Hoo grave deposit. In *The Sutton Hoo Ship Burial, 3: The hanging bowls, silver vessels and domes-tic objects* (A.C. Evans, ed.). BMP, London.

BIMSON, M. and FREESTONE, I.C. (1983) An analytical study of the relationship between the Portland Vase and other Roman cameo glasses. *J. Glass Stud.*, **25,** 55–69, Corning Museum of Glass, Corning, NY.

BIMSON, M. and FREESTONE, I.C. (eds) (1987) *Early Vitreous Materials*. British Museum Occasional Papers, **56**, London.

BIMSON, M. and WERNER, A.E. (1964a) The danger of heating glass objects. *J. Glass Stud.*, **6,** 148–50.

BIMSON, M. and WERNER, A.E. (1964b) Scientific exami-nation of ancient glass. *Ann 3e. Congr. Journ. Int. Verre*, Damascus, AIHV, Liège, pp. 200–9.

BIMSON, M. and WERNER, A.E. (1967) Two problems in ancient glass: opacifiers and Egyptian core material. *Ann 4e. Congr. Journ. Int. Verre*, Ravenne–Venise, AIHV, Liège, pp. 262–6.

BIMSON, M. and WERNER, A.E. (1969) Problems in Egyptian core glasses. *Studies in Glass History and Design*, Sheffield, 121–2.

BIMSON, M. and WERNER, A.E. (1971) Notes on a suggested technique for the consolidation of fragile excavated glasses. *Proc. 9th Int. Congr. Glass*, Versailles, pp. 63–5.

BIRINGUCCIO (1540) Quoted by Turner, W.E.S. (1956a); see also SMITH, C.S. and GNUDI, M.T. (1942) and Chapter 14, Concerning Glass and All Other Semi-materials in General, pp. 126-33, in *Pirotechnica*. Cambridge, Mass., 1959 (a Renaissance treatise on smelting and metalworking).

BLECK, R.D. (1967–1979) *Bibliographie der Archaeo-logisch-Chemischen Literatur*, **1** (1967), **2** (1968), **3** (1971), **4** (1979), Weimar, Germany.

BLY, J. (ed.) (1986) *Is it Genuine?* Mitchell Beazley, London.

BOHM, C. (1998) *Crizzling Glass* [in Swedish collections] *Revisited*. Unpublished paper given at the *ICOM–CC Interim Meeting of the Working Group on Glass, Ceramics and Related Materials*, Vantaa, Finland.

BONTEMPS, G. (1868) *Guide du Verrier*, Paris.

BOON, G.C. (1966) Roman window-glass from Wales. *J. Glass. Stud.*, **8,** 41–5, Corning Museum of Glass, Corning, NY.

BORBELY-KISS, I., FUELOEP, Z., KISS, A.Z., KOLTAY, E. and SZABO, G. (1994) The PIXE–PIGE method for the classification of late Roman glass sealings. *Nuclear Instruments and Methods in Physics Research B*, **85,** 836–9.

BOVINI (1964) Les anciens vitraux de l'eglise Sainte-Vital a Ravenne. *Ann. 3e Congr. Journ. Int. Verre*, Damascus, AIHV, Liège, pp. 85–90.

BRAIN, C. (1992) Glass reconstruction materials and techniques. In *Glass and Enamel Conservation*, UKIC, Occasional Papers, **11,** 15–17, London.

BRAIN, C. (1999) Using glass luminosity to study 17th century English drinking glass. *Proceedings of Current Research on the History of Glass through Scientific Analysis*. UKIC, London.

BRANDA, F., LAUDISIO, G., CONSTARTINI, A. and PICCI-OLI, C. (1999) Weathering of Roman glass. A new hypothesis of pit formation on glass surfaces. *Glass Technol.*, **40** (3), 89–91.

BRETZ, S. and RYSER, F. (2000) Kleines Handbuch der Hinterglasmalerei (Petit manuel de la peinture sous verre). In Glanzlichter. Die Kunst der Hinterglasmalerei. Exhibition catalogue. Musée Suisse du Vitrail Romont/Museum in der Burg Zug.

BREWSTER, D. (1855) On the phenomenon of decom-posed glass. *Trans. Brit. Assoc. Adv. Sci*, 10.

BREWSTER, D. (1863) On the structure and optical phenomena of ancient decomposed glass. *Phil. Trans. R.. Soc. Edinb.*, 193–204.

BRILL, R.H. (1962) A note on the scientists' definition of glass. *J. Glass Stud.*, **4,** 127–38.

BRILL, R.H. (1963) Ancient Glass. *Scientific American*, November, pp. 120–30.

BRILL, R.H. (1965) The chemistry of the Lycurgus Cup. *Proc. 7th Int. Congr. Glass*, Brussels, Paper No. 223.

BRILL, R.H. (1967a) Lead isotopes in ancient glass. *Ann. 4e Congr. Journ. Int. Verre*, Ravenne–Venise, AIHV, Liège, pp. 255–61.

BRILL, R.H. (1967b) Information for persons submitting samples [for lead isotope analysis]. *Ann. 4e Congr. Journ. Int. Verre*, Ravenne–Venise, AIHV, Liège, p. 261.

BRILL, R.H. (1968) The scientific examination of ancient glass. *Proc. 8th Int. Congr. Glass*, London, 47–68.

BRILL, R.H. (1970a) Lead and oxygen isotopes in ancient objects. *Phil. Trans. R. Soc, Lond*, **A.269**, 143–64.

BRILL, R.H. (1970b) Some chemical observations on the cuneiform glass making texts. *Ann. 5e Congr. Journ. Int. Verre*, Prague, AIHV, Liège, pp. 319–36.

BRILL, R.H. (1970c) The chemical interpretation of the texts. In *Glass and Glassmaking in Ancient Mesopotamia* (Oppenheim *et al.*, eds), pp. 105–28. Corning Museum of Glass, Corning, NY.

BRILL, R.H. (1971a) Chemical-analytical round-robin of four synthetic ancient glasses. *Proc. 9th Int. Congr. on Glass*, Versailles, pp. 93–110.

BRILL, R.H. (1972) Incipient crizzling in some early glasses. *JAIC*, **12**, 46–7.

BRILL, R.H. (1973) Analysis of some finds from the Gnalic wreck. *J. Glass Stud.*, **15**, 93–7.

BRILL, R.H. (1975) Crizzling-a problem of glass cons. *Preprints of the Contributions to the Stockholm Congress on Conservation in Archaeology and the Applied Arts* (D. Leigh, A. Moncrieff and W.A. Oddy, eds), pp. 121–34. IIC, London.

BRILL, R.H. (1978) Use of equilibrated silica gel for the protection of glass with incipient crizzling. *J. Glass Stud.*, **20**, 100–18.

BRILL, R.H. (1988) Scientific Investigations. In G.D. Weinburg, *Excavations at Jalamie: Site of a Glass Factory in Late Roman Palestine*. University of Missouri, Columbia, pp. 257–94.

BRILL, R.H. (1995) Appendix 3: Chemical analysis of some glass fragments from Nishapur in the Corning Museum of Art. In *Nishapur: Glass of the Early Islamic Period*, pp. 211–13.

BRILL, R.H. (1999) Chemical analyses of early glasses, **1** *The Catalogue*. **2** *The Tables*. **3** *The Interpretation of the Results*, Corning Museum of Glass, Corning, NY

BRILL. R.H. and BARNES, I.L. (1988) The examination of some Egyptian glass objects. In *Researches in the Arabah, 1959–1984, I: The Egyptian Mining Temple at Timna* (B. Rothenburg, ed.), pp. 217–23. London Institute for Archaeometallurgy, London.

BRILL, R.H., AIKEN, C.A., NOVICK, D.T. and ERRETT, F.E. (1990) Conservation problems of Zwischengoldglas. Part 1: Examination and Analyses. *J. Glass Stud.*, **22**, 12–35.

BRILL, R.H. BARNES, I.L. and ADAMS, B. (1974) Lead isotopes in some ancient Egyptian objects. *Rec. Advances in Science and Technology of Materials*, **3** (A. Bishay, ed.), pp. 9–25. Plenum Press, New York.

BRILL, R.H., BARNES, I.L. and JOEL, E.C. (1991) Lead isotope studies of early Chinese glass. In *Scientific Research in Early Chinese Glass*. Corning Museum of Glass, Corning, NY.

BRILL, R.H., FLEISCHER, R.L., PRICE, P.B. and WALKER, R.M. (1964) The fission-track dating of man-made glasses: preliminary results. *J. Glass Stud.*, **6**, 151–5.

BRILL, R.H. and HANSON, V.P. (1976) Chemical analyses of Amelung glasses. *J. Glass Stud.*, **18**, 216–38.

BRILL, R.H. and HOOD, H.P. (1961) A new method of dating ancient glass. *Nature*, **189**, 12–14.

BRILL, R.H. and MARTIN, J.H. (1991) *Scientific Research in Early Chinese Glass*. Corning Museum of Glass, Corning, NY.

BRILL, R.H. and MOLL, S. (1961) The electron beam microanalysis of ancient glass. *Recent Advances in Conservation*. Butterworth, Oxford, 145–51. (Also shortened version in *Advances on Glass Technology* (1963), 293–302.)

BRILL, R.H., SHIELDS, W.R. and WAMPLER, J.M. (1970) New directions in lead isotope research. In *Application of Science in Examination of Works of Art* (W.J. Young, ed.), pp. 73–84.

BRILL, R.H. and WOSINSKI, J.P. (1965) A huge slab of glass in the ancient necropolis of Beth She'arim. *Proc. 7th Int. Congr. on Glass*, Brussels, Paper No. 219.

BRUCE, J. (1979) *Work in Progress. Glassblowing: a Manual of Basic Technology*. Crafts Council and Jane Bruce, London.

BRUCE-MITFORD, R. (1975) *The Sutton-Hoo Ship Burial*, **3**, *The Hanging Bowls, Silver Vessels and Domestic Objects* (A.C. Evans, ed.). BMP, London.

BRUNDLE, C.R., EVANS, A.C. and WILSON, S. (1992) *Encyclopaedia of Materials Characterization, Materials Characterization Series, Surfaces, Interfaces and Thin Films*. Butterworth-Heinemann, Boston, Mass.

CABLE, M. (1998) The operation of wood fired glass melting furnaces. In *The Prehistory and History of Glassmaking Technology*, (P. McCray, ed.), *Ceramics and Civilisation*, **VIII**, 315–29. American Ceramics Society, Columbus, Ohio.

CABLE, M. and SMEDLEY, J.W. (1987) Liquidus temperatures and melting characteristics of some early container glasses. *Glass Technol.*, **28**, 94–8.

CALDARARO, N. (1997) Conservation treatments of paintings on ceramics and glass: two case studies. *Stud. Conserv.*, **23** (3), 157–64.

CAVAILLÉ, D., VIALLA, R., LEVELUT, C., VACHER, R., Le BOURIS, E. and GY, R. (1998) Internal stresses in silico-soda-lime glasses investigated by Brillouin scattering. *Proc. 18th Int. Congr. Glass*, San Francisco, CD-ROM, Paper No. 3 in Group D6, 17.

CHAMBON, R. (1963) L'evolution des procedes de fabrication manuelle de verre a vitres du dixieme siècle a nos jours. In *Advances in Glass Technology, Part 2*, (Matson, F.R. and Rindone, G.E. eds), pp. 165–78. Plenum Press, New York.

CHANCE, J.F. (1919) *A History of the Firm of Chance Brothers and Co., Glass and Alkali Manufacturers*. Privately printed, London.

CHARLESTON, R.J. (1958) Glass. In *A History of Technology*, **III**, *From the Renaissance to the Industrial Revolution, c.1500–c.1750* (C. Singer *et al.* eds), Oxford.

CHARLESTON, R.J. (1959) English glassmaking and its spread from the XVIIth to the middle of the XIXth Century. *Ann Ier Congr. Journ. Int. Verre*, AIHV, Liège, pp. 155–65.

CHARLESTON, R.J. (1960) Lead in glass. *Archaeometry*, **3**, 1–4.

CHARLESTON, R.J. (1962) Some tools of the glassmaker in medieval and renaissance times with special reference to the glassmaker's chair. *Glass Technol.*, **3**, 107–11.

CHARLESTON, R.J. (1963) Glass 'cakes' as raw material and articles of commerce. *J. Glass Stud.*, **5**, 54–67.

CHARLESTON, R.J. (1964) Wheel engraving and cutting; some early equipment: 1. Engraving. *J. Glass Stud.*, **6**, 83–100.

CHARLESTON, R.J. (1965) Wheel engraving and cutting;

some early equipment: II Water power and cutting. *J. Glass Stud.*, **7**, 41–54.

CHARLESTON, R.J. (1967) The transport of glass in the 17th to 18th centuries. *Ann 4e. Congr. Journ. Int. Verre*, Ravenne–Venise, pp. 183–92, AIHV, Liège, France, 1968.

CHARLESTON, R.J. (1972) Enamelling and gilding on glass. *Glass Circle* (R.J. Charleston, W. Evans and A. Polak, eds), pp. 18–32. Newcastle.

CHARLESTON, R.J. (1977) A brief survey of the history of glass and glassmaking. *An Illustrated Dictionary of Glass* (H. Newman, ed.), pp. 9–14. Thames and Hudson, London.

CHARLESTON, R.J. (1978) Glass furnaces through the ages. *J. Glass Stud.* **20**, 9–33.

CHARLESWORTH, D. (1977) Roman window glass from Chichester, Sussex. *J. Glass Stud.*, **19**, 182.

CHASE, W.T. (1971) Egyptian blue as a pigment and ceramic material. *Science and Archaeology* (R.H. Brill, ed.), pp. 80–91. MIT Press, Cambridge, Mass.

CHILD, D.G. (1990) *World Mirrors, 1650–1990*, London.

CHIRNSIDE, R.C. and PROFFITT, P.M.C. (1963) The Rothschild Lycurgus Cup; an analytical investigation. *J. Glass Stud.*, **5**, 18–23.

CHUN, F.S. FENG, S., SINGH, J.P., YUEH, F.Y., RIGSBY, J.T.III., MONTS, D.L. and COOK, R.L. (2000) Glass composition measurement using laser induced breakdown spectrometry. *Glass Technol.*, **41** (1), 16–21.

CLARK, D.E., PANTANO, C.G. and HENCH, L.L. (1979) *Corrosion of Glass*. Books for Industry, New York.

CLARKE, H.G. (1928) *The Story of English Glass Pictures, 1690–1810*. London.

COLLONGUES, R. (1974) Sur le phénomène de corrosion des vitraux. *ENSCP Convention*, 11 pp. typescript.

COLLONGUES, R. (1977) La corrosion des vitraux. *Les Monuments Historiques de la France*, Nr. 1, 14–16.

COLLONGUES, R. and PEREZ-Y-JORBA, M. (1973) Sur le phénomène des vitraux. Part 1 (Abstract No. 182 in *CVMA News Letter*, **13**).

COLLONGUES, R., PEREZ-Y-JORBA, M., TILLOCA, G. and DALLAS, J-P. (1976) Nouveaux aspects du phénomène des vitraux anciens des églises françaises. *Verres et Réfract.* **30**, 43–55.

COOPER, M. (1998) *Laser Cleaning in Conservation*. Butterworth-Heinemann, Oxford.

COPPIETERS-MOLS, J. (1999) Les peintures sur verre – propositions de materiaux et techniques de restauration. In *Preprints of Triennial Meeting of ICOM—CC*, Lyon, France, pp. 787–92.

CORNING MUSEUM OF GLASS (1976) Conservation of opus sectile panels from Kenchreai. Unpublished work report.

CORNING MUSEUM OF GLASS (1992) *Reverse Painting on Glass*. The Ryser Collection: Exhibition Catalogue. New York: Corning Museum of Glass.

CORVAIA, C., MACLEOD, I.D. and HARLEY, C. (1996) Conservation of glass recovered from shipwreck sites. *Preprints of the 11th Triennial Meeting of ICOM–CC* (J. Bridgland, ed.). Edinburgh, **1**, 884–90. James & James, London.

COSGROVE, M.G. (1974) *The Enamels of China and Japan. Champlevé and Cloisonné*. Robert Hale.

COX, G.A. and FORD, B.A. (1989) The corrosion of glass on the sea bed. *J. Mater. Sci.*, **24**, 3146–53.

COX, G.A. and FORD, B.A. (1993) The long term corrosion of glass by ground water. *J. Mater. Sci.* **28**, 5637–47.

COX, G.A. and KHOOLI, A.R. (1992) The natural corrosion of glass; the formation and structure of plugs. *Glass Technol.*, **33**, 60–2.

COX, G.A., HEAVENS, O.S., NEWTON, R.G. and POLLARD, A.M. (1979) A study of the weathering behaviour of medieval glass from York Minster. *J. Glass Stud.*, **21**, 54–75.

COX, G.A. and POLLARD, A.M. (1977) X-ray fluorescence analysis of ancient glass: the importance of sample preparation. *Archaeometry*, **19**, 45–54.

CRAMP, R. (1968) Glass finds from the Anglo-Saxon Monastery at Monkwearmouth and Jarrow. *Stud. Glass Hist. Des.*, 16–19.

CRAMP, R. (1975) Window glass from the monastic site of Jarrow: Problems of interpretation. *J. Glass Stud.*, **17**, 88–95.

CRONYN, J.M. (1992) *The Elements of Archaeological Conservation*. Routledge, London and New York.

CRONYN, J.M., FOLEY, K. and HUNTER, K. (1987) Principles of conservation of enamels. In *From Pinheads to Hanging Bowls, the Identification, Deterioration and Conservation of Applied Enamel and Glass Decoration on Archaeological Artefacts* (L. Bacon and B. Knight, eds). UKIC, London.

CROSSLEY, D.W. (1967) Glassmaking in Bagot's Park, Staffordshire, in the sixteenth century. *Post-Med. Archaeol.*, **1**, 44–83.

CROSSLEY, D.W. (1972) The performance of the glass industry in sixteenth century England. *Econ. Hist. Rev., 2nd series*, **25**, 421–33.

CROSSLEY, D.W. (1998) The English glassmaker and his search for materials in the 16th and 17th centuries. In *The Prehistory and History of Glassmaking Technology* (P. McCray, ed.), *Ceramics and Civilisation*, **VIII**, 167–79. American Ceramics Society, Columbus, Ohio.

CROSSLEY, D.W. (1999) Fragments from the field – aspects of sampling of glass-working residues. In *Current Research on the History of Glass through Scientific Analysis*, London.

CROSSLEY, D.W. and ABERG, F.A. (1972) Sixteenth century glassmaking in Yorkshire; excavations of furnaces at Hutton and Rosedale, North Riding. 1968–71. *Post-Med. Archaeol.*, **6**, 107–59.

DANDRIDGE, P. and WYPISKI, M.T. (1992) Preliminary technical study of medieval Limoges enamels. In *Materials Issues in Art and Archaeology*, **III**, Pittsburgh. PA, The Materials Research Society, pp. 817–26.

DAVIDSOHN, A. and MILWIDSKY, S.M. (1978) *Synthetic Detergents*, 6th edn. Godwin, London and John Wiley, New York.

DAVISON, S. (1984) A review of adhesives and consolidants used on glass antiquities. *Preprints of Contributions to the Paris Congress on Adhesives and Consolidants* (N.S. Bromelle, E.M. Pye, P. Smith, P.G. Thomson, eds), pp. 191–4. IIC, London.

DAVISON, S. (1988) Cut glass chandeliers; dismantling, cleaning. recording and restoring. *Preprints of the contributions to the UKIC 30th Anniversary Conference* (V. Todd, ed.), pp. 90–3. UKIC, London.

DAVISON, S. (1992) The conservation of a Louis XIV glass table-top. *Glass and Enamel Conservation*, UKIC Occasional Papers **11**, 3–5, London.

DAVISON, S. (1998) Reversible fills for transparent and translucent materials. *JAIC*, **37**, 35–47.

DAVISON, S. and JACKSON, P.R. (1985) The restoration of flat glass; four case studies. *The Conservator*, **9**, 10–13.

DAWSON, P.T., HEAVENS, O.S. and POLLARD, A.M. (1978) Glass surface analysis by Auger electron spectroscopy. *J. Phys. C: Sol. Stat Phys.*, **11**, 2183–93.

DEPASSIOT, M-C. (1997) *Le Collage du verre, l'usure du temps; la restauration des objects du patrimonie.* Musée archaelogique de Saint-Romain-en-Gal et les auteurs, pp. 108–9.

DIDEROT, D. et D'ALEMBERT, J. le ROND (1751–1771) *Dictionnaire Raisonné des Sciences, des Arts, et des Metièrs.* Diderot, Paris.

DODWELL, C.R. (1961) *The Various Arts.* Nelson, London (Translation of Theophilus' *De Diversis Artibus*).

DOPPELFELD, A. (1965) Die Kölner Glasöfen vom Eigelstein. *Proc. 7th Int. Congr. Glass Brussels.* New York, Paper No. 236.

DOUGLAS, R.W. and FRANK, S. (1972) *A History of Glassmaking.* Foulis, Henley-on-Thames.

DOVE, S. (1981) Conservation of glass-inlaid bronzes and lead curses from Uley, Gloucestershire. *The Conservator*, **5**, 31–5.

DOWLING, J. (1999) Removal and installation of mirrors for the British Gallery Project. *V&A Cons. J.*, **33**, 8–9. (Victoria and Albert Museum, London.)

DOWMAN, E.A. (1970) *Conservation in Field Archaeology.* Methuen, London.

DOWN, J.L. (1986) The yellowing of epoxy resin adhesives, report on high-intensity light ageing. *Studies in Conservation*, **31**, 159–70.

DUBIN, L.S. (1987) *The History of Beads.* Thames and Hudson, London.

DUNCAN, G.S. (1960) *Bibliography of Glass* [to 1940]. Dawsons, London.

EARL, N. (1999) The investigation of glass deterioration as a result of storage systems for waterlogged archaeological glass. In *The Cons. of Glass and Ceramics: Research, Practice and Training.* (N.H. Tennent, ed.), pp. 96–113. James and James, London.

EL-NADY, A.B.M., ZIMMER, K. and ZARY, G. (1985) Spectographical analysis of medieval glass by means of inductively coupled plasma and glow discharge sources. *Spectrochimica Acta*, **40**, 999–1004.

EL-SHAMY, T.M. (1973) The chemical durability of $K_2O–CaO–MgO–SiO_2$ glasses. *Phys. Chem. Glasses*, **14**, 1–5.

EL-SHAMY, T.M., LEWINS, J. and DOUGLAS, R.W. (1972) The dependence on the pH of the decomposition of glasses by aqueous solutions. *Glass Technol.*, **13**, 81–7.

EL-SHAMY, T.M., MORSI, S.E., TAKI-ELDIN, H.D. and AHMED, A.A. (1975) Chemical durability of $Na_2O–CaO–SiO_2$ glasses in acid solutions. *J. Non-Cryst. Solids*, **19**, 241–50.

EMELEUS, V.M. (1960) Beta-ray back scattering. A simple method for the quantitative determination of the lead oxide in glass, glaze and pottery. *Archaeometry*, **3**, 5–9.

EMERY, M.J. (1991) *Techniques in Reverse Glass Painting.* Quality Printing, Pittsfield, Mass.

ENGLE, A. (1973a) 3000 years of glassmaking on the Phoenician Coast. *Readings in Glass History*, **No. 1**, 1–26. (Phoenix Publications, Jerusalem.)

ENGLE, A. (1973b) A semantic approach to glass history. *Readings in Glass History*, **No. 1**, 81–4. (Phoenix Publications, Jerusalem.)

ENGLE, A. (1974) The De Gands of Ghent. *Readings in Glass History*, **No. 4**, 42–54. (Phoenix Publications, Jerusalem.)

ERNSBERGER, F.M. (1977) Mechanical properties of glass. *Proc. 11th Int. Congr. Glass, Prague: Survey Papers,* Vol. 1, 293–321.

ERNSBERGER, F.M. (1980) The role of molecular water in the diffusive transport of protons in glass. In *Phys. Chem. Glasses*, **21**, 146–9.

ERRETT, R.F. (1972) The repair and restoration of glass objects. *JAIC* **12**, 48–9.

ERRETT, R.F., LYNN, M. and BRILL, R.H. (1984) The use of silanes on glass. In *Preprints of the Contributions to the Paris Congress on Adhesives and Consolidants* (N.S. Bromelle, E.M. Pye, P. Smith and G. Thomson, eds), pp. 185–90. IIC, London.

ESCRITT, J. and GREENACRE, M. (1972) Note on toxic gases in polyurethane foam. *Studies in Conservation*, **17**, 134.

ESHØJ, B. (1988) *Glas: Historie, Teknologi, Opbyning, Nedbrydning, Konsiervering,* Konservatorskolen. Det Kongelige Danske Kunstakademi.

ESWARIN, R. (1982) *Reverse Paintings on Glass: The Ryser Collection.* The Corning Museum of Glass, Corning, NY.

ETHRIDGE, E.C., CLARK, D.E. and HENCH, L.L. (1979) Effects of glass surface area to solution volume ratio on glass corrosion. *Glass. Technol.*, **20**, 35–40.

EVANS, W., ROSS, C., WERNER, A. (1995) *Whitefriars Glass: James Powell, and Sons, of London.* Museum of London.

FELLER, R.L. (1972) Problems in the investigation of picture varnishes. In *Conservation of Painting and the Graphic Arts.* Proceedings of the IIC Conference, Lisbon, pp. 201–9.

FENN, J. (1987) Deterioration of glass trade beads, or glass beads in soapy bubbles. *Proceedings of the ICOM Triennial Conference*, pp. 189–91.

FERNANDEZ NAVARRO, J.M. and La IGLESIA, A. (1994) Estudio de la Coloracion Roja y Amarilla de Vidrios de la Catedral de Toledo. *Boletin de la Sociedad Ceramica y Vidrio*, **33**, 864-8.

FERRAZZINI, J.C. (1977) Untersuchungen über eine neue in Chartres angewandte Methode zur Reinigung von mittelelterlichen Glasgemälde. *Maltechnik* **83**, 145–54. (Abstract in *CVMA News Letter* **23**, item 3.2, 3 December, 1976.)

FIELDS, J. (2000) Replacing Synperonic N. *Cons. News*, **72**, 3. (UKIC, London.)

FIORENTINO, P. and BORELLI, L.V. (1975) A preliminary note on the use of fillers and adhesives in the restoration of glass. *Stud. Cons.* **20**, 201–5. (IIC, London.)

FIORENTINO-RONCUZZI, I. (1967) Traditions et progrès dans les materiaux vitraux de la mosaique. In *Ann. 4e Congr. Int. Journ. Verre,* Ravenne–Venise, AIHV, Liège, pp. 230–8.

FIORENTINO-RONCUZZI, I. (1970) Dating and analysis of mosaics. *Ann. 4e Congr. Int. Journ. Verre*, Ravenne–Venise, AIHV, Liège, pp. 353–6.

FISHER, P. (1988) Advances in the restoration of glass vessels. In *Preprints of the Contrib. to the UKIC 30th Anniversary Conference* (V. Todd, ed.), pp. 81–3. UKIC, London.

FISHER, P. (1991) The restoration of historical enamels. Les Arts du Verre, Historie, Techniques et Conservation. In *Journées d'Études de la SFIIC,* Nice, France, pp. 181–91.

FISHER, P. (1992) HXTAL NYL-1, an epoxy resin for the conservation of glass. *Glass and Enamel Conservation,* UKIC Occasional Papers No. 11, pp. 6–9. UKIC, London.

FISHER, P. and NORMAN, K. (1987) A new approach to the reconstruction of two Anglo-Saxon beakers. *Stud. in Cons.,* **32**, 49–58.

FITZ, S. (1981) A new method of cleaning browned medieval glass. In *Preprints of the 6th Triennial Meeting of ICOM–C.C.,* Ottawa, Canada.

FITZ, S., FITZ-ULRICH, E., FRENZEL, G., KRÜGER, R. and KUHN, H. (1984) *Die Einwirkung von Luft-unvereinigungen auf ausgewälte Kunstwerke mittelalter-liche Glasmalerei.* Deutsches Museum, Munich.

FLEMING, S.J. and SWANN, C.P. (1994) Roman onyx glass. A study of production recepies and colorants, using PIXE spectrometry. *Nuclear Instruments and Methods in Physics Research B,* **85**, 864–8.

FLORIAN, M.L.E. (1979) Letter to R.G. Newton, dated 16 February 1987.

FOLEY, K. and HUNTER, K. (1987) The Lincoln Hanging Bowl. In *From Pinheads to Hanging Bowls; the Identification, Deterioration and Conservation of Applied Enamel and Glass Decoration on Archaeological Artefacts,* (L. Bacon and B. Knight, eds). UKIC, London.

FORBES, R.J. (1961) Glass throughout the ages. *Philips Tech. Rev.,* **22**, 282–99.

FORBES, R.J. (1966) *Studies in Ancient Technology.* Leyden, The Netherlands.

FOWLER, J. (1881) On the process of decay in glass and, incidentally, on the composition and texture at different periods, and the history of its manufacture. *Archaeologia,* **46**, 65–162.

FRANK, S. (1982) *Glass and Archaeology.* Academic Press, London.

FRANK, S. (1984) Gold ruby glass. In *Glass Technol.* **25**, 47–50.

FREESTONE, I.C. (1991) Looking into Glass, in *Science and the Past* (Bowman, S. ed.) pp. 37–56, British Museum Publications, London.

FREESTONE, I.C. (1993) Compositions and origins of glasses from Romanesque champlevé enamels. In Stratford, N., *Catalogue of Material Enamels in the British Museum,* **II** *Northern Romanesque Enamel,* pp. 37–45. BMP, London.

FREESTONE, I.C. (1999) Ancient Glass and Modern Science – Building on the legacy of W.E.S. Turner, 13th Turner Memorial Lecture, 1999. University of Sheffield.

FREESTONE, I.C. (2001) Post depositional changes in archaeological ceramics and glass. In *Handbook of Archaeological Sciences* (D.R. Brothwell and A.M. Pollard, eds). John Wiley & Sons Ltd, Chichester.

FREESTONE, I.C. and BIMSON, M. (1995) Early Venetian enamelling on glass: technology and origins. In *Materials Issues in Art and Archaeology* **IV,** (P.B. Vindiver *et al.,* eds), pp. 352, 415–31. Materials Research Soc. Symp. Proc., Pittsburgh.

FREESTONE, I.C. and GORIN-ROSEN, Y. (1999) The great glass slab at Bet She'arim Israel. An early Islamic glass-making experiment? *J. Glass Stud.,* **41**, 105–16.

FREESTONE, I.C. and STAPLETON, G.P. (1998) Composition and technology of Islamic enamelled Glass. In *Islamic Gilded and Enamelled Glass of the Middle East* (R. Ward, ed.), pp. 122–8. BMP, London.

FREESTONE, I.C., BIMSON, M. and BUCKTON, D (1990) Compositional categories of Byzantine glass tesserae. *Ann. 11ᵉ Congr. Assoc. Int. Hist. Verre,* AIHV, Amsterdam, pp. 271–9.

FREESTONE, I.C., HUGHES, M.J. and STAPLETON, G.P. (1999) Compositional studies of some Saxon glass. In *Proceedings of Current Research on the History of Glass through Scientific Analysis,* London.

FREMERSDORF, F. (1930) Die Herstellung der Diatreta, *Schumaker Festschrift,* Mainz, pp. 295–300.

FRENZEL, G. (1970) La conservation des vitreaux anciens **II.** Le nettoyage, 4 pp. typescript (Abstract **No. 153** in Newton 1982b).

FRIEDMAN, I., SMITH, R.L. and CLARK, D. (1963) Obsidian dating. In *Science in Archaeology. A Comprehensive Survey of Progress and Research* (D. Bothwell and E. Higgs, eds), pp. 47–58. Thames and Hudson, London.

FRODL-KRAFT, E. (1967) Restaurierung und Erforschung, 1, Die Südrose von Maria Strassengel. *Osterr. Zeits. Kunst. Denkm.* **21**, 192–7.

FRODL-KRAFT, E. (1970) Konservierungsprobleme mitte-lalterlicher Glasmalerein. *Ann. 5ᵉ Congr Int. Hist. Verre,* Prague, pp. 357–70. AIHV, Liège.

FRODL-KRAFT, E. (1971) Restaurierung und Sicherung Die Bildfenster der Wassenkirche. In *Osterr. Zeits. Kunst. Denkm.,* **25**, 70–3.

GABRIEL, J.H. (2000) *The Gilbert Collection: Micromosaics.* Philip Wison, London.

GAIROLA, T.R. (1960) *Handbook of Chemical Conservation of Museum Objects.* Department of Museology, Maharaja Sayajirao, University of Baroda.

GARLAKE, M. (1969) Recovery and treatment of fragile artefacts from an excavation. *S. Afr. Archaeolog. Bull.,* **24**, 61–2.

GASPARETTO, A. (1965) Les fouilles de Torcello et leur apport a l'histoire de la verrerie de la Vénétie dans le Haut Moyen Age. *Proc. 7th Int.. Congr. Glass,* Brussels, New York, Paper No. 239.

GASPARETTO, A. (1967) A proposito dell' officina vetraria Torcellana – forni e sistemi diffusione antiche. *J. Glass Stud.* **9**, 50–75.

GASPARETTO, A. (1973) Verres Venitiens du moyen age. *Proc. 10th Int. Congr. Glass,* Kyoto, pp. 9–21 to 9–29 and 15–90.

GEILMANN, W. (1956) Beiträge zur Kenntnis alter Gläser IV Die Zersetzung der Gläser im Boden. *Glastech. Berlin.* **29**, 156–168.

GEILMANN, W. (1960) Beiträge zur Kenntnis alter Gläser VI Eine eigenartige Verwitterungs-erscheinung auf Römichen Glass-scheiben. *Glastech. Berlin.,* **33**, 291–6.

GEILMANN, W. and BRUCKBAUER, T. (1954) Beiträge zur Kenntnis alter Gläser. II. Der Mangangehalt alter Gläser. *Glastech. Berlin,* **27**, 456–9.

GERMAIN-BONNE, D., BIRON, I. and TROCELLIER, P. (1996) The degradation of fifteenth- and sixteenth-century painted enamel. In *Preprints of 11ᵗʰ Triennial Meeting of ICOM–CC,* Edinburgh, Scotland, pp. 826–32.

GIBSON, P. and NEWTON, R.G. (1974) A study on cleaning painted and enamelled glass in an ultrasonic bath. *Br. Acad. CVMA Occasional Papers,* **Part 1**, 70–8.

GILARD, P. and DUBRUL, L. (1937) The calculation of the physical properties of glass III. The index of refraction. *Trans. J. Glass Technol.*, **21**, 476–88.

GODFREY, E.S. (1975) *The Development of English Glassmaking 1560–1640*, Oxford.

GOLDSTEIN, S.M. (1977) Forgeries and reproductions of ancient glass in Corning. *J. Glass Stud.*, **19**, 40–62.

GOODMAN, C.H.L. (1987) A new way of looking at glass. *Glass Technol.*, **28**, 19–29.

GORIN-ROSEN, Y. (1993) Halera, Bet Eli'ezer; in English Edition of *Hadashot Arkheologiyot*, **No. 100**, 42–3, Jerusalem.

GORIN-ROSEN, Y. (1997) Glass Workshop in the Bet She'an Excavation Project. 1992–1994. In (G. Mazor and R. Bar-Nathan, eds), in English Edition of *Hadashot Arkheologiyot*, **No. 105** (Jerusalem), 27–9.

GRAHAM, K.W. (1976) Examination and treatment of Hinterglasmalerei or reverse paintings on glass. In Conference Papers, Cooperstown Training Programme, USA, pp. 1–8.

GRATUZE, B. and BARRANDON, J-N. (1990) Islamic glass weights and stamps: analysis using nuclear techniques. *Archaeometry*, **32**, 155–62.

GREEN, P. (1979) Tracking down the past. *New Scientist*, **84** (1182), 624–6.

GREEN, L.R. and HART, F.A. (1987) Colour and chemical composition in ancient glass: An examination of some Roman and Wealdon glass by means of ultravisible–infrared spectrometry and electron micro-probe analysis. *J. Archaeol. Sci.*, **14**, 271–82.

GROSE, D.F. (1977) Early blown glass. *J. Glass Stud.* **19**, 9–29.

GUIDO, M. (1977) *The Glass Beads of the Prehistoric and Roman Periods in Britain and Ireland*. London.

GÜNTHER, R. (1961a) Die Entwicklung der Glasschmeltzwanennofen. *Glastechn. Berlin*, **34**, 417–82.

GÜNTHER, R. (1961b) Rauchgaskegel auf alten glashütten. *Glastechn. Berlin*, **34**, 559–62.

HABEREY, W. (1963) Die Glasindustrie im Römichen Rheinland. In *Advances in Glass Technology, Part 2* (F.R. Matson and G.E. Rindone, eds), pp. 349–58. New York.

HADSUND, P. (1993) The tin–mercury mirror: its manufacturing technique and deterioration processes. *Stud. in Cons.*, **38**, (1).

HALL, E.T., BANKS, M.S. and STERN, J.M. (1964) Uses of X-ray fluorescence analysis in archaeology. *Archaeometry*, **7**, 84–9.

HALL, E.T. and SCHWEIZER, F. (1973) X-ray fluorescence analysis of museum objects: a new instrument. 1. A non-dispersive X-ray isoprobe. In *Archaeometry*, **15**, 53–7, 74–6.

HANCOCK, R.G., CHAFE, A. and KENYON, I. (1994) Neutron activation analysis of sixteenth and seventeenth–century blue glass trade beads from the Eastern Great Lakes of North America. *Archaeometry*, **36**, 253–66.

HARDEN, D.B. (1936) *Roman Glass from Karanis, Found by the University of Michigan Archaeological Expedition in Egypt (1924–1929)*. University of Michigan Press.

HARDEN, D.B. (1956) Glass vessels in Britain and Ireland AD 400–1000. In *Dark Age Britain: Studies presented to E.T. Leeds* (D.B. Harden, ed.), pp. 132–67. London.

HARDEN, D.B. (1959) New light on Roman and Early Medieval window glass. *Glastechn. Berlin*, **32K**, **VIII**/8 – **VIII**/16.

HARDEN, D.B. (1961) Domestic window glass. Roman, Saxon, and Medieval. In *Studies in Building History: Essays in Recognition of the work of B.H. St J. O'Neil* (E.M. Jope, ed.). pp. 39–63. Odhams, London

HARDEN, D.B. (1963) The Rothschild Lycurgus Cup: addenda and corrigenda. *J. Glass Stud.*, **5**, 9–17.

HARDEN, D.B. (1968) Ancient glass I: Pre-Roman. *Archaeolog. J.*, **125**, 46–72 (*).

HARDEN, D.B. (1969a) Ancient glass II: Roman. *Archaeolog. J.*, **126**, 44–77 (*).

HARDEN, D.B. (1969b) Medieval glass in the West. *Proc. 8th Int. Congr. Glass*, pp. 97–111, Sheffield.

HARDEN, D.B. (1971) Ancient glass III: Post-Roman. *Archaelog. J.*, **128**, 78–117 (*) [The three articles marked (*) were re-issued in 1997].

HARDEN, D.B. (1973) In *Excavations at Shakenoak Farm, near Wilcote, Oxfordshire, Part IV* (A.C.C. Brodribb, A.R. Hands and D.R. Walker, eds), privately printed and available from Dr A.R. Hands, Exeter College, Oxford.

HARDEN, D.B. (1974) Window glass from the Romano-British bath-house at Garden Hill, Hartfield, Sussex. *Antiquaries J.*, **54**, 280–1.

HARDEN, D.B., PAINTER, K.S., PINDER-WILSON, R.H. and TAIT, H. (1968) *Masterpieces of Glass*. Trustees of the British Museum, London.

HARDEN, D.B. and TOYNBEE, J.M.C. (1959) The Rothschild Lycurgus Cup. *Archaeologia*, **97**, 179–212.

HARTMANN, G., KAPPEL. I., GROTE, K. and ARNDT, B. (1997) Chemistry and technology of prehistoric glass from Lower Saxony and Hesse. *J. Arch. Sci.*, **24**, 547–59.

HARRINGTON, J.C. (1952) *Glassmaking at Jamestown*. Richmond Va.

HAWTHORNE, J.H., and SMITH, C.S. (1963) *On Divers Arts: the Treatise of Theophilus*, 2nd edn, University of Chicago Press, 1979. [The foremost medieval treatise on painting, glassmaking and metalwork.]

HAYNES, D.E.L. (1975) *The Portland Vase*, Trustees of the British Museum.

HEALTH & SAFETY EXECUTIVE (UK) (2000) INDG 307 Hydrofluoric acid poisoning – Recommendations on First Aid Procedures. HSE, London.

HEDGES, R. and NEWTON, R.G. (1974) Use of the 'Isoprobe' for studying the chemical composition of some 12th century glass from York Minster. *Br. Acad. C.V.M.A. Occasional Papers*, Part 1, 79–93.

HEDVALL, J.A., JAGITSCH, R. and OLSEN, G. (1951) Uber das Problem der Zerstörung antiker Gläser. II. Mitteilung. Uber die Belegung von Glasoberflächen mit Schutzfilmen. *Trans. Chalmers Inst. Technol.*, **No. 118**, Göteborg.

HEJDOVÁ, J. (1965) Comments on archaeological finds in the field of glassmaking in Czechoslovakia. *Czechoslovak Glass Rev.*, **12**, 353.

HENCH, L.L. (1975a) Characterization of glass. *Characterization of Materials in Research, Ceramics, and Polymers* (J.J. Burke and V.I. Weiss, eds), Ch. 8, pp. 11–51. Syracuse, NY.

HENCH, L.L. (1975b) Characterization of glass corrosion and durability. *J. Non-Cryst. Sol.* **19**, 27–39.

HENCH, L.L. (1977) Physical chemistry of glass surfaces. In *Proc. 11th Congr. Int. Comm. Glass*, Prague, Survey Papers, **II**, 343–69.

HENCH, L.L. (1982) Glass surfaces. *J. Physique Colloque, C.9. Supplement to No. 12*, **43**, C9–625 to C9–636.

HENCH, L.L. and CLARK, D.E. (1978) Physical chemistry of glass surfaces. *J. Non-Cryst. Sol.* **28**, 83–105.

HENCH, L.L. and SANDERS, D.M. (1974) Analysis of glass corrosion. *The Glass Industry*, Feb. and Mar., 12, 13, 16, 18, 19.

HENCH, L.L., NEWTON, R.G. and BERNSTEIN, S. (1979) Use of infrared reflection spectroscopy in analysis of durability of medieval glasses, with some comments on conservation procedures. *Glass Technol.*, **20**, 144–8.

HENDERSON, J. (1985) The raw materials of early glass production. *Oxford J. Archaeology*, **40**, 267–91.

HENDERSON, J. (1988) Electron microprobe analysis of mixed alkali glasses. *Archaeometry*, **30**, 77–91.

HENDERSON, J. (1991) Chemical characterisation of Roman glass vessels, enamels and *tesserae.*. In *Materials Issues in Art and Archaeology II*. Materials Research Society Symposium Proceedings, **185**, 601–7.

HENDERSON, J. (1993a) Technological characteristics of Roman enamels. *Jewellery Stud.*, **5**, 65–76.

HENDERSON, J. (1993b) Aspects of early medieval glass production in Britain. *Ann 12e Congr. Assoc. Int. Verre.* AIHV, Liège, pp. 247–59.

HENDERSON, J. (1995) An investigation of early glass production at Raqqa, Syria. In *Materials Issues in Art & Archaeology*, IV, *Mats. Res. Soc. Proc.* **352**, 433–443.

HEYWORTH, M.P., HUNTER, J.R., WARREN, S.E. and WALSH, J.N. (1989) I.C.P.S. and glass: the multi-element approach. In *Neutron Activation and Plasma Emission Spectrometric Analysis in Archaeometry* (M.J. Hughes, M.R. Cowell and D.R. Hook, eds), British Museum Occasional Paper 82, 143–154. BMP, London.

HOFFMAN, P. (1994) Analytical determination of colouring elements and of their compounds in glass beads from graveyards of the Merowings' time. In *Fresenius' J. Analyt. Chem.*, **349**, 320–33.

HOGAN, I. (1993) An improved method of making supportive resin fills for glass. *Cons. News*, **50**, 29–30. UKIC, London.

HOGG, S.E.T., McPHAIL, D.S., ROGERS, P.S. and OAKLEY, V.L. (1998) Mono-functional organo-silanes as candidates for treatments of crizzling glasses. In *Preprints of the ICOM-CC Working Group on Glass, Ceramics & Related Materials* (A. Paterakis, ed.), pp. 53–7. EVTEK Institute of Arts and Design, Vantaa, Finland.

HOGG, S.E.T., McPHAIL, D.S., OAKLEY, V.L. and ROGERS, P.S. (1999) Modern instrumental methods for the study of the deterioration of vessel glass. In *The Conservation of Glass and Ceramics: Research, Practice and Training* (N.H. Tennent, ed.), pp. 42–55. James and James, London.

HOLDEN, A. (1991) The museum approach to the conservation/restoration of stained glass. In *Les Arts du Verre: Histoire, Technique et Conservation*. Journées d'Études de la SFIIC, Paris, pp. 69–74.

HOLLISTER, P. (1974) The glazing of the Crystal Palace. *J. Glass Stud.* **16**, 95–110.

HORIE, C.V. (1987) *Materials for Conservation*. Butterworths, London.

HORTON-JAMES, D., WALSTON, S. and ZOUNIS, S. (1990) Evaluation of the stability, appearance and performance of resins for adhesion of flaking paint on ethnographic objects. *Stud. Cons.*, **36**, 203–21.

HOSFORTH, J. and DAVISON, P. (1988) Conserving Ndebele Beadwork. *Am. Mus. Nat. Hist.*, 85–95.

HOWARTH, J.T., SYKES, R.F. and TURNER, W.E.S. (1934) A study of the fundamental reactions in the formation of soda–lime–silica glasses. *Trans. J. Soc. Glass Technol.*, **18**, 290–308.

HUDSON, A.P. and NEWTON, R.G. (1976) A means for the *in situ* identification of medieval glass by the detection of its natural radioactivity. *Archaeometry*, **18**, 229–32.

HUGGINS, M.I. and SUN, K-H. (1946) Calculation of density and optical constants of a glass from its composition in weight percentage. *J. Soc. Glass Technol.* **30**, 333–42.

HUGHES, M.J. (1987) Materials, deterioration and analysis. In *From Pinheads to Hanging Bowls, the Identification, Deterioration and Conservation of Applied Enamel and Glass Decoration on Archaeological Artefacts* (L. Bacon and B. Knight, eds). UKIC, London.

HUME, I.N. (1976) Archaeological excavations on the site of John Frederick Amelung's New Bremen Glass manufactury, 1962–1963. *J. Glass Stud.* **18**, 138–215.

HUNTER, J.R. (1977) Glass fragments from the vicarage garden, Brixworth. *J. Brit. Arch. Assoc.*, 104–7.

HUNTER, J.R. (1981) The medieval glass industry. In *Medieval Industry* (D.W. Crossley, ed.), pp. 1430–50. CBA Research Report 40, London.

HUNTER, J.R. and HEYWORTH, M. (1999) *The Hamwich Glass*. Council for British Archaeology, London.

HUNTLEY, D.J. and BAILEY, D.C. (1978) Obsidian source identification by thermoluminescence. *Archaeometry*, **20**, 159–70.

HURST-VOSE, R. (1980) *Glass*. Collins, London.

HUTCHINSON, M.E. (1981) An experimental method for consolidating excavated medieval glass. Contributions to the Seminar on Medieval Glass Technology and Medieval Glaziers, Urban Research Committee of the Council for British Archaeology and Corpus Medii Aevi.

IBRAHIM, L., SCRANTON, R. and BRILL, R.H. (1976) The panels of *opus sectile* in glass. *Kenchreî – Eastern Part of Corinth*, vol. 2. E.J. Brill, Leiden, The Netherlands.

ICCROM (1983) Conservation in situ.: mosaics. No. 3, Aquileia (Rome).

ICI (1977) *Polyurethanes, General, Isocyanates, Hazards and Safe Handling Procedures*, 4th edn. ICI Technical Information, U93, London.

ILIFFE, C.J.A. and NEWTON, R.G. (1976) Using triangular diagrams to understand the behaviour of medieval glasses. *Verres et Réfract.* **30**, 30–4.

INTERNATIONAL COMMISSION ON GLASS (1972–1979) *The Chemical Durability of Glass; a Bibliographic Review of the Literature*. Institut National du Verre, Charleroi, **1**, 1972; **2**, 1973; **3**, 1979.

JACKSON, C.M. and SMEDLEY, J.W. (1999) Raw materials and glass recipes – glassmaking in Staffordshire in the 14th–16th centuries. In *Proceedings of Current Research on the History of Glass through Scientific Analysis*. London.

JACKSON, C.M., HUNTER, J.R., WARREN, S.E. and COOL, H.E.M. (1991) The analysis of blue–green glass and glassy waste from two Romano–British glass-working sites. In *Archaeometry '90*, Basle (E. Pernicka and G. A Wagner, eds), pp. 295–305. Birkhauser Verlag, Germany.

JACKSON, C.M., NICHOLSON, P.T. and GNEISINGER, W. (1998) Glassmaking at Tell El Amarna: an integrated approach. *J. Glass Stud.*, **40**, 11–23.

JACKSON, L. (ed.) (1996) *Whitefriars Glass: The Art of James Powell & Sons*. Richard Dennis.

JACKSON, P.R. (1982a) A doweling technique for glass restoration. *The Conservator*, **6**, 33–5.

JACKSON, P.R. (1982b) Resins used in glass conservation. In *Proc. Symp. Resins and Cons.*, 10.1–10.7, SSCR, Edinburgh University, Extra Mural Department, Edinburgh, Scotland.

JACKSON, P.R. (1983) Restoration of an Italic glass *oinchoe* with Technovit 4004a. *The Conservator*, **7**, 44–7. UKIC, London.

JACKSON, P.R. (1984) Restoration of glass antiquities. In *Preprints of the 7th Triennial Meeting of ICOM–CC*. Copenhagen, Denmark, 84.20. 13–7.

JACKSON, P.R. (1985) Restoration of the Auldjo Jug. *Ann. 9e. Congr. Assoc.Hist. Verre*. AIHV, Liège.

JACKSON, P.R. (1987) The Hampton Court fire – rescuing pier glasses. In: Recent Advances in the Conservation and Analysis of Artefacts. *Proceedings of the University of London Institute of Archaeology Jubilee Conservation Conference*.

JACKSON, C.M., NICHOLSON, P.T. and GNEISSINGER, W. (1998) Glassmaking at Tell el-Amarna: an integrated approach. *J. Glass Stud.*, **40**, 15–23.

JANTZEN, C.M. and PLODINEC, M.J. (1984) Thermodynamic model of natural, medieval, and nuclear waste glass durability. *J. Non-Cryst. Sol.*, **67**, 207–23.

JOHNSTON, R.H. (1975) Master glassblowers of Heart, Afghanistan: some archaeological relationships. *77th General Meeting of the Archeology Institute of America*, **22**.

KARL, F. (1970) Behandlung korrodierter geschliffener Gläser. *Arbeitsblätter für Restauratoren*, **2**, Gruppe 5, 17–19.

KEISER, H.B. (1937) *Die deutsche Hinterglasmalerei*. Munich.

KENYON, G.H. (1967) *The Glass Industry of the Weald*. Leicester University Press.

KENYON, I., HANCOCK, R.G.V. and AUFREITER, S. (1995) Neutron activation analysis of AD 1660–1930 European copper-coloured blue glass trade beads from Ontario, Canada. *Archaeometry*, **37**, 323–37.

KERR, J. (1991) *The Repair and Maintenance of Historic Glass*. Church House Publishing.

KLEITZ, M.O. (1991) La peinture sur verre, technologie, degradation, problems de restauration de la couche picturale. In *Les Arts du Verre: Histoire, Technique et Conservation*. Journées d'Etude de la SFIIC, Paris, 117–33.

KNAIPP, F. (1988) *Hinterglas-Kunste. Eine Bildokumentation*. Linz and Munich.

KNIGHT, B. (1999) Excavated window glass – a neglected resource? In *Preprints of the Contributions to the Copenhagen Congress on Archaeological Conservation and its Consequences* (A. Roy and P. Smith, eds), pp. 96–104. IIC, London.

KNOWLES, J.A. (1959) Decay of glass, lead and iron in ancient stained glass windows. *J. Brit. Soc, Master Glass Painters*, **12**, 70–6.

KOCK, J. and SODE, T. (1995) *Glass, Glass Beads and Glassmakers in Northern India*. Thot Press, Vanlose, Denmark.

KOEZUKA, T. and YAMASAKI, K. (1998) Investigation of some K2O–PbO–SiO2 glasses excavated in Japan. *Proc. 18th Int. Congr. Glass,* San Francisco, CD-ROM, Paper No. 1 in Group B3, 1–4.

KOOB, S.P. (1981) Consolidation with acrylic colloidal dispersions. In *Preprints of the 9th Annual Meeting of the AIC*, pp. 86–94. JAIC, Philadelphia and Washington.

KOOB, S.P. (1982) The instability of cellulose nitrate adhesives. *The Conservator*, **6**, 31–4.

KOOB, S.P. (2000) New techniques for the repair and restoration of ancient glass. In *Preprints of the Contributions to the Melbourne Conference on Tradition and Innovation: Advances in Conservation* (Roy, A. and Smith, P. eds), pp. 92–5. IIC, London.

KOOB, S.P. BRILL, R.H. and THIMME, D. (1996) The Kenchrei *opus sectile* panels revisited: a comparison and assessment of previous treatments. In *Preprints of the Contributions to the Copenhagen Congress on Archaeological Conservation and its Consequences* (A. Roy and P. Smith, eds), pp. 105–10. IIC, London.

KORDAS, G. (ed.) (2002) Hyalos–Vitrum–Glass. *Proceedings of the First International Conference on the History, Technology and Conservation of Glass and Vitreous Materials in the Hellenistic World*. Rhodes, 2001.

KRAWCZYK-BÄRSCH, E., DÄBRITZ, S. and HAUFFE, W. (1998) The characterization of the weathering process in medieval glass by scanning electron microscopy in combination with ion beam slope cutting. *Proc. 18th Int. Congr. Glass,* San Francisco, CD-ROM, Paper No. 11 in Group B1, 61–6.

KUNCKEL, VON LOEWENSTEIN (1679) *Ars Vetrarii Experimentalis*. Leipzig, Germany.

LABINO, D. (1966) The Egyptian sand core technique: a new interpretation. *J. Glass Stud.*, **8**, 124.

LAL, B.B. (1962–63) Chemical preservation of ancient glass. *Ancient India*, **18–19**, 230–80.

LAMBERT, J.B., McLAUGHLIN, C.D. and CARTER, G.F. (1978) Analysis of early Egyptian glass by atomic absorption and X-ray photoelectron spectroscopy. *Archaeological Chemistry. 2. Advances in Chemistry Series*. **171**. American Chemical Society, New York.

LAMM, C.J. (1941) *Oriental Glass of Medieval Date Found in Sweden and the Early History of Lustre Painting*. Kungl. Vitterhets Hist. och Antik. Akad. Handlingar, del 50:1, Stockholm, Sweden.

LANFORD, W.A. (1977) Glass hydration: a method of dating glass objects. *Science*, **166**, 975–6.

LANFORD, W.A. (1986) Ion beam analysis of glass surfaces: dating, authentication and conservation. *Nucl. Inst. Meth.*, **B14**, 123–6.

LANG, J. and PRICE, J. (1975) Iron tubes from a late Roman glassmaking site at Mérida (Badajoz), Spain. *J. Archaeol. Sci.*, **2**, 289–96.

LANMON, D.P. and PALMER, A.M. (1976) John Frederick Amelung and the New Bremen Glasmanufactury. *J. Glass Stud.* **18**, 14–137.

LANZ, H. and SEELIG, L. (ed.) (1999) *Farbig Kostbarkeiten Aus Glas, Kabinettstucke der Zurcher Hinterglasmalerei, 1600–1650*. Exhibition catalogue, Bayerisches Nationalmuseum, Munchen und Schwizerisches Landesmuseum, Zurich.

LANZ, H. and SEELIG, L. (2000) *Glanzlichter. Die Kunst der Hinterglasmalerei*. Exhibition catalogue. Musée Suisse du Vitrail Romont/Museum in der Burg Zug.

LARNEY, J. (1975) *Restoring Ceramics*, pp. 100–2. Barrie and Jenkins, London.

LAVOISIER, A.J. (1770) Action of water on glass. *Mem. Acad. Sci. (Paris)*, **73**, 90.

LEE, L., SEDDON, G. and STEPHENS, F. (1982) *Stained Glass*. Mitchell Beazley, London.

LEWIS, G.D. (1973) *The South Yorkshire Glass Industry*, 2nd edn. Sheffield City Museum.

LÎBIETE, J. (1998) Conservation of the Daugmale Castle Mound Beads. In *Preprints of the Interim Meetings of the ICOM-CC. Working Group Glass, Ceramics and Related Materials* (A. Paterakis, ed.). EVTEK Institute of Arts and Design, Vantaa, Finland.

LIEFKES, R. (1997) *Glass*. V&A Publications, London.

LILLIE, H.R. (1936) Stress release in glass, a phenomenon involving viscosity as a variable with time. *J. Am. Ceram. Soc.*, **19**, 45–54.

LILYQUIST, C. and BRILL, R.H. (1993) Glassy materials, glass and lead isotope analyses of some objects from Egypt and the Near East. In *Studies in Early Egyptian Glass*. The Metropolitan Museum of Art, New York.

LINDSEY, H. (2000) Protective packaging: an introduction to the materials used to produce archival quality boxes, folders, sleeves, and envelopes. *Journal of the Society of Archivists* **21**, (1) 87–103.

LONGWORTH, G., TENNENT, N.H., TRICKER, M.J. and VISHNAVA, P.P. (1982) Iron-57 Moessbauer spectral studies of medieval stained glass. *J. Archaeol. Sci.*, **9**, 261–73.

LOUBENGAGER, A.W. (1931) Weathering of glass. *J. Am. Ceram. Soc.*, **14**, 833–6.

LOUGHEED, S. and SHAW, J. (1986) Deteriorating glass beads on ethnographic objects. In *The Care and Preservation of Ethnographic Materials*. CCI, Canada, pp. 109–13.

McCRAY, W.P., OSBORNE, Z.A. and KINGERY, W.D. (1995) The technology of Venetian girasole glass. In *Material Issues in Art and Archaeology*, II (Vandiver, P.B. *et al.*, eds). Pittsburgh, PA, The Materials Research Society.

McGOVERN, P.E., FLEMING, S.J. and SWANN, C.P. (1991) The beads from tomb B10aB27 at Dinkha Tepe and the beginning of glassmaking in the ancient Near East. *Am. J. Archaeol.* **95**, 395–402.

McGRATH, R., FROST, A.C. and BECKETT, H.E. (1961) *Glass in Architecture and* MACLEHOSE, L.S. (trans.) (1907) *Vasari on Technique – Georgio Vasari*, pp. 253–7. Dover Inc., New York.

MacLEOD, C. (1987) Accident or design? George Ravenscroft's patent and the invention of lead-crystal glass. *Technol. Cult.*, **28**, 776–803.

MACLEOD, I.D. and BENG, E.H. (1998) Analysis and interpretation of glass artefacts from 17th–19th century Dutch and colonial Australian shipwrecks. In *Proceedings of the ICOM–CC Working Group, Ceramics and Related Materials* (A. Paterakis, ed.). EVTEK Institute of Arts and Design, Vantaa, Finland.

MACLEOD, I.D. and DAVIES, J.A. (1987) Deterioration of glass, stone and ceramics. In *Preprints of the ICOM–CC 8th Triennial Meeting* (J. Bridgland, ed.), pp. 1003–7. GCI, Los Angeles.

Decoration. Architectural Press, London.

MADSEN, H.B. (1972) A new product for mending glass. *Stud. Glass Conserv.*, **17**, 131–2.

MAJEWSKI, E.J. (1973) Conservation of archaeological material at Sardis, Turkey. *Bull. Am. Inst. Cons.*, **13**, 99–104.

MANSFIELD, C.R., LAUGHLIN, A.W., CREMERS, D.A. and FERRIS, M.J. (1998) Real-time analysis of glass and glass raw materials using LIBS. *Proc. 18th Int. Congr. Glass, San Francisco*, CD-ROM, Paper No. 1 in Group A3, 1–9.

MÅNSSON, P. (*circa* 1520) *Glaskonst*. Modern translation by R. Geete, Stockholm, 1913–15.

MARCHINI, G. (1972) L'afflaiblissement de la grisaille, de long des plombs *Compt. Rend. 8e Colloque, York*, CVMA, **46**.

MARSCHNER, H. (1977) Zur Lochfrass corrosion an Mittelalterlichen Fensterglasern. *DGG Meeting in Frankfurt* (Abstract No. 289 in *CVMA News Letter* **26**).

MARTIN, J.H. (ed.) (1977) *The Corning Flood: Museum Underwater*. Corning Museum of Glass, Corning, NY.

MARTIN, M.G. (1985) *Els vitralls cloisonné de Barcelona*. Museum of Modern Art, Barcelona.

MARYON, H. (1971) *Metalwork and Enamelling: A Practical Treatise on Gold and Silversmiths' Work and their Allied Crafts*, 5th rev. edn. Dover Inc., New York.

MASS, J.L. (1999) Instrumental methods of analysis applied to the Conservation of Ancient and Historic Glass. In *The Conservation of Glass and Ceramics: Research, Practice and Training*. (N.H. Tennent, ed.), pp. 15–41. James and James, London.

MASS, J.L., STONE, R.E. and WYPYSKI, M.T. (1998) The mineralogical and metallurgical origins of Roman opaque coloured glasses. In *The Prehistory and History of Glassmaking Technology* (P. McCray, ed.), *Ceramics and Civilisation*, **VIII**, 121–44. American Ceramics Society, Columbus, Ohio.

MEHLMAN, F. (1982) *The Phaidon Guide to Glass*. Phaidon Press, London.

MEIGH, E. (1972) *The Story of the Glass Bottle*. C.E. Ramsden and Co., Stoke-on-Trent.

MELUCCO, A. (1971) *Vetro-materiali vitrei. Problemi di conservazioni*, (Urbain, ed) Sec. IV. Uff. de Min. per il coordinamento della ricerca scientifica e technologica, Bologna.

MERRETT, C. (1662) *The Art of Glass* (translation of Antonio Neri, *L'Arte Vetraria*), London.

MERRIFIELD, M.P. (1849) *Original Treatises on the Arts of Painting*, 2 vols. John Murray, London. (Reprinted by Dover Inc., New York, 1966.)

MESSINGER II, J.M. and LANSBURY, P.T. (1989) Controlling the refractive index of epoxy resins. *JAIC,* **28**, 127–36.

MIRTI, P., CASOLI, A. and APPOLONIA, L. (1993) Scientific analysis of Roman glass from Augusta Pretoria. *Archaeometry*, **35**, 225–40.

MOHYUDDIN, I. and DOUGLAS, R.W. (1960) Some observations on the anelasticity of glasses. *Phys. Chem. Glasses*, **1** (3), 7–86.

MONCRIEFF, A. (1971) Polyurethane foaming resins. *Stud. Cons.*, **16**, 119.

MONCRIEFF, A. (1975) Problems and potentialities in the conservation of vitreous materials, In *Preprints of the Contributions to the Stockholm Congress: Conservation in Archaeology and the Applied Art*, (D. Leigh, A. Moncrieff, W.A. Oddy and P. Pratt, eds), pp. 99–104. IIC, London.

MONEY, J.H. (1976) *Fourth Interim Report on Excavations in the Iron Age Hill Fort and Romano-British Iron-Working Settlement at Garden Hill, Hartfield, Sussex*, Fig. 8.

MOODY, B.E. (1988) The life of George Ravenscroft. *Glass Technol.*, **29**, 198–209.

MOOREY, P.R.S. (1994) *Ancient Mesopotamian Materials and Industries: The Archaeological Evidence*. Oxford University Press, Oxford.

MORGÓS, A., NAGY, L. and PALOSSY, L. (1984) New silicone rubber mould-making materials. The addition-type silicone rubbers. In *Preprints of the 7th Triennial Meeting of the ICOM-CC*. Copenhagen, pp. 84.20.19–84.20.20.

MORTIMER, C. (1993) Analyses of glass and glassworking waste from the collections of the Guildford Museum Ancient Monuments Laboratory Report, **106/93**, English Heritage, London.

MORTIMER, C. (1995) The glass working evidence from Old Broad Street, London. In (D.R. Hook *et al.*, ed.) *Trade and Discovery*. British Museum Occasional Paper 109. BMP, London.

MORTIMER, M.M. (2000) *The English Glass Chandelier*. The Antique Collector's Club.

MURGATROYD, J.B. (1942) The significance of surface marks on fractured glass. *J. Glass Technol.*, **26**, 155–71.

NAVARRO, J. (1999) Moving displays: four methods of mounting ceramics and glass objects in drawers. In *Preprints of the 12th Triennial Meeting of ICOM–CC*, Lyons (J. Bridgland, ed.), pp. 793–8. EVTEK Institute of Arts and Design, Vantaa, Finland.

NERI, A. (1612) *Dell 'Arte Vetraria* (translated by Christopher Merrett, *The Art of Glass*). London.

NEWMAN, H. (1977) *An Illustrated Dictionary of Glass*. Thames and Hudson, London.

NEWTON, R.G. (1966) Some problems in the dating of ancient glass by counting the layers in the weathering crust. *Glass Technol.*, **7**, 22–5.

NEWTON, R.G. (1969) Some further observations on the weathering crusts on ancient glass. *Glass Technol.*, **10**, 40–2.

NEWTON, R.G. (1970) Metallic gold and ruby glass. *J. Glass Stud.* **12**, 165–70.

NEWTON, R.G. (1971a) The enigma of the layered crusts on some weathered glasses, a chronological account of the investigations. *Archaeometry*, **13**, 1–9.

NEWTON, R.G. (1971b) A preliminary examination of the suggestion that pieces of strongly coloured glass were articles of trade in Iron Age Britain. *Archaeometry*, **13**, 11–16.

NEWTON, R.G. (1971c) Glass trade routes in the Iron Age? In *Proceedings of the 9th International Congress on Glass, Versailles. Art. Hist. Comm.*, pp. 197–204.

NEWTON, R.G. (1972) Stereoscan views of weathering layers on a piece of ancient glass. *Glass Technol*, **13**, 54–6.

NEWTON, R.G. (1974a) Recovery of lost or faded decoration on painted glass. *Brit. Acad. CVMA Occasional Papers, Part 1*, pp. 68–9, 87–9.

NEWTON, R.G. (1975) Arty Facts (Presidential Address). *Glass Technol.*, **16**, 103–6.

NEWTON, R.G. (1976) The effects of medieval glass paint. *Stained Glass*, **71**, 226–30.

NEWTON, R.G. (1978) Colouring agents used by medieval glassmakers. *Glass Technol.*, **19**, 59–60.

NEWTON, R.G. (1979) Sulphur dioxide and medieval stained glass. In *Sulphur Emissions and the Environment*, pp. 311–13, 500–1. London, Society of Chemical Industry, Water and Environmental Group.

NEWTON, R.G. (1982a) Unusual effects of the weathering of ancient glass. *Crown in Glory* (P. Moore, ed.), pp. 73–80. Jarrold.

NEWTON, R.G. (1982b) *The Deterioration and Conservation of Painted Glass. A Critical Bibliography*. British Academy and Oxford University Press, Occasional Papers, II.

NEWTON, R.G. (1985a) The durability of glass: a review. *Glass Technol.*, **26**, 21–38.

NEWTON, R.G. (1985b) W.E.S. Turner: recollections and developments [The Eighth Turner Memorial Lecture]. In *Glass Technol.*, **26**, 93–103.

NEWTON, R.G. (1987) Air pollution damage. *Profess. Stained Glass*, **7**, 14, 15, 17, 19, 21.

NEWTON, R.G. (1988) Who invented covered pots? *Glass Technol.*, **29**, 49–50.

NEWTON, R.G. (1992) The future of the Ballidon glass burial experiment. *Glass Technol.*, **33** (5), 179–80.

NEWTON, R.G. (1996) Fact or fiction: can cold glass flow under its own weight, and what happens to stained glass windows? *Glass Technol.*, **37** (4), 143.

NEWTON, R.G. and BETTEMBOURG, J-M. (1976) Effects of repeated condensation. *CVMA News Letter*, **21**, 9–21.

NEWTON, R.G. and BRILL, R.H. (1983) A 'weeping' glass bowl at the Ashmolean Museum. *J. Glass Stud.*, **23**, 93–9.

NEWTON, R.G. and DAVISON, S. (1989, 1996) *Conservation. of Glass*. Butterworth-Heinemann, Oxford.

NEWTON, R.G. and FUCHS, D. (1988) Chemical analyses and weathering of some medieval glass from York Minster. *Glass Technol.*, **29**, 43–8.

NEWTON, R.G., HOLLOWAY, D.G. and HENCH, L.L (1981) A note on the 'spontaneous cracking' of ancient glass. *Ann. 8e Congr. Assoc. Verre,* London and Liverpool, pp. 355–67, 385. AIHV, Liège.

NEWTON, R.G. and RENFREW, C. (1970) British faience beads reconsidered. In *Problems in European Prehistory* (C. Renfrew, ed.), pp. 293–303. Edinburgh University Press, Edinburgh.

NEWTON, R.G. and SEDDON, A.B. (1992) The durability of a silicate glass in the presence of a saturated leachant. *Corrosion Science*, **23**, 617–26.

NEWTON, R.G. and SEDDON, A.B. (1999) Organic coatings for medieval glasses. In *The Conservation of Glass and Ceramics: Research, Practice and Training* (N.H. Tennent, ed.), pp. 66–71. James and James, London.

NEWTON, R.G. and SHAW, G. (1988) Another unsolved problem concerning weathering layers. *Glass Technol.*, **29**, 78–9.

NEWTON, R.G. and WERNER, A.E. (1974) Definition of the term 'devitrification'. *Brit Acad. CVMA Occasional Papers*, Part I, No. 100.

NICHOLSON, P.T. (1993) *Egyptian Faience and Glass*. Shire Egyptology Series, **19**. Shire Publications, Princes Risborough, Bucks.

NICHOLSON, P.T. (1995) Glassmaking and glassworking at Armarna: some new work. *J. Glass Stud.* **37**, 11–19.

NICHOLSON, P.T. (1997) Early glass and glazing in Egypt: new excavations at Tell el Amarna. *Archaeological Sciences, 1995* (Slater, Slater and Gowlett, eds). Oxbow Monograph 64, Oxford.

NICHOLSON, P.T. and JACKSON, C.M. (1998) Kind of blue. Glass of the Amarna period. In *The Prehistory and*

History of Glassmaking Technology. (P. McCray, ed.), *Ceramics and Civilisation,* **VIII**, 105–20. American Ceramics Society, Columbus, Ohio.

NICHOLSON, P.T., JACKSON, C.M. and TROTT, K.M. (1997) The Ulu Burun glass ingots, cylindrical vessels and Egyptian glass. *J. Egypt. Archaeol.,* **83**, 143–53.

NIGHTINGALE, G. (1998) Glass and the Mycenaean palaces of the Aegean. In *The Prehistory and History of Glassmaking Technology* (P. McCray, ed.), *Ceramics and Civilisation,* **VIII**, 205–26. American Ceramics Society, Columbus, Ohio.

NISHIMURA, S. (1971) Fission track dating of archaeological materials from Japan. *Nature,* **230**, 242–3.

NOBLE, J.V. (1969) The technique of Egyptian faience. *Am. J. Arch.,* **73**, 435–9.

NOONAN, T., KOVALEV, R. and SHERMAN, H. (1998) The development and diffusion of glassmaking in pre-Mongol Russia. In *The Prehistory and History of Glassmaking Technology* (P. McCray, ed.), *Ceramics and Civilisation,* **VIII**, 293–314. American Ceramics Society, Columbus, Ohio.

NORTHWOOD, J. (1924) Noteworthy productions of the glass craftsman's art. **I**. The reproduction of the Portland Vase. *J. Soc. Glass Technol.,* **8**, 82–92.

NOVIS, W.E. (1975) The lifting of mosaic pavements. In *Contributions to the Stockholm Congress on Conservation in Archaeology and the Applied Arts* (D. Leigh, A. Moncrieff, W.A. Oddy and P. Pratt, eds), pp. 143–6. Stockholm, Sweden.

NYLÉN, E. (1975) Documentation and presentation. *Fornvännen,* **70**, 213–23.

OAKLEY, V. (1999) Five years on: A re-assessment of aspects involved in the conservation of glass objects for a new gallery at the Victoria and Albert Museum. In *The Conservation of Glass and Ceramics: Research, Practice and Training* (N.H. Tennent, ed.), pp. 217–28. James and James, London.

ODDY, W.A. and CARROLL, S. (1999) Reversibility – does it exist? *British Museum Occasional Paper No. 135.*

OLIN, J.S., THOMPSON, B.A. and SAYRE, E.V. (1972) Characterisation of medieval window glass by neutron activation analysis. In *Developments in Applied Spectroscopy, 10,* pp. 33–55. Plenum Press, New York.

OLIVE, J and PEARSON, C. (1975) The conservation of ceramics from marine archaeological sites. In *Preprints of the Contributions to the Stockholm Congress on Conservation in Archaeology and the Applied Arts* (D. Leigh, A. Moncrieff, W.A. Oddy and P. Pratt, eds), pp. 63–6. IIC, London.

OLIVER, R. (1999) The Stupendous Chandelier. *V.&A. Cons J.* (Victoria and Albert Museum, London).

OLSEN, D.A., JOHNSON, R.E., KIVEL, J. and ALBERS, F.C. (1969) Kinetics of leaching of lead glass by ethylenediamine tetra-acetic acid. *J. Am, Ceram. Soc.,* **52**, 318–22.

OPPENHEIM, A.L. (1973) A note on research in Mesopotamian glass. *J. Glass Stud.* **15**, 9–11. OPPENHEIM, A.L., BRILL, R.H., BARAG, D. and VON SALDERN, A. (1970) *Glass and Glassmaking in Ancient Mesopotamia.* Corning Museum of Glass, Corning, New York.

PAGE, J-A. (1998) Crizzling: a curatorial point of view. *Proc. 18th Int. Congr. Glass,* San Francisco, CD-ROM, Paper No. 2 in Group B2, 7–13.

PANNELL, J. (1990) Conservation of glass at Bodrum Museum of Underwater Archaeology. In *Proceedings of the 1st Anatolian Glass Symposium,* 1988 (TSCFAS, Information and Document Center, ed.) Istanbul, Turkey.

PANTANO, C.G., ROSSI-WILCOX, S. and LANGE, D. (1998) The Glass Flowers. In *The Prehistory and History of Glassmaking Technology* (P. McCray, ed.), *Ceramics and Civilisation,* **VIII**, 761–78. American Ceramics Society, Columbus, Ohio.

PAPE, T. (1933) An Elizabethan glass furnace. *The Connoisseur,* 172 ff.

PETTANATI, S. (1978) I vetri graffiti et I vetri dipinti. Musie Civico di Torino, Turin.

PAUL, A. (1977) Chemical durability of glasses: a thermodynamic approach. *J. Mater. Sci,.* **12**, 2246–68.

PAUL, A. (1978) Influence of complexing agents and nature of the buffer solution on the chemical durability of glass. Part 1. Theoretical discussion. *Glass Technol.,* **19**, 162–5.

PAUL, A. and YOUSSEFI, A. (1978) Influence of complexing agents, and nature of the buffer solution, on the chemical durability of glass. Part 2. EDTA, ethyl alcohol and sugar in the leach solution. *Glass Technol.,* **19**, 166–70.

PAZAUREK, G.E. (1903) *Kranke Gläser.* Reichenberg.

PEARSON, C. (1975) On-site conservation requirements for marine archaeological excavations. In *Proceedings of the ICOM Sessions on Conservation,* Venice, 75/13/2.

PEARSON, C. (1987) *Conservation of Marine Archaeological Objects.* Butterworth-Heinemann, Oxford.

PELOUZE, T.J. (1867) Sur le verre. *CR. Acad. Sci. (Paris),* **64**, 53–66.

PELTENBURG, E.J. (1987) Early faience: recent studies, origins and relations with glass. In *Early Vitreous Materials* (M. Bimson and I.C. Freestone, eds), *British Museum Occasional Paper No. 56,* 5–29.

PEREZ-ARRANTEGUI, J., CEPRIÁ, G., ABADÍAS, O., USÓN, A., ARANDA, C. and CASTILLO, J.R. (2000) Voltammetry of immobilised microparticles: a nondestructive tool for materials characterisation. In *The 32nd International Archaeometry Symposium,* Abstract No. 299. Mexico City.

PEREZ-Y-JORBA, M., DALLAS, J-P., BAUER, C., BAHEZRE, C. and MARTIN, J.C. (1980) Deterioration of stained glass by atmospheric corrosion and micro-organisms. *J. Mater. Sci.,* **15**, 1640–7.

PEREZ-Y-JORBA, M., DALLAS, J-P., COLLONGUES, R., BAHEZRE, C. and MARTIN, J.C. (1978) Etude de l'alteration des vitraux anciens par microscopie électronique à bayalage et microsonde. *Silicates Industrielles,* **43**, 89–99.

PEREZ-Y-JORBA, M., TILLOCA, G., MICHEL, D. and DALLAS, J-P. (1975) Quelques aspects du phénomène de corrosion des vitraux anciens des èglises françaises. *Verres et Réfract.,* **29**, 53–63.

PERROT, P.N. (1971) A 'tank' furnace at Somelaria (Es-Samariya), Israel. *Proc. 9th Int.. Congr. Glass, Art. Hist. Comm.,* pp. 51–61.

PETERMANN, R. (1969) Nachbildung antiker Gläser. *Arbeitsblätter für Restauratoren,* **1** (18), 9–14.

PETRICIOLI, S. (1973) The Gnalic Wreck: the glass. *J. Glass Stud.,* **15**, 85.

PETRIE, W.M.F. (1894) *Tell el-Amarna.* Methuen, London.

PEYCHES, I. (1952) The viscous flow of glass at low temperatures. *Trans. J. Soc. Glass Technol.*, **36**, 164–80.

PIERCY, R.C.M. (1978) Mombassa wreck excavation, Second Preliminary Report. *Int. J. Naut. Archaeol. Underwater Expl.*, **7** (4), 310–19.

PILOSI, L. and WYPISKI, M.Y. (1998) Two ancient glasses with modern decoration in the Metropolitan Museum of Art. *Proc. ICOM–CC, Working Group, Ceramics and Related Materials* (A. Paterakis, ed.). EVTEK Institute of Arts & Design, Vantaa, Finland.

PINDER-WILSON, R.H. (1968) Pre-Islamic, Persian and Mesopotamian, Islamic and Chinese [glasses]. In *Masterpieces of Glass* (D.B. Harden *et al.* eds). Trustees of the British Museum, London.

PLENDERLEITH, H.J. and WERNER, A.E.A. (1976) *Conservation of Antiquities and Works of Art*, 2nd edn. Oxford University Press, Oxford.

PLINY (AD 77) *Natural History*, **10**, Book xxxvi (translated by Eicholz (1962) Loeb Classical Library, p. 190, also William Heinemann, London, p.65).

POLLARD A.M. (1979) X-ray fluorescence and surface studies of glass with application to the durability of medieval window glass. Unpublished PhD thesis, University of York.

PRICE, J. (1992) Retrieving the larger structure: ideas and case studies in lifting technology. In *Retrieval of Objects from Archaeological Sites* (R. Payton, ed.). Archetype Publications, London.

QUINTON, J.C. (1998) The conservation of an 18th century pier glass mirror at Hampton Court Palace. In *Proceedings of the ICOM–CC Working Group on Glass, Ceramics and Related Materials* (A. Paterakis, ed.). EVTEK Institute of Arts and Design, Vantaa, Finland.

RAUCH, F. (1985) Applications of ion beam analysis to solid state reactions. *Nucl. Inst. Meth.*, **B10/11**, 746–50.

RAW, F. (1955) The long-continued action of water on window-glass: weathering of the medieval glass at Weoley Castle, Birmingham. *Trans. J. Soc. Glass Technol*, **39**, 128–33.

REILLY, J.A. and MORTIMER, M.M. (1998) The care and conservation of glass chandeliers. *JAIC*, **37**, 149–72.

REISMAN, S.N. and LUCAS, D. (1978) Recommendations for the treatment of glass objects retrieved from an underwater environment (unpublished report).

REUREN, T., PUSCH, E. and HEROLD, A. (1998) Glass colouring works within a copper-centred industrial complex in Late Bronze Age Egypt. In *The Prehistory and History of Glassmaking Technology*, (P. McCray, ed.), *Ceramics and Civilization*, **III**, 227–50. American Ceramics Society, Columbus, Ohio.

RICHEY, W.D. (1975) Chelating agents – a review. In *Preprints of the Contributions to the Stockholm Congress on Conservation. in Archaeology and the Applied Arts* (D. Leigh, A. Moncrieff, W.A. Oddy and P. Pratt, eds), pp. 229–343. IIC, London.

RICHTER, R.W. (1998) Crizzling in enamels – a museums laboratory study of the relevant factors and phenomena. *Proc. 18th Int. Congr. Glass*, San Francisco, CD-ROM, Paper No. 1 in Group B1, p. 2.

RITZ, G.M. (1972) *Hinterglasmalerei, Geschichte, Erscheinung, Technik.* Georg D.W. Callwey, Munich.

ROBERTS, J.D. (1984) Acrylic colloidal suspensions as pre-consolidants for waterlogged archaeological glass. In *Preprints of the 7th Triennial Meeting of the ICOM–CC*, Copenhagen, **84**, 20–1.

ROGERS, J. (1980) The approach to the restoration of the Music Room, Brighton Pavilion following arson in 1975. *The Conservator*, **4**.

ROGERS, P., McPHAIL, D.S., RYAN, J. and OAKLEY, V.L. (1993) A quantitative study of decay processes of Venetian glass in a museum environment. *Glass Technol.*, **34**, 67–8.

RÖMICH, H. (1999a) Historic glass and its interaction with the environment. In *The Conservation of Glass and Ceramics: Research, Practice and Training* (N.H. Tennent, ed.), pp. 5–14. James and James, London.

RÖMICH, H. (1999b) Laboratory experiments to simulate corrosion on stained glass windows. In *The Conservation of Glass and Ceramics: Research, Practice and Training.* (N.H. Tennent, ed.), pp. 57–65. James and James, London.

RÖMICH, H., AERTS, A., JANSSENS, K. and ADAMS, F. (1998) Simulation of corrosion phenomena of glass objects on model glasses. *Proc. 18th Int.. Congr. Glass*, San Francisco, CD-ROM, Paper No. 7 in Group B1, 36–41.

ROOKSBY, H.P. (1959) An investigation of ancient opal glasses, with special reference to the Portland Vase. *Trans. J. Soc. Glass Technol.*, **4**, 285–8.

ROOKSBY, H.P. (1962) Opacifiers in opal glasses throughout the ages. *Gen. Elec. Co. Sci. J.*, **29**, 20–6.

ROOKSBY, H.P. (1964) A yellow cubic lead tin oxide opacifier in ancient glasses. *Phys. Chem. Glasses*, **5**, 20–5.

ROOSMA, M. (1969) The glass industry of Estonia in the 18th and 19th centuries. *J. Glass Stud.*, **11**, 70–2.

RYAN, J. (1995) Chemical stabilization of weathered glass surfaces. A new approach to glass conservation. *V.&A. Cons. J.*, **16**, 6–9.

RYAN, J., McPHAIL, D., ROGERS, P. and OAKLEY, V. (1993) Glass deterioration in the museum environment. *Chemistry and Industry*, **13**, 498–501.

RYAN, J., McPHAIL, D., ROGERS, P. and OAKLEY, V. (1996) Glass deterioration in the museum environment. A study of the mechanisms of decay using secondary ion mass spectrometry. In *Preprints of the 11th ICOM–CC. Triennial Meeting, Edinburgh*, pp. 839–44. James and James, London.

RYSER, F. (1991) *Verzauberte Bilder. Die Kunst der Malerei hinter Glas von der Antike bis zum 18 Jahrhundert.* Verlag Kilinkhardt and Bierman, Munich.

RYSER, F. and SALMEN, B. (eds) (1995) *Amelierte Stuck uff Glas/Hinder Glas Gemäld. Historien und Gemald. Hinterglaskunst von der Antike bis zur Neuzeit.* Exhibition catalogue. Schloßmuseum Murnau.

SALEM, A.A., GRASSERBAUER, M. and SHREINER, M. (1994) Study of the corrosion processes in glass from Scandinavia and Britain, PACT. *Journal of the European Study Group on the Physical, Chemical and Mathematical Techniques Applied to Archaeology*, **7**, 401–11.

SALMEN, B. (ed.) (1997) *Glas Glanz Farbe. Vielfalt barocker Hinterglaskunst im Europa des 17 und 18 Jahrhunderts.* Exhibition Catalogue. Schloßmuseum Murnau.

SANDERS, D.M. and HENCH, L.L. (1973) Surface roughness and glass corrosion. *Ceram. Bull.*, **52**, 666–9.

SAYRE, E.V. (1963) The intentional use of antimony and

manganese in ancient glasses. In *Advances in Glass Technology, Part 2* (F.R. Matson and G.E. Rindone, eds), pp. 263–82. New York.

SAYRE, E.V. (1965) Summary of the Brookhaven program of analysis of ancient glass. *Application of Science in Examination of Works of Art.* 145–54, Seminar, Boston.

SAYRE, E.V. and SMITH, R.. (1961) Compositional categories of ancient glass. *Science*, **133**, 1824–6 (No. 3467).

SAYRE, E.V. and SMITH, R.W. (1974) Analytical studies of ancient Egyptian glass. In *Recent Advances in Science and Technology of Materials*, **3** (A. Bishay, ed.), pp. 47–70. Plenum Press, New York.

SCHACK VON WITTENAU, C. (1998) 'Sick' glasses – a case for the Veste Coburg. *Proc. 18th Congr. Glass*, San Francisco (CD-ROM).

SCHÄFER, F.W. (1968) Two pragmatic views on 'Vasa Dietrata'. *J. Glass Stud.*, **10**, 176–7.

SCHÄFER, F.W. (1969) Wiederherstellung eines Diatrietetglases in Römicher Schlifftechnik. *Studies in Glass History and Design*, pp. 125–6. Sheffield.

SCHOFIELD, P.F., CRESSEY, G., HOWARD, P.W. and HENDERSON, C.N.B. (1995) Origin of colour in iron and manganese containing glasses investigated by synchrotron radiation. *Glass Technol.*, **36**, 89–94.

SCHOLES, S.R. (1929) Density factors for soda lime glasses. *J. Am. Ceram. Soc.*, **12**, 753–5.

SCHOLZE, H. (1977) *Glas, Natur, Structur und Eigenschaften*, 2nd edn. Springer Verlag, Berlin.

SCHOLZE, H. (1978) Characterisierung 'kranker' gläser. Contribution to the *Projektgruppe 'Glas' Meeting in Bonn* (Abstract No. 336, in *CVMA News Letter*, **28**).

SCHOLZE, H., HELMREICH, D. and BAKARDJIEV, I. (1975) Untersuchungen über des Verhalten von Kalk–Natron Gläsern in verdunten Säuren. *Glastech. Berlin*, **48**, 237–46.

SCHOTT, F.L. (1998a) Zur Festigung der Wurzburger Tischplatten und anderen Hinterglasmalerein. In *Ausst. Kat. Gemalt hinter Glas, Bayerisches National Museum, Munchen*. Munchen u. Wurzburg.

SCHOTT, F.L. (1998b) Eglomise – Technik und Konservervierung. *Restauro*, 9–17. Callweg-Verlag, Munich.

SCHOTT, F.L. (1999) Restaurierung von drei Hinterglasmalereigefassen. In *Ausst. Kat. Gemalt hinter Glas, Bayerisches Nationalmuseum, Munchen*. Munchen u. Wurtzburg.

SCHREINER, M. (1987) Analytical investigations of medieval glass paintings. In *Recent Advances in the Conservation and Analysis of Artefacts* (Proceedings of the Institute of Archaeology Jubilee Conservation Conference, pp. 73–8. London.

SCHREINER, M.R., PROHASKA, I., RENDL, J. and WEIGEL, G. (1999) Leaching studies of potash–lime–silica glass with medieval compositions. In *The Conservation of Glass and Ceramics: Research, Practice and Training* (N.H. Tennent, ed.), pp. 72–83. James and James, London.

SCHREINER, M.R., STINGEDER, G. and GRASSERBAUER, M. (1984) Quantitative characterization of the surface layers on corroded medieval glass with SIMS. *Fresnius' Zeitschr. Analyt. Chem.*, **319**, 600–5.

SCHREURS, J.W.H. and BRILL, R.H. (1984) Iron- and sulphur-related colours in ancient glass. *Archaeometry*, **29**, 199–209.

SCHRÖDER, H. and KAUFMANN, R. (1959) Schutzschichten für alte Gläzer. In *Beiträge zur Angewanten Glasforschung* (E. Schott, ed), pp. 355–61. Stuttgart.

SCHULER, F. (1959a) Ancient glassmaking techniques. The molding process. *Archaeology*, **12**, 47–52.

SCHULER, F. (1959b) Ancient glassmaking processes. The blowing technique. *Archaeology*, **12**, 116–22.

SCHULER, F. (1962) Ancient glassmaking processes. The Egyptian core-vessel process. *Archaeology*, **51**, 32–7.

SCHULER, F. (1963) Ancient glassmaking techniques. Egyptian fused miniature mosaics. In *Advances in Glass Technology*, Part, 2 (F.R. Matson and G.E. Rindone, eds), p. 206. Plenum Press, New York.

SCHULZE, G. (1977) Chemisch–analytische Untersuchungen an Glasfunden aus der Kunckel Hütte. Contribution to the DGG Meeting in Frankfurt (Abstract No. 297 in *CVMA. News Letter* **26**).

SCHUSTER, R. (1980) *Hinterglasbilder aus Außergerfild in Böhmerwald*. Grafenau.

SCHUSTER, R. (1983) *Hinterglasbilder der Neukirchener Schule*. Grafenau.

SCHUSTER, R. (1984) *Das Raimundsreuter Hinterglasbild. Geschischte der Raimundsreuter Hinterglasmalerei und ihres Einflußgebietes*. Grafenau.

SCHWARZ, M.D. (ed.) (1974) *American Glass from the Pages of Antiques, I. Blown and Molded*. The Pyne Press.

SCHWEIG, B. (1973) *Mirrors: A Guide to the Manufacture of Mirrors and Reflecting Surfaces*. Pelham Books, London.

SCOTT, A.S. (1932) Apparent decay of ancient glass at Wells Cathedral. *J. Brit. Soc. Master Glass Painters*, **4**, 171.

SCRANTON, R. (1967) Glass pictures from the sea. *Archaeology*, **20** (3), 165–73.

SEASE, C. (1981) The case against using soluble nylon in conservation work. *Stud. Cons.*, **26**, 102–10. IIC, London.

SEASE, C. (1988) *A Conservation Manual for the Archaeologist*. Archeological Research Tools, **4.** Institute of Archeology, University of California, Los Angeles.

SEELA, J. (1974) The early Finnish glass industry. *J. Glass Stud.*, **16**, Fig. 3, 65.

SEIBEL, F. (2000) Technologie Römicher Glashütten im Rheinland. *Glastech. Berlin Glass Sci. Technol.* **73**, (1) N1–N6.

SEIDLER, R. (1987) *The Use of Silanes for the Consolidation of Paintings on Glass*. University of Delaware, USA.

SELLNER, C. (1977) Untersuchungen an Waldgläsern mit Elektronen–spinresonanz. In Contribution to the *Projektgruppe 'Glas' Meeting in Würzburg* (Abstract No. 298 in *CVMA News Letter* **26**).

SELLNER, C., OEL, H.J. and CAMARA, B. (1979) Untersuchungen alter Gläzer (Waldglas) auf Zusammenhang von Zusammenzetzung, Farbe und Schmelzatmosphäre mit der Elektronenspektroscopie und der Elektronenspinresonanz (ESR) *Glastech. Berlin*, **52**, 255–64.

SHAW, G. (1965) Weathered crusts on ancient glass. *New Scientist*, **21**, 290–1.

SHORTLAND, A. (1999) Early Egyptian glass – evidence for trade and tribute. In *Proceedings of Current Research on the History of Glass through Scientific Analysis*. London.

SHORTLAND, A.J. and TITE, M.S. (1998) The interdependence of glass and vitreous faience production at Armana. In *The Prehistory and History of Glassmaking Technology* (P. McCray, ed.), *Ceramics and Civilisation*, **VIII**, 251–68. American Ceramics Society, Columbus, Ohio.

SIMPSON, H.E. (1953) Some factors affecting the testing of surface durability of glass. *J. Am. Ceram. Soc.*, **36**, 143–6.

SINGLEY, K. (1998) *The Conservation of Archaeological Artefacts from Freshwater Environments*. Lake Michigan Maritime Museum, South Haven, Michigan.

SIROIS, P.J. (1999) The deterioration of glass trade beads from Canadian ethnographic and textile collections, In *The Conservation of Glass and Ceramics: Research, Practice and Training* (N.H. Tennent, ed.), pp. 84–95. James and James, London.

SLOAN, J.L. (1993) *Conservation of Stained Glass in America: A Manual for Studios and Caretakers*. Art in Architecture Press, USA.

SMEDLEY, J.W., JACKSON, C.M. and BOOTH, C.A. (1998) Back to roots: the raw materials, glass recipes, and glassmaking practices of Theophilus. In *The Prehistory and History of Glassmaking Technology* (P. McCray, ed.), *Ceramics and Civilisation*, **VIII**, 145–165. American Ceramics Society, Columbus, Ohio.

SMITH, C.S. and GNUDI, M.T. (1942) *The Pirotechnica of Vannoccio Biringuccio*. American Institute of Mining and Metallurgical Engineering, New York.

SMITH, R.W. (1963) Archaeological evaluation of analyses of ancient glass. In *Advances in Glass Technology*, Part 2 (F.R. Matson and G.E. Rindone, eds), pp. 283–90. Plenum Press, New York.

SMITH, R.W. (1963a) Archaeological evaluation of analyses of ancient glasses. In *Advances in Glass Technology*, Part 2 (F.R. Matson and G.E. Rindone, eds), pp. 283–90. Plenum Press, New York.

SMITH, R.W. (1963b) The analytical study of glass in archaeology. In *Science in Archaeology* (D. Brothwell and E. Higgs, eds), pp. 519–28. Thames and Hudson, London.

SMITH, S. (1996) The manufacture and conservation of Egyptian faience. In *Preprints ICOM–CC 11th Triennial Meeting, Edinburgh*, pp. 845–50. ICOM, London.

SMITHSONIAN INSTITUTION (1969) *Glass Goblet Excavated from a Privy*. Conservation–Analytical Laboratory, USA.

SODE, T. (1996) *Anatolske Glasperler*. Thot Press, Vanlose, Denmark.

SODE, T. and SCHNELL, U. (1998) Contemporary faience makers in Quarna, Egypt. In *Preprints Interim Meeting ICOM–CC Working Group on Ceramics, Glass and Related Materials* (A. Paterakis, ed.). EVTEK Institute of Arts and Design, Vantaa., Finland.

SOMMER-LARSON, A. (1999) Conservation of three glass chandeliers from Konigsberg Church, Norway. In *The Conservation of Decorative Arts* (V. Horie, ed.), pp. 35–42. Archetype Publications, UKIC, London.

SPEEL, E. (1984) *Popular Enamelling*, London.

STAFFELBACH, G. (1951) *Geschichte der Luzerner Hinterglasmalerei*. Luzern.

STAHL, C.J. (1915) *Dekorative Glasmalerei, Unterglasmalerei und mahlen auf Glas*. In *Chemisch und Tecknisch Bibliotek*, **354**. Vienna and Leipzig.

STAUDE, H. (1972) Die Technik des Zussammensetzens und Ergänzens antiker Gläzer. *Arbeitsblätter für Restauratoren*, **1**, Gruppe 5, 20–7.

STEINBRUCKER, C. (1958) Artikel Eglomise. In *Reallexikon zur Deuytschen Kunstgeschichte*, **4**, 749ff.

STERN, E.M. (1998) Interaction between glassworkers and ceramiscists. In *The Prehistory and History of Glassmaking Technology* (P. McCray, ed.), *Ceramics and Civilisation*, **VIII**, 183–204. American Ceramics Society, Columbus, Ohio.

STEVELS, J.M. (1960) New light on the structure of glass. *Philip's Tech. Rev.*, **22**, 300–11.

STONE, J.F.S. and THOMAS, L.C. (1956) The use and distribution of faience in the ancient East and prehistoric Europe. *Proc. Prehist. Soc.*, **22**, 37–84.

STRAHAN, D. (2001) Uranium in glass, glazes and enamels: history, identification and handling. *Stud. Cons.* **46**, 181–195.

STRONG, D. and BROWN, D. (1976) *Roman Crafts*. Duckworth, London.

SWANN, C.P., McGOVERN, P.E. and FLEMING, S. J. (1990) Colorants used in Ancient Egyptian glassmaking: specialised studies using PIXE spectrometry. *Nuclear Instruments and Methods in Physics Research, B*, **45**, 199–209.

TABACZYNSKA, E. (1968) Remarks on the origin of the Venetian glassmaking center. *Proc. 8th Int. Congr. Glass, Studies in Glass History and Design*, pp. 20–3.

TAIT, H. (1968) Glass in Europe from the Middle Ages to 1862. In *Masterpieces of Glass* (D.B. Harden *et al.*, eds). Trustees of the British Museum, London.

TAIT, H. (1979) *The Golden Age of Venetian Glass*. BMP, London.

TAIT, H. (ed.) (1991) *Five Thousand Years of Glass*. BMP, London.

TAYLOR, T.H. (1984) *In situ* repair of architectural glass. In *Preprints of the Contributions to the Paris Congress on Adhesives and Consolidants* (N S. Bromelle, M. Pye, P. Smith and G. Thomson, eds), pp. 202–4. IIC, London.

TECHMER, K.S. and RÄDLEIN, E. (1998) TEM and AFM studies on the alteration of natural glasses. *Proc. 18th Int. Congr. Glass*, San Francisco, CD-ROM, Paper No. 9 in Group C4, 49–51.

TENNENT, N.H. (1981) Fungal growth on medieval glass. *J. Br. Soc. Master Glass Painters*, **17**, 64–8.

TENNENT, N.H. and TOWNSEND, J.H. (1984a) The significance of the refractive index of adhesives for glass repair. In *Preprints of the Contributions to the Paris Congress on Adhesives and Consolidants* (N.S. Bromelle, E.M. Pye, P. Smith and G. Thomson, eds), pp. 205–12. IIC, London.

TENNENT, N.H. and TOWNSEND, J.H. (1984b) Factors affecting the refractive index of epoxy resins. *Preprints of the 7th Triennial Meeting of ICOM–CC*, Copenhagen, pp. 84.20.26 to 84.20.28.

TENNENT, N.H., McKENNA, P., LO, K.K.N., McLEAN, G. and OTTAWAY, J.M. (1984b) Major, minor and trace element analysis of medieval stained glass by flame atomic absorption spectrometry. *N Archaeological Chemistry III* (Advances in Chemistry Series), **205**, 133–50.

THEOBALD, W. (1933) *Technik des Kunsthandwerks im zehnten Jahrhundert des Theophilus*, Berlin.

THEOPHILUS, PRESBYTER. (*circa* 1140) *Schedula Divers*

Artium (Treatise on Diverse Arts) (translated as *On Divers Arts*, Dodwell (1961) and by Hawthorne and Smith (1963)).

THOMSON, G. (1998) *The Museum Environment*, 2nd edn. Butterworth-Heinemann, London.

THOMPSON, R.G. (1925) *On the Chemistry of the Ancient Assyrians*. London.

THORENSEN, L. (1998) The use of glass in the glyptik arts. In *Preprints of the ICOM–CC Working Group: Ceramics, Glass and Related Materials* (A. Paterakis, ed.). EVTEK Institute for Arts & Design, Vantaa, Finland.

THORNTON, J. (1981) A transfer treatment technique for Hinterglasmalerei. *JAIC*, **20**, 28–35.

THORNTON, J. (1990) A light box apparatus for the repair of glass. *Stud. Cons.*, **35** (2), 107–9.

THORPE, W.A. (1938) The prelude to European cut glass *Trans. J. Soc. Glass Technol.*, **22**, 5–37.

THORPE, W.A. (1961) *English Glass*, 3rd edn, p. 99. London.

TITE, M.S. and BIMSON, M. (1987) Identification of early vitreous materials. In *Recent Advances in the Conservation and Analyses of Artefacts: Proceedings of the Jubilee Conservation Conference of the Institute of Archaeology*, pp. 81–5. University of London Press.

TITE, M.S., BIMSON, M. and FREESTONE, I. C. (1983) Egyptian faience: an investigation of the methods of production. *Archaeometry*, **23**, 17–27.

TITE, M.S., BIMSON, M. and MEEKS, N.G. (1981) Technological characterisation of Egyptian Blue. In *Actes du XX Symposium International d'Archaeometrie III (et Analyse) Review d'Archaeometrie*, Supplement, 296–301.

TONINATO, T. (1984) Technology and tradition in Murano glassmaking. *Glass in Murano*, 20–40. Venice.

TREMAIN, D. (1988) Reverse-glass prints: their history, techniques and conservation. *Proc. Symp. 88, CCI*, pp. 143–52.

TURNER, W.E.S. (1930) The scientific basis of glass melting. *J. Soc. Glass Technol.*, **14**, 368–93.

TURNER, W.E.S. (1954a) Studies in ancient glass and glass-making processes. Part 1. Crucibles and melting temperatures employed in ancient Egypt at about 1370 BC. *Trans. J. Soc. Glass Technol.*, **38**, 436–44.

TURNER, W.E.S. (1954b) Studies in ancient glass and glass-making processes. Part II. The composition, weathering characteristics and historical significance of some Assyrian glasses of the eighth to sixth centuries BC, from Nimrud. *Trans. J. Soc. Glass Technol.*, **38**, 445–56.

TURNER, W.E.S. (1956a) Studies in ancient glasses and glass-making processes. Part III. The chronology of the glassmaking constituents. *Trans. J. Soc. Glass Technol.*, **40**, 39–52.

TURNER, W.E.S. (1956b) Studies in ancient glasses and glass-making processes. Part IV. The chemical composition of ancient glasses. *Trans. J. Soc. Glass Technol.*, **40**, 162–86.

TURNER, W.E.S. (1956c) Studies in ancient glasses and glass-making processes. Part V. Raw materials and melting processes. *Trans. J. Soc. Glass Technol.*, **40**, 276–300.

TURNER, W.E.S. (1957a) Antichi vetri opali, il supposto effeto opalizzante del biossido di stagna. *Vetro e Silicati*, **2**, 27–30.

TURNER, W.E.S. (1957b) Ancient sealing wax red glasses. *J. Egyptian Arch.*, **43**, 110–12.

TURNER, W.E.S. (1959) Studies in ancient glasses and glass-making processes. Part VI. The composition and physical characteristics of the glasses of the Portland Vase. *Trans. J. Soc. Glass Technol.*, **43**, 262–84.

TURNER, W.E.S. (1962) A notable British seventeenth-century contribution to the literature of glassmaking. *Glass Technol.*, **3**, 201–13.

TURNER, W.E.S. (1963) The tercentenary of Neri–Merrett's 'The Art of Glass'. *Advances in Glass Technology*, Part 2 F.R. Madson and G.E. Rindone, eds), pp. 181–201. Plenum Press, New York.

TURNER, W.E.S. and ROOKSBY, H.P. (1959) A study of the opalising agents in ancient opal glasses throughout three thousand four hundred years. *Glastech. Ber.*, **32K**, VIII/17–VIII/28.

TURNER, W.E.S. and ROOKSBY, H.P. (1961) Further historical studies, based on X-ray diffraction methods, of the reagents employed in making opal and opaque glasses. *J. Röm.–German. Zentralmuseums (Mainz)*, **VIII**, 1–6.

VANDIVER, P.B. (1992) Corrosion and conservation of ancient glass and ceramics. In *Corrosion of Glass Ceramics and Ceramic Superconductors* (D.E. Clark and B.K. Zoitas, eds), pp. 393–430. Noyes Publications, Park Ridge, NJ.

VANDIVER, P.B. and KINGERY, W.D. (1986) Egyptian faience. The first high-tech ceramic. In *High Technology Ceramics* (W. Kingery, ed.), *Ceramics and Civilization*, **III**, 19–34. American Ceramics Society, Columbus, Ohio.

VANDIVER, P.B., GIBSON, McG. and McMAHON, A. (1995) Glass manufacture in the late third millenium BC at Nippur in Iraq. In *The Ceramics Cultural Heritage: Proceedings of the International Symposium 'The Ceramics Heritage' of the 8ᵗʰ CIMTEC–World Ceramics Congress & Forum on New Materials*, Florence, Italy. *Monogr. Mater. Soc.*, **2**, 331–41.

VANDIVER, P.B., SWANN, C.P. and CRANMER, D. (1991) A review of mid-second millennium BC Egyptian glass technology at Tell El-Amarna. In *Material Issues in Art and Archaeology*, **II**, 609–16. The Materials Research Society, Pittsburgh, PA.

VERITÁ, M. (1985) L'invenzione del cristallo Muranese: una verifica analytica delle fonti storiche *Rivista delle Stazione Sperimentale del Vetro*, **1**, 17–36.

VERITÁ, M. (1995) Analytical investigation of European enamelled beakers of the 13th and 14th centuries. *J. Glass Stud.* **37**, 83–98.

VERITÁ, M. (2001) Technology and deterioration of vitreous mosaic *tesserae*. *Rev. Cons.*, **1**, 65–76.

VERITÁ, M., BASSO, R., WYPYSKI, M.T. and KOESTLER, R.J. (1994) X-ray microanalysis of ancient glassy materials: a comparative study of wavelength dispersive and energy dispersive techniques. *Archaeometry*, **36**, 241–51.

VINCENT, J. (1556) *La Pyrotechnie. traduite d'Italien en Français par feu Maitre Jaques Vincent*, p. 90. Claude Fremy, Paris.

VOLF, M.B. (1977) *Jaroslav Brychta*. Zivé sklo, Prague.

VON SALDERN, A. (1970) Originals – reproductions – fakes. *Ann. 5ᵉ Congr. Assoc. Hist. Verre*, Prague, pp. 299–318. AIHV, Liège.

VON SALDERN, A. (1974) *Gläser der Antike*, Museum für Kunst und Gewerbe, Hamburg.

VOS-DAVIDSE, L. (1969) Note of the reversible glueing of broken glass objects. *Stud. Conserv.*, **4**, 183.

WAKEFIELD, H. (1963) Methods of packing in the Victoria and Albert Museum. In *Recent Advances in Conservation* (G. Thomson, ed.), pp. 16–18. Butterworths, London.

WALLACE, K. (1976) Examination and treatment of *Hinterglasmalerei,* or reverse paintings on glass. Unpublished paper, National Gallery of Art, Ottawa, Canada.

WALTERS, H.V. and ADAMS, P.B. (1975) Effects of humidity on the weathering of glass. *J. Non-Cryst. Sol.*, **19**, 183–99.

WARD, C. (1998) Sadana Island shipwreck: final; season. *INA Quarterly*, **25**, no. 3, 3–6.

WARREN, P. (1981) *Irish Glass.* Faber and Faber, London.

WATKINSON, D. and LEIGH, D. (1978) Polyurethane foam: a health hazard. *Cons. News*, IIC–UHG, **No. 6**, 7–8.

WATKINSON, D. and NEAL, V. (ed.) (1998) *First Aid for Finds.* Rescue/UKIC Archaeology Section and Museum of London, UKIC, London.

WATTS, D.C. (1999) Some London glasshouses in the 17th to 19th centuries, and their particular association with the Thames South Bank. In *The Guild of Glass Engravers Spring Newsletter 1999*, pp. 4–9.

WEDEPOHL, K.H. (1993) Herstellung mittelalterlicher und antiker Gläser. *Abh. Akad. Wissenschaften Lit.* Mainz, Germany.

WEDEPOHL, K.H., WINKELMANN, W. and HARTMANN, G. (1997) Glasfunde aus der karolingischen Pfalz in paderborn und die frühe Holzasche–Glasherstellung. In *Ausgrabungen und Funde in Westfalen–Lippe* (Munster), Germany, 9/A, pp. 41–53.

WEIER, L.E (1973) The deterioration of inorganic materials under the sea. *Bull. Inst Arch. (London)*, **11**, 131–63.

WEINBERG, G.D. (1975) A medieval mystery: Byzantine glass production. *J. Glass Stud.*, **17**, 127–41.

WEINTRAUB, S. (1998) Crizzling: microclimate control solutions. *Proc. 18th Int. Congr. Glass*, San Francisco, CD-ROM, Paper No. 3 in Group B1, pp. 13–17.

WERNER, A.E., BIMSON, M. and MEEKS, N.D. (1975) The use of replica techniques and the scanning electron microscope in the study of ancient glass. *J. Glass Stud.*, **17**, 158–60.

WEYL, W.A. (1951) *Coloured Glasses.* Society of Glass Technology, Sheffield.

WEYL, W.A. and MARBOE, E.C. (1967) The constitution of glasses, a dynamic interpretation. In *Surface Chemistry Silicate Glasses.* 3 vols, 23, 1010–270. Wiley, New York.

WHARTON, G. and OLDKNOW, C. (1987) The conservation of an eighteenth century glass medallion beaker. In *The Conservator*, **11**, 42–5. UKIC, London.

WICKS, S. (1985) *Jewellery Making Manual.* Little, Brown, London.

WIECK, T. (1981) *Glas als Bildträger. Historische Techniken und ihre Anwendung ohne Berücksichtigung von Scmelzvefahren.* Diplomarbeit, Institut fur Tech-nologie der Malerei, Staatliche Akademie der Bildenden Künste. Stuttgart.

WIEDERHORN, S.M. (1967) Influence of water vapor crack propagation in soda–lime glass. *J. Am. Ceram. Soc.*, **50**, 407–14.

WIHR, R. (1963) Repair and reproduction of ancient glass. *Recent Advances in Conservation*, pp. 152–5. Butterworths, London.

WIHR, R. (1968) Möglichkeiten der Restaurierung und Nachbildung der antiker Gläser, mittels giessbarer Kunststoffe. *Arbeitsblätter für Restauratoren,* Gruppe 5, 1–12.

WIHR, R. (1977) *Restaurierung von Keramik und Glas.* Callwey, Munich.

WILLIAMS, N. (1989) *The Breaking and Re-making of the Portland Vase.* BMP, London.

WILLISTON, S.S. and BERRETT, K.R. (1978) Preliminary notes on setting down paint flaking from glass. *JAIC*, **18**, 46–8.

WILLS, G. (1965) *English Looking Glasses, 1670-1820.* London.

WINTER, A. (1965) Alteration des surfaces des verres anciens. *Proc. 8th Int. Congr. Glass*, Brussels, Paper No. 229, 12 pp.

WOOD, E.S. (1965) A medieval glasshouse at Blunden's Wood, Hambledon, Surrey. *The Surrey Arch. Collections*, **64**, 54–79.

WOSINSKI, J.F. and BRILL, R.H. (1969) A petrographic study of Egyptian and other cored vessels. In *Studies in Glass History and Design: Proc. 8th Int. Congr. Glass*, Sheffield. 123–4.

WULFF, H.S., WULFF, H.W. and KOCH, L. (1968) Egyptian faience, a possible survival in Iran. In *Archaeology*, **21**, 98–107.

YABUKI, H., YABUKI, S. and SHIMA, M. (1973) Fission track dating of man-made glasses from Ali Tar Cavern vestiges. In *Scientific Papers of the Institute of Physical and Chemical Research*, **67**, 41–2.

YALOURIS, N. (1968) An unreported use of some Mycenean paste beads. *J. Glass Stud.*, **10**, 9–16.

YPEY, J. (1960–1961) Das Bergen von stuck angegriffen Glas Während einer Ausgrabung mit Hilfe einer Kunstharzlösung. *Ber. van de Rijsdienst voor het oudheikundig Bodeminders*, **10–11**, 363–9.

YPEY, J. (1965) The conservation of disintegrated glass during the excavation. *Proc. 7ᵇ Int. Congr. Glass*, Brussels, paper No. 227, 3 pp.

ZACHARIASEN, W.H. (1932) The atomic arrangement in glass. *J. Am. Ceram. Soc.*, **54**, 3841–51.

ZECCHIN, L (1987) Il recettario Dardin. In *Un Codice Vetrario del Seicento Transcritto e Commentato.* Statzione Sperismentale del Vetro, Murano, Italy.

ZIMMER, K. (1988) Spectrographical investigation of Hungarian glass finds. *Archaeometrical Research in Hungary*, pp. 131–40. Budapest National Centre of Museums.

Index

AAS (atomic absorption spectrometry), 237
Abbasid dynasty (Islamic glass), 27
Abbé (optical glassmaker), 117
Ablebond 342-1 (epoxy adhesive), 212, 276, 296
Abies balsam (Canada balsam), 205
Abrasion:
    damage by, 170, *Fig. 4.4, 4.5*
Accelerated ageing tests, 196–7
Acetaldehyde acid, 309
Acetic acid, 262, 309, 333, 334
Acetates, effects of, 182
Acetone, 256, 270, 272, 278, 314
Acid, attack on glass, 170, 175, 190, 197
    etching of glass, 101
Acid-free tissue, 259, 312, 316
Acre, Palestine (glassmaking in), 22
Acrylic polymers, 205, 216–7, *Fig. 5.10*
Acryloid B-72 (see Paraloid B-72)
Active conservation, 242
Adam, Robert and James (archtect designers), 70
Adhesion (theory of), 205
Adhesives, 204–6, *Fig. 5.1*
AES (Auger Emission spectrometry), 235
'Agar Quf, Mesopotamia (Iraq), 93
Aggry (aggri, see Beads)
Airbrasive cleaning, 256, 262
Air-twist stems or bubbles (decorative), 42, 106, *Fig. 3.24*
Agate glass, 76
Agricola, Georgius (writer of glassmaking), 147, 148, 149, 161
Alabastron (vessel type), 19, *Fig. 2.2*
Albert Memorial The, London (glass jewels on), 275
Alcohol (solvent), 316
Aleppo, Syria (glassmaking in), 27, 30, 101
Alexandria, Egypt (glassmaking in), 22, 27, 30, 79, 98, 102
Algae (removal of), 203
Alkali, 73, 74, 139, 141, 176, 180–1, 193
    attack on glass (see De-alkalization)
    Source of (plant ash), 74–5, 137, 143, 186
Alloa , Scotland (cone furnace), 166
Alloway, New Jersey (USA) (glassworks), 46
Aloplast (modelling material), 220, 294, 295–7
Altare, Italy (glassmaking in), 80
Aluminium, 319
    foil, 246, 247, 248
Aluminium oxide (alumina) in glass:
    (emery, corundum, bauxite), 7, 76, 177, 223
Amalgam, 58, 334, 335
Amber glass, 8
Amelierung, 57, 340

Amelung, New Bremen, USA, (glasshouse), 46, 158–9, *Fig. 3.70*
Amelung, Johann Frederick (glassmaker), 158–9
Amiens, France (glassmaking in), 30
Aminocarboxylic acids, 201, *Fig. 5.3*
Amines, effects of, 182
Ammonia, 225, 331
Ammonium hydrogen carbonate, 202
Amphorisk (vessel type), 21
Amsterdam, Netherlands, 36
Amsterdam, The (shipwreck), 187
Ancient glasses (definition of), 1–3
Anelasticity (internal friction), 11, 12
Anglo-Venetian glass, 111
Anions, 5
Animal glues, 203
Anisotropy, 229
Annealing, 12, 86–87
    annealing furnace, 160
Antimony, 1, 77, 78, 79, 136, 237
    as decolorizer, 9
    as opacifier, 10
    in mirror making, 134
Antioch (modern *Antakya*), *Turkey,* 18
Antwerp, Belgium, 37
Aqua regia, 9
Aquamanile (vessel type), 33
Aquarel paints, 343
Aquileia, Italy (glassmaking in), 30
Aphrodisias (Roman writer), 62
Apollonia, Israel (glassmaking site), 143
Application technique (Egyptian faience), 85
Araldite adhesives (AY193/HY956), 225, 276, 306, 307
Araldite 2020, 212, 276
Arbogast machine, 48, 117
Arsenic, 136
    oxide (decolourizer), 9, 77
Archae-o-Derm (PVC), 219
Archetto (drill for engraving), 97
Arrêt du Conseil d'Etat, 129
Argon atmosphere, 314
Argy-Rousseau, Gabriel (glass paste), 91
Art Nouveau glass, 48, 49
Ars Experimentalis (Experiments in the Art of Glass), 159
Artsorb silica gel, 317
Aryballos (vessel type), 21, *Fig. 2.2*
Ascension windows, *Le Mans cathedral, France,* 64
Ashurbanipal (cuneiform library of), 135
Astarte (figurine of), 90, *Fig. 3.7*
Atmospheric pollution, effect of, 171, 173, 174, 190, Fig. 4.24

Atomic force microscopy, 241
Augsburg Bible (illustration in), 163
Augsburg Cathedral, Germany (windows in), 64
Auldo Jug, The (cameo glass), 22, 98, 294–7, 304
Aventurine glass (decorative red), 33, 76
AYAF (polyvinyl acetate), 225–6

Baccarat , France (glass paperweights from), 94
Back-matching corrosion (on windows), 192
Badajoz, Spain (glassmaking site), 141
Badarian civilization (Egypt), 18, 85
Baghdad Iraq (glassmaking in), 27
Bagot's Park, Staffordshire (furnace sites), 155
Baia, Naples, Italy (glass from), 187
Bailey & Saunders (glassmakers)71
Ballidon, Derbyshire (glass burial experiment), 198
Ballotini (glass beads) (*see Cloisonné* glass windows), 338
Barcelona, Spain (glassmaking in), 30, 57
Barias, Israel (glassmaking site), 143
Barilla (source of alkali), 39, 80
Barium in glass:
    barium oxide, 76
    barium sulphide (barytes or heavy spar), 76
Barovier, Ercole, (glassmaker), 49
Basilica of S. Maria Assunta, Torcello, Italy (mosaics), 144
Battledore (glass shaping tool), 104
Baumgartner, Wolfgang (glass painter), 57
Bauxite (aluminium hydroxide), 76
Beads, 87–88, 235, 236, 237, 262, *Fig. 3.3, 3.4*
Beauvais, France, (glassmaking in), 30
Bedacryl 122X , 217
Beechwood (fuel or source of alkali), 75, 79,
Beijing, China (glassmaking in), 29
Beilby (William & Mary, glass enamellers & gilders), 43, 113, 115
Belfast, Northern Ireland (glassmaking in), 45, 166
*Belfast Newsletter, The*166
Belus River (R.. Na'aman, Palestine, *source of sand*), 16, *22, 73, 143*
Benckert, Hermann (glass decorator), 112
Beta-ray back scattering test, 240
Bet She'arim, Palestine (glassmaking site), 3, 102, 142–3
Beva 371 (adhesive), 343
Bianconi, Gian-Ludovico (author), 150
Biedermeier glasses (decorative), 43, 44
Bierschieben (celebration windows), 65
Biocides, 199, 203
Biringuccio (writer on glassmaking), 146, 147, 148, 149, 151
Bismuth (in mirror making), 134
Bishopp, Hawley, (glassmaker), 40
Bisseval (medieval glassmaking family), 17
Blaschka, Leopold, Rudolph, glass figures, 318, *Fig. 7.55, 7.56*
Bloom on glass, 273, 274, 318, *Fig. 4.30*
Blore Park, Staffs (furnace site), 155
Blowpipe (blow iron, for glassblowing), 105
Blue Vase, The (cameo glass, in Naples), 98
Blunden's Wood, Surrey, (furnace site), 154–156, *Fig. 3.61, 3.62, 3.63*
Bocca/boccarello (furnace mouth), 145, 148, 149
Bohemian glass, 34, 37, 77, 100
Bone, Henry (glass enameller), 52

Bone beads, 319
Bontemps (glassmaker), 117, 130, 165
Boric oxide (boron, in glass), 4, 74
Boshan, China (glassmaking site), 4, 28
Boston Glass Manufacturing Co., 47
Boulsovier, Thomas, 69
Bracchio/bracchia (measurement), 146
Brewster (investigator into glass), 174
Bridging oxygen atoms, 4–5, 253
Brighton Pavilion, Sussex (chandeliers in), 71, 323
Brillouin light scattering (test), 241
Bristol glass, 58
Brittleness, 14
Brixworth, Northamptonshire (glass from), 128
Broad glass (see Cylinder glass)
Broc à glaces (see Ice glass)
Brown's Hospital, Canterbury (glass jewels in windows), 132
Brunswick, Germany (glass engraving in), 36
Brychta, Jaroslav (glass figure maker), 318–9
Bubblewrap (packing material), 312
Buckholt, Wiltshire, (furnace site), 158
Burial experiments (of glass) (see *Ballidon*)
Burmese glass (decorative), 44, 48
Burne-Jones, Sir Edward (window designer), 65
Butanone (hydrophilic solvent), 270
Butteri, G.M., (wallpainting of glass furnace), 148, 149
Butvar-B (polyvinylbutyral), 219
Byzantine glass/mosaics, 26

Cage cups (see *Diatreta*)
Caistor St. Edmund, Norfolk (furnace site), 142
Calaton CA7, & CB (see Soluble nylon)
Calcedonio (chalcedony glass, decorative), 76
Calcium antimonate (opalising agent), 10
Calcium chloride, 314
Calcium fluoro-phosphate (opalising agent), 10
Calcium gluconate (HF antidote), 203
Calcium (lime, in glass), 17, 139, 176, 200, 202
    oxide, 5, 60, 73, 81, 180, 309
    hydroxide (slaked lime), 86
    limestone, 89
    sulphate, 221
Calculi (quartz pebbles), 74
Calgon (polyphosphate cleaning agent), 201, 202
Calaton CA 7 CB (soluble Nylon), 211
Cam, Jean le(glassmaker), 39
Cameo glass, 21, 29, 98–100, 106–7, Fig. 3.19
Cames lead strips for stained glass (see Leading)
Campania, Italy (glassmaking centre), 22
Canada balsam (*abies balsama*), 205
Candelabra and candlesticks, 68–9
Canosa, Apulia, Italy (glass from), 116, Fig. 2.3, 3.32,
Canton, China (glasspainting in), 58
Canqueray, Philippe de (glassmaker), 129
Capella Palatine, Palermo, Italy (mosaics in), 60
Carbon dioxide, 190
Carbon disulphide, 262
Carbon-sulphur amber glass, 8
Carbonate precipitation (at sea), 171, 189–190
Carbon tetrachloride, 314
Carbowax 6000 (polyethylene glycol wax), 245, 266
Carder, Frederick (glassmaker), 48
Carleon, S. Wales (Roman window glass), 62, 126

Carlsberg, C.W. (illustrator), 167
Carré, Jean le (glassmaker), 38, 63, 154
Cartellina (thin sheet of glass), 60
Cartoon, 65
Casing, cupping, 106–7
　(see also Cameo glass)
Cassiterite (see Tin oxide)
Cast glass sheets, 130
Casting in moulds, 91–2
Casting materials, 90
Catcliffe, Yorkshire (cone furnace), 166
Catechol (complexing agent), 263
Cations, 5
Cavalet (or crown), iron ring around Glory-hole, 149
Cave relievo (engraving), 98
Cellosolve (ethylene glycol monoethyl ether), 341, 342
Celluloid (cellulose nitrate), 211
Cellulose nitrate, 275, 319
　(see also HMG, Durofix, Duco cement)
Cementation (Egyptian faience), 84
Chair (glassformer's workplace), 102
Champlevé (enamelling technique), 51, 52, 119, 122
Chagall, Marc (artist), 65
Chance Bros. (glassmakers), 117, 129, 130
Chandeliers, 69–72
　conservation, 320–332, *Fig. 7.59, 7.60*
　de crystal, 71
　dismantling, 326–330, *Fig.7.62, 7.63, 7.64*
　examination, 324–6
　recording, 328, Fig. 7.61
Chandelles (tallow candles), 69
Chartres Cathedral, France (windows in), 63
Chelating (sequestering) agents,
　for cleaning, 199, 200–1, 337, *Fig. 5.1*
Chemical analysis, 239
Chemical deterioration of glass, 173–182
Chemical tests (for identifying soluble salts), 252–3
Chichester, Sussex (early crown glass in), 128
Chiddingfold, Sussex, 156, 158
　church windows, 337
　furnace site, 46
Chinese glass, 28, 58, 59, 178, 231, 238, 316
　painting on mirrored glass, 333
Chinoiserie (decorative style), 37, 42, 43, 72
Chloride ion (detection of), 252–3
Chromium oxide (chromate & bichromate, in glass), 78
Chrystoleum (backed photographs), 54
Chunk glass (newly-made, made for export), 29, 82, 142, *Fig. 3.1*
Cire perdue (see Lost wax process)
Citrates (effect of), 182
Clay (see Potters' clay)
Cleaning glass:
　agents, 199
　on site, 257–8, *Fig. 7.8, 7.9*
　in the laboratory, 260–3, *Fig. 7.12*
　historic glass, 271
Clichy, France (glasss paperweights from), 94
Clingfilm, 225, 247
Cloisonné glass, 54, 66–7, 317, 337–8, *Fig. 7.68*
Cobalt (in glass), 73, 76, 237, 319, *Fig. 1.7*
Coefficient of expansion, 13, *Table 5.1*
Colchester, Essex (Roman glass), 26
Cold painting (decorative), 54, 113

Cold working (abrading, cutting, grinding), 95–8, 176, *Fig. 2.3, 2.10, 3.15*
Colemanite (hydrated calcium borate), 44
Colloidal suspension (of metals), 8, 76, 138
Cologne, Germany, 25, 30
Colourants:
　for glass, 6, 73, 74, 114, 115, 143, 177, 223
　for filling materials, 223
Commercial restoration, 308
Complexing (chelating) agents, 182, 194
Composition of glass, effect on decay, 176
Conchae (shells), 74
Condensation, effect on glass, 174, 183, 192
Conductivity meter, 251
Conqueror, J. (glassmaker), 130
Consolidation, 204–6, 263–270, 314, 336, 341, *Fig. 7.14, 7.15, 7.16, 7.17*
　system, definition of, 264
Constantinople (Istanbul), Turkey, 26, 31, 32, 62
Copper (in glass), 8, 73, 76, 77, 131, 139, 225
　chloride, 86
　copper oxide, 86
　cuprous oxide, 10, 136, 138
Copper foil (for repair), 337, 338
Copper-ruby glass, 8
Cordoba, Spain (Roman glass), 26
Core forming (technique), 18, 88–9, *Fig. 2.1, 2.2, 3.5, 3.6*
Corinth, Greece (glassmaking site), 30, 31
Cork, Eire (glassmaking in), 45
Corning Mus. of Glass (USA), 254, 255, 316
Corning Glassworks (USA), 116
Correx board (packaging material), 226, 311
Cotton wool (Surgical cotton; cotton buds), 259, 261, 278, 280, 315
Counter enamelling (see Enamelling)
Coupling agents (silanes), 205
Coventry Cathedral, Warwickshire, 65
Covered pots (for melting glass), 167
Cracks in glass, 183, 233, 259, 280, 334
Craquelure (decorated glass), 33, 49
Cristallo (colourless glass), 30. 32, 80, 178
Crystallum (crystallina), (Roman term for crystal glass), 79
Cristobalite (type of silica), 1, 86
Crizzling (of glass), 179, 191, 280, 310, 314–7, *Fig. 4.17*
Cross, Henri & Jean (sculptors), 91
Crown glass (Normandy-, spun-glass), 61, 63, 128–9
Crucibles, 73, 82, 140
Crutched Friars, London (glasshouse), 148
Cryla acrylic paints, 344
Crystal Palace, London (window glass in), 43, 63, 71, 117
Culbin, Scotland (glass beads from), 85
Cullet (re-usable glass), 73, 75, 80, 83, 86, 182
Cuneiform tablets (in Assyria), 9, 82, 86, 135–7
Cupping (see Cameo glass)
Cut-line, 65
Cyanoacrylate adhesives, 205, 217–8, 276, 280, *Fig. 5.11*
Cylinder-, Broad- Spread-, Muff-glass, 61, 63, 126–8, 291, *Fig. 3.43*
Czechoslovakia (Czech Republic), 71, 154, 158

Dalle de verre (slab glass), 66
Damascus, Syria (glassmaking), 27, 28, 30
Dammar resin, 276

Dammouse, Albert (glass paste), 91
Damp storage of church windows, 191
Daphne Ewer, The (cold painting on), 113–4, *Fig. 3.30*
Daraa, Syria,
Darduin, Giovanni (glassmaker), 80
Darmstad, Germany,
Darney Forest, France,
Daruvar, Zagreb, Yugoslavia (cage cup from), 96
Daugmale castle mound, Latvia (glass beads from), 262
Daum glass (decorative)49
Daumengläser (vessel vessel), 35, 110, *Fig. 2.15*
Davenport's Patent Glass (decorative), 111
Davidson & Co. (glass manufacturers), 44
De-alkalisation (leaching), 174, 175, 179, 196
De Coloribus et Artibus Romanorum (On the Colours & Arts of the Romans), 153
Decorchement, Francois (glass paste), 91
De Re Metallica (glassmaking text), 147, 148
Decalomania (decorative technique), 54
Decanters (conservation), 273, 304
Decolorizers for glass, 7, 78–9
Deka fabric dyes (use of), 306
Density (of glasses), 14, 231, *Fig. 1.8, 1.11*
Dental wax (use of), 220, 280–292
Denton, Manchester (glassworks site), 77
Der Blau Reiter (the blue rider, glasspainter's group), 57
Derm-O-Plast SG Normaal (PVC), 219, 245
De la Pirotechnia, 146
Desalination of glass, 250–253, *Fig. 7.5*
    monitoring of, 251–2, *Fig. 7.6*
Desolv 292 (solvent), 279
Detergents, 200
Deterioration of glass:
    atmospheric pollution, 190, *Fig. 4.13*
    blackening of the surface, 186, 193, *Fig. 4.24, 4.27*
    deterioration layers, 240, *Fig. 6.3*
    dulling, 183, *Fig. 4.19*
    encrustations, 171, *Fig.4.8, 4.9, 6.1*
    flaking, 183
    iridescence, 260
    milky or enamel like weathering, 184, *Fig. 4.22*
    previous treatment, 194, *Fig. 4.4, 4.10, 4.11, 4.12*
    stains and residues, 171, *Fig. 4.6*
    surface pits and crusts, 190–1, 196
    spontaneous cracking, 183–4, *Fig. 4.20, 4.21*
Devitrification, 11
Devitrite, 3
Dextrins, 205
Di pinto freddo (cold painting), 113
Diamond point engraving (decorative technique), 31, 33, 42, 96, 115, *Fig. 3.16*
Diatreta (cage cups), 96, 308
Dichloromethane (solvent), 272, 279
Dichroism (optical colour effect), 8, 237
Diderot (author of *Encyclopédie*, illustrations of glassmaking)150, 164, 165,
Diploica lanescans Ach., (micro-organism), 193
Displaying glass, 309–11
Divalent alkaline earth cations, 5
Dollond (optical glass maker), 117
Domes (glass, repairing), 290–2
Dor, Palestine (modern Israel) (glassmaking site), 143
Dow Corning Clear Seal (mastic), 257
Dowelling (repair technique), 281, 284, *Fig. 7.27*

Dresden, Germany (glass engraving in), 36
Drottengina af Sverige (shipwreck, glass from), 187
Dry artists' pigments, 284
DSIMS (dynamic secondary ion mass spectrometry), 238
Dublin, Eire (glassmaking in), 45, 68, 166
Duco cement (cellulose nitrate), 211, 263, 275
Due Lettere di Signor Marchese Scipione, 150, *Fig. 3.9*
Maffei (furnace illustration in), 150
Dunstable Swan, The (enameeled brooch), 52
Durofix (cellulose nitrate), 211, 263, 275
Durol-Polier-Fluat SD (fluoro-silicate), 269
Dyers Cross, Sussex (glassmaking site), 64

Edkins, Michael (glass enameller & gilder), 113, 115
Edison (glass light bulbs), 117
Edrei , Syria,
EDTA (ethylene diamine salt), 194, 200, 201–2, 263
EDS (energy-dispersive X-ray spectrometry), 234
Efflorescence (Egyptian faience), 84
*Egermann, Frederick (glassmaker), 37
Eglomisé, 54, 58, 340
Egyptian Blue (pigment), 2, 3
Egyptian:
    beads, 82, 85–6, 319, *Fig. 3.2, 3.3*
    deterioration & conservation of, 313–4, 315
    faience, 2, 81, 83–5, 242, *Fig. 7.53, 7.54*
    glass, 19, 138–141, 191
    -Islamic glass, 7, *Fig. 1.6*
Ehlipakku (Ancient Egyptian raw glass), 139
Eichensfeld, Germany (glassmaking in), 79
Eigelstein, Germany (glassmaking site), 142
El Djem, Tunisia (mosaic depicting glass), 102
Electro-float (glassmaking technique), 130
Electron beam analysis, 233, 234
Elizabethtown, Pennsylvania, USA (glasshouse), 46
Ellison Glassworks, 44
Emery (polish), 97
Emission spectrography, 239
EPMA (electron probe micro-analysis), 235
Enamels (vitreous coatings on metal), 1, 3, 51–3, 118–123, 234, 310, 317, 321–2, *Fig. 3.33*backing (counter -), 50
    bassetaille, 51, 52, 121, *Fig. 3.37*
    champlevé, 51, 52, 119, 122, *Fig. 3.36*
    cloisonné, 51, 52, 62, 119, 122, 125, 322, *Fig. 3.34*
    counter, 50
    damage to, 321–2, *Fig. 7.57, 7.58*
    dipped, 119
    en plein, 52
    en resille sur verre, 52, 122
    en ronde bosse, 52, 120, 122
    en taille d'epergne, 119
    filigree, 120
    lavoro di basso relievo, 52–
    painted, 122, 237, Fig. 3.38
    plique à jour, 51, 52, 120, 322, *Fig. 3.35*
    Surrey enamelling, 52
Enamelling (vitreous paint on glass), 42, 43, 113
    decay of, 192, *Fig. 4.29*
Enclyclopédie (glass manufacturing), 150, 151, 164, 167
Engraved glass, 37, 42
    -gold glass, 54
Ennion (Sidonian glassmaker), 23
Ensell, George (glassmaker), 150

Environment, effects on glass, 174, 182–194
  partially desiccated, 243
  dry, 243
  saturation, 243
Environmental control, 316–17
Epotek 301-2 (epoxy adhesive), 212, 276, 343
Epoxy resins, 205, 207, 211–15, 223, 276, 278, 280, 281, 284, 285, 286, 303, 319, 322, 343, *Table 5.2, Fig. 5.7, 5.8*
EPR (electron paramgagnetic resonance) (see ESR)
Eraclius (Medieval historian), 153
Eridu, Mesopotamia, 138
ESCA (electron spectroscopy for chemical analysis) (see XPS)
Escomb, Durham (glass from), 128
ESR (electron spin resonance), 239
Ethanol (ethyl alcohol), 203, 262, 270
Ethazote (inert foam, packing material), 225
Ethics of conservation, 242
Ethyl alcohol, 262
Etruria, Italy, 21
Evelyn, John (diarist), 74
Excavated glass, dry, wet, 243
Examination of glass, 228–231, 26, *Fig. 6.2*
Excise Act (see Glass-)

Faber, Johann Ludwig (glass decorator), 113
Fabergé, Peter Carl (enameller), 51–52
Facet cutting, 100–101
Façon de Venise, 32, 34, 35, 37, 38, 39, 80, 96, 102, 110
Façon de l'Angleterre, 41
Faenza, Italy, 3
Faience (see Egyptian faience)
Fakes (see Replicas and forgeries)
Faraday, Michael 193
Ferric oxide, 6, 331
Ferrous oxide, 6
Ferrous sulphide, 193
Fernfold, Sussex (furnace site), 154
Ferramenta (in windows), 66, 336
Fictive temperature, 11
Filigrana (decorative technique)33, 107–109, *Fig. 3.25*
Fire-cracking, 1.17
Fission track dating, 240
Flammability of solvents, 203
Flashed glass, 8, 131
Flat glass sheets, 130, *Fig. 3.44*
Flint, 1
Flint glass (see Lead glass)
Float glass, 130
Florence, Italy (glassmaking in), 30
Fluorescence (in UV), 236
Fluorspar (in glass), 78
Fluxes (in glassmaking), 73, 118, 177
Fondo d'oro (gold design), 54, 116, 124, *Fig. 2.7*
Forest glass, 29, 37, 114, 160
Forest of Darney, Vosges, France, 17
Forgeries (see Reproductions and fakes)
Formaldehyde, 309
Formalose (moulding material), 221
Formic acid, 309
Fornax vitr (glass furnace), 145
Fossiles harenae (Roman term for sandstones), 74

Fourcault machine (sheet glass), 118
Fourier transform infrared microscopy, 253
Fraches (conveyor belt), 150
Fracture analysis, 232
*Fraunhofer Institute für Silicatsforchung*317
Freshwater environment, 186
Freezing, soil block, 247
  beads, 321
Fritsche, William (glass engraver), 44
Fritting, 81
Fucus versiculosus (marine algae, Mn in), 78
Fuel (for glassmaking furnaces), 73–40, 79, 80
Fufeng, China (glass from), 28
Fulgurite (natural form of silica), 1
Fumed silica, 284
Furnace:
  ancient Mesopotamia, 137–8
  ancient Egyptian, 139141, *Fig. 3.47*
  Roman, 141–2, *Fig. 3.49*
  cone, 163–68, *Fig. 3.21, 3.78, 3.79, 3.80*
  northern, 151–63, *Fig. 3.61, 3.62, 3.63, 3.64, 3.65, 3.74*
  reverbatory, 146
  southern, 144–51, *Fig.3.52, 3.53, 3.54, 3.55, 3.56, 3.57, 3.8, 3.59, 3.60*
  tank, 142–43, 145, *Fig. 3.50*
  verrerie en bois, *Fig. 3.57, 3.58*
Fusing (powdered glass), 90–1
Fustat, Egypt (glassmaking in), 27
Fynebond (epoxy resin), 210, 212, 276

Gablonz, Czech Republic, 212, 276
Gagiana (shipwreck), 30
Galla Placidia, Ravenna (mosaics in), 60
Galliano (pigment), 59
Gallé, Emille, 48, 91, 100
  -glass, 49
Gallo, Andrea & Domenica (mirror makers), 62
Gap filling (see Restoration)
Garden Hill, Sussex (Roman window glass from), 126
Gatchell, Jonathan (glass manufacturer), 45
Gate, Simon (glass artist), 49
Gatherer (part of glassmakers' team), 102
Gaul (Roman France, glassmaking in), 26
Gawber, Yorkshire (glass cone), 166
German sheet glass (see Cylinder glass)
Gernheim, Germany (glass cone), 166
Ghost images (of deterioration on windows), 193
Giles, James (engraver & decorator), 42, 115
Gilding, 23, 27–8, 33, 42, 115–7, 340
Girandoles, 68, 69
Girasole glass (Venetian), 235
Glasborn, Spessart, Germany (glassworks site), 7
Glass:
  abrading95–8
  beads, 87–8
  on textiles & ethnographic materials, 319–21
  blowing (invention of), 101, *Fig. 3.48, 3.51*
  bull's eye, 62
  bulk (mass) glass, 176–80, 229–30
  crizzling (see Weeping glass)179
  cold working, abrading, cutting, grinding, 95–8
  decoration:
    abrasion, 176

Glass (*cont.*)
  addition of glass blobs & trails, 110, *Fig. 2.8, 2.9*
    tooling, 110, *Fig. 3.27*
    Davenport's patent glass, 111
    enamelling (see Enamelling)
    gilding (see Gilding)
    grinding, 95–8
    ice glass, 111
  definition of, 1, *Fig. 1.3, 1.4, 1.5*
  disease (see Weeping glass)
  Excise Act of, 42, 45, 70
  forming, 81, 86
  fritting, 81
  fusing, 319
  grinding, 95–8, *Fig. 3.8*
  making, 81, 86
  melting, 86
  of flint (lead glass), 40
  paste (*pâte de verre, pâte de riz*), 91
  seals (Roman), 236
  Sellers Company, 39, 40
  sick (see Weeping glass)
  surfaces, 176, 195–6, 228–9, *Fig. 4.31*
  transition temperature (see Viscosity)
  waste, 182, 234
  weeping179
Glassfibre surfacing tissue, 285
  matting, 295
Glassine (silicone paper), 265
Glassmaking families (medieval), 17, 41
Glassworkers' tools, 102, *Fig. 3.22*
Glastonbury, Somerset (glassworks site), 153
Glaze, 2, 3, 139–41, 322, Fig. 1.2
Glazing (windows), 63, 317
Glenluce, Scotland (glass beads from), 85
Glory Hole (part of furnace), 129, 144, 148
Glyptic (see Cold-working techniques)88
Gnalic Wreck (Yugoslavia), 30
Goddard's Silver Dip and Foam, 331
Gold ruby glass, 8, 9
Gordion, Turkey, 79
Gob-fed machine (for glassmaking), 118
Gotha, Germany (glass engraving in), 36
Graal glass (decorative), 49
Grand feu (enamelling furnace), 51
Gravel Lane, London (glassworks site), 157, Fig. 3.66, 3.67
Great Casterton, Leicestershire (Roman Site), 184
Great Trade Exhibition (of 1851), 43
Greenhouse effect, The, 43
Greener & Company (glass manufacturers)44
Greenwood, Frans (stipple engraver), 97
Grey Eye Temple, Lebanon, 83
Grinding (see Cold working)
Grisaille (painting effect), 52, 56, 61, 65, 132
Grünenplan, Germany (glassworks site), 159
Grozing66
Guide de Verrier (Guide for the glassmaker), 165
Guildford, Surrey (glassmaking site), 64
Guinand (glassmaker), 117
Gumley, John (glass seller), 69
Guilloche, 51
Gurgan, Mesopotamia, Gypsum (weathering product), 190

Haaretz Collection of Glass, Israel, 27

Hackle marks (from fracture), 15
Hadera, Israel, 142
Haematinum (red glass), 10
Hald, Edvard (glass artist), 49
Hall-in-Tyrol, Austria (glass decoration in), 96, 115
Halsinelle (hooks or supports), 147, 148
Hallorenglas (type of medieval beer glass), 112
*Hama, Syria*101
Hambacher Forest area of Germany (glassmaking sites), 142
Hamwic (Southampton), 75,
Hampton Court Palace, Surrey (chandeliers in), 323, 333
Han Dynasty, China (glassmaking in), 28, 178
Hanover, Germany, 159, 166
Hard glass (definition), 12
Hardness of glass, 14
Hartfield, E. Sussex (widow glass from), 62, 127
Harrapan faience, 313
Hartley, James (glassmaker), 130
Hasanlu, Anatolia,
Haughton Green, Manchester (furnace site), 164, *Fig. 3.77*
Heating glass,
Heemskirk, Willem von (glass engraver), 38
Heindert, Luxembourg (furnace site), 157
Helgö, Sweden,
Helmback, Abraham (glass decorator), 113
Hellenistic glass,
Henley-on-Thames, Berkshire (glassworks site), 40
Heart, Afghanistan (glassworking site)74
Henriksdorp, Sweden (furnace site), 163
Heraclius (Roman historian), 116
*Hilsborn, Grunenplan, Germany*7
Hill, John (glass manufacturer), 45
Hinterglasmalerei (*reverse painting on glass*), 33, 53, 54, 55, 56, 57, 58, 114, 270, 39–344, Fig. 3.31, 7.71, 7.72
HMG (cellulose nitrate adhesive), 211, 263, 267, 275, 278, 279, 301, 307, 313, 318
HMS Sapphire (Newfoundland wreck), 193
Hochschnitt (cutting technique), 65, 98, *Fig. 3.18*
Hofkellereiglas (type of beer glass), 112
Hope, Sir John (diarist), 116
Hot melt preparations (moulding), 221
HST (heat shrinkable tubing), 311
Humidity (effect on glass), 174, 182, 191, 197, 315
Humpen glasses (Bohemian beer glasses), 35, 112, 114, 162
Hutton, Yorkshire (furnace site), 157
HXTAL NYL-1 (epoxy adhesive), 212, 215, 307, 322
Hyalith (black) glass, 37, 77, 88–90
Hyaloplastic (see Hot working techniques)
Hydration rind dating, 240
Hydrochloric acid, 203, 262, 274
Hydrofluoric acid (for glass etching), 101, 123, 203, 274, 308
Hydrogen glass,
Hydrogen peroxide, 202–3
Hydrogen sulphide, 186
Hydroxybiphenyl (biocide), 203
Hydroxycarbolic acids (chelating agents), 202, *Fig. 5.4*
Hyttekaer, Denmark (furnace site), 163

IBSCA (ion beam spectrochemical analysis), 240–1

Ice glass (decorative technique), 49, 111, *Fig. 2.14, 3.28*
ICP-OES (inductively coupled plasma optical emission spectrometry), 237
ICPMS (inductively coupled plasma mass spectrometry), 237
Igel ('hedgehog' shape) glass, 30
Immersion techniques for refractive index, 232
Impact cone (from glass fracture), 15, 233, *Fig. 1.12*
Impact damage, 170, *Fig. 1.12, 1.13*
IMS (Industrial Methylated Spirit), 225, 250, 261, 272, 314, 331, 334, 335
Index of dispersion, 14
Infra red (IR) photography, 231
Inlays in furniture, 18
Inorganic glasses, 1
Insoluble salts (identification of), 252–3
Institute of Nautical Archaeology (American), 82, 187, 257
Intaglio engraving, 27, 98, 100
Ions, and ion exchange (see De-alkalisation)
Iridescence:
    natural, 174–5, 183, 185, 260, 269
    produced artificially (decorative), 115
Irish glass, 44–6, 100
Iron (in glass), 76, 186, 223, 319
Iron-manganese amber glass, 8, 73
IRRS (Infra-red reflection spectroscopy), 226, 240
Ishgar (plant ash), 74
Isinglas (fish glue), 318
Islamic glass, 26, 27, 28, 115
Isotopic ratio analysis, 238
Ivory beads, 319
Jacobite glasses, *Fig. 3.17*
Jacobs, Lazarus (glass gilder), 115
Jamestown , Virginia, USA (glasshouse site), 46, 147
Japanese mulberry tissue, 270
Jarrow, Northumbria (Saxon glassworking), 75, 130, 184, 337
Jeanette Glassworks, Pennsylvania, USA, 48
Jemdet Nasr phase (Mesopotamia), 18
Jerash, Palestine (window glass from), 128
Jesse Tree Window, *Regensburg Cathedral, Germany*, 132
Jones, Robert (Regency designer), 71
Josephus (Roman historian), 16
Junkersfelde, Westphalia, Germany (furnace site), 163

Kaltmalerei (cold painting), 113
Kandinsky, Wassily (glass painter), 57
Kangxi, Chinese emperor (glassmaking under), 28
Karanis, Egypt, 102
Karlova Hut, Czech Republic, 158
Karlsruhe, Germany,
Kas, Turkey, (Bronze Age site), 187, 257
Kassel, Germany (glass engraving in), 36
Kempak (packing material), 312
Kenchreai, Corinth, Greece (opus sectile), 61, 124–5, 187, 253–7
Khorfush (Egyptian, vitrified material), 141
Kimble Glass Company, 47
Kimmeridge, Dorset (glasshouse site), 157–8, 163, 164, *Fig. 3.69*
King's Lynn, Norfolk (source of sand), 40

King Sargon of Assyria (*aryballos*), 95
Kirdford church, Sussex (windows in), 337
Klucel C (hydroxyl-propylcellulose), 341
Knightons, Alfold, Surrey (glassworks site), 155, *Fig. 3.64*
Knops (decoration on stem of wine glasses), 32
Knossos, Crete, 138
Kny, Frederick (glass engraver), 44
Kongsberg, Norway (chandeliers from), 71–2
Kraron G1650 (plasticizer), 342
Krautstrunk (cabbage stalk prunts), 30
Kreybich, George Franz (glass engraver), 100
Kubu images (Assyrian glassmaking), 136
Kunstammlungen der Vest Coburg, Germany, 37,
Kunckel, Johann (glassmaker), 8, 36, 150, 159, 160, 163, 164, 168
    kiln of, *Fig. 3.71, 3.72*
Kurfurstenhumpen, (decorated thin beer glasses), 35
Kuttrof (German beaker), 35
Kythera, Island of, Greece (shipwreck), 187

Labino, Dominic (glassblower), 49
Lacrymae Batavicae (see PrinceRupert's drops)
La Farge, John (window glass maker), 65
La Grandja de San Idelfonso, Spain (glass decorating in), 115
La Tene I Period, 88
Lacquers, 204–6, 269, 319
Lalique, René (glass maker), 49
Lambeth, London (see Gumley, John)
Lampshades, 67–8
Lampworking, 108, *Fig. 3.26*
Lanterns, 67–8
Lapiz lazuli, 81
Laser cleaning (ablation), 274
Larmes de verre (see Prince Rupert's drops)
Latticino (latticinio) (decorative technique), 107
Lattimo (decorative technique), 49, 57, 107
*Lavoisier, A .J.*174
Leaching (see De-alkalization)
Le Mans Cathedral, France (windows in), 63
Leading (in windows), 66, 131, 192, 336
    lead-line (windows), 65
Lead in glass, lead silica glass, 9, 10, 12, 40, 47, 134, 176, *Fig.1.8*
    arsenate, 235
    basic lead carbonate, 80
    lead crystal glass, 100
    lead oxide, 60, 74, 76, 80
    lead, red, 76, 80
    lead sulphide, 262
    lead, white (basic lead carbonate), 76, 80
    litharge, 9, 80
Lead isotopes in glass, 238
Lechatelerite (a natural glass), 1, 2
Lehman, Caspar (glass engraver), 36
Lehr (or Leer) (annealing furnace), 149, 150, 151
Lemington glass cone, Newcastle-on-Tyne, 166
Libbey, E.D. (glass manufacturer), 47
LIBS (laser induced breakdown spectroscopy), 241
Lichens (on glass), 193
Lepraria flavia Arch. (micro-organism), 193
Liège, Belgium (glassmaking in), 30, 37
Lifting materials (on excavations), 224
Lime in glass (see Calcium)

Limoges, France, 52, 122, 321
Linnet-hole, 160
Liquidus temperature, 3
Liquitex (acrylic pigments), 257
Lissapol (non-ionic detergent), 200
Litharge (lead oxide), 9, 76
Lithium (in glass), 8
Littleton, Harvey (glassmaker), 49
Lobmeyer, J.J. (glass manufacturer), 45
Loetz glassworks, Czech Republic, 48
London (Roman glass from), 26
London Gazette, The, 166
Longe, George (glassmaker), 45
Lorraine, France, 38, 62, 63
Lorsch, Germany,
Lost wax process (*cire perdue*), 91, Fig. 3.9
Low Countries (glass from), 36, 38, 62, 113
Lubbers glassmaking machine, 128
Lumella (*occhio*, furnace hole), 149
Lustre painting, 27, 114–5
Lycurgus Cup (*diatreta*), 8, 96, 237

Magnes lapis (Roman term for limestone), 74, 79
Magnesia in glass, 5, 76, 77, 180, 186, 223
   magnesium oxide, 5, 309
   chloride, 317
Malachite (copper corrosion), 83
Mancetter (UK Roman furnace site), 26, 142
Mandeville, Sir John (illustrator of glassmaking), 153, 157, 162, 168
Manganese in glass, 75, 76, 77, 78, 86, 186, 223
   as decoloriser, 7, 76
   dioxide, 77, 78
Mannheim, Pennsylvania, USA (glasshouse), 46
Mansell, Sir Robert, 38, 39
Månsson, Peder (writer on glassmaking), 143
Maranyl (soluble Nylon), 211
Manufacturing defects (in glass), 170
Marble Hill House, London (glass fanlight in), 63
Marcasite (in mirror making), 134
Marking glass, 258–9, *Fig. 7.10*
Marlik, Mesopotamia (mosaic glass from), 93
Marine environment, glass in, 186–190, *Fig. 4.26, 4.27*
   fouling organisms (on glass), 189, *Fig.4.28*
Marmot, Maurice (glassmaker), 49
Marvering (shaping hot glass), 89
Masonite (support), 225, 226
Mass spectrographic analysis, 233, 237
Matting (painting technique), 192
Mattioli, Alessio (mosaic maker), 50
MDF (medium density fibre board), 333
Medici, Francesco I de' (studio wallpainting depicting glass), 148
Melinex (polyester film), 335, 336, 344
Mekku (ancient Egyptian raw glass), 139
Melting point, 3
Menorah, 24, 25
Mercury (amalgam for mirrors), 133–5
Merrett (translator of *Neri*), 149, 156–7, 166, 167
Mesopotamia (glassmaking in), 17–9, 27, 135–138, 177, 234
   transparent glasses, 137
   opal glasses, 138
Metal corrosion deposits on buried glass, 172, 317

Metal 'staples' (bridges for support), 278
Metallic oxides (see Colourants for glass)
Methanol, 203
Methyl methacrylate, 216–7
Metropolitan Museum of Art, New York (glass in), 308
Mezzotints, 58–9
Michelfeld, Austria (glass reliquary from), 30
Micromesh (cushioned abrasives), 290
Micro-mosaics, 49–51, 52, 322, *Fig. 2.17*
Micro-organisms on glass, 193, 203
Microscope (use of), 228, 308
Middlewich, Cheshire (glassmaking site), 142
Mildner, Johann Josef (glass decorator), 117
Millefiori glass (decorative), 33, 52, 88, 94–5, 123, *Fig. 2.13, 3.13, 3.14*
Milliput (epoxy putty), 284
Millville, New Jersey, USA, 47
Mineral acids, 203
'Mirror area' (of fractured glass), 15
Mirrors, 62, 133–5, 317, 332–6, *Fig. 3.46, 7.65, 7.66*
   painting on, 54, *Fig.7.67, 7.72*
Modelling materials, 220
Modifiers (see Network modifiers)
Mohn, Samuel (father & son, glass decorators), 113
Mohs' scale of hardness, 14
Molar glass compositions, 180–1, *Table 4.1, 4.2*
Monks Riborough, Buckinghmshire (church windows), 337
Monkwearmouth, Durham (monastic window glass), 128
Mombasa, S. Africa (ship-wreck, glass from), 249
Monte Casino, Italy (library of), 144
Monte Lecco, Italy (glassmaking site), 145, 146
Morris, William (arts & crafts designer), 65, 100
Mortar (glass embedded in), 172
Mosaic glass, 18, 21, 22, 52, 91, *Fig. 2.5, 3.10, 3.11*
Mosaico in piccolo (see Micromosaics)
Mosaic tesserae, 30, 54, 59–60, *Fig. 3.39, 3.42*
Mosque lamps, 27, 116, *Fig. 2.11*
Mould:
   blowing, 105–9
   flash lines, 308
   making materials,
      dental wax, 286–92, *Fig. 7.33, 7.34, 7.35, 7.36*
      silicone rubber, 292, *Fig. 7.37, 7.38, 7.39, 7.40*
   piece mould, 299–301, Fig. 7.43
   pressing, 286
Mount Carmel, Palestine, 16
Mount Washington, USA (glass factory), 44
Mounting fragmentary glass, 284, *Fig. 7.28, 7.51*
Mowital B20H (PVB), 219
Muff glass (see Cylinder glass)
Muffle kiln, 52, 132
   (see also *Petit feu*)
Mulvaney, Charles (glass manufacturer), 45
Münter, Gabriele (glass painter), 57
Murano, Italy (glassmaking in), 30, 38, 49, 52, 80, 94
Mutissu (Assyrian); m*attara* (Syrian), rake, 137
Mycenaean glass, 18, 87

N-methylmethoxy Nylon (see Soluble Nylon)
Na'aman, river (see Belus, river)
NAA (neutron activation analysis), 236–7
Naga plant (Assyrian source of alkali)136
Nailsea Bristol (glassworks), 77
Namur, France (glassmaking in), 74

Navarre, Henri (glassmaker), 49
Natron (Egyptian source of alkali), 74
Nef (vessel type), 33, *Fig. 2.12*
Nebou, Louis Lucas de (glassmaker), 62
Nejsum, Denmark (furnace site), 163
Neri, Antonio (glassmaker and author), 81, 149, 150, 160
Netherlands (glass engraving), 115
Network dissolution, 175–6
Network formers and modifiers, 3, 4, 73, 176, 171, 177
Netzglas (decorative),
Nevers, Frances (glass figures from), 317
New Bremen, Maryland (furnace site),
Newcastle upon Tyne, Northumbria,
    glass from, 37, 38, 41, 42, 43, 113
    source of sand, 40
Nickel oxide (millerite, in glass), 78
Nimrud, Mesopotami (glassmaking in), 27, 79, 138
Nineveh, Mesopotamia, (glassmaking in), 27, 174
Nishapur, ancient Persia (Iran), (glassmaking in), 27
Nitrate ion, detection of, 252
Nitric acid, 203, 314
Nitromors (solvent), 279
    Superstrip, 279
Nitrum (Roman term for soda), 74
Non-bridging ions, 5, 175, 253
Norland Optical (UV setting) adhesive, 217
Norman slabs, 66, 129, *Fig. 3.43*
North American glass, 46–8
Northwood, Harry, 48
    John, 44, 48, 99
Nostangen, Norway (glass furnace), 167
Notsjö, Finland (glass furnace), 159
Nuppen (German, prunts), 30
Nuremberg, Germany (glass engraving in), 35, 36, 37, 57
Nylon fishing line, 310, 311

Obernkirchen, Germany (glass cone), 166
Obsidian (volcanic glass), 1, 15, 16, 319, *Fig. 1.1*
Ochsenkopfglas (type of enamelled beaker), 112
Occhio (*lumella*), eye, 136–7
OEL (Occupational Exposure Limits), 203
Offhand blowing (glassforming procedure), 102
Oil gilding,
Oinochoe (jug), 21, 304–6, *Fig. 2.2, 7.47*
Olympia, Greece (glass from), 90
Ontario Glass manufacturing Co., Canada, 47
Onyx glass (artificial opal), 76, 236
Opacifying agents, 10, 223, *Table 1.1*
Opalescent enamel, 51
Opnaim's red glass,
Oppitz, Paul (glass engraver), 44
Optical methods of analysis, 237
Optical properties of glass, 13
Opticon UV57 adhesive, 217
Opus sectile, 23, 54, 58, 60, 123, 124, 125, 126, 187, 253–7, *Fig. 3.40, 3.41*
Oratorio of St Rocco, Altare, Italy (picture of a glassmaking furnace), 145
Organic solvents, 199, 203
Organo-silanes (see Silanes)
Orrefors, Sweden, 49
Osler, T&C (glass manufacturers), 43, 71
Ostia, Sicily, 124

Overshot glass (see Ice glass)
Owens suction glassmaking machine, 118
Oxidation, 6
Oxidation state methods of analysis, 233, 238
Oxonium ion (H3O+),
Oxyfume 12 (fumigant), 256
Oxygen isotopes in glass, 238
Packaging:
    materials, 225–6
    methods, 244, 312–3, *Fig. 7.52*
    archaeological glass (see Storage)
Padua, Italy, 56
Paillons (decoration beneath enamel), 51
Painted enamel (on metal), 51
Paintings on mirrored glass, 58
Painted and stained glass windows, 130–3, 237
Pala d'oro, St. Marks, Venice, Italy, 52
Palm House, Kew Gardens, London (Glass panes in), 63
Palmo (unit of measurement), 146
Palmyra, Syria, 101
Panacide (disinfectant), 310
Paperweights, 94–5, 106
Paraison, (gathering of molten glass), 103
Paraloid:
    B-48N, 311
    B-67314, 342
    B-72211, 219, 250, 266, 267, 268, 276, 285, 311, 312, 313, 314, 317, 318, 336, 342, 344
    B-99314
Particle methods of analysis, 236
Passementerie, 69
Passglas (vessel type), 30, 35
Passive conservation, 242
Pâte-de-riz and *Pâte-de-verre* (see Glass paste)
Pattern moulding (technique), 105
Paviken, Sweden,
Peach Bloom (decorative), 48
Peckitt, William (glassmaker), 133
Pearlised glass (decorative), 319, 320
PEG 4000 (polyethylene glycol) wax, 267
Penarth, S. Wales (source of sand), 141?
Penrose, George & William (glass manufacturers), 45
Perrot, Bernard (glassmaker), 61
Perry & Co. (chandelier makers), 70, 71
Perspex (US Plexiglas, acrylic sheet), 242, 292, 302, 304, 314
Pertusaria Leucosora Nyl (micro-organism), 193
Petit feu (enamelling kiln), 50, 119, 132
Pettenkofer Process, 342
Pfauen Island, Berlin, Germany (glasshouse), 9
pH value, 175, 176, 189, 202, 263, 315, 331
Phase-separated glass, 6
Phidias (ancient glassmaker), 90
Phiolarius (type of vessel), 31
Phosphate (intermediate & effect of), 177
Phosphorous, 4
Photo-activated adhesives, 205
Photographic images on glass, 54, 338–9, *Fig. 7.69, 7.70*
Photography of glass, 231, 244
Physical damage of glass, 169–71, 182, *Fig. 4.2, 4.3*
PIGME (proton-induced gamma ray emission), 321
Pilkington (glassmakers), 118, 130
PIXE (particle induced x-ray emission), 236, 321
Plain glazing (windows), 336–7

Pit formation, 183
Plant ash (source of alkali), 29, 86, 143
Plastazote LD45 (inert polyester foam), 225, 245, 259, 3, 311, 334
Plaster of Paris (gypsum), 221, 225, 247, 294, 299–302
Plasticine (US Plastilina, modelling compound), 220, 301
Plate glass (patent plate, improved cylinder glass), 130
Plastogen G (polymethacrylate), 223
Pleichroism (displays different polariscope colours), 229
Plexigum 24 (polybutyl methacrylate), 217, 269
Plexisol P550, 342
Plextol D466 (acrylic resin dispersion), 342
Pliny the Elder (Roman historian), 16, 22, 59, 74, 77, 79, 82
Po, River, Italy, 20, 24
Pocatky, Czech Republic, 154
Pokal (vase type),
Polariscope, 229
Poli, Flavio (glassworker), 49
Polyethylene glycol wax, 224
Polyester resins, 205, 215, 220, 222, 276, 285, 286, 297, *Fig. 5.9*
Polythene (self-seal) bags, 244, 260, 265
Polythene sheet, 248
Polyethylene foam, 225
Polymers, deterioration of, 208
Polymethyl methacrylate, 208, 216–7, 314
  resins, 222–3
Polyphosphates, 201, *Fig. 5.2*
Polyurethane foam, 224–5, 247
Polyurethane resin, 205, 218, 247–8
Polyvinyl acetate, 208, 219, 224, 225
Polyvinyl alcohol, 287, 289, 295, 299
Polyvinyl chloride, 208, 219, 224, 225
Pompeii, Italy (glass windows from), 126
Pontil (glassformer's tool), 102
Portland Vase (cameo glass), 99, 273, *Fig. 7.20, 3.19*
Potash (in glass), 7, 73
Potash glass, 118, 143, 175, 176, 177, 180, 183, 186, 233
Potassium, 317
Potassium carbonate, 81
Potassium hydroxide, 262
Pot-coloured glass, 76, 131
Potash glass, 118, 143, 175, 176, 177, 180, 183, 186, 233
Potichimanie (decorative technique), 54
Potsdam, Berlin, Germany, 36
Potters' clay (modelling material), 220, 297–8
Powell, J. (see Whitefriars Glassworks)
Precipitation (effect of), 182
Preissler, Ignatius (glass decorator), 37
Press-moulded glass, 47–8
Pressure sensitive tape,
  damage by, 172
  use of, 225, 276, 284, 303, 343
Preussler, Christian (glass enameller), 162, *Fig. 3.75*
Primal (acrylic emulsions),
  AC-235, 267, 270
  WS-12, 267, 270
  WS-24, 269
  WS-50, 267, 270
Prince Rupert's Drops, 12
Proclamation Touching Glass (of 1614), 38, 63, 163
Profilometer (flatness measuring device).240
Propan-2-ol (hydrophilic solvent), 261, 270

Prophet windows (see Augsburg cathedral)
Protons, 175
Prudentius (Roman poet), 62
Prunted beakers, 30
Ptolomais ('Akko), Palestine, 16
PTFE (polytetrafluoroethylene), 222
Pumice (volcanic glass), 1, 97
Punty (*pontil*) (glassmakers' tool), 102
Purple of Cassius, 36
PVA release agent, 303
PVA-AYAA (conslidant), 270, 342
PVAC (polyvinyl acetate), 208, 249–50, 255, 275
PVAL (polyvinyl alcohol),
PVB (polyvinyl butyral), 262
PVC (polyvinyl chloride), 208, 219, 224, 225, *Fig. 5.14*
Pyrex glass, 118

Qantir, Egypt, 139
Qing Dynasty (glass from), 316
Quarry (window pane), 337
Quartz (source of silica), 1, 3, 4, 14, 29, 71, 81, 97, 139
Quentglaze (polyurethane), 247

Radiation monitoring of potash glass, 238
Radiocarbon dating, 240
Ramla, Israel (glassmaking site), 143
Ramos, Felix (glass engraver), 65
Raqqa, Syria (glassmaking site), 143
Ravenna, Italy (mosaics from), 123
Ravenscroft, George (glassmaker), 10, 39, 40, 178, *Fig. 2.16*
Reamer (glassworkers' tool), 104
Rebel 2000 (paints), 344
Recording and documentation of glass, 227–8
Red glass, 8, 9
Reduced pressure (vacuum impregnation), 265
Reduction, 6
Refractive index, 207–8, *Table 1.2, 1.11*
  measurement of, 231–2, 281
Regency Period (in Britain), 70
Reichadlerhumpen (type of beaker), 35, *Fig. 2.15*
Reichenau, Austria (glasshouse), 162, 163, *Fig. 3.76*
Regalrez 1094 (resin), 342
Rejdice, Czech Republic (glasshouse), 154
Relative humidity (RH), 183, 184, 315, 316, 317
Release agents, 221–2, 300
Removal of glass,
  from the ground, 244–
  immobiliztion of glass, 245
  immobilization of a soil block, 246, *Fig. 7.2, 7.3*
  freezing a soil block, 247, 249
  from a marine or freshwater environment, 249
Removal of glass kilns, 248
Removal of previous repair/restoration materials, 271–3, *Fig. 7.18, 7.19, 7.20, . 7.23, 7.24, 7.25, 7.26*
Repair:
  of archaeological glass, *Fig. 7.13*
  of historic glass, 275
Replicas and fakes, 308–9, *Fig. 7.48, 7.49*
Repton, Derbyshire (glass from), 128
Re-setting excavated window glass, 337
Restoration of glass, 271, 284–308
  commercial, 308
  detachable gapfills304–306, *Fig. 7.47*

filling losses in opaque glass284, *Fig. 7.29, 7.30*
filling tiny losses284–5
partial restoration285, *Fig. 7.31*
gapfilling with casts from moulds taken off the
   original glass, 286–290, *Fig. 7.32, 7.33, 7.34*
gapfilling with casts from a mould taken from a clay
   model or a previous restoration, 297–303, *Fig.
   7.41, 7.42, 7.43, 7.44*
gapfilling where the interior of a vessel is inaccessible
   for working, 303–304, *Fig. 7.45, 7.46*
Reticelli, 75, 94, *Fig. 3.12*
Retouching paint, 343
Retouching lacquers, 223–4
Reverse paintings (on glass), 54–56, 339–344, *Fig. 7.71*
Reverse foil engraving, 56, *Fig. 2.18*
Reversibility of polymers, 208–9
Rhineland, Germany (glassmaking in), 25
Rhodes, island of, Greece, 83, 257
Rhodorsil 11504A (silicone rubber), 296
Rib marks (from fracture), 15
Rice Harris & Sons (glass manufacturers), 44
Richardsons (glass manufacturers), 44
Rigger (sable tracing brush), 131
Rishpon, Palestine, 102
Riss (painting outline), 55
River Euphtaes (Iraq), 137
Rivenhall church, Essex,
Roche, Captain Philip *(glassmaker)*, 166
Rock crystal (quartz), 13
Roemer glasses (beakers with large bowl), 35, *Fig. 2.15*
   Roman glassmaking, 141–2
   (see also Glassmaking in the Roman Empire)
Rosedale, Yorkshire (furnace site), 157, *Fig. 3.68*
Rosenborg Castle, Copenhagen (mirrors in), 333
Rouen Cathedral, France, 65
Rousseau, Eugène, 48
Royal Gold Cup, The, 121
Rummer (large beer glass), 35
Rüsselbecher (claw-beaker), 29
Rustin's Clear Plastic Coating (urea formaldehyde), 223

San. Apollinare in Classe, Ravenna (mosaics in), 60
San. Cosmo, Rome (mosaics in), 60
San. Damiano, Rome (mosaics in), 60
St. Chapelle, Paris (windows in), 63
St. Cuthbert's Window, York Minster, 132
St. Gobain, France (glass manufacturing), 62
St. John's Church, Stamford, Canterbury (jewels in
   windows), 132
St. Louis, France (glass paperweights from), 94
St. Michael's Church, York (window in), 132
St. Weonard's, Herefordshire (glassmaking site), 155
Sabellico, Marc Antonio, 94
Sadana Island, Red Sea, Egypt, 187
Sala, Jean (glassmaker), 49
Salicornia kali (source of alkali)74, 85
Salsola kali (source of alkali), 85, 136
Samara, Mesopotamia (Iraq, glassmaking in), 27
San Idelfonso, Royal Palace of, Madrid, 65
San Marco, Venice, 17
San Sophia, Constantinople, 60
San Vitale, Ravenna (mosaics in), 30, 60, 63, 129
Sand blasting, 101
Sand moulding109

Sandwiched gold leaf, 21, 116–7, *Fig. 2.4, 3.32*
Sang, Jacob (glass engraver), 36, 38
Santocel (fumed silica), 292
Saranwrap (PVC film), 225, 247
Sanfirico (see *Zanfirico*),
Sardis, Turkey (glass from), 270
Sargon, king of Assyria (alabastron of), 95
Sarosel room (part of furnace complex), 150
Sassanian period (Islamic glass), 97
SA/V (surface area/volume ratio), effect of, 176, 197
Schaper, Johan (*schwarzlot* enameller), 35, 112
Schedula Diversum Artium (Treatise on Diverse Arts),
   152
Schurterre, John (glassmaker), 64
Schwannbardt, George (glass engraver), 36
Schwartzlot (black enamel decoration), 35
Science Museum, London (model in), 151, 152
Sconces (wall lights), 68
Scopas (release agent), 222
Scotch Magic Tape 810, 276, 343
Scotchtint (solar refelcetive film), 335
Scratches, effect of, 184
Seawater (see Marine environment)
Seed (bubbles in glass), 80, 81, 170
Selenium in glass, 78
Sellotape, 307
SEM (scanning electron microscope), 234, 308
SEM-EDS (energy dispersive X-ray spectrometry), 234–5
SEM-WDS (wavelength dispersive X-ray analysis) (see
   EPMA)
SEM/EDXRA270
Sequestering agents (see Chelating agents)
Sepiolite clay, 201
Serçe Liman wreck (Turkey), 28, 82, 83, 257
Servitor (part of glassformer's team), 102, 149
Shading (glasspainting technique), 192
Shakenoak Farm, Oxfordshire (Roman site), 127
Shellac, 204, 205, 222, 330
Sidon, Syria, 22, 26, 30, 102
Siebel, Franz Anton, 113
Siemens regenerative furnace, 117
Silanes, 205–7, 218, 266, 315, *Fig. 5.5, 5.13*
Silastic E RTV (silicone rubber),
Silcoset 105 (silicone rubber), 296
Silesia (glass cutting in), 171
Silhouettes on glass, 54, *Fig. 2.19*
Silica in glass, 3, 73, 74, 138, 176, 177, 223
Silica gel, 315, 316
Silicate deposits on glass during burial, 171
Silicone release agent, 222
Silicone rubber (moulding material), 218, 221, 292–303
Silver nitrate, 133
   in mirror making, 134
Silver stain, 64, 65, 66, 130–3, 192
Siraf, Persian Gulf (glassmaking centre), , 27
SIMS (secondary ion mass spectroscopy), 236, 237
Skenarice, Czech Republi (furnace site), 154
Slagelse, Denmark (glass from), 268
Smalti (cakes of glass), 50, 59
Smalti filati (glass threads), 50
Smear shading (painting technique), 66, 192
Smithsonian Institution, Washington, 316
Snake thread trailing (decorative technique), 25
Soda crystals, 74

Soda glass, 73, 74, 81, 83, 86, 118, 143, 175, 176, 177, 180, 183, 231, 233
Sodium bicarbonate, 86
  carbonate, 74, 81, 82, 86, 137
  chloride, 74, 86
  nitrate, 74
  sesquicarbonate, 74
  sulphate, 74
Solarisation, 193
Soluble nylon (consolidant), 211, 313
Soluble salts, effects of, 187
Song Dynasty, China (glassmaking in), 28
Solvol Autosol (fine abrasive paste), 290
Specific gravity, 14
Specula (blown glass window), 61
Springing (of glass), 170, 280
Sprungli, Hans Jacob (glass painter), 57
Stabilisers (see Network modifiers)
Staffordshire, UK (glassmaking in), 79
Stained glass, 130, 171, *Fig. 3.45*
Stangenglas (German beaker type), 35, 112, *Fig. 2.15*
Stassfurt, Germany (source of potash), 80
Steigel, 'Baron' (glassmaker), 46
Steatite, 81
Steinkrug, Hanover, Germany (glass cone), 166
Stenbult, Denmark (furnace site), 163
Stevens & Willimas (glassmakers), 44
'Sticky Wax' (see Waxes)
Stipple engraving (decorative technique), 38, 97
Stipple painting, 66
Stonea, Cambridgeshire (Roman window glass from), 62, 126
Stones (inclusions) in glass, 81, 170, *Fig. 4.1*
Stones of Venice (John Ruskin), 308
Storage of glass:
  dry or treated, 259–60, *Fig. 7.11*
  and display of historic glass, 309–311
  of paintings in reverse on glass, 344
  weeping glass, *Fig. 7.50*
  wet glass, 244–5, *Fig. 7.1, 7.4, 7.16*
Stourbridge, Worcestershire (glassmaking in), 43, 44, 166
Strabo (Roman historian), 78
Strain and stress (caused by adhesives), 207
Strain detection of, 232
Striae (cords seen in glass), 170, 229, 230
'Striking' (of colour in glass), 8
Sumerian words for glassmaking (Akkadian trans.), 135–6
  abnu (glass mix)137
  abussu(plant ash)136
  *anzabhu (b-su)*138
  bab kuri (door)137
  bilhu glass mix)137
  bit kuri (house of furnaces)136
  dabtu(crucible)137
  immanakku (ground quartzite pebbles)136
  kuri sa ibni (furnace), 136
  kuri sa siknat enait-pel-sa (furnace), 136
  kuri sa takkanni (furnace arch), 136
  mutirru (*mattara*, Syrian, *rutabulum,* glassmakers' rake), 137
  naga plant (plant source of soda), 136
  nimedu (stilt), 137
  sipparuarhu (fast bronze)136

su'lu (ladle), 137
taptu zakatu (crucible), 137
urudu hi (slow copper), 136
zuku (frit), 135, 136
Sulphate ion, detection of, 252
Sulphur deposits on buried glass, 171
Sulphur dioxide, 190
Sulphur-reducing bacteris, 186, 188
Sulphuric acid, 101, 203
Superficial disfigurement of glass, 171–3
Supporting glass during repair, 276, *Fig. 7.21, 7.22*
Surrey enamelling (see Enamelling)
Susa, Iran, 21
Sussita, Palestine (ancient Hyppos), 102
Sutton Hoo, Suffolk, 260
Swann, Sir Joseph (glassmaker), 117
Swiss enamelling (see Enamelling)
Synperonic N (non-ionic detergent), 200
Syriste, Czech Republic, 154
Taccbardia lacca (see Shellac)
Taffel offen (table oven), 162
*Tamerlane (Timur)*112
Tara, Eire,
Tazza (type of bowl),
Technovit 4004A (polymethyl methacrylate resin), 223, 304
Tektites (natural glass), 1
Tell al Rima, Iraq (glass mosaic from), 93, *Fig. 3.11*
Tell el Amarna, Egypt, 18, 138, 139, 236
Tell 'Umar, Mesopotamia?
TEM (transmission electron microscope),
Temperature, effect of, 197 316
Tesserae (mosaic components), 23, 26, 30, 50, 59, 60, 117, 124
  en grisaille (micromosaic), 50
Thermal expansion, 13, *Fig. 1.10*
  shock damage, 170
Thermal history (of a glass), 10
Thermodynamics, 197
Theophilus (writer on glassmaking), 60, 113, 126, 132, 152– 53, 157
Thetford, Essex (glass from), 129
Thornham Hall, Suffolk (chandelier from), 69
Thornton, John (window maker), 64
Three-mould process,
Thuret, André (glassmaker), 49
Tiberias, Palestine, 102
Tiefschnitt (engraving), 98
Tiffany, Louis Comfort (glassmaker), 48, 100
Tin amalgam (mirror making), 134, 333
Tin oxide (cassiterite, opalising agent), 10, 77, 333, *Table 1.1*
Tinsholt, Denmark (furnace site), 163
  monoxide (romarchite), 333
Tiseur (part of the glassformers' team),
TL (thermoluminescence dating), 240
TLV (Threshold Limit of Toxicity), 203
Toledo cathedral, Spain (windows in), 239
Toledo, Spain (glasspainting in), 57
Toluene (solvent), 225
Tongs (glassformers' tool), 105
Topkapi Palace, Istanbul (windows in), 64
Torcello, Italy (furnace site), 123, 144
Tourlaville, France (glass manufacturing), 57

Toutin, Henri & Jean (enamellers), 62
Toxicity of solvents, 203–4
Trace elements in glass223
Traprain Law, Scotland (glass from), 86
Travels (illustrations of glassmaking), 153
Trestenhult, Sweden *(furnace site), 160, 162,* Fig. 3.73
Triangular diagram, 180–1, *Fig. 4.18*
Tridymite (a form of silica), 1
Trichlorethylene, 203, 225
Triton (non-ionic detergent), 200
Turquoise, 83
Tut-ankh-amen (glass head-rest of), 95, 115
Tuthmosis III (glassmaking under), 18, 19
    glass jug of, 112, *Fig. 2.1*
Twycross church, Leicestershire,
Tylose MH 300 (methyl cellulose), 341
Tyre, Syria (glasshouse site), 26

Ultrasonic cleaning, 262
Ultra-violet light, 340
    curing adhesives, 205, 217–8, *Fig. 5.12*
    examination of glass by, 230, 308
    UV-VIS (ultra-violet & visible spectroscopy), 239
Ulu Burun, Turkey (shipwreck, glass from), 82, 187, 257, *Fig. 3.1*
Unguentarium vessel type), 25, 90, 102
Universal indicator papers, 231
Uranium glass, 49
Uppark House, Sussex (chandeliers from), 323

Vacuum impregnation, 265, 269
Vacuum tweezers, use of, 279
Van Dyke (style of cutting), 70
Vann Copse, Hambledon, Surrey (furnace site), 155, *Fig. 3.65*
Vaseline (release agent), 298, 301
Vauxhall, London (glassmaking in), 58
Vel-Mix (gap filler), 256
Venice, Italy, 17, 31–4, 65, 77, 96, 115
Vermiculite (packing material), 296
Verre:
    *craquelé*111
    de fougère (bracken glass), 29
    de Nevers, 109
    églomisé, 54, 58, 116
    façon de Lorraine, 128, 158
    frisée, 109
    verre en table, 128
Ververi Bityska, Czech Republic (furnace site), 153
Verzelini, Jacob (glassmaker), 38, 39, 69, 96
Vesuvius, Mount, Italy (eruption of), 24
Vetro:
    @pi:a fili, 107
        filigranato, 107
    a ghiacccio (ice glass), 111
    a reticello, 107, 108
    a retorti, 108
    corroso (modern ice glass), 111
    a redelexo (a redexin), 107
    de trina, 107
Victoria & Albert Museum, London (glass in), 310, 315, 316
Vinac B-7, 342
Vinamold (PVCmoulding material), 221

Vinamul 6815 (PVC emulsion), 267
Vinyl polymers, 218–220
Viscosity of molten glass, 10, 11–12, 81, *Fig. 1.9*
    annealing point, 11, 12
    fictive temperature, 11
    liquidus temperature, 3
    softening point, 11
    strain point, 11, 73, 170
    transition point (Tg)/temperaure11, 13
    of adhesives, 219
    working point, 11
Visitello, Christopher (glassmaker), 167
Visual examination of glass, 228
Visscher, Anna Roemer (engraver), 38
Vitre mania, 54
Vitrum (Roman term for glass), 32, 79
    in massa et rudus (crude lump glass), 32
    purum (pure glass), 79
Voltammetry of immobilized microparticles, 24
Volturnus River, Italy, 16, 73
Von Eiff, Wilhelm (glassmaker), 65
Vosschemie (polyester) resin, 306

Wachsausschmelzfahren (see Lost wax process)
Wadi Natrun, Egypt (source of soda), 74
Waldglas (see Forest glass)
Ware Collection of glass, The, 318
Warmbrunn, Germany (glass engraving in), 36
Washing sound glass, 273
Water:
    cleaning with, 199–200
    content of glass, 243–4
    effect on glass, 174
Waterford, Eire (glassworks), 45, 68·
Waxes:
    beeswax, 204, 276, 343
    cerecine, 276
    dental (for moulds), 303, 304, *Fig. 7.33, 7.34, 7.35, 7.36*
    natural, 204
    paraffin, 343
    polyethylene, 245, 266
    'sticky wax', 276, *Fig. 7.21, 7, 22b*
    use of wax or wax/resin mixture, 343
Webb, Thomas & Son (glass manufacturers), 44
Wedgwood, Josiah (ceramic manufacturer), 99
Weeping glasses, 242, 191, 309, 314–7, *Fig. 4.15, 4.16, 7.50*
Weimar, Germany (glass engraving in), 36
Wells Cathedral, Somerset (window glass in), 190
Welwyn Garden City, Hertfordshire, 10
Wemyss, Scotland (glasshouse), 166
Wetland burial sites, 182
Wheaton Glass Company, New Jersey, USA, 47
Wheel cutting (wheel engraving), 38, 97–8, *Fig. 3.17, 3.18, 3.20*
Whitefriars Glass (see Powell)44, 61
White Spirit (solvent), 272
Wilderspool, Cheshire (glassmaking site), 142
Winchester House (cone furnace), 166
Window glass, 61–7, 126–33, 155, 162, 235, 237, 317
Windsor Castle, Berkshire, (window glass in), 62
Winterthur, Delaware, USA (chandelier from), 70
Wissembourg, Germany

Wistar, Caspar & Richard (glassmakers), 46
Wollastonite (devitrification product), 3
Woodall, George (glass decorator), 44
Woodchester, Gloucestershire, 156
Woodhouse, George (glassmaker), 44
Wroxeter, Shropshire (glassmaking site), 26, 197

X-ray examination methods (of glass), 233, *Fig. 7.49*
X-radiographs, 227, 230–1
XPS (X-ray photo-electron spectrometry), 255, 309
  -ESCA (electron spectrometry for chemical analysis), 236
XRD (X-ray diffraction analysis), 186, 235
XRF (X-ray fluorescence analysis), 236
X-ray tomography, 241
Xylene (solvent), 272

Yellow Mesopotamian glass, 9
York Minster (window glass in), 132, 133, 177, 191
Yuan Dynasty, China (glassmaking in), 28

Zachariasen, W. H., 3
Zanfirico (*sanfirico,* twisted stems), 107
Zapon (cellulose nitrate), 314
Zeilburg glasshouse, Bohemia, 162
Zeiss, Carl (optical glassmaker), 117
Želený Brod Museum, Czech Republic (glass in), 318
Zephiran chloride (antidote for HF), 203
Zirconia (in glass), 78
Zuytdorp (shipwreck) 270
Zweizel (glasscutter), 96
Zwischengoldglas, (decorative technique), 36, 117